Rick Steves'
GERMANY
& AUSTRIA
2008

D0972342

GERMANY & AUSTRIA

═A24═	Freeway/Autobahn
	Major Roads
	Major Rail Line
✈	Airport
St. Goar	Recommended Location*
Bebra	Just Passing Through**
■	Ruin, Museum, Other Point of Interest
⛫	Castle/Monument/Palace

* Black locations are places of interest to tourists, sized by importance.

** Gray locations are not places of interest to tourists and are sized by population.

0 km	50	100 km
0 miles		50 miles

POLAND

Neustrelitz
A19
Sachsenhausen ■
Tegel ✈
Spandau ✈ **Berlin** Frankfurt an der Oder
-ndenburg ● Potsdam ✈ Schönefeld Rzepin
Sanssouci Palace
A2 A9 A13
Gorzow Wielkopolski
A11
A10
A12
● Wittenberg
Zielona Góra
-ssau
Elbe Cottbus
A15
Zary
Lauchhammer
A13 A4
Bolesławiec
Leipzig Moritzburg ⛫
Meissen ● Bautzen ● **Görlitz** ● Zgorzelec
Dresden S I L E S I A
S A X O N Y Bad Schandau Zittau
-auchau A4 Chemnitz Seiffen Děčín
A72 Ústí nad Labem
■ Litoměřice
Plauen ● Terezín
Ruzyně ✈ Hradec Kralove
Svidnica
Opole
● Nysa
Nachod
Karlovy Vary **Prague** ✈
Cheb Mariánské Lázně Kutná Hora ● Lichkov **Štramberk**
-Marktredwitz E50 Karlštejn Castle **Olomouc**
Plzeň ● **CZECH REPUBLIC** Kromeriz ●
A93 B O H E M I A E50 E65 M O R A V I A Zlin ●
Furth Tabor ● **Brno**
Český Kubice ● Veselí nad Lužnicí ● Telč ● Breclav ●
Regensburg Slavonice ● Kuty ●
Ober- České Budějovice ● Český Velenice Gmünd **SLOVAKIA**
traubling A3 **Český Krumlov** ●
-23 A92 Passau ● Summerau W A C H A U Krems ●
Danube Durnstein ● Grinzing ● **Vienna** ✈
-I A **Linz** Mauthausen ● Melk ● Schönbrunn ✈ **Bratislava**
Attnang Puchheim St. Valentin Puchberg ● Palace Eisenstadt ●
Herrenchiemsee ⛫ Chiemsee A1 Schneeberg A2 Sopron ● ■ Esterhazy Palace
-nheim A8 **Salzburg** ● Bad Ischl **A U S T R I A**
Berchtesgaden ● Hallstatt ● S A L Z K A M M E R G U T Selzthal ● **Szombathely** ●
Kufstein ● Hallein ● Stainach Irdning ● Bruck an der Mur ●
A12 Zell am See ● Leoben ●
Wörgl ● Kitzbühel ● Piber ● **Graz** ●
-nterhornalm Badgastein ● A10 **HUNGARY**
MI Grossglockner Pass Spielfeld ●
-ner Pass Lienz ● Spittal ● A9
Dobbiaco ● **Klagenfurt** ✈ Maribor ● Nagykanizsa ●
A L P E D I S I U S I Villach ● Ptuj ●
-astelrotto ● Cortina Tarvisio Vršič 1 t Pass Bled/Lesce ● **SLOVENIA** **CROATIA**
Jesenice ●

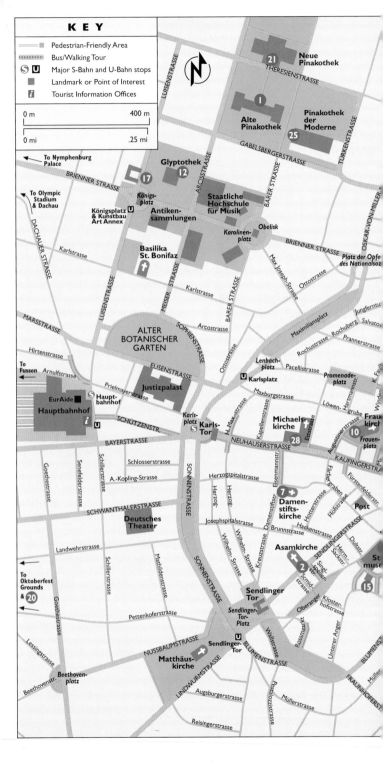

MUNICH

- Alte Pinakothek
- Asam Church
- Bavarian National Museum
- Beer and Oktoberfest Museum
- To Chinese Pagoda Beer Garden
- Cuvilliés Theater
- Damenstift Church
- **8** Deutsches Museum
- **9** English Garden
- **10** Frauenkirche
- **11** Fünf Höfe Shops
- **12** Glyptothek
- **13** Haus der Kunst
- **14** Hofbräuhaus
- **15** Jewish History Museum
- **16** Kunsthalle Art Center
- **17** Lenbachhaus
- **18** Marienplatz
- **19** Munich City Museum
- **20** To Museum of Transportation
- **21** Neue Pinakothek
- **22** New Town Hall & Glockenspiel
- **23** Odeonsplatz
- **24** Old Town Hall
- **25** Pinakothek der Moderne
- **26** Residenz Museum
- **27** Residenz Treasury
- **28** St. Michael's Church
- **29** St. Peter's Church
- **30** Viktualienmarkt

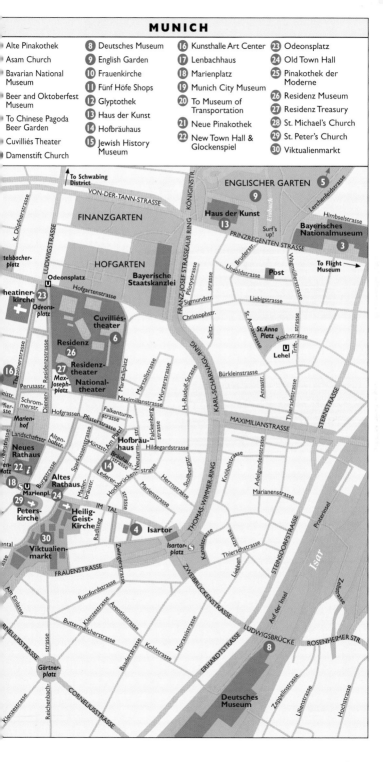

BERLIN

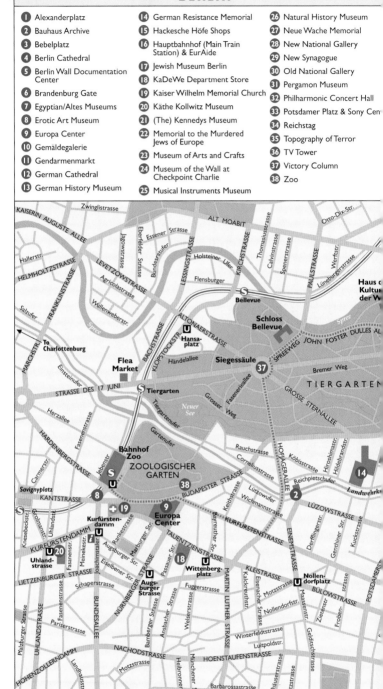

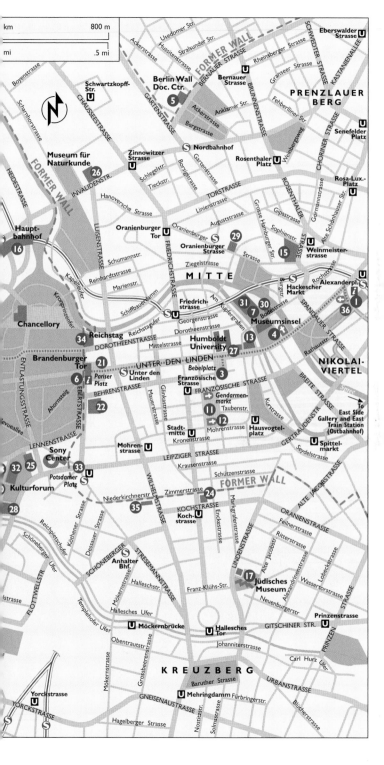

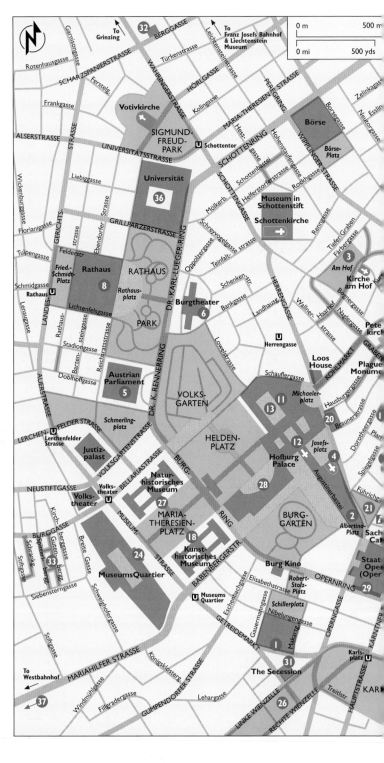

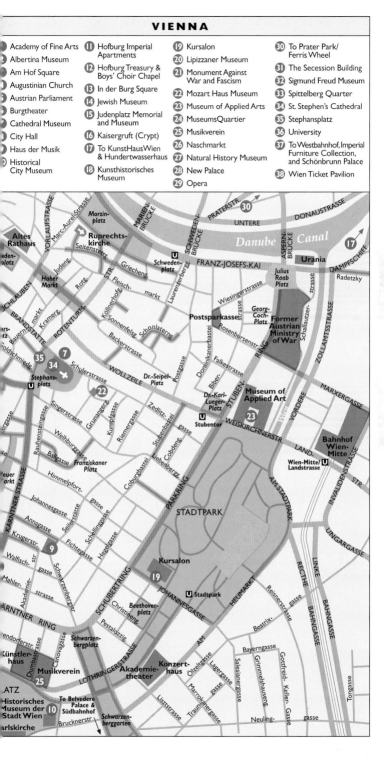

VIENNA

Rick Steves'

GERMANY
& AUSTRIA
2008

AVALON
TRAVEL

CONTENTS

Top Destinations in Germany & Austria

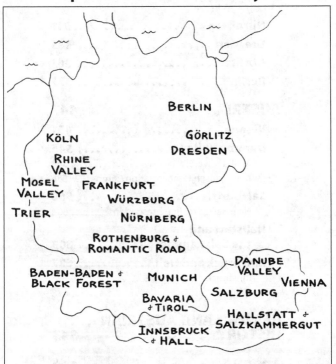

INTRODUCTION

In many ways, Germany and Austria are Teutonic twins, offering alpine scenery, dramatic castles, cobbled quaintness, and tasty wurst and strudel. But Germany is more of a mover and shaker, emerging from its tumultuous history to lead the way for the new united Europe in the 21st century. Meanwhile, Austria is content to bask in its good living and opulent past as the former head of one of Europe's grandest empires. Taken together, the two countries are intriguing and rewarding for you to explore.

This book breaks Germany and Austria into their top big-city, small-town, and rural destinations. It then gives you all the information and opinions necessary to wring the maximum value out of your limited time and money. If you plan a month or less in this region and have a normal appetite for information, this book is all you need. If you're a travel-info fiend, this book sorts through all the superlatives and provides a handy rack upon which to hang your supplemental information.

Experiencing this region's culture, people, and natural wonders economically and hassle-free has been my goal for three decades of traveling, tour guiding, and travel writing. With this new edition, I pass on to you the lessons I've learned, updated for your trip in 2008.

The places I cover are balanced to include a comfortable mix of cities and villages, mountaintop hikes and forgotten Roman ruins, sleepy river cruises and sky-high gondola rides. While you'll find the predictable biggies (such as Rhine castles, Mozart's house, chunks of the Berlin Wall, and the Vienna Opera), I've also mixed in a healthy dose of Back Door intimacy (a thrilling Austrian mountain luge, a soak in a Black Forest mineral spa, a beer with Bavarian monks, and a ramble through traffic-free alpine towns). I've been selective, including only the most exciting sights. For example, there are dozens of quaint villages in Austria's Salzkammergut Lake District. I take you to only the most charming: Hallstatt. And of the many castles in the Mosel Valley, I guide you to the best: Burg Eltz.

The best is, of course, only my opinion. But after spending a third of my adult life exploring and researching Europe, I've developed a sixth sense for what travelers enjoy. The places featured in this book will make anyone want to slap-dance and yodel.

About This Book

Rick Steves' Germany & Austria is your friendly Franconian, your German in a jam, a tour guide in your pocket.

This book is organized by destinations, each one a mini-vacation on its own, filled with exciting sights and homey, affordable places to stay. In the following chapters, you'll find:

Planning Your Time, a suggested schedule with thoughts on how best to use your limited time.

Orientation includes tourist information, tips on public transportation, local tour options, helpful hints, and an easy-to-read map designed to make the text clear and your arrival smooth.

Self-Guided Walks take you through interesting neighborhoods, with a personal tour guide in hand.

Sights provides a succinct overview of the most important sights, arranged by neighborhood, with ratings:

▲▲▲—Don't miss.

▲▲—Try hard to see.

▲—Worthwhile if you can make it.

No rating—Worth knowing about.

Sleeping describes my favorite hotels, from budget deals to splurges.

Eating serves up good-value restaurants, ranging from inexpensive pubs to fancier options.

Transportation Connections to nearby destinations by train, bus, and plane. It also includes route tips for drivers, with recommended roadside attractions along the way.

The **German and Austrian History** chapter introduces you to some of the key people and events in these nations' complicated pasts, making your sightseeing that much more meaningful.

The **appendix** is a traveler's tool kit, with a handy packing checklist, recommended books and films, instructions on how to use the telephone, useful phone numbers, and the procedure for dealing with lost credit cards. You'll also find detailed information on driving and public transportation, as well as a climate chart, festival list, a hotel reservation form, and German survival phrases.

Study this book and put together the plan of your dreams.

Then have a great trip! Traveling like a temporary local and taking advantage of the information here, you'll get the absolute most out of every mile, minute, and euro. As you visit places I know and love, I'm happy you'll be meeting some of my favorite Europeans.

PLANNING

Trip Costs

Five components make up your trip cost: airfare, surface transportation, room and board, sightseeing and entertainment, and shopping and miscellany.

Airfare: A basic round-trip flight from the US to Frankfurt should cost $600 to $1,300 (even cheaper in winter), depending on what city you fly from and when. Always consider saving time and money in Europe by flying "open jaw" (flying into one city and out of another; for instance, into Frankfurt and out of Vienna).

Surface Transportation: For a three-week whirlwind trip of all my recommended destinations, allow $650 per person for public transportation (trains and buses) or $750 per person (based on two people sharing) for a three-week car rental, parking, gas, and insurance. Car rental is cheapest when reserved from the US. Train passes are normally sold only outside of Europe. You may save money by simply buying tickets as you go (see "Transportation," page 674).

Room and Board: You can travel comfortably in this region on an average of $100 a day per person for room and board (less in small towns, more in big cities such as Berlin or Vienna). A $100-a-day budget allows $10 for lunch, $15 for dinner, $5 for beer and *Eis* (ice cream), and $70 for lodging (based on two people splitting the cost of a $140 double room that includes breakfast). That's doable. Students and tightwads eat and sleep on $40 a day ($20 per hostel bed, $20 for meals and snacks).

Sightseeing and Entertainment: In big cities, figure $9 to $13 per major sight (Munich's Deutsches Museum-$11, Vienna's Kunsthistorisches Museum-$13), $3 to $5 for minor ones, and $25 to $50 for bus tours and splurge experiences (such as concert tickets, alpine lifts, and conducting the beer-hall band). An overall average of $25 a day works for most. Don't skimp here. After all, this category is the driving force behind your trip—you came to sightsee, enjoy, and experience Germany and Austria.

Shopping and Miscellany: Figure $2 per postcard, coffee, beer, and ice-cream cone. Shopping can vary in cost from nearly nothing to a small fortune. Good budget travelers find that this category has little to do with assembling a trip full of lifelong and wonderful memories.

Germany and Austria:
Best Three-Week Trip by Car

Day	Plan	Sleep in
1	Fly into Frankfurt, to the Rhine	Bacharach
2	Rhine Valley	Bacharach
3	To Baden-Baden via the Mosel Valley	Baden-Baden
4	Relax and soak in Baden-Baden	Baden-Baden
5	Drive through the Black Forest	Staufen
6	To the Tirol	Reutte
7	Bavaria and castles	Reutte
8	To Hallstatt via Innsbruck and Hall	Hallstatt
9	Hallstatt and Salzkammergut Salzkammergut Lake District	Hallstatt
10	To Vienna via Schönbrunn Palace	Vienna
11	Vienna	Vienna
12	To Salzburg via Melk and Mauthausen	Salzburg
13	Salzburg	Salzburg
14	To Munich	Munich
15	Munich	Munich
16	To Rothenburg via the Romantic Road	Rothenburg
17	Rothenburg	Rothenburg
18	To Nürnberg	Nürnberg
19	To Dresden	Dresden
20	To Berlin	Berlin
21	Berlin	Berlin
22	Fly home	

Note: This itinerary is designed to be done by car, but could be done by train with some modifications: Take the train from Baden-Baden to Rothenburg, spend the night, take the train

When to Go

The "tourist season" runs roughly from May through September.

Summer has its advantages: best weather, snow-free alpine trails, very long days (light until after 21:00), and the busiest schedule of tourist fun.

Travel during "shoulder season" (May, June, Sept, and early Oct) is easier and a bit less expensive. Shoulder-season travelers get minimal crowds, decent weather, the full range of sights and tourist fun spots, and the ability to grab a room almost whenever and wherever they like—often at a flexible price. Also, in fall, fun harvest and wine festivals enliven many towns and villages.

to Munich, visit Bavaria and the castles (possibly as a day trip from Munich), see all of the Austrian sights (Salzburg, Hallstatt, Mauthausen, Melk) on the way to Vienna, and take a night train from Vienna to Berlin (skipping Dresden and Nürnberg).

Winter travelers find concert seasons in full swing, with absolutely no tourist crowds, but some accommodations and sights are either closed or run on a limited schedule. Confirm your sightseeing plans locally, especially when traveling off-season. The weather can be cold and dreary, and nightfall draws the shades on sightseeing well before dinnertime. You may find the climate chart in the appendix helpful.

Sightseeing Priorities

Depending on the length of your trip, and taking geographic proximity into account, the following are my recommended priorities.

Major Holidays and Weekends

Popular places are even busier on weekends, and holidays can bring many businesses to a grinding halt. Plan ahead and reserve your accommodations and transportation well in advance. Mark these dates in red on your travel calendar: New Year's Day, Easter (March 23 in 2008), Oktoberfest in Munich (Sept 20–Oct 5), Christmas, December 26, and New Year's Day. Also check the list of festivals and holidays on page 684 of the appendix.

3 days:	Munich, Salzburg
5 days, add:	Rhine Valley, Rothenburg
7 days, add:	Bavaria and Tirol
10 days, add:	Berlin
14 days, add:	Vienna, Hallstatt, Danube Valley
16 days, add:	Baden-Baden, Black Forest
More time:	Choose among Würzburg, Mosel Valley, Trier, Frankfurt, Köln, Nürnberg, Dresden, Görlitz, and Innsbruck/Hall.

(The itinerary and map on pages 4 and 5 include nearly everything on this list.)

Travel Smart

Your trip to Germany and Austria is like a complex play—easier to follow and to really appreciate on a second viewing. While no one does the same trip twice to gain that advantage, reading this book in its entirety before your trip accomplishes much the same thing.

Design an itinerary that enables you to visit the various sights at the best possible times. As you read this book, make note of festivals and when sights are closed. Saturday mornings are like weekday mornings, but at lunchtime, many shops close down through Sunday. Sundays have the same pros and cons as they do for travelers in the US (special events, limited hours, closed shops and banks, limited public transportation, no rush hours). Popular destinations are even more popular on weekends.

To give yourself a little rootedness, minimize one-night stands. It's worth a long drive after dinner to be settled into a town for two nights. B&Bs are also more likely to give a good price to someone staying more than one night.

Be sure to mix intense and relaxed periods in your itinerary. Every trip (and every traveler) needs at least a few slack days. Pace yourself. Assume you will return.

Reread this book as you travel, and visit local tourist information offices. Upon arrival in a new town, lay the groundwork for

Know Before You Go

Your trip is more likely to go smoothly if you plan ahead.

Since **airline carry-on restrictions** are always changing, visit the Transportation Security Administration's website (www.tsa.gov/travelers) for an up-to-date list of what you can bring on the plane with you...and what you have to check. Remember to arrive with plenty of time to get through security.

Call your **debit and credit card companies** to let them know the countries you'll be visiting, so that they'll accept (and not deny) your international charges. Confirm your daily withdrawal limit; consider asking to have it raised so you can take out more cash at each ATM stop.

Be sure that your **passport** is valid at least six months after your ticketed date of return to the US. If you need to get or renew a passport, it can take up to three months (for more on passports, see www.travel.state.gov).

Book your rooms well in advance if you'll be traveling during any major **holidays,** such as Oktoberfest (see "Major Holidays and Weekends," page 6). It's also smart to reserve rooms for your first night and during high season. Check if you'll be visiting **Frankfurt** and **Köln** during convention season (see page 214 and 305), and consider changing your dates in those cities to avoid peak prices.

To get tickets to **Neuschwanstein Castle,** email, go online, or phone ahead (a minimum of 24 hours before your visit) to avoid the long lines (see page 100 for tips).

For **Munich,** make a reservation in advance if you'd like a free BMW factory tour (see page 67).

Tickets for the music-packed **Salzburg Festival** (late July through August) can go fast. Consider buying tickets ahead if there's a specific event you want to see (for details, see page 586).

In **Vienna,** while there are always plenty of live **classical music** options available without advance booking, the major events can be booked out for weeks. While same-day standing-room tickets are sometimes available, booking will guarantee you a seat to see the **Lipizzaner Stallions** (see page 488), the **Vienna Boys' Choir** (see page 518), and performances at the **Opera** (see page 473).

If you're planning on **renting a car** in Austria, you're required to carry an International Driver's Permit (available at your local AAA office for $15 plus two passport photos; www.aaa.com). An International Driver's Permit is recommended, though not mandatory, for Germany.

Just the FAQs, Please

Whom do I call in case of emergency?
Dial 112 for police or medical emergencies in both Germany and Austria.

What if my credit card is stolen?
Act immediately. See "Damage Control for Lost Cards," page 664, for instructions.

How do I make a phone call to, within, and from Germany and Austria?
For detailed dialing instructions, refer to page 667.

How can I get tourist information about my destination?
Germany and Austria have national tourist information offices in the US (see page 659) and offices in virtually every destination covered in this book. Note that Tourist Information is abbreviated **TI** in this book.

What's the best way to pack?
Light. For a recommended packing list, see page 689.

Does Rick have other resources that could help me?
For more on Rick's guidebooks, public television series, free audiotours, public radio show, website, guided tours, travel bags, accessories, and railpasses, see page 660.

Are there any updates to this guidebook?
Check www.ricksteves.com/update for changes to the most recent edition of this book.

a smooth departure; write down the schedule for the train or bus you'll take when you depart.

Plan ahead for laundry, picnics, and Internet stops. Get online at Internet cafés or your hotel to research transportation connections, confirm events, check the weather, and get directions to your next hotel. Buy a phone card and use it for reservations, reconfirmations, and double-checking hours.

Connect with the culture. Enjoy the hospitality of the Germanic people. Slow down and ask questions—most locals are eager to point you in their idea of the right direction. Keep a notepad in your pocket for organizing your thoughts. Wear your money belt, and learn the local currency and how to estimate prices in dollars. Those who expect to travel smart, do.

PRACTICALITIES

Red Tape: You need a passport—but no visa or shots—to travel in Germany and Austria. Your passport must be valid for at least six months beyond the time you leave. Pack a photocopy of your

Can you recommend any good books or movies for my trip?
For suggestions, see pages 662–664.

Do you have information on driving, train travel, and flights?
See pages 674–684 in the appendix.

How much do I tip?
Relatively little. For tips on tipping, see page 665.

Will I get a student or senior discount?
While discounts are not listed in this book, some sights are discounted for seniors (loosely defined as those who are retired or willing to call themselves a senior), youths (ages 8–18), students, groups of 10 or more, and families.

How can I get a VAT refund on major purchases?
See the details on page 666.

Do Germany and Austria use the metric system?
Yes. A liter is about a quart, four to a gallon. A kilometer is six-tenths of a mile. I figure kilometers to miles by cutting them in half and adding back 10 percent of the original (120 km: 60 + 12 = 72 miles, 300 km: 150 + 30 = 180 miles). For more metric conversions, see page 686.

passport in your luggage in case the original is lost or stolen. Even as borders fade, when you change countries, you must still change telephone cards, postage stamps, and *Unterhosen*.

Time: In Europe—and in this book—you'll use the 24-hour clock. It's the same through 12:00 noon, then keep going: 13:00, 14:00, and so on. For anything over 12, subtract 12 and add p.m. (14:00 is 2:00 p.m.).

Germany and Austria, like most of continental Europe, is generally six/nine hours ahead of the East/West coasts of the US. The exceptions are the beginning and end of Daylight Saving Time: Europe "springs forward" the last Sunday in March (two weeks after most of North America), and "falls back" the last Sunday in October (one week before North America). For a handy online time converter, try www.timeanddate.com/worldclock.

Business Hours: Most stores throughout Germany and Austria are open from about 9:00 until 18:00–20:00 on weekdays, but close early on Saturday (generally between 12:00 and 17:00, depending on whether you're in a town or a big city), and are almost always closed on Sunday. By German law, stores must close by 22:00, but very few stay open that late, and some shutter their doors as early as 18:30. Laws in both countries make exceptions for shops in train stations, which often have grocery stores that are open daily until late.

Catholic regions, including Bavaria, shut down during religious holidays. Turkish-owned shops are often open later than other stores. Many museums and sights are closed on Monday.

Medical Help: If you get sick, do as the locals do and go to a pharmacist. They can help you with most any ailment. If a pharmacy is closed, a sign near the door indicates the nearest pharmacy that's open.

Watt's Up? Europe's electrical system is different from North America's in two different ways: the shape of the plug (two round prongs) and the voltage of the current (220 volts instead of 110 volts). For your North American plug to work in Europe, you'll need an adapter, sold inexpensively at travel stores in the US. As for the voltage, most newer electronics or travel appliances (such as hair dryers, laptops, and battery chargers) automatically convert the voltage—if you see a range of voltages printed on the item or its plug (such as "110–220"), it'll work in Europe. Otherwise, you can buy a converter separately in the US (about $20).

News: Americans keep in touch via the *International Herald Tribune* (published almost daily via satellite throughout Europe). Every Tuesday, the European editions of *Time* and *Newsweek* hit the stands with articles of particular interest to travelers. Sports addicts can get their daily fix online or from *USA Today*. Good websites include www.europeantimes.com and http://news.bbc.co.uk. Many hotels have CNN or BBC television channels available.

MONEY

Banking

Throughout Europe, cash machines (ATMs) are the standard way for travelers to get local currency. Bring plastic—credit and/or debit cards—along with several hundred dollars in hard cash as an emergency backup. It's smart to bring two cards, in case one gets demagnetized or eaten by a temperamental machine. Traveler's checks are a waste of time (long waits at slow banks) and a waste of money (in fees).

Cash from ATMs

To use a cash machine to withdraw money from your account, you'll need a debit card (ideally with a Visa or MasterCard logo for maximum usability), plus a PIN code. Know your PIN code in numbers; there are only numbers—no letters—on

---

Exchange Rate

I list prices in euros for Germany and Austria.

1 euro (€) = about $1.30

To convert prices in euros to dollars, add about 30 percent: €20 = about $26, €50 = about $65. Just like the dollar, the euro is broken down into 100 cents. You'll find coins ranging from 1 cent to 2 euros, and bills from 5 euros to 500 euros.

So that €65 German cuckoo clock is about $85, and the €90 taxi ride through Vienna is...uh-oh.

European keypads.

Before you go, verify with your bank that your card will work overseas, and alert them that you'll be making withdrawals in Europe; otherwise, the bank may not approve transactions if it perceives unusual spending patterns.

Try to take out large sums of money to reduce your per-transaction bank fees. If the machine refuses your request, don't take it personally. Just try again and select a smaller amount.

The German word for "cash machine" is *Bankomat* or *Geldautomat*. Many ATMs don't issue receipts with your transaction. In case you need a bank in Germany, they're generally open Monday through Friday 8:00 to 12:00 and 14:00 to 16:00; in Austria, Monday through Friday 8:00 to 15:00 and until 17:30 on Thursday.

Keep your cash safe. Thieves target tourists. Use a money belt—a pouch with a strap that you buckle around your waist like a belt, and wear under your clothes. A money belt provides peace of mind, allowing you to carry lots of cash safely. Don't waste time every few days tracking down a cash machine—withdraw a week's worth of money, stuff it in your money belt, and travel!

Credit and Debit Cards

For purchases, Visa and MasterCard are more commonly accepted than American Express. Just like at home, credit or debit cards work easily at larger hotels, restaurants, and shops, but smaller businesses prefer payment in local currency (in small bills—break large bills at a bank or larger store).

Credit and debit cards—whether used for purchases or ATM withdrawals—often come with additional, tacked-on "international transaction" fees of up to 3 percent plus $5 per transaction. To avoid unpleasant surprises, call your bank or credit-card company before your trip to ask about these fees.

Note that receipts show your credit-card number; don't toss

these thoughtlessly. If your cards are lost or stolen, see page 664 for advice on what to do.

SIGHTSEEING

Sightseeing can be hard work. Use these tips to make your visits to Germany and Austria's finest sights meaningful, fun, fast, and painless.

Plan Ahead

Set up an itinerary that allows you to fit in all your must-see sights. Most sights keep stable hours, but you can easily confirm the latest by checking with the local TI.

Don't put off visiting a must-see sight—you never know when a place will close unexpectedly for a holiday, strike, or restoration. If you'll be visiting during a holiday, find out if a particular sight will be open by phoning ahead or visiting its website.

When possible, visit key museums first thing (when your energy is best) and save other activities for the afternoon. Hit the highlights first, then go back to other things if you have the stamina and time.

Depending on the sight, there are ways to avoid crowds. This book offers tips on specific sights, such as Neuschwanstein Castle. Try visiting very early, at lunch, or very late. Evening visits are usually peaceful, with fewer crowds.

At the Sight

All sights have rules, and if you know about these in advance, they're no big deal.

Some important sights have metal detectors or conduct bag searches that will slow your entry.

Most museums require you to check daypacks and coats. They'll be kept safely. If you have something you can't bear to part with, stash it in a pocket or purse. If you don't want to check a small backpack, carry it under your arm like a purse as you enter. From a guard's point of view, a backpack is generally a problem while a purse is not.

Cameras are normally allowed, but not flashes or tripods (without special permission). Flashes damage oil paintings and distract others in the room. Even without a flash, a handheld camera will take a decent picture (or buy postcards or posters at the museum bookstore). Video cameras are usually allowed.

Some museums have special exhibits in addition to their permanent collection. Some exhibits are included in the entry price, while others come at an extra cost (which you may have to pay even if you don't want to see the exhibit).

Many sights rent audioguides, which generally offer excellent recorded descriptions of the art. If you bring along your own pair of headphones and a Y-jack, two people can sometimes share one audioguide and save. Guided tours (widely ranging in quality) are most likely to occur during peak season.

Expect changes—paintings can be on tour, on loan, out sick, or shifted at the whim of the curator. To adapt, pick up any available free floor plans as you enter, and ask museum staff if you can't find a particular painting.

Most important sights have an on-site café or cafeteria (usually a good place to rest and have a snack or light meal). The WCs are free and generally clean.

Museums have bookstores selling postcards and souvenirs. Before you leave, scan the postcards and thumb through the biggest guidebook (or skim its index) to be sure you haven't overlooked something that you'd like to see.

Most sights stop admitting people 30–60 minutes before closing time, and some rooms close early (generally about 45 minutes before the actual closing time). Guards usher people out, so don't save the best for last.

Every sight or museum offers more than what is covered in this book. Use the information in this book as an introduction—not the final word.

SLEEPING

I favor accommodations (and restaurants) handy to your sightseeing activities. Rather than list hotels scattered throughout a city, I choose two or three favorite neighborhoods and recommend the best accommodations values in each, from $17 bunk beds to fancy-for-my-book $250 doubles.

While accommodations in Germany and Austria are fairly expensive, they are normally very comfortable and come with breakfast. Plan on spending $100 to $140 per hotel double in big cities, and $50 to $80 in towns and in private homes.

A triple is much cheaper than a double and a single. While hotel singles are most expensive, B&Bs (called *Pensions*) have a flat per-person rate. Hostels and dorms always charge per person. Especially in private homes, where the boss changes the sheets, people staying several nights are most desirable. One-night stays are sometimes charged extra.

I look for places that are friendly; clean; a good value; located in a central, safe, quiet neighborhood; English-speaking; and not mentioned in other guidebooks. I'm more impressed by a handy location and a fun-loving philosophy than hair dryers and shoe-shine machines.

Sleep Code

(€1 = about $1.30)

To help you sort easily through these listings, I've divided the rooms into three categories based on the price for a standard double room with bath:

$$$ **Higher Priced**
$$ **Moderately Priced**
$ **Lower Priced**

To give maximum information in a minimum of space, I use the following code to describe the accommodations. Prices listed are per room, not per person. Unless otherwise noted, English is spoken and breakfast is included. You can assume a hotel takes credit cards unless you see "cash only" in the listing.

When there is a range of prices in one category, that means the price fluctuates with the season; the prices and seasons are posted at or near the hotel desk.

S = Single room (or price for one person in a double).
D = Double or twin. Double beds are usually big enough for nonromantic couples.
T = Triple (generally a double bed with a single).
Q = Quad (usually two double beds).
b = Private bathroom with toilet and shower or tub.
s = Private shower or tub only (the toilet is down the hall).

According to this code, a couple staying at a "Db-€85" hotel would pay a total of €85 (about $110) for a double room with a private bathroom and an included breakfast. The staff speaks English and credit cards are accepted.

I also like local character and simple facilities that don't cater to American "needs." Obviously, a place meeting every criterion is rare, and all of my recommendations fall short of perfection—sometimes miserably. But I've listed the best values for each price category, given the above criteria. The very best values are family-run places with showers down the hall and no elevator.

You should find most prices listed in this book to be good through 2008 (except for major holidays and festivals—see page 684). Prices can soften off-season, for stays of two nights or longer, or for payment in cash (rather than by credit card). Always mention that you found the place through this book—many of the hotels listed offer special deals to our readers.

Unless I note otherwise, the cost of a room includes a breakfast (sometimes continental, but often buffet). The price is usually posted in the room. Before accepting, confirm your understanding of the complete price.

B&Bs

Staying in a B&B *(Pension)* can be a great way to save money over sleeping in a bigger (and more expensive) hotel. Throughout Germany and Austria, people rent out rooms *(Zimmer)* in their homes to travelers. Look for *Zimmer Frei* or *Privat Zimmer* signs. These are very common in areas popular with travelers (such as Germany's Rhine, Romantic Road, and southern Bavaria, and Austria's Tirol and Salzburg). In Germany, signs will clearly indicate whether they have available rooms (green) or not (orange). Booking direct saves both you and your host the cut the TI takes.

You'll get your own key to a private room that's clean, comfortable, and simple, though usually homey. Some B&Bs are like mini-hotels, with a separate entrance and several rooms, each with a private bath. Other B&Bs are family homes with spare bedrooms (the rooms sometimes lack sinks, but you have free access to the bathroom and shower in the home). Most B&Bs include a hearty continental breakfast.

*Pension*s and *Gasthofs* are similarly priced small, family-run hotels. Don't confuse *Zimmer* with the German *Ferienwohnung*, which is a self-catering apartment rented out by the week or fortnight.

Making Reservations

Given the quality of the gems I've found for this book, I'd recommend that you reserve your rooms in advance, particularly if you'll be traveling during peak season. Book several weeks ahead, or as soon as you've pinned down your travel dates. Note that some holidays merit your making reservations far in advance (see "Major Holidays and Weekends" sidebar on page 6).

Some travelers make reservations as they travel, calling hotels or B&Bs a few days to a week before their visit. If you prefer the flexibility of traveling without any reservations at all, you'll have greater success snaring rooms if you arrive at your destination early in the day. When you anticipate crowds, call hotels at about 9:00 on the day you plan to arrive, when the hotel clerk knows who'll be checking out and just which rooms will be available.

To make a reservation in advance, contact hotels directly by email, phone, or fax. Email is the clearest and most economical way to make a reservation. In addition, many hotel websites now have online reservation forms. If phoning from the US, be mindful of time zones (see page 9). Most hotels listed are accustomed to English-only speakers.

To ensure you have all the information you need for your

reservation, use the form in this book's appendix (also at www .ricksteves.com/reservation).

When you request a room for a certain time period, use the European style for writing dates: day/month/year. Hoteliers need to know your arrival and departure dates. For example, for a two-night stay in July, I would request "2 nights, arrive 16/07/08, depart 18/07/08." Consider in advance how long you'll stay; don't just assume you can extend your reservation for extra days once you arrive.

If you don't get a reply to your email or fax, it usually means the hotel is already fully booked.

If the response from the hotel gives its room availability and rates, it's not a confirmation. You must tell them that you want that room at the given rate.

The hotelier will sometimes request your credit-card number for a one-night deposit. While you can email your credit-card information (I do), some people prefer to share that personal info via phone call, fax, or secure online reservation form (if the hotel has one on its website).

If you must cancel your reservation, it's courteous to do so with as much advance notice as possible (simply make a quick phone call or send an email). Family-run hotels and B&Bs lose money if they turn away customers while holding a room for someone who doesn't show up. Understandably, some hoteliers bill no-shows for one night. Hotels in larger cities such as Berlin sometimes have strict cancellation policies (for example, you might lose a deposit if you cancel within two weeks of your reserved stay, or you might be billed for the entire visit if you leave early); ask about cancellation policies before you book.

Always reconfirm your room reservation a few days in advance from the road. Most places will hold a room until 16:00, but if you'll be arriving later, let them know.

On the small chance that a hotel loses track of your reservation, bring along a hard copy of their emailed or faxed confirmation.

Camping and Hosteling

There are plenty of great campgrounds and I don't list any of them in this book. Campers can manage with Let's Go listings (see "Other Guidebooks," page 662) and help from the local TI (ask for a regional camping listing). Your hometown travel bookstore should also have guidebooks on camping in Europe. You'll find campgrounds just about everywhere you need them. Look for *Campingplatz* signs. You'll meet lots of Europeans—camping is a popular, middle-class-family way to go. Campgrounds are cheap ($6–10 per person), friendly, safe, more central and convenient than rustic, and rarely full.

Hostelers can take advantage of the wonderful network of hostels. Follow signs marked *Jugendherberge* (with triangles) or with the logo showing a tree next to a house. Generally, travelers without a membership card ($28 per year, sold at hostels in most US cities or online at www.hiusa.org, US tel. 202/783-6161) are admitted for an extra $5.

Hostels are open to members of all ages. For decades, Bavaria's official hostels were the only ones in Europe that enforced a maximum age limit of 26. But now, even this has been relaxed, and everyone is welcome (though some slow-to-change Bavarian hostels may still place some restrictions or charge slightly higher rates for older travelers). Hostel bunks usually cost $10–20 per night (cheaper for those under 27, plus $4 sheet rental if you don't have your own). Many hostels serve good, cheap meals and/or provide kitchen facilities. If you plan to stay in hostels, bring your own sheet. While many hostels have a few doubles or family rooms available upon request for a little extra money, plan on gender-segregated dorms with 4- to 20-beds per room. Hostels can be idyllic and peaceful, but school groups can raise the rafters. School groups are most common on summer weekends and on school-year weekdays. I like small hostels best. While many hostels may say over the telephone that they're full, most hold a few beds for people who drop in, or they can direct you to budget accommodations nearby.

EATING

Germanic cuisine is heavy, hearty, and—by European standards—inexpensive. Though it's tasty, it can get monotonous if you fall

into the schnitzel or wurst-and-potatoes rut. Be adventurous. Each region has its specialties, which, though not cheap, are often good values.

There are many kinds of restaurants. Hotels often serve fine food. A *Gaststätte* is a simple, less-expensive restaurant. For smaller portions, order from the *kleine Hunger* (small hunger) section of the menu.

Ethnic restaurants provide a welcome break from Germanic fare. Foreign cuisine is either the legacy of a crumbled empire (Hungarian and Bohemian, from which Austria gets its goulash and dumplings) or a new arrival to feed the many hungry-but-poor guest workers. Italian, Turkish, and Greek food are good values.

The cheapest meals are found in department-store cafeterias,

Schnell-Imbiss (fast-food) stands, university cafeterias *(Mensas)*, and hostels. For a quick, cheap bite, have a deli make you a *Wurstsemmel*—a meat sandwich. Especially in big cities, you'll see kiosks everywhere selling inexpensive *Döner Kebab*s (or just *Döner* for short)—a Turkish-style pita sandwich with chopped-up, slow-roasted meat (similar to a Greek gyro).

Most restaurants tack a menu onto their door for browsers and have an English menu inside. Only a rude waiter will rush you. Good service is relaxed (slow to an American). In Germany and Austria, you might be charged for bread you've eaten from the basket on the table; have the waiter take it away if you don't want it. To wish others "Happy eating!" offer a cheery *"Guten Appetit!"* When you want the bill, say, *"Zahlen* (TSAH-lenn), *bitte."* For tips on tipping, see page 665.

For most visitors, the rich pastries, wine, and beer provide the fondest memories of Germanic cuisine. The wine (85 percent white) from the Mosel, Rhine, and Danube river valleys and eastern Austria is particularly good. Order wine by the *Viertel* (quarter-liter, or 8 oz.) or *Achtel* (eighth-liter, or 4 oz.). You can say, *"Ein Viertel Weisswein* (white wine), *bitte* (please)." Order it *süss* (sweet), *halb trocken* (medium), or *trocken* (dry). *Rotwein* is red wine and *Sekt* is German champagne. Menus list drink size by the tenth of a liter, or deciliter (dl). Ask for a *Weinschorle* and you'll get a spritzer—white wine pepped up with a little sparkling water.

The Germans enjoy a tremendous variety of great beer. The average German, who drinks 40 gallons of beer a year, knows that *dunkles* is dark, *helles* is light, *Flaschenbier* is bottled, and *vom Fass* is on tap. *Pils* is barley-based, *Weizen* or *Hefeweizen* is wheat-based, and *Malzbier* is the malt beer that children learn with. *Radler* is half beer and half lemon-lime soda. When you order beer, ask for *eine Halbe* for a half-liter (not always available) or *eine Mass* for a whole liter (about a quart).

Tap water—which many waiters aren't eager to bring you—is *Leitungswasser.* They would rather you buy *Mineralwasser (mit/ohne Gas,* with/without carbonation). Popular soft drinks include *Apfelschorle* (half apple juice, half sparkling water) and *Spezi* (Coke and orange soda).

TRAVELING AS A TEMPORARY LOCAL

We travel all the way to Europe to enjoy differences—to become temporary locals. You'll experience frustrations. Certain truths that we find "God-given" or "self-evident," such as cold beer, ice in drinks, bottomless cups of coffee, hot showers, and bigger being better, are suddenly not so true. One of the benefits of travel is the eye-opening realization that there are logical, civil, and

---

How Was Your Trip?

Were your travels fun, smooth, and meaningful? If you'd like to share your tips, concerns, and discoveries, please fill out the survey at www.ricksteves.com/feedback. I value your feedback. Thanks in advance—it helps a lot.

---

even better alternatives.

Americans tend to be noisy in public places, such as restaurants and trains. My Germanic friends place a high value on speaking quietly in these same places. Listen while on the bus or in a restaurant—the place can be packed, but the decibel level is low. Try to remember this nuance, and soften your speaking voice as a way of respecting their culture.

If there is a negative aspect to the image Europeans have of Americans, it's that we are big, loud, aggressive, impolite, rich, superficially friendly, and a bit naive.

Given our reluctance to work with the world on climate change issues, Europeans don't respond well to Americans complaining about being too hot or too cold. Bring a sweater in winter, and in summer, be prepared to sweat a little like everyone else.

While Europeans look bemusedly at some of our Yankee excesses—and worriedly at others—they nearly always afford us individual travelers all the warmth we deserve. Judging from all the happy feedback I receive from travelers who have used this book, it's safe to assume you'll enjoy a great, affordable vacation—with the finesse of an independent, experienced traveler.

Thanks, and *gute Reise!*

BACK DOOR TRAVEL PHILOSOPHY
From *Rick Steves' Europe Through the Back Door*

Travel is intensified living—maximum thrills per minute and one of the last great sources of legal adventure. Travel is freedom. It's recess, and we need it.

Experiencing the real Europe requires catching it by surprise, going casual..."Through the Back Door."

Affording travel is a matter of priorities. (Make do with the old car.) You can travel—simply, safely, and comfortably—nearly anywhere in Europe for $100 a day plus transportation costs. In many ways, spending more money only builds a thicker wall between you and what you came to see. Europe is a cultural carnival, and, time after time, you'll find that its best acts are free and the best seats are the cheap ones.

A tight budget forces you to travel close to the ground, meeting and communicating with the people, not relying on service with a purchased smile. Never sacrifice sleep, nutrition, safety, or cleanliness in the name of budget. Simply enjoy the local-style alternatives to expensive hotels and restaurants.

Extroverts have more fun. If your trip is low on magic moments, kick yourself and make things happen. If you don't enjoy a place, maybe you don't know enough about it. Seek the truth. Recognize tourist traps. Give a culture the benefit of your open mind. See things as different but not better or worse. Any culture has much to share.

Of course, travel, like the world, is a series of hills and valleys. Be fanatically positive and militantly optimistic. If something's not to your liking, change your liking. Travel is addictive. It can make you a happier American as well as a citizen of the world. Our Earth is home to six and a half billion equally important people. It's humbling to travel and find that people don't envy Americans. Europeans like us, but, with all due respect, they wouldn't trade passports.

Globe-trotting destroys ethnocentricity. It helps you understand and appreciate different cultures. Regrettably, there are forces in our society that want you dumbed down for their convenience. Don't let it happen. Thoughtful travel engages you with the world—more important than ever these days. Travel changes people. It broadens perspectives and teaches new ways to measure quality of life. Rather than fear the diversity on this planet, travelers celebrate it. Many travelers toss aside their hometown blinders. Their prized souvenirs are the strands of different cultures they decide to knit into their own character. The world is a cultural yarn shop, and Back Door travelers are weaving the ultimate tapestry. Join in!

GERMANY

GERMANY

Deutschland

Deutschland is energetic, efficient, and organized—it's Europe's muscleman, both economically and wherever people line up (Germans have a reputation for pushing ahead). Its bustling cities hold 85 percent of its people, and average earnings are among the highest in the world. Ninety-seven percent of the workers get one-month paid vacations, and, during the other 11 months, they create a Gross Domestic Product (GDP) that's about one-quarter of the United States'. Germany has risen from the ashes of World War II to become the world's fifth-largest industrial power. Germany also shines culturally, beating out all but two countries in production of books, Nobel laureates, and professors.

Though its East–West division lasted about 40 years, historically Germany has been divided between north and south. Northern Germany was barbarian, is predominantly Protestant, and tackles life aggressively, while southern Germany was Roman, is largely Catholic, and enjoys a more relaxed tempo. The romantic American image of Germany is beer-and-pretzel Bavaria (probably because that was "our" sector after the war). This historic North–South division is less pronounced these days as Germany becomes a more mobile society. The big tasks facing Germany today include its continual efforts to revive the former East Germany and to strengthen the country's economy while maintaining its generous social services.

Germany's tourist route today—Rhine, Romantic Road, Bavaria—was yesterday's trade route, connecting its most thriving medieval cities. Germany as a nation is just 130 years old. In 1850, there were 35 independent countries in what is now Germany. In medieval times, there were 300, each with its own weights, measures, coinage, king, and lottery.

Many visitors can't help but associate Germany with its dark Nazi past. While a small neo-Nazi skinhead element still survives in the back alleys of German society, for the most part the nation has evolved into a surprisingly progressive, almost touchy-feely place. A genuine sense of shame and responsibility for World

Germany

War II and the Holocaust pervades much of German society, and the last few generations of German kids have been raised to fully understand their nation's destructive role in the 20th century. If you visit a concentration camp memorial, you'll likely see several field-trip groups of German teens, and other reminders of the Nazi chapter are everywhere: Imagine sitting down after dinner and watching *Schindler's List* or *Band of Brothers* on national TV... featuring your grandparents as the bad guys. As Germany leads the way in forming a healthy European Union—with peace, unity, tolerance, and human rights as its central motivations—it seems that most Germans are trying to make up for the ugliness their

Germany

Germany Almanac

Official Name: Bundesrepublik Deutschland, or simply Deutschland.

Population: Germany's 82 million people (four times the population of Texas) are largely of Teutonic DNA (90 percent), plus a small but significant minority (2.5 percent) of Turkish-descended citizens. A third of Germans are Catholic, a third Protestant, and a third unaffiliated or Muslim.

Latitude and Longitude: 51°N and 9°E. The latitude is similar to Alberta, Canada.

Area: At 138,000 square miles, Germany is slightly smaller than Montana and about half the size of Texas. It's bordered by nine countries.

Geography: The terrain gradually rises—from flat land in the north to the rugged Alps in the south, culminating in the 9,700-foot Zugspitze mountain. The climate is temperate.

Biggest Cities: The capital city of Berlin has 3.4 million people, followed by Hamburg's 1.7 million and Munich's 1.3 million.

Economy: With a GDP of $2.5 trillion—similar to America's Midwest states combined—Germany is Europe's largest economy. Still, the GDP per capita is $31,500, or about 25 percent less than America's. Their high-tech industries pump out iron and steel (ThyssenKrupp), cars (BMW, Daimler, Volkswagen), chemicals and drugs (Bayer), and global electronics (Siemens, T-Mobile/Deutsche Telekom). There are 1,280 breweries, but much of the production is consumed locally. Germany trades almost equally with a half-dozen neighboring countries, and the United States.

Since the 1990 reunification, Germany's economy has been burdened by the cost (about $70 billion a year) of integrating the

ancestors subjected Europe to not so long ago.

All over Germany (and much of Catholic Europe), you'll likely see written on doorways a mysterious message: "20 + C + M + B + 08." This is marked in chalk on Epiphany (January 6), the Christian holiday celebrating the arrival of the Magi to adore the newborn Baby Jesus. In addition to being the initials of the three wise men (Caspar, Melchior, and Balthazar), the letters also stand for the Latin phrase *Christus mansionem benedicat*—"May Christ bless the house." The little crosses separating the letters remind all who enter that the

former East Germany into the modern West. Germany's expensive social security system gets even costlier as the population ages. Thanks to powerful trade unions, workers get good benefits, but unemployment seems permanently fixed at 10 percent. Recently, the deficit has even exceeded the 3-percent-of-GDP level required to be a euro currency member.

Government: Germany's September 2005 elections were extremely close, with no single party, left or right, sweeping to victory. Conservative Chancellor Angela Merkel now heads a coalition government that leans slightly to the right. A small but powerful minority party, the Greens, presses the pro-environment agenda. Germany's chancellor, similar to the prime minister in other countries, is not elected directly by the people but is the head of the lead party in parliament. The less-powerful president (Horst Köhler) is also elected by parliament. The legislative branch includes the *Bundestag* (613 seats, elected by both direct and proportional representation) and the *Bundesrat* (69 votes by local officials of Germany's 16 states).

Flag: Deutschland's flag is composed of three horizontal bands of (starting from the top) black, red, and gold.

The Average *Deutsche*: The average German is 42 years old—six years older than the average American—has 1.39 kids, and will live to be almost 79. He or she lives in a household with two other people, watches 2.5 hours of TV a day, spends 20 minutes reading the daily newspaper, and says the word *der* more often than any other word. The average German drinks a pint of beer every 32 hours, which is slightly less than the average Irish or Czech.

house has been blessed in this year (20+08). Epiphany is a bigger deal in Catholic Europe than in the US. The holiday includes gift-giving, feasting, and caroling door to door—often collecting for a charity organization. Those who donate get their doors chalked up as in thanks, and these marks are left on the door through the year.

Germans eat lunch and dinner about when we do. Order house specials whenever possible. Pork, fish, and venison are good, and don't miss the bratwurst and sauerkraut. Potatoes are the standard vegetable, but *Spargel* (giant white asparagus) is a must in-season (early summer). The bread and pretzels in the basket on your table often cost extra. When I need a break from pork, I order the *Salatteller* (big, varied dinner-size salad). Great beers and white wines abound. Go with whatever beer is on tap.

Gummi bears are local gumdrops with a cult following (look for the Haribo brand), and Nutella is a chocolate-hazelnut spread that may change your life.

When it comes to drink, the Germans enjoy an embarrassment of riches. In addition to being famous for their excellent brew and rowdy beer halls, Germany is also known for its fine wine—from the sweet, white "Rhine wines" to some good reds. For more on German consumption, see page 17 in this book's Introduction.

Germany

MUNICH

München

Munich, Germany's most livable and "yuppie" city, is also one of its most historic, artistic, and entertaining. It's big and growing, with a population of 1.3 million. Until 1871, it was the capital of an independent Bavaria. Its imperial palaces, jewels, and grand boulevards constantly remind visitors that this was once a political and cultural powerhouse. And its straightforward, somewhat sterile street plan reminds us that 75 years ago it provided a springboard for Nazism, and 60 years ago it lost a war. Today, Munich is a city of the 21st century, but still respects its past—in 2008, the city celebrates its 850th birthday, with the theme "Building Bridges" (with a summer full of festivities, including three separate festivals: June 14–15, July 19–20, and August 1–3).

Orient yourself in Munich's old center with its colorful pedestrian mall. Immerse yourself in Munich's art and history—crown jewels, Baroque theater, Wittelsbach palaces, great paintings, and beautiful parks. Munich evenings are best spent in frothy beer halls, with their oompah, bunny-hopping, and belching Bavarian atmosphere. Pry big pretzels from buxom, no-nonsense beer maids.

Planning Your Time

Munich is worth two days, including a half-day side-trip to Dachau. If necessary, its essence can be captured in a day (walk the center, tour a palace and a museum, and enjoy a beer-filled evening). Those in a hurry and without a car can see "Mad" King Ludwig's castles (covered in the Bavaria and Tirol chapter) as a day trip from Munich by tour. Even Salzburg (1.5–2 hours one-way by train) is within day-tripping distance.

ORIENTATION

(area code: 089)

The tourist's Munich is circled by a ring road (site of the old town wall) marked by four old gates: Karlstor, also known as Stachus (near the main train station—the Hauptbahnhof), Sendlinger Tor, Isartor (near the river), and Odeonsplatz (no surviving gate, near the palace). Marienplatz marks the city's center. A great pedestrian-only zone (Kaufingerstrasse and Neuhauserstrasse) cuts this circle in half, running nearly from Karlstor and the train station through Marienplatz to Isartor. Orient yourself along this east–west axis. Ninety percent of the sights and hotels I recommend are within a 20-minute walk of Marienplatz and each other.

Despite its large population, Munich feels small. This big-city elegance is possible because of a law that no building can be taller than the church spires. Despite ongoing debate about changing this policy, there are still no skyscrapers in downtown Munich.

Tourist Information

Munich has two outlets for tourist information: the official TIs, and the handy travel agency called EurAide.

Official TIs

Munich has two helpful TIs (www.muenchen-tourist.de). One is in front of the **main train station** (with your back to the tracks, walk through the central hall, step outside, and turn right; April–Oct Mon–Sat 9:00–20:00, Sun 10:00–18:00; Nov–March Mon–Sat 9:00–18:30, Sun 10:00–18:00; tel. 089/233-0300). The other TI is on Munich's main square, **Marienplatz,** below the glockenspiel (Mon–Fri 10:00–20:00, Sat 10:00–16:00, closed Sun).

At either TI, pick up brochures and a city map (€0.30, often free in hotel lobbies) and confirm your sightseeing plans. Consider the *Monatsprogramm* (€1.65, German-language list of sights and events calendar) and the free, twice-monthly magazine *In München* (in German, lists all movies and entertainment in town). The TI can book you a room (you'll pay about 15 percent here, then pay the rest at the hotel), but you'll get a better value with my recommended hotels—contact them directly. If you're interested in a Panorama/Gray Line tour of the city or to nearby castles (described on page 34), don't buy your ticket at the TI; instead, buy discounted tickets for these same tours at EurAide (see next section).

The **City Tour Card,** which covers public transportation and stingy sightseeing discounts on minor sights, is a bad deal (€10/1 day, €19/3 days, available at TIs or EurAide, validate before using). Two or more people traveling on a Munich "partner" all-day transit pass blow this deal out of the water (see "Getting Around

Munich," page 31).

If the line at the TI is bad, go to EurAide.

EurAide

The industrious, eager-to-help EurAide office in the main train station is a godsend for Eurailers and budget travelers (June–Sept

daily 7:45–12:45 & 14:00–18:00; Oct–May Mon–Fri 8:00–12:00 & 13:00–16:00, closed Sat–Sun; with your back to track 19, head toward the main entrance, and turn left before the pretzel stand down the hallway—the EurAide office is on the left; tel. 089/593-889, fax 089/550-3965, www .euraide.com, see www.euraide.com /ricksteves for Rhine cruise schedules and other useful information). EurAide sells a €0.50 city map and offers a free, information-packed newsletter, *The Inside Track* (described on page 31; it's always available in a rack at their door).

EurAide helps 600 visitors per day in the summer; do your homework, have a list of questions ready, and keep in mind that they're busiest in the morning. Chances are that your questions are already answered by their *Inside Track* newsletter—scan it first. Alan Wissenberg and his EurAide staff know your train-travel and accommodations questions and have answers in clear American English. The German rail company pays them to help you design your train travels, and they make reservations and sell tickets, *couchettes*, and sleepers for the train at the same price as at the station ticket windows.

EurAide also sells tickets for Panorama/Gray Line city tours (see page 34), as well as for tours to Neuschwanstein and Linderhof castles (see page 38). EurAide offers a discount on these tickets with this book in 2008.

Arrival in Munich

By Train: Munich's main train station (Hauptbahnhof) is a sight in itself—one of those places that can turn an accountant into a fancy-free vagabond. Expansion of the S-Bahn subway system in 2008 could turn the main hall into a construction site, but trains won't be affected.

For a quick rest stop, Burger King's toilets (upstairs, €0.30) are as pleasant and accessible as its hamburgers. More toilets are downstairs near track 26 (clean, but €1.10). Check out the bright and modern complex of **restaurants** and shops opposite track 14. For a quick train picnic, I shop at **Yorma's,** by track 26 and outside the station, next to the TI. The **k presse + buch** shop (across from track 23) is great for English-language books, newspapers, and magazines, including *Munich Found* (informative English-speaking residents' monthly, €3). You'll find two **tourist information** offices (the city TI and EurAide—see "Tourist Information" above) and **lockers** (€2, at tracks 18, 26, and 31). **Car-rental agencies** are up the steps opposite track 21 (Mon–Fri 7:00–21:00, Sat–Sun 8:00–17:00). A **pharmacy** is out the front door to the left, at the corner of Luisenstrasse and Elisenstrasse (Mon–Fri 8:00–19:00, Sat 9:00–14:00, closed Sun, tel. 089/595-444). A quiet, non-smoking **waiting room** *(Warteraum)* is open to anybody (across from track 23 and up the escalator), but the nearby, plush **DB Lounge** is only for those with a first-class ticket issued by DeutscheBahn (railpasses don't get you in).

Subway lines, trams, and buses connect the station to the rest of the city (though many of my recommended hotels are within walking distance of the station). If you get lost in the underground maze of subway corridors while you're simply trying to get to the train station, follow the signs for *DB* (DeutscheBahn) to surface successfully. Watch out for the hallways with blue ticket-stamping machines in the middle—these lead to the subway, where you could be fined if nabbed without a validated ticket.

By Plane: There are two good ways to connect Munich Airport and downtown Munich: subway or airport bus. You can take an easy 40-minute ride on the S-1 or S-8 **subway,** which runs every 20 minutes between the airport and Marienplatz (€9, or free with a validated and dated railpass). Or hop on the Lufthansa **airport bus,** which links the airport with the main train station (€10, 3/hr, 45 min, buses depart train station 5:10–19:50, buy tickets on bus; at the station, buses line up near taxi stands facing Arnulfstrasse—from inside the station, exit near track 26). Airport info: tel. 089/97500, www.munich-airport.de.

Helpful Hints

Museum Hours: The Alte Pinakothek, Munich City Museum, Jewish Museum, Pinakothek der Moderne, Lenbachhaus, Glypothek, Bavarian National Museum, Beer and Oktoberfest Museum, and Dachau Concentration Camp are closed on Monday. The Neue Pinakothek closes Tuesday. The art galleries are generally open late one night a week. On Sunday, the Pinakotheks and Bavarian National Museum cost just €1 apiece, but you'll pay extra for the usually free audioguides.

Useful Phone Numbers: Pharmacy—tel. 089/595-444 (Mon–Fri 8:00–19:00, Sat 9:00–14:00, closed Sun, near train station on the corner of Luisenstrasse and Elisenstrasse); EurAide train info—tel. 089/593-889; American Express—tel. 089/2280-

1465 (no train tickets, Mon–Fri 9:30–17:30, Sat 9:30–12:30, closed Sun, near Karlsplatz at Promenadeplatz 6); Taxi—tel. 089/21610.

Internet Access: There's plenty of online access in Munich. **EasyInternetcafé** dominates the scene, with great rates and an ideal location near the train station (open 24 hours daily, 500 terminals and a convenient phone center with cheap international rates, opposite station's main entrance at Bahnhofplatz 1). **Munich Walk**'s offices also offer Internet access (on Marienplatz at Weinstrasse 6, and near Isartor at Thomas-Wimmer-Ring 1—look for *Tourist info* sign, tel. 089/2423-1767).

Laundry: A handy self-service **Waschcenter** is a 10-minute walk from the train station (€6.50/15 lbs, €11/25 lbs, drop-off service for €8–16 depending on load size, daily 7:00–23:00, English instructions, Paul-Heyse-Strasse 21, near intersection with Landwehrstrasse, tel. 089/531-311).

Bikes and Pedestrians: Signs painted on the sidewalk or blue-and-white street signs show which side of the sidewalk is designated for pedestrians and which is for cyclists. The strip of pathway closest to the street is usually reserved for bikes. Pedestrians wandering into the bike path may hear the cheery ding-ding of a cyclist's bell just before being knocked unconscious by a local biker.

Private Driver: Johann Fayoumi is reliable and speaks English (€50/hr, mobile 0174-183-8473, johannfayoumi@gmail.com).

Car Rental: Several car-rental agencies are located upstairs at the train station, opposite track 21 (Mon–Fri 7:00–21:00, Sat–Sun 9:00–17:00).

The Inside Track **Train Travelers' Newsletter:** Anyone traveling by train should pick up this wonk-ish yet brilliant quarterly newsletter published by Alan Wissenberg at EurAide (free, always available in a rack by the EurAide door—see EurAide listing under "Tourist Information," above). You'll find all the tedious but important details on getting to Neuschwanstein, Dachau, Nymphenburg, and Prague; the ins and outs of supplements and reservations necessary for railpass-holders; a daily schedule of various tours in Munich; and (of course) plenty of tips on how to take advantage of EurAide's services.

What's with Monaco? People walking around with guidebooks to Monaco aren't lost. "Monaco" means "Munich" in *Italiano*.

Getting Around Munich

Much of Munich is walkable. To reach sights away from the city center, use the efficient tram, bus, and subway systems. Taxis are honest and professional, but expensive and generally unnecessary (except perhaps to avoid the time-consuming trip by tram and foot to Nymphenburg Palace).

By Public Transit

Subways are called U-Bahns or S-Bahns (actually an underground-while-in-the-city commuter railway). Subway lines are numbered (for example, S-3 or U-5). Eurailpasses are good on the S-Bahn (but not the U-Bahn), but if you use a flexipass, it'll cost you a travel day.

The entire system (bus/tram/subway) works on the same tickets, sold at TIs and in the subway at booths and easy-to-use ticket machines (which take coins and €5 and €10 bills). There's a wide array of ticket types. A **regular ticket** *(Einzelfahrkarte)* costs €2.20 and is good for two hours in one direction, including changes. For the shortest rides (1 or 2 stops, no transfer), buy the €1.10 *Kurzstrecke* ("short stretch") ticket. The €5 **all-day pass** *(Single Tageskarte)* is a great deal for a single traveler. For small groups, the €9 **partner** all-day pass *(Partner Tageskarte)* is an even better deal—it covers all public transportation for up to five adults and a dog (two kids count as one adult, so two adults, six kids, and a dog can travel with this ticket). The **XXL ticket** includes the extended transportation network, which covers the trip to Dachau Concentration Camp (€6.70/1 person, €11.80/partner ticket). For longer stays, consider a **three-day ticket** (€12.30/1 person, €21/partner ticket for the gang), but be aware that the three-day ticket does not include transportation to Dachau. All-day and multi-day passes are valid until 6:00 the following morning.

Partner tickets—while seemingly impossibly cheap—are for real. Read it again and do the arithmetic. Even two people traveling together save money. And for groups, it's a real steal. The only catch is you've got to stay together.

You must stamp your ticket with the date and time prior to using it (for all-day or multi-day passes, you only have to stamp it the first time you use it). For the subway, punch your ticket in the blue machine *before* going down to the platform. For buses and trams, stamp your ticket once on board. Plainclothes ticket-checkers enforce this honor system, rewarding freeloaders with stiff €40 fines. For more information, call tel. 089/4142-4344 or see www.mvv-muenchen.de. There's a transit customer service center at Marienplatz (Mon–Fri 9:00–20:00, Sat 9:00–16:00, closed Sun, underground—directly beneath Beck's department store).

Important: All S-Bahn lines connect the Hauptbahnhof (main station) with Marienplatz (main square). If you want to use the S-Bahn and you're either at the station or at Marienplatz, follow signs to the S-Bahn (U is not for you), and concern yourself

Central Munich

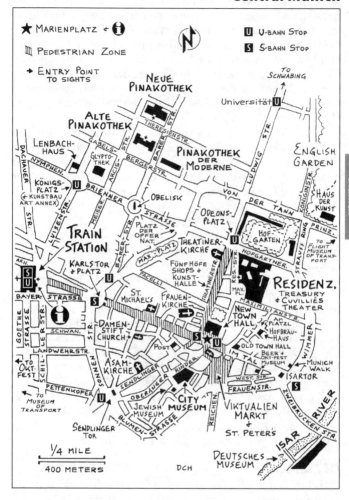

★ MARIENPLATZ + ⓘ

▥ PEDESTRIAN ZONE

➔ ENTRY POINT TO SIGHTS

Ⓤ U-BAHN STOP

Ⓢ S-BAHN STOP

Munich

only with the direction (Hauptbahnhof/Pasing or Marienplatz). "Direction" in German is *Richtung*.

By Bike

Level, compact, and featuring plenty of bike paths, Munich feels good on two wheels. You can rent bikes quickly and easily at the train station from **Radius Tours,** which offers a 10 percent discount on rentals to my readers with this book in 2008 (city bikes–€3/hr, €14.50/day, €17/24 hrs, €25/48 hrs, mountain bikes 25 percent more, €50 cash or credit-card deposit, ask about self-guided bike-tour info, mid-April–mid-Oct daily 9:30–18:00, closed in bad weather mid-Oct–mid-April, in front of track 32, tel. 089/596-113, www .radiusmunich.com). At the other end of the tourist zone (near the river and Isartor), **Munich Walk** also rents bikes (€3/hr, €15/24 hrs, 2-hour minimum, open daily 24 hours, near Isartor at Thomas-Wimmer-Ring 1, storefront says *Tourist info*, tel. 089/2423-1767, www.munichwalktours.de). Both outfits have maps and good advice, and both offer bike tours (mentioned below). Also see the "Bikes and Pedestrians" warning under "Helpful Hints," page 30.

For a longer trip, consider this great day on a bike: English Garden to Olympic Park, then along the canal to Nymphenburg Palace, around the palace grounds, and back to the center (in 30 min) via Arnulfstrasse, which has a bike path the entire way. Or consider the Isar River bike ride described on page 68.

TOURS

Munich has three major tour companies. **Panorama/Gray Line** specializes in bus tours of the city and to the Bavarian castles of "Mad" King Ludwig (Neuschwanstein and Linderhof; tel. 089/5490-7560, www.msr-muc.de; you'll get a discount on these tours if you buy tickets at EurAide—see "Tourist Information" earlier in this chapter). The two other major companies compete directly with each other, offering walking tours, bike tours, and day trips to Dachau Concentration Camp and Neuschwanstein Castle. In my experience, they're comparable: **Radius Tours** (office in the main train station, in front of track 32, tel. 089/5502-9374, www .radiusmunich.com) and **Munich Walk** (near Isartor at Thomas-Wimmer-Ring 1, tel. 089/2423-1767, www.munichwalktours.de). Both Radius Tours and Munich Walk offer €1 off any of their walking tours with this book in 2008.

Of Munich

Walking Tours—**Radius Tours** runs two city walking tours daily April through October (fewer tours off-season): "Munich Highlights" (at 10:00, 2 hours) and "Hitler and the Third Reich" (at 15:00, 2.5 hours). Their guides are reliably good. Each tour costs €10 and departs from the Radius office (in front of track 32 at the train station). There's no need to register—just show up. They also offer an educational "Bavarian Beer and Food" tour that includes a visit to the Beer and Oktoberfest Museum (see page 47), samples of five varieties of the sudsy stuff, and regional food (€22; Tue, Thu, and Sat at 18:00; also Fri at 18:00 mid-April–mid-Oct; 3 hours).

Munich Walk offers similar walks: a "City Walk" (€10, May–mid-Oct daily at 10:45 and 14:45) and "Hitler's Munich" tour (€10, April–Oct daily at 10:00; fewer tours off-season). Their

"Beer and Brewery" tour (like the Radius Tour version, above) is more mature than your typical hard-partying pub crawl. You visit Munich's oldest brewery to learn, eat, and drink in the city that made beer famous. The price includes three different beers, and ends at the Hofbräuhaus—or at Oktoberfest if you time it right (€17, May–mid-Sept daily at 18:15, fewer tours off-season, 3.5 hours). All Munich Walk tours depart from under the glockenspiel on Marienplatz; no reservations are necessary.

New Munich advertises free walking tours. This youthful outfit (which started with the same guerilla business plan in Berlin) has an irreverent, boisterous approach to walking tours—it's basically an hour of entertainment sprinkled with some historical "facts." The first basic tour is free (although you'll be hit up for tips, as that's how their guides are paid). They sell the other standard Munich tours. Their nightly pub crawl offers a fun way to make drunken friends from around the world. For details, see their free magazine (all over town) or go to www.newmunich.com.

Local Guides—I've had great days with three good guides, each charging the same prices (€110/2 hrs, €130/3 hrs): **Georg Reichlmayr,** tel. 08131/86800, mobile 0170-341-6384, www.muenchen-stadtfuehrung.de, info@muenchen-stadtfuehrung.de), **Monika Hank** (tel. 089/311-4819, monika.hank@web.de), and **Renate Suerbaum** (mobile 0179-205-7759, renate@suerbaum.de). They helped me with much of the historical information in this chapter, and Georg was my sidekick on the Munich episode of my public television series.

Bike Tours—**Mike's Bike Tours,** popular with the college crowd, are four-hour frat parties on wheels. The tours are slow-paced and the guides are better comedians than historians, but you do ride through the English Garden (€24, tips encouraged, bikes provided, 1-hour break in Chinese Tower beer garden, at least 1 tour daily, mid-April–Aug at 11:30 and 16:00, March–mid-April and Sept–mid-Nov at 12:30, no need to reserve, meet under tower of Old Town Hall on Marienplatz; for schedule, call tel. 089/651-4275 or mobile 0172-852-0660, visit www.mikesbiketours.com, or pick up brochure at TI). **Munich Walk** also offers a bike tour (€22/3.5 hrs, April–Oct daily at 11:15), and is unique in offering private guided bike tours to small groups at any time (€22 per person for groups of at least four). Team up with a small gang, then call 089/2423-1767 and set a date.

Quickie Orientation City Bus Tour—**Panorama/Gray Line Tours** offers many itineraries, including one-hour orientation bus tours (departs from Hertie department store, Elisenstrasse 3, directly in front of train station). This tour is actually well worthwhile—sitting upstairs on the topless double-decker bus, you'll see lots of things missed by the typical visitor wandering around

Munich at a Glance

In the Center

▲▲▲**Deutsches Museum** Germany's version of our Smithsonian Institution, with 10 miles of science and technology exhibits. **Hours:** Daily 9:00–17:00. See page 60.

▲▲**Marienplatz** Munich's main square, at the heart of a lively pedestrian zone, watched over by New Town Hall (and its glockenspiel show). **Hours:** Always open; glockenspiel jousts daily at 11:00 and 12:00, plus 17:00 May–Oct. See page 39.

▲▲**Hofbräuhaus** World-famous beer hall, worth a visit even if you're not chugging. **Hours:** Daily 9:00–24:00. See page 46.

▲▲**Residenz Museum** The elegant family palace of the Wittelsbachs, awash with Bavarian opulence. **Hours:** Daily April–mid-Oct 9:00–18:00, mid-Oct–March 10:00–16:00. See page 48.

▲▲**Residenz Treasury** One thousand years of Wittelsbach family crowns and royal knickknacks. **Hours:** Daily April–mid-Oct 9:00–18:00, mid-Oct–March 10:00–16:00. See page 51.

▲▲**Alte Pinakothek** Bavaria's best painting gallery, with a wonderful collection of European masters from the 14th through the 19th centuries. **Hours:** Tue–Sun 10:00–18:00, Tue until 20:00, closed Mon. See page 53.

▲**Viktualienmarkt** Munich's "small-town" open-air market, perfect for a quick snack or meal. **Hours:** Mon–Sat, *Biergarten* open until late, closed Sun. See page 44.

▲**Munich City Museum** The city's history in five floors. **Hours:** Tue–Sun 10:00–18:00, closed Mon. See page 47.

▲**Neue Pinakothek** The Alte's twin sister, with paintings from 1800 to 1920. **Hours:** Thu–Mon 10:00–18:00, Wed 10:00–20:00, closed Tue. See page 56.

▲**Pinakothek der Moderne** Hip contemporary-art museum near the Alte and Neue Pinakotheks—with a building as interesting as the art. **Hours:** Tue–Sun 10:00–18:00, Thu until 20:00, closed Mon. See page 57.

▲**Lenbachhaus** Collection of Blaue Reiter (Blue Rider) Expressionism. **Hours:** Tue–Sun 10:00–18:00, closed Mon. See page 57.

▲**English Garden** The largest city park on the Continent, packed with locals, tourists, surfers, and nude sunbathers. (I'd rate this ▲▲ on a bike.) **Hours:** Always open. See page 58.

▲**Beer and Oktoberfest Museum** Charming medieval house with exhibit exploring Munich's brewing tradition and the story behind its world-famous annual party. **Hours:** Tue–Sat 13:00–17:00, closed Sun–Mon. See page 47.

St. Michael's Church Renaissance church housing Baroque decor and a crypt of 40 Wittelsbachs. **Hours:** Church—daily 9:00–19:00, Thu until 21:00 and Sun until 22:00; crypt—Mon–Fri 9:30–16:30, Sat 9:30–14:30, closed Sun, less off-season. See page 40.

Frauenkirche Huge, distinctive twin-domed church looming over the city center. **Hours:** Church—daily 7:00–19:00; tower climb—April–Oct Mon–Sat 10:00–17:00, closed Sun and Nov–March. See page 40.

St. Peter's Church Munich's oldest church, packed with relics. **Hours:** Church—long hours daily; spire climb—Mon–Fri 9:00–18:30, Sat–Sun 10:00–18:30, off-season until 17:30. See page 41.

Away from the Center

▲▲**Nymphenburg Palace** The Wittelsbachs' impressive summer palace featuring a hunting lodge, coach museum, fine royal porcelain collection, and vast park. **Hours:** Daily April–mid-Oct 9:00–18:00, mid-Oct–March 10:00–16:00. See page 63.

▲▲**Dachau Concentration Camp** Notorious Nazi camp on the outskirts of Munich, now a powerful museum. **Hours:** Tue–Sun 9:00–17:00, closed Mon. See page 69.

▲**Museum of Transportation** Deutsches Museum annex devoted to travel. **Hours:** Daily 9:00–17:00. See page 61.

▲**Olympic Park** Munich's 1972 Olympic stadium, now a lush park with a view tower and swimming pool. **Hours:** Grounds always open; tower daily 9:00–24:00, pool daily 7:00–23:00. See page 67.

▲**Andechs Monastery** Baroque church, hearty food, and Bavaria's best brew, in the countryside near Munich. **Hours:** *Biergarten* open daily 10:00–22:00, last meal order 20:00, church open until 18:00. See page 69.

the center. It complements the information in this book beautifully. The live guide narrates in German and English. Just show up and pay the driver, or get a small discount (of €1–2) by picking up your ticket in advance at EurAide. Choose from a basic, one-hour "Express Circle" that heads past the Pinakotheks, Marienplatz, and Karlsplatz; or the more interesting "Grand Circle" that lasts 90 minutes longer and also includes the Nymphenburg Palace, Olympia Park, and the Schwabing neighborhood (€13 Express tour, €18 Grand tour, daily in season on the hour 10:00–17:00, tel. 089/5502-8995, www.sightseeing-munich.com).

From Munich

"Mad" King Ludwig's Castles—Two spectacular Bavarian castles, Neuschwanstein and Linderhof, make a logical day trip from Munich. For more on these destinations, see the Bavaria and Tirol chapter.

Panorama/Gray Line Tours offers rushed all-day bus tours of the two castles that also include 30 minutes in Oberammergau (€49, discount with this book in 2008 if you buy your ticket at EurAide, castle admissions-€15 extra, daily April–Oct, no tours Mon Nov–March). In summer, it's wise to purchase tickets a day ahead. Tours meet at 8:10 and depart at 8:30 from the Hertie department store (across from the station). While **Munich Walk** advertises a similar tour, they're simply selling tickets for this Panorama/Gray Line trip.

Radius Tours runs all-day tours to Neuschwanstein Castle by train (€32 with this book in 2008, €25 with railpass, castle admission-€9 extra, departs daily mid-April–Sept at 9:30 from in front of track 32 at train station, you're home by 19:00, book ahead; Oct–mid-April tours run Mon, Wed, and Sat at 10:30; tel. 089/5502-9374, www.radiusmunich.com). This tour is basically an escort on public transportation (not really necessary, but it allows you to avoid the ticket line at the castle if you don't have a reservation—see "Neuschwanstein Castle" in the Bavaria chapter, page 98).

Dachau Concentration Camp—Radius Tours offers English-language-only tours of the camp year-round (€21 includes the €6.70 cost of public transportation, €3 discount with this book in 2008; June–July Tue–Sun at 9:15, 11:00, and 12:30; April–May and Aug–mid-Oct Tue–Sun at 9:15 and 12:30; mid-Oct–March Tue–Sun at 11:00; no tours Mon, when camp is closed; depart from Radius office in Munich station—in front of track 32, it's smart to confirm times, but you can just show up, allow 5 hours round-trip). **Munich Walk** does a similar tour (€21 includes €6.70 transport costs, May–Oct Tue–Sun at 10:20 and 13:15, Nov–March Tue–Sun at 10:30, April Tue–Sun at 13:15, no tours Mon). While several other companies do Dachau tours, only Radius, Munich Walk, and New Munich are allowed to actually guide inside the camp.

SIGHTS AND ACTIVITIES

Central Munich

▲▲**City Views**—Downtown Munich's three best city viewpoints (all described in this section) are from the tops of: St. Peter's Church (stairs only), Frauenkirche (stairs plus elevator), and New Town Hall (elevator).

▲▲**Marienplatz and the Pedestrian Zone**—Riding the escalator out of the subway into sunlit Marienplatz ("Mary's Square")

gives you a fine first look at the glory of Munich: great buildings bombed flat and rebuilt, outdoor cafés, and people bustling and lingering like the birds and breeze with which they share this square. Notice the ornate facades of the gray, pointy Old Town Hall and the Neo-Gothic New Town Hall, with its beloved glockenspiel.

The **New Town Hall** (Neues Rathaus), built from 1867 until 1906, dominates the square. Munich was a very royal city. Notice the politics of the statuary. The 40 statues—though sculpted only in 1900— decorate New Town Hall not with civic leaders, but with royals and blue-blooded nobility. Because this building survived the bombs and had a central location, it served as the US military headquarters in 1945.

The New Town Hall is famous for its **glockenspiel**—only 100 years old—which "jousts" daily at 11:00 and 12:00 all year (also

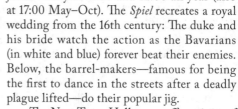

at 17:00 May–Oct). The *Spiel* recreates a royal wedding from the 16th century: The duke and his bride watch the action as the Bavarians (in white and blue) forever beat their enemies. Below, the barrel-makers—famous for being the first to dance in the streets after a deadly plague lifted—do their popular jig.

The New Town Hall tower offers **views** of the city (€2, elevator from under glockenspiel, Mon–Fri 9:00–19:00, Sat–Sun 10:00–19:00, tearoom; possibly still closed after 2007 renovation).

Marienplatz is marked by a statue of the **Virgin Mary,** moved here in 1638 from its original location in the Frauenkirche out of thanks that the Swedes didn't sack the town during their occupation. It was also a rallying point for the struggle against the Protestants. The cherubs are fighting against the four great biblical enemies of civilization: war, hunger, disease, and the wrong faith. The serpent represents the "wrong faith," a.k.a. Martin Luther.

The **Old Town Hall** (Altes Rathaus; at the right side of square as you face New Town Hall) was completely destroyed by WWII bombs and later rebuilt. Ludwig IV, an early Wittelsbach who was Holy Roman Emperor (back in the 14th century), stands in the center of the facade. He donated this great square to the people. On the bell tower, find the city seal with its monk and towers. Munich flourished because, in its early days, all salt trade had to stop here on Marienplatz.

Back at Marienplatz, the **pedestrian mall** (Kaufingerstrasse and Neuhauserstrasse) leads you through a great shopping area, past carnivals of street entertainers and good old-fashioned slicers and dicers, the towering twin-domed Frauenkirche (built in 1470, rebuilt after WWII), and several fountains, to Karlstor and the train station. As one of Europe's first pedestrian zones, the mall enraged shopkeepers when it was built in 1972 for the Olympics. Today, it is Munich's living room. Nearly 9,000 shoppers pass through it each hour. The shopkeepers are happy...and merchants nearby are begging for their streets to become traffic-free. Imagine this street in hometown USA.

Three Churches near Marienplatz—In the pedestrian zone around Marienplatz are three noteworthy churches: St. Michael's, the Frauenkirche, and St. Peter's. Each was heavily bombed in World War II, and each displays photos of that destruction near its entrance. To locate these churches: As you face New Town Hall, St. Michael's is a few blocks down the pedestrian street to your left; the Frauenkirche is the big twin-domed church at 10 o'clock; and St. Peter's is over your right shoulder.

St. Michael's Church, while one of the first great Renaissance buildings north of the Alps, has a brilliantly Baroque interior. The crypt contains 40 stark royal tombs, including the resting place of King Ludwig II, the "mad" king still loved by Romantics (church entry free, daily 9:00–19:00, Thu until 21:00, Sun until 22:00; crypt-€2, Mon–Fri 9:30–16:30, Sat 9:30–14:30, closed Sun, less off-season; frequent concerts—check the schedule outside).

The twin onion domes of the 500-year-old **Frauenkirche** (Church of Our Lady) are the symbol of the city. While much of the church was destroyed during World War II (see photos just inside the entrance, on the right), the towers survived and the rest has been gloriously restored (free, daily 7:00–19:00). It was built in Gothic style, but money problems meant the domes weren't added until Renaissance times. Late-Gothic buildings in Munich were generally built of brick—easy to make locally and cheaper and faster to use than stone. This church was constructed in a remarkable 20 years.

It's located on the grave of Ludwig IV (who died in 1348). His big, black, ornate tomb (now in the back) was originally in front at the high altar. Standing in the back of the nave, notice how your eyes go right to the altar...Christ...and (until recently) Ludwig. Those Wittelsbachs—always trying to be associated with God. In fact, this alliance was instilled in people through the prayers they were forced to recite: "Virgin Mary, mother of our duke, please protect us."

You can ascend the tower for the city's highest public viewpoint, at 280 feet (€3, 86 steps to elevator, April–Oct Mon–Sat 10:00–17:00, closed Sun and Nov–March). On many Wednesday evenings in summer, you can catch an organ concert here (€8, 19:00, tickets available at München Ticket office inside Marienplatz TI).

St. Peter's Church, the oldest in town, overlooks Marienplatz from its perch near the Viktualienmarkt. It's built on the hill where Munich's original monastic inhabitants probably settled. Outside, notice the old tombstones plastered onto the wall—a reminder that in the Napoleonic age, the cemeteries surrounding most city churches were (for hygienic and practical space reasons) dug up and moved. Inside, check out the photos of the bomb damage (near the entrance). Then look at the marvelously restored altar and ceiling frescoes—possible with the help of Nazi catalog photos (see "Munich Bombed" page 46).

Munich has more relics than any city outside of Rome. For more than a hundred years, it was the pope's bastion against the rising tide of Protestantism in northern Europe during the Reformation. Favors done in the defense of Catholicism earned the Wittelsbachs neat relic treats. For instance, check out the tomb of Mundita (second side chapel on left as you enter). She's a second-century martyr whose remains were given to Munich by Rome as thanks and a vivid reminder that those who die for the cause of the Roman Church go directly to heaven without waiting for Judgment Day.

It's a long climb to the top of the spire (306 steps, no

The History of Munich

Born from Salt (1100–1500)

Munich began in the 12th century when Henry the Lion (Heinrich der Löwe) muscled in on the lucrative salt trade, burning a rival's bridge over the Isar River and building his own near a monastery of "monks"—München. (The town's coat of arms features the Münchner Kindl, a boy in monk's robes, though these days, he's portrayed by a young woman.) Henry built walls and towers, opened a market, and peasants flocked in from the countryside. Marienplatz—then as now—was the center of town, and the crossroads of the Salzstrasse (Salt Road) from Salzburg to Augsburg.

After Henry's death, the town was taken over by an ambitious merchant family, the Wittelsbachs (1240), and became the capital of the region (1255). Munich-born Louis (or Ludwig) IV (1282–1347) was elected king of Germany and Holy Roman Emperor, temporarily making Munich a major European capital. (See Ludwig IV's tomb in the Frauenkirche, page 41, and his statue on the Altes Rathaus, page 40.)

By the 1400s, Munich's maypole-studded market bustled with trade. Besides salt, Munich gained a reputation for beer. Over 30 breweries pumped out the golden liquid that lubricated trade and traders. The Bavarian Beer Purity Law assured quality control. Wealthy townspeople erected the twin-domed Frauenkirche and the Altes Rathaus on Marienplatz, and the Wittelsbachs built a stout castle that would eventually become the cushy Residenz. When the various regions of Bavaria united in 1506, Munich (pop. 14,000) was the natural capital.

Religious Wars, Plagues, Decline (1500–1800)

While Martin Luther and the Protestant Reformation raged in northern Germany, Munich became the ultra-Catholic heart of the Counter Reformation. The devout citizens poured enormous funds into building the massive St. Michael's Church (1583) as a home for the Jesuits, and into the Residenz (early 1600s) as home of the Wittelsbachs. Both were showpieces of conservative power and the Baroque and Rococo styles.

During the Thirty Years' War, the Catholic city was surrounded by Protestants (1632). The Wittelsbachs surrendered quickly and paid a ransom, sparing the city from pillage, but it was soon hit by the bubonic plague. After it passed, the leaders erected the Virgin's column on Marienplatz to thank God for only killing 7,000 citizens. (Munich's many plagues are also remembered today when the glockenspiel's barrel-makers do their daily dance to ward off the plague.)

The double whammy of invasion and plague left Munich bankrupt and powerless, overshadowed by the more powerful

Hapsburgs of Austria. The Wittelsbachs took their cultural cues from France (Nymphenburg Palace is a mini-Versailles), England (the English Garden), and Italy (the Pitti Palace–inspired Residenz). While the rest of Europe modernized and headed towards democracy, Munich remained conservative and backward.

The Kings—Max I, Ludwig I, Max II, Ludwig II (1800–1900)

When Napoleon's army of French revolutionaries surrounded the city (1800), the Wittelsbachs once again surrendered hospitably. Napoleon rewarded the Wittelsbach "duke" with more territory and a royal title—"king." Maximilian I (r. 1806–1825) now ruled the Kingdom of Bavaria, an independent nation bigger than Switzerland, with a constitution and a parliament. When Max's popular son Ludwig got married (September 1810), it touched off a two-week celebration that became an annual event—Oktoberfest.

As king, Ludwig I (r. 1825–1848) set about rebuilding the capital in the Neoclassical style we see today. He tore down the medieval walls and ramshackle houses and replaced them with grand buildings of columns and arches (including the Residenz and Alte Pinakothek, to house the family's paintings). Connecting these were broad boulevards and plazas for horse carriages and promenading citizens (Ludwigstrasse and Königsplatz). Ludwig established the university and built the first railway line, making Munich (pop. 90,000) a major transportation hub and budding industrial city.

In 1846, the skirt-chasing King Ludwig (see the Nymphenburg's Gallery of Beauties, page 65) came under the spell of a notorious Irish dancer named Lola Montez. He made her his mistress and fawned over her in public, scandalizing Munich. The Münchners resented the way she spent their tax money and dominated their king (she supposedly inspired the phrase "Whatever Lola wants, Lola gets"). In 1848, when all of Europe was swept by a tide of revolution, the citizens rose up and forced Ludwig to abdicate. His son Maximilian II (r. 1848–1864) continued Ludwig's enlightened program of rebuilding and modernizing while studiously avoiding Spanish dancers from Ireland.

In 1864, 18-year-old Ludwig II (r. 1864–1886) became king. He immediately invited the composer Richard Wagner to Munich, planning a lavish new opera house to stage Wagner's operas. Munich did not like the idea, and Ludwig did not like Munich. For most of his reign, Ludwig avoided the Residenz and Nymphenburg and lived in the Bavarian countryside building castles at Munich taxpayer expense. (For more on "Mad" King Ludwig II, his castles, and his mysterious death, see page 99.)

(continued on next page)

The History of Munich *(continued from previous page)*

In 1871, Bavaria became part of the newly united Germany and, overnight, Berlin overtook Munich as Germany's power center. But turn-of-the century Munich was culturally rich, birthing the abstract art of Wassily Kandinsky, Paul Klee, and the Blue Rider group.

Wars, Nazis, Rebuilding (1900–2000)

World War I devastated Munich. Poor, hungry, disillusioned, unemployed Münchners roamed the streets. Extremists from the left and right battled for power. In 1918, a huge mob marched to the gates of the Residenz and drove the Wittelsbachs out of the city, ending nearly 800 years of continuous rule. In quick succession, the prime minister was gunned down, Communists took power, and the army restored the old government. In the chaos, one fringe group emerged—the Nazi party, centered around the charismatic war veteran Adolf Hitler.

Hitler—an Austrian who'd settled in Munich—made stirring speeches in Munich's beer halls (including the Hofbräuhaus) and galvanized the city's disaffected. On November 8–9, 1923, the Nazis launched a coup d'état known as the Beer Hall Putsch. They kidnapped the mayor, and Hitler led a mob to overthrow the German government in Berlin. The march got as far as Odeonsplatz before Hitler was arrested and sent to prison in nearby Landsberg. Though the Nazis eventually gained power in Berlin, they remembered their roots, dubbing Munich "Capital of the Movement." The Nazi headquarters stood near today's

elevator)—much of it with two-way traffic on a one-lane staircase—but the view is dynamite (€1.50, Mon–Fri 9:00–18:30, Sat–Sun 10:00–18:30, off-season until 17:30, last exit 30 min after closing). Try to be two flights from the top when the bells ring at the top of the hour, and then, when your friends back home ask you about your trip, you'll say, "What?"

▲**Viktualienmarkt**—Early in the morning, you can still feel small-town Munich here, long a favorite with locals for fresh produce and good service (open Mon–Sat, food stalls open late, closed Sun). The most expensive real estate in town could never really support such a market, but the town charges only a percentage of the gross income, enabling these old-time shops to carry on (and keeping fast-food chains out).

obelisk on Brienner Strasse, Dachau was chosen as the regime's first concentration camp, and Odeonsplatz was designated as a place where all who passed by were required to make the Nazi salute.

During World War II, Munich was pummeled mercilessly by air raids, leveling nearly half the city. After the war, with generous American aid, the Münchners rebuilt. Unlike other German cities, Munich took care to preserve the original street plan and recreate the medieval steeples, Neo-Gothic facades, and Neoclassical buildings. They blocked off the city center to cars, built the people-friendly U-Bahn system, and opened up Europe's first pedestrian-only zone (Kaufingerstrasse and Neuhauserstrasse).

The 1972 Olympic Games, featuring a futuristic stadium and a squeaky-clean city, were to be Munich's postwar statement that it had arrived. However, the Games turned tragic when a Palestinian terrorist group stormed a dormitory and kidnapped (and eventually killed) 11 Israeli athletes. In 1989, when Germany reunited, Berlin once again became the focal point of the country, relegating Munich to the role of sleepy Second City.

Today's Munich is rich—home to BMW and Siemens, and a producer of software, books, movies, and the latest fashions. It's consistently voted one of Germany's most-livable cities—safe, clean, cultured, a university town, built on a people scale, and close to the beauties of nature. Though it's the capital of Bavaria and a major metropolis, Munich's low-key atmosphere has led Germans to dub it *Millionendorf*—the "village of a million people."

The huge maypole is a tradition. Fifteenth-century town market squares posted a maypole decorated with various symbols to explain which crafts and merchants were doing business in the market. Munich's maypole shows the city's six great brews and the crafts and festivities associated with brewing. (You can't have a kegger without coopers—find the merry barrel-makers.)

Munich's breweries each take turns here—notice the beer counter. Changing every day or two, a sign *(Heute im Ausschank)* announces which of the six Munich beers is being served. Here, unlike at other *Biergartens*, you can order half a liter (for shoppers who want to have a quick sip and then keep on going).

The Viktualienmarkt is ideal for a light meal (see page 82). Or, for a more expensive selection, try the...

Alois Dallmayr Delicatessen—When the king called out for dinner, he called Alois Dallmayr. As you enter, read the black plaque with the royal seal by the door: *Königlich Bayerischer Hof-Lieferant* ("Deliverer for the King of Bavaria and his Court"). This place

Munich Bombed

As World War II drew to a close, it was clear that Munich would be destroyed. Hitler did not allow the evacuation of much of the town's portable art treasures and heritage—a mass emptying of churches and civil buildings would have caused hysteria and been a statement of no confidence in his leadership. While museums were closed (and could be systematically emptied over the war years), public buildings were not. Rather than save the treasures, the Nazis photographed everything. What the bombs didn't get was destroyed by 10 years of rain and freezing winters. The first priority after the war was to get roofs over the ruined buildings. Only now, more than 60 years after the last bombs fell, are the restorations—based on those Nazi photographs—finally being wrapped up.

Shortly after World War II, German cities established commissions to debate how they'd rebuild their cities: restoring the old towns or bulldozing and going modern. While Frankfurt voted to bulldoze (hence its Manhattan-like feel today), Munich voted—by a close margin—to rebuild its old town. Buildings cannot exceed the height of the church spires. Today, Munich has no real shopping malls. Instead, its downtown is vital, filled with people who come to shop.

became famous for its exotic and luxurious food items: tropical fruits, seafood, chocolates, fine wines, and coffee. Catering to royal and aristocratic tastes (and budgets), it's still the choice of Munich's old rich. Today, it's most famous for its coffee, dispensed from fine hand-painted Nymphenburg porcelain jugs (Mon–Sat 9:30–19:00, closed Sun, Dienerstrasse 14, behind New Town Hall).

▲▲**Hofbräuhaus**—Whether or not you slide your lederhosen on its polished benches, it's a great experience just to see the world's most famous beer hall in all its rowdy glory. As you wander, look for the following: Various *Stammtisch* signs (meaning "reserved") hang above tables where different clubs meet regularly; don't sit here unless you're specifically invited. Racks of locked steins, made of pottery and metal, are for regulars. You'll see locals stuffed into lederhosen and dirndls; giant gingerbread cookies that sport romantic messages; and postcards of the new German (and apparently beer-drinking) pope. The men's room has two dozen urinals around a vomitorium. The bouncer at the door nabs 20 to 50 people (mostly Italians, he says) trying to steal mugs as souvenirs. The staircase to the left of the entrance displays historic old Hofbräuhaus photos and prints (daily 9:00–24:00, live oompah music during lunch and dinner, a 5-min walk northeast of Marienplatz at Platzl 6). For more details, see page 81.

▲**Beer and Oktoberfest Museum (Bier- und Oktoberfest-museum)**—Get a frothy take on history at this charming new museum, where exhibits and interesting artifacts outline the centuries-old quest for the perfect beer (apparently perfected in Munich) and the origins of the city's Oktoberfest celebration. The oldest house in the city center, the museum's home is noteworthy in itself, with the same old beams and low, low doorways that it's had since 1347. If friendly, lederhosened Lukas—who runs the place—can fit through those doorways, anyone can. The museum also has its own restaurant...which serves beer, of course (€4; museum open Tue–Sat 13:00–17:00, closed Sun–Mon; restaurant open Tue–Sat 17:00–24:00, closed Sun–Mon; between Isartor and Viktualienmarkt at Sterneckerstrasse 2, tel. 089/2423-1607, www.bier-und-oktoberfestmuseum.de).

▲**Munich City Museum (Münchner Stadtmuseum)**—Five floors of exhibits tell the story of life in Munich through the centuries (including the history of "monk culture," the development of National Socialism, and WWII), illustrated with paintings, photos, and models. As it underwent an extensive renovation in 2007, prices and times could change (probably €4, free on Sun, open Tue–Sun 10:00–18:00, closed Mon, few English descriptions, no crowds, bored and playful guards, 3 blocks off Marienplatz at St.-Jakobs-Platz 1, tel. 089/2332-2370, www.stadtmuseum-online.de). The museum's Stadt Café is handy for a good meal (see page 86).

Jewish History Museum (Jüdisches Museum München)—Munich's new Jewish History Museum anchors a revitalized Jewish quarter, which includes a synagogue, kindergarten and day school, children's playground, kosher restaurant, and bookstore. The cube-shaped museum's small permanent exhibit, one floor underground, focuses on Jewish life in Munich. While there's not much to see, what's there is well presented. The two floors of temporary exhibits, always very Munich-specific, might justify the entry fee—check to see what's on (€6, Tue–Sun 10:00–18:00, closed Mon, across the street from the Munich City Museum at St.-Jakobs-Platz 16, tel. 089/96096, www.muenchen.de/juedisches-museum).

Rococo Churches—Near the Munich City Museum, the private church of the Asam brothers **(Asamkirche)** is a gooey, drippy, Baroque-concentrate masterpiece by Bavaria's top two Rococonuts. A few blocks away, the small **Damenstift Church** has a sculptural rendition of the Last Supper so real that you feel you're not alone (at intersection of Altheimer Ecke and Damenstiftstrasse, a block south of the pedestrian street).

The Residenz

For a long hike through corridors of gilded imperial Bavarian grandeur, tour the Wittelsbachs' family palace (largely rebuilt after World War II). The Wittelsbachs, who ruled Bavaria for more than 700 years, modeled the front of their enormous palace on the Medici family's Pitti Palace in Florence. The sprawling place evolved from the 14th through the 19th centuries—as you'll see on the charts near the entrance. Whatever happened to the Wittelsbachs, the longest continuously ruling family in European history? They're still around—but since they're no longer royalty, most of them have real jobs now.

Cost, Hours, Location: €6 each to visit the Residenz Museum (palace apartments) and the Treasury, including audioguides; the €9 combo-ticket covers both and is valid all day, so you can leave the building for lunch and come back. The Halls of the Nibelungen are free. All parts of the palace are open daily April–mid-Oct 9:00–18:00, mid-Oct–March 10:00–16:00, last entry 30 min before closing. The complex is located three blocks north of Marienplatz.

Information: Your ticket includes a free English audioguide. For more in-depth information, consider the €10 English guidebook, but don't bother with the dry €3 version. Tel. 089/290-671, www.schloesser.bayern.de.

Orientation: While impressive, the Residenz can be confusing for visitors. Enter the complex from the main entrance on Max-Joseph-Platz (at the corner of the palace nearest Marienplatz) or from the entrance on Residenzstrasse. Just inside the main entrance are the Halls of the Nibelungen (free) and the ticket booth for the Residenz Museum and the Treasury (which are located in separate wings, but share the same ticket booth).

Halls of the Nibelungen (Nibelungensäle)—The mythological scenes in these fascinating halls were the basis of Wagner's *Der Ring des Nibelungen*. Wagner and "Mad" King Ludwig were friends and spent time hanging out here (c. 1864). These very images could well have inspired Wagner to write his *Ring* and Ludwig to build his "fairy-tale castle," Neuschwanstein. Even if you're not touring the rest of the Residenz, note that these rooms are free to enter.

▲▲Residenz Museum (Residenzmuzeum)—This museum includes the most spectacular halls and private apartments in the Wittelsbachs' palace complex. It's the best place to get a glimpse of the opulent lifestyle of Bavaria's late, great royal family.

❸ Self-Guided Tour: Since it's so big, different sections of the Residenz Museum are open in the mornings and in the afternoons (after 13:30 in summer, 12:30 in winter). Leave the ticket office to your right (without going back outside), and follow the *Rundgang* signs. This self-guided tour is designed to coincide with the afternoon route (a little more interesting than the morning). Due to ongoing renovations, either tour route can change without notice. To help you find the highlights, I have numbered the rooms as they appear on the official map (free at entry), though be warned the rooms themselves aren't all numbered.

Shell Grotto (Room 6, actually outside, ground floor): This artificial grotto was an exercise in man controlling nature—a celebration of humanism.  Renaissance humanism was a big deal when this was built in the 1550s. Imagine the ambience here during that time, with Mercury—the pre-Christian god of trade and business—overseeing the action, and red wine spurting from the mermaid's breasts and dripping from Medusa's head in the courtyard. The strange structure is made from Bavarian freshwater shells. This palace was demolished by WWII bombs. After the war, people had no money to contribute to the reconstruction—but they could gather shells. All the shells you see here were donated by small-town Bavarians as the grotto was rebuilt according to Nazi photos (see "Munich Bombed" sidebar, page 46). To the right of the shells, the door marked *OO* leads to public toilets.

Antiquarium (Room 7, ground floor): In the mid-16th century, Europe's royal families (such as the Wittelsbachs) collected  and displayed busts of emperors—implying a connection between themselves and the ancient Roman rulers. Given the huge demand for these Classical statues in the courts of Europe, many of the "ancient busts" are fakes cranked out by crooked Romans. Still, a third of the statuary you see here is original. This was, and still is, a festival banquet hall. Two hundred dignitaries can dine here, surrounded by allegories of the goodness of just rule on the ceiling. Notice the small paintings around the room—these survived the bombs because they were painted in arches. Of great historic interest, these paintings show 120 Bavarian villages as they looked in 1550. Even today, when a Bavarian historian wants a record of how his village once looked, he comes here. Notice the town of Dachau in 1550 (above the door on the right as you leave).

Gallery of the Wittelsbach Family (Room 4, ground floor): This room is from the 1740s (about 200 years younger than the Antiquarium). All official guests had to pass through here to meet the duke. The family tree in the center is labeled "genealogy of an imperial family." A big Wittelsbach/Hapsburg rivalry was worked out through 500 years of marriages and wars—when weddings failed to sort out a problem, they had a war. Opposite the tree are portraits of Charlemagne and Ludwig IV, each a Holy Roman Emperor and each wearing the same crown (now in Vienna). Ludwig IV was the first Wittelsbach HRE—an honor used for centuries to substantiate the family's claim to power. You are surrounded by a scrapbook covering 738 years of the Wittelsbach family.

Allied bombs took their toll on this hall. Above, the central ceiling painting is restored, but since there were no photos of the other two ceiling paintings, those spots remain empty. On the walls, notice how each painting was hastily cut out of its frame. Museums were closed in 1939 and would gradually be evacuated in anticipation of bombings. But public buildings like this palace could not prepare for the worst. Only in 1944, when bombs were imminent, was the last-minute order given to slice each portrait out of its frame and hide them all away.

Nymphenburg Porcelain (Room 5, at the end of the family gallery, ground floor): In the 18th century, a royal family's status was bolstered by an in-house porcelain works (like Meissen for the Wettins in Dresden). The Wittelsbach family had their own Nymphenburg porcelain made for the palace. Notice how the mirrors give the effect of infinite pedestals with porcelain vases. If this inspires you to own some Nymphenburg porcelain, it's for sale at the Nymphenburg boutique at Odeonsplatz (see "Shopping," page 73).

Reliquary (Room 95, upper floor, often closed in the morning): Meet St. John the Baptist and his mother, Elizabeth (#47 and #48—skulls on jeweled pillows). The case in the center contains skeletons of three babies from the slaughter of the innocents in Bethlehem (when Herod, in an attempt to kill the baby Jesus, ordered all sons of a certain age killed).

Chapel (ground-floor Room 89, but also viewable from upper-floor room 96, likely closed in the morning): Dedicated to Mary, this late-Renaissance/early-Baroque gem was the site of "Mad" King Ludwig's funeral after his mysterious murder—or suicide—in 1886. (He's buried in St. Michael's Church; see page 40.) While Ludwig was not popular in the political world, he was beloved by his people, and the funeral drew huge crowds. "Mad" King Ludwig's grandfather (Ludwig I) was married here in 1810. After the wedding ceremony, carriages rolled his guests to a rollicking reception, which turned out to be such a hit that it became an annual tradition—Oktoberfest.

Private Chapel of Maximilian I (Room 98, upper floor, probably closed in the morning): Maximilian I, the dominant

Bavarian figure in the Thirty Years' War, built one of the most precious rooms in the palace. The miniature pipe organ (from about 1600) still works. The room is sumptuous, from the gold leaf and the fancy hinges to the stucco marble. (Stucco marble is fake marble—a special mix of stucco, applied and polished. Designers liked it because it was less expensive than real marble and the color could be controlled.) Note the post-Renaissance perspective tricks decorating the walls; they were popular in the 17th century.

Precious Rooms (Rooms 55–62, upper floor): The Wittelsbachs were always trying to keep up with the Hapsburgs, and this long string of ceremonial rooms was all for show. The decor and furniture are Rococo. The family art collection, now in the Alte Pinakothek, once decorated these walls. The bedroom (Room 60) was the official sleeping room, where the duke would publicly go to bed and awaken, à la Louis XIV.

Red Room (Room 62, upper floor): The ultimate room is at the end of the corridor—the coral red room from 1740. (Coral red was *the* most royal of colors in Germany.) Imagine visiting the duke and having him take you here to ogle at miniature copies of the most famous paintings of the day, painted with one-haired brushes. Notice the fun effect of the mirrors around you—the corner mirrors make things go forever and ever.

▲▲**Residenz Treasury (Schatzkammer)**—The Treasury, next door to the Residenz, shows off a thousand years of Wittelsbach crowns and knickknacks. Vienna's jewels are better, but this is Bavaria's best, with fine 13th- and 14th-century crowns and delicately carved ivory and glass (for cost and hours, see page 48).

⊙ **Self-Guided Tour:** A long clockwise circle through the eight rooms takes you chronologically through a thousand years of royal treasure. (It's a one-way system—getting lost is not an option.) Your ticket includes an English audioguide, but I've explained the highlights below.

The oldest jewels in the first room are 200 years older than Munich itself. Many of these came from various prince-bishop collections when they were secularized (and their realms came under the rule of the Bavarian king from Munich) in the Napoleonic Era (c. 1800). The tiny mobile altar allowed a Carolingian king (from Charlemagne's family of kings) to pack light in 890—and still have a little Mass while on the road.

In Room 3, study the reliquary with St. George killing the dragon—sparkling with more than 2,000 precious stones (#58). Get up close (it's OK to walk around the rope posts)...you can almost hear the dragon hissing. It was made to contain the relics of St. George, who never existed (Pope John Paul II declared him nothing more than a legend). If you could lift the miniscule visor, you'd see that the carved ivory face of St. George is actually the Wittelsbach duke (the dragon represents the "evil" forces of Protestantism).

In the next room (#4), notice the vividly carved ivory crucifixes from 1630 (#157 and #158, on the right). These incredibly realistic sculptures were done by local artist Georg Petel, a friend of Peter Paul Rubens (whose painting of Christ on the cross—which you'll see across town in the Alte Pinakothek—is Petel's obvious inspiration). Look at the flesh of Jesus' wrist pulling around the nails.

Continue into Room 5. The freestanding glass case (#245) holds the never-used royal crowns of Bavaria. Napoleon ended the Holy Roman Empire and let the Wittelsbach family rule as kings of Bavaria. As a sign of friendship, this royal coronation gear was made in Paris by the same shop that made Napoleon's crown. But before the actual coronation, Bavaria joined in an all-Europe anti-Napoleon alliance, and suddenly these were too French to be used.

Cuvilliés Theater—Attached to the Residenz is the Cuvilliés Theater, dazzling enough to send you back to the days of divine monarchs. It's been under renovation, but is due to reopen in the summer of 2008—ask at the TIs or ticket desk for more information.

Near the Residenz

Hofgarten—The elegant people's state garden (Hofgarten) is a delight on a sunny afternoon. The "Renaissance" temple center-piece has great acoustics (and usually a musician performing for tips from lazy listeners). The lane leads to a building that houses the government of Bavaria and the Bavarian war memorial, which honors the fallen *heroes* of  World War I, but only the *fallen* of World War II. The venerable old **Café Tambosi**—with a Viennese elegance inside and a relaxing garden setting outside—is a good antidote to all the beer halls (daily 8:00–24:00, Odeonsplatz 18, tel. 089/298-322).

Getting There: To get to the Hofgarten, face the Residenz entrance, then go left around the Residenz one long block to the palace's original entryway (flanked by the second set of lions—rub their noses for good luck) and enter the complex. After the first arch, bear left across the courtyard and cut through the entry of the Egyptian collection into the park.

Odeonsplatz and Nearby—This square near the Hofgarten is a part of the grand, imperial Munich vision. The church on

Odeonsplatz (Theatinerkirche) contains nearly all the Wittelsbach tombs. The loggia in the Hofgarten (honoring Bavarian generals) is modeled in the Florentine Renaissance style. A Roman-type triumphal arch hovers in the distance to the north (at the end of Ludwigstrasse). And to the west, a grand axis (Brienner Strasse) heads towards the Greek-inspired museum quarter.

Brienner Strasse: From Odeonsplatz, look (or wander) down

Brienner Strasse to get a taste of the Wittelsbachs' ambitious city planning. At Karolinenplatz, the black obelisk commemorates the 30,000 Bavarians who marched with Napoleon to Moscow and never returned. Beyond that is the grand Königsplatz, or "King's Square," with its stern Neoclassicism, evocative of ancient Greece (and home to Munich's cluster of art museums, described below).

On the way to this imperial splendor, Brienner Strasse goes through a square called **Platz der Opfer des Nationalsozialismus** ("Square of the Victims of Nazism"). Nearby, you'll find two former Nazi administration buildings; one is now the music academy, though it's still very much fascist in its architecture. A plaque on the street explains the buildings' history.

Munich's Cluster of Art Museums

This cluster of blockbuster museums (Alte, Neue, and Moderne Pinakotheks; Lenbachhaus; Glyptothek; and Brandhorst) displays art spanning from the 14th century to modern times. The Glyptothek and Lenbachhaus are on Königsplatz, while the three Pinakothek museums and the Brandhorst sit around a grassy square just to the northeast. The Pinakotheks are a 10-minute walk from the nearest U-Bahn stops, but handy tram #27 whisks you right there from Karlsplatz (near the train station).

▲▲Alte Pinakothek

Bavaria's best painting gallery (the "Old Art Gallery," pronounced ALL-tuh pee-nah-koh-TAYK) shows off a world-class collection of European masterpieces from the 14th to 19th centuries, starring the two tumultuous centuries (1450–1650) when Europe went from medieval to modern. See paintings from the Italian Renaissance (Raphael, Leonardo, Botticelli, Titian) and the German Renaissance it inspired (Albrecht Dürer). The Reformation of Martin Luther eventually split Europe into two subcultures—Protestants and Catholics—with their two distinct art styles (exemplified by Rembrandt and Rubens, respectively).

Alte Pinakothek

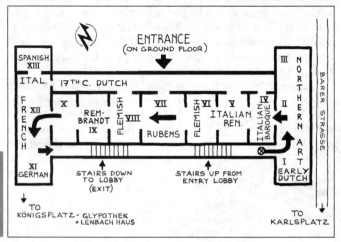

Cost, Hours, Location: €5.50, €1 on Sun, open Tue–Sun 10:00–18:00, Tue until 20:00, closed Mon, last entry 30 min before closing, free and excellent audioguide (€4 on Sun), obligatory lockers, no flash photos, U-2 or U-8: Königsplatz, Barer Strasse 27, tel. 089/2380-5216, www.pinakothek.de/alte-pinakothek.

○ Self-Guided Tour: From the ticket counter, head toward the back wall and walk up the stairway to the left. All the paintings we'll see are on the upper floor, which is laid out like a barbell. Start at one fat end and work your way through the "handle" to the other end. Along the way you'll find the following paintings, roughly in this order.

German Renaissance—Room II: Albrecht Altdorfer's *The Battle of Issus (Schlacht bei Issus)* shows a world at war. Masses of soldiers are swept along in the currents and tides of a battle completely beyond their control, their confused motion reflected in the swirling sky. We see the battle from a great height, giving us a godlike perspective. Though the painting depicts Alexander the Great's victory over the Persians (find the Persian king Darius turning and fleeing), it could as easily have been Germany in the 1520s. Christians were fighting Muslims, peasants battled masters, and Catholics and Protestants were squaring off for a century of conflict. The armies melt into a huge landscape, leaving the impression that the battle goes on forever.

Albrecht Dürer's larger-than-life *Four Apostles* (*Johannes und Petrus* and *Paulus und Marcus*) are saints of a radical new religion—Martin Luther's Protestantism. Just as Luther challenged Church authority, Dürer—a friend of Luther's—strips these saints of any rich clothes, halos, or trappings of power and gives them down-to-earth, human features: receding hairlines, wrinkles, and suspicious eyes. The inscription warns German rulers to follow the Bible rather than Catholic Church leaders. The figure of Mark—a Bible in one hand and a sword in the other—is a fitting symbol of the dangerous times.

Dürer's *Self-Portrait in Fur Coat (Selbstbildnis im Pelzrock)* looks like Jesus Christ but is actually 28-year-old Dürer himself, gazing out, with his right hand solemnly giving a blessing. This is the ultimate image of humanism: the artist as an instrument of God's continued creation. Get close and enjoy the intricately braided hair, the skin texture, and the fur collar. To the left of the head is Dürer's famous monogram—"A.D." in the form of a pyramid.

Italian Renaissance—Room IV: With the Italian Renaissance—the "rebirth" of interest in the art and learning of ancient Greece and Rome—artists captured the realism, three-dimensionality, and symmetry found in classical statues. Leonardo da Vinci's *Virgin and Child (Maria mit dem Kind)* need no halos—they radiate purity. Mary is a solid pyramid of maternal love, flanked by Renaissance-arch windows that look out on the hazy distance. Baby Jesus reaches out to play innocently with a carnation, the blood-colored symbol of his eventual death.

Raphael's *Holy Family at the Canigiani House (Die hl. Familie aus dem Hause Canigiani)* takes Leonardo's pyramid form and runs with it. Father Joseph forms the peak, with his staff as the strong central axis. Mary and Jesus (on the right) form a pyramid-within-the-pyramid, as do Elizabeth and baby John the Baptist on the left. They all exchange meaningful contact, safe within the bounds of the stable family structure.

In Botticelli's *Lamentation over Christ (Die Beweinung Christi)*, the Renaissance "pyramid" implodes, as the weight of the dead Christ drags everyone down, and the tomb grins darkly behind them.

Room V: In Titian's *Christ Crowned with Thorns (Die Dornenkronung)*, a powerfully built Christ sits silently enduring torture by prison guards. The painting is by Venice's greatest Renaissance painter, but there's no symmetry, no pyramid form, and the brushwork is intentionally messy and Impressionistic. By the way, this is the first painting we've seen done on canvas rather than wood, as artists experimented with vegetable oil–based paints.

Rubens and Baroque—Room VII: Europe's religious wars split Europe in two—Protestants in the northern countries, Catholics in the south. (Germany itself was split, with Bavaria remaining Catholic.) The Baroque style popular in Catholic countries features large canvases, bright colors, lots of flesh, rippling motion, wild emotions, grand themes...and pudgy winged babies, the sure sign of Baroque. This room holds several canvases by the great Flemish painter Peter Paul Rubens.

In Rubens' 300-square-foot *Great Last Judgment (Das Grosse Jüngste Gericht)*, Christ raises the righteous up to heaven (left side) and damns the sinners to hell (on the right). This swirling cycle of nudes was considered risqué and kept under wraps by the very monks who'd commissioned it.

Rubens and Isabella Brant shows Rubens with his first wife, both of them the very picture of health, wealth, and success. They lean together unconsciously, as people in love will do, with their hands clasped in mutual affection. When his first wife died, 53-year-old Rubens found a replacement—16-year-old *Hélène Fourment,* shown in her wedding dress. You may recognize Hélène's face in other Rubens paintings.

The Rape of the Daughters of Leucippus (Der Raub der Tochter des Leukippos) has many of Rubens' most typical elements—fleshy, emotional, rippling motion; bright colors; and a classical subject. The legendary twins Castor and Pollux crash a wedding and steal the brides as their own. The chaos of flailing limbs and rearing horses is all held together in a subtle X-shaped composition. Like the weaving counterpoint in a Baroque fugue, Rubens balances opposites.

Notice that Rubens' canvases were—to a great extent—cranked out by his students and assistants from small "cartoons" the master himself made (displayed in the next room).

Room IX: From Holland, Rembrandt van Rijn's *Six Paintings from the Life of Christ* are a down-to-earth look at supernatural events. The *Adoration (Die Anbetung der Hirten)* of Baby Jesus takes place in a 17th-century Dutch barn with ordinary folk as models. The canvases are dark brown, lit by strong light. The *Adoration*'s light source is the Baby Jesus himself—literally the "light of the world." In the *Deposition (Kreuzabnahme),* the light bounces off Christ's pale body onto his mother Mary, showing how his death also hurts her. The drama is underplayed, with subdued emotions. Looking on is a man dressed in blue—a self-portrait of Rembrandt.

▲Neue Pinakothek

The Alte Pinakothek's sister is a twin building across the square, showing off paintings from 1800 to 1920: Romanticism, Realism, Impressionism, *Jugendstil,* Claude Monet, Pierre-Auguste Renoir, Vincent van Gogh, Francisco Goya, and Gustav Klimt (€5.50, €1 on Sun, open Thu–Mon 10:00–18:00, Wed 10:00–20:00, closed Tue, well-done audioguide is usually free but €4 on Sun, classy Café Greco in basement spills into park and offers fine salads, U-2 or U-8: Theresienstrasse, Barer Strasse 29 but enter on Theresienstrasse, tel. 089/2380-5195, www.pinakothek.de/neue-pinakothek).

▲Pinakothek der Moderne

This museum picks up where the other two leave off, covering the 20th century. Four permanent displays (graphics, design, architecture, and paintings) are layered within the striking minimalist architecture. You'll find works by Pablo Picasso, Salvador Dalí, Joan Miró, René Magritte, Max Beckmann, Max Ernst, and abstract artists. The big, white, high-ceilinged building itself is worth a look. Even if you don't pay to visit the exhibits, step into

the free entrance hall to see the sky-high atrium and the colorful blob-column descending the staircase (€9.50, €1 on Sun, open Tue–Sun 10:00–18:00, Thu until 20:00, closed Mon, U-2 or U-8: Königsplatz, Barer Strasse 40, tel. 089/2380-5360, www.pinakothek.de/pinakothek-der-moderne). This far-out collection offers little information in English—including no English audioguide—but some temporary exhibits may have an English flyer; ask at the information desk.

Museum Brandhorst

Due to open in spring of 2008, this museum (on the same city block as the larger Pinakothek der Moderne) houses a collection of works from the last six decades, with a special focus on the 1990s (prices and times will probably resemble nearby museums, U-2 or U-8: Königsplatz, Barer Strasse 29, tel. 089/2380-5104, www.museum-brandhorst.de).

▲Lenbachhaus

Housed in a beautiful, late 19th-century Tuscan-style villa (owned by painter Franz von Lenbach), this museum features the most complete collection of the early Modernist movement known as

Blaue Reiter (Blue Rider), a branch of Expressionism that flourished from 1911 to 1914. When Wassily Kandinsky, Paul Klee, Franz Marc, Gabriele Münter, and some of their art-school cronies got fed up with being told how and what to paint, they formed the Blaue Reiter around a common ideology: to strive for new forms that expressed spiritual truth. Already controversial in their own day, their work was later targeted by the Nazis as *entartete Kunst* ("degenerate art"). As you tour the museum, trace Kandinsky's progression from his earlier, more realistic works to the complete abstraction he's best known for. Münter, Kandinsky's lover and a great painter in her own right, donated her entire private collection (90 paintings and 330 other works) to Lenbachhaus in 1957, putting this little museum on the world art map (€5–10 depending on exhibits, Tue–Sun 10:00–18:00, closed Mon, worthwhile €3 audio-guide, €8 guidebook is a nice souvenir but otherwise unnecessary, small café, U-2 or U-8: Königsplatz, Luisenstrasse 33, enter through small archway, tel. 089/2333-2000, www.lenbachhaus .de). Your Lenbachhaus admission includes the Kunstbau modern art gallery in the Königsplatz U-Bahn station.

Glyptothek
A collection of Greek and Roman sculpture started by King Ludwig I, the Glyptothek includes the famous *Barberini Faun,* statues from the Greek Classical period, funerary monuments of wealthy Athenian families, and pediments of the Temple of Aegina. For a Who's Who of ancient celebrities, visit the Room of Ancient Portraits, where you'll come face to face with Alexander the Great and other luminaries from ancient political and philosophical spheres (€3.50, €1 on Sun, not much in English so invest in the worthwhile €1 guidebook, Tue–Sun 10:00–17:00, Thu until 20:00, closed Mon, U-2 or U-8: Königsplatz, on Königsplatz, tel. 089/286-100).

In and near the English Garden
▲**English Garden (Englischer Garten)**—Munich's "Central Park," the largest on the Continent, was laid out in 1789 by an American. More than 100,000 locals commune with nature here on sunny summer days. The park stretches three miles from the center, past the university to the trendy and bohemian Schwabing quarter. For the best quick visit, follow the river from the surfers (under the bridge just past Haus der Kunst) downstream into the

garden. Just beyond the hilltop temple (walk up for a postcard view of the city), you'll find the big Chinese-pagoda beer garden and other places to enjoy a drink or a meal (see page 83). A rewarding respite from the city, the park is especially fun—and worth ▲▲—on a bike under the summer sun and on warm evenings (for

Green Munich

Although the capital of a very conservative part of Germany, Munich has long been a liberal stronghold. For nearly two decades, the city council has been controlled by a Social Democrat/Green Party coalition. The city policies are pedestrian-friendly—you'll find most of the town center closed to normal traffic, with plenty of bike lanes and green spaces. Talking softly and hearing birds rather than motors, it's easy to forget you're in the center of a big city. On summer Mondays, the peace and quiet makes way for "blade Monday"—when streets in the center are closed to cars and as many as 30,000 in-line skaters swarm around town in a giant rolling party.

bike rental, see page 33; unfortunately, there are no bike-rental agencies in or near the park). Caution: While local law requires sun-worshippers to wear clothes on the tram, the park is sprinkled with buck-naked sunbathers—quite a shock to prudish Americans (they're the ones riding their bikes into the river and trees).

Haus der Kunst—Built by Hitler as a temple of Nazi art, this bold and fascist building is now an impressive shell for various temporary art exhibits. Ironically, the art now displayed in Hitler's "house of art" is the kind that annoyed the Führer most—modern (€5–9 per exhibit, combo-ticket for €12 if there are two exhibits, daily 10:00–20:00, Thu until 22:00, little information in English but some exhibits may have English handouts, at south end of English Garden, tram #17 or bus #100 to Nationalmuseum/Haus der Kunst, Prinzregentenstrasse 1, tel. 089/211-270, www.hausderkunst.de).

Just beyond the Haus der Kunst, where Prinzregentenstrasse crosses the Eisbach canal, you can watch adventure-seekers actually surfing in the rapids created as the small river tumbles underground.

Bavarian National Museum (Bayerisches Nationalmuseum)—This tired but interesting collection features Tilman Riemenschneider carvings, manger scenes, traditional living rooms, and old Bavarian houses (€7, €1 on Sun, open Tue–Sun 10:00–17:00, Thu until 20:00, closed Mon, tram #17 or bus #100 to Nationalmuseum/Haus der Kunst, Prinzregentenstrasse 3, tel. 089/211-2401, www.bayerisches-nationalmuseum.de).

Deutsches Museum

Germany's answer to our Smithsonian Institution, the Deutsches Museum traces the evolution of science and technology. The main branch of the Deutsches Museum is a centrally located, must-see sight. The two side branches—the Museum of Transportation and the Flight Museum—are located outside the city center, but are worth the effort for enthusiasts. You can pay separately for each museum, but all three are covered by one €15 combo-ticket. Since this ticket has no time limit, you can spread out your visits to the various branches over your entire stay.

▲▲▲Deutsches Museum (Main Branch)

Enjoy wandering through well-described rooms of historic airplanes (Hitler's "flying bomb" from 1944), spaceships, mining, the harnessing of wind and water power, hydraulics, musical instruments, printing, chemistry, computers, clocks, and astronomy...it's the Louvre of technical know-how. The museum is designed to be hands-on; if you see a button, push it. But with 10 miles of exhibits from astronomy to zymurgy, even those on roller skates will need to be selective.

Cost, Hours, Information: €8.50, €15 combo-ticket includes Museum of Transportation and Flight Museum, daily 9:00–17:00, worthwhile €4 English guidebook, self-service cafeteria, tel. 089/21791, www.deutsches-museum.de. Most sections of the museum are well-described in English. The much-vaunted high-voltage demonstrations (3/day, 15 min, all in German) show the noisy creation of a five-foot bolt of lightning.

Getting There: Take the S-Bahn to Isartor, then walk 300 yards over the river, following signs.

◉ Self-Guided Tour: First head to the **mines,** which trace the history of mining since prehistoric times (mines closed during daily German-language tours at 9:45 and 13:45). As you follow the spiral stairs down to the mines, notice the 19th-century miners' chapel on the left. (Also notice the handy WC on the right.) While descriptions of the mines are only in German, the reconstructions of coal, potash, and salt mines are still impressive. It's a fun, haunted house–type experience, with creepy life-like miners tucked away in dark corners. Enjoy the photo ops, like the chairlift that used to transport miners. (Hop in!) Apart from the fun and games, the museum has made great efforts to include realistic, accurate details to show what rigorous, dangerous work mining has always been. When you emerge from the mines, skip the mineral oil and natural gas section *(Erdöl und Erdgas)* and follow the signs for *Ausgang* (exit).

The fascinating, compact exhibit on **marine navigation** (on the ground floor) has models of sail, steam, and diesel vessels, from early canoes to grand sailing ships. Take the staircase down into the galley, below the main floor, to check out how life on passenger ships has changed—and don't miss the bisected U1 submarine. This first German submarine, dating from 1906, has been in the museum since 1921.

Flying high above the masts of the marine navigation exhibit is the section on **aeronautics** (first floor). Displays cover the most basic airborne flights (flying insects and seed pods), Otto Lilienthal's 1891 successful efforts to imitate bird flight, and the development of hot-air balloons and gas-powered zeppelins. Many of the planes here are original, including the Wright brothers' Type A (1909), fighters and cargo ships from the two World Wars, and the first functioning helicopter, made in 1936. Climb into the planes whenever permitted, and try out the flight simulator.

The **astronautics** exhibit is located on the second floor. Back in the 1920s, Germany was working on rocket-propelled cars and sleds. Germany's research provided the US and Soviet space teams with much of their technical know-how. Here, you can peer at models of the A4 (one of the first remote-controlled rockets/weapons, from World War II), motors from the American Saturn rockets, and various space capsules, including Spacelab. The main focus is the walk on the moon, the Apollo missions, and the dogs-in-space program (monkeys, too)...but if you've ever been curious about space underwear, you'll find your answer here. Skip the nearby Altamira Caves exhibit, a replica of the 15,000-year-old drawings found in a cave in northern Spain; they're so dark that you can barely see anything.

The third floor traces the **history of measurement,** including time (from a 16th-century sundial and an 18th-century clock to a scary Black Forest wall clock complete with grim reaper), weights, geodesy (surveying and mapping), and computing (from 18th-century calculators to antiquated computers from the 1940s and 1950s).

On your way to the state-of-the-art **planetarium** (worth a visit if open, requires €2 extra ticket, lecture in German), poke your head out into the **sundial garden** located above the third floor. Even if you're not interested in sundials, this is a great place for a view of the surrounding landscape. On a clear day, you can see the Alps.

▲Museum of Transportation (Verkehrszentrum)

You don't need to be an engineer or race-car driver to get a kick out of this fun museum. The Deutsches Museum celebrated its 100th anniversary in 2003 by opening this annex across town that shows off all aspects of transport, from old big-wheeled bikes to Benz's first car (a three-wheeler from the 1880s) to sleek ICE super-trains. It's housed in a recently renovated early 20th-century conference hall and three giant hangar-like exhibition halls near the Oktoberfest grounds, a.k.a. Theresienwiese.

Cost, Hours, Location: €5, €15 combo-ticket includes

Deutsches Museum and Flight Museum, daily 9:00–17:00, Thu until 20:00, Theresienhöhe 14a, U-4 or U-5: Schwanthalerhöhe, tel. 089/2179-529, www.deutsches-museum.de.

Tours: The free tours Sat–Sun at 14:30 (kid-focused) and 15:30 (general) are primarily in German, but English-speaking guides are happy to share.

◐ Self-Guided Tour: True to the Deutsches Museum's interactive spirit, the Museum of Transportation is totally hands-on, and comes with plentiful English explanations. Without getting too academic, it traces the physiological and socioeconomic origins of motion and travel, from basic human and animal anatomy (try to identify those paw prints) to nomadic herders and camel caravans. What would our lives be like without transportation? Exhibits show how modes of transportation developed from sheer necessity into entertainment and competition, from Neolithic "bone" skates (predecessors to today's Rollerblades), to 19th-century Lapland skis, to today's snowboards and fast cars.

Hall 1 takes an inside-out look at Munich's public-transportation system—ride the tram and marvel at the cross-section of the intricate and multi-layered subway system.

Hall 2 gives you a look at the development of transportation for the sake of overland travel. While it focuses primarily on trains, don't miss the chance to climb into the old carriage. The metal track simulates what it would feel like to travel in the 18th century over different terrain (grass and cobblestones—pretty uncomfortable). Admire the Maffei S3/6, a.k.a. "The Pride of Bavaria" (in its heyday the fastest steam engine, at nearly 80 miles per hour); the clever old postal train (complete with a mail slot on the side); and the 1950s panorama bus that shuttled eager tourists to fashionable destinations like Italy.

Hall 3 is all about fun: motorcycles, bicycles, skis, and race cars. Famous prewar models include the deluxe Mercedes Benz 370 (1930s) and the Auto Union Type C "Grand Prix" race car. Other tiny racers—which resemble metal pickles to the uninitiated—include the 1950s Mercedes Benz 300 SLR and the famous Messerschmitt 200. You'll also find early 18th-century bicycles based on Leonardo da Vinci's drawings. Before the invention of the pedal crank, bikes were just silly-looking scooters for adults.

Flight Museum (Flugwerft Schleissheim)

Fans of all things winged will enjoy the Deutsches Museum's Flight Museum, with more than 50 planes, helicopters, gliders, and an original Europa rocket housed in a historical aerodrome on a former military airfield. Inside the museum is the glass-walled workshop where visitors can watch as antique planes are restored (€5, €15 combo-ticket includes Deutsches Museum and

Greater Munich

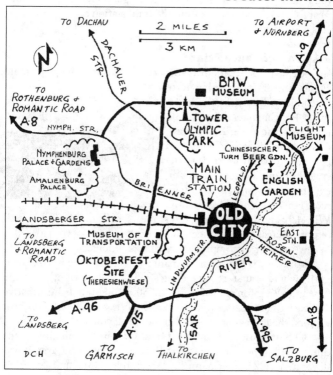

Museum of Transportation, daily 9:00–17:00, about 8 miles outside of town, take S-1 direction: Freising Flughafen and get off at Oberschleissheim, Effnerstrasse 18, tel. 089/315-7140, www.deutsches-museum.de).

Nymphenburg Palace Complex

Nymphenburg Palace and the surrounding one-square-mile park are good for a royal stroll or bike ride. Here you'll find a pair of palaces, the Royal Stables Museum, and playful extras such as a bathhouse, pagoda, and artificial ruins.

Cost and Hours: €10 for everything, less for each of the six individual parts. All sights are open daily April–mid-Oct 9:00–18:00, mid-Oct–March 10:00–16:00. The park is open daily 6:00–dusk. Tel. 089/179-080, www.schloesser.bayern.de.

Getting There: The palace is three miles northwest of central Munich. Getting there from the center is easy, if a bit time-consuming: Take tram #17 from Karlstor (20 min to palace) or the train station (15 min to palace) to the Schloss Nymphenburg stop. From the bridge by the tram stop, you'll see the palace, but you'll have to walk another 10 minutes to get there. A pleasant bike path follows Arnulfstrasse from the train station all the way to the palace (a 30-min pedal).

▲▲Nymphenburg Palace

In 1662, after 10 years of trying, the Bavarian ruler Ferdinand Maria and his wife, Henriette Adelaide of Savoy, finally had a son, Max Emanuel. In gratitude for a male heir, Ferdinand gave this land to his Italian wife, who proceeded to build an Italian-style Baroque palace. Their son expanded the palace to today's size. For 200 years, this was the

Wittelsbach family's summer escape from Munich. (They still refer to themselves as princes and live in one wing of the palace.) If "Wow!" is your first impression, that's intentional.

Your visit is limited to 16 main rooms on one floor: the Great Hall (where you start), the King's Wing (to the right), and the Queen's Wing (on the left). The €2.50 audioguide is informative and easy to use (better than the €6 English guidebook). For most visitors, the following self-guided tour is all you'll need.

◆ **Self-Guided Tour:** The **Great Hall** in the middle was the dining hall. One of the grandest Rococo rooms in Bavaria, it was decorated by Zimmermann (of Wieskirche fame) and Cuvilliés in about 1760. The painting on the ceiling shows Olympian gods keeping the peace (the ruler's duty).

The **King's Wing** (right of entrance) has walls filled with Wittelsbach portraits and stories. In the second room straight ahead, notice the painting showing the huge palace grounds, with Munich (and the twin onion domes of the Frauenkirche) three miles in the distance. Imagine the logistics when the royal family—with their entourage of 200—decided to move out to the summer palace. The Wittelsbachs were high rollers because, from 1624 until 1806, a Wittelsbach was one of seven electors of the Holy Roman Emperor. In 1806, Napoleon ended that institution and made the Wittelsbachs kings. (Note: For simplicity, I often refer to the Wittelsbachs as kings and queens, even though before 1806, these rulers were technically electors—and some were even Holy Roman Emperors.)

In the **Queen's Wing** (left of entrance), enter the first room, then head to the right to find the very red room. You'll see the founding couple, Henriette Adelaide and Ferdinand Maria (after the Counter-Reformation, Bavarian men were named Maria—but his high heels and leggings were another story altogether). The inlaid table was a wedding present. The real pay-off, this palace, didn't come until Henriette (who was 14 when married) got pregnant. The green room is the ceremonial bedroom. The painting to the right of the bed shows Max Emanuel as a kid in a double portrait with his older sister. Both are dressed in the latest French fashions.

King Ludwig I's Gallery of Beauties, near the end of the long hall in the Queen's Wing, is decorated with portraits of 36 beautiful women—all of them painted by Joseph Stieler from 1827 to 1850. King Ludwig I was a consummate girl-watcher who prided himself on the ability to appreciate beauty regardless of social rank. He would pick the prettiest women from the general public and invite them to the palace for a portrait. The women range in status from royal princesses to a humble cobbler's daughter...but Ludwig seemed to prefer brunettes. The portraits reflect the modest Biedermeier style, as opposed to the more flamboyant Romanticism of the same period. If only these creaking floors could talk. Something about the place feels highly sexed, in a Prince Charles kind of way.

The next rooms are decorated in the Neoclassical style of the Napoleonic Era. At the rope, see the room where Ludwig II was born (August 25, 1845). Royal births were carefully witnessed. The mirror allowed for a better view. While Ludwig's death was shrouded in mystery (see page 99), his birth was well-documented.

Amalienburg Palace

Three hundred yards from the palace, hiding in the park (ahead and to the left as you go through to back of palace), you'll find one of the finest Rococo buildings in all of Europe. In 1734, Elector Karl Albrecht had this hunting lodge built for his wife, Maria Amalia—another Rococo jewel designed by Cuvilliés and decorated by Zimmermann. Above the pink-and-white grand entryway, notice Diana, goddess of the chase, flanked by busts of satyrs. Look for the perch atop the roof where the queen would do her shooting. Behind a wall in the garden, dogs would scare non-flying pheasants. When they jumped up in the air above the wall, the sporting queen—as if shooting skeet—would pick the birds off.

Tourists enter this tiny getaway through the back door. The first room has doghouses under gun cupboards. Next, in the fine yellow-and-silver bedroom, see Vulcan forging arrows for amorous cupids at the foot of the bed. The bed is flanked by portraits of Karl Albrecht and Maria Amalia—decked out in hunting attire. She liked her dogs. The door under the portrait leads to stairs to the rooftop pheasant-shooting perch.

The mini–Hall of Mirrors is a blue-and-silver commotion of Rococo nymphs designed by Cuvilliés in the mid-1700s. Cuvilliés, short and hunchbacked, showed a unique talent for art and was sent to Paris to study. In the next room, paintings show court festivities, formal hunting parties, and no-contest kills (where the animal is put at an impossible disadvantage—like shooting fish in a barrel). Finally, the kitchen is decorated with Chinese picnics on blue Dutch tiles.

Royal Stables Museum (Marstallmuseum)

This huge garage is lined with gilded Cinderella coaches. The highlight is just inside the entrance: the 1742 Karl Albrecht coronation coach. When the Elector Karl Albrecht was chosen as Emperor, he rode in this coach, drawn by eight horses. Kings only get six.

Wandering through the collection, you can trace the evolution of 300 years of coaches—getting lighter and with better suspension as they were harnessed to faster horses. The carousel for the royal kids made development of dexterity fun—lop off noses and heads and toss balls through the snake. The glass case is filled with accessories.

In the room after the carousel, find the painting on the right of "Mad" King Ludwig on his sleigh at night. In his later years, Ludwig was a Howard Hughes–type recluse who stayed away from the public eye and only went out at night. (At his nearby Linderhof Palace, he actually had a hydraulic-powered dining table that would rise from the kitchen below, completely set for the meal—so he wouldn't be seen by his servants.) In the next room, you'll find Ludwig's actual sleighs. Next to them is the coach designed for his wedding, but it was never used. Ludwig's over-the-top coaches were Baroque. But this was 1870. The coaches, like the king, were in the wrong century. Notice the photos (c. 1865, in the glass case) of Ludwig with the Romantic composer Richard Wagner. Ludwig cried on the day Wagner was married. Hmmm.

Across the passage from the museum entrance, the second hall is filled with coaches for everyday use. Upstairs is a collection of **Nymphenburg porcelain** (described by an English loaner booklet at the entrance). Historically, royal families such as the Wittelsbachs liked to have their own porcelain plants to make fit-for-a-king plates, vases, and so on. The Nymphenburg palace porcelain works is still in operation. Ludwig ordered the masterpieces of his royal collection (now at the Alte Pinakothek) to be copied in porcelain for safekeeping into the distant future. Take a close look—these are exquisite.

The Olympic Park and Nearby

▲**Olympic Park (Olympiapark München)**—Munich's great 1972 Olympic stadium and sports complex is now a lush park. You can get a good look at the center's striking "cobweb" style of architecture while enjoying the park's picnic potential. In addition, there are several activities on offer at the park, including a tower with a commanding but so-high-it's-boring view from 820 feet (Olympiaturm, €4, daily 9:00–24:00, last trip 23:30, tel. 089/3066-8585) and an excellent swimming pool (Olympia-Schwimmhalle, €3.50, daily 7:00–23:00, last entry 22:00, tel. 0180-179-6223, www.olympiapark -muenchen.de).

With the construction of Munich's new soccer stadium for the 2006 World Cup, the Olympic Park has been left in the past. It will now melt into the neighborhood as simply a fine park and swimming pool. To zip up its image, the park is offering roof-climbing tours with a dizzying zip-cord finale (the TI has details). To reach the park, take U-3 to Olympia-Zentrum direct from Marienplatz.

BMW Museum—The futuristic museum at the BMW headquarters will likely reopen in early 2008 after a four-year remodel. A glass-and-steel building encloses a floating urban streetscape with exhibits highlighting BMW design and technology through the years, and includes a good look at rare cult models. Ask the TI for updates on status, cost, and hours (possibly €2, daily 10:00–20:00, last entry 45 min before closing, U-3: Olympia-Zentrum, tel. 089/3822-5652, www.bmw-museum.de). The Deutsches Museum's Museum of Transportation has a much better old-car exhibit (see page 61). True BMW fans should call or register online several weeks in advance for factory tours (free, 2.5 hrs, by appointment, books up fast July–Aug, same tel. as above, www.bmw-werk -muenchen.de).

Near Munich

For day trips to many Bavarian destinations, including the first three listed here, consider traveling by train with the **Bayern-Ticket.** It covers up to four people from Munich anywhere in Bavaria and back for only €27 (valid until 3:00 in the morning on the day after purchase, not valid before 9:00 Mon–Fri, www.bayern-takt.de). The ticket is explained in *The Inside Track* newsletter and sold at EurAide—see page 31). Note that on weekdays, the Bayern ticket is only valid after 9:00—so if you're visiting "Mad" King Ludwig's Castles, you'll need to plan your entrance time accordingly.

▲▲▲"Mad" King Ludwig's Castles—The spectacular Neu-schwanstein and Linderhof castles make a great day trip. Your easiest option is to take a tour (see page 34). Without a tour, only Neuschwanstein is easy (2 hrs by train to Füssen, then 10-min bus ride to Neuschwanstein). Or spend the night there. For all the details, see the Bavaria and Tirol chapter, page 88.

▲▲Nürnberg—A new express train gets you to Nürnberg in about an hour (departures several times an hour), making this very historic city a viable day trip from Munich. For information, see the Nürnberg chapter, page 311.

▲Berchtesgaden—This resort, near Hitler's Eagle's Nest get-away, is easier as a day trip from Salzburg (just 12 miles away); see page 604.

▲Isar River Bike Ride—Munich's river, lined by a gorgeous park, leads bikers into the pristine countryside in just a few minutes. From downtown (easy access from the English Garden or Deutsches Museum), follow the riverside bike path south (upstream) along the east (left) bank. You can't get lost. Just stay on the lovely bike path. It crosses the river after a while, passing tempting little *Biergartens* and lots of Bavarians having their brand of fun—including gangs enjoying Munich's famous river party rafts. Go as far as you like, then retrace your route to get home. The closest bike rental is at Munich Walk, near Isartor (see page 33).

▲**Andechs Monastery**—This monastery crouches quietly with a big smile between two lakes just south of Munich. For a fine Baroque church in a rural Bavarian setting at a monastery that serves hearty food and perhaps the best beer in Germany, consider a short side-trip here. The cafeteria terrace offers first-class views and second-class prices (*Biergarten* open daily 10:00–22:00, last meal order 20:00, church open until 18:00, tel. 08152/3760). Reaching Andechs from Munich without a car is frustrating (take the S-5 train to Herrsching, then catch a shuttle bus or taxi, or hike 3 miles). Don't miss the stroll up to the church, where you can sit peacefully and ponder the striking contrasts a trip through Germany offers.

▲▲**Dachau Concentration Camp Memorial (KZ-Gedenkstätte Dachau)**—Dachau was the first Nazi concentration camp (1933). Today, it's the most accessible camp for travelers and an effective voice from our recent but grisly past, pleading "Never again." A visit here is a valuable experience and, when approached thoughtfully, well worth the trouble. After this most powerful sightseeing experience, many people gain  more respect for history and the dangers of mixing fear, blind patriotism, and an evil government. You'll likely see lots of students here, as all German schoolchildren are required to visit a concentration camp. It's interesting to think that a couple of generations ago, people greeted each other with a robust *"Sieg Heil!"* Today, almost no Germans know the lyrics of their national anthem, and German flags are a rarity outside of major soccer matches.

Cost and Hours: Free, Tue–Sun 9:00–17:00, last entry 30 min before closing, closed Mon except holidays.

Information and Tours: For maximum understanding, rent the €3 audioguide and consider the English guided walk (€3; May–Sept daily at 13:30, also at 12:00 on weekends; Oct–April Sat–Sun and Thu at 13:30; 2.5 hours, call 08131/669-970 or ask at door to confirm), or take a tour from Munich (see page 38). The extensive website is www.memorial-site-dachau.org.

Getting There: Dachau is a 45-minute trip from downtown

Dachau

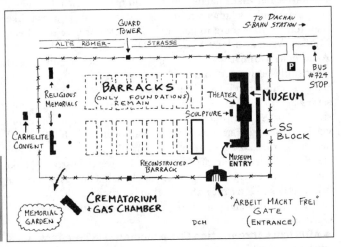

Munich. Take S-2 (direction: Petershausen) to Dachau, then from the station, catch bus #724 or #726 (Dachau-Ost) to KZ-Gedenkstätte (the camp). The XXL ticket covers the entire trip, both ways (€6.70/1 person, €11.80/partner ticket). Drivers follow Dachauer Strasse from downtown Munich to Dachau-Ost, then follow the *KZ-Gedenkstätte* signs.

The Town: The town of Dachau is more pleasant than its unfortunate association with the camp (TI tel. 08131/75286). With 40,000 residents, located midway between Munich and its airport, it's now a high-priced and in-demand place to live.

Orientation: A visit to the Dachau memorial consists of the museum, the bunker behind the museum, the restored barracks, and a pensive walk across the huge but now-empty camp to the shrines and crematorium at the far end. Upon arrival, pick up the €0.50 mini-guide, consider the excellent €2 booklet, and note when the next documentary film in English will be shown (20 min, normally shown at 11:30 and 15:30, verify times on board as you enter museum).

Background: In the 1930s, the camp was outside the town, surrounded by a mile-wide restricted area. A huge training center stood next to the camp. While a relatively few 32,000 inmates died in Dachau between 1933 and 1945 (in comparison, more than a million were killed at Auschwitz in Poland), the camp is notorious because the people who ran the entire concentration-camp system were trained here. Given the strict top-down Nazi management style, it's safe to assume that most of the demonic innovations for Hitler's mass killing originated at Dachau. This was a work camp, where inmates were used for slave labor. It was also a departure point for people shipped to gas chambers in the east, mostly in Nazi-occupied Poland—where most of the mass murder took place (conveniently distant, far out of view of the German public).

Few realize that Dachau actually housed people longer *after* the war than during the war. After liberation, the fences were taken down, but numerous survivors who had nowhere else to go stayed. The camp later served as a prison for camp officials convicted in the Dachau trials. Still later, it housed refugees from Eastern Europe. Until the 1960s, it was like a small town, with a cinema, shops, and so on.

◑ **Self-Guided Tour:** You enter, like the inmates did, through the infamous **iron gate** with the taunting slogan *Arbeit macht frei* ("Work makes you free"). The **museum**—which tries valiantly to personalize the plight of the inmates—is thoughtfully described in English. Computer touch-screens let you watch early newsreels. The **theater** shows a powerful documentary movie (see above for times).

The **bunker** behind the theater was for "special prisoners," such as failed Hitler assassins and politicians who challenged Nazism. It contains an exhibit on the notorious SS (you have direct access to the bunker after the movie lets out, otherwise walk around museum past the *Arbeit macht frei* sign.)

The big **square** between the museum and the reconstructed barracks was used for roll call. Twice a day, the entire camp population assembled here. They'd stand at attention until all were accounted for. If someone was missing (more likely dead than escaped), everyone would have to stand—often through the night—until the person was located.

Beyond the two reconstructed **barracks** (one is open to the public—where you can rent an audioguide), a long walk takes you past the foundations of the other barracks to four places of meditation and worship (Jewish, Catholic, Protestant, and Russian Orthodox). Beyond that is a Carmelite Convent.

To the left of the shrines, a memorial garden surrounds the camp **crematorium.** Look at the smokestack. You're standing on ground nourished by the ashes of those who died at Dachau. While the Dachau gas chamber is like those at other concentration camps, this one was never used.

EXPERIENCES

Oktoberfest

The 1810 marriage reception of King Ludwig I was such a success that they made it an annual bash. These days, the Oktoberfest lasts more than two weeks (Sept 20–Oct 5 in 2008), starting on the third Saturday in September and usually ending on the first

Sunday in October (but never before Oct 3—the day Germany celebrates its recent reunification).

Oktoberfest kicks things off with an opening parade of more than 6,000 participants. Every night, it fills eight huge beer tents with about 6,000 people each. A million gallons of beer later, they roast the last ox.

It's best to reserve a room early, but if you arrive in the morning (except Fri or Sat) and haven't called ahead, the TI can normally help. The Theresienwiese fairground (south of the main train station), known as the "Wies'n," erupts in a frenzy of rides, dancing, and strangers strolling arm-in-arm down rows of picnic tables while the beer god stirs tons of beer, pretzels, and wursts in a bubbling cauldron of fun. The triple-loop roller coaster must be the wildest on earth (best before the beer-drinking). During the fair, the city functions even better than normal. It's a good time to sightsee, even if beer-hall rowdiness isn't your cup of tea. For details, see www.oktoberfest.de.

If you're not visiting while the party's on, don't worry: You can still dance to oompah bands, dunk huge pretzels, and show off your stein-hoisting skills any time of year at Munich's classic beer halls, including the venerable **Hofbräuhaus** (see page 46). Also in the city center, the **Beer and Oktoberfest Museum** gives an enjoyable historical take on the festival (see page 47).

SHOPPING

You'll find beer steins to take home at shops on the pedestrian zone by St. Michael's Church and at the gift shops that surround the Hofbräuhaus. Münchners take their shoes very seriously; the pedestrian zone abounds with shoe stores featuring everything from expensive Italian models to Birkenstocks (substantially cheaper here than in the US).

Here are a few areas and stores to consider:

On Marienplatz: Beck's has been a local institution since 1861, when it began meeting the needs of the royal family, including "Mad" King Ludwig. This shop has long been to fabrics what Alois Dallmayr is to fine food (see page 45). Today, it's an upscale department store, with stationery, cosmetics, and its own clothing label and designer duds (Mon–Sat 10:00–20:00, closed Sun). If you're facing the glockenspiel on New Town Hall, look to your right—you can't miss it on the corner. Also on Marienplatz is the **Hugendubel** bookstore, with an extensive selection of English-language books (Mon–Sat 9:30–20:00, closed Sun, coffee shop on top floor).

Weinstrasse/Theatinerstrasse: Shoppers will want to stroll from Marienplatz down the pedestrianized Weinstrasse, which becomes Theatinerstrasse. As you walk down Weinstrasse (it runs alongside the left of New Town Hall, as you face it), look for **Fünf Höfe** on your left—named for its five courtyards and filled with Germany's top shops (open until 20:00, www.fuenfhoefe .de). Soon after is the **Kunsthalle,** a big bank-sponsored art center with excellent temporary exhibits and impressive events (daily 10:00–20:00, Theatinerstrasse 8, tel. 089/224-412, www .hypo-kunsthalle.de). Note how its Swiss architects (who also designed Munich's grand new soccer stadium for the 2006 World Cup) play with light and color. Even if you're not a shopper, wander through the Kunsthalle to appreciate the architecture. Theatinerstrasse spills out onto Odeonsplatz, where you'll find the **Nymphenburg Porcelain Store** (Mon–Fri 10:00–18:30, Sat 10:00–16:00, closed Sun, Odeonsplatz 1, tel. 089/282-428).

Maximilianstrasse: For the most exclusive shops, stroll this street. Ludwig I made the grand but very impersonal Ludwig-strasse. As a reaction to this unpopular street by this unpopular king, his son Maximilian built a street designed for the people and for shopping. It leads from the National Theater over the Isar River to the Bavarian Parliament (which you can see from the theater end).

SLEEPING

Unless you hit Munich during a fair, convention, or big holiday, you can sleep reasonably here. Lots of student hotels around the station house anyone who's young at heart for €20, and it's easy to find a fine double with breakfast in a good basic hotel for €80. I've listed accommodations in two neighborhoods: within a few blocks of the central train station (Hauptbahnhof) and in the old center. Many of these places have complicated, slippery pricing schemes. I've listed the normal non-convention, non-festival prices. There are major conventions about 30 nights a year—prices increase from 20 percent to as much as 300 percent during Oktoberfest (Sept 20–Oct 5 in 2008; reserve well in advance). Prices can also go up slightly for smaller conventions. On the other hand, during slow times, you may be able to do better than the rates listed here—always ask.

Sleep Code

(€1 = about $1.30, country code: 49, area code: 089)
S = Single, **D** = Double/Twin, **T** = Triple, **Q** = Quad, **b** = bathroom, **s** = shower only. Unless otherwise noted, credit cards are accepted, a buffet breakfast is included, there is no air-conditioning, and English is spoken.

To help you sort easily through these listings, I've divided the rooms into three categories based on the price for a standard double room with bath:

$$$ **Higher Priced**—Most rooms €100 or more.
$$ **Moderately Priced**—Most rooms between €70–100.
$ **Lower Priced**—Most rooms €70 or less.

Near the Train Station

Budget hotels cluster in the area immediately south of the station. It feels seedy after dark (erotic cinemas and men with moustaches in the shadows), but it's dangerous only for those in search of trouble. Neighborhoods in the old center (see page 77) might feel more comfortable to many readers.

$$$ **King's Hotel First Class,** a fancy 90-room business-class hotel, is an elegant splurge that becomes a good deal on weekends. You'll get a lobby with chandeliers and carved wooden ceilings, rooms with canopy beds, and a well-polished staff (Sb-€140, Db-€160, or Db-€100 Fri–Sun, prices higher during Oktoberfest and other events, breakfast-€15, air-con, 500 yards north of station at Dachauer Strasse 13, tel. 089/551-870, fax 089/5518-7300, www .kingshotels.de, 1stclass@kingshotels.de). Their sister hotel (around the corner), $$$ **King's Center Hotel,** also rents fine business-class canopy-bed rooms, but is less plush (Sb-€99, Db-€130, or Db-€75 Fri–Sun, breakfast-€12, Marsstrasse 15, tel. 089/515-530, www.kingshotels.de, center@kingshotels.de).

$$$ **Alpen Hotel,** a once-grand old hotel with a pleasant breakfast terrace and other gorgeous public spaces close to the train station, rents 57 simple, comfortable, slightly overpriced rooms (Sb-€110, small Db-€140, big Db-€160, Adolf-Kolping-Strasse 14, tel. 089/559-330, fax 089/559-33100, www.alpenhotel-muenchen .de, info@alpenhotel-muenchen.de).

$$ **Hotel Europäischer Hof** is a huge, impersonal business hotel with 158 decent rooms. They have four categories of rooms, ranging from fairly cheap to outrageous (official rates are sky-high, but actual rates are usually closer to S-€50, Sb-€85, D-€60, Db-€100; 10 percent discount on prevailing rate in 2008 with this book and advance reservation, *or* if you pay cash—no double discounts;

Hotels near the Train Station

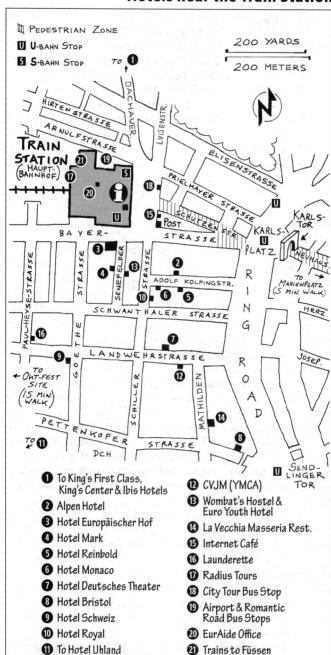

- **1** To King's First Class, King's Center & Ibis Hotels
- **2** Alpen Hotel
- **3** Hotel Europäischer Hof
- **4** Hotel Mark
- **5** Hotel Reinbold
- **6** Hotel Monaco
- **7** Hotel Deutsches Theater
- **8** Hotel Bristol
- **9** Hotel Schweiz
- **10** Hotel Royal
- **11** To Hotel Uhland
- **12** CVJM (YMCA)
- **13** Wombat's Hostel & Euro Youth Hotel
- **14** La Vecchia Masseria Rest.
- **15** Internet Café
- **16** Launderette
- **17** Radius Tours
- **18** City Tour Bus Stop
- **19** Airport & Romantic Road Bus Stops
- **20** EurAide Office
- **21** Trains to Füssen

no discounts during conventions, major events, and Oktoberfest weekends; non-smoking rooms, family rooms, free Internet access, Bayerstrasse 31, tel. 089/551-510, fax 089/5515-11444, www.heh.de, info@heh.de). They also run **$$ Hotel Mark** around the corner, with a similar institutional-slumbermill ambience—large lobby, dim hallways, and 95 plain, cheaper rooms (high official rates, but normal rates usually about S-€50, Sb-€75, D-€60, basic Db-€80, ask for 10 percent discount described above, Senefelderstrasse 12, tel. 089/559-820, fax 089/5598-22444, www.hotel-mark.de, mark@heh.de).

$$ Hotel Reinbold has 64 sunny rooms in a great location on a quiet street close to the station. Enjoy their huge breakfast spread in the winter garden. Hardworking manager Johannes promises these special cash-only rates with this book in 2008 (Sb-€61, Db-€81, Tb-€91, elevator, Adolf-Kolping-Strasse 11, tel. 089/5999-3902, fax 089/5999-3994, www.eckelmann-hotels.de, info@hotel-reinbold.de).

$$ Hotel Monaco is a delightful and welcoming little hideaway, tucked inside the fifth floor of a giant, nondescript building two blocks from the station. Emerging from the elevator, you're warmly welcomed by Christine into her flowery, cherub-filled oasis. It's homey, with 24 clean and fresh rooms (Sb-€45–70, Db-€55–90, prices higher during Oktoberfest and other events, Schillerstrasse 9, entrance on Adolf-Kolping-Strasse, tel. 089/545-9940, fax 089/550-3709, www.hotel-monaco.de, info@hotel-monaco.de).

$$ Hotel Deutsches Theater, also managed by the Hotel Reinbold's Johannes, is a brass-and-marble-filled place with 28 tight, modern, three-star rooms. The back rooms face the courtyard of a neighboring theater—when there's a show, there can be some street noise (Sb-€65, Db-€85, Tb-€95, these rates promised in 2008 with cash and this book, prices higher during events, pricier suites, non-smoking floor, Landwehrstrasse 18, tel. 089/545-8525, fax 089/5458-5261, www.hoteldeutschestheater.de, info@hoteldeutschestheater.de).

$$ Hotel Bristol has 57 comfortable but slightly overpriced business-class rooms. While a longer walk from the station, it's pleasantly located just across the street from Sendlinger Tor (Sb-€79, Db-€89, Tb-€109, €10 cheaper on weekends, more expensive during events, hearty buffet breakfast, non-smoking rooms, free Internet access and Wi-Fi, elevator, one U-Bahn stop from station, U-1 or U-2: Sendlinger Tor, Pettenkoferstrasse 2, tel. 089/5434-8880, fax 089/5434-888111, www.bristol-munich.de, info@bristol-munich.de).

$$ Hotel Schweiz is built like a bomb shelter, but is a good value. Solid and efficient, it comes with a warm welcome, 57 new-feeling rooms, and a tasty breakfast (Sb-€58, Db-€75, Tb-€90, non-smoking rooms, Internet access, from the station walk 2 blocks down Goethestrasse to #26, tel. 089/543-6960, fax 089/5436-9696, www.hotel-schweiz.de, info@hotel-schweiz.de).

$$ Hotel Ibis is a big, plain, efficient chain hotel that offers 200 simple but comfortable little industrial-strength staterooms for a good price to businesspeople on a tight per diem (Sb-€66–72, Db-€81–87, cheaper prices are for Fri–Sun, breakfast-€9.50, non-smoking rooms, air-con, Dachauer Strasse 21, tel. 089/551-930, fax 089/5519-3102, www.ibishotel.com, h1450@accor.com).

$$ Hotel Royal is perhaps the best value in its price range (if you don't mind the strip joints flanking the entry). While a bit institutional, it's clean, fresh, efficient, entirely non-smoking, and plenty comfortable. Most importantly, it's energetically run by Pasha and Changiz. Each of its 40 rooms is fresh and bright (Sb-€49–59, Db-€69–79, Tb-€79–109, prices higher during Oktoberfest and other events, book direct for a 10 percent discount off the prevailing price with this book in 2008, ask for a room on the quiet side, Internet access and Wi-Fi, Schillerstrasse 11a, tel. 089/591-021, fax 089/550-3657, www.hotel-royal.de, info @hotel-royal.de).

$ The CVJM (YMCA), open to all ages, rents 85 beds in modern rooms (S-€35, D-€60, T-€82.50, €27.50/bed in a shared triple, those over 26 pay about 10 percent more, cheaper for 3 nights or more and in winter, €5/night per person more during Oktoberfest, free showers, Landwehrstrasse 13, tel. 089/552-1410, fax 089/550-4282, www.cvjm-muenchen.org, hotel@cvjm-muenchen.org).

$ Wombat's Hostel, casual and welcoming anyone young at heart, seems to be the best option near the station for budget backpackers. They have cheap doubles and six- to eight-bed dorms with lockers, a bar open until 2:00 in the morning, a relaxing and peaceful winter garden, all the normal services, and creative management. All bedrooms are fresh and modern, with good bathrooms (dorm bed-€24, Db-€68, breakfast-€4, cheaper off-season, open 24 hours, a block from the station at Senefelderstrasse 1, tel. 089/5998-9180, www.wombats-hostels.com, office@wombats-munich .de).

$ Euro Youth Hotel is a hostel near the train station with no age limit (dorm bed-€12.50, D-€45, great breakfast, within a block of train station at Senefelderstrasse 5, tel. 089/5990-8811, www .euro-youth-hotel.de).

In the Old Center

$$$ Mercure München Altstadt Hotel is a huge, impersonal, basic business-class hotel with all the modern comforts on a boring street very close to the Marienplatz action. If you want an

Central Munich Hotels and Restaurants

1. Mercure München Altstadt Hotel
2. Hotel Blauer Bock
3. Hotel am Viktualienmarkt
4. Pension Lindner
5. Hotel Atlanta
6. Hotel Münchner Kindl
7. Hofbräuhaus
8. Weisses Bräuhaus
9. Suppenküche
10. To Augustiner Beer Garden
11. Jodlerwirt Pub
12. Nürnberger Bratwurst Glöckl am Dom & Andechser am Dom
13. Altes Hackerhaus
14. Spatenhaus
15. To Chinesischer Turm Biergarten & Seehaus
16. Glockenspiel Café & Hugendubel Bookstore
17. Alois Dallmayr Deli
18. Buxs Self-Service Vegetarian Restaurant
19. Forum Speisecafé
20. Stadt Café (in City Museum)
21. Prinz Myshkin Veggie Rest.
22. Riva Bar Pizzeria
23. Café Tambosi
24. Nymphenburg Porcelain Store
25. Beer & Oktoberfest Museum
26. Munich Walk Office

American-style hotel room buried deep in Munich for a good price, this place has 70 of them (Sb-€100–110, Db-€110–120 for most days, breakfast-€13, non-smoking floors, air-con, a block south of the pedestrian zone at Hotterstrasse 4, tel. 089/232-590, fax 089/2325-9127, www.mercure.com, h3709@accor.com).

$$$ Hotel Blauer Bock, formerly a dormitory for Benedictine monks, has been on the same corner across from the Munich City Museum since 1841. It's a little pricey and feels spartan, but offers clean, decent rooms and a straightforward pricing system (the same prices every day of the year). Breakfast is served in its very mod and sleek restaurant next door, though most of the decor feels like the monks still run the place (S-€45–53, Sb-€64–72, D-€72–78, Db-€100–118, Tb-€130–135, Qb-€155, Sebastianplatz 9, tel. 089/231-780, fax 089/2317-8200, www.hotelblauerbock.de, info @hotelblauerbock.de).

$$ Hotel am Viktualienmarkt, located just a block off of the market, was recently renovated by Elke Glöckle and her daughter Stephanie. Light-colored wood gives the rooms a fresh, clean feeling. The prices are very good for this central location (Sb-€40–48, Db-€85–98, Tb-€98–115, Qb-€115–130, extra bed-€25, lower prices are for Fri–Sun, prices about €50 more during Oktoberfest, 10 percent higher during other events, no elevator, Utzschneiderstrasse 14, tel. 089/231-1090, fax 089/2311-0955, www.hotel-am-viktualienmarkt.de, reservierung@hotel-am -viktualienmarkt.de).

$$ Pension Lindner is clean, quiet, and modern, with 10 pastel-bouquet rooms, mediocre plumbing, and—at times—indifferent service (S-€39, D-€55–60, Ds-€65–70, Db-€75–85, these special prices promised with this book through 2008, prices higher during Oktoberfest and other events, cash preferred, reception and breakfast in café below, elevator, Dultstrasse 1, tel. 089/263-413, fax 089/268-760, www.pension-lindner.com, info@pension-lindner .com, Marion Sinzinger).

$$ Hotel Atlanta is conveniently located 50 yards from the Sendlinger Tor U-Bahn stop and a 10-minute walk from Marienplatz. Its 20 rooms are split between two buildings connected by a peaceful patio. To minimize street noise, ask for a room in the older back building (S-€40, Ss-€55, Sb-€70, Ds-€70, Db-€80–90, prices higher during Oktoberfest and other events, Sendlingerstrasse 58, tel. 089/263-605, fax 089/260-9027, www .hotel-atlanta.de, info@hotel-atlanta.de).

$$ Hotel Münchner Kindl is jolly, with 22 decent rooms above a friendly neighborhood bar (S-€45, Db-€90, Tb-€115, Qb-€130, these prices through 2008 with this book, lower rates possible in summer—ask, rooms €25 more during Oktoberfest and other events; non-smoking rooms, no elevator, night noises travel up central courtyard, no air circulation in courtyard-facing rooms so they can get hot in summer, Damenstiftstrasse 16, tel. 089/264-349, fax 089/264-526, www.hotel-muenchner-kindl.de, reservierung@hotel-muenchner-kindl.de, Renate Dittert).

Away from the Center

$$ Hotel Uhland is a stately mansion that rents 31 delightful rooms in a safe-feeling residential neighborhood near the Theresienwiese Oktoberfest grounds. It's been in the same wonderful Hauzenberger family for 50 years (Sb-€70–85, small Db-€85, big Db-€95, Tb-€120, save about €10 a night by booking through their website, great family rooms and deals, non-smoking floor, Wi-Fi, free parking; from station, take bus #58 to Georg-Hirth-Platz, or walk 15 minutes: go up Goethestrasse and turn right on Pettenkoferstrasse, cross Georg-Hirth-Platz to Uhlandstrasse and find #1; tel. 089/543-350, fax 089/5433-5250, www.hotel-uhland.de, info@hotel-uhland.de).

$ Munich's venerable **International Youth Camp Kapuzinerhölzl** (a.k.a. "The Tent") offers 400 spots on the wooden floor of a huge circus tent and never fills up. You'll get a mattress (€7.50) or bed (€10.50), or pitch your own tent (€5.50/tent plus €5.50/person). Blankets, hot showers, lockers, self-service laundry, and Wi-Fi are all included; breakfast is a few euros extra. It can be a fun but noisy experience—kind of a cross between a slumber party and Woodstock. There's a cool table-tennis-and-Frisbee atmosphere throughout the day, nightly campfires, and no curfew (open mid-June–mid-Oct only, prices a little higher during Oktoberfest, Internet access, bikes-€8/day, catch tram #17 from train station for 17 minutes to Botanischer Garten, direction Amalienburgstrasse, and follow the crowd down Franz-Schrank-Strasse, tel. 089/141-4300, www.the-tent.com, cu@the-tent.de).

EATING

Munich cuisine is best seasoned with beer. You have two basic choices: beer halls such as the Hofbräuhaus, where you'll find music and tourists; or the mellower beer gardens, where you'll find the Germans. I'm here for the beer-garden fun. But when the *Wurst und Kraut* get to be too much for you, Munich has more Michelin-star restaurants than any other German city, plus a galaxy of good, more affordable alternatives.

In beer halls, beer gardens, or at the Viktualienmarkt, try the most typical meal in town: *Weisswurst* (white-colored veal sausage) with *süsser Senf* (sweet mustard), a salty *Brezel* (pretzel), and *Weissbier* ("white" wheat beer). Another traditional favorite is *Obatzda* (a.k.a. *Obatzter*), a mix of soft cheeses and butter with paprika and raw onions that's spread on bread. *Brotzeit,* meaning "time for bread," gets you a wooden platter of cold cuts, cheese, and pickles and is a good option for a light dinner. Also unique and memorable is a *Steckerlfisch*—fish on a stick (great with a pretzel and a big beer).

Beer Halls and Beer Gardens

These are my favorite places to sip or chug some Munich brew. For tips on enjoying this quintessential Munich experience, see the "Munich's Beer Scene" on page 82.

The **Hofbräuhaus** (HOFE-broy-howse) is the world's most famous beer hall. Although it's grotesquely touristy, it's a Munich

must. Even if you don't eat here, check it out; it's fun to see 200 Japanese people drinking beer in a German beer hall...across from a Hard Rock Café. Germans go for the entertainment—to sing "Country Roads," see how Texas girls party, and watch tourists try to chug beer (daily 9:00–24:00, music during lunch and dinner, Platzl 6, 5-min walk from Marienplatz, tel. 089/290-1360, www .hofbraeuhaus.de). You can drop by anytime for the €20 buffet, order a light meal (my favorite: €6.60 for *ein paar Schweinswurst mit Kraut*—two pork sausages with sauerkraut), or just order a drink. They only sell beer by the one-liter mug, or *Mass* (€6.20). And they sell 10,000 of these liters every day. The Hofbräuhaus is the only beer hall in town offering regular live oompah music. This music-every-night atmosphere is thick, and the fat, shiny-leather bands even get church mice to stand up and conduct three-quarter time with breadsticks. They also host a gimmicky folk evening in the upstairs *Festsaal* (second floor) nightly from 19:00 to 22:30. Walk up the stairs to the left of the entrance just to see the historic old Hofbräuhaus photos and prints. For more on this Munich institution, see page 46.

Weisses Bräuhaus is much less rowdy than the Hofbräuhaus, but still very touristy. It's famous as the birthplace of Weissbier (fizzy, unfiltered wheat beer). The menu features a full selection of very traditional Bavarian specialties. While the food menu is in English, the drink menu—with a huge and confusing variety of beers—is only in German. The food is very good here, and you'll pay a few extra euros for the history (€5–14 main dishes, daily 9:00–24:00, between Marienplatz and Isartor, 2 blocks from Hofbräuhaus at Im Tal 7, tel. 089/290-1380). Hitler met with fellow fascists here in 1920, when his Nazi party had yet to ferment.

Munich's Beer Scene

In Munich's beer halls *(Bräuhäuser)* and beer gardens *(Biergartens)*, meals are inexpensive, white radishes are salted and cut in delicate spirals, and surly beer maids pull mustard packets from their cleavage.

Beer gardens go back to the days when monks brewed their beer and were allowed to sell it directly to the thirsty public. They stored their beer in cellars under courtyards kept cool by the shade of bushy chestnut trees. Eventually, tables were set up, and these convivial eateries evolved. The tradition (complete with chestnut trees) survives, and any real beer garden will keep a few tables (identified by not having a tablecloth) available for customers who buy only beer and bring in their own food.

Huge liter beers (called *ein Mass* in German, or *"ein pitcher"* in English) cost about €6. You can order your beer *helles* (light but not "lite"—which is what you'll get if you say *"ein* beer"), *dunkles* (dark), or *Radler* (half lemon-lime soda, half beer). Beer gardens have a deposit system for their big glass steins: You pay €1 extra, and when you're finished, you can take the mug to the return man for your refund, or leave it on the table and lose your money. (Men's rooms come with vomitoriums.)

Many beer halls have a cafeteria system. Eating outside is made more pleasant by the *Föhn* (warm winds that come over the Alps from Italy), which gives this part of Germany 30 more days of sunshine than the North—and sometimes even an Italian ambience. (Many natives attribute the city's huge increase in outdoor dining to global warming.)

Beer halls take care of their regular customers. You'll notice many *Stammtische* (tables reserved for regulars and small groups, such as the "Happy Saturday Club"). They have a long tradition of being launch pads for grassroots action. The Hofbräuhaus was the first place Hitler talked to a big crowd.

The **Viktualienmarkt Beer Garden** taps you into about the best budget eating in town (closed Sun, see page 44). Countless stalls surround the beer garden and sell wurst, sandwiches, produce, and so on. This B.Y.O.F. tradition goes back to the days when monks served beer but not food. To picnic, choose a table without a tablecloth. This is a good spot to grab a typical Munich *Weisswurst* and some beer. The self-service **Suppenküche** (soup kitchen) is fine for a small, cozy, sit-down lunch (€4–6 soup meals,

Mon–Fri 10:00–19:00, Sat 9:00–17:00, closed Sun; go straight into market 50 yards from the intersection of Frauenstrasse and Reichenbachstrasse, look on the left for green shop with red sign).

Augustiner Beer Garden is a sprawling haven for well-established local beer-lovers on a balmy evening. For a true under-the-leaves beer garden packed with Münchners—many of whom claim that Augustiner is the best beer in town—this is very good (daily 10:00–24:00, food until 22:00, across from train tracks, 3 loooong blocks from station, away from the center at Arnulfstrasse 52, tram #17, taxis always waiting at the gate).

Tiny **Jodlerwirt** is a smart-alecky, yodeling kind of pub. The food is great, and the ambience is as Bavarian as you'll find. Avoid the basic ground-floor bar and climb the stairs into the action. Good food and lots of belly laughs...completely incomprehensible to the average tourist (Tue–Sat 18:00–3:00 in the morning, food until 23:00, closed Mon except in Sept–April, always closed Sun, accordion act nightly from 20:30, between Hofbräuhaus and Marienplatz at Altenhofstrasse 4, tel. 089/221-249).

Nürnberger Bratwurst Glöckl am Dom, popular with tourists, offers a classier, fiercely Bavarian evening. Dine outside under the trees or in the dark, medieval, cozy interior—patrolled by wenches and spiked with antlers. I come here to enjoy the explosively tasty little *Nürnberger* sausages (€9–15 dinners, daily 10:00–24:00, at the rear of the twin-domed Frauenkirche, Frauenplatz 9, tel. 089/291-9450).

The trendier **Andechser am Dom,** on the same breezy square, serves Andechs beer and great food to appreciative regulars. Münchners favor the dark beer (ask for *dunkles*), but I love the light *(helles)*. The €10.50 *Gourmetteller* is a great sampler of their specialties (€5–15 main dishes, daily 10:00–24:00, Weinstrasse 7, reserve during peak times, tel. 089/298-481).

Altes Hackerhaus is popular with locals—especially the workers from the newspaper—for its traditional *Bayerischer* (Bavarian) fare with a fancier feel. It offers a small courtyard and a fun forest of characteristic nooks festooned with old-time paintings and posters (€10–20 meals, €5–10 wurst dishes, daily 10:00–24:00, Sendlinger Strasse 14, tel. 089/260-5026).

Spatenhaus is the opera-goers' beer hall, serving more elegant food in a woodsy, traditional setting since 1896. Or eat outside, on the square facing the opera and palace. It's pricey, but you won't find better-quality *Biergarten* cuisine (€20 meals, daily 9:30–24:00, on Max-Joseph-Platz opposite opera, Residenzstrasse 12, tel. 089/290-7060).

In the English Garden

For outdoor ambience and a cheap meal, spend an evening at

the English Garden's **Chinesischer Turm** (Chinese pagoda) **Biergarten.** You're welcome to B.Y.O. food and grab a table, or buy from the picnic stall *(Brotzeit)* right there. Don't bother to phone ahead—they have 6,000 seats. This is a fine opportunity to try a *Steckerlfisch,* sold for €9 at a separate kiosk (daily, long hours in good weather, usually live music, tel. 089/3838-7327, www .chinaturm.de; take tram #17 from main train station or Sendlinger Tor to Tivolistrasse, or U-3 or U-6 to Universität). **Seehaus im Englischen Garten** is famous among Münchners for its idyllic lakeside setting and excellent Mediterranean and traditional cooking. It's dressy and a bit snobbish, and understandably filled with locals who fit the same description. Choose from classy indoor or lakeside seating (€20–25 meals, daily 10:00–24:00, a pleasant 15-min hike into the English Garden—located on all the city maps—or tram #44 or taxi to the doorstep, Kleinhesselohe 3, tel. 089/3816-130). **Seehaus Beer Garden,** adjacent to the fancy Seehaus restaurant, is a less expensive, more casual beer garden with all the normal wurst, kraut, pretzels, and fine beer at typical prices. What makes this spot special: You're buried in the English Garden, enjoying the fine lakeside setting (daily, long hours from 11:00 when the weather's fine).

Non-Beer Hall Restaurants

Man does not live by beer alone. Well, maybe some do. But for the rest of us, I recommend the following alternatives to the beer-hall scene.

On or near Marienplatz

With a Bird's-Eye Marienplatz View: **Glockenspiel Café** is good for a coffee or a meal with a view down on the Marienplatz action. There are several dining zones. Locals like the sunroof, but regardless of the weather, I grab a seat overlooking Marienplatz (Mon–Sat 10:00–24:00, Sun 10:00–19:00, ride elevator from Rosenstrasse entrance, opposite glockenspiel at Marienplatz 28, tel. 089/264-256). For a quicker and less crowded option, go to the Starbucks-style café on the top floor of **Hugendubel** bookstore (described under "Shopping" on page 73).

An Elegant Picnic or Café: The crown in **Alois Dallmayr**'s emblem indicates that the royal family assembled its picnics at this historic and expensive delicatessen. Explore this dieter's purgatory and put together a royal picnic to munch in the nearby Hofgarten. A classy but pricey café serves light meals on the ground floor (Mon–Sat 9:30–19:00, closed Sun, behind New Town Hall, Dienerstrasse 14). For more information, see page 45.

A Budget Picnic: To save money, browse at Dallmayr's but buy in the basement **supermarkets** of the **Kaufhof** stores across

Flöss **Party Rafts**

Münchners love a good time out in nature with friends. Nowhere is this lifestyle on better display than the local tradition called the *Flöss*—party rafts that local groups rent to float down the Isar River on warm days from May to early September. These log rafts come complete with oompah bands, merry revelers, and a keg of Munich's finest suds—Bavaria meets Huckleberry Finn. The *Flöss* tradition goes back to the time when the Isar was a vital artery in the growth of Munich. For centuries, rafts have been used to transport logs, salt, and other goods as well as passengers down the river. Today, rafters put in south of town

at Wolfratshausen and leave the river at Thalkirchen. There are two atmospheric riverside *Biergartens* where you enjoy a beer out in nature and watch the *Flöss* flotillas float by. Each takes a little effort to get to, but it's worth it to see this unique Bavarian pastime.

Gasthof Hinterbrühl is five miles southwest of Munich (Sat–Thu 9:30–22:30, closed Fri, Hinterbrühl 2, tel. 089/794-494, www.gasth-hinterbruehl.de). Take U-3 to Thalkirchen. Cross the street and hop on bus #135 five stops to Hinterbrühl. Or, to reach the *Biergarten* on foot, cross the street from the Thalkirchen station and find the path along the river that leads 15 minutes past the campground.

Brückenwirt is about two miles farther upriver, where the Isar has an even more alpine feel. Take S-7 to Hollriegelskreuth and walk down Karl von Lindestrasse to the path that snakes down to the river. Just before you get to the river, you'll see the high Grünwalder Bridge. Consider a detour onto the bridge to get some great views of the rafts below. Then retrace your steps and head down to Brückenwirt on the river, and grab a table outside. From the S-Bahn station, allow 15 minutes down, 20 minutes back up...plus another five minutes for every *Mass* you drink (daily 10:00–24:00, closed Mon Sept–April, Grünwalderbrücke 1, tel. 089/793-0167, www.brueckenwirt.de).

Marienplatz or at Karlsplatz (Mon–Sat 9:30–20:00, closed Sun), or the **Minimal** at Fünf Höfe (Mon–Sat 7:00–20:00, closed Sun).

Trendy Eateries South of Marienplatz

The area south of Marienplatz is becoming a kind of Soho, with lots of fun shops, wine bars, and bistros handy for a healthy and quick lunch. All of these recommended restaurants are located on the map on page 78, except for the last one (La Vecchia Masseria), which is on the map on page 75.

Buxs Self-Service Vegetarian Restaurant is a cafeteria where you'll find exactly what you want—as long as it's vegetarian. Fill a plate with your choice of organic soups, salads, and hot dishes, then pay by weight (about €10 for a meal, Mon–Fri 11:00–18:45, Sat 11:00–15:00, closed Sun, non-smoking, at bottom end of Viktualienmarkt at Frauenstrasse 9, tel. 089/291-9550).

Forum Speisecafé—young, stylish, and without a hint of tourism—features international cuisine. It's famous for its creative breakfasts (served all day long) and for its imaginative weekly specials posted outside on the chalkboard (€6 lunches available 11:00–14:30, €10 dinners, open daily 8:00–24:00, later Fri–Sat, smoky interior or breezy outdoor seating, corner of Corneliusstrasse and Müllerstrasse, tel. 089/268-818).

Stadt Café is a lively, smoky diner/café serving great daily specials (€5–8) and an inventive menu of Italian, German, salads, and vegetarian dishes. This high-energy, no-frills restaurant and its cobbled courtyard are packed with enthusiastic local eaters, newspaper-readers, and coffee-sippers. In the summer, try a refreshing *Hollerblüten-Schorle*—elderflower spritzer, served with mint (daily 10:00–24:00, in Munich City Museum, St.-Jakobs-Platz 1, tel. 089/266-949).

Prinz Myshkin is everybody's favorite upscale vegetarian eatery in the old center. You'll find a clever, appetizing selection of €8–15 plates. The decor is modern, the arched ceilings are cool, the outside seating is on a quiet street, and the clientele is entirely local (daily 11:30–23:00, non-smoking section doesn't quite work, Hackenstrasse 2, tel. 089/265-596).

Riva Bar Pizzeria is a long, skinny bar with an open oven popping out great pizzas to a crowd of young Münchners. It's very popular for its fresh, homemade-quality pizzas, pastas, and salads. There's a crowded dining area in back and a few pleasant tables outside on the busy sidewalk (€7–11 pizzas, Mon–Sat 8:00–24:00, Sun 12:00–24:00, 50 yards toward Marienplatz from Isartor at Im Tal 44, tel. 089/220-240).

La Vecchia Masseria serves simple Italian food inside amid a cozy Tuscan farmhouse decor, or outside in a beautiful flowery courtyard. Try the €24 tasting *menu* (daily 11:30–23:00, reservations smart, cash or AmEx only, near train station, Mathildenstrasse 3, tel. 089/550-9090, fax 089/550-9091).

TRANSPORTATION CONNECTIONS

Munich is a super transportation hub (one reason it was the target of so many WWII bombs). Train info: tel. 11861 (€0.60/min). For quick help at the main train station, stop by the train service counter in front of track 18. For better English and more patience, drop by EurAide in a small hallway off the main entryway (with your back to track 19, head toward the main entrance; before the pretzel stand, turn left—the EurAide office is on the left; see page 29). For flight information, see page 30.

From Munich by Train to: **Füssen** (hourly, 2 hrs; for a Neuschwanstein Castle day trip, depart at 6:50 and arrive at 9:00 with transfer in Buchloe; or go direct at 8:52 and arrive at 10:55—confirm times at station), **Reutte,** Austria (hourly, 2.5–3.5 hrs, transfer in Garmisch, Pfronten-Steinach, or Kempten), **Oberammergau** (nearly hourly, 1.75 hrs, change in Murnau), **Salzburg,** Austria (hourly, 1.5–2 hrs), **Berchtesgaden** (roughly hourly, 2.5–3 hrs, most with change in Salzburg or Freilassing, many with connection to bus), **Nürnberg** (2–3/hr, 1–1.25 hrs), **Würzburg** (1–2/hr, 2 hrs), **Rothenburg** (hourly, 2.5–3.5 hrs, 2–3 transfers), **Frankfurt** (hourly, 3 hrs) and **Frankfurt Airport** (2/hr, 3.5 hrs, a few with change in Mannheim), **Dresden** (about hourly, 5.75–6.25 hrs, transfer in Leipzig or Nürnberg), **Berlin** (hourly, 5.75 hrs, a few with change in Nürnberg), **Vienna** (3/day direct, 4.25 hrs; otherwise about hourly, 5–5.75 hrs, transfer in Salzburg), **Venice** (3–5/day, 7 hrs, may change in Verona), **Paris** (4/day, 6–7 hrs, 1–3 changes), **Prague** (2/day direct, 6/day with changes, 6–7 hrs). Night trains run daily to Berlin, Vienna, Venice, Florence, Rome, Paris, Amsterdam, Budapest, Milan (via Switzerland), Copenhagen, and Prague (at least 7 hours to each city). To use a railpass for a night train to Italy, your pass must include all countries on the train route (i.e., Austria or Switzerland). Otherwise, you must buy a ticket covering the entire trip.

Romantic Road Bus: For information on the Romantic Road bus tour, which connects "Mad" King Ludwig's castles, Munich, Dinkelsbühl, Rothenburg, and the Rhine, see page 182.

BAVARIA AND TIROL

Two hours south of Munich, between Germany's Bavaria and Austria's Tirol, is a timeless land of fairy-tale castles, painted buildings shared by cows and farmers, and locals who still yodel when they're happy.

In Germany's Bavaria, tour "Mad" King Ludwig II's ornate Neuschwanstein Castle, Europe's most spectacular. Stop by the Wieskirche, a textbook example of Bavarian Rococo bursting with curly curlicues, and browse through Oberammergau, Germany's woodcarving capital and home of the famous Passion Play.

In Austria's Tirol, hike to the ruined Ehrenberg castle,

scream down a ski slope on an oversized skateboard, and then catch your breath for an evening of traditional music or dancing.

In this chapter, I'll cover Bavaria first, then Tirol. Austria's Tirol is easier and cheaper than touristy Bavaria. My favorite home base for exploring Bavaria's castles is actually in Austria, in the town of Reutte. Füssen, in Germany, is a handier home base for train travelers.

Planning Your Time

While Germans and Austrians vacation here for a week or two at a time, the typical speedy American traveler will find two days' worth of sightseeing. With a car and more time, you could enjoy

Highlights of Bavaria and Tirol

three or four days, but the basic visit ranges anywhere from a long day trip from Munich to a three-night, two-day visit. If the weather's good and you're not going to Switzerland on your trip, be sure to ride a lift to an alpine peak.

By Car: Here's a good one-day circular drive from Reutte: 7:30–Breakfast; 8:00–Depart hotel; 8:30–Arrive at Neuschwanstein to pick up tickets (which you reserved a few days earlier—see page 100) for the two castles—Neuschwanstein and Hohenschwangau; 9:00–Tour Hohenschwangau; 11:00–Tour Neuschwanstein; 13:00–Drive to the Wieskirche (20-min stop) and on to Linderhof Castle; 14:30–Tour Linderhof; 16:30–Drive along scenic Plansee lake back into Austria; 17:30–Back at hotel;

19:00–Dinner at hotel and perhaps a folk evening. In peak season, you might arrive later at Linderhof to avoid the crowds. Off-season (Oct–March), start your day an hour later, since Neuschwanstein and Hohenschwangau don't open until 10:00.

The next morning, you could stroll through Reutte, hike to the Ehrenberg ruins, and ride the luge on your way to Innsbruck, Munich, Switzerland, Venice, or wherever.

By Public Transportation: Train travelers can use Füssen as a base and bus or bike the three miles to Neuschwanstein. Reutte is connected by bus with Füssen (except Sat–Sun; taxi €30 one-way). If you're based in Reutte, you can bike to the Ehrenberg ruins (just outside Reutte) and to Neuschwanstein Castle/Tegelberg luge (90 min). A one-way taxi from Reutte to Neuschwanstein costs about €35. Or, if you stay at the recommended Gutshof zum Schluxen hotel, it's a one-hour hike through the woods to Neuschwanstein.

Getting Around Bavaria and Tirol

By Car: This region is ideal by car. All the sights are within an easy 60-mile loop from Reutte or Füssen. Even if you're doing the rest of your trip by train, consider renting a car in Füssen for the day here (€62/day; see "Car Rental," page 93).

By Public Transportation: It can be frustrating. Local bus service in the region is spotty for sightseeing. If you're rushed and without wheels, Reutte, the Wieskirche, Linderhof, and most of the luge rides are probably not worth the trouble (though the Tegelberg luge near Neuschwanstein is within walking distance of the castle and served regularly by bus).

Füssen, with hourly train connections to and from Munich (2-hour trip, some with transfer in Buchloe), is three miles from Neuschwanstein Castle, easily reachable by bus or bike (see page 97).

Reutte is a 35-minute bus ride from Füssen (Mon–Fri 6/day, none Sat–Sun, less off-season, €3.40; taxis from Reutte to the castles are €35 one-way; to Füssen, €30). Ask your hotel to help you find the most up-to-date schedule.

Buses also run from Füssen to **Oberammergau** (6/day, less off-season, 1.5 hr, transfer in Echelsbacher Brücke; bus often marked *Garmisch*, confirm with driver that bus will stop in Oberammergau). From Munich, visiting Oberammergau directly by train is easier (nearly hourly, 1.75 hrs, change in Murnau or Oberau) than going to Füssen to catch the bus.

Füssen to Linderhof by public transportation will burn most of a valuable sightseeing day; you'll spend more time on the bus (or waiting for it) than you will at the castle. Skip Linderhof—or rent a car for the day. If you must go, take an early bus to Oberammergau (see connections above), which has direct bus connections to Linderhof (4/day in summer, less off-season, 30 min).

The **Wieskirche** is relatively easy to reach from Füssen by bus (4–5/day, 40–50 min each way, more frequently with a transfer in Steingaden). But, as with Linderhof, you'll spend more time on the bus—and waiting for the return bus—than you'll spend actually enjoying the church.

Confirm all bus schedules in Füssen: Check the big board at the bus stop across from the train station, buy the indispensable bus timetable (€0.30, *OVG Fahrpläne der Linienbusse*) at the TI or train station, check online at www.rva-bus.de, or call 08362/939-0505. For longer-distance bus trips (such as to Garmisch or Linderhof), you'll save money if you buy a *Tagesticket* (day pass).

If you'll be taking a lot of trains in Bavaria (for example, day-tripping from Munich to the castles), consider the **Bayern-Ticket** (covers up to four people from Munich to anywhere in Bavaria and back for only €27/day, not valid Mon–Fri before 9:00; for more information, see page 67 in the Munich chapter).

By Tour: If you're interested only in Bavarian castles, consider an all-day organized bus tour of the Bavarian biggies as a side-trip from Munich (see page 38 in the Munich chapter).

By Bike: This is great biking country. Shops in or near train stations rent bikes for €8–15 per day. The ride from Reutte to Neuschwanstein and the Tegelberg luge (90 min) is great for those with the time and energy.

By Thumb: Hitchhiking, always risky, is a slow-but-possible way to connect the public-transportation gaps.

Füssen

Füssen has been a strategic stop since ancient times. Its main street sits on the Via Claudia Augusta, which crossed the Alps (over the Brenner Pass) in Roman times. The town was the southern terminus of a medieval trade route now known among modern tourists as the "Romantic Road." Dramatically situated under a renovated castle on the lively Lech River, Füssen recently celebrated its 700th birthday.

Unfortunately, Füssen is overrun by tourists in the summer. Traffic can be exasperating. Apart from Füssen's cobbled and arcaded town center, there's little real sightseeing here. The striking-from-a-distance **Castle** (Hohes Schloss) houses a boring picture gallery. The mediocre **City Museum** (Kloster St. Mang) in the monastery below the castle exhibits lifestyles of 200 years ago and the story of the monastery, and offers displays on the

Füssen

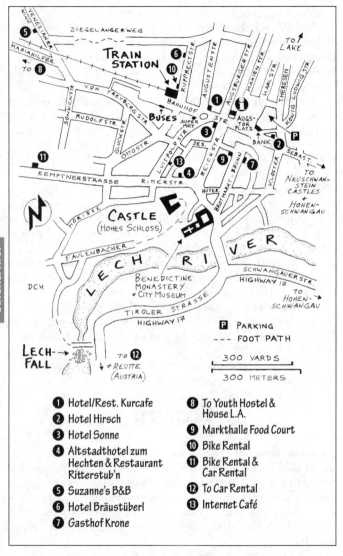

Füssen

1 Hotel/Rest. Kurcafe

2 Hotel Hirsch

3 Hotel Sonne

4 Altstadthotel zum Hechten & Restaurant Ritterstub'n

5 Suzanne's B&B

6 Hotel Bräustüberl

7 Gasthof Krone

8 To Youth Hostel & House L.A.

9 Markthalle Food Court

10 Bike Rental

11 Bike Rental & Car Rental

12 To Car Rental

13 Internet Café

P PARKING

- - - FOOT PATH

300 YARDS

300 METERS

development of the violin, for which Füssen is famous (€2.50, €3 includes castle gallery; April–Oct Tue–Sun 11:00–17:00, closed Mon; Nov–March Fri–Sun 13:00–16:00, closed Mon–Thu; English descriptions, free WC outside entrance, tel. 08362/903-146).

Halfway between Füssen and the border (as you drive, or a woodsy walk from the town) is the **Lechfall,** a thunderous waterfall (with a handy WC).

ORIENTATION

(area code: 08362)

Füssen's train station is a few blocks from the TI, the town center (a cobbled shopping mall), and all my hotel listings (see "Sleeping"). If necessary, the **TI** can help you find a room (June–mid-Sept Mon–Fri 9:00–18:30, Sat 10:00–14:00, Sun 10:00–12:00, less off-season, one free Internet terminal, 3 blocks down Bahnhofstrasse from station, tel. 08362/93850, fax 08362/938-520, www.fuessen.de). After hours, the little self-service info pavilion (7:00–24:30) near the front of the TI features an automated room-finding service.

Arrival in Füssen: Exit left as you leave the train station (lockers available, €2–3) and walk a few straight blocks to the center of town and the TI. To get to Neuschwanstein or Reutte, catch a bus from in front of the station.

Helpful Hints

Internet Access: Try **Videoland** (€2/30 min, €3/hr, Mon–Wed and Fri–Sat 9:00–23:00, Sun 9:00–21:00, closed Thu, Luitpoldstrasse 11, tel. 08362/38300).

Bike Rental: The easiest location is **Bike Station,** sitting right where the train tracks end (€8/24 hrs, May–Sept Mon–Fri 9:00–18:30, Sat 9:00–14:00, Sun 9:00–12:00 in good weather, closed Oct–April, mobile 0176-2205-3080). **Rad Zacherl** has a bigger selection, but a less convenient location (€8/24 hrs, mountain bikes-€15/24 hrs, passport number for deposit; Mon–Fri 9:00–12:00 & 14:00–18:00, Sat 9:00–13:00, closed Sun; three-quarters of a mile out of town at Kemptener Strasse 26, tel. 08362/3292). For a strenuous but enjoyable 20-mile loop trip, see page 103.

Car Rental: Peter Schlichtling is quite central, with reasonable prices (€62/day, includes insurance, Mon–Fri 8:00–18:00, Sat 9:00–12:00, closed Sun, Kemptener Strasse 26, tel. 08362/922-122, www.schlichtling.de). **Auto Osterried/Europcar** rents at similar prices, but is an €8 taxi ride away from the train station (daily 8:00–19:00, across river from Füssen at Tiroler Strasse 65, tel. 08362/6381).

SLEEPING

Though I prefer sleeping in Reutte (see page 109), convenient Füssen is just three miles from Ludwig's castles and offers a cobbled, riverside retreat. It's very touristy, but it has plenty of rooms. All recommended accommodations are within a few blocks of the train station and the town center. Parking is easy at the station.

Sleep Code

(€1 = about $1.30, country code: 49, area code: 08362)
S = Single, **D** = Double/Twin, **T** = Triple, **Q** = Quad, **b** = bathroom,
s = shower only. Unless otherwise noted, credit cards are
accepted, English is spoken, and breakfast is included. The
€1.35 per person, per night "tourist tax" is not included in
these rates.

To help you sort easily through these listings, I've divided
the rooms into three categories, based on the price for a standard double room with bath:

$$$ Higher Priced—Most rooms €100 or more.
$$ Moderately Priced—Most rooms between €60–100.
$ Lower Priced—Most rooms €60 or less.

Bavaria/Tirol

Prices listed are for one-night stays. Most hotels give about 5 to
10 percent off for two-night stays—always request this discount.
Competition is fierce, and off-season prices are soft. High season
is mid-June through September. Rooms are generally about 12 percent less in shoulder season and much cheaper in off-season. To
locate these hotels, see the map on page 92.

$$$ Hotel Kurcafe is deluxe, with 30 spacious rooms and
all of the amenities. The standard rooms are comfortable, and the
newer, bigger rooms have elegant touches and fun decor—like
canopy drapes and cherubic frescoes over the bed (Sb-€89, stan-
dard Db-€109–125, bigger Db-€135–149 depending on size,
Tb-€135, Qb-€149, 4-person suite-€179–209, €10 more for week-
ends and holidays, ask about package deals, cheaper off-season,
non-smoking rooms, elevator, parking-€5–9/day, carries some
US newspapers, on tiny traffic circle a block in front of station at
Bahnhofstrasse 4, tel. 08362/930-180, fax 08362/930-1850, www
.kurcafe.com, info@kurcafe.com, Schöll family).

$$$ Hotel Hirsch is a big, romantic, old tour-class hotel with
53 rooms on the main street in the center of town. Their standard
rooms are fine, and their theme rooms are a fun splurge (Sb-€62–
82, standard Db-€113–133, theme Db-€135–165, depends on room
size and demand, cheaper Nov–March and during slow times, only
the expensive theme rooms are non-smoking, family rooms, elevator, free parking, Kaiser-Maximilian-Platz 7, tel. 08362/93980, fax
08362/939-877, www.hotelhirsch.de, info@hotelhirsch.de).

$$$ Hotel Sonne, in the heart of town, rents 51 stylish and
spacious rooms (Sb-€92–122, Db-€117–158, Tb-€136–169, Qb-
175–185, higher prices are for huge rooms in the new wing, cheaper
Oct–mid-May, non-smoking rooms, elevator, free Internet

terminal in lobby, free sauna, parking-€2.50–4.50/day, kitty-corner from TI at Prinzregentenplatz 1, tel. 08362/9080, fax 08362/908-100, www.hotel-sonne.de, info@hotel-sonne.de).

$$ Altstadthotel zum Hechten, with 35 rooms, offers all the modern comforts in a friendly, traditional shell right under Füssen Castle in the old-town pedestrian zone (Sb-€54, Db-€89, Tb-€114, Qb-€136, get a discount in 2008 if you reserve by email and mention this book, cheaper off-season, beds can be short, non-smoking rooms, fun miniature bowling alley in basement, free parking; from TI, walk down pedestrian street and take second right to Ritterstrasse 6; tel. 08362/91600, fax 08362/916-099, www.hotel-hechten.com, hotel.hechten@t-online.de, Pfeiffer and Tramp families).

$$ Suzanne's B&B is run by a plainspoken, no-nonsense American woman who strikes some travelers as a brusque drill sergeant. Suzanne runs a tight ship, offering travel advice, local cheese, a children's yard, a gorgeous garden, laundry (€25/load), and bright, woody, spacious rooms (Db-€90, huge Db with water-bed and balcony-€95, Tb-€120, Qb-€156, suite from €120 can hold up to 10—ask for details; cash only, non-smoking, Internet access-€5/hr; exit station right and backtrack 2 blocks along tracks, cross tracks at Venetianerwinkel to #3; tel. 08362/38485, fax 08362/921-396, www.suzannes.de, svorbrugg@t-online.de). Her kid-friendly attic loft has very low ceilings (you'll crouch), a private bathroom (you'll crouch), and up to six beds (attic special: €73/2 people, €105/3 people, €130/4 people).

$$ Hotel Bräustüberl has 16 decent rooms at fair rates attached to a gruff, musty, old beer hall–type place. Don't expect much service (Db-€84, cash only, Rupprechtstrasse 5, 1 block from station, tel. 08362/7843, fax 08362/923-951, www.brauereigasthof-braeustueberl.de, brauereigasthof-fuessen@t-online.de).

$ Gasthof Krone, a rare bit of pre-glitz Füssen in the pedestrian zone, has dumpy halls and stairs and 12 big, worn-but-clean time-warp rooms at good prices (S-€28, D-€52, extra bed-€26, extra bed for kids under 12-€20, €3 more per person for 1-night stays, reception in medieval-themed restaurant, closed Nov–June; from TI, head down pedestrian street and take first left to Schrannengasse 17; tel. 08362/7824, fax 08362/37505, www.krone-fuessen .de, info@krone-fuessen.de).

$ Füssen Youth Hostel, a fine, German-run place, welcomes travelers (€18 dorm beds in 2- to 6-bed rooms, D-€56, €3 more for non-members, includes breakfast and sheets, guests over age 26 allowed only if there's room, non-smoking, laundry-€3.20/load, dinner for a few euros, bike rental, office open 7:00–12:00 & 17:00–23:00, until 22:00 off-season, from station backtrack 10 min along tracks, Mariahilfer Strasse 5, tel. 08362/7754, fax 08362/2770, www.fuessen.jugendherberge.de, jhfuessen@djh-bayern.de).

$ House L.A. has three very basic but clean rooms at youth-hostel prices, a 20-minute walk from the station (D-€40, light breakfast served in room; from station, follow Von Freybergstrasse until it turns into Welfenstrasse, #39 is on the left, also rents rooms at Wachsbleiche 2; tel. 08362/607-366, mobile 0170-624-8610, fax 08362/38534, www.housela.de, info@housela.de).

EATING

Füssen's old town and main pedestrian drag are lined with a variety of eateries. The first three listings cluster on Ritterstrasse, just under the castle, off the top of the main street.

Restaurant Ritterstub'n offers delicious, reasonably priced fish, salads, fondue, veggie plates, and a fun kids' menu (€6–12 plates, Mon 17:00–23:00, Tue–Sun 11:30–14:30 & 17:30–23:00, Ritterstrasse 4, tel. 08362/7759). Demure Gabi serves while her husband cooks.

Wirtshaus and **Schencke** are two restaurants located within the recommended Altstadthotel zum Hechten. They dish up hearty, traditional Bavarian fare and specialize in pike *(Hecht)* pulled from the Lech River, served with a tasty, fresh herb sauce (€8–13 plates, daily 10:00–22:00, tel. 0836/91600, Ritterstrasse 6).

Hotel Kurcafe's fine restaurant, right on Füssen's main traffic circle, has good weekly specials, plus a tempting bakery (daily 11:30–14:30 & 17:30–21:30, choose between a traditional dining room and a pastel winter garden, live Bavarian zither music most Fri–Sat during dinner, Bahnhofstrasse 4, tel. 08362/930-180).

The **Markthalle** food court, just across the street from Gasthof Krone, offers a wide selection of reasonably priced, non-wurst items. Located in an old corn warehouse from 1483, it's now home to a fishmonger; Chinese, Turkish, and Italian delis; a fruit stand; a bakery; and a wine bar. Buy your food from one of the vendors, park yourself at any one of the tables, then look up and admire the Renaissance ceiling (Mon–Fri 7:30–18:30, Sat 7:30–14:00, closed Sun, corner of Schrannengasse and Brunnengasse).

Picnic Supplies: Bakeries and *Metzger*s (butcher shops) abound and frequently have ready-made sandwiches. For groceries, try the **Plus** supermarket at the roundabout on your way into town from the train station (Mon–Sat 8:30–20:00, closed Sun).

TRANSPORTATION CONNECTIONS

From Füssen to: Neuschwanstein (1–2 buses/hr, 10 min, €1.60 one-way, €3.20 round-trip; taxis cost €9 one-way), **Oberammergau** (6 buses/day, fewer off-season, 1.5 hrs), **Reutte** (Mon–Fri 6 buses/

day, none Sat–Sun, 35 min, €3.40 one-way; taxis cost €30 one-way), **Munich** (hourly trains, 2 hrs, some change in Buchloe), **Innsbruck** (5 trains/day, 4.25 hrs, change in Munich). Train info: tel. 11861 (€0.60/min).

Romantic Road Buses: The northbound Romantic Road bus departs Füssen at 10:10; the southbound bus arrives Füssen at 19:35 (bus stops at train station). A railpass gets you a 60 percent discount on the Romantic Road bus (without using up a day of a flexipass). For more information, see page 182 in the Rothenburg chapter.

The Best of Bavaria

Within a short drive of Füssen or Reutte, you'll find some of the most enjoyable—and most tourist-filled—sights in Germany. The otherworldly castles of Neuschwanstein and Hohenschwangau capture romantics' imaginations, the ornately decorated Wieskirche puts the faithful in a heavenly mood, and the little town of Oberammergau overwhelms visitors with cuteness. Yet another impressive castle (Linderhof) and a sky-high viewpoint (the Zugspitze) round out Bavaria's top attractions.

The most popular tourist destinations in Bavaria are the "King's Castles" *(Königsschlösser)*. With fairy-tale turrets in a fairy-tale alpine setting built by a fairy-tale king, they are understandably beloved.

Planning Your Time

The well-organized visitor can have a great four-hour visit. Others will just stand in line and possibly not even see the castles. The key: Phone ahead for a reservation (details below) or arrive by 8:00 to wait in line for tickets (you'll have time to see both castles, consider fun options nearby—mountain lift, luge course, or Füssen town—and get out by early afternoon). Off-season (Oct–June), you have a little more flexibility, but it's still a good idea to get an early start (try to arrive by 9:00).

Getting There

If arriving by **car,** note that road signs in the region refer to the sight as *Königsschlösser,* not Neuschwanstein. There's plenty of parking (all lots-€4.50). Get there early, and you'll park where you like. Lot 4—past the ticket center and next to the lake—is my favorite.

From **Füssen,** those without cars can catch the roughly hourly **bus** (€1.60 one-way, €3.20 round-trip, 10 min, note times carefully on the meager schedule, catch bus at train station), take a **taxi** (€9 one-way), or ride a rental **bike** (2 miles).

From **Reutte,** take the bus to Füssen (Mon–Fri 4/day, none Sat–Sun, €3.40, 35 min; more connections via train to Pfronten-Weissbach then bus to Füssen—2/day Mon–Fri, 6/day Sat–Sun, 1–1.5 hrs), then hop a city bus to the castle.

For a romantic twist, hike or mountain-bike from the trailhead at the recommended hotel **Gutshof zum Schluxen** in Pinswang (see page 118). When the dirt road forks at the top of the hill, go right (downhill), cross the Austria–Germany border (marked by a sign and deserted hut), and follow the narrow paved road to the castles. It's a 60- to 90-minute hike or a great circular bike trip (allow 30 min; cyclists can return to Schluxen from the castles on a different 30-min bike route via Füssen).

SIGHTS

The King's Castles

▲▲▲Neuschwanstein Castle

Imagine "Mad" King Ludwig as a boy, climbing the hills above his dad's castle, Hohenschwangau (see next page), dreaming up the ultimate fairy-tale castle. He had the power to make his dream concrete and stucco. Neuschwanstein (noy-SHVAHN-shtine) was designed by a painter first...then an architect. It looks medieval, but it's only about as old as the Eiffel Tower. It feels like something you'd see at a home show for 19th-century royalty. Built from 1869 to 1886, it's the epitome of the Romanticism popular in 19th-century Europe. Construction stopped with Ludwig's death (only a third of the interior was finished), and within six weeks, tourists were paying to go through it.

Today, guides herd groups of 60 through the castle, giving an interesting—if rushed—30-minute tour. You'll go up and down more than 300 steps, through lavish Wagnerian dream rooms, a royal state-of-the-19th-century-art kitchen, the king's gilded-lily bedroom, and his extravagant throne room. You'll visit 15 rooms with their original furnishings and fanciful wall paintings. After the tour, you'll see a room lined with fascinating drawings (described in English) of the castle plans, construction, and drawings from 1883 of Falkenstein—a whimsical, over-the-top, never-built castle that makes Neuschwanstein look stubby. Falkenstein occupied Ludwig's fantasies the year he died.

"Mad" King Ludwig

A tragic figure, Ludwig II (a.k.a. "Mad" King Ludwig) ruled Bavaria for 23 years until his death in 1886 at the age of 41. Politically, his reality was to "rule" either as a pawn of Prussia or a pawn of Austria. Rather than deal with politics in Bavaria's capital, Munich, Ludwig frittered away most of his time at his family's hunting palace, Hohenschwangau. He spent much of his adult life constructing his fanciful Neuschwanstein Castle—like a kid builds a tree house—on a neighboring hill upon the scant ruins of a medieval castle. Although Ludwig spent 17 years building Neuschwanstein, he lived in it only 172 days.

Ludwig was a true Romantic living in a Romantic age. His best friends were artists, poets, and composers such as Richard Wagner. His palaces are wallpapered with misty medieval themes—especially those from Wagnerian operas. Eventually he was declared mentally unfit to rule Bavaria and taken away from Neuschwanstein. Two days after this eviction, Ludwig was found dead in a lake. To this day, people debate whether the king was murdered or committed suicide.

Following the tour, a 20-minute slide show (alternating German and English) plays continuously. If English is on, pop in. If not, it's not worth waiting for.

Mary's Bridge (Marienbrücke)—Before or after the Neuschwanstein tour, climb up to Mary's Bridge to marvel at Ludwig's castle, just as Ludwig did. This bridge was quite an engineering accomplishment 100 years ago. From the bridge, the frisky can hike even higher to the *Beware—Danger of Death* signs and an even more glorious castle view. (Access to the bridge is closed in bad winter weather, but many travelers walk around the barriers to get there—at their own risk, of course.) For the most interesting descent from Neuschwanstein (15 min longer but worth it, especially with new steel walkways and railings that make the slippery area safer), follow signs to the Pöllat Gorge *(Pöllatschlucht)*.

▲▲Hohenschwangau Castle

Standing quietly below Neuschwanstein, the big, yellow Hohenschwangau (hoh-en-SHVAHN-gow) Castle was Ludwig's boyhood home. Originally built in the 12th century, it was ruined by Napoleon. Ludwig's father, Maximilian, rebuilt it, and you'll see it as it looked in 1836. It's more lived-in and historic, and excellent 30-minute tours actually give a better glimpse of Ludwig's life than the more-visited and famous Neuschwanstein Castle tour.

Neuschwanstein and Hohenschwangau Castles

Bavaria/Tirol

NOTE: MAP NOT TO SCALE
BORDER TO ALPSEE PARKING = 3 MILE DRIVE.
ALPSEE PARKING TO NEUSCH. = 30 MIN. HIKE.
TRAILS ARE SLIPPERY WHEN WET.

— ROAD
- - - TRAIL
P PARKING

❶ Alpenhotel Meier
❷ Romantic Pension Albrecht
❸ Beim "Landhannes" Rooms
❹ Sonnenhof Rooms
❺ Festspielhaus & Bike Path Start

Visiting the Castles

Cost and Hours: Each castle costs €9, a *Königsticket* for both castles costs €17, and children under 18 (accompanied by an adult) are admitted free (castles open April–Sept daily from 9:00 with last tour departing at 18:00, Oct–March daily from 10:00 with last tour at 16:00).

Getting Tickets for the Castles: Every tour bus in Bavaria converges on Neuschwanstein, and tourists flush in each morning from Munich. A handy reservation system (described below) sorts out the chaos for smart travelers. Tickets come with admission times. To tour both castles, you must do Hohenschwangau first (logical, since this gives a better introduction to Ludwig's short life). You'll get two tour times: Hohenschwangau and then, two hours later, Neuschwanstein. If you miss your appointed tour time, you can't get in.

If you arrive late and without a reservation, you'll spend two

hours in the ticket line and may find all tours for the day booked. A **ticket center** for both Neuschwanstein and Hohenschwangau is located at street level between the two castles (daily April–Sept 8:00–17:00, Oct–March 9:00–15:00, last tickets sold for Neuschwanstein 1 hour before closing, for Hohenschwangau 30 min before closing). Tickets purchased at the ticket center are for that day only. First tours start at about 9:00 (or 10:00 Oct–March). Arrive by 8:00 in summer, and you'll likely be touring by 9:00. Warning: During the summer, tickets for English tours can run out by 16:00.

It's best to **reserve ahead** in peak season (July–Sept, especially Aug). You can make reservations a minimum of 24 hours in advance by contacting the ticket office by phone (tel. 08362/930-830), e-mail (info@ticket-center-hohenschwangau.de), or booking online (www.ticket-center-hohenschwangau.de). Tickets reserved in advance cost €1.80 extra (per person, per castle), and ticket holders must be at the ticket office well before the appointed entry time (30 min before for Hohenschwangau, 1 hour before for Neuschwanstein—this allows you sufficient time to make your way up to the castle). Remember that many of the businesses are owned by the old royal family, so they encourage you to space the two tours longer than necessary in hopes that you'll spend a little more money. Insist on the tightest schedule—with no lunch break—if you don't want too much down time.

Services: The helpful TI, bus stop, ATM, stamp machine, WC (€0.50, handy change machine outside), and telephones cluster around the main intersection (**TI** hours are sporadic, but generally open daily May–Sept 11:00–19:00, Oct–April 11:00–17:00, tel. 08362/819-765, www.schwangau.de). The "village" at the foot of Europe's Disney castle feeds off the droves of hungry, shop-happy tourists. The Bräustüberl cafeteria serves the cheapest grub (often with live folk music). The Alpsee lake is ideal for a picnic, but there are no grocery shops nearby. Your best bet is to get food go from one of the many bratwurst stands (between the ticket center and TI) for a lazy lunch at the lakeside park or in one of the old-fashioned rowboats (rented by the hour in summer).

Getting to the Castles: From the ticket booth, Hohenschwangau is an easy 10-minute climb, and Neuschwanstein is a steep 30-minute hike. To minimize hiking to Neuschwanstein, you can take a shuttle bus (from in front of Hotel Lisl, just above ticket office and to the left) or horse-drawn carriage (from in front of Hotel Müller, just above ticket office and to the right), but neither gets you to the castle doorstep. The frequent shuttle buses drop you off near Mary's Bridge, leaving you a steep 10-minute downhill walk from the castle—be sure to see the view from Mary's Bridge before hiking down (€1.80 up, €2.60 round-trip not worth it since you have to hike up to bus stop for return trip). Carriages (€5 up, €2.50 down) are slower than walking and stop below Neuschwanstein, leaving you a five-minute uphill hike. Note: If it's less than an hour until your Neuschwanstein tour time, you'll need to hike, and even at a brisk pace, it still takes 30 minutes. For a less-strenuous, varied, and economical plan, ride the bus to Mary's Bridge for the view, hike down to the castle, and then catch the carriage from there back down.

Near the Castles

▲**Tegelberg Gondola**—Just north of Neuschwanstein is a fun play zone around the mighty Tegelberg gondola. Hang gliders circle like vultures. Their pilots jump from the top of the Tegelberg gondola. For €15 round-trip (€9 one-way), you can ride the lift to the 5,500-foot summit (daily Dec–Oct 9:00–17:00, closed Nov, 4–5/hr, last ride up at 16:30, in bad weather call first to confirm, tel. 08362/98360). On a clear day, you get great views of the Alps and Bavaria and the vicarious thrill of watching hang gliders and paragliders leap into airborne ecstasy. Weather permitting, scores of adventurous Germans line up and leap from the launch ramp at the top of the lift. With one leaving every two or three minutes, it's great for spectators. Thrill-seekers with exceptional social skills may talk themselves into a tandem ride with a paraglider. From the top of Tegelberg, it's a steep 2.5-hour hike down to Ludwig's castle. Avoid the treacherous trail directly below the gondola. At the base of the gondola, you'll find a playground, a cheery eatery, and a very good luge ride (below).

▲**Tegelberg Luge**—Next to the Tegelberg Gondola is a luge course. A luge is like a bobsled on wheels (for more details, see "Luge Lesson" sidebar on page 114). This stainless-steel track is heated, so it's often dry and open, even when drizzly weather shuts down the concrete luges. It's not as scenic as Austria's Biberwier luge (see page 114), but it's handy (€2.50/ride, 6-ride sharable card-€10, July–Sept daily 10:00–18:00, otherwise same hours as gondola, in winter sometimes opens late due to wet track, in bad weather call first to confirm, tel. 08362/98360). A funky cable system pulls riders (in their sleds) to the top without a ski lift.

▲**Royal Crystal Baths (Königliche Kristall-Therme)**—This pool/ sauna complex just outside Füssen is the perfect way to relax on a rainy day, or to cool off on a hot one. The downstairs contains two heated indoor pools and a café; outside you'll find a shallow kiddie pool, a lap pool, a heated "Kristallbad" with massage jets and a whirlpool, and a salty mineral bath. The extensive saunas upstairs are well worth the few extra euros, as long as you're OK with nudity. (Swimsuits are required in the downstairs pools, but *verboten* in the upstairs saunas.) You'll see pool and sauna rules in German all over, but don't worry—just follow the locals' lead. To enter the baths, first choose the length of your visit and your focus (big outdoor pool only, all ground-floor pools but not the saunas, or the whole enchilada—a flyer explains all the prices in English). You'll get a wristband and a credit-card-sized ticket with a bar code. Insert that ticket into the entry gate, and keep it—you'll need it to get out. Enter through the yellow changing stalls—where you'll change into your bathing suit—then choose a storage locker (€1 coin deposit). When it's time to leave, reinsert your ticket in the gate—if you've gone over the time limit, feed extra euros into the machine (€8.50/2 hrs, €12.20/4 hrs, €15.80/day, saunas-€4, towel rental-€2, bathing suit rental-€3, daily 9:00–22:00, Fri–Sat until 23:00, nude swimming everywhere Tue and Fri after 19:00; from Füssen, drive, bike, or walk across the river, turn left toward Schwangau, and then, about a mile later, turn left at signs for *Kristall-Therme*, Am Ehberg 16, tel. 08362/819630).

Bike Ride Around Forggensee—On a beautiful day, nothing beats a bike ride around the bright-turquoise Forggensee lake. This 20-mile ride is almost exclusively on bike paths, with just a few stretches on country roads. Locals swear that going clockwise is less work, but either way has a couple of strenuous uphill parts. Still, the amazing views of the surrounding Alps will distract you from your churning legs—so this is still a great way to spend the afternoon. Rent a bike (see page 93), pack a picnic lunch, and figure about three hours round-trip. From Füssen, follow *Festspielhaus* signs; once you reach the theater, follow *Forggensee Rundweg* signs. From the theater, you can also take a boat ride on the Forggensee (€7/50 min, 6/day; €9.50/2 hrs, 6/day; fewer departures Nov–May, confirm schedule at Füssen TI, tel. 08362/921-363).

SLEEPING

In Hohenschwangau, near Neuschwanstein Castle

(€1 = about $1.30, country code: 49, area code: 08362)

Inexpensive farmhouse *Zimmer* (B&Bs) abound in the Bavarian countryside around Neuschwanstein, offering drivers a decent value. Look for *Zimmer Frei* signs ("room free," or vacancy). The going rate is about €50 to €65 for a double, including breakfast.

$$ Alpenhotel Meier is a small, family-run hotel with 18 rooms in a bucolic setting within walking distance of the castles, just beyond the lower parking lot (Sb-€48–58, Db-€80–88, Tb-€110, 5 percent discount with cash and this book in 2008, cheaper for longer stays, non-smoking rooms, all rooms have porches or balconies—some with castle views, family rooms, sauna, elevator, easy parking, just before tennis courts at Schwangauer Strasse 37, tel. 08362/81152, fax 08362/987-028, www.alpenhotel-allgaeu.de, info@alpenhotel-allgaeu.de, Frau Meier).

$$ Romantic Pension Albrecht, in the shadow of Neuschwanstein, offers seven rooms in a historic home. Just a three-minute walk from the ticket booth, you enjoy proximity to the castle without all the hustle and bustle. This charming house is a little tired—but at 102 years old, you would be, too. Many of the rooms have balconies, and friendly Frau Strauss—who welcomes her guests as her mother did before her—is happy to share her garden with you (Sb-€39, Ds-€57, Db-€67, cheaper for 4-night stays, cash only, free parking, Pfleger Rothut Weg 2, tel. & fax 08362/81102, www.albrecht-neuschwanstein.de, info@albrecht -neuschwanstein.de).

$ Beim "Landhannes" is a 200-year-old working dairy farm run by Johann and Traudl Mayr. They rent six creaky but fresh and sunny rooms, and keep flowers on the balconies, big bells and antlers in the halls, and cows in the yard (Sb-€30, Db-€60, 20 percent discount for 3 or more nights, apartment with kitchen, cash only, poorly signed in the village of Horn on the Füssen side of Schwangau, look for the farm 100 yards in front of Hotel Kleiner König, Am Lechrain 22, tel. & fax 08362/8349, www.landhannes .de, mayr@landhannes.de).

$ Sonnenhof is a big, woody, old house with four spacious, traditionally decorated rooms (all with balconies) and a cheery garden. It's a 15-minute walk through the fields to the castles (S-€35, D-€50, Db-€60, cash only; at Pension Schwansee on the Füssen–Neuschwanstein road, follow the small lane 100 yards to Sonnenweg 11; they'll pick you up from the train station if you request ahead, tel. 08362/8420, Frau Görlich).

Wieskirche

Germany's greatest Rococo-style church, this "Church in the Meadow" is newly restored and looking as brilliant as the day it floated down from heaven. It's worth ▲▲. Overripe with decoration but bright and bursting with beauty, this church is a divine droplet, a curly curlicue, the final flowering of the Baroque movement.

Cost and Hours: Donation requested, summer daily 8:00–19:00, winter daily 8:00–17:00, parking-€1, tel. 08862/932-930, www.wieskirche.de.

Getting There: The Wieskirche is 30 minutes north of Neuschwanstein. The Romantic Road bus tour stops here for 30 minutes—but only on the northbound route from Munich to Frankfurt. Southbound buses stop here to pick up and drop off only on request. For information on taking the bus from Füssen to the Wieskirche, see page 91 in "Getting Around Bavaria and Tirol," earlier in this chapter. By car, head north from Füssen, turn right at Steingaden, and follow the signs. Take a commune-with-nature-and-smell-the-farm detour back through the meadow to the parking lot.

❍ **Self-Guided Tour:** This pilgrimage church is built around the much-venerated statue of a scourged (or whipped) Christ, which supposedly wept in 1738. The carving—too graphic to be accepted by that generation's church—was the focus of worship in a peasant's barn. Miraculously, it shed tears—empathizing with all those who suffer. Pilgrims came from all around. A tiny and humble chapel was built to house the statue in 1739. (You can see it where the lane to the church leaves the parking lot.) Bigger and bigger crowds came. Two of Bavaria's top Rococo architects, the Zimmermann brothers, were commissioned to build the Wieskirche that stands here today.

Follow the theological sweep from the altar to the ceiling: Jesus whipped, chained, and then killed (notice the pelican above

the altar—recalling a pre-Christian story of a bird that opened its breast to feed its young with its own blood); the painting of a baby Jesus posed as if on the cross; the sacrificial lamb; and finally, high on the ceiling, the resurrected Christ before the Last Judgment. This is the most positive depiction of the Last Judgment around. Jesus, rather than sitting on the throne to judge, rides high on a rainbow—a symbol of forgiveness—giving any sinner the feeling that there is still time to repent, with plenty of mercy on hand. In the back, above the pipe organ, notice the empty throne—waiting for Judgment Day—and the closed door to paradise.

Above the entrances to both side aisles are murky glass cases with 18th-century handkerchiefs. People wept, came here, were healed, and no longer needed their hankies. Walk up either aisle flanking the high altar to see votives—requests and thanks to God (for happy, healthy babies, and so on). Notice how the kneelers are positioned so that worshippers can meditate on scenes of biblical miracles painted high on the ceiling and visible through the ornate tunnel frames. A priest here once told me that faith, architecture, light, and music all combine to create the harmony of the Wieskirche.

Two paintings flank the door at the rear of the church. One shows the ceremonial parade in 1749 when the white-clad monks of Steingaden carried the carved statue of Christ from the tiny church to its new big one. The second painting, from 1757, is a votive from one of the Zimmermann brothers, the artists and architects who built this church. He is giving thanks for the successful construction of the new church.

If you can't visit the Wieskirche, visit one of the other churches that came out of the same heavenly spray can: Oberammergau's church (see below), Munich's Asamkirche, Würzburg's Hofkirche Chapel (at the Residenz), the splendid Ettal Monastery (free and near Oberammergau), and, on a lesser scale, Füssen's cathedral.

Route Tips for Drivers: If you're driving from the Wieskirche to Oberammergau (below), you'll cross the **Echelsbacher Bridge,** which arches 230 feet over the Pöllat Gorge. Thoughtful drivers let their passengers walk across (for the views) and meet them at the other side. Any kayakers? Notice the painting of the traditional village woodcarver (who used to walk from town to town with his art on his back) on the first big house on the Oberammergau side, a shop called Almdorf Ammertal. It has a huge selection of overpriced carvings and commission-hungry tour guides.

Oberammergau

The Shirley Temple of Bavarian villages, and exploited to the hilt by the tourist trade, Oberammergau wears way too much makeup. If you're passing through anyway, it's a ▲ sight—worth a wander among the half-timbered *Lüftlmalerei* houses frescoed (in a style popular throughout the town in the 18th century) with biblical scenes and famous fairy-tale characters.

Tourist Information: The TI is at Eugen-Papst-Strasse 9A (Mon–Fri 9:00–18:00, Sat 9:00–12:00, Sun 10:00–12:00; Nov–May closed Sun; tel. 08822/92310, www.oberammergau.de).

Getting There: From Füssen to Oberammergau, six buses run daily (fewer in winter, 1.5 hrs). Trains run from Munich to Oberammergau (nearly hourly, 1.75 hrs, change in Murnau or Obergau). Drivers entering the town from the north should cross the bridge, take the second right, and park in the free lot a block beyond the TI. Leaving town, head out past the church and turn toward Ettal on Road 23. You're 20 miles from Reutte via the scenic Plansee. If heading to Munich, Road 23 takes you to the autobahn, which gets you there in less than an hour.

SIGHTS

Oberammergau Church—Visit the town church, a poor cousin of the one at Wies. This church looks richer than it is. Put your hand on the "marble" columns. If they warm up, they're fakes—"stucco marble." Wander through the graveyard. Ponder the deaths that two wars dealt Germany. Behind the church are the photos of three Schneller brothers, all killed within two years in World War II.

Passion Play—Still making good on a deal the townspeople struck with God when they were spared devastation by the Black Death several centuries ago, once each decade Oberammergau presents its Passion Play. For 100 summer days in a row, the town performs an all-day dramatic story of Christ's crucifixion (in 2000, 5,000 people attended per day). Until the next performance, in 2010, you'll have to settle for reading the book, seeing Nicodemus tool around town in his VW, or browsing through the theater's exhibition hall (€4, €6 combo-ticket includes Heimatmuseum, German tours March–Oct daily 10:00–16:00, Dec–Feb weekends only except daily for a week before and after Christmas, no tours in Nov, tel. 08822/945-8833). English speakers get little respect here, with only two theater tours a day scheduled (April–Oct at 11:00 and 14:00). They may do others if you pay the €25 or gather 20 needy English speakers.

Local Arts and Crafts—Browse through woodcarvers' shops—small art galleries filled with very expensive whittled works. The beautifully frescoed **Pilate's House** on Ludwig-Thomas-Strasse is a living workshop full of woodcarvers and painters in action (free; April–Oct Tue–Sat 13:00–18:00, closed Sun–Mon; Advent weekends and two weeks after Christmas 13:00–17:00, closed rest of year). Or see folk art at the town's **Heimatmuseum** (€4, €6 combo-ticket includes Passion Play theater, April–Oct and Dec–Jan Tue–Sun 10:00–17:00, closed Mon; closed Nov and Feb–March).

SLEEPING

(€1 = about $1.30, country code: 49, area code: 08362)

$$ Gasthof zur Rose is a big, central, family-run place with 21 rooms (Sb-€38, Db-€62, Tb-€77, Qb-€86, kids under 14 cheaper—ask, Dedlerstrasse 9, tel. 08822/4706, fax 08822/6753, www.hotel-oberammergau.de, gasthof-rose@t-online.de).

$ Hotel Bayerischer Löwe is central, with a good restaurant and 18 comfortable rooms (Db-€58, cash only, Dedlerstrasse 2, tel. 08822/1365, fax 08822/882, www.bayerischerloewe.com, gasthof .loewe@freenet.de, Reinhofer family).

$ Frau Magold's three bright and spacious rooms are twice as nice as the cheap hotel rooms, for much less money (Db-€44, cash only, immediately behind Gasthof zur Rose at Kleppergasse 1, tel. & fax 08822/4340, no English spoken).

$ The **youth hostel,** on the river, is a short walk from the center (€17.50 beds, includes taxes, breakfast, and sheets, tel. 08822/4114, fax 08822/1695, jhoberammergau@djh-bayern.de).

More Sights in Bavaria

▲▲Linderhof Castle—This homiest of "Mad" King Ludwig's castles is small and comfortably exquisite—good enough for a minor god. Set in the woods 15 minutes from Oberammergau and surrounded by fountains and sculpted, Italian-style gardens, it's the only palace I've toured that actually had me feeling envious. Don't miss the grotto, located outside and uphill from the palace; 25-minute tours are included with the palace ticket (€7, daily April–Sept 9:00–18:00, Oct–March 10:00–16:00, last tour 30 min before closing; English tours on request; parking-€2.50, fountains often erupt on the half-hour, tel. 08822/92030). Plan for lots of walking and a two-hour stop to fully enjoy this royal park. Pay at the entrance and get an admission time. Visit outlying sights in the garden to pass any wait time. The palace, freshly refurbished inside and out, is glorious. But without a car, getting to (and home from) Linderhof is a royal headache—skip it (but diehards can find details under "Getting Around Bavaria and Tirol," page 90).

▲▲Zugspitze—The tallest point in Germany is a border crossing. Lifts from Austria and Germany travel to the 9,700-foot summit of the Zugspitze. You can straddle the border between two great nations while enjoying an incredible view. Restaurants, shops, and telescopes await you at the summit.

On the German side, the 75-minute trip from Garmisch costs €47 round-trip; family discounts are available (buy a combo-ticket for cogwheel train to Eibsee and cable-car ride to summit, drivers can park for free at cable-car station at Eibsee, daily 8:15–14:15 to go up, last cable car down at about 16:30, tel. 08821/7970, www .zugspitze.de). Allow plenty of time for afternoon descents: If bad weather hits in the late afternoon, cable cars can be delayed at the summit, causing tourists to miss their train from Eibsee back to Garmisch. Hikers enjoy the easy six-mile walk around the lovely Eibsee (German side, 5 min downhill from cable car).

On the Austrian side, from the less-crowded Talstation Obermoos above the village of Erwald, the tram zips you to the top in 10 minutes (€32 round-trip, cash only, goes every 20 min, daily 8:40–16:40 except closed April–mid-May and most of mid-Oct–Nov, drivers follow signs for *Tiroler Zugspitze,* Austrian tel. 05673/2309, www.zugspitze.com).

The German ascent from Garmisch is easier for those without a car, but buses connect the Erwald train station and the Austrian lift nearly every hour.

Reutte

Reutte (ROY-teh, with a rolled *r*), a relaxed Austrian town of 5,700, is located 20 minutes across the border from Füssen. It's far from the international tourist crowd, but popular with Germans and Austrians for its climate. Doctors recommend its "grade 1" air. Reutte's one claim to fame with Americans: As Nazi Germany was falling in 1945, Hitler's top rocket scientist, Werner von Braun, joined the Americans (rather than the Russians) in Reutte. You could say the American space program began here.

Reutte isn't featured in any other American guidebook. While its generous sidewalks are filled with smart boutiques and lazy cof-

feehouses, its charms are subtle. It was never rich or important. Its castle is ruined, its buildings have painted-on "carvings," its churches are full, its men yodel for each other on birthdays, and its energy is spent soaking its Austrian and German guests in *Gemütlichkeit*. Most guests stay for a week, so the town's attractions are more time-consuming than thrilling. If the weather's good, hike to the mysterious Ehrenberg ruins, ride the luge, or rent a bike. For a slap-dancing bang, enjoy a Tirolean folk evening. For accommodations, see page 115.

ORIENTATION

Tourist Information
Reutte's TI is a block in front of the train station (Mon–Fri 8:00–12:00 & 14:00–17:00, no midday break July–Aug, Sat 8:30–12:00, closed Sun, tel. 05672/62336, from Germany dial 00-43-5672/62336, www.reutte.com). Go over your sightseeing plans, ask about a folk evening, pick up city and biking maps and the *Sommerprogramm* events schedule (in German only), and ask about discounts with the hotel guest cards. Their free informational booklet has a good self-guided town walk.

Helpful Hints
Laundry: There isn't an actual launderette in town, but the recommended hotels Maximilian and Ernberg let even

non-guests use their self-service machines (see page 117). Or stay at the recommended Gutshof zum Schluxen or the local campground, which both have washing machines and dryers.

Bike Rental: Try **Intersport** (€15/day, Mon–Fri 9:00–18:00, Sat 9:00–17:00, closed Sun, Lindenstrasse 25, tel. 05672/62352), or check at Hotel Maximilian.

SIGHTS AND ACTIVITIES

▲▲Ehrenberg Castle Ensemble (Festungsensemble Ehrenberg)

Just a mile outside of Reutte are the brooding ruins of four castles that once made up the largest fort in Tirol (built for defense against the Bavarians). Today, these castles are gradually being turned into a European Castle Museum, showing off 500 years of military architecture in one swoop. The European Union is helping fund the project because it promotes the heritage of a multinational region—Tirol—rather than a country (the EU's vision includes a zone of regions rather than nations).

Three of the castles cluster together; the fourth (Fort Claudia) is across the valley (an hour by foot on the *Wanderweg*). All four were once connected by walls. The first three—the easiest and most interesting to visit—are described below, from lowest to highest. New signs throughout the castle complex will help you find your way and explain some background on the region's history, geology, geography, culture, flora, and fauna.

Getting to the Castle Ensemble: The Klause, Ehrenberg, and Schlosskopf castles are on the road to Lermoos and Innsbruck. These are a pleasant walk or a short bike ride from Reutte; bikers can use the *Radwanderweg* along the Lech River (the TI has a good map).

▲Klause Valley Fort—At the parking lot at the base of the ruin-topped hill, you'll find the recently modernized remains of a Gothic fortification. It was located on the medieval salt road (which used to be the ancient Roman road, Via Claudia Augusta). Beginning in the 14th century, the fort controlled traffic and levied tolls on all who passed through this strategic valley. Today, it houses a 30-minute **multimedia show** about the castles (€6.80, €9.50 combo-ticket includes museum—see below, daily in English at 13:00). You'll sit inside the shell of the old castle while the 2,000-year history of this valley's fortresses is projected on the old stone walls and modern screens around you. There's also an extensive family-friendly **museum** about the castle ensemble (€6.80, €9.50

Reutte

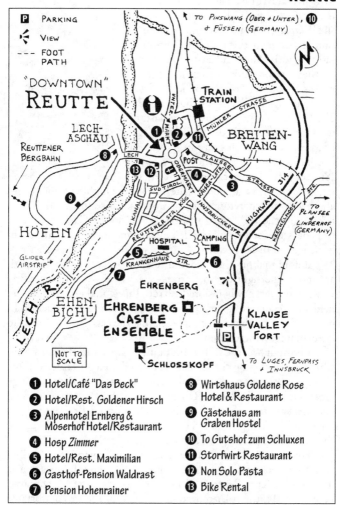

- **1** Hotel/Café "Das Beck"
- **2** Hotel/Rest. Goldener Hirsch
- **3** Alpenhotel Ernberg & Moserhof Hotel/Restaurant
- **4** Hosp Zimmer
- **5** Hotel/Rest. Maximilian
- **6** Gasthof-Pension Waldrast
- **7** Pension Hohenrainer
- **8** Wirtshaus Goldene Rose Hotel & Restaurant
- **9** Gästehaus am Graben Hostel
- **10** To Gutshof zum Schluxen
- **11** Storfwirt Restaurant
- **12** Non Solo Pasta
- **13** Bike Rental

combo-ticket includes multimedia show, €16 family pass for 2 adults and unlimited kids, plentiful English signage; mid-Dec–Oct daily 10:00–17:00, closed Nov–mid-Dec, tel. 05672/62007, www.ehrenberg.at). If you're hungry, drop by the nearby café/guest house, Gasthof Klause (closed Mon except in Aug), which offers a German-language flier and a wall painting of the intact castle.

▲▲**Ehrenberg Ruins**—Ehrenberg, a 13th-century rock pile, provides a great contrast to King Ludwig's "modern" castles and a super opportunity to let your imagination off its leash. Hike up 30 minutes from the parking lot for a great view from your own private ruins. Facing the hill from the parking lot, find the gravelly road at the *Klause* sign. Follow the road to the saddle between the two hills. From the saddle, notice how the castle stands high on the horizon. This is Ehrenberg (which means "Mountain of Honor"), the first of the four ensemble castles, built in 1296. Thirteenth-century castles were designed to stand boastfully tall. With the advent of gunpowder, castles dug in. Notice the **ramparts** around you. They are from the 18th century. Approaching Ehrenberg cas-

tle, look for the small door to the left. It's the night entrance (tight and awkward, therefore safer against a surprise invasion). While hiking up the hill, you go through two doors. Castles allowed step-by-step retreat, giving defenders time to regroup and fight back against invading forces.

Before making the final and steepest ascent, follow the path around to the right to a big, grassy courtyard with commanding views and a fat, newly restored **turret.** This stored gunpowder and held a big cannon that enjoyed a clear view of the valley below. In medieval times, all the trees approaching the castle were cleared to keep an unobstructed view.

Look out over the valley. The pointy spire marks **Breitenwang,** which was a stop on the ancient Via Claudia Augusta. In A.D. 46, there was a Roman camp there. In 1489, after the Reutte bridge crossed the Lech River, Reutte (marked by the onion-domed church) was made a market town and eclipsed Breitenwang in importance. Any gliders circling? They launch from just over the river in Höfen (see "Flying and Gliding," page 113).

For centuries, this castle was the seat of government—ruling an area called the "judgment of Ehrenberg" (roughly the same as today's "district of Reutte"). When the emperor came by, he stayed here. In 1604, the ruler moved downtown into more comfortable quarters, and the castle was no longer a palace.

Now climb the steep hill to the top of the castle. Take the high ground. There was no water supply here—just kegs of wine, beer, and a cistern to collect rain.

Ehrenberg repelled 16,000 Swedish soldiers in the defense of Catholicism in 1632. Ehrenberg saw three or four other battles, but its end was not glorious. In the 1780s, a local businessman bought the castle in order to sell off its parts. Later, when vagabonds moved in, the roof was removed to make squatting miserable. With the roof gone, deterioration quickened, leaving this evocative shell and a whiff of history.

▲**Schlosskopf**—If you have energy left after conquering Ehrenberg, hike up another 30 minutes to the mighty Schlosskopf ("Castle Head"). When the Bavarians captured Ehrenberg in 1703, the Tiroleans climbed up to the bluff above it to rain cannonballs down on their former fortress. In 1740, a mighty new castle—designed to defend against modern artillery—was built on this same sky-high strategic location. By the end of the 20th century, the castle was completely overgrown with trees—you couldn't see it from Reutte. But today the trees are shaved away, and the castle has been excavated. In 2005, the Castle Ensemble project reconstructed the original equipment used to build this fortress (such as wooden cranes)—and then began using those same means to restore parts of it. By the spring of 2008, Schlosskopf should be finished (ask at TI), and the 18th-century construction equipment will be retired and become part of the exhibit.

In Reutte

Folk Museum (Heimatsmuseum/Grünes Haus)—Reutte's Heimatmuseum, offering a quick look at the local folk culture and the story of the castles, is more cute than impressive. Ask to borrow the packet of information in English (€2, May–Oct Tue–Sun 10:00–16:00, closed Mon and Nov–April, in the bright-green building on Untermarkt, around corner from Hotel Goldener Hirsch, tel. 05672/72304).

▲▲**Tirolean Folk Evening**—Ask the TI or your hotel if there's a Tirolean folk evening scheduled. During the summer (July–Aug), nearby towns (such as Höfen) occasionally put on an evening of yodeling, slap dancing, and Tirolean frolic worth the €8 to €10 and short drive. Off-season, you'll have to do your own yodeling. There are also weekly folk concerts featuring the local choir or brass band in Reutte's park (free, July–Aug only, ask at TI). For listings of these and other local events, pick up a copy of the German-only *Sommerprogramm* schedule at the TI.

▲**Flying and Gliding**—For a major thrill on a sunny day, drop by the tiny airport in Höfen across the river, and fly. A small single-prop plane can buzz the Zugspitze and Ludwig's castles and give you a bird's-eye peek at Reutte's Ehrenberg ruins (2 people for 30 min-€110, 1 hour-€220, tel. 05672/63207, phone rarely answered and then not in English, so your best bet is to show up at the Höfen airport on good-weather afternoons). Or, for something more angelic, how about *Segelfliegen*? For €40, you get 30 minutes in a glider for two (you and the pilot, €60/1 hour). Just watching the towrope launch the graceful glider like a giant, slow-motion rubber-band gun is exhilarating (May–mid-Sept 12:00–19:00, sometimes in April and Oct if not too snowy, in good but breezy weather only, find someone in the know at the "Thermic

Luge Lesson

Taking a wild ride on a luge (pronounced "loozh") is a quint-essential alpine experience. It's also called *Sommerrodelbahn*, or "summer toboggan." To try one of Europe's great cheap thrills (€2–6), take the lift up to the top of a mountain, grab a wheeled, sled-like go-cart, and scream back down the mountainside on a banked course. Then take the lift back up to the top and start all over again.

Luge courses are highly weather-dependent, and can close at the least hint of rain. If the weather's questionable, call ahead to confirm that your preferred luge is open. Stainless-steel courses are more likely to stay open in drizzly weather than concrete ones.

Operating the sled is simple: Push the stick forward to go faster, pull back to apply brakes. Even a novice can go very, very fast. Most are cautious on their first run, speed demons on their second...and bruised and bloody on their third. A woman once showed me her journal illustrated with her husband's dried five-inch-long luge scab. He disobeyed the only essential rule of luging: Keep both hands on your stick. To avoid getting into a bumper-to-bumper traffic jam, let the person in front of you get way ahead before you start. You'll emerge from the course with a windblown hairdo and a smile-creased face.

Ranch," tel. 05672/71550, mobile 0676-557-1085, Segelflugverein Ausserfern).

Reuttener Bergbahn—This mountain lift swoops you high above the tree line to a starting point for several hikes and an alpine flower park, with special paths leading you past countless varieties of local flora. Unique to this lift is a barefoot hiking trail *(Barfusswanderweg)*, designed to be walked without shoes—no joke (€9 one-way, €13 round-trip, flowers best in late July, lift usually mid-June–Oct daily 9:00–12:00 & 13:00–17:00, tel. 05672/62420, www.reuttener-seilbahnen.at).

Near Reutte

▲▲Luge Course *(Sommerrodelbahn)*—Near Lermoos, on the road from Reutte to Innsbruck, you'll find the Biberwier *Sommerrodelbahn*. At 4,250 feet, it's the longest in Austria (20 min from Reutte, just past Lermoos—Biberwier is the first exit after a long tunnel). The only drawbacks are its short season and hours, and its proclivity for shutting down sporadically and at the slightest bit of rain (€6.50/1 ride, €17.60/3 rides, €27.60/5 rides, late May–mid-Oct daily 9:00–16:30, closed mid-Oct–late May, tel. 05673/2111, regional TI is more likely to have info in English—tel. 05673/20000). Nearby in Bichlbach, another luge—this one shorter, but steeper—may be open (call ahead to regional TI listed on page 109). If you're without a car, these are not worth the trouble (consider the luge near Neuschwanstein instead—see "Tegelberg Luge," page 102).

▲**Fallerschein**—Easy for drivers and a special treat for those who may have been Kit Carson in a previous life, this extremely remote log-cabin village is a 4,000-foot-high, flower-speckled world of serene slopes and cowbells. Thunderstorms roll down the valley like it's God's bowling alley, but the pint-size church on the high ground, blissfully simple in a land of Baroque, seems to promise that this huddle of houses will survive, and the river and breeze will just keep flowing. The couples sitting on benches are mostly Austrian vacationers who've rented cabins here. Many of them, appreciating the remoteness of Fallerschein, are having affairs.

Sleeping in Fallerschein: **$ Lottes Fallerscheiner Stube** is a family-friendly mountain-hut restaurant with a low-ceilinged attic space that has basic beds for up to 17 sleepy hikers. The accommodations aren't fancy, but if you're looking for remote, this is it (dorm bed-€9, sheets-€4, open May–Oct only, closed Tue, wildlife viewing deck, tel. 05632/2140, www.alpe-fallerschein.at, Gapp family).

Getting to Fallerschein: From Reutte, it's a 45-minute drive. Take road 198 to Stanzach (passing Weisenbach am Loch, then Forchach), then turn left toward Namlos. Follow the L21 Berwang road for about five miles to a parking lot. From there it's a two-mile walk down a drivable but technically closed one-lane road.

SLEEPING

In and near Reutte
(€1 = about $1.30, country code: 43, area code: 05672)
Reutte is a mellow Füssen with fewer crowds and easygoing locals with a contagious love of life. Come here for a good dose of Austrian ambience and lower prices. Those with a car should make their home base here; those without should consider it but plan very carefully. (To call Reutte from Germany, dial 00-43-5672, then the local number.) You'll drive across the border without stopping. Reutte is popular with Austrians and Germans, who come here year after year for one- or two-week vacations. The hotels are big, elegant, and full of comfy, carved furnishings and

creative ways to spend lots of time in one spot. They take great pride in their restaurants, and the owners send their children away to hotel-management schools. All include a great breakfast, but few accept credit cards. Most hotels give about a 5 percent discount for stays of two nights or longer.

The Reutte TI has a list of 50 private homes that rent out generally good rooms *(Zimmer)* with facilities down the hall, pleasant communal living rooms, and breakfast. Most charge €20 per person per night and speak little or no English. Reservations are nearly impossible for one- or two-night stays, but short stops are welcome if you just drop in and fill available gaps. As these are all family-run places, it is especially important to cancel in advance if your plans change. Most places charge about €1.50 extra for heat in winter (worth it). I've listed a few favorites below, but the TI can always find you a room when you arrive.

Reutte is surrounded by several distinct "villages" that basically feel like suburbs—many of them, such as Breitenwang (described below), within easy walking distance of the Reutte town center. While there are some good hotels in central Reutte itself, these nearby communities are also worth considering. If you want to hike through the woods to Neuschwanstein Castle, stay at Gutshof zum Schluxen (listed on page 118). To locate the recommended accommodations, see the map on page 111.

In Central Reutte

$$ Hotel "Das Beck" offers 16 clean, sunny, modern rooms (many with balconies) in the heart of town. It's a great value, and guests are personally taken care of by Hans, Inge, and Pipi. Enjoy their homemade marmalade at breakfast in the open kitchen/coffee bar or on the sunny patio. Their small café offers tasty snacks and specializes in Austrian and Italian wines (Sb-€42–45, Db-€68, Tb-€82–89, Qb-€105, family rooms, non-smoking rooms, Internet access, free parking, they'll pick you up from the station, Untermarkt 11, tel. 05672/62522, fax 05672/625-2235, www.hotel-das-beck.at, info@hotel-das-beck.at).

$$ Hotel Goldener Hirsch, located in the center of Reutte just two blocks from the station, is a grand old hotel renovated with Tirolean *Jugendstil* flair. It boasts 56 rooms and one lonely set of antlers (Sb-€58–62, Db-€85–90, Db suite-€90–98, Tb-€125–135, Qb-€140–145, 2-night discounts, family rooms, elevator, restaurant—see "Eating," later in this section, tel. 05672/62508, fax 05672/625-087, www.goldener-hirsch.at, info@goldener-hirsch.at; Monika, Helmut, and daughters Vanessa and Nina).

In Breitenwang

Right next door to Reutte is the older and quieter village of

Breitenwang (with good *Zimmer* and a fine bakery). It's a 20-minute walk from the Reutte train station (at post office round-about, follow Planseestrasse past onion dome to pointy straight dome, near the two hotels; the Hosps—as well as other B&Bs—are along unmarked Kaiser-Lothar-Strasse, the first right past this church).

$$ Alpenhotel Ernberg is run with great care by friendly Hermann, who combines Old World elegance with modern touches. Nestle in for some serious coziness among the carved-wood eating nooks and tiled stoves (Sb-€45, Db-€78, less for longer stays, self-service laundry for €7—also available for non-guests, restaurant, Planseestrasse 50, tel. 05672/71912, fax 05672/191-240, www.ernberg.at, info@ernberg.at).

$$ Moserhof Hotel has 30 new-feeling rooms plus an elegant dining room (Sb-€52, Db-€84, these special rates promised with this book in 2008—ask for the Rick Steves discount when you reserve, extra bed-€35, most rooms have balconies, elevator, Internet access-€3/hr, restaurant, free parking, Planseestrasse 44, tel. 05672/62020, fax 05672/620-2040, www.hotel-moserhof.at, info@hotel-moserhof.at, Hosp family).

Zimmer: **$ Walter and Emilie Hosp** rent three rooms in a comfortable, quiet, and modern house two blocks from the Breitenwang church steeple (D-€42, D-€38 for 2 nights or more, T-€60, Q-€80, cash only, Kaiser-Lothar-Strasse 29, tel. 05672/65377).

In Ehenbichl, near the Ehrenberg Ruins

The next three listings are a bit farther from central Reutte, a couple miles upriver in the village of Ehenbichl (under the Ehrenberg ruins). From central Reutte, go south on Obermarkt and turn right on Kög, which becomes Reuttener Strasse, following signs to *Ehenbichl*.

$$ Hotel Maximilian is a great value. It includes free bicycles, table tennis, a children's playroom, a pool table, and the friendly service of Gabi, Monika, and the rest of the Koch family. They host many special events, and their hotel has lots of wonderful extras such as a sauna and a masseuse (Sb-€45–50, Db-€74–84, ask for these special Rick Steves prices when you reserve, family deals, elevator, free Internet access and Wi-Fi, laundry service for €12—or €16 for non-guests, good restaurant, tel. 05672/62585, fax 05672/625-8554, www.maxihotel.com, info@hotelmaximilian.at). They rent cars to guests only (1 Renault, 1 VW van, book in advance) and bikes to anyone (€6/half-day, €10/day).

$ Gasthof-Pension Waldrast, separating a forest and a meadow, is run by the farming Huter family. The place feels hauntingly quiet and has no restaurant, but it does offer 10 nice rooms with sitting areas and castle-view balconies (Sb-€37, Db-€60, Tb-€75, Qb-€95; discounts with this book in 2008: 5 percent for 2 nights, 10 percent for 3 nights or more; cash only, all rooms non-smoking, free parking; less than 1 mile from Reutte, just off main drag toward Innsbruck, past campground and under castle ruins on Ehrenbergstrasse; tel. & fax 05672/62443, www.waldrasttirol .com, info@waldrasttirol.com).

$ Pension Hohenrainer, a big, quiet, no-frills place, is a good value with 12 modern rooms and some castle-view balconies (Sb-€24–29, Db-€48–54, €3 per person extra for 1-night stays, cheaper for longer stays and in April–June and Sept–Oct, cash only, family rooms, non-smoking rooms, free Internet access, restaurant across the street, follow signs up the road behind Hotel Maximilian into village of Ehenbichl, tel. 05672/62544 or 05672/63262, fax 05672/62052, www.hohenrainer.at, hohenrainer@aon.at).

In Other Villages near Reutte

$$ Wirtshaus Goldene Rose, while officially in the village of Lechaschau, is only about a 10-minute walk from the center of Reutte. This no-nonsense, sprawling, traditional hotel—complete with antlers and portraits of the *Kaiser*—makes a good home base for those spending several days in the area who want amenities such as easy parking, Internet access, a restaurant, and a sauna (Sb-€40-45, Db-€80–85, from downtown Reutte cross bridge and take the first right, Dorfstrasse 2, tel. 05672/62411, fax 05672/624-117, www .hotel-goldene-rose.at, info@hotel-goldene-rose.at, Klotz family).

$ The homey **Gästehaus am Graben hostel** has two to six beds per room and includes breakfast and sheets. Frau Reyman and her son Rudy keep the place traditional, clean, and friendly, and serve a great €7 dinner for guests only. This is a super value, and the castle views are fantastic. If you've never hosteled and are curious (and have a car or don't mind a bus ride), try it. The double rooms are hotel-grade, and they accept non-members of any age (dorm bed-€21, Db-€54, cash only, non-smoking rooms, Internet access, laundry service, no curfew, closed April and Nov–mid-Dec, less than 2 miles from Reutte, bus connection to Neuschwanstein via Reutte; from downtown Reutte, cross bridge and follow main road left along river, or take the bus—hourly until 19:30, ask for Graben stop, no buses Sun; Graben 1, tel. 05672/626-440, fax 05672/626-444, www.hoefen.at, info@hoefen.at).

In Pinswang

The village of Pinswang is closer to Füssen (and Ludwig's castles), but still in Austria.

$$ Gutshof zum Schluxen, run by helpful Hermann, gets the "Remote Old Hotel in an Idyllic Setting" award. This family-friendly working farm offers modern rustic elegance draped in goose down and pastels, and a chance to pet a rabbit and feed the deer. "Mad" King Ludwig himself is said to have slept here. Its picturesque meadow setting will turn you into a dandelion picker, and its proximity to Neuschwanstein will turn you into a hiker; the castle is just an hour's hike away—see page 98 (Sb-€45, Db-€84, extra person-€22, 10 percent discount for 4 nights or more, Internet access and Wi-Fi, self-service laundry, mountain-bike rental, good restaurant, fun bar, between Reutte and Füssen in village of Pinswang, free pickup from Reutte or Füssen, call ahead if you'll arrive after 18:00, tel. 05677/8903, fax 05677/890-323, www .schluxen.com, welcome@schluxen.com).

EATING

In Reutte

The hotels here take great pride in serving local cuisine at reasonable prices to their guests and the public. Rather than go to a cheap restaurant, try a hotel. Most offer €8 to €14 dinners from 18:00 to 21:00 and are closed one night a week. Reutte itself has plenty of inviting eateries, including traditional, ethnic, fast food, grocery stores, and delis.

Restaurant Goldener Hirsch, located in the hotel of the same name (recommended under "Sleeping"), offers local specialties in a traditional setting. If you need a break from Tirolean food, try the tasty vegetable plate, *Gemüseplatte* (€8–13 entrées, Tue–Sun 11:00–14:00 & 17:30–22:30, closed Mon, Mühlerstasse 1, tel. 05672/62508).

Wirtshaus Goldene Rose is known for its grill and game specialties, as well as its wine cellar. Go here for a fancy dinner of regionally inspired dishes featuring fresh asparagus, mushrooms, or whatever's in season. Families will feel comfortable here, too (€9–18 plates, daily 12:00–14:00 & 17:30–21:30, Dorfstrasse 2, tel. 05672/62411, fax 05672/624-117, www.hotel-goldene-rose.at, info @hotel-goldene-rose.at).

Alpenhotel Ernberg, Moserhof Hotel, and **Hotel Maximilian** also offer fine restaurants (see "Sleeping").

Storfwirt is *the* place for a quick lunch or light dinner. You can get the usual sausages here, as well as baked potatoes and salads. Check for daily lunch or dinner specials (€3–7 meals, Mon–Fri 8:30–15:00, Sat 9:00–14:30, closed Sun, Schrettergasse 15, tel. 05672/62640).

Non Solo Pasta, just off the traffic circle, is a local favorite for Italian food (€7–10 entrées, Mon–Fri 11:30–14:00 & 18:00–23:00, Sat 18:00–23:00, closed Sun, Lindenstrasse 1, tel. 05672/72714).

Picnic Supplies: **Billa** supermarket has everything you'll need (across from TI, Mon–Fri 8:00–19:00, Sat 8:00–17:00, closed Sun).

TRANSPORTATION CONNECTIONS

From Reutte by Train to: Garmisch (every 2 hrs, 1 hr), **Innsbruck** (every 2 hrs, 2.5 hrs, change in Garmisch), **Munich** (hourly, 2.5–3.5 hrs, change in Garmisch or Kempten).

By Bus to: Füssen (Mon–Fri 4/day, none Sat–Sun, 35 min, €3.40, buses depart from in front of the train station, pay driver; more connections via train to Pfronten-Weissbach then bus to Füssen—2/day Mon–Fri, 6/day Sat–Sun, 1–1.5 hrs). Taxis cost €30 one-way.

By Car from Germany into Reutte: Skip the north *(Nord)* exit and take the south *(Süd)* exit into town. While Austria requires a toll sticker for driving on its highways (€8/10 days, buy at the border, gas stations, car-rental agencies, or *Tabak* shops), those just dipping into Tirol from Bavaria do not need one.

Bavaria/Tirol

BADEN-BADEN AND THE BLACK FOREST

Combine Edenism and hedonism as you explore this most romantic of German regions and dip into its mineral spas. The Black Forest, or *Schwarzwald* in German, is a range of hills stretching 100 miles north–south along the French border from Karlsruhe to Switzerland. Its highest peak is the 4,900-foot Feldberg. Because of its thick forests, people called it black.

Until the last century, the Schwarzwald was cut off from the German mainstream. The poor farmland drove medieval locals to become foresters, glassblowers, and clockmakers. Strong traditions continue to be woven through the thick dialects and thatched roofs. On any Sunday, you will find Germans in traditional costumes coloring the Black Forest on *Volksmärsche* (group hikes—open to anyone; for a listing, visit www.volksmarch.com).

Popular with German holiday-goers and those looking for some serious R&R, the Black Forest offers clean air, cuckoo clocks, cherry cakes, cheery villages, and countless hiking possibilities.

The area's two biggest tourist traps are the tiny Titisee (a lake not quite as big as its tourist parking lot) and Triberg, a small town filled with cuckoo-clock shops. In spite of the crowds, the drives are scenic, the hiking is *wunderbar,* and the attractions listed in this chapter are well worth a visit.

The two major (and very different) towns are Baden-Baden in the north and Freiburg in the south. Their proximity to France lends both cities a sunny elegance. Freiburg is the Black Forest's capital and university town. Baden-Baden is Germany's grandest 19th-century spa resort. Stroll through its elegant streets and casino. Soak in its famous baths.

The Black Forest

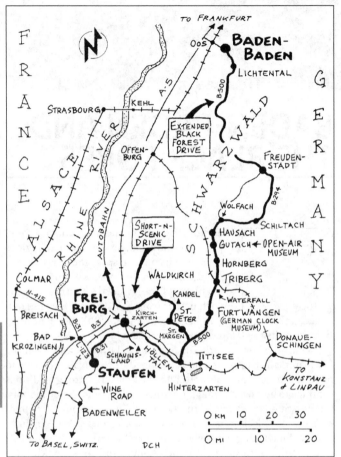

Planning Your Time

Save a day and two nights for Baden-Baden. Tour Freiburg, but sleep in charming and overlooked Staufen. By train, Freiburg and Baden-Baden are easy, as is a short foray into the forest from either. With more time, do the small-town forest medley between the two.

If you're driving, do the whole cuckoo thing—a night in Staufen, a busy day touring north, and two nights and a relaxing day in Baden-Baden. Try this blitz itinerary from Staufen by car: 9:00–Enjoy the town of Staufen, 11:00–Take the scenic drive to Furtwangen and tour the German Clock Museum, 13:00–Drive to the Black Forest Open-Air Museum and tour it, 17:00–Drive to Baden-Baden, 19:00–Arrive in Baden-Baden for some spa time (last entry 20:00).

Baden-Baden

Of all the high-class resort towns I've seen, Baden-Baden (population 50,000) is the easiest to enjoy in jeans with a picnic. The town makes a great first stop in Germany, especially for honeymooners (1.5 hours from Frankfurt's airport, direct trains every 2 hours).

Baden-Baden was the playground of Europe's high-rolling elite 150 years ago. Royalty and aristocracy would come from all corners to take the *Kur*—a soak in the curative (or at least they feel that way) mineral waters—and enjoy the world's top casino. Wrought-iron balconies on handsome 19th-century apartment buildings give Baden-Baden an elegant, Parisian feel.

The town remains popular today. How popular? Hoteliers in typical convention towns expect that 85 percent of their guests will need single rooms and 15 percent will need doubles. As spouses insist on coming to conventions held in Baden-Baden, hoteliers flip-flop those figures, anticipating that 85 percent of the demand will be for doubles.

Along with conventioneers, this lush resort town attracts a middle-class crowd consisting of tourists in search of a lower pulse, and Germans enjoying the fruits of their generous health-care system.

ORIENTATION

(area code: 07221)

Baden-Baden is made for strolling with a poodle. Except for the train station, youth hostel, and a recommended hotel on the opposite side of town, everything that matters is clustered within a 10-minute walk between the baths and the casino.

The station is in a suburb called Baden-Oos, three miles from the center but easily connected with the center by bus. Although you'll barely notice if you just stick around the center, Baden-Baden is actually a long, skinny town, strung out over several miles along the narrow valley of the Oosbach river. The river empties out into the Rhine plain below the train station. The train station is at the lower (northern) end of the valley, and the Lichtentaler Abbey at the upper end, 18 stops away on bus #201. The casino and center of town are about halfway between, at the point where a small side valley joins the Oosbach. The church, castle, baths, and oldest sections of town are a few blocks uphill on the north slope of this side valley.

Tourist Information

Baden-Baden's TI is in the ornate Trinkhalle building. Pick up the free monthly events program, *Baden-Baden Aktuell,* with an

excellent fine-print, fold-out map. The TI has enough recommended walks and organized excursions to keep the most energetic vacationer happy. If you're headed into the countryside,
consider the good €1 *Outline Map* and the €5 Black Forest guidebook (Mon–Sat 10:00–17:00, Sun 14:00–17:00, WC-€0.50, tel.
07221/275-200, www.baden-baden.com).

The TI shares space with a café (see page 138) and an agency
that sells tickets to performances in town (theater, opera, orchestra,
and musicals; Tue–Sat 10:00–18:00, Sun 14:00–17:00, closed Mon).
Another TI is on the B-500 autobahn exit at Schwarzwaldstrasse
52 (Mon–Sat 9:00–18:00, Sun 9:00–13:00).

Arrival in Baden-Baden

Walk out of the train station (lockers at platform 1, €1.50–3) and
catch bus #201 in front of the kiosks on your right (€2 single ticket;
see "Getting Around Baden-Baden"). Get off in about 15 minutes at the 11th stop, Leopoldsplatz, usually also announced as
Stadtmitte ("center of town"). Allow €16 for a taxi from the train
station to the center.

Helpful Hints

Shopping: The big **Wagner Galerie** has just about everything,
including a modern supermarket and a post office (Mon–Sat
9:00–19:00, closed Sun, at north end of Lange Strasse).

Horse Races: Book well in advance if you'll be visiting Baden-
Baden during its horse races (mid–May and late Aug in 2008,
www.baden-galopp.de).

Internet Access: There are two good 10-terminal, late-hours
places on either end of town: **Internet and Callshop** in the
north (€1/30 min, daily 10:00–22:00, Lange Strasse 54, tel.
07221/398-400) and **Weblounge** in the south (€2.40/hr,
Mon–Thu 10:00–22:00, Fri–Sun 12:00–22:00, Eichstrasse 3,
near Augustaplatz, tel. 07221/281-230).

Laundry: Bring lots of €1 coins to **SB-Waschcenter** (€7 per
load, Mon–Sat 7:30–21:00, last load 18:00, closed Sun; from
Sophienstrasse go up Stephanienstrasse, then left on steeply
uphill Scheibenstrasse, then down the alley, Scheibenstrasse
14; tel. 07221/24819).

Bike Rental: You can rent cheap bikes at the parking-garage office
under the casino (€1/2 hours, €2.50/6 hours, €5/12 hours, leave
€20 and driver's license as deposit, half-price with *Kurkarte*
discount card you'll get from your hotel—described on page
135, rental daily 8:00–18:00, return until 20:00; enter garage
and find section A, space 52—easiest way down is from stairs
off Kaiserallee marked *Kasse/Garage;* tel. 07221/277-203).

Train Info: The **Derpart** travel agency, between Leopoldsplatz

Baden-Baden

Baden-Baden

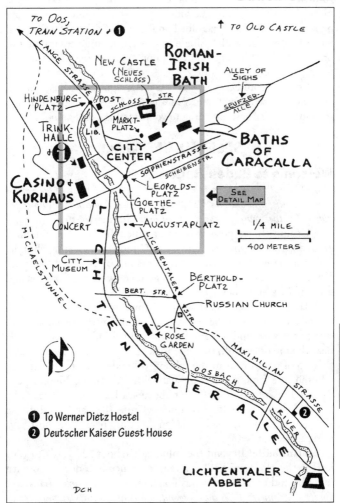

To Werner Dietz Hostel
Deutscher Kaiser Guest House

and the casino, posts a train schedule outside. They'll charge you a €3 fee to answer your train questions and/or sell you a ticket—which is pricey but saves you a trip to the station (Mon–Fri 9:00–18:00, Sat 10:00–14:00, closed Sun, Sophienstrasse 1B).

Getting Around Baden-Baden

Within town, only one bus matters. Bus #201 runs straight through Baden-Baden, connecting the train station in Oos, the town center, and the Lichtentaler Abbey at the southeast end of town (every

10 min until 19:00, then about every 20 min until around midnight; buy tickets from machines at stops or from driver: €2 per person, €4.50 24-hour pass for 1 adult, €6.80 24-hour family pass, bus info at www.kvv.de). Single tickets are valid for 90 minutes in one direction. With bus #201, you don't need to mess with downtown parking.

Locals recommend bus #208 as a fun sightseeing bus. Hop on anywhere in the center, and you'll take a big scenic loop through the outlying regions, returning to your starting point an hour later.

SELF-GUIDED WALK

Welcome to Baden-Baden

• *This walk starts at the casino, loops through the old town to both of the famous baths, and ends back at the river where you can stroll up to the abbey. In other words, it covers everything. Start on the steps of the...*

Casino: The impressive building called the *Kurhaus* is wrapped around a grand casino. Built in the 1850s in wannabe-French style, it was declared "the most beautiful casino" by Marlene Dietrich. You can tour it in the morning and gamble away the afternoon and evening (described below).

To get a visual overview of the town from the casino, stand on the steps between the second and third big white columns and survey the surroundings from left to right: Find the ruined castle near the top of the hill, then the rock-climbing cliffs, the new castle (top of town) next to the salmon-colored spire of the Catholic Church (the famous baths are just behind that), the Merkur peak (marked by a tower, 2,000 feet above sea level, easy to reach by bus and funicular—described below), and the bandstand in the Kurhaus garden. The Baden-Baden orchestra plays here most days (free, usually at 16:00).

Trinkhalle: Beyond the colonnade (about 100 yards to your left) is the old Trinkhalle—a long entrance hall decorated with nymphs and romantic legends (explained in the book, *Trinkhalle Baden-Baden: Its Tales and Legend,* sold inside for €9), serving as the home for the TI, a recommended café, and a ticket agency.

Wander its fancy portico studying the romantic paintings which spa-goers a century ago could really relate to.

• *From the Trinkhalle, walk down the steps, tip your hat to Kaiser Wilhelm (no moustache jokes), and go over the river. Walk one block inland, then go left on the pedestrian Lange Strasse. After a block, take a hard right, and climb up Hirschstrasse (under the "Bad" Hotel zum Hirsch skybridge) until you hit a big church.*

Catholic Church and Market Platz: Baden-Baden's Catholic Church looks over the marketplace which has marked the center of town since Roman times. You're actually standing upon the "emperor's spa." While it's not open to the public, city officials don oxygen masks and descend once a year (through the square metal hatch in the cobbles) to clean its sumptuous marble.

Because it sits atop the spa, the Catholic Church is muggy and warm all year. There are no heaters inside. In the winter, the floor stones are designed to transmit the natural spa heat. Because the air in the nave is at a steady 85 percent humidity level, the wooden pews have to be replaced twice a century; all the art consists of copies (originals are stored safely in the regional museum); and it smells musty.

Towering above the square you can see the edge of the "new castle." It's owned by a Kuwaiti woman who hopes to turn it into a fabulous five-star hotel at the cost of €500 million (if she can overcome the hurdles that come with renovating a historic building).

From the Church to the Museum: Behind the church, walk under a modern art installation holding jugs 20 yards high (reminders of the Roman spa which once stood here) and down a cobbled lane. Because the soil is spa-warmed, the vegetation is lush—Mediterranean pines and orange trees. At the end (top of stairs), enjoy the **viewpoint;** Baden-Baden's high-rent district—nicknamed Paradise—climbs the hills opposite.

Take the steps down to a water spigot called **Fettquelle** (literally "rich water source"). Taste the spa water. It's 105 degrees—as hot as a spa open to the public can legally be. Until recently, this was a practical source of hot water. Older locals remember being sent here to fetch hot water for their father's shave.

Find the **statue** on the lawn 50 yards farther. She's got her rear to the modern fun baths (Baths of Caracalla) and is eyeing the luxurious old-school Roman-Irish Bath (both described in "Experiences," below).

• *Return halfway to the Fettquelle spigot and take the stairs down into the parking level to the small…*

Ancient Spa Museum: This spa, now in ruins, was built for Roman soldiers to use. While just one room—most of which you can see through the big windows, it's worth the €2.50 admission only if you want to use the included headphone to learn the engineering and story of the ancient spa. As it was just for soldiers, this spa is just a simple terra-cotta structure with hollow walls and elevated floors to let the heat circulate (Tue–Sun 11:00–13:00 & 14:00–17:00, closed Mon).

• *Leaving the museum, jog left and head down…*

Gernsbacherstrasse: Walking down Gernsbacherstrasse, note the heritage of 2,000 years of guests housed, fed, and watered here at the spa. Fyodor Dostoyevsky, Mark Twain, Johannes Brahms, and Russian princes all called this neighborhood home in its 19th-century heyday. Germany's oldest tennis and golf clubs were created here in the 19th-century for the English community.

The late 20th-century German health-care system was very, very good for Baden-Baden. The government provided lavishly for spa treatment for its tired citizens. Now, doctors must make the case to insurance companies that their patients are more than tired…actually sick. And the insurance company then says where they'll go. The government still pays for up to three weeks to recreate in a spa like this—but patients must go to the spa that is recommended and sleep in its clinic. If they want to sleep in a hotel, they lose their government funding—the gig is up.

• *After two blocks, you hit Sonnenplatz. Jog left, and at the corner (which has a little gifty shop selling all the local specialties), continue right down Sophienstrasse where a signpost directs you to Lichtentaler Allee.*

Sophienstrasse: This street enjoys the reliable shade of a long row of chestnut trees. In the 1870s, when it was lined exclusively by hotels, it was the town's aristocratic promenade. Back then there were 15,000 bedrooms for rent in Baden-Baden, triple what the city has today. (Note the bus stop just before Leopoldsplatz, where buses #204 and #205 go to the Merkur funicular—described on page 131.)

• *Sophienstrasse leads into…*

Leopoldsplatz: This square was, until 1985, a main traffic hub with 30,000 cars muscling through it each day. Now a 1.5-mile long tunnel takes the east–west traffic under the city, and the peace and quiet you'd expect in a spa town has returned. Actually, Baden-Baden had to get rid of the noise and pollution caused by the traffic in order to maintain its top rating as a spa resort. Lose that, and Baden-Baden would lose half its business. The modern art decorating this square (and streets and squares throughout the city) rotates, as many artists want the exposure that an open-air exhibit in Baden-Baden brings.

• *From Leopoldsplatz, head left on Lichtentaler Strasse. You'll pass the venerable Café König (on right, described in "Eating"), antique shops (on left), and fine little malls. The big fountain in the distance marks Augustaplatz. Head toward it. At the fountain, go right, through the park and over the petite bridge, where you'll come to a sweet riverside strolling path called Lichtentaler Allee (described on page 131). From here the casino is to your right. A stroll to the left—down Lichtentaler Allee—takes you to the rose garden, City Museum (a humble but well-*

displayed collection of artifacts and etchings showing the history of the spa town in an elegant old mansion), and out to Lichtentaler Abbey. You choose which way to go. My walk is done.

SIGHTS

▲▲**Casino and Kurhaus**—Baden-Baden's classy building called the *Kurhaus* contains a grand casino. Built in the 1850s, it was

inspired by the Palace of Versailles, and is filled with rooms honoring French royalty who never set foot in the place. But many other French people did. Gambling was illegal in 19th-century France... just over the border. The casino is licensed on the condition that it pays 92 percent of its earnings to the state. The amount of revenue it generates to help the state fund social services is a mystery, but insiders estimate that it's more than $30 million a year. The staff of 150 is paid by tips from happy gamblers.

You can visit the casino on a guided tour in the mornings, when it's closed to gamblers (see below), but the casino is most interesting to see in action, after 14:00. You can gamble if you want, but a third of the visitors come only to people-watch under the chandeliers. The scene is more subdued than at an American casino; anyone showing emotion is a tourist. Lean against a gilded statue and listen to the graceful reshuffling of personal fortunes. Do some imaginary gambling or buy a few chips at the window near the entrance (an ATM is nearby).

The casino is open for gambling daily from 14:00 to 2:00 in the morning (Fri–Sat until 3:00, €3 entry, €1.50 entry with *Kurkarte* discount card from your hotel—see page 135, €2 minimum bet, €10,000 maximum bet, no tennis shoes, tie and coat and collared shirt required and can be rented for €11 with an €11 deposit, passport required—driver's license isn't enough, under 21 not admitted, no photos, liveliest after dinner and later, pick up English history and game rules as you enter, tel. 07221/30240, www.casino-baden-baden.de).

Lower rollers and budget travelers can try their luck downstairs at the casino's €1 slot machines, called *Automatenspiel* (€1 entry fee or included in €3 casino admission, same hours, no dress code, no passport needed).

Casino Tour: The casino gives 30-minute German-language tours every morning, departing from 9:30 to 11:30 (€4, 2/hr, Nov–March from 10:00; some guides speak English, or call ahead and

Baden-Baden

Central Baden-Baden

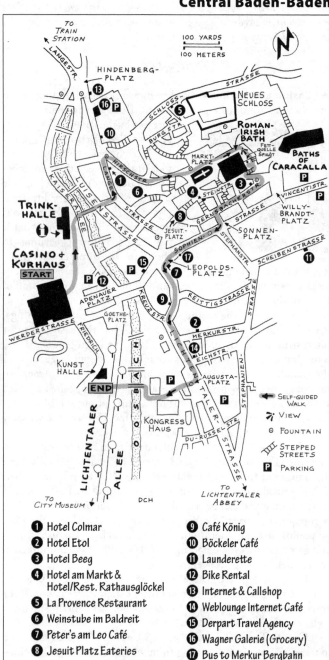

1. Hotel Colmar
2. Hotel Etol
3. Hotel Beeg
4. Hotel am Markt & Hotel/Rest. Rathausglöckel
5. La Provence Restaurant
6. Weinstube im Baldreit
7. Peter's am Leo Café
8. Jesuit Platz Eateries
9. Café König
10. Böckeler Café
11. Launderette
12. Bike Rental
13. Internet & Callshop
14. Weblounge Internet Café
15. Derpart Travel Agency
16. Wagner Galerie (Grocery)
17. Bus to Merkur Bergbahn

pay €15 extra per group for an English tour—tel. 07221/30240, or just pick up the paltry English brochure). Even camera-toting peasants in T-shirts, shorts, and sandals are welcome on tours.

▲▲**Strolling Lichtentaler Allee**—Imagine yourself in top hat and tails as you promenade down the famous Lichtentaler Allee, a pleasant, picnic-perfect, 1.5-mile-long lane. You'll stroll through a park along the babbling, brick-lined Oosbach river, past old mansions and under hardy oaks and exotic trees (street-lit all night), to the historic Lichtentaler Abbey, a Cistercian convent founded in 1245. At the elitist tennis courts, cross the bridge into the free Art Nouveau rose garden (*Gönneranlage,* 100 labeled kinds of roses, great lounge chairs, best in early summer). Either walk the whole length round-trip, or take city bus #201 one-way (runs between downtown and Klosterplatz, near the abbey). Many bridges cross the river, making it easy to shortcut to bus #201 anytime. Biking is another option (see "Bike Rental," page 124), but you'll have to stay on the road in the bike lane, since the footpath is only for pedestrians.

Russian Baden-Baden—Many Russians, including Dostoyevsky and Tolstoy, flocked to Baden-Baden after the czars banned gambling in their motherland. Many lost their fortunes, borrowed a pistol, and did themselves in on the "Alley of Sighs" (Seufzerallee, past the baths just off Sophienstrasse/Vincentistrasse). You'll find a Russian **church** just south of the center (€1, daily 10:00–18:00, services normally Sat 17:00–20:00 and Sun 9:40–11:30, near *Gönneranlage* rose garden across river from Lichtentaler Allee, or take bus #201 to Bertholdplatz stop). While the church dates from about 1900 and was quiet for generations, the current boom in the Russian population here has the church livelier than ever.

Many of Baden-Baden's top hotels are now Russian-owned. Throughout Europe floods of ultra-wealthy Russians are buying up urban property. While some mayors object, others see the money pouring into their towns as good for their economy and ask no questions. Baden-Baden is a favorite among Russians. While more Americans visit Baden-Baden, Russians—who stay longer—account for more overnights each year. You'll see Russian on multilingual signs around town.

▲**Funicular to Merkur**—For a delightful trip to a hilltop overlooking Baden-Baden, summit Merkur. Catch bus #204 or #205 from the city center (departing Sophienstrasse, just off Leopoldsplatz, normally hourly at :26 and :52, ride 11 min to end of line) through the ritzy "Paradise" neighborhood to the base of the Merkur Bergbahn. Catch the funicular to the 2,000-foot summit of Merkur (€4 round-trip, March–Dec daily 10:00–22:00, closed Jan–Feb). At the top you can enjoy a meal or drink (restaurant daily 10:00–18:00) and, if the weather's good (with winds from the south or west), you can watch the paragliders leap into ecstasy. From here there are lots of confusing trails and an easy paved lane taking you back to the base of the Merkur Bergbahn (4.2 miles, signposted *Merkurbahn Talstation*). From the bottom of the funicular, buses depart back to Baden-Baden twice hourly (at :09 and :37).

Mini–Black Forest Walks—Baden-Baden is at the northern end of the Black Forest. If you're not going south, but want a taste of Germany's favorite woods, consider one of several hikes from town. The TI has suggested routes and details enabling you to choose the right walk or hike.

EXPERIENCES

The Baths

Baden-Baden's two much-loved but very different baths stand side by side in a park at the top of the old town. The Roman-Irish Bath is traditional, stately, indoors, not very social, and extremely relaxing...just you, the past, and your body. The perky, fun, and modern Baths of Caracalla are half the price, indoor and outdoor, and more social. Caracalla is better in the sunshine. Roman-Irish is fine anytime. Some hotels sell discounted tickets (10–15 percent off) to one or both of the baths—ask at your hotel.

At either bath, your admission ticket works like a subway token—you need it to get out. If you overstay your allotted time, you pay extra. You can relax while your valuables are stowed in very secure lockers. Both baths share a huge underground Bäder-Garage, which is free (for the first 2 hours, then €1/hr) if you validate your parking ticket before leaving either bath.

▲▲▲Roman-Irish Bath (Friedrichsbad)

The highlight of most visits to Baden-Baden is a sober two-hour ritual called the Roman-Irish Bath. Friedrichsbad pampered the rich and famous in its elegant surroundings when it opened 120 years ago. Today, this steamy world of marble, brass columns, tropical tiles, herons, lily pads, and graceful nudity welcomes gawky tourists as well as locals. For €29, you get up to three hours and the works (€21 without the 10-minute massage).

Read this carefully before stepping out naked: In your changing cabin, load all your possessions onto the fancy hanger. Then hang it in the locker across the way, slip your card into the lock, and strap the key around your wrist. (If taking a massage, strap your plastic massage "coupon" to your wrist.) As you enter (in the "body crème" room), check your weight on the digital kilo scale. Do this again as you leave to see how much you sweated off. You will lose a kilo...all in sweat. The complex routine is written (in English) on the walls with recommended time—simply follow the room numbers from 1 to 15. Instructions are repeated everywhere. For the first couple of stops only, you will use plastic slippers (marked with European sizes) and a towel (given to you by the attendant for the hot-room lounges—for hygienic reasons and because the slats are too hot to sit on without the towel).

Take a shower. Grab a towel and put on plastic slippers before hitting the warm-air bath for 15 minutes and the hot-air bath for five minutes. Shower again. If you paid extra, take the soap-brush massage—rough, slippery, and finished with a good Teutonic spank. Play Gumby in the shower; lounge under sunbeams in one of several thermal steam baths; and glide like a swan under a divine dome in a royal pool (one of three "mixed" pools—the reason many Americans miss out on this experience). Don't skip the cold plunge. Dry in warmed towels and lie on a bed for 30 minutes, thinking prenatal thoughts, in the mellow, yellow, silent room. You don't appreciate how clean you are after this experience until you put your dirty socks back on. (Bring clean ones.)

All you need is money. You'll get a key, locker, and towel, and hair dryers are available (daily 9:00–22:00, last admission 3 hours before closing if you're getting a massage, 2 hours before otherwise; men and women together Tue, Wed, Fri–Sun; women separate Mon and Thu—see below; Römerplatz 1, tel. 07221/275-920, www.carasana.de). If you wear glasses, there are trays throughout for you to park them, but it's more relaxing if you can go without.

About the dress code: It is always nude. Men and women use parallel and nearly identical facilities. During "mixed" times, men and women share only three pools in the center. On Mondays and Thursdays, two of the shared pools are reserved for women only, but the biggest pool is still used by both men and women (if they choose). Shy bathers should avoid Sundays, when all of the rooms are mixed, including the steam and massage rooms. If you're concerned, there is no ogling going on. It's a very classy and respectful ritual—and a shame to miss because of the nudity.

Afterward, before going downstairs, browse through the Roman artifacts upstairs in the Renaissance Hall (also accessible to non-bathers), sip just a little of the terrible but "magic" hot water *(Thermalwasser)* from the elegant fountain, and stroll down the broad royal stairway, feeling, as they say, five years younger—or at least 2.2 pounds lighter.

Baden-Baden

▲▲Baths of Caracalla (Caracalla Therme)

For a more modern experience, spend a few hours at the Baths of Caracalla, a huge palace of water, steam, and relaxed people (daily 8:00–22:00, last entry at 20:30, sometimes closed for 2 weeks in June or July for renovation, kids under 6 not allowed, those 6 to 14 must be with parents—it's not really a splashing and sliding kind of pool, tel. 07221/275-940, www.carasana.de).

Here you need to bring a towel (or pay €5 plus a €10 deposit to rent one) and a swimsuit (shorts are OK for men). Buy a card (€13/2 hours, €15/3 hours, €17/4 hours, 10 2-hour entries for repeat visits or to split among a group cost €110) and put it in the locker to get a key. Change clothes, strap the key around your wrist, and go play. Your key gets you into another poolside locker if you want to lock up glasses or money for a tan or a drink. Bring your towel to the pool (there are plenty of places to stow it). The baths are an indoor/outdoor wonderland of steamy pools, waterfalls, neck showers, Jacuzzis, hot springs, cold pools, lounge chairs, saunas, a cafeteria, and a bar. After taking a few laps around the fake river, you can join some kinky Germans for water spankings (you may have to wait a few minutes to grab a vacant waterfall). Then join the gang in the central cauldron. The steamy "inhalation" room seems like purgatory's waiting room, with a misty minimum of visibility, filled with strange, silently aging bodies.

Nudity is limited to one zone upstairs. The grand spiral staircase leads to a naked world of saunas, tanning lights, cold plunges, and sunbathing outside on lounge chairs. At the top of the stairs everyone stows their suit in a cubbyhole and wanders around with their towel (some are modest and wrapped; others just run around buck naked). There are three eucalyptus-scented saunas of varying temperatures (80, 90, and 95 degrees) and two saunas in outdoor log cabins (with mesmerizing robotic steam-makers). Follow the instructions on the wall. Towels are required, not for modesty but to separate your body from the wood benches. The highlight is the Arctic bucket in the shower room. Pull the chain. Only rarely will you feel so good. And you can do it over and over.

SLEEPING

The TI can nearly always find you a room—but don't use the TI for places listed here, or you'll pay more. Go direct! The only tight times are during the horse races (mid–May and late Aug,

---

Sleep Code

(€1 = about $1.30, country code: 49, area code: 07221)
S = Single, **D** = Double/Twin, **T** = Triple, **Q** = Quad, **b** = bathroom,
s = shower only. Unless otherwise noted, credit cards are
accepted, English is spoken, and breakfast is included.

To help you sort easily through these listings, I've divided
the rooms into three categories based on the price for a standard double room with bath:

$$$ **Higher Priced**—Most rooms €90 or more.
 $$ **Moderately Priced**—Most rooms between €70–90.
  $ **Lower Priced**—Most rooms €70 or less.

---

www.baden-galopp.de). If you arrive by train, just hop on bus
#201, which goes to the center of town (and recommended hotels),
and then follows the river to the Lichtentaler Abbey (and another
hotel). Hotel am Markt is a great value and worth calling in
advance.

All hotels and pensions are required to extract an additional
€2.80 per person, per night "spa tax." This comes with a "guest
card" *(Kurkarte)*, offering small discounts on tourist admissions
around town (including casino entry and bike rental). If you're
coming into town by car or foot, look for the helpful green signs
that direct you to each hotel by name.

In the Center, near the Casino

For locations, see the map on page 130.

$$$ Hotel Colmar, run with a personal touch by Hilde and
Shaso Özcan and family, rents 26 pastel-elegant rooms, some
with balconies (Sb-€78–85, Db-€98, 2-room apartment Db-€118,
extra bed-€35, 10 percent discount with cash and this book, non-
smoking rooms, elevator, parking-€11/day, Lange Strasse 34, tel.
07221/93890, fax 07221/938-950, www.hotel-colmar.de, info
@hotel-colmar.de).

$$$ Hotel Etol, located on a quiet courtyard among indus-
trial-looking buildings, recalls its past as a bathtub factory for the
czars of Russia. Its friendly staff and central location make this
a winning choice. The 18 modern rooms, all named after towns
in the area, will particularly appeal to minimalists, but lots of
natural light and cheerful carpets keep them inviting to all (Sb-
€75–95, Db-€90–110, all rooms non-smoking, €5/day parking,
Merkurstrasse 7, tel. 07221/973-470, fax 07221/9734-7111, www
.hotel-etol-badenbaden.de, info@hotel-etol-badenbaden.de).

In the Center, Uphill by the Baths

$$$ Hotel Beeg rents 15 attractive and comfortable rooms, run from a delectable pastry shop/café on the ground floor. It's wonderfully situated on a little square in a pedestrian zone and faces the baths, though the staff can be a bit formal (Sb-€85, Db-€109, balcony-€10 extra, apartment Tb-€150, elevator, reception in café, on Römerplatz at Gernsbacher Strasse 44, tel. 07221/36760, fax 07221/367-610, hccbeeg@t-online.de, Herr Beeg).

$$ Hotel am Markt is a warm, 25-room, family-run hotel with all the comforts a commoner could want in a peaceful, central, nearly traffic-free location, two cobbled blocks from the baths (S-€30–32, Sb-€42–47, D-€62–65, Db-€76–80, Tb-€95–100, extra bed-€15, Wi-Fi, Marktplatz 18, tel. 07221/27040, fax 07221/270-444, www.hotel-am-markt-baden.de, info@hotel-am-markt-baden.de, Herr und Frau Bogner-Schindler and Frau Jung). For romantics, the church bells blast charmingly through each room every quarter hour from 6:15 until 22:00; for others, they are a nuisance. Otherwise, quiet rules. The ambience and the clientele make having breakfast or just killing time on their small terrace a joy.

$$ Hotel Rathausglöckel, around the corner and below the Hotel am Markt at Steinstrasse 7, is a 16th-century guest house with nine cozy rooms and steep stairs (Sb-€60, Db-€70–85, third person-€20, 2-room apartment with kitchen-€80–150, depending on number of people and length of stay, Wi-Fi, church bells every 15 min 6:15–22:00, parking-€6/day, tel. 07221/90610, fax 07221/906-161, www.rathausgloeckel.de, info@rathausgloeckel.de, kind Michael Rothe).

Outside the Center

The following two listings are a few stops from the center by bus #201 (for locations, see map on page 125).

$ Deutscher Kaiser is a big, traditional guest house with 22 simple and spacious old rooms, run by no-nonsense Frau Peter. Herr Peter cooks fine local-style meals in the hotel restaurant (€7–15, restaurant closed Mon–Tue). It's two doors from the Eckerlestrasse stop of bus #201 (6/hr, 10 min from center, 20 min from train station) or a 25-minute stroll from the city center down polite Lichtentaler Allee—cross the river at the green *Restaurant Deutscher Kaiser* sign, then turn right (S-€35, Sb-€47–49, D-€46–49, Db-€61–69, family rooms, often impressive discounts on their website, non-smoking rooms, Wi-Fi, free and easy parking, Hauptstrasse 35, tel. 07221/72152, fax 07221/72154, www.hoteldk.de, info@hoteldk.de). Drivers: From the autobahn, skip the town center by following *Congress* signs into Michaelstunnel. Take the tunnel's first exit, then another right at the end of the exit (direction: Lichtental). Outside, the hotel is about a half-mile down on the left. From the Black Forest, follow *Zentrum* signs. Just 10 yards after the Aral gas station, turn left down the small road to Hauptstrasse.

$ Werner Dietz Hostel, between the station and the center, is big, modern, and has the cheapest beds in town (€18 per bed in 4- to 6-bed dorms, €3 less for 2 nights or more, €3 more if you're over 26, adult non-members pay €3 extra, S/D rooms €5 extra per person, includes sheets and breakfast, cash only, 23:30 curfew, Hardbergstrasse 34, tel. 07221/52223, www.jugendherberge -baden-baden.de, info@jugendherberge-baden-baden.de). To reach the hostel from the train station or downtown, take bus #201 to Grosse Dollenstrasse (also announced as *Jugendherberge*), six stops from the station or five from downtown; it's a steep, well-marked, 10-minute climb from there. Drivers should call the hostel for careful directions.

EATING

Dining with Elegance and Atmosphere

Hotel Rathausglöckel's restaurant, personal and homey, has long had a good reputation for great food. The setting is understated Old World elegance (but all indoors—a negative if the weather is really hot). Michael serves well-presented traditional cuisine with good vegetarian options and is happy to explain the day's specials (€7–19 entrées, Thu–Sun 11:30–14:00 & 18:00–21:30, Wed 18:00–21:30, closed Mon–Tue, reservations smart, Steinstrasse 7, tel. 07221/90610).

La Provence makes dining a memorable experience. Stepping into one big high-energy room under vaulted arches, you feel this is a winner. It has a dark, romantic setting with tight and tangled tables. Their creative menu features Spanish, French, and Italian dishes, including big €10 dinner salads and an unforgettable €15 "La Provence" appetizer plate (€15–22 entrées, Mon–Fri 17:00–23:00, Sat–Sun 12:00–23:00, reservations smart, from Marktplatz hike up to Schlossstrasse 20, tel. 07221/216-515). As there are no outside tables, this is also hot when it's hot.

Weinstube im Baldreit, with both a cozy cellar and a leafy back courtyard, is best for a hot evening. Dining here, I feel like a pampered salamander in a Monet terrarium. While her French man (Philippe) cooks wonderful regional dishes, Nicole is happy to explain the daily specials—which aren't on the English menu. The priority here is near-gourmet food at great prices. Reservations are smart (€8–18 meals, Mon–Sat 12:00–14:00 & 17:00–22:00, closed Sun; several entrances: from Lange Strasse 10, walk up Küferstrasse, look for *Weinstube* signs and enter under archway, Küferstrasse 3; tel. 07221/23136).

Simple Meals

Peter's am Leo Café is a fun self-service place offering salads, pasta, fish, omelets, pastries, and views over a busy square. (Try to snare one of the outdoor tables.) This is where commoners pile their plates high. The lively staff dons lederhosen for Oktoberfest, Hawaiian shirts in sunny weather, and striped shirts for the horse races (€5–6 entrées, Mon–Fri 6:30–19:00, Sat 6:30–18:00, Sun 8:00–19:00, free coffee and tea refills, on Leopoldsplatz at Sophienstrasse 10, tel. 07221/392-817).

Eateries on Jesuit Platz: **Gasthaus Löwenbräu** is a sloppy, rude Bavarian *Biergarten* slinging good beer and basic schnitzel fare under a vine-covered trellis. Across the street, several decent restaurants offer curbside tables—great for people-watching. And just up Gernsbacherstrasse from here (at #17), the **Lotus Chinese Restaurant** serves big cheap portions and has a few cute outdoor tables (daily 11:00–23:00).

Prime People-Watching Cafés

Café König is *the* place to spend too much for an elegant, 19th-century cup of coffee and a slice of Black Forest cake. At the counter, you can buy pastry and candy to go (daily 8:30–18:30, fine shady patio, look for sign with squiggly script, just before Augustaplatz at Lichtentaler Strasse 12, tel. 07221/23573).

In der Trinkhalle, a café that shares the handsome Trinkhalle building with the TI, has comfy leather sofas, international newspapers and magazines, and a casino-view terrace (daily 10:00–24:00, Kaiserallee 3, tel. 07221/302-905).

Böckeler Café has good cakes and outdoor tables along a lively pedestrian street (Mon–Fri 8:00–18:30, Sat–Sun 9:30–18:00, Lange Strasse 40–42, tel. 07221/949-594).

TRANSPORTATION CONNECTIONS

From Baden-Baden by Train to: Freiburg (hourly, 45 min, sometimes 90 min with a change in Offenburg), **Triberg** (hourly, 70 min), **Munich** (hourly, 4 hrs, some direct but most with 1–2 changes), **Frankfurt** (2/hr, 1.5 hrs, most with a change in Mannheim or Karlsruhe), **Frankfurt Airport** (every 2 hrs direct, 1.5 hrs; or hourly with a change in Karlsruhe, 1.5 hrs), **Bacharach** (hourly, 3 hrs, 1–3 changes), **Strasbourg** (almost hourly, 30 min direct or 60–90 min with 1 change), **Bern** or **Zürich** (every 1–2 hrs, 3 hrs, change in Basel). Train info: tel. 11861 (€0.60/min).

Freiburg

Freiburg im Breisgau is worth a quick look, if for nothing else than to appreciate its thriving center and very human scale. Bikers and hikers seem to outnumber cars, and trams run everywhere. This "sunniest town in Germany," with 30,000 students, lacks must-see attractions but offers the pleasures of a university town: small shops, cozy cafés, fine food, and fewer tourists than Baden-Baden.

Freiburg (FRY-burg), bombed nearly flat in 1944, skillfully put itself back together. This capital of the Schwarzwald, exuding an "I could live here" appeal, is surrounded by lush forests and filled with environmentally aware people so dedicated to solar power that they host an annual Intersolar trade fair.

Marvel at the number of pedestrian-only streets. Freiburg's trademark is its system of *Bächle*, tiny streams running down each street. These go back to the Middle Ages (serving as fire protection, cattle refreshment, and a constantly flushing disposal system). Local lore says that if you fall into a *Bächle,* you are destined to marry a Freiburger. A sunny day turns any kid-at-heart into a puddle-jumper. Enjoy the ice cream and street-singing ambience of the cathedral square, which has a great produce and craft market (Mon–Sat 7:30–13:00, biggest Wed and Sat, closed Sun). To get a glimpse of the historic Altstadt (old town), be sure to stroll down the street named Gerberau and marvel at 15th-century houses and medieval city gates (Martinstor and Schwabentor).

ORIENTATION

(area code: 0761)

Tourist Information
Freiburg's busy but helpful TI has free city maps and sells better maps for €1, as well as several city guidebooks that aren't necessary for a short stay (the €4 guide has tons of practical information, the €5 city guide with photos has the most info on sights, and the €7 book is geared toward students spending a semester in Freiburg, with lots of bar and nightlife suggestions). The TI also offers a room-booking service (€3 per booking for Freiburg and Black Forest area), walking tours in German and English (€7, 2 hours,

May–Oct Sun–Fri at 10:30, Sat at 10:00, none off-season), and lots of information on the Black Forest region (including yet another €5 book; TI open June–Sept Mon–Fri 9:30–20:00, Sat 9:30–17:00, Sun 10:00–12:00; Oct–May Mon–Fri 9:30–18:00, Sat 9:30–14:30, Sun 10:00–12:00; tel. 0761/388-1880, www.freiburg.de).

Arrival in Freiburg

The bustling train station has lockers (€2–4 lockers by track 1B, or try the high-tech ones—with English instructions—in the station hall), a high-tech WC (€0.80), and a helpful *Reisezentrum* that dispenses rail info and sell tickets (Mon–Sat 6:30–20:00, Sun 7:30–20:00). The bus station is next door.

Walk out of the train station, cross the street, and head straight up the tree-lined boulevard called Eisenbahnstrasse (passing the post office). Within three blocks, you'll take an underpass beneath a busy road. On the other side, it becomes Rathausgasse; follow it and take a left where it intersects with Universitätsstrasse to find the TI on Rathausplatz.

Helpful Hints

Internet Access and Laundry: Get online at **Tee Online** (€3.50/ hr, Mon–Sat 9:00–21:00, Sun 10:00–21:00, Grünewaldstrasse 19) or at **Uni Kopie + Druck** (€3.50/hr, Mon–Fri 8:30–19:00, Sat 9:30–16:00, closed Sun, Niemensstrasse 11). Or do your laundry while surfing the Net at **Wash Tours** (€6/load, Internet access-€3/hr, Mon–Fri 9:00–19:00, Sat 9:00–18:00, closed Sun, access from passage at Grünewaldstrasse 19, tel. 0761/288-866, www.washtours.com). All three are close to Martinstor.

Bike Rental: Mobile, by the station, rents bikes and has free route maps (€5/3 hrs, €9.50/6 hrs, €12.50/24 hrs, €50 cash and passport for deposit, daily 5:00–24:00; from station, cross tram bridge over train tracks to round building on left and walk downstairs; Wentzingerstrasse 15, tel. 0761/292-7998, www .mobile-freiburg.com).

Getting Around Freiburg

The city center (including all my recommended hotels) is completely walkable, though you might want to use a taxi or a tram to haul luggage from the station. Trams are also useful to reach outlying sights such as Schauinsland (€2 per ride, €4.80 for 24-hour pass).

SIGHTS

▲**Cathedral (Münster)**—This impressive church, completed in 1513, took more than three centuries to build, and ranges in style from late Romanesque to lighter, brighter Gothic. It was virtually the only building in town to survive WWII bombs. The lacy tower *(Münsterturm),* considered by many the most beautiful around, is as tall as the church is long...and not worth the 329-step ascent (tower–€1.50, Mon–Sat 9:30–17:00, Sun 13:00–17:00). From this lofty perch, watchmen used to scan the town for fires. While you could count the 123 representations of Mary throughout the church, most  gawk at the "mooning" gargoyle (facing the entrance, walk around the right and look at the second butt-ress)...and wait for rain.

Take a clockwise spin around the cathedral to appreciate the hodgepodge of architectural styles, ranging from 15th-century charming to 20th-century ugly (since much of the north side of the square was bombed flat in World War II). The fountain was moved here from another location in 1970. Noteworthy buildings include the Kornhaus (1489), which has served as a granary and theater. The ornate Historisches Kaufhaus (1532), across from the church, was the trading and customs center in the 16th century and briefly housed the state parliament after the war. The pale yellow Haus zum Ritter has morphed from a clubhouse for local knights to the residence of the archbishop, and today it remains property of the cathedral.

If you follow Buttergasse (just left of the Historisches Kaufhaus) to Schustergasse, jog right and immediately right, you'll end up at the...

Augustiner Museum—While this museum is undergoing extensive renovation (until the end of 2008, though some exhibits remain open), it feels more like a warehouse of crosses, goblets, and broken statuary. When completed, it is slated to be the Upper Rhine Region's most significant collection of Black Forest art and culture. There are no descriptions in English as of yet, but most of the collection is self-explanatory. The highlights are a close-up look at some of the Münster's original medieval stained glass and statuary, as well as Wentzinger's *Immaculata,* a two-foot-tall terra-cotta statue from the 18th century (free while under renovation, €2–5 for special exhibits, Tue–Sun 10:00–17:00, closed Mon, 2 blocks south of cathedral in big yellow building on Augustinerplatz,

Freiburg

tel. 0761/201-2531).

The area around Augustinerplatz is the heart of the Gerberau district, popular with locals. It's quieter and filled with little galleries and restaurants that are less expensive than on the Marktplatz. There's a great playground for kids and a beer garden just around the corner. From here, it's a five-minute walk to the base of Schlossberg.

Schlossberg (Castle Hill)—Schlossberg towers over the east end of Freiburg's old town. It was named Castle Hill because a 17th-century fort once stood here, built by the French to control the citizens of Freiburg during a period of French occupation. Schlossberg today is popular for its views over the city. Though the old fort is long gone, a new modern lookout tower (100 feet high) stands where the French Fort d'Aigle (eagle tower) once stood.

To get to the top of Schlossberg, you can either hike or take an elevator from Schwabentor, the half-timbered tower at the east end of the old town. From the tower, look for the footbridge on Oberlinden street. Cross the bridge and hike up 10 minutes (to the left). You can also continue straight through the tunnel to the free elevator *(Aufzug)*. At the top of the elevator and trail, you'll come to the restaurant Greiffenegg Schlössle (see "Eating" on page 144). From there, walk another seven minutes up to the viewpoint. To continue 20 more minutes to the Fort d'Aigle lookout tower from the viewpoint, walk the level path to the left (with your back to the benches), then veer right uphill at the big white cross (look for small silver signs pointing through forest).

Schauinsland—Freiburg's own mountain, while little more than an oversized hill, is nine miles southeast of the center. This viewpoint, which won't wow Americans from Colorado, offers the handiest panorama view of the Schwarzwald for those without wheels. The gondola system—one of Germany's oldest—was designed for Freiburgers relying on public transportation (€11.50 round-trip, €26 family ticket includes 2 adults and up to 4 kids, daily July–Sept 9:00–18:00, Oct–June 9:00–17:00; catch tram #2—direction Günterstal—from town center to the end, then take bus #21 seven stops to Talstation stop for gondola; tel. 0761/292-930, www.bergwelt-schauinsland.de). At the 4,000-foot summit, you'll find a view restaurant, pleasant circular walks, and the Schniederli Hof, a 1592 farmhouse museum. A tower on a nearby peak offers an even more commanding Black Forest view.

Nightlife—Night owls flock around the Martinstor in the area affectionately called Freiburg's "Bermuda Triangle." Take the street to your right just before going through the gate and get sucked in. Look at the Burger King ahead of you; mischievous Puck does a little dance and plays the pan pipes. He's a fitting mascot for a district known for its fun, colorful bars.

SLEEPING

(€1 = about $1.30, country code: 49, area code: 0761)
Though I prefer nights in sleepy Staufen (see page 146), many will enjoy a night in lively Freiburg. Prices include breakfast, and English is spoken. Hotel Alleehaus offers the most value for your money.

Near the Center
All the listings below are in or within a few blocks of the old town.

$$$ Schwarzwälder Hof is just steps from the cathedral, with odd bits of art in the hallways and 45 rooms over a reasonably priced restaurant. Ask for one of the new modern rooms (S-€45, Ss-€45, Sb-€60, D-€75, Ds-€75, Db-€95–98, Tb-€110–120, includes free local transport card, Wi-Fi, parking-€9/day, Herrenstrasse 43, walk 15 min from station or take tram #1 three stops to Oberlinden, tel. 0761/38030, fax 0761/380-3135, www .shof.de, info@shof.de, Engler family).

$$ Hotel Alleehaus is tops. It has 19 comfy rooms with modern furniture and decorations at the south edge of the center, on a quiet, leafy street in a big house that feels like home. It's warmly run by Bernd, Claudia, and their team (S-€49, Sb-€68–75, small Db-€85, larger Db-€99, Tb-€135, Qb-€154, reception closed 19:30–6:00, call by 18:00 if arriving later than 19:30, good buffet breakfast, non-smoking rooms, parking-€6/day, Marienstrasse 7, near intersection with Wallstrasse, from station walk 20 min or take tram #3 or #5 three stops to Holzmarkt, tel. 0761/387-600, fax 0761/387-6099, www.hotel-alleehaus.de, wohlfuehlen @hotel-alleehaus.de).

$$ Hotel am Stadtgarten, on the north side of town (a 20-min walk from the station), rents 73 comfortable rooms in two buildings across the street from each other. Sprightly owner Paul Niehaus lived in New York City in the 1960s...and has the accent to prove it (Sb-€64–84, Db-€79–99, higher prices depend on which building, season, and size; extra bed-€27, bike rental-€9/day; parking-€8/day on lot, €12/day in garage; coupons for local restaurants and discounts for walking tours, Bernhardstrasse 5, at intersection with Karlstrasse, near Siegesdenkmal stop on tram line #2—you'll have to change trams if coming from the station, tel. 0761/282-9002, fax 0761/282-9022, www.hotelamstadtgarten.de, kontakt @hotelamstadtgarten.de).

Near the Train Station
$$$ Hotel Barbara has 21 fine and bright rooms (Sb-€69–79, Db-€92–115, extra bed-€20, prices €10 higher during fairs, nearby

parking garage-€9/day, on quiet street 2 min from station, head toward TI but turn left at post office to Poststrasse 4, tel. 0761/296-250, fax 0761/26688, www.hotel-barbara.de, mail@hotel-barbara.de, friendly Erika and Armin Wahl).

Hostels

$ Black Forest Hostel has 105 of the cheapest beds in town. Run by friendly Tania, with a young, bohemian attitude, it's bare-bones simple (€13–16 per person in 21-bed rooms, €17–21 per person in 11-bed rooms, S-€28, D-€46, sheets-€3, sleeping bags OK, cash only, no curfew, no smoking in rooms, lockers, Internet access-€2/hr, self-service kitchen, laundry-€4, Kartäuser Strasse 33—look for anchor sign and go down driveway; 20-min walk from station or take tram #1—direction: Littenweiler—to Oberlinden stop, then walk 10 more min; tel. 0761/881-7870, fax 0761/881-7895, www.blackforest-hostel.de, backpacker@blackforest-hostel.de). If full, they might direct you to the much larger, more distant **$ Freiburg Youth Hostel** at Kartäuser Strasse 151 (dorm bed-€20.80, includes sheets, €3 more for travelers over 26, tel. 0761/67656, www.jugendherberge-freiburg.de, info@jugendherberge-freiburg.de).

EATING

Freiburg has plenty of dining options. I've listed a few good places in the town center, and a couple atop the scenic Schlossberg.

In the Center

Hausbrauerei Feierling brews its own beer and also serves fine meals. On warm summer evenings, their *Biergarten* across the street offers cool, leafy shade and a bustling atmosphere (€5–12 entrées, daily 11:00–24:00, Gerberau 46, tel. 0761/243-480).

Sichlschmied is a good option rain or shine. Its alcoves and cluttered interior give it a cozy living-room feel and its creekside seating can't be beat (be careful not to confuse it with neighboring, lesser-value restaurant). For easygoing regional cuisine, good value, and a family-friendly ambience, come here (€7–15 plates, daily 12:00–22:00, Insel 1 but enter on Marienstrasse, tel. 0761/35037).

Tacheles appeals to student-size appetites (big) and budgets (small). Who knew that schnitzel could be prepared in literally a dozen different ways? Here at the self-proclaimed *"Schnitzel Paradies,"* they serve up big schnitzels (€1 extra for *Pute*—turkey—instead of the traditional pork), a salad, and your choice of a side dish (french fries, *Spätzle*, and so on) for a mere €5.50 for lunch or €6.90 for dinner (after 18:00). The pub downstairs, a favorite hangout, can be crowded and smoky; instead, opt for the quiet courtyard seating upstairs (Mon–Sat 11:00–24:00, Sun 15:00–

24:00, also vegetarian options, nightly drink specials listed on menu under *Tagesschau*, live *Fussball* broadcasts Sat–Sun nights, Grünwalderstrasse 17, tel. 0761/319-6669).

Kleiner Meyerhof, around the corner from the TI, offers typical German food, with regional specialties and reasonable prices (€7–17 entrées, daily 10:00–24:00, kitchen closes at 22:00, Rathausgasse 27, tel. 0761/26941).

At **UC/Uni-Café,** join the cerebral grad-student crowd for cheap salads, sandwiches, and breakfasts—have a cappuccino outside on the square, or pop inside to drink beer and watch a *Fussball* match on the flat-screen TV (€4–8 salads and sandwiches, Mon–Sat 8:00–23:00, Sun 10:00–23:00, Niemensstrasse 7, at Universitätsgasse, tel. 0761/383-355).

Chang Thai is where students satisfy their Asian-food cravings (Mon–Sat 12:00–23:00, Sun 13:00–22:30, Grünwalderstrasse 21).

Aran ("bread" in Celtic) is committed to getting back to basics. Their signature organic dark sourdough, topped with fresh spreads from curried chicken to spicy pepper cream cheese, makes a great light lunch. Other menu items include hot sandwiches, daily soups, baked potatoes, smoothies, and yogurt and müsli parfaits. Sit inside and feel "designy" or relax outside in the bamboo oasis (€3–10 plates, daily May–Oct 8:30–23:00, Nov–April 8:30–19:00, Salzstrasse 29, tel. 0761/290-9664).

On Freiburg's Schlossberg

For directions on getting to these scenic eateries, see "Schlossberg (Castle Hill)," page 142.

Greiffenegg Schlössle offers rooftop views over Freiburg, but the meals are expensive and worth it only if you can get a table on the terrace in good weather (€17–25 entrées, daily 11:00–24:00, reservations smart, tel. 0761/32728). Consider instead their self-service, open-air **Biergarten Kastaniengarten,** just above the restaurant (€6–8 entrées, open April–Oct in good weather, same hours and phone). Cheaper yet, consider a picnic at the Schlossberg viewpoint.

TRANSPORTATION CONNECTIONS

The full name of the town—and the station—is Freiburg im Breisgau, often abbreviated as "Freiburg (Brsg)" on schedules.

From Freiburg to Staufen: There are hourly trains to Staufen (fewer on Sun, 30 min; transfer in Bad Krozingen and take the slick light rail to Staufen; last Bad Krozingen–Staufen train leaves at about 22:00 Mon–Sat and 20:00 on Sun, or 19:00 most nights in the direction from Staufen to Freiburg, but you can take a shared

Freiburg

taxi between Staufen and Bad Krozingen for €10—call taxi 30 min before you need it, tel. 07633/5386). For local bus schedules, see www.sweg.de.

By Train to: Baden-Baden (hourly, 45 min, sometimes 90 min with a change in Offenburg), **Munich** (hourly, 4.5 hrs, 1 change), **Basel** (hourly, 45 min), **Bern** (hourly, 2 hrs, transfer in Basel), **Frankfurt** (hourly, 2 hrs, mostly direct, some require change in Mannheim). Train info: tel. 11861 (€0.60/min).

Staufen

Staufen im Breisgau makes a peaceful and delightful home base for your exploration of Freiburg and the southern trunk of the Black Forest. Hemmed in by vineyards, it's small and off the beaten path, with a quiet pedestrian zone of colorful old buildings bounded by a happy creek that actually babbles.

Tourist Information: The TI, on the main square in the Rathaus, has a good (German-only) map of the wine road (Mon 9:00–12:30 & 14:00–18:00, Tue–Thu until 17:30, Fri until 17:00, Sat 9:30–12:00, closed Sun, tel. 07633/80536, www.staufen .de, touristik@staufen.de).

Arrival in Staufen: Everything I list is within a 10-minute walk of the station (no lockers, but try Bahnhof Hotel—see "Sleeping and Eating"). To get to town, exit the station with your back to the pond and angle right up Bahnhofstrasse. Turn right at the post office onto Hauptstrasse for the town center, hotels, and TI.

SIGHTS

There's little to do in Staufen but enjoy the marketplace atmosphere, hike through the vineyards to the ruined castle overlooking the town, and savor a good dinner with local wine. Visiting with the local vintners in town as you taste their wine is popular. My favorite Staufen activity is to browse the super-quaint lanes and then hang out with Lotte at the Bahnhof Hotel.

Cyclists and joy-drivers tour the **Wine Road** (Badische Weinstrasse) with Staufen as a springboard. The Wine Road through this part of Germany staggers from Staufen through the tiny towns of Grunern, Dottingen, Sulzburg, and Britzingen, before collapsing in Badenweiler. If you're in the mood for some tasting, look for *Winzergenossenshaft* signs, which invite visitors in to taste and buy wines, and often to tour a winery.

SLEEPING AND EATING

(€1 = about $1.30, country code: 49, area code: 07633)
The TI has a list of B&Bs (their prices listed are for one night, but most places don't like one-nighters). The following hotels are fine for stays of one night (or more). Except for the last listing, breakfast is included.

$$ Gasthaus Krone, on the main pedestrian drag, has nine rooms that gild the lily but offer a good value in this price range (Sb-€65, Db-€85, Tb-€105, balconies, parking, Hauptstrasse 30, tel. 07633/5840, fax 07633/82903, www.die-krone.de, info @die-krone.de; Kurt Lahn, who looks a bit like Dan Rather, speaks a little English). Its **restaurant** appreciates vegetables and offers wonderful splurge meals (closed Sat).

$$ Hotel Hirschen, with a storybook location in the old pedestrian center, is family-run, with 15 plush and thoughtfully appointed rooms, balconies, and a big roof deck (Sb-€60, Db-€78, Tb-€105, elevator, free and easy parking, on main pedestrian street at Hauptstrasse 19, cozy restaurant open Wed–Sun, tel. 07633/5297, fax 07633/5295, www.hirschen-staufen.de, for reservations on short notice it's best to fax, Dieter and Isabelle). They have a huge luxury penthouse for four to six people (€140–150).

$ Hotel Sonne, at the edge of the pedestrian center, offers eight newly renovated rooms with Italian flair. Friendly Antonio is particularly proud of his **restaurant**—which offers a nice break from traditional *deutsche Küche,* serving tasty pizzas and Italian fare (Sb-€50, Db-€65, Tb-€85; continue straight past Hotel Krone, turn right at T intersection, and take second left on Mühlegasse to reach Albert-Hugard-Strasse 1; tel. 07633/95300, fax 07633/953-014).

$ Bahnhof Hotel is the cheapest, simplest place in town, with a dynamite castle view from the upstairs terrace, a self-service kitchen, a *kleine* washing machine for guests, and €7 dinners served on its tree-shaded patio or in its antler-filled **restaurant** (S-€21, D-€41, no breakfast, across from train station, tel. 07633/6190, no English spoken). Seven comfortable and cheery rooms right out of Grandma's house share two bathrooms. At night, master of ceremonies Lotte makes it the squeeze-box of Staufen. People come from all around to party with Lotte, so it can be noisy at night. If you want to eat red meat in a wine barrel under a tree, this is the place. For stays of three nights or longer, ask her about the rooms next door (Sb-€30, Db-€40).

The Best of the Black Forest

▲▲Short and Scenic Black Forest Joyride (by Car or Train and Bus)

This pleasant loop from Freiburg takes you through the most representative chunk of the area, avoiding the touristy, overcrowded Titisee.

By Car: Leave Freiburg on Schwarzwaldstrasse (signs to *Donaueschingen*), which becomes scenic road B-31 down the dark Höllental ("Hell's Valley") toward Titisee. Turn left at Hinterzarten onto road B-500, follow signs to St. Märgen and then to St. Peter—one of the healthy, go-take-a-walk-in-the-clean-air places that doctors actually prescribe for people from all over Germany. There's a fine four-mile walk between St. Märgen and St. Peter, with regular buses to bring you back.

To continue your drive from St. Peter, you can wind through idyllic Black Forest scenery up to Mt. Kandel. At the summit is the Berghotel Kandel. You can park here and take a short walk to the 4,000-foot peak for a great view. Then the road winds steeply through a dense forest to Waldkirch, where a fast road takes you to the Freiburg Nord autobahn entrance. With a good car and no stops, you'll get from Staufen/Freiburg to Baden-Baden via this route in three hours.

By Train and Bus: Trains run twice hourly from Freiburg to Kirchzarten Bahnhof, where bus #7216 goes to St. Peter and St. Märgen. Get off at St. Peter, hike four miles to St. Märgen, and bus/train back to Freiburg (€3.40 one-way, or consider the Regio Pass: €9.60/1 adult or €15/up to 5 adults for 24 hours on all regional transportation, including within Freiburg and Badenweiler). If you're staying overnight in the area, ask your hotel or pension about the KONUS guest card, which allows you to travel on the region's public transit for free. The regional bus information office has all the details on getting around the area (turn right out of Freiburg train station and walk 100 yards, tel. 0761/368-0388 during business hours; after hours, call 01805-779-966 for €0.12/min, or call Freiburg TI, tel. 0761/388-1880).

Town of St. Peter: The **TI,** just next to the Benedictine Abbey (private), can recommend a walk (TI open April–Oct Mon–Fri 9:00–12:00 & 15:00–17:00, Sat in July–Aug 10:00–12:00; Nov–March Mon–Fri 9:00–12:00; closed Sun year-round and Sat Sept–June; Klosterhoff 11, tel. 07660/910-224). Sleep at the traditional old **$$ Gasthof Hirschen** on the main square (Sb-€39–44, Db-€66–82, Tb-€87–97, Qb-€110, parking-€3.60/day, St. Peter/Hochschwarzwald, Bertoldsplatz 1, tel. 07660/204, fax 07660/1557, www.gasthof-hirschen.de, info@gasthof-hirschen.de), or consider **$ Pension Kandelblick** (D-€50, cash only, Seelgutweg 5, tel. 07660/349).

▲▲Extended Black Forest Drive

Of course, you could spend much more time in the land of cuckoo clocks and healthy hikes. For a more thorough visit, still connecting with Baden-Baden, try this drive: As described above, drive from Staufen or Freiburg down Höllental. After a short stop in St. Peter, wind up in Furtwangen with the impressive **German Clock Museum** (Deutsches Uhrenmuseum, €4, daily April–Oct 9:00–18:00, Nov–March 10:00–17:00, tel. 07723/920-2800, www .deutsches-uhrenmuseum.de). More than a chorus of cuckoo clocks, this museum traces (in English) the development of clocks from the Dark Ages to the Space Age. It has an upbeat combo of mechanical musical instruments as well. By car, continue on to...

Triberg—Deep in the Black Forest, Triberg is famous for its Gutach Waterfall (which falls 500 feet in several bounces, €2 to see it) and, more importantly, the **Black Forest Museum,** which gives a fine look at the costumes, carvings, and traditions of the local culture (€4.50, daily 10:00–17:00, Wallfahrtstrasse 4, tel. 07722/4434, www.schwarzwaldmuseum.de). Touristy as Triberg is, it offers an easy way for travelers without cars to enjoy the Black Forest (TI located in Black Forest Museum, tel. 07722/866-490, www.triberg.de). Next, head toward the...

▲Black Forest Open-Air Museum (Schwarzwälder Freilichtmuseum Vogtsbauernhof)—This excellent museum offers the best look at this region's traditional folk life. (Note: It's different from the similarly named museum in Triberg, described above.) Built around one grand old farmhouse, the museum is a collec-

tion of several old farms filled with exhibits on the local dress and lifestyles. Make time for the grain mill (€6, daily April–Nov 9:00–18:00, until 20:00 in Aug, last entry 1 hour before closing, closed Dec–March, English descriptions and €5 guidebook, north of Triberg, through Hornberg to Hausach/Gutach on road B33, tel. 07831/93560, www .vogtsbauernhof.org). The surrounding shops and restaurants are awfully touristy, but are a fair source for local specialties. Skip the indoor restaurant and instead try your *Frikadelle* (a spiced pork-and-beef patty) or *Schupfnudeln* (potato-based noodles, served fried up with sauerkraut) at the outdoor stands. Don't be shy to try a little of everything; the friendly ladies ladling the portions will fill up your plate with whatever you point to and charge about €5–6). Be sure to indulge in a creamy piece of Schwarzwald Kirschtorte.

Continue north through Freudenstadt, the capital of the northern Black Forest, and on to the Schwarzwald-Hochstrasse, which takes you along a ridge through 30 miles of pine forests before dumping you right on Baden-Baden's back porch.

ROTHENBURG AND THE ROMANTIC ROAD

The Romantic Road takes you through Bavaria's medieval heartland, a route strewn with picturesque villages, farmhouses, onion-domed churches, Baroque palaces, and walled cities. The Romantic Road is the most scenic way to connect Frankfurt with Munich. Clearly marked for drivers, and well-described in a free brochure available at any TI, the route technically runs from Würzburg south to Füssen. Car travelers can follow the signposts, meandering from one medieval town to the next. No trains run along the entire Romantic Road, but rail travelers can linger for a night or two in Rothenburg (ROE-tehn-burg), the most interesting town along the route.

Countless travelers have searched for the elusive "untouristy Rothenburg." There are many contenders (such as Michelstadt, Miltenberg, Bamberg, Bad Windsheim, and Dinkelsbühl), but none holds a candle to the king of medieval German cuteness. Even with crowds, overpriced souvenirs, Japanese-speaking night watchmen, and, yes, even *Schneeballen*, Rothenburg is best. Save time and mileage and be satisfied with the winner.

Rothenburg
(Rothenburg ob der Tauber)

In the Middle Ages, when Frankfurt and Munich were just wide spots on the road, Rothenburg ob der Tauber was a free imperial city. With a whopping population of 6,000, it was one of Germany's largest. Today, it's her best-preserved medieval walled town, enjoying tremendous tourist popularity without losing its charm.

During Rothenburg's heyday, from 1150 to 1400, it was a strategic stop on the trade routes between northern and southern Europe. Today, the great trade is tourism: Two-thirds of the townspeople are employed to serve you. While 2.5 million people visit each year, a mere 500,000 spend the night. Rothenburg is yours after dark, when the groups vacate and the town's floodlit cobbles wring some romance out of any travel partner.

Too often, Rothenburg brings out the shopper in visitors before they've had a chance to see the historic town. True, this is a fine place to do your German shopping, but appreciate Rothenburg's great history and sights, too.

Planning Your Time

If time is short, you can make just a two- to three-hour midday stop in Rothenburg, but the town is really best appreciated after the day-trippers have gone home. Spend at least one night in Rothenburg (hotels are cheap). With two nights and a day, you'll be able to see more than the essentials and actually relax a little.

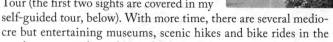

Rothenburg in one day is easy, with four essential experiences: the Medieval Crime and Punishment Museum, Tilman Riemenschneider's wood carving in St. Jakob's Church, a walk along the city wall, and the entertaining Night Watchman's Tour (the first two sights are covered in my self-guided tour, below). With more time, there are several mediocre but entertaining museums, scenic hikes and bike rides in the nearby countryside, and lots of cafés and shops.

Rothenburg is very busy through the summer and in the Christmas Market month of December. Spring and fall are a joy, but it's pretty bleak from January through March—when most locals are hibernating or on vacation. Many shops stay open on Sundays during the tourist season, but close on Sundays in November and from Christmas to Easter.

There are several Rothenburgs in Germany, so make sure you are going to Rothenburg ob der Tauber (not "ob der" any other river). People actually drive or ride the train to nondescript Rothenburgs by accident, so be careful.

ORIENTATION

(area code: 09861)

To orient yourself in Rothenburg, think of the town map as a human head. Its nose—the castle garden—sticks out to the left,

Rothenburg

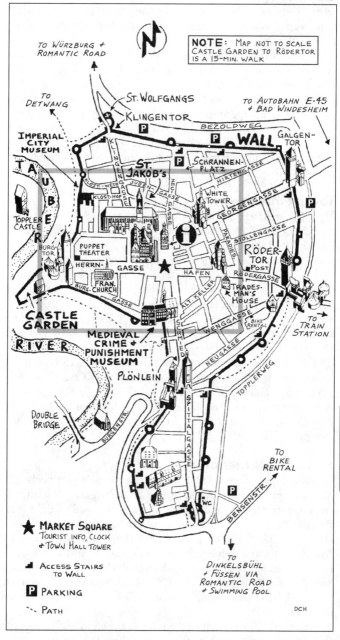

NOTE: MAP NOT TO SCALE
CASTLE GARDEN TO RÖDERTOR
IS A 15-MIN. WALK

TO WÜRZBURG &
ROMANTIC ROAD

TO DETWANG

ST. WOLFGANGS

KLINGENTOR

TO AUTOBAHN E-45
& BAD WINDESHEIM

BEZOLDWEG

WALL

GALGEN-TOR

IMPERIAL CITY MUSEUM

ST. JAKOB'S

SCHRANNEN-PLATZ

HIRTENGASSE

TAUBER

TOPPLER CASTLE

KLOST-WETH

KLINGEN

JUDEN-GASSE

HEU-GASSE

WHITE TOWER

GEORGENGASSE

KLOST-HOF

PUPPET THEATER

HERRN-GASSE

BURG-TOR

STOLLENGASSE

PARADIES

RÖDER-TOR

Post

RÖDERGASSE

HAFEN

ALT KELLER

TRADES-MAN'S HOUSE

TO TRAIN STATION

FRAN.-CHURCH

BURG-GASSE

CASTLE GARDEN

WENGGASSE

BIKE RENTAL

RIVER

SCHMIED

NEUGASSE

MEDIEVAL CRIME & PUNISHMENT MUSEUM

PLÖNLEIN

TOPPLERWEG

DOUBLE BRIDGE

BURGENSTR.

SPITTALGASSE

TO BIKE RENTAL

WC

BENSENSTR.

★ MARKET SQUARE
TOURIST INFO, CLOCK & TOWN HALL TOWER

ACCESS STAIRS TO WALL

P PARKING

⋰⋱ PATH

TO
DINKELSBÜHL
& FÜSSEN VIA
ROMANTIC ROAD
& SWIMMING POOL

DCH

Rothenburg

and the skinny lower part forms a wide-open mouth, with the hostel and some of the best hotels in the chin. The town is a delight on foot. No sights or hotels are more than a 15-minute walk from the train station or each other.

Most of the buildings you'll see were in place by 1400. The city was born around its long-gone castle—built in 1142, destroyed in 1356—which was located where the castle garden is now. You can see the shadow of the first town wall, which defines the oldest part of Rothenburg, in its contemporary street plan. A few gates from this wall still survive. The richest and biggest houses were in this central part. The commoners built higgledy-piggledy (read: picturesque) houses farther from the center, but still inside the present walls.

Tourist Information

The TI is on Market Square (May–Oct Mon–Fri 9:00–18:00, Sat–Sun 10:00–15:00; Nov–April Mon–Fri 9:00–12:00 & 13:00–17:00, Sat 10:00–13:00, closed Sun; Marktplatz 2, tel. 09861/404800, www.rothenburg.de). If there's a long line, just raid the rack where they keep all the free pamphlets. The free *Map & Guide* comes with a walking guide to the town. The free *RoTour* monthly guide lists all the events and entertainment (in German only; also look for current concert listing posters here and at your hotel). Ask about the daily English walking tour at 14:00 (€6, April–Oct and Dec; see "Tours," page 156). The TI has one free Internet terminal (15-min maximum). Visitors who arrive after closing can check the handy map highlighting which hotels have rooms available, with a free direct phone connection to them; it's just outside the door. A better town map is available free with this book at the Friese shop, two doors west from the TI (toward St. Jakob's Church; see "Shopping," page 167).

Arrival in Rothenburg

By Train: It's a 10-minute walk from the station to Rothenburg's Market Square (following the brown *Altstadt* signs, exit left from station, turn right on Ansbacher Strasse, and head straight into the Middle Ages). Day-trippers can leave luggage in station lockers (€2, on platform) or at the Friese shop on Market Square. Arrange train and couchette/sleeper reservations at the combined ticket office and travel agency in the station (Mon–Fri 9:00–18:00, Sat 9:00–13:00, closed Sun, tel. 09861/7711). Free WCs are behind the snack bar next door to the station. Taxis wait at the station (€5 to any hotel).

By Car: While much of the town is closed to traffic, anyone with a hotel reservation can drive in and through pedestrian zones to get to their hotel. But driving in town can be a nightmare, with many narrow, one-way streets. If you're packing light, just park outside the walls and walk five minutes to the center. Parking lots line the town walls: P1 costs €5 per day; P5 and the south half of P4 are free. Only those with a hotel reservation can park within the walls after hours (but not during festivals). The easiest way to enter and leave Rothenburg is generally via Spitalgasse and the Spitaltor (south end).

Helpful Hints

Festivals: Rothenburgers dress up in medieval costumes, and *Biergartens* spill out into the street to celebrate Mayor Nusch's Meistertrunk victory (May 9–12 in 2008; see story of the draught that saved the town under "Meistertrunk Show" on page 157, more info at www.meistertrunk.de). This touristic town dreams up a festival whenever possible: 2008 will celebrate the 600-year anniversary of Mayor Toppler's death.

Christmas Market: Rothenburg is dead in November, January, and February, but December is its busiest month—the entire town cranks up the medieval cuteness with concerts and costumes, shops with schnapps, stalls filling squares, hot spiced wine, giddy nutcrackers, and mobs of ear-muffed Germans. Christmas markets are big all over Germany, and Rothenburg's is considered one of the best. The festival takes place each year during Advent, the four weeks leading up to the last Sunday before Christmas (Nov 30–Dec 21 in 2008). Virtually all sights listed in this chapter are open longer hours during these four weeks. Try to avoid Saturdays and Sundays, when big-city day-trippers really clog the grog.

Internet Access: When it comes to getting online, Rothenburg is still pretty medieval. Few hotels have phones in the rooms or offer Internet access. The **TI** has one free terminal for brief use (maximum 15 min). **Passage 12** offers a free Internet terminal upstairs among the cuckoo clocks. **Inter@Play,** the only Internet café in town, has eight fast terminals and kids playing video games (€.50/10 min, €3/hr, daily 8:00–24:00, 2 blocks down Hafengasse from Market Square and around the corner to the left at Milchmarkt 3, see map on page 158, tel. 09861/935-599).

Laundry: A handy launderette is near the station, off Ansbacher Strasse (€5.50/load, includes soap, English instructions, opens at 8:00, last load Mon–Fri at 18:00, Sat at 14:00, closed Sun, Johannitergasse 9, tel. 09861/2775).

Haircuts: At **Salon Wack** (pronounced vack, not wack), Horst speaks English and does a nice cut for men and women (about €11, Tue–Fri 8:00–12:00 & 13:30–18:00, Sat 9:30–14:00, closed Sun–Mon, in the old center just off Wenggasse at Goldene

Ringgasse 8, tel. 09861/7834).

Swimming: Rothenburg has a fine modern recreation center with an indoor/outdoor pool *(Hallenbad)* and sauna. It's just a few minutes' walk south of town down the road towards Dinkelsbühl (adults–€3.50, kids–€2, swimsuit and towel rental–€2 each, Mon 14:00–21:00, Tue–Thu 9:00–21:00, Fri–Sun 9:00–18:00, Nördlinger Strasse 20, tel. 09861/4565).

Bike Rental: You can rent a bike and follow the suggested route on page 167. **Fahrradhaus Krauss** is a big bike shop that rents 8-gear bikes. It's cheap, reliable, and right in the old town (€2/2 hrs, €4/4 hrs, €8/24 hrs, no helmets, Tue–Fri 9:00–18:00, Sat 9:00–13:00, closed Sun–Mon, Wenggasse 42, tel. 09861/3495).

TOURS

▲▲Night Watchman's Tour—This tour is flat-out the most entertaining hour of medieval wonder anywhere in Germany. The Night Watchman (a.k.a. Hans-Georg Baumgartner) jokes like a medieval Jerry Seinfeld as he lights his lamp and takes tourists on his rounds, telling slice-of-gritty-life tales of medieval Rothenburg (€6, free for kids, mid-March–Dec nightly at 20:00 in English, meet at Market Square, www .nightwatchman.de). This is the best evening activity in town.

Old Town Historic Walk—The TI offers 90-minute guided walking tours in English (€6, April–Oct and Dec daily at 14:00, departs from Market Square). While the Night Watchman's Tour is fun, take this tour for the serious side of Rothenburg's history, and to make sense of the town's architecture. The tours are completely different, and it would be a shame not to take advantage of this informative tour just because you took the other.

Private Guides—A local historian can really bring the ramparts alive. Prices are standardized (€53/90 min, €70/2 hrs). Gisela Vogl (tel. 09861/4957, werner.vogl@t-online.de) and Anita Weinzierl (tel. 09868/7993, anitaweinzierl@aol.com) are both good. Martin Kamphans, a potter, also works as a guide (tel. 09861/7941, www .stadtfuehrungen-rothenburg.de, kamphans@t-online.de). Other guides are available—just send an e-mail to the TI to reserve (info@rothenburg.de).

Horse-and-Buggy Rides—These farm boys, who are generally about as charming as their horses, give a relaxing 30-minute clip-clop through the old town, starting from Market Square or Schrannenplatz. Good luck negotiating a fair price (private buggy for €30–50, or wait for one to fill up for €6 per person).

SELF-GUIDED WALK

Welcome to Rothenburg

This one-hour circular walk weaves Rothenburg's top sights together.

• *Start the walk on Market Square.*

➲**Market Square Spin Tour:** Stand at the bottom of Market Square (10 feet below the wooden post on the corner) and spin 360 degrees clockwise, starting with the Town Hall tower. Now do it again, this time more slowly, following these notes:

Town Hall and Tower: Rothenburg's tallest spire is the **Town Hall tower** (Rathausturm). At 200 feet, it stands atop the old Town Hall, a white, Gothic, 13th-century building. Notice the tourists enjoying the best view in town from the black top of the tower (€1 and a rigorous but interesting climb, 214 steps, narrow and steep near the top—watch your head, April–Oct daily 9:30–12:30 & 13:00–17:00, closed Nov–March, enter on Market Square through middle arch of new Town Hall). After a fire burned down part of the original building, a new Town Hall was built alongside what survived of the old one (fronting the square). This half of the rebuilt complex is in the Renaissance style from 1570.

Meistertrunk ("Master Draught") Show: At the top of Market Square stands the proud Councillors' Tavern (clock tower from 1466). In its day, the city council—the rich guys who ran the town government—drank here. Today, it's the TI and the focus of most tourists' attention when the little doors on either side of the clock flip open and the wooden figures (from 1910) do their thing. Be on Market Square at 11:00, 12:00, 13:00, 14:00, 15:00, 20:00, 21:00, or 22:00 for the ritual gathering of the tourists to see the less-than-breathtaking reenactment of the Meistertrunk story:

In 1631, the Catholic army took the Protestant town and was about to do its rape, pillage, and plunder thing. As was the etiquette, the mayor had to give the conquering general a welcoming drink. The general enjoyed a huge tankard of local wine. Feeling really good, he told the mayor, "Hey, if you can drink this entire three-liter tankard of wine in one gulp, I'll spare your town." The mayor amazed everyone by drinking the entire thing, and Rothenburg was saved.

While this is a nice story, it was dreamed up in the late 1800s for a theatrical play designed (effectively) to promote a romantic image of the town. In actuality, if Rothenburg was spared, it happened because it bribed its way out of a jam. It was occupied and

Rothenburg Self-Guided Walk

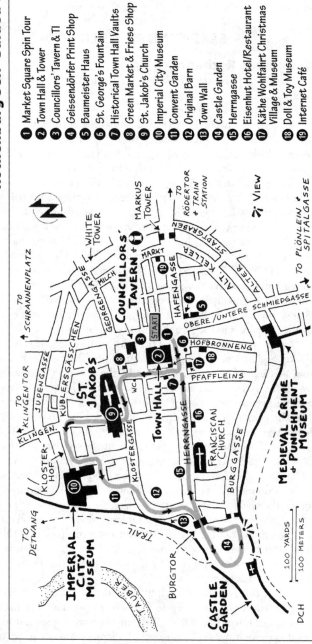

1. Market Square Spin Tour
2. Town Hall & Tower
3. Councillors' Tavern & TI
4. Geissendörfer Print Shop
5. Baumeister Haus
6. St. George's Fountain
7. Historical Town Hall Vaults
8. Green Market & Friese Shop
9. St. Jakob's Church
10. Imperial City Museum
11. Convent Garden
12. Original Barn
13. Town Wall
14. Castle Garden
15. Herrngasse
16. Eisenhut Hotel/Restaurant
17. Käthe Wohlfahrt Christmas Village & Museum
18. Doll & Toy Museum
19. Internet Café

ransacked several times in the Thirty Years' War, and it never recovered—which is why it's such a well-preserved time capsule today.

Hint: For the best show, don't watch the clock; watch the open-mouthed tourists gasp as the old windows flip open. At the late shows, the square flickers with camera flashes.

Bottom of Market Square: On the bottom end of the square, the cream-colored building on the corner has a fine **print shop** (upstairs—see "Shopping," page 167). Adjoining that is the **Baumeister Haus,** featuring a famous Renaissance facade with statues of the seven virtues and the seven vices—the former supporting the latter. The statues are copies; the originals are in the Imperial City Museum (listed below). The green house below that is the former home of the 15th-century Mayor Toppler (it's now the recommended Gasthof Goldener Greifen).

Keep circling to the big 17th-century **St. George's fountain.** The long metal gutters slid, routing the water into the villagers' buckets. Rothenburg had an ingenious water system. Built on a rock, it had one real source above the town which was plumbed to serve a series of fountains; water flowed from high to low through Rothenburg. Its many fountains had practical functions beyond providing drinking water (some were stocked with fish on market days and during times of siege). Water was used for fighting fires, and because of its plentiful water supply—and its policy of requiring relatively wide lanes as fire breaks—the town never burned entirely, as so many neighboring villages did.

Two fine buildings behind the fountain show the old-time lofts with warehouse doors and pulleys on top for hoisting. All over town, lofts were filled with grain and corn. A year's supply was required by the city so they could survive any siege. The building behind the fountain is an art gallery showing off the work of local artists (free, Tue–Sun 14:00–18:00, closed Mon). To the right is Marien Apotheke, an old-time pharmacy mixing old and new in typical Rothenburg style.

The broad street running under the Town Hall tower is **Herrngasse** (also see end of tour, page 163). The town originated with its castle (built in 1142 but now long gone; only the castle garden remains). Herrngasse connected the castle to Market Square. The last leg of this circular walking tour will take you from the castle garden up Herrngasse to where you now stand. For now, walk a few steps down Herrngasse and stand by the arch under the Town Hall tower (between the new and old town halls). On the left wall are the town's measuring rods—a reminder that medieval Germany was made of 300 independent little countries, each with its own weights and measures. Merchants and shoppers knew that these were the local standards: the rod (4.3 yards), the *Schuh* (or shoe, roughly a foot), and the *Ell* (from elbow to fingertip—four inches longer than mine...try it). Notice the protruding cornerstone. These are all over town—originally to protect buildings from reckless horse carts (and vice versa).

• *Under the arch, you'll find the...*

Historical Town Hall Vaults (Historiengewölbe): This grade-schoolish little museum, rated ▲, gives a waxy but interesting look at Rothenburg during the Catholics-vs.-Protestants Thirty Years' War. With helpful English descriptions, it offers a look at "the fateful year 1631," a replica of the mythical Meistertrunk tankard, and a dungeon complete with three dank cells and some torture lore (€2, April–Oct daily 9:30–17:30, closed Nov–March, tel. 09861/86751).

• *Leaving the museum, turn left (past a much sketched and photographed venerable door), and walk through the courtyard to a square called...*

Green Market (Grüner Markt): Once a produce market, it's now a parking lot that fills with Christmas shops during December. Notice the clay-tile roofs. These "beaver tail" tiles became standard after thatched roofs were outlawed to prevent fires. Today, all of the town's roofs are made of these. The little fences keep the snow from falling, and catch tiles that blow off during storms. The free public WC is on your left, the recommended **Friese shop** (see "Shopping," page 167) is on your right, and straight ahead is St. Jakob's Church.

Outside the church, you'll see 14th-century statues (mostly original) showing Jesus praying at Gethsemane, a common feature of Gothic churches. The artist is anonymous, because in the Gothic age (pre–Albrecht Dürer) artists were just nameless craftspeople working only for the glory of God. Five yards to the left (on the wall), notice the nub of a sandstone statue—a rare original, looking pretty bad after 500 years of weather and, more recently, pollution. Most original statues are now in the city museum. The better-preserved statues you see on the church are copies.

• *If it's your wedding day, take the first entrance. Otherwise, use the second (downhill) door to enter...*

St. Jakob's Church: Built in the 14th century, this church (rated ▲▲) has been Lutheran since 1544. The interior was "purified" by Romantics in the 19th century—cleaned of everything Baroque or not original, and refitted in the Neo-Gothic style. (For example, the baptismal font and the pulpit above the second pew *look* Gothic, but are actually Neo-Gothic.) The stained-glass windows behind the altar (most colorful in the morning light) are originals from the 1330s. Entrance costs €2 (April–Oct and Dec Mon–Sat 9:00–17:30, Sun 10:30–17:30; Nov and Christmas–March daily 10:00–12:00 & 14:00–16:00; free helpful English info sheet, concerts and tour schedule posted on the door).

At the back of the church, take the stairs that lead up behind the pipe organ. In the loft, you'll find the artistic highlight of Rothenburg and perhaps the most wonderful wood carving in all of Germany: the glorious 500-year-old, 35-foot-high *Altar of the Holy Blood*. Tilman Riemenschneider, the Michelangelo of German woodcarvers, carved this from 1499 to 1504 to hold a precious rock-crystal capsule, set in a cross that contains a scrap of tablecloth miraculously stained in the shape of a cross by a drop of communion wine. It's a realistic commotion, showing that Riemenschneider—while a High Gothic artist—was ahead of his time. Below, in the scene of the Last Supper, Jesus gives Judas a piece of bread, marking him as the traitor, while John lays his head on Christ's lap. Everything is portrayed exactly as described in the Bible. On the left: Jesus enters Jericho, with the shy tax collector Zacchaeus looking on from his tree. Notice the fun attention to detail—down to the nails on the horseshoe. On the right: Jesus prays in the Garden of Gethsemane. Notice how Judas, with his big bag of cash, could be removed from the scene—illustrated by photos on the wall nearby—as was the tradition for the four days leading up to Easter.

Head back down the stairs to the church's main hall. Go up front to take a close look at the main altar (from 1466, by Friedrich Herlin). Below Christ are statues of six saints. St. James (Jakob in German) is the one with the shell. He's the saint of pilgrims, and this church was a stop on the medieval pilgrimage route to Santiago ("St. James" in Spanish) de Compostela in Spain. Study the painted panels—ever see Peter with spectacles? Around the back of the altarpiece (upper left) is a painting of Rothenburg's Market Square in the 15th century—looking much like it does today, with the exception of the full-Gothic Town Hall (as it was before the big fire of 1501). Notice Christ's face on the veil of Veronica (center of back side). It follows you as you walk from side to side—it must have given the faithful the religious heebie-jeebies four centuries ago.

The small altar to the left is also worth a look. It's a century older than the main altar. Notice the unusual Trinity: the Father and Son are literally bridged by a dove, which represents the Holy Spirit. Stepping back, you can see that Jesus is standing on a skull—clearly "overcoming death."

Before leaving the front of the church, notice the old medallions above the carved choir stalls. They feature the coats of arms of Rothenburg's leading families and portraits of city and church leaders.

Rothenburg

• *Leave the church and, from its outside steps, walk around the corner to the right and under the chapel (built over the road). Go two blocks down Klingengasse and stop at the corner of Klosterhof street. Looking down Klingengasse, you see the...*

Klingentor: This cliff tower was Rothenburg's water reservoir. From 1595 until 1910, a copper tank high in the tower provided clean spring water (pumped up by river power) to the privileged. To the right of Klingentor is a good stretch of wall rampart to walk. To the left, the wall is low and simple, lacking a rampart because it guards only a cliff. Now find the shell decorating a building on the street corner next to you. That's the symbol of St. James (pilgrims commemorated their visit to Santiago de Compostela with a shell), indicating that this building is associated with the church.

• *Turn left down Klosterhof, passing the shell and, on your right, the colorful Altfränkische Weinstube (see "Eating," page 175), to reach the...*

Imperial City Museum (Reichsstadt-Museum): You'll get a scholarly sweep through Rothenburg's history at this museum, rated ▲▲. The museum is housed in the former Dominican convent. Cloistered nuns used the lazy Susan embedded in the wall (to the right of museum door) to give food to the poor without being seen.

Highlights include *The Rothenburg Passion,* a 12-panel series of paintings from 1492 showing scenes leading up to Christ's crucifixion (in the *Konventsaal*); an exhibit of Jewish culture through the ages in Rothenburg *(Judaika);* a 14th-century convent kitchen *(Klosterküche)* with a working model of the lazy Susan and a massive chimney; romantic paintings of the town *(Gemäldegalerie);* the fine Baumann collection of weapons and armor; and sandstone statues from the church and Baumeister Haus (the seven vices and seven virtues). Follow the *Rundgang Tour* signs (€3, daily April–Oct 9:30–17:30, Nov–March 13:00–16:00, English info sheet and descriptions, Klosterhof 5, tel. 09861/939-043, www .reichsstadtmuseum.rothenburg.de).

• *Leaving the museum, go around to the right and into the Convent Garden (when locked at night, continue straight to the T-intersection and see the barn three doors to the right).*

Convent Garden: This spot is a peaceful place to work on your tan...or mix a poisoned potion (free, same hours as museum). Enjoy the herb garden. Monks and nuns, who were responsible for concocting herbal cures in the olden days, often tended herb gardens. Smell (but don't pick) the *Pfefferminze, Juniper* (gin), *Chamomilla* (disinfectant), and *Origanum.* Don't smell the plants in the poison corner (potency indicated by the number of crosses... like spiciness stars in a Chinese restaurant).

• *Exit opposite from where you entered, angling left through the nuns' garden (site of the now-gone Dominican church), eventually leaving via an arch at the far end. Looking to your left, you'll see the back end of an...*

Original Barn: This is the back side of a complex that fronts Herrngasse. Medieval Germans often lived in large structures like this that were like small villages in themselves, with a grouping of buildings and open spaces. The typical design included a house, a courtyard, a stable, a garden, and, finally, a barn. Notice how the bulging wall is corseted by a brace with iron washers. Crank on its nuts and the building will stand up straight.

• *Now go downhill to the...*

Town Wall: This part of the wall (view through bars, look to far right) takes advantage of the natural fortification provided by the cliff, and is therefore much smaller than the ramparts. Angle left along the wall to the big street (Herrngasse), then right under the Burgtor tower. Notice the tiny "eye of the needle" door cut into the big door. If trying to get into town after curfew, you could bribe the guard to let you through this door (which was small enough to keep out any fully armed attackers).

• *Step through the gate and outside the wall. Look around and imagine being locked out in the year 1400. This was a wooden drawbridge (see the chain slits above). Notice the "pitch nose" mask—designed to pour boiling Nutella on anyone attacking. High above is the town coat of arms: a red castle* (roten Burg).

Castle Garden (Burggarten): The garden before you was once that red castle (destroyed in the 14th century). Today, it's a picnic-friendly park. The chapel (50 yards into the park on the left) is the only bit of the original castle to survive. It's now a memorial to local Jews killed in a 1298 slaughter. A few steps beyond that is a grapevine trellis that provides a fine picnic spot. If you walk all the way out to the garden's far end, you'll find a great viewpoint (well past the tourists, and considered the best place to kiss by romantic local teenagers). But the views of the lush Tauber River Valley below are just as good from the top end of the park. Facing the town, on the left, a path leads down to the village of Detwang (you can see the church spire below)—a town even older than Rothenburg (for a walk to Detwang, see "A Walk in the Countryside," page 166). To the right is a fine view of the fortified Rothenburg and the "Tauber Riviera" below.

• *Return to the tower, cross carefully under the pitch nose, and hike back up Herrngasse to your starting point.*

Herrngasse: Many towns have a Herrngasse, where the richest patricians and merchants (the *Herren*) lived. Predictably, it's your best chance to see the town's finest old mansions. Strolling back to Market Square, you'll pass the old-time puppet theater (German only, on left), the Franciscan church (from 1285, oldest in town, on right), and the hippie Sawasdee shop (where the Night

Watchman spends his days dreaming of his next trip to Thailand while his girlfriend sells what they've imported, as well as "Night Watchman mementos," Herrngasse 23). The house at #18 is the biggest patrician house on the street. The family, which has lived here for three centuries, disconnected the four old-time doorbells. Their door—big enough to allow a carriage in (with a human-sized door cut into it)—is typical of the age. To see the traditional house-courtyard-stables-garden-barn layout, pop into either #14 (now an apartment block) or—if that's closed—the shop across the street, at #11. The Eisenhut Hotel, Rothenburg's fanciest, is worth a peek inside (see "Eating," page 175). The Käthe Wohlfahrt Christmas shops (at Herrngasse 1 and 2, see "Shopping," page 167) are your last, and perhaps greatest, temptations before reaching your starting and ending point: Market Square.

SIGHTS AND ACTIVITIES

Museums Within a Block of Market Square

▲▲Medieval Crime and Punishment Museum (Mittelalterliches Kriminalmuseum)—This museum is the best of its kind, specializing in everything connected to medieval criminal justice.

Learn about medieval police, medieval criminal law, and above all, instruments of punishment and torture—even a special cage complete with a metal gag for nags. The museum is more eclectic than its name, and includes exhibits on general history, superstition, biblical art, and temporary displays in a second building. Follow the yellow arrows—the one-way traffic system makes it hard to double back. Exhibits are tenderly described in English (€4, daily April–Oct 9:30–18:00, Nov and Jan–Feb 14:00–16:00, Dec and March 10:00–16:00, last entry 45 min before closing, fun cards and posters, Burggasse 3–5, tel. 09861/5359, www.kriminalmuseum.rothenburg.de).

▲Doll and Toy Museum (Puppen- und Spielzeugmuseum)—These two floors of historic *Kinder* cuteness are a hit with many. Pick up the free English binder (just past the entry curtain) for an extensive description of the exhibits (€4, family ticket-€10, daily March–Dec 9:30–18:00, Jan–Feb 11:00–17:00, just off Market Square, downhill from the fountain at Hofbronnengasse 11–13, tel. 09861/7330, kath.engels@web.de).

▲German Christmas Museum (Deutsches Weihnachtsmuseum)—This excellent museum, upstairs in the giant Käthe

Wohlfahrt Christmas Village shop, tells the history of Christmas decorations. There's a unique and thoughtfully described collection of Christmas-tree stands, mini-trees sent in boxes to WWI soldiers at the front, early Advent calendars, old-time Christmas cards, 450 clever ways to crack a nut, and a look at tree decorations through the ages—including the Nazi era and when you were a kid. The museum is not just a ploy to get shoppers to spend more money, but a serious collection managed by professional curator Felicitas Höptner (€4, April–Dec daily 10:00–17:30, Jan–March Sat–Sun 10:00–17:30 and irregularly on weekdays, Herrngasse 1, tel. 09861/409-365, www.germanchristmasmuseum.com). You can visit the museum at the €2.50 student rate with this book in 2008—if you promise to learn something.

More Sights and Activities in Rothenburg

▲▲**Walk the Wall**—Just longer than a mile and a half around, providing great views and a good orientation, this walk can be done by those under six feet tall and without a camera in less than an hour. The hike requires no special sense of balance. This walk is covered and is a great option in the rain. Photographers go through lots of film, especially before breakfast or at sunset, when the lighting is best and the crowds are fewest. The best fortifications are in the Spitaltor (south end). Walk from there counterclockwise to the "forehead" (note on the Rothenburg map how the town outline looks like

a head). Climb the Rödertor en route. The names you see along the way are people who donated money to rebuild the wall after World War II, and those who've recently donated €1,000 per meter for the maintenance of Rothenburg's heritage. You can enter or exit the ramparts at nearly every tower.

▲**Rödertor**—The wall tower nearest the train station is the only one you can climb. It's worth the 135 steps for the view and a short but fascinating rundown on the bombing of Rothenburg in the last weeks of World War II, when the east part of the city was destroyed (€1, pay at top, unreliable hours, usually open April–Oct daily 10:00–16:00, closed Nov–March, WWII photos have English translations). If you climb this, you can skip the more claustrophobic Town Hall tower climb.

▲▲**The Allergic-to-Tourists Wall and Moat Walk**—For a quiet and scenic break from the tourist crowds and a chance to appreciate the marvelous fortifications of Rothenburg, consider this hike:

From the Castle Garden, go right and walk outside the wall to Klingentor. At Klingentor, climb up to the ramparts and walk on the wall past Galgentor to Rödertor. Then descend, leave the old town, and hike through the park (once the moat) down to Spitaltor. Explore the fortifications here before hiking a block up Spitalgasse, turning left to pass the youth hostel, popping back outside the wall, and heading along the upper scenic reaches of the "Tauber Riviera" and above the vineyards back to the Castle Garden.

▲Tradesman's House (Alt-Rothenburger Handwerkerhaus)— See the everyday life of a Rothenburger in the town's heyday in this restored 700-year-old home (€2.20; Easter–Oct Mon–Fri 11:00–17:00, Sat–Sun 10:00–17:00; Nov–Dec daily 14:00–16:00; closed Jan–Easter; Alter Stadtgraben 26, near Markus Tower, tel. 09861/94280).

St. Wolfgang's Church—This fortified Gothic church is built into the medieval wall at Klingentor. Its dungeon-like passages and shepherd's-dance exhibit are pretty lame (€1.50, April–Sept Wed–Mon 10:00–13:00 & 14:30–17:00, Oct until 16:00, closed Tue and Nov–March).

Near Rothenburg

▲A Walk in the Countryside

From the *Burggarten* (castle garden), head into the Tauber Valley. With your back to town, go down the hill, exiting the castle garden on your left. Once outside of the wall, walk around, keeping the castle and town on your right. The trail becomes really steep, taking you down to the wooden covered bridge on the valley floor. Across the bridge, the road goes left to Toppler Castle and right (downstream, with a pleasant parallel footpath) to Detwang.

Toppler Castle (Topplerschlösschen) is cute, skinny, sky-blue, and 600 years old, and it was the castle/summer home of the medieval Mayor Toppler. The tower's top looks like a house—a

sort of tree fort for grownups. It's in a farmer's garden, and it's open whenever he's around and willing to let you in (€1.50, normally Fri–Sun 13:00–16:00, closed Mon–Thu and Nov, 1 mile from town center at Taubertalweg 100, tel. 09861/7358). People say the mayor had this valley-floor escape to get people to relax about leaving the fortified town...or to hide a mistress.

To extend your stroll, walk back to the bridge and follow the river downstream to the peaceful village of **Detwang.** One of the oldest villages in Franconia, Detwang dates from 968. Like Rothenburg, it has a Riemenschneider altarpiece in its church.

Franconian Bike Ride

To get a fun, breezy look at the countryside around Rothenburg, rent a bike from Fahrradhaus Krauss (see "Helpful Hints," page 156). For a pleasant half-day pedal, escape the old town through Rödertor, bike along Topplerweg to Spitaltor, and follow the curvy road down into the Tauber Riviera. Turn right at the yellow *Leutzenbronn* sign to cross the double-arcaded bridge. From here a peaceful road follows the river downstream to **Detwang,** passing the cute Topplerschlösschen (described above). From Detwang, follow the main road to the old mill, and turn left to follow the *Liebliches Taubertal* bike path signs as far up the Tauber River (direction: Bettwar) as you like. After 2.5 miles, you'll arrive in the sleepy farming town of **Bettwar;** claim a spot among the chickens and the apple trees for a picnic or have a drink at one of the two restaurants in town.

Franconian Open-Air Museum (Fränkisches Freilandmuseum)

A 20-minute drive from Rothenburg—in the undiscovered "Rothenburgy" town of Bad Windsheim—is an open-air folk museum that, compared with others in Europe, is a bit humble. But it tries very hard and gives you the best look around at traditional rural Franconia (€5, daily March–Sept 9:00–18:00, Oct–Dec 10:00–16:00, closed Jan–Feb, last entry 1 hour before closing, tel. 09841/66800, www.freilandmuseum.de).

SHOPPING

Be warned...Rothenburg is one of Germany's best shopping towns. Do it here and be done with it. Lovely prints, carvings, wineglasses, Christmas-tree ornaments, and beer steins are popular. Rödergasse is the old town's everyday shopping street. There is also a modern shopping center across the street from the train station.

Christmas Souvenirs

Rothenburg is the headquarters of the **Käthe Wohlfahrt** Christmas trinkets empire, which is spreading across the half-timbered reaches of Europe. In Rothenburg, tourists flock to two Käthe Wohlfahrt stores (at Herrngasse 1 and 2, just off Market Square). Start with the **Christmas Village** (Weihnachtsdorf) at Herrngasse 1. This Christmas wonderland is filled with enough twinkling lights to require a special electrical hookup. You're greeted by instant

Christmas mood music (best appreciated on a hot day in July) and American and Japanese tourists hungrily filling little woven shopping baskets with €5 to €8 goodies to hang on their trees. Let the spinning flocked tree whisk you in, but pause at the wall of Steiffs, jerking uncontrollably and mesmerizing little kids. (OK, I admit it, my Christmas tree sports a few KW ornaments.) The **Christmas Museum** upstairs is described under "Sights and Activities" (page 164). The smaller **Christmas Market** (Weihnachtsmarkt), across the street at Herrngasse 2, specializes in finely crafted wooden ornaments. A third, much smaller store is at Untere Schmiedgasse 19. Note: Prices are padded with tour-guide incentives (all stores open Mon–Sat 9:00–18:00, May–Dec also most Sun 10:00–18:00, Jan–April generally closed Sun, tel. 09861/4090, www.wohlfahrt .com). Käthe started the business in Stuttgart in 1963, and it's now run by her son Harald Wohlfahrt, who lives in Rothenburg.

Traditional German Souvenirs

The **Friese shop** has been welcoming readers of this book for more than 20 years (on the smaller square just off Market Square, west of TI, on corner across from free public WC). Cuckoo with friendliness, trinkets, and souvenirs, it gives shoppers with this book tremendous service: a 10 percent discount, 19 percent tax deducted if you have it mailed, and a free map (normally €1.50). Anneliese Friese, who runs the place with her sons Frankie and Berni and grandson Rene, charges only her cost for shipping, and lets tired travelers leave their bags in her back room for free. If he's not busy, ask Rene to show you pictures of the local American football team he played on. For fewer crowds and more attentive service, visit after 14:00 (Mon–Sat 8:30–17:00, Sun 9:30–17:00, Grüner Markt 8, tel. 09861/7166, fax 09861/936-619, friese-kabalo@gmx.de).

Passage 12, a huge, more commercial souvenir shop with a vast selection of steins, knives, and noisy clocks, is just a block below Market Square at Obere Schmiedgasse 12 (April–Dec Mon–Sat 9:00–19:00, Sun 10:00–19:00; Jan–March Mon–Sat 10:00–18:00, closed Sun; tel. 09861/8196). Martina, the manager, promises a 10 percent discount on prices (which are not always clearly marked) with this book in 2008. Customers can check their email for free upstairs among the cuckoo clocks (and stock up on ice at the machine by the door).

Werkstattladen Lebenshilfe sells tasteful, original, unconventional souvenirs made in sheltered workshops by disabled Germans. It's a tiny shop down the side street behind Herrngasse 10 (daily 10:30–18:00, Jan–April closed Sun, Kirchgasse 1, tel. 09861/938-401).

Romantic Prints: The Ernst Geissendörfer print shop has sold fine prints, etchings, and paintings here since 1908. In 2008, show this book and Frau Geissendörfer will offer 10 percent off marked prices on all cash purchases (or minimum €50 credit-card purchases) plus a free shot of German brandy to sip while you browse (May–Dec Mon–Sat 10:00–18:00, Sun 10:00–17:00; Jan–April Mon–Sat 10:00–18:00, closed Sun; enter through teddy-bear shop on corner of Market Square, Hafengasse, and Obere Schmiedgasse; Obere Schmiedgasse 1, go up one floor, tel. 09861/2005, www.geissendoerfer.de).

Wine Stuff: For characteristic wineglasses, winemaking gear, and the real thing from the town's oldest winemakers, drop by the **Weinladen am Plönlein** (daily 9:00–18:00, Untere Schmiedgasse 27—see "Wine-Drinking in the Old Center," page 179, for info on wine-tasting). Although Rothenburg is technically in Bavaria, the region around Rothenburg is called *Franken* (Franconia). You'll recognize Franconian wines by the shape of the bottle—short, stubby, and round.

Books: A good bookstore is at Rödergasse 3, on the corner of Alter Stadtgraben (Mon–Sat 9:00–18:30, Sun 11:00–18:30, Jan–April closed Sun).

Mailing Your Goodies Home: You can get handy yellow €2.50 boxes at the old town **post office** (Mon–Fri 9:00–13:00 & 14:00–17:30, Sat 9:00–12:00, closed Sun, inside photo shop at Rödergasse 11). The main post office is in the shopping center across from the train station.

Pastries: Those who prefer to eat their souvenirs browse the *Bäckereien* (bakeries). Their succulent pastries, pies, and cakes are

pleasantly distracting...but skip the bad-tasting Rothenburger *Schneeballen.* Unworthy of the heavy promotion they receive, *Schneeballen* are bland pie crusts crumpled into a ball and dusted with powdered sugar or frosted with sticky-sweet glop. There's little reason to waste your pleasure on a *Schneeball* when you can enjoy a curvy *Mandelhörnchen* (almond crescent), a triangular *Nussecke* (nut bar), a round *Florentiner* cookie, a couple of fresh *Krapfen* (like jelly doughnuts), or even just a soft, warm German pretzel.

SLEEPING

Rothenburg is crowded with visitors, but most are day-trippers. Except for the rare Saturday night and festivals (see "Festivals," page 155), finding a room is easy throughout the year. If you want to splurge, you'll snare the best value by paying extra for the biggest

---

Sleep Code

(€1 = about $1.30, country code: 49, area code: 09861)
S = Single, **D** = Double/Twin, **T** = Triple, **Q** = Quad, **b** = bathroom,
s = shower only. Unless otherwise noted, credit cards are accepted, English is spoken, and breakfast is included.

To help you sort easily through these listings, I've divided the rooms into three categories, based on the price for a standard double room with bath:

$$$ Higher Priced—Most rooms €65 or more.
  $$ Moderately Priced—Most rooms between €40–65.
    $ Lower Priced—Most rooms €40 or less.

---

and best rooms at the hotels I recommend.

Many hotels and guesthouses will pick up tired heavy-packers at the station. If you're driving and unable to find where you're sleeping, stop and give them a call. They will likely come rescue you. Keep your key when out late. Rothenburg's hotels are small, and often lock the front entrance at about 22:00, asking you to let yourself in through a side door.

You may be greeted at the station by *Zimmer* skimmers who have rooms to rent. If you have reservations, resist them and honor your reservation. But if you haven't booked ahead, you could try talking one of these eager beavers into giving you a bed-and-breakfast room for a youth-hostel price. Be warned: These people are notorious for taking you to distant hotels and then charging you for the ride back if you decline a room. The automated hotel vacancy board at the TI (described on page 154) is another option for those without reservations.

In the Old Town

$$$ Gasthof Goldener Greifen, once Mayor Toppler's home, is a big, traditional, 600-year-old place with 15 large rooms and all the comforts. It's run by a helpful family staff and creaks with rustic splendor (small Sb-€38, Sb-€48, small Db-€60, big Db-€82, Tb-€97–102, Qb-€117–122, 10 percent off for 3-night stays, full-service laundry-€8, free and easy parking, half a block downhill from Market Square at Obere Schmiedgasse 5, tel. 09861/2281, fax 09861/86374, www.gasthof-greifen-rothenburg.de, info@gasthof-greifen-rothenburg.de, Brigitte and Klingler family). The family also has a couple of loaner bikes free for guests, and runs a good restaurant, serving meals in the back garden or dining room.

$$$ Hotel Gerberhaus, a classy and stylish hotel in an old building, is warmly run by Inge and Kurt and daughter Deborah,

Rothenburg Accommodations

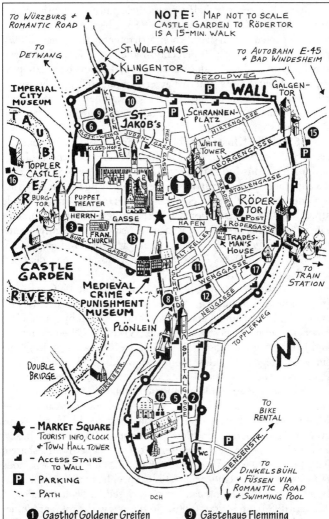

NOTE: MAP NOT TO SCALE
CASTLE GARDEN TO RÖDERTOR
IS A 15-MIN. WALK

- ★ – **MARKET SQUARE**
  TOURIST INFO, CLOCK
  & TOWN HALL TOWER
- ◢ – **ACCESS STAIRS**
  TO WALL
- 🅿 – **PARKING**
- ⋱ – **PATH**

DCH

① Gasthof Goldener Greifen
② Hotel Gerberhaus
③ Hotel Kloster-Stüble
④ Hotel Spitzweg
⑤ Gasthof zur Goldenen Rose
⑥ Hotel Altfränkische
  Weinstube am Klosterhof
⑦ Pension Elke
⑧ Hotel Café Uhl

⑨ Gästehaus Flemming
⑩ Gästehaus Viktoria
⑪ Gästehaus Raidel
⑫ Pension Pöschel
⑬ Frau Liebler Rooms
⑭ Rossmühle Youth Hostel
⑮ Hotel Hornburg
⑯ Pension Fuchsmühle
⑰ Bike Rental

Rothenburg

who mix modern comforts into 20 bright and airy rooms while maintaining a sense of half-timbered elegance. Enjoy the pleasant garden in back (Sb-€56, Db-€69–98, Tb-€119–129, Qb-€145, prices depend on room size; 2-room apartment with kitchen-€109/2 people, €155/4 people; 10 percent off and a free *Schneeball* if you stay 2 nights and pay cash, non-smoking, 4 rooms have canopied 4-poster *Himmel* beds, Internet access, laundry-€7, Spitalgasse 25, tel. 09861/94900, fax 09861/86555, www.gerberhaus.rothenburg .de, gerberhaus@t-online.de). The downstairs café and *Biergarten* serve good soups, salads, and light lunches.

$$$ Hotel Kloster-Stüble, deep in the old town near the castle garden, is my classiest listing. Rudolf does the cooking, while Erika—his fun and energetic first mate—welcomes guests. Twenty-one rooms fill two medieval buildings, connected by a modern atrium. The hotel is just off Herrngasse on a tiny side street (Sb-€52–72, traditional Db-€82, bigger and more modern Db-€112, Tb-€108–128, see website for suites and family rooms, kids under age 5 free, Internet access, Heringsbronnengasse 5, tel. 09861/938-890, fax 09861/6474, www.klosterstueble.de, hotel @klosterstueble.de).

$$$ Hotel Spitzweg is a rustic-yet-elegant 1536 mansion (never bombed or burned) with 10 big rooms, open beams, and endearing hand-painted antique furniture. It's run by gentle Herr Hocher, whom I suspect is the former Wizard of Oz—now retired and in a very good mood (Db-€85, Tb-€100, family suite, non-smoking, elegant breakfast room, free parking, tel. 09861/94290, Paradeisgasse 2, www.hotel-spitzweg.de, info@hotel-spitzweg.de).

$$ Gasthof zur Goldenen Rose is a classic, 12-room, family-run place—simple, traditional, comfortable, and a great value—where scurrying Karin serves breakfast and stately Henni keeps everything in good order. Flowers spill out of the window boxes, and there's a peaceful back garden. A few cheaper rooms share a bath (S-€22, D-€38, Ds-€48, Db-€50–55, some triples; spacious family apartment-€110/4 people, €130/5 people, €150/6 people; kid-friendly, streetside rooms can be noisy, closed Jan–Feb, Spitalgasse 28, tel. 09861/4638, fax 09861/86417, www.thegoldenrose.de, info@thegoldenrose.de). The family also serves good, reasonably priced meals (restaurant closed Tue eve and Wed).

$$ Hotel Altfränkische Weinstube am Klosterhof is *the* place for well-heeled bohemians. Mario, Hanne, and their lovely daughter Viktoria rent six cozy rooms above their dark and evocative pub in a 600-year-old building. It's an upscale, *Lord of the Rings* atmosphere, with TVs, modern showers, open-beam ceilings, and canopied four-poster beds (Sb-€48, Db-€59, bigger Db-€69, Db suite-€79, Tb-€79, prefer cash, kid-friendly, off Klingengasse at Klosterhof 7, tel. 09861/6404, fax 09861/6410, www.romanticroad

.com/altfraenkische-weinstube). Their pub is a candlelit classic—and a favorite with locals, serving hot food to Hobbits until 22:30, and closing at 1:00 in the morning. Drop by on Wednesday evening (19:00–24:00) for the English Conversation Club (see "Meet the Locals," page 179).

$$ Pension Elke, run by the spry Erich Endress and his son Klaus, rents 12 bright, airy, and comfy rooms above the family grocery store. Guests who jog are welcome to join Klaus on his half-hour run around the city every evening at 19:30 (S-€28, Sb-€38, D-€42–48, Db-€60–65, depends on size, extra bed-€15, 10 percent discount with this book through 2008 when you stay at least 2 nights, cash only; reception in grocery store until 19:00, otherwise go around corner to back of building and ring bell at top of stairs; near Markus Tower at Rödergasse 6, tel. 09861/2331, fax 09861/935-355, www.pension-elke-rothenburg.de, info @pension-elke-rothenburg.de).

$$ Hotel Café Uhl offers 12 fine rooms over a bakery (Sb-€30–45, Db-€50–72, prices depend on room size, third person-€18, fourth person-€14, 10 percent discount with this book and cash in 2008, reception in café, parking-€4/day, closed Jan, Plönlein 8, tel. 09861/4895, fax 09861/92820, www.hotel-uhl.de, info@hotel-uhl .de, Paul and Robert the baker).

$$ Gästehaus Flemming has seven tastefully modern, fresh, and comfortable rooms and a peaceful garden behind St. Jakob's Church (Sb-€45, Db-€59, Tb-€79, cash only, non-smoking rooms, Klingengasse 21, tel. 09861/92380, fax 09861/976-384, www.gaestehaus-flemming.de, gaestehaus-flemming@ t-online.de, Regina).

$$ Gästehaus Viktoria is a cheery little place right next to the town wall. Its three rooms overflow with furniture, ribbons, and silk flowers, and lovely gardens surround the house (Db-€55–65, larger Db suite-€75, ask about family specials and their romantic apartment, cash preferred, a block from Klingentor at Klingenschutt 4, tel. 09861/87682, www.romanticroad.com /gaestehaus-viktoria, Hanne).

$$ Gästehaus Raidel rents 12 large rooms in a 500-year-old

house filled with beds and furniture, all handmade by friendly Norry Raidel himself. The ramshackle ambience makes me want to sing the *Addams Family* theme song—but the place has a rare, time-passed family charm (S-€24, Sb-€39, D-€49, Db-€59, Tb-€70, cash only, Wenggasse 3, tel. 09861/3115, Norry asks you to use the reservations form at www.romanticroad.com/raidel). Norry plays in a Dixieland band, invented a fascinating hybrid saxophone/trombone called the Norryphone, and loves to jam.

$$ Pension Pöschel is simple and friendly, with six plain rooms in a concrete but pleasant building, and an inviting garden out back. Only one room has a private shower and toilet (S-€22, D-€40, Db-€45, T-€55, Tb-€60, small kids free, cash only, Wenggasse 22, tel. 09861/3430, www.pensionpoeschel.de, pension.poeschel@t-online.de, Bettina).

$ Frau Liebler rents two large, modern, ground-floor rooms with kitchenettes. They're great for those looking for real privacy—you'll have your own room fronting a quiet cobbled lane just below Market Square (Db-€40, extra bed-€10, 10 percent discount for 2 or more nights with this book in 2008, breakfast-€5, cash only, laundry-€5, behind Christmas shop at Pfaffleinsgässchen 10, tel. 09861/709-215, fax 09861/709-216).

$ Rossmühle Youth Hostel—This charming hostel, run since 1981 by Eduard Schmitz, rents 186 beds in two buildings. While it's mostly four- to six-bed dorms, they also have 15 doubles. Reception is in the droopy-eyed building—formerly a horse mill, it was used when the old town was under siege and the river-powered mill was inaccessible (dorm bed-€19, bunk-bed Db-€44, includes breakfast and sheets, all-you-can-eat dinner-€5.40, self-serve laundry including soap-€5, entrance on Rossmühlgasse, tel. 09861/94160, fax 09861/941-620, www.rothenburg.jugendherberge.de, jhrothenburg@djh-bayern.de).

Outside the Wall

$$$ Hotel Hornburg, a grand 1903 mansion, is close to the train station, a two-minute walk outside the wall. With groomed grounds, gracious sitting areas, and 10 spacious, tastefully decorated rooms, it's a super value (Sb-€53–72, Db-€71–103, Tb-€95–120, ground-floor rooms, non-smoking rooms, family-friendly, avoid if you're allergic to dogs, free Internet access and Wi-Fi, parking-€5/day; if walking, exit station and go straight on Ludwig-Siebert-Strasse, then turn left on Mannstrasse until you're 100 yards from town wall; if driving, the hotel is across from parking lot P4; Hornburgweg 28, at intersection with Mannstrasse, tel. 09861/8480, fax 09861/5570, www.hotel-hornburg.de, info@hotel-hornburg.de, friendly Gabriele and Martin).

$$ Pension Fuchsmühle is a guest house in a renovated old mill on the river below the castle end of Rothenburg, across from the Toppler Castle. It feels rural, but is a pleasant (though steep) 15-minute hike to Market Square. Alex and Heidi Molitor, a young couple, offer free tours of the mill (in use until 1989) and run a used-book business on the side. Eight bright, modern, light-wood rooms fill the building's three floors (Sb-€40, Db-€60, Tb-€85, Qb-€110, 6-bed apartment-€150, extra bed-€18, €5 less if you stay 3 nights, non-smoking, healthy farm-fresh breakfasts, piano, parking, free pickup at station if you call ahead, flashlights provided for your walk back after dark, Taubertalweg 103, tel. 09861/92633, www.fuchsmuehle.de, fuchsmuehle@t-online.de).

EATING

Many restaurants take a mid-afternoon break, and stop serving lunch at 14:00 and dinner as early as 20:00. My recommendations are all within a five-minute walk of Market Square. While all survive on tourism, many still feel like local hangouts. Your choices are typical German or ethnic. A good dish to try is *Maultaschen*. This Swabian ravioli smuggles meat in a big piece of pasta—a custom that some say started as a culinary trick used by Catholics to eat meat when it wasn't allowed. Any bakery will sell you a sandwich for a couple euros.

Traditional German Restaurants

Eisenhut Restaurant, in Hotel Eisenhut, is a fine place for a dress-up splurge with surprisingly reasonable prices. You'll enjoy elegantly presented dishes, both traditional and international, with formal service. Sit in their royal dining room or on their garden sun terrace (€17–24 main dishes, fixed-price meals from €25, Herrngasse 3, tel. 09861/7050).

Zur Goldenen Rose is a hardworking eatery in a small hotel at the south end of the old town. Reno cooks up traditional German fare at great prices as Henni stokes your appetite (Tue 11:00–14:00, Thu–Mon 11:00–14:00 & 17:30, last order at 20:30, closed Tue eve and Wed, leafy garden terrace out back open in sunny weather, Spitalgasse 28, tel. 09861/4638).

Gasthof Goldener Greifen is in a historic building just off the main square. The Klingler family serves quality Franconian food to in-the-know locals at a good price...and with a smile. The wood is ancient and polished from generations of happy use, and the ambience is practical rather than posh—and that's just fine with me (€7–15 entrées, €11 three-course daily specials, supercheap kids' meals, Mon–Sat 11:30–21:30, Sun 11:30–14:00, Obere Schmiedgasse 5, tel. 09861/2281).

Bürgerkeller is a typical European cellar restaurant with a quiet, calming atmosphere, medieval murals, and pointy pikes. Without a burger in sight (*Bürger* means "townsman"), Harry Terian and his family pride themselves on quality local cuisine, offering a small but inviting menu and reasonable prices. Harry likes oldies, and you're welcome to look over his impressive playlist

Rothenburg

Rothenburg Restaurants

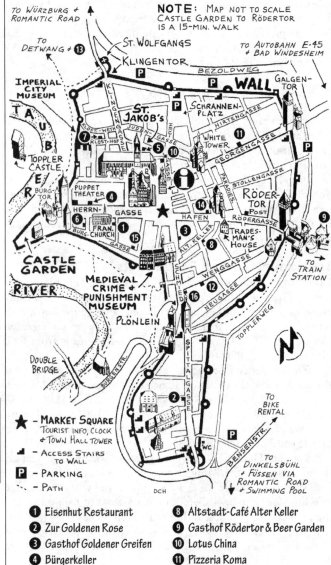

NOTE: MAP NOT TO SCALE
CASTLE GARDEN TO RÖDERTOR
IS A 15-MIN. WALK

TO WÜRZBURG &
ROMANTIC ROAD

TO
DETWANG & 13

St. WOLFGANGS

KLINGENTOR

TO AUTOBAHN E-45
& BAD WINDESHEIM

BEZOLDWEG

WALL

GALGEN-
TOR

IMPERIAL
CITY
MUSEUM

A
U
B
E
R

TOPPLER
CASTLE

BURG-A-
TOR

St.
JAKOB'S

KLINGENGASSE

KLOST-WETH-G

KLOST-HOF

JUDEN-GASSE

SCHRANNEN-
PLATZ

HIRTENGASSE

WHITE
TOWER

GEORGENGASSE

HEU-GASSE

PARADIES

STOLLENGASSE

RÖDER-
TOR

POST

RODERGASSE

PUPPET
THEATER

HERRN-
GASSE

FRAN.
CHURCH

BURG-GASSE

CASTLE
GARDEN

RIVER

MEDIEVAL
CRIME &
PUNISHMENT
MUSEUM

PLÖNLEIN

DOUBLE
BRIDGE

BURGERSTR.

HAFEN

ALT-KELLER

SCHMIED-GASSE

WENGGASSE

NEUGASSE

TRADES-
MAN'S
HOUSE

TOPPLERWEG

TO
TRAIN
STATION

SPITTALGASSE

N

★ - MARKET SQUARE
TOURIST INFO, CLOCK
& TOWN HALL TOWER

◢ - ACCESS STAIRS
TO WALL

P - PARKING

⋰ - PATH

TO
BIKE
RENTAL

WC

BENSENSTR.

TO
DINKELSBÜHL
& FÜSSEN VIA
ROMANTIC ROAD
& SWIMMING POOL

DCH

1 Eisenhut Restaurant

2 Zur Goldenen Rose

3 Gasthof Goldener Greifen

4 Bürgerkeller

5 Reichs-Küchenmeister

6 Hotel Restaurant
Klosterstüble

7 Altfränkische Weinstube
am Klosterhof

8 Altstadt-Café Alter Keller

9 Gasthof Rödertor & Beer Garden

10 Lotus China

11 Pizzeria Roma

12 Döner Kebap Shop

13 To Unter den Linden Beer Garden

14 Eis Café D' Isep (Ice Cream)

15 Trinkstube zur Hölle

16 Restaurant Glocke

and request your favorite music (€6–12 entrées, cash only, Thu–Tue 11:30–14:00 & 18:00–21:00, closed Wed, a few sidewalk tables, near bottom of Herrngasse at #24, tel. 09861/2126).

Reichs-Küchenmeister is a forgettable, big-hotel restaurant, but on a balmy evening, its pleasant, tree-shaded terrace overlooking St. Jakob's Church is hard to beat. Their *Vesperbrett* plate is a fine selection of cold cuts (€8–17 entrées, daily 11:00–22:00, Kirchplatz 8, tel. 09861/9700).

Hotel Restaurant Klosterstüble, on a small street off Herrngasse near the castle garden, is a classy place for delicious and beautifully presented traditional cuisine. Chef Rudy's food is better than his English, so head waitress Erika makes sure communication goes smoothly. The shady terrace is nice on a warm summer evening. I prefer their traditional dining room to the stony, sleek, modern room (€10 entrées, daily 11:00–14:00 & 18:00–21:00, Heringsbronnengasse 5, tel. 09861/938-890).

Altfränkische Weinstube am Klosterhof seems designed for gnomes to celebrate their anniversaries. At this very dark pub, classically candlelit in a 600-year-old building, Mario whips up gourmet pub grub (€6–12 entrées, hot food served 18:00–22:30, closes at 1:00 in the morning, off Klingengasse at Klosterhof 7, tel. 09861/6404). If you'd like dinner company, drop by on Wednesday evening, when the English Conversation Club has a big table reserved from 19:00 on (see "Meet the Locals—English Conversation Club," below). You'll eat well and with new friends—both travelers and locals.

Altstadt-Café Alter Keller is just right for a light meal near the center, but tucked away from the crowds. Eat indoors under walls festooned with old pots and jugs, or outdoors on a quiet little square. Herr Hufnagel, a baker and pastry chef, whips up a tempting array of cakes, pies, and giant meringue cookies, while gracious Christine makes sure you understand your options (€3 goulash soup with bread, €5–7 main dishes, Sat–Thu 11:00–20:00, Sun 11:00–18:00, closed Fri, Alter Keller 8, tel. 09861/2268).

Gasthof Rödertor, just outside the wall through the Rödertor gate, is a lively place where Rothenburgers go for a hearty meal at a good price. Their passion is potatoes—the menu is dedicated to spud cuisine (€6–11 entrées, daily 11:30–14:00 & 17:30–22:30, Ansbacher Strasse 7, tel. 09861/2022). They also run a popular *Biergarten* (see below).

Breaks from Pork and Potatoes

Lotus China is a peaceful world apart, serving good Chinese food (€8–10 entrées, selection of €6 two-course lunch specials, daily 11:30–14:30 & 17:30–23:00, 2 blocks behind TI near church, Eckele 2, tel. 09861/86886).

Pizzeria Roma is smoky because it's the locals' favorite for €6.50 pizza and pastas with good Italian wine. The Magrini family moved here from Tuscany in 1970 (many Italians immigrated to Germany in those years) and they've been cooking pasta for Rothenburg ever since (Thu–Tue 11:30–24:00, closed Wed and mid-Aug–mid-Sept, Galgengasse 19, tel. 09861/4540, Ricardo).

The **Döner Kebab** shop at Wenggasse 4, just off Untere Schmiedgasse, serves cheap and tasty food to go. This tiny place offers what must be the best €3 hot meal in Rothenburg (daily 11:00–21:00, tel. 09861/92417).

Picnic Goodies: A small **grocery store** is in the center of town at Rödergasse 6 (Mon–Fri 7:30–19:00, Sat 7:30–18:00, April–Dec also Sun 10:00–18:00, closed Sun Jan–March). **Supermarkets** are outside the wall: Exit the town through Rödertor, turn left through the cobbled gate, and cross the parking lot to reach the Comet supermarket, or head to the even bigger one in the shopping center across from the train station (Mon–Fri 8:00–20:00, Sat 8:00–18:00, closed Sun).

Beer Gardens *(Biergartens)*

Rothenburg's *Biergartens* can be great fun, but they're only open when the weather is balmy.

Unter den Linden, a bohemian yet family-friendly *Biergarten* in the valley along the river, is worth the 20-minute hike on a pleasant evening (daily in season with decent weather, 10:00–22:00 and sometimes later, self-service food and good beer, call first to confirm it's open, tel. 09861/5909). As it's in the valley on the river, it's cooler than Rothenburg; bring a sweater. Take a right outside the Burgtor, then a left on the footpath toward Detwang; it's at the bottom of the hill on the left.

Gasthof Rödertor, just outside the wall through the Rödertor gate, runs a backyard *Biergarten* that's great for a rowdy crowd, cheap food, and good beer (May–Sept daily 17:00–24:00, look for wooden gate, tel. 09861/2022). If the *Biergarten* is closed, their indoor restaurant (described earlier) is a good value.

Dessert

Eis Café D' Isep, with a pleasant "Venetian minimal" interior, is the town's ice-cream parlor, serving up cakes, drinks, fresh-fruit ice cream, and fancy sundaes (daily 9:30–22:00, closed mid-Oct–mid-Feb, 1 block off Market Square at Hafengasse 17, run by Paolo and Paola D'Isep). Their sidewalk tables are great for lazy people-watching.

Wine-Drinking in the Old Center

Trinkstube zur Hölle ("Hell") is dark and foreboding, offering a thick wine-drinking atmosphere, pub food, and a few main dishes. It's small and can get painfully touristy in summer (daily 17:00–24:00, closed Sun Jan–March, a block past Medieval Crime and Punishment Museum on Burggasse, with the devil hanging out front, tel. 09861/4229).

Mario's **Altfränkische Weinstube am Klosterhof** (see "Traditional German Restaurants," page 175) is the liveliest place, and the clear favorite with locals for an atmospheric drink or late meal. When every other place is asleep, you're likely to find good food, drink, and energy here.

Eisenhut, behind the fancy hotel of the same name on Herrngasse, is a good bet for gentle and casual *Biergarten* ambience within the old center (also listed under "Traditional German Restaurants," above).

Restaurant Glocke, a *Weinstube* (wine bar) popular with locals, is run by Rothenburg's oldest wine-makers, the Thürauf family. The menu, which has a very extensive wine list, is in German only because the friendly staff wants to explain your options in person. Their €4.20 deal, which lets you sample five Franconian wines, is popular (€10–15 entrées, Mon–Sat 10:30–23:00, Sun 10:30–14:00, Plönlein 1, tel. 09861/958-990).

Meet the Locals—English Conversation Club

For a rare chance to mix it up with locals who aren't selling anything, bring your favorite slang and tongue twisters to the English Conversation Club at Mario's Altfränkische Weinstube am Klosterhof (Wed 19:00–24:00, Hermann the German and his sidekick Wolfgang are regulars; see restaurant listing under "Traditional German Restaurants," above). This group of intrepid linguists has met more than 1,000 times. Consider arriving early for dinner, or after 21:00, when the beer starts to sink in, the crowd grows, and everyone seems to speak that second language a bit more easily.

TRANSPORTATION CONNECTIONS

From Rothenburg ob der Tauber by Train: A tiny branch train line connects Rothenburg to the outside world via **Steinach** in 14 minutes (generally 1/hr from Rothenburg at :06 and from Steinach at :35). If you plan to arrive in Rothenburg in the evening, note that the last train from Steinach to Rothenburg departs at about 20:30. All is not lost if you arrive in Steinach after the last train. The German government believes in providing public transport to its visitors, as well as its citizens—so it subsidizes the

Rothenburg

taxi fare to Rothenburg. To use this handy service, called AST *(Anrufsammeltaxi)*, you make an appointment with a participating taxi service (call 09861/2000 or 09861/7227) at least an hour in advance (2 hours ahead is better), and they'll drive you from Steinach to Rothenburg for the train fare (about €3.60/person) rather than the regular €25 taxi fare.

From Steinach by Train to: Würzburg (hourly, 50 min), **Nürnberg** (hourly, 1–1.5 hr, most change in Ansbach or Neustadt an der Aisch), **Munich** (hourly, 2.25–3 hrs, 1–2 changes), **Frankfurt** (hourly, 3 hrs, change in Würzburg), **Berlin** (hourly, 5 hrs, 2 changes).

Train connections in Steinach are usually quick and efficient (trains to and from Rothenburg generally use track 5). The station at Steinach is not staffed, but has touch-screen terminals for fare and schedule information and ticket sales. Visit the ticket office in Rothenburg, or as a last resort call for train info at tel. 11861 (€0.60/min).

From Rothenburg by Bus: The Romantic Road bus stops at Schrannenplatz in Rothenburg each afternoon (April–Oct) on its way between Frankfurt and Munich (and vice versa). See the schedule and tour description below.

The Romantic Road

The Romantic Road (Romantische Strasse) winds you past the most beautiful towns and scenery in Germany's medieval heartland.

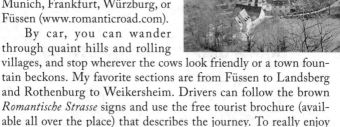

Once Germany's north–south trade route, it connected the Rhine to the Roman road that crossed the Alps south of Munich. Now it's the most scenic way to connect the dots between Rothenburg and Munich, Frankfurt, Würzburg, or Füssen (www.romanticroad.com).

By car, you can wander through quaint hills and rolling villages, and stop wherever the cows look friendly or a town fountain beckons. My favorite sections are from Füssen to Landsberg and Rothenburg to Weikersheim. Drivers can follow the brown *Romantische Strasse* signs and use the free tourist brochure (available all over the place) that describes the journey. To really enjoy the countryside, give yourself an extra day or two. If you're driving with limited time, just zero in on Rothenburg by autobahn.

The Romantic Road is the oldest and most famous of Germany's two dozen signposted scenic routes. Others celebrate

Romantic Road Bus Schedule

The Romantic Road bus runs daily April through October.
Every day, one bus goes north to south (Frankfurt to Munich),
and another follows the same route south to north (Munich to
Frankfurt). Along the way, both buses pass through towns and
attractions such as Würzburg, Rothenburg, the Wieskirche,
and Füssen. You can begin or end your journey at any of
these stops. The following times include only the main stops,
based on the 2007 schedule. Check the full schedule at www
.romanticroadcoach.de for any changes.

North to South

Depart Frankfurt	8:00
Arrive Würzburg.	9:30
Depart Würzburg	10:00
Arrive Rothenburg	12:15
Depart Rothenburg.	12:45
Arrive Dinkelsbühl	13:40
Depart Dinkelsbühl.	14:10
Arrive Wieskirche*	18:55
Depart Wieskirche	18:55
Arrive Füssen.	19:35
Depart Füssen	19:35
Arrive Munich	21:15

South to North

Depart Munich.	8:15
Arrive Füssen.	10:00
Depart Füssen	10:10
Arrive Wieskirche	11:15
Depart Wieskirche	11:45
Arrive Dinkelsbühl	16:15
Depart Dinkelsbühl.	16:35
Arrive Rothenburg	17:30
Depart Rothenburg.	18:00
Arrive Würzburg.	19:30
Depart Würzburg	19:30
Arrive Frankfurt	21:00

* stops only on request

The Romantic Road

toys, porcelain, architecture (Swabian Baroque or brick Gothic), clocks, and baths—and there are now two separate *Spargelstrassen* (asparagus roads). The "Castle Road" that runs between Rothenburg and Mannheim sounds intriguing, but it's nowhere near as interesting.

The Romantic Road Tour Bus

The Deutsche Touring company runs buses daily between Frankfurt and Munich in each direction (April–Oct, tel. 069/790-3230, www.romanticroadcoach.de). The bus leaves only once a day in each direction, stopping in most places only long enough to give you just a glimpse of what's there. Consider the bus only if you'd like to see most or all of the hard-to-reach villages en route, or if you prefer a 13-hour scenic bus ride to the four-hour fast train between Frankfurt and Munich. Most Romantic Roadsters, however, are happier visiting fewer places, and at their own pace. If that's more your style, the bus is only useful for its direct connections between two stops poorly served by public transportation (such as Dinkelsbühl and the Wieskirche; see "Public Transportation Along the Romantic Road").

If you do take the bus, confirm departures and arrivals when you buy your ticket—schedules aren't posted, and special events can temporarily change bus-stop locations and schedules.

The location of the bus stop in each town is listed on the bus brochure and website. The stops are not well-signed. The drivers usually hand out maps and brochures and play a tape-recorded narration of the journey highlights in English. The time in each town (about 30 min in Rothenburg and 20–30 min in Dinkelsbühl; just long enough to use the WC at a few other attractions) is too brief to really see the place, but long enough to slow down the overall journey. You can join or leave the trip where you like, but if you choose to stay at a particular stop, you'll have to wait until tomorrow for the next bus—or find another way to your next destination. If you prefer urban sights and speedy trains, this can seem like a glorified Greyhound ride with a beverage service (free coffee, €1 for cold drinks).

The entire ride (Frankfurt to Munich) costs €98 (pay cash on the bus). Shorter segments cost less (for example, Würzburg to Rothenburg is €14). Students and seniors—without a railpass—get a 10 percent discount.

You can get a 60 percent discount on your bus ticket if you have a German railpass, Eurailpass, or Eurail Selectpass (if Germany is one of your selected countries). You do not have to use a travel day of a flexipass to get this discount; if bus drivers say it takes a travel day, set them straight.

Bus reservations are almost never necessary. But they are free and easy, and, technically, without one you can lose your seat to someone who has one (reserve online at www.romanticroadcoach.de, or call 069/790-3230).

Public Transportation Along the Romantic Road

The Romantic Road has good, frequent train coverage for its major destinations (Rothenburg, Würzburg, and Füssen), but no coverage for small, out-of-the-way sights, such as the Wieskirche. With limited time, focus on **Rothenburg** and **Würzburg** (in that order) as your best introduction to the Romantic Road.

If you have lots of time, you can get to many of the Romantic Road sights by train, or by a train-and-bus combination. Trains between **Füssen** and **Augsburg** leave hourly and take two hours (half of these are direct). **Nördlingen** is a 30-minute trip off the main line that connects Rothenburg to Augsburg (change in Donauwörth, trains run hourly, €4.60). **Weikersheim,** on the northern end of the route, is an hour from Würzburg by hourly trains (half of these are direct).

Only three stops not served by trains are worth considering (listed in order of wow-value):

1. The **Wieskirche** (outside Füssen, see page 104). City buses run from Füssen to the Wieskirche (4–5/day, 40–50 min each way, more frequently with a transfer in Steingaden). But as I mention in the Bavaria chapter, you'll spend more time in transit than you will visiting the church.

2. The town of **Dinkelsbühl** (midway along the route). To get to Dinkelsbühl, take the train to Ansbach, then the easy one-hour bus that leaves hourly from Ansbach's train station (about €7).

3. The **Herrgottskirche,** in Creglingen, near Weikersheim. Creglingen is a half-hour from both Rothenburg and Weikersheim by local buses, which drop you off a mile's walk from the Herrgottskirche (to/from Rothenburg: 3/day Mon–Fri only, €3.30, change in Archshofen; to/from Weikersheim: 6/day Mon–Fri, 4/day Sat, no buses on Sun, €4.60).

SIGHTS

Along the Romantic Road

These sights are listed from north to south.

▲▲**Würzburg**—With its fancy palace and chapel, historic Würzburg can make a good overnight stop (see next chapter).

Weikersheim—This untouristy town has a palace with fine Baroque gardens (luxurious picnic spot), a folk museum, and a picturesque town square.

▲**Herrgottskirche**—This peaceful church is graced with Tilman Riemenschneider's greatest carved altarpiece (Easter–Oct daily 9:15–17:30, less off-season, tel. 07933/508, www.herrgottskirche .de). Across the street is the Fingerhut (thimble, literally "finger hat") museum (€2, April–Oct daily 9:00–18:00, less off-season, tel. 07933/370, www.fingerhutmuseum.de). The southbound Romantic Road bus stops here for 10 minutes, long enough to see one or the other. The church and museum are a mile south of Creglingen (TI tel. 07933/631, www.creglingen.de).

▲▲▲**Rothenburg**—See page 151 for information on Germany's best medieval town.

▲**Dinkelsbühl**—Rothenburg's little sister is cute enough to merit a short stop. A moat, towers, gates, and beautifully preserved medieval wall surround this town. Dinkelsbühl's his-

---

Maypoles

Along the Romantic Road, and throughout Bavaria, you'll see colorfully ornamented maypoles decorating town squares (see an example on page 44). Many are painted in Bavaria's colors, white and blue. The decorations that line each side of the pole, which symbolize the craftspeople and businesses of that community, are festively replaced each May Day. Traditionally, rival communities try to steal each other's maypole. Locals guard their new pole night and day as May Day approaches. Stolen poles are ransomed only with lots of beer for the clever thieves.

---

tory museum is meager and without a word of English. The Kinderzeche children's festival celebrates the success of the local children who pleaded with the Swedish army during the Thirty Years' War, convincing them to spare the town. The festival turns Dinkelsbühl wonderfully on end for a week at the end of July (www .kinderzeche.de). The helpful **TI** on the main street sells maps with a short walking tour and can help find rooms (Mon–Fri 9:00–18:00, Sat 10:00–13:00 & 14:00–16:00, Sun 10:00–13:00, less off-season, tel. 09851/90240, www.dinkelsbuehl.de).

Sleeping in Dinkelsbühl: Consider **$$$ Hotel Palmengarten,** run by the Danner-Bohl family (Sb-€34–46, Db-€62–76, Tb-€77–88, parking garage-€5/day, Untere Schmiedgasse 14, tel. 09851/57670, fax 09851/7548, www.sonne-palmengarten.de, info @sonne-palmengarten.de).

Nördlingen—Known for its 15-mile-wide valley, which is an impact crater blasted out by a meteor 15 million years ago, Nördlingen also gained fame as the "grain basket" because of its rich soil. Apollo astronauts did research and field training here; if you visit the museum dedicated to the study of the meteor (Riesenkrater Museum), so can you (Tue–Sun 10:00–12:00 & 13:30–16:30, closed Mon, Eugene-Shoemaker-Platz 1, tel. 09081/273-8220, www.rieskrater-museum.de).

Augsburg—Founded more than 2,000 years ago by Emperor Augustus, Augsburg enjoyed its heyday in the 15th and 16th centuries. Today, it's Bavaria's third largest city. The old town is pleasant, especially the small streets below the main square, where streams diverted from the river Lech run alongside pedestrians (www.augsburg.de).

Landsberg am Lech—Like many towns in this area, Landsberg (on the river Lech) has its roots in the salt trade. Every four years, the town returns to its medieval roots and hosts the Ruethenfest. The town, founded the same year as Munich (1158), was shaped by the architect Dominikus Zimmerman (of Wieskirche fame). Adolf Hitler wrote *Mein Kampf* while serving his prison sentence here after the Beer Hall Putsch of 1923 (when Hitler and his followers unsuccessfully attempted to take over the government of Bavaria).

Rottenbuch—This nondescript village has an impressive church in a lovely setting. The bus stops here only on request.

▲▲**Wieskirche**—This is Germany's most glorious Baroque–Rococo church, beautifully restored and set in a sweet meadow. Heavenly! Romantic Road buses stop here for 30 minutes—but only on the northbound Munich-to-Frankfurt run. Southbound buses will pick up and drop off here, but only on request. (See page 104 of the Bavaria and Tirol chapter.)

Füssen—This town, three miles from the stunning Neuschwanstein Castle, is worth a stop on any sightseeing agenda. (See page 91 of the Bavaria and Tirol chapter for description and accommodations.)

WÜRZBURG

A historic city—though freshly rebuilt since World War II—Würzburg is worth a stop to see its impressive prince-bishop's Residenz, the bubbly Baroque chapel (Hofkirche) next door, and the palace's sculpted gardens. Surrounded by vineyards and filled with atmospheric *Weinstuben* (wine bars), this tourist-friendly town is easy to navigate by foot or streetcar. Today, 25,000 of its 130,000 residents are students—making the town feel young and very alive.

Planning Your Time

Würzburg has a few hours' worth of sightseeing. Begin at the Residenz (prince-bishop's palace), then take my self-guided walk through town to the Old Main Bridge. With more time, hike up to the hilltop Marienberg Fortress across the bridge.

ORIENTATION

(area code: 0931)

Tourist Information

Würzburg's helpful TI is in the Rococo-style Falken Haus on Market Square (May–Oct Mon–Fri 10:00–18:00, Sat–Sun 10:00–14:00; April and Nov–Dec same hours but closed Sun; Jan–March Mon–Fri 10:00–16:00, Sat 10:00–13:00, closed Sun; Marktplatz, tel. 0931/372-398, www.wuerzburg.de). Their free *Visitor's Guide* pamphlet and map covers the tourist's Würzburg well. The TI books rooms for free (in person only, not by phone), sells detailed maps for biking through the local wine country, and offers a one-hour

---

Würzburg's Beginnings

The city was born centuries before Christ at an easy-to-ford part of the Main River under an easy-to-defend hill. A Celtic fort stood where the fortress stands today. Later, three Irish missionary monks came here to Christianize the local barbarians. In A.D. 686, they were beheaded, and their relics put Würzburg on the pilgrimage map. About 500 years later, when the town was the seat of a bishop, Holy Roman Emperor Frederick Barbarossa came here to get the bishop's OK to divorce his wife. The bishop said "No problem," and the emperor thanked him by giving him secular rule of the entire region of Franconia. From then on, the bishop was also a prince, and the prince-bishop of Würzburg answered only to the Holy Roman Emperor.

---

walking tour in English (€5, June–Oct daily at 18:30). If you'll be continuing on the Romantic Road (see previous chapter), the TI has the *Romantische Strasse* brochure and a list of car-rental options. The TI also sells the Würzburg Welcome Card, offering minimal discounts on a few sights and restaurants (€2/7 days).

Arrival in Würzburg

By Train: Würzburg's train station is user-friendly and filled with handy services (coin-op lockers in main hall, WCs between main hall and tunnel to platforms). Walk out of the train station to the small square in front. A big **city map** board provides a quick orientation (on small building to the right). Farther right is the **post office** and the **Romantic Road bus stop** (track 13, curb closest and parallel to station building, look for very small and faded *Touring* sign and schedule).

From the cul-de-sac in front of the station, **trams** #1, #2, #3, or #5 take you one stop to recommended hotels (except Hotel-Pension Spehnkuch, which is near the station) or two stops to Market Square and the TI. By **foot,** cross over the busy Röntgenring and head up the shop-lined Kaiserstrasse. For the **Residenz,** it's either a 15-minute walk or a short bus ride (on #14, #16, #20, #26, or #28).

By Car: Drivers entering Würzburg can keep it simple by following signs to the *Residenz*, and parking in the vast cobbled square that faces the palace.

Helpful Hints

Festivals: Würzburg—always clever when it comes to trade— schedules its three annual festivals (wine, Mozart, and the Kiliani-Volksfest) in rapid succession to keep things busy

Würzburg

from June 1 through late July.

Internet Access: Try the **Stadtbücherei** (library), located in the same building as the TI, on Market Square (€1/20 min plus €4 deposit, Mon–Fri 10:00–18:00, Thu until 19:00, Sat 10:00–15:00, closed Sun, check in with info desk on first floor, Falken Haus, Marktplatz).

Bike Rental: Fahrrad Körner rents bikes right in the old town, a five-minute walk north of the cathedral (Bronnbachergasse 3, tel. 0931/52340). Less central is **Velo-Momber,** several blocks south of the Old Main Bridge (Mon–Fri 10:00–18:00, Sat 9:00–13:00, closed Sun, Landwehrstrasse 13, tel. 0931/12627, www.velo-momber.de).

Local Guide: Maureen Aldenhoff, who grew up in Liverpool but has been married to a German for 30 years, gives good private walking tours (€80/2 hrs, €100/3 hrs, €185/full day, tel. 0931/52135, maureen.aldenhoff@web.de).

Getting Around Würzburg

You can easily walk to everything but the hilltop Marienberg Fortress. For public transit, the same tickets work on all city bus or tram lines (including the bus up to the fortress). Your options include a single ticket (*Einzelfahrschein*, €2, good for 90 min in one direction with transfers) or a day pass (*Tageskarte Solo*—€4.10 for one person; or *Tageskarte Familie*—€8.30 for two adults and kids under age 15). You can buy either type of ticket from the bus driver or at a streetside machine. Tickets are only valid if you stamp them, using the little box inside the tram or bus (stamp it only the first time for a day pass). For transit info, call tel. 0931/362-320.

SELF-GUIDED WALK

Welcome to Würzburg

This brief walk gets you from the Residenz, which you may want to tour first (described under "Sights," below), to the Old Main Bridge (Alte Mainbrücke) via the key old-town sights.

• *Begin at the fountain in front of the Residenz palace.*

Fountain of Franconia: In 1814, the prince-bishop got the boot, and the region of Franconia was secularized and given to the Bavarian Wittelsbach dynasty. Technically, Franconia is a part of Bavaria, but that status is as controversial as Ireland being part of Great Britain (never call a Franconian a Bavarian). This statue—a gift from the townspeople to their then-new royal family—turns its back to the palace and faces the town. It celebrates the artistic and intellectual genius of Franconia with statues of three great hometown boys (a medieval bard, the woodcarver Tilman Riemenschneider, and the Renaissance painter Matthias Grünewald).

• *If Franconia hopped down and ran 300 yards ahead down Hofstrasse, she'd hit the twin-spired cathedral. Meet her there.*

St. Kilian's Cathedral (Dom): This building's core is Romanesque (1040–1188), with Gothic spires and Baroque additions to the transepts. Enter through the back (the end nearest you, on the right-hand side).

Destroyed in World War II, the cathedral was rebuilt in the 1960s. Before 1945, the entire church was slathered in Baroque stucco decor, as the apse is today. The nave has a cohesive design, progressing from the menorah (representing the Old Testament) in the back, past tombstones of centuries of prince-bishops and a crucified Jesus (above the high altar), to the apse, where a resurrected Christ welcomes you into a hopeful future. The skulls of Würzburg's three favorite saints—those Irish monks martyred in the seventh century—lie in a box on the altar (for more on the

Central Würzburg

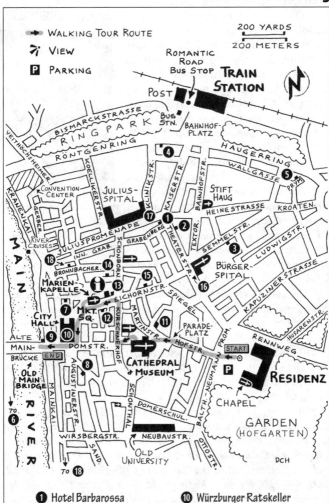

- ➊ Hotel Barbarossa
- ➋ Hotel Schönleber
- ➌ Sankt Josef Hotel
- ➍ Hotel-Pension Spehnkuch
- ➎ Babelfish Hostel
- ➏ To Youth Hostel
- ➐ Zum Stachel Weinhaus
- ➑ Backöfele
- ➒ Alte Mainmühle
- ➓ Würzburger Ratskeller
- ⓫ Martinsklause & Martinz
- ⓬ Café Schönborn
- ⓭ Café Michel
- ⓮ Weinstube Maulaffenbäck
- ⓯ Pasta e Olio
- ⓰ Weinstube Bürgerspital
- ⓱ Juliusspital
- ⓲ Bike Rentals (2)

Würzburg

monks, see sidebar on page 188).

There's a fine memorial to the 15th-century Prince-Bishop Rudolf von Scherenberg, whose name means "scissors man" (see his coat of arms). Scherenberg ruled until he was 94 years old. Carved by Tilman Riemenschneider, this tombstone is an example of late-Gothic realism. Back then, it was outrageous to portray an old bishop as...an old bishop (looking at the tombstone, you can tell he needs dentures). The next prince-bishop, whose tomb is to the right of Scherenberg's, saw how realistic his predecessor's was, and insisted on having an idealized portrait (also by Riemenschneider) done to his satisfaction before he died. (He's looking unbelievably good.)

• *Leave the church through the side door, behind Mr. Scissors. Riemenschneider's tomb is on the church wall just outside the door. Stepping outside, look up at the three martyrs (before they were beheaded), turn left, and go into the museum.*

Cathedral Museum (Museum am Dom): The museum features a poignant combination of old and new religious art. It pairs 11th- to 18th-century works with modern interpretations, sprinkles it all with a Christian theme, and wraps it in a shiny new building (€3.50, €4.50 combo-ticket includes Cathedral Treasury, April–Oct Tue–Sun 10:00–18:00, Nov–March Tue–Sun 10:00–17:00, closed Mon year-round, tel. 0931/3866-5600, www.museum-am-dom.de).

• *Upon leaving, hook right through a tunnel, which emerges on a delight-ful urban scene. Domstrasse leads down to the spire of the City Hall and the Old Main Bridge (where this walk will end). On your left you'll see a sign for the **Cathedral Treasury** (Domschatz, €2, €4.50 combo-ticket includes Cathedral Museum, Tue–Sun 14:00–17:00, closed Mon, tel. 0931/386-261). But we're looping right. Go a block up Kurschner Hof. On your right, you'll pass the entrance to the...*

Neumünster Basilica: Like the cathedral, this church has a Romanesque body with a Baroque face. Go up the stairs to take a look inside, then continue up the street, noticing the vineyards in the distance. Appreciate this quiet pedestrian zone. Locals wouldn't have it any other way—electric trolleys, bikes, and pedestrians.

• *Enter the square on the left with the lacy, two-tone church.*

Market Square (Marktplatz): Imagine this square during the wine fest in June, with 75 vintners showing off their best wines, or during the Christmas market, when the square is full of quaint stalls selling holiday goodies. The fancy yellow-and-white Rococo-designed Falken Haus (House of the Falcon) once had three different facades. To fix it, the landlady gave a wandering band of stucco artists a chance to show their stuff...and ended up with this (inside are the TI and a prizewinning library with Internet access).

• *Set your eyes on the church.*

Marienkapelle: The two-tone, late-Gothic church was the merchants' answer to the prince-bishop's cathedral. Since Rome didn't bankroll the place, it's ringed with "swallow shops" (like swallows' nests cuddled up against a house)—enabling the church to run little businesses. The sandstone statues (replicas of Riemenschneider originals) depict the 12 apostles and Jesus. Walk downhill along the church to the lower marketplace, where the city's produce market bustles daily except Sunday (May–Oct 8:00–16:00). The famous Adam and Eve statues (flanking the side entrance to the church) show off Riemenschneider's mastery of the human body. Continue around the church to the west portal (main entrance), where the carved Last Judgment shows kings, ladies, and bishops—some going to heaven, others making up the chain gang bound for hell, via the monster's mouth. (This was commissioned by those feisty town merchants tired of snooty blue-bloods.) Continue around to the next entry to see the Annunciation, with a cute angel Gabriel telling Mary (who is a virgin, symbolized by the lilies) the good news. Notice how God whispers through a speaking tube as baby Jesus slips down and into her ear.

• *Go back around to the lower market (Adam-and-Eve side) and leave—passing the obelisk—in the direction of the yellow building. Follow Schustergasse, a pedestrian lane lined with shops that leads back to Domstrasse. The cathedral is on your left, while the City Hall and bridge are to the right. Head for the City Hall's tower.*

City Hall (Rathaus): Würzburg's City Hall is relatively humble because of the power of the prince-bishop. A side room (facing the building, around the left side, free, always open) holds the Gedenkraum 16. März 1945. This is a memorial to the 20-minute Allied bombing that created a firestorm, destroying (and demoralizing) the town on March 16, 1945—just six weeks before the end of World War II. Check out the sobering model, and ponder the names (lining the ceiling) of those killed. As you leave, notice the horizontal lines cut into the archway on your right. These mark the flood waters *(Hochstand des Maines)* of the years 1342, 1682, and 1784.

• *Now, find the bridge.*

Old Main Bridge (Alte Mainbrücke): This isn't the town's "main" (as in primary) bridge; rather, it spans the Main (pronounced "mine") River, which also flows through Frankfurt.

The bridge, from 1133, is the second-oldest in Germany. The 12 statues lining the bridge are Würzburg saints and prince-bishops.

Walk to the St. Kilian statue (with the golden sword)—one of the three monks who are shown being beheaded in the Residenz palace's Chapel (Hofkirche). Stand so that you can't see the white power-plant tower and enjoy the best view in town. Marienberg Fortress caps the hill. Squint up at Kilian pointing to God...with his head on.

The hillside is blanketed with grapevines destined to become the fine Stein Franconian wine. Johann Wolfgang von Goethe, the German Shakespeare, ordered 900 liters of this vintage annually. A friend once asked Goethe what he thought were the three most important things in life. He said, "Wine, women, and song." The friend then asked, "If you had to give one up, which would it be?" Without hesitating, Goethe answered "Song." Then, when asked what he would choose if he had to give up a second, Goethe paused and said, "It depends on the vintage."

• *Your walking tour is over. From here, consider paying a visit to the fortress on the hill above you (described under "Sights") or have lunch at the Alte Mainmühle restaurant, with a terrace overlooking the bridge (see "Eating," page 199).*

SIGHTS

Würzburg's Residenz

Würzburg's opulent palace and its associated sights—the Chapel (Hofkirche) and garden—are the town's main attraction.

▲▲**Residenz Palace**—This Franconian Versailles features grand rooms, 3-D art, and a massive (and recently restored) fresco by Giovanni Battista Tiepolo. Restoration work continues in the Imperial Hall, which will be closed to visitors until 2009.

Cost, Hours, Location: €5, daily April–Oct 9:00–18:00, Nov–March 10:00–16:00, last entry 30 min before closing, no photos, tel. 0931/355-170 or 0931/355-1712. Don't confuse the Residenz (a 15-min walk southeast of the train station) with Marienberg Fortress (on the hilltop across the river). The Residenz is the far more important sight to visit. Easy parking is available in front of the Residenz (€2 for first hour, €1 each  additional hour, pay at the machine marked *Kasse* before you leave your car).

Tours, Information, Services: English tours, offered May through October daily at 11:00 and 15:00, include the normally closed South Wing, which has the five best rooms (45 min, call

Würzburg

ahead or tell the cashier you want to join the English tour, covered in entry price, but tips are welcome if the guide is good). The only other way to see the South Wing is to be trapped on a German tour (3/hr). If you can't make either scheduled English departure, call to see if any private English groups are scheduled that you can join. The €5 English guidebook is dry and lengthy. Few English descriptions are provided in the Residenz; follow the self-guided tour, below, for an overview. On the right as you exit the ticket office, you'll find free WCs and €1 storage lockers.

Residenz Grounds: The elaborate Chapel (Hofkirche) is next door (as you exit the palace, go left), and the entrance to the picnic-worthy garden is just beyond (for more on both, see below).

❂ Self-Guided Tour: The following self-guided tour gives you the basics to appreciate this fine palace.

• *Begin at the entrance.*

1. Vestibule: This area functioned as a grand circular drive-way—just right for six-horse carriages to drop off their guests at the base of the stairs. The elegant stairway comes with low steps, enabling high-class ladies to glide gracefully up, heads tilted back to enjoy Europe's largest and grandest fresco opening up above them. Hold your lady's hand high and get into the ascending rhythm. Enjoy the climb.

• *Ascend the stairs and look up at the...*

2. Tiepolo Fresco: In 1752, the Venetian master Giovanni Battista Tiepolo was instructed to make a grand fresco illustrating the greatness of Europe, Würzburg, and the prince-bishop. And he did—in only 13 months. Find the four continents, each symbolized by a woman on an animal and pointing to the prince-bishop in the medallion above Europe. America—desperately uncivilized—sits naked with feathers in her hair on an alligator among severed heads. She's being served hot chocolate, a favorite import and nearly a drug for Europeans back then. Africa sits on a camel in a land of trade and fantasy animals (based on secondhand reports, and therefore inaccurate). Asia rides her elephant (with the backward ear) in the birthplace of Christianity and the alphabet. And Europe is shown as the center of high culture—Lady Culture points her brush not at Rome, but at Würzburg. The prince-bishop had a healthy ego. The ceiling features Apollo and a host of Greek gods, all paying homage to the PB.

3. The White Hall: This hall, actually gray, was kept plain to punctuate the colorful rooms on either side. It's a Rococo-stucco fantasy. (The word "Rococo" comes from the Portuguese word for the frilly rocaille shell.)

• *Straight ahead is the palace gift shop. Continue to your left, following signs for* Rundgang.

4. The Imperial Hall: Unfortunately, this glorious hall will be covered in scaffolding until 2009. (During the restoration period, you can learn about the process through an exhibit under the scaffolding.)

When it's open, this hall is the ultimate example of Baroque: harmony, symmetry, illusion, and the bizarre; lots of light and mirrors facing windows; and all with a foundation of absolutism (a divine monarch, inspired by Louis XIV). If it happens to be open, take a moment to marvel at all the 3-D tricks in the ceiling. Here's another trick: As you enter the room, look left and check out the dog in the fresco. When you get to the window, have another look... notice that he has gotten older and fatter while you were crossing the hall. The room features three scenes: On the ceiling, find Father Main (the local river) amusing himself with a nymph. The two walls tell more history. On one, the bishop presides over the marriage of a happy Barbarossa (whose bride was actually 12 years old, unlike the woman in the painting, who looks considerably older; for more on Barbarossa, see the sidebar on page 188). The bishop's power is demonstrated through his oversized fingers (giving the benediction) and through the details of his miter, which—unlike his face—is not shown in profile to allow you to see his coat of arms. Opposite that is the pay-off: Barbarossa, now the Holy Roman Emperor, gives the bishop Franconia and the secular title of prince. From this point onward, the prince-bishop rules. Also in the Imperial Hall, the balcony offers a great vantage point for surveying the Italian section of the garden (explained on page 197).

5. The North Wing: This wing is a string of lavish rooms—evolving from fancy Baroque to fancier Rococo—used for the prince-bishop's VIP guests. It's a straight shot, with short English descriptions in each room to the Green Room in the corner.

6. The Green Lacquer Room: This room is named for its silver-leaf walls, painted green. The Escher-esque inlaid floor was painstakingly restored after WWII bombings. Have fun multiplying in the mirrors before leaving. The nearby hall (look for the exit sign) shows photos of the city in rubble in 1945—and craftsmen bringing the palace back to its original splendor soon after. The little four-foot-tall doors were used by tiny servants who stoked the stoves, unseen from this hallway.

▲▲ **Chapel (Hofkirche)**—This sumptuous chapel was for the exclusive use of the prince-bishop (private altar upstairs with direct entrance to his residence) and his court (ground floor). The decor and design is textbook Baroque. Architect Johann Balthasar Neumann was stuck with the existing walls. His challenge was to bring in light and create symmetry—essential to any Baroque work. He did it with mirrors and hidden windows. All the gold is real—if paper-thin—gold leaf. The columns are "manufactured marble," which isn't marble at all but marbled plaster. This method was popular because it was uniform, economical, and the color could be controlled. Pigment was mixed into plaster, which was rolled onto the stone or timber core of the column. This half-inch veneer was then polished. You can tell if a "marble" column is real or fake by resting your hand on it. If it warms up...it's not marble. The faded painting high above the altar shows three guys in gold robes losing their heads (for more on these martyred Irish monks, see sidebar on page 188). The two side paintings are by the great fresco artist Tiepolo. Since the plaster wouldn't dry in the winter, Tiepolo spent his downtime painting with oil (free, daily April–Oct 9:00–18:00, Nov–March 10:00–16:00, closed during Sun 10:00 Mass and on Catholic holidays; facing the palace, use separate entrance at far right just before garden entrance).

Residenz Garden—One of Germany's finest Baroque gardens is a delightful park (enter next to the chapel). By definition, Baroque gardens have three sections: English, French, and Italian. The French section is just inside the gate. It typically features statues of Greek gods (with lots of kidnapping action), carefully trimmed 18th-century yew trees, and an orangerie. The English section (to the right) is like a rough park. The Italian section, directly behind the palace around to the left, is grand—à la Versailles—but uses terraces to create the illusion of spaciousness (since it was originally hemmed in by the town wall). A modern feature has been added (WCs in the far-right corner).

Marienberg Fortress (Festung Marienberg)

This 13th-century fortified retreat was the original residence of Würzburg's prince-bishops. After being stormed by the Swedish army during the 17th-century Thirty Years' War, the fortress was rebuilt in Baroque style. The fortress contains two museums: a **City History Museum** (Fürstenbaumuseum, €4, €5 combo-ticket for both museums, April–mid-Oct Tue–Sun 9:00–18:00, closed Mon and mid-Oct–March, tel. 0931/355-1750) and the **Mainfränkisches Museum,** which highlights the work of Riemenschneider, Germany's top wood-carver and onetime mayor of Würzburg (€3, €5 combo-ticket for both museums, few English explanations, €3 audioguide, April–Oct Tue–Sun 10:00–17:00, Nov–March Tue–Sun 10:00–16:00, closed Mon year-round, tel. 0931/205-940, www.mainfraenkisches-museum .de; Riemenschneider fans will also find his work throughout Würzburg's many churches). The **fortress grounds** (free) provide

Würzburg

fine city views. The gift shop sells a good €2.60 guide explaining the fortress' history, courtyard buildings, and museums. For restaurants at the fortress, see "Eating."

Getting to Marienberg Fortress: Take bus #9 (€2 one-way, covered by *Tageskarte* passes, runs daily 10:00–18:00 every 40 min, departs from Residenzplatz and Barbarossaplatz/Juliuspromenade). To walk, cross the Old Main Bridge and follow small *Festung Marienberg* signs to the right uphill for a heart-thumping 20 minutes (signs pointing left indicate a longer, more gradual path through vineyards).

SLEEPING

Würzburg's good-value hotels provide a stress-free first or last night when flying into or out of Frankfurt. Hourly trains connect Würzburg and Frankfurt's airport in 90 minutes.

Near Theaterstrasse

These hotels cluster within a block on Theaterstrasse, a seven-minute walk from the train station. Head up Kaiserstrasse to the circular awning at Barbarossaplatz and angle left, toward KFC, for Theaterstrasse. In these hotels, quieter rooms are in back, front rooms have street noise, and all rooms are entertained by church bells.

$$ Hotel Barbarossa, tucked peacefully away on the fourth floor, rents 18 simple, comfortable rooms (S-€30, Ss-€40, Sb-€50, Db-€80, Tb-€90, these discounted prices promised with this book and cash in 2008, elevator, across from KFC at Theaterstrasse 2, tel. 0931/321-370, fax 0931/321-3737, marchiorello@t-online.de, Martina Marchiorello).

$$ Hotel Schönleber has 32 good rooms, but is a lesser value than my other higher-priced listings (S-€42, Sb-€60–65,

---

Sleep Code

(€1 = about $1.30, country code: 49, area code: 0931)
S = Single, **D** = Double/Twin, **T** = Triple, **Q** = Quad, **b** = bathroom, **s** = shower only. Credit cards are accepted, English is spoken, and breakfast is included.

To help you sort easily through these listings, I've divided the rooms into two categories, based on the price for a standard double room with bath:

$$ Higher Priced—Most rooms €80 or more.
$ Lower Priced—Most rooms less than €80.

D-€62, Ds-€68, Db-€80–100 depending on size, Tb-€108, elevator, Theaterstrasse 5, tel. 0931/304-8900, fax 0931/16012, www .hotel-schoenleber.de, reservierung@hotel-schoenleber.de).

Elsewhere in Würzburg

The first three listings are closer to the station; the fourth is across the river.

$$ Sankt Josef Hotel has 33 fine rooms and a pleasant breakfast room (Sb-€50–55, Db-€80–100 depending on size, non-smoking rooms, reserve ahead for parking-€8/day, left off Theaterstrasse to Semmelstrasse 28, tel. 0931/308-680, fax 0931/308-6860, www.hotel-st-josef.de, hotel.st.josef@t-online.de, Herr and Frau Casagrande speak some English). The hotel also has a restaurant (€6–14 plates, Thu–Tue from 17:00, Sat–Sun also open for lunch 11:00–14:30, closed Wed).

$ Hotel-Pension Spehnkuch, the best budget hotel near the station, overlooks a busy street but is quiet behind double-paned windows. It's friendly, simple, clean, and comfortable, but can be smoky (S-€34, D-€56, T-€78–81, cash only; if canceling, call 72 hours in advance; 3-min walk from station: exit station and take a right onto the first street, walk 500 feet to Röntgenring 7, on first floor; tel. 0931/54752, fax 0931/54760, www.pension-spehnkuch .de, info@pension-spehnkuch.de, Markus).

$ Babelfish Hostel, just a five-minute walk from the station, welcomes travelers of all ages. This laid-back place is clean and feels safe. There's no breakfast, but you can store food and whip up your own treats in the community kitchen (€16-dorm beds, D-€45, sheets-€2.50, laundry-€4; free coffee, tea, parking, lockers, and Internet access; wheelchair-accessible, bike rental-€5/day; exit the station, cross over Röntgenring, and turn left for Prymstrasse 3; tel. 0931/304-0430, fax 0931/304-3632, www.babelfish-hostel .de, info@babelfish-hostel.de).

$ Würzburg's official youth hostel, across the river, has 226 beds (€17 per bed in 4- to 10-bed rooms, includes sheets and breakfast, non-members-€3 extra, cash only, must be under age 27, family rooms, lunch and dinner available, 1:00 curfew; 20-min walk from station, cross Old Main Bridge and turn left on Saalgasse to Burkarderstrasse 44; tel. 0931/42590, jhwuerzburg@djh-bayern.de).

EATING

In the Center

Zum Stachel, Würzburg's oldest *Weinhaus*, originated as the town's tithe barn—where people deposited 10 percent of their produce as tax. In 1413, it began preparing the produce and selling wine. Today, it's a worthy splurge, serving gourmet Franconian meals in an elegant stone-and-ivy courtyard and woody dining room. The ceiling depicts a medieval *Stachel* (mace) in deadly action (€20–24 entrées, daily 11:00–23:00, reservations smart for this dressy place; from Marktplatz head toward river, turn right on Gressengasse to intersection with Marktgasse; Gressengasse 1, tel. 0931/52770).

Backöfele is a fun hole-in-the-wall (literally). Named "The Oven" for its entryway, this place is a hit with Germans, offering a rustic menu full of local specialties (€6–16 entrées, daily 12:00–24:00, reservations smart; with your back to the City Hall, go straight on Augustinerstrasse, take the first left onto Wolfhartsgasse, then the first right to Ursulinergasse 2; tel. 0931/59059).

Alte Mainmühle, on the bridge in a converted mill, is a great place to end your walking tour. On a warm day, nothing beats a cold beer on their deck, which overlooks the river and the fortress—choose from their sunny top-floor terrace or the shade below. They have fresh fish specials (try their *Forelle* or *Zanderfilet*) and traditional fare with a Franconian twist. Their homemade sourdough bread *(Natursauerteigbrot)* is a delicious nod to their milling history (€7 wurst plates, €13–20 entrées, Mon–Sat 9:00–24:00, Sun 10:00–24:00, kitchen open daily 11:00–22:30, Mainkai 1, tel. 0931/16777).

At **Würzburger Ratskeller,** enjoy traditional Franconian farmers' food, and choose from three seating options: an inviting courtyard (weather permitting), a stately restaurant, or a cozy multi-room *Weinstube* below (€7–15 entrées, daily 11:30–24:00, reservations smart, next to City Hall at Langgasse 1, tel. 0931/13021).

At **Martinsklause,** a 12th-century cellar near the cathedral, the bar is an old confessional and the booths are made from cut-up church pews. You'll find local wines and specialties on the menu (€6–12 entrées, Tue–Sun 18:00–24:00, closed Mon, Martinstrasse 21, tel. 0931/353-9290). Upstairs, **Martinz** serves a long list of sweet and savory pancakes *(Pfannkuchen),* salads, steaks, and soups (€4–9 entrées, daily 8:30–24:00). In good weather, try their *Biergarten* terrace.

Café Schönborn, in the shadow of the Marienkapelle on Market Square, is a good place for a light lunch (soups and salads), a bottomless cup of coffee (virtually unheard-of in Germany, served here until 11:00), people-watching, or a late-night drink with the hip crowd. The inside can be loud and smoky, but the outside seating is great (€3–8 light meals, Mon–Sat 8:30–24:00, Sun 10:00–24:00, live jazz on Thu nights, Marktplatz 30, tel. 0931/404-4818).

Café Michel, across the square, is a quieter, more family-oriented tea house, serving soups, small sandwiches, cakes, tea, coffee, and—until 16:00—inexpensive egg breakfasts. This place has been around since 1911 (€2–5 plates, Mon–Sat 8:00–18:00, Sun 10:00–18:30, Marktplatz 11, tel. 0931/53776).

Weinstube Maulaffenbäck, tucked away in an alley off the cathedral, is a tiny and characteristic place for cheap Franconian meals and good wine. If you order wine, you are welcome to bring your own food—they'll provide the plate and fork. This is an old tradition unique to Würzburg: Local bakeries *(Bäckerei)* found they could make an extra buck by serving wine to thirsty customers who were waiting for fresh bread. In keeping with this tradition, stop at the butcher shop next door (conveniently owned by the same family, Mon–Fri 7:30–18:00, Sat 8:00–14:00, closed Sun) to pick up great cold cuts before finding a table (€5–7 entrées, April–Oct Mon–Sat 10:00–24:00, Nov–March Mon–Sat 16:00–23:00, closed Sun year-round, Maulhardgasse 9, tel. 0931/52351).

Pasta e Olio, a few blocks east of Market Square, is where Signora Aucone serves up fresh pasta to those on the go. Because the pasta is made here daily, the menu is limited, but usually includes a pasta dish, lasagna, a vegetarian option, and mixed antipasti. Place your order, then stand at one of the counters to eat (€4 plates, Mon–Sat 11:00–17:00, Sun 11:00–15:00, Eichhornstrasse 6, tel. 0931/16699).

At Marienberg Fortress

A self-service cafeteria/*Biergarten* next to the Mainfränkisches Museum has typical sausage-and-pretzel fare (€4–8 meals). The fancier *Burggaststätte*, next to the City History Museum, is a lesser value (€6–10 meals, same hours as museum, closed Mon, tel. 0931/47012).

Wine-Drinking to Support the Needy

Würzburg has several large wineries that produce the area's distinctive, bulbous *Bocksbeutel* bottles. These institutions, originally founded as homes for the old and poor, began making wine to pay the bills. Today, these grand Baroque complexes, which still make wine and serve the needy, have restaurants, wine shops, and extensive wine cellars (for serious buyers only).

After more than 600 years, the **Bürgerspital** now cares for about a hundred local seniors, funding its work by selling its wine. Its characteristic restaurant and wine bar are right downtown. The funky little **Hockerle** pub adjacent to the **wine store** is a time warp, filled with locals munching B.Y.O. sandwiches while sipping wine sold by the glass—as explained on its blackboard (Mon–Fri 9:00–18:00, Sat 9:00–15:00, closed Sun, corner of Theaterstrasse and Semmelstrasse at Theaterstrasse 19, tel. 0931/350-3403, www .buergerspital.de). Its **Weinstube Bürgerspital** is a classy, candlelit restaurant with a cloistered feel and gorgeous courtyard seating

(€4–8 entrées, daily 10:00–24:00, Theaterstrasse 19, tel. 0931/352-880).

Another delightful option is the **Juliusspital,** which has updated its traditional roots with a slightly modern, Mediterranean feel. The courtyard is especially popular (daily 10:00–24:00, kitchen closes at 22:00, Juliuspromenade 19, tel. 0931/54080).

TRANSPORTATION CONNECTIONS

From Würzburg by Train to: Rothenburg (hourly, just longer than 1 hr total, transfer in Steinach; 50 min to Steinach—the tiny Steinach–Rothenburg train often leaves from track 5 shortly after the Würzburg train arrives—then 14 min from Steinach to Rothenburg), **Frankfurt Airport** (1–2/hr, 1.5 hrs), **Nürnberg** (2–3/hr, 1 hr), **Munich** (1–2/hr, 2 hrs, usually with 1 or 2 changes), **Köln** (hourly, 3.5 hrs), **Berlin** (hourly, 4 hrs, 1 change). Train info: tel. 11861 (€0.60/min).

FRANKFURT

Frankfurt, while a bit low on Old World charm, offers a good look at today's no-nonsense, modern Germany. There's so much more to this country than castles and old cobbled squares. Cosmopolitan Frankfurt is a business hub of the united Europe, giving it a special sophistication and spice. Especially in the area around the train station, you'll notice the fascinating multi-ethnic flavor of the city. A third of its 650,000 residents carry foreign passports. For years, Frankfurt was a city to avoid... but today, it has a unique energy that makes it worth a look.

Planning Your Time

You might fly into or out of Frankfurt am Main, or at least pass through—this glossy city links the best wine-and-castles stretch of the Rhine to the north with the fairy-tale Romantic Road to the south. Even two or three hours in Frankfurt leaves you with some powerful impressions. The city's great sights are a 20-minute walk from its train station, which is a 12-minute train ride from its airport. At a minimum, wander the old town area (Römerberg) and head up to the top of the Main Tower for commanding city views. With more time or an overnight, Frankfurt has plenty of museums and other attractions to choose from.

ORIENTATION

(area code: 069)

Frankfurt, a forest of skyscrapers perched on the banks of the Main (pronounced "mine") River, has been dubbed Germany's "Mainhattan." The city is Germany's trade and banking capital,

leading the country in sky-scrapers (mostly bank head-quarters)...and yet, a third of Frankfurt is green space.

The convention center (Messe), the red light dis-trict, and most of the sky-scrapers are near the train station. Beyond that zone (to the east) is Frankfurt's old town, with the Römerberg, or central market square, as its focal point. Across the river, the south bank of the Main is lined with Frankfurt's top museums, and beyond that is Sachsenhausen, the characteristic restaurant zone.

Note that most museums are closed Monday and most are open until 20:00 on Wednesday (confirm at any TI).

Tourist Information

Frankfurt has several TIs. The handiest is inside the train station's main entrance, offering an abundance of brochures and a free hotel-booking service (Mon–Fri 8:00–21:00, Sat–Sun 9:00–18:00, tel. 069/2123-8800, www.frankfurt-tourismus.de). You'll find other TIs on Römerberg's square (Mon–Fri 9:30–17:30, Sat–Sun 10:00–16:00), on the pedestrian shopping street Zeil, and at the airport. At any TI, buy the city/subway map (the basic €0.50 ver-sion is fine—skip the detailed €1 map) and consider the *Frankfurt Welcome* brochure (€0.50). The TI also offers bus tours of the city (see "Tours").

Discount Deals: Two discount passes compete for your atten-tion, both sold at local TIs. The **Museum Ticket** gets you free entry into 26 museums (€12, valid 2 days). The **Frankfurt Card** gives you a transit pass (including connections to and from the airport), 50 percent off all major museums, and 25 percent off the city bus tour, which virtually pays for the pass (€8/1 day, €12/2 days). If you're touring like mad for a day, the Frankfurt Card can be worthwhile.

Arrival in Frankfurt

By Train: The Frankfurt main train station (Hauptbahnhof) bustles with travelers. The TI is in the main hall just inside the front door. Baggage check (€5/day, Mon–Fri 6:30–19:30) and lockers are in the main hall across from the TI. More lockers are near the escalators across from track 18, and at track 24 across from the post office (P.O. open Mon–Fri 7:00–19:30, Sat 8:00–16:00, closed Sun, does not accept packages, automatic stamp machine outside—€1 for postcard to US or Canada). WCs (€0.70) are under track 9/10. Inquire about train tickets in the *Reisezentrum* across from track 9 (Mon–Fri 6:00–22:00, Sat–Sun 7:00–22:00). Above the *Reisezentrum* is a peaceful lounge with a snack bar, clean WCs, telephones, and a children's play area (free entry with train ticket or railpass, free coffee and juice in first-class lounge). Pick up a snack at the good food court across from tracks 4 and 5. There's a 24-hour Internet café at the other end of the station (€0.02/minute). The station is a five-minute walk from the convention center (Messe), a three-minute subway ride or 20-minute walk from the center, or a 12-minute shuttle train from the airport.

By Plane: See "Frankfurt's Airport," page 219.

Getting Around Frankfurt

By Subway: Frankfurt's subway is easy to use, but a 10-minute wait for a train can be normal. From the train station, follow signs for *U-Bahn* (*U*, blue) or *S-Bahn* (*S*, green). Buy your tickets *(Fahrkarten)* from an RMV machine. Tickets are issued with a validating stamp already on them, and are only valid immediately after they're bought. Find your destination on the chart, key in the number, choose your ticket type, then pay. Choose *Einzelfahrt* for a regular single ticket (€2), *Kurzstrecke* for a short ride (€1.40, 3 stops or less), *Tageskarte Frankfurt* for an all-day pass (€5.40 without the airport, €8.40 with), or *Gruppenkarte* for an all-day group ticket for up to 5 adults (€8.40 without the airport, €13.70 with). An individual one-way ticket to the airport costs €3.55 (no group rate for airport-only trips).

By Taxi: A taxi stand is just outside the main entrance of the train station to your left. An average ride to the Römerberg square should cost you €7 (or up to €10 in slow traffic). To get to the airport from any of my recommended hotels, count on at least €25.

TOURS

City Bus Tour—The basic city bus tour gives a 2.5-hour orientation to Frankfurt, including Römerberg and a visit to either the Goethe House or (summer only) the observation deck of the Main Tower (€25, 25 percent discount with Frankfurt Card, recorded narration, April–Oct daily at 10:00 and 14:00, Nov–March daily at 14:00). The bus picks up at the Römerberg TI first, then 15 minutes later at the Frankfurt train station TI.

Local Guide—Elisabeth Lücke loves her city and shares it very well (€55/hr, reserve in advance, tel. 06196/45787, mobile 0173-913-3157, www.elisabeth-luecke.de, elisabeth.luecke@t-online.de).

SELF-GUIDED WALK

Welcome to Frankfurt's Römerberg

This sightseeing walk focuses on Römerberg, Frankfurt's lively market square, and begins at the train station (because that's where you'll likely arrive in Frankfurt). Allow 30 to 60 minutes, depending on whether you walk to the square from the station.

• *You'll probably start at the...*

Train Station: This is Germany's busiest train station: 350,000 travelers make their way to 25 platforms to catch 1,800 trains every day. While it was big news when it opened in the 1890s, it's a dead-end station, which, with today's high-speed trains, makes it outdated. In fact, the speedy ICE trains are threatening to bypass Frankfurt altogether unless it digs a tunnel to allow for a faster pass-through stop (a costly project that is now in the discussion stage).

• *To get to Römerberg, it's a 20-minute walk (up Kaiserstrasse), a €7–10 taxi ride, or three-minute subway ride. To take the subway, buy a ticket (see "Getting Around Frankfurt," above) and follow signs to* U-4 *(direction: Seckbacher Landstrasse) or* U-5 *(direction: Preungesheim). Choose the track with the closest* Nächste Abfahrt *(next departure) time and go two stops to Römerberg. Exit the station following* Römerberg *signs (not* Domplatz*). As you surface, you'll see the tall, red tower of St. Bartholomew's Cathedral behind you, where we'll end this walk. For now, walk around the building in front of you and downhill to...*

Römerberg: Frankfurt's market square, a ▲ sight, was the birthplace of the city. The Town Hall *(Römer)* houses the *Kaisersaal,* or Imperial Hall, where Holy Roman Emperors celebrated their coronations. Today, the *Römer* houses the city council and mayor's office. The cute row of half-timbered houses (rebuilt in 1983) opposite the *Römer* is typical of Frankfurt's quaint old center before World War II.

• *Walk past the red-and-white church downhill toward the river to Frankfurt's...*

History Museum (Historisches Museum): Most won't want to hike through the actual museum upstairs, which has two floors of artifacts, paintings, and displays—with very little English explanation (possibly closed for renovation in 2008, otherwise €4, Tue–Sun 10:00–18:00, Wed until 21:00, closed Mon, Saalgasse 19, tel. 069/2123-5599, www.historisches-museum.frankfurt.de). However, the models in the ground-floor annex are fascinating (€1, follow signs to *Altstadtmodelle,* English film and explanations).

Frankfurt

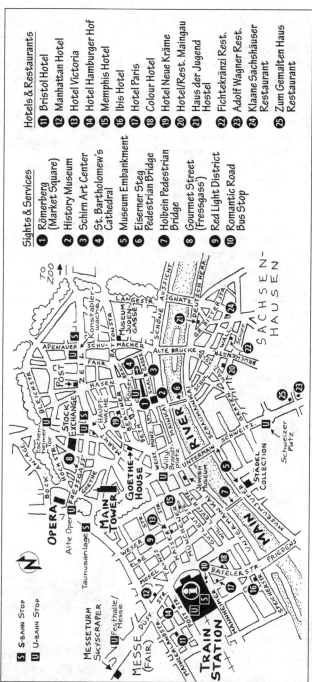

Hotels & Restaurants

⑪ Bristol Hotel
⑫ Manhattan Hotel
⑬ Hotel Victoria
⑭ Hotel Hamburger Hof
⑮ Memphis Hotel
⑯ Ibis Hotel
⑰ Hotel Paris
⑱ Colour Hotel
⑲ Hotel Neue Kräme
⑳ Hotel/Rest. Maingau
㉑ Haus der Jugend Hostel
㉒ Fichtekränzi Rest.
㉓ Adolf Wagner Rest.
㉔ Klaane Sachshäuser Restaurant
㉕ Zum Gemalten Haus Restaurant

Sights & Services

① Römerberg (Market Square)
② History Museum
③ Schirn Art Center
④ St. Bartholomew's Cathedral
⑤ Museum Embankment
⑥ Eiserner Steg Pedestrian Bridge
⑦ Holbein Pedestrian Bridge
⑧ Gourmet Street (Fressgass')
⑨ Red Light District
⑩ Romantic Road Bus Stop

S S-Bahn Stop
U U-Bahn Stop

The big model in the middle of the room shows the town in the 1930s. Study the maps of medieval Frankfurt. The wall surrounding the city was torn down in the early 1800s to make the ring of parks and lakes you see on your modern map. The long, densely packed row of houses on the eastern end of town was Frankfurt's Jewish ghetto from

1462 to 1796. The five original houses that survive comprise one of the city's two Jewish Museums (described on page 212)—Frankfurt was the birthplace of Anne Frank and the Rothschild banking family.

Go up the steps and see the horror that befell the town in 1940, 1943, and on the "fatal night" of March 23, 1944. This last Allied bombing accomplished its goal of demoralizing the city. Find the facade of the destroyed Town Hall—where you just were. The film behind this model is a good 15-minute tour of Frankfurt through the ages (ask them to change the language for you—*"Auf Englisch, bitte?"*).

• *Leaving the museum, turn right to...*

Saalgasse: Literally "Hall Street," this lane of postmodern buildings echoes the higgledy-piggledy buildings that stood here

until World War II. In the 1990s, famous architects from around the world were each given a ruined house of the same width and told to design a new building to reflect the building that stood there before the war. As you continue down the street, guess which one is an upside-down half-timbered house with the stars down below. (Hint: Animals are on the "ground floor.")

Saalgasse leads to some ancient Roman ruins in front of St. Bartholomew's Cathedral (turn left when you first see the cathedral). The grid of stubs was the subfloor of a Roman bath (allowing the floor to be heated). The small monument in the middle of the ruins commemorates the 794 meeting of Charlemagne

(king of the Franks and the first Holy Roman Emperor) with the local bishop—the first official mention of a town called Frankfurt. When Charlemagne and the Franks fled from the Saxons, a white deer led them to the easiest place to cross the Main—where the Franks could ford the river—hence, Frankfurt. The skyscraper with the yellow emblem in the distance is the tallest office block in Europe (985 feet). The shorter, glassy building next to it, also with a red-and-white antenna, is the Main Tower (open to the public—recommended and described later).

• *Behind the Roman ruins is...*

St. Bartholomew's Cathedral (Kaiserdom): Ten Holy Roman Emperors were elected and crowned in this cathedral between 1562 and 1792. The church was destroyed in World War II, rebuilt, and reopened in 1955. Walk around the front of the church and enter on the side opposite the river. Twenty-seven scenes from the life of St. Bartholomew (*Bartholomäus* in German) flank the high altar and ring the choir. Everything of value was moved to safety before the bombs came. But the delightful red-sandstone chapel of Sleeping Mary (to the left of the high altar), carved and painted in the 15th century, was too big to move—so it was fortified with sandbags. The altarpiece and fine stained glass next to it survived the bombing (free, Sat–Thu 9:00–12:00 & 14:30–20:00, Fri 15:00–20:00). An in-depth English booklet about the cathedral is available for €2.50 in the adjoining Dom Museum (€2, same hours as cathedral, not particularly interesting).

• *From the cathedral, it's a short walk to the Zeil, Frankfurt's lively department store–lined pedestrian boulevard (leading to the Opera and Main Tower, described later). Or circle back through the Römerberg to visit more old-town sights.*

SIGHTS

Near Römerberg

Paulskirche—Dominating a big square just across the street from Römerberg, this church is known as the "cradle of German democracy." It was here, during the political upheaval of 1848, that the first freely elected National Assembly met and the first German Constitution was drafted, paving the way for a united Germany in 1871. Following its destruction by Allied bombs on March 18, 1944, the church became the first historic building in the city to be rebuilt. Around the outside of the building, you'll see reliefs honoring people who contributed to the German nation, including Theodor Heuss, the first president, and John F. Kennedy, who spoke here on June 25, 1963.

Schirn Art Center (Schirn Kunsthalle)—Opened in 1986, this facility has quickly become one of Europe's most respected homes to modern and contemporary art. Rotating exhibits pay homage to everything and everyone from Kandinsky and Kahlo to contemporary artists, movements, and topics (€6–8 depending on exhibits, Tue–Sun 10:00–19:00, Wed–Thu until 22:00, closed Mon, Römerberg, tel. 069/299-8820, www.schirn-kunsthalle.de).

▲**Goethe House (Goethehaus)**—Johann Wolfgang von Goethe (1749–1832), a scientist, minister, poet, lawyer, politician, and playwright, was a towering figure in the early Romantic Age. His birthplace, now a fine museum, is a five-minute walk northwest of Römerberg. It's furnished as it was in the mid-18th century, when the boy destined to become the "German Shakespeare" grew up here (€5, €2 high-tech but easy-to-use and informative audioguide, €1.50 English booklet has same info as free laminated cards—worthwhile only as a souvenir, Mon–Sat 10:00–18:00, Sun 10:00–17:30; 15-min walk from Hauptbahnhof up Kaiserstrasse, turn right on Am Salzhaus to Grosser Hirschgraben 23; tel. 069/138-800, www.goethehaus-frankfurt.de).

Borrow a laminated card at the bottom of the stairs for a refreshingly brief commentary on each of the 16 rooms. Since nothing's roped off and there are no posted signs, it's easy to picture real people living here. Goethe's father dedicated his life and wealth to cultural pursuits, and his mother told young Johann Wolfgang fairy tales every night, stopping just before the ending so that the boy could exercise his own creativity. Goethe's family gave him all the money he needed to travel and learn. His collection of 2,000 books was sold off in 1795. Recently, 800 of these have been located and repurchased by the museum (you'll see them in the library). This building honors the man who inspired the Goethe-Institut, dedicated to keeping the German language strong.

In the Skyscraper Zone, Northwest of Römerberg

Many of Frankfurt's skyscrapers—including the Main Tower, with its observation deck (see below)—cluster between the Römerberg and the train station. In this area, you'll also find some of Frankfurt's best shopping and fine dining.

▲**Main Tower**—Finished in 2000, this tower houses the Helaba Bank and offers the best public viewpoint from a Frankfurt skyscraper. A 45-second, ear-popping elevator ride—and then 50 stairs—takes you to the 55th floor, 650 feet above the city.

Cost, Hours, Location: €4.60; April–Sept Sun–Thu 10:00–21:00, Fri–Sat 10:00–23:00; Oct–March Sun–Thu 10:00–19:00,

Fri–Sat 10:00–21:00; last entry 30 min before closing, enter at Neue Mainzer Strasse 52, near corner of Neue Schlesingerstrasse, tel. 069/3650-4777.

❶Self-Guided Spin-Tour: Here, from Frankfurt's ultimate viewpoint, survey the city circling clockwise, starting with the biggest skyscraper (with the yellow emblem).

1. Commerzbank Building: Designed by Norman Foster (of Berlin Reichstag and London City Hall fame), the Commerzbank building was finished in 1997. It's 985 feet high, with nine winter gardens spiraling up its core. Just to the left is Römerberg—the old town center. Look to the right (clockwise).

2. European Central Bank: The blue-and-gold euro symbol (€) decorates the front yard of the Euro Tower, home of the European Central Bank (a.k.a. "City of the Euro"). Its 1,000 employees administer the all-Europe currency from here. Typical of skyscrapers in the 1970s, it's slim—to allow maximum natural light into all workplaces inside. The euro symbol in the park was unveiled on January 1, 2002, the day the euro went into circulation in the first 12 Eurozone countries.

The **Museum Embankment** (see page 213) lines Schaumainkai on the far side of the Main River, just beyond the Euro Tower.

3. Airport: The Rhine–Main airport, in the distance, is the largest employment complex in Germany (62,000 workers). Frankfurt's massive train station dominates the foreground. From the station, the grand Kaiserstrasse cuts through the city to Römerberg.

4. Messe: The Frankfurt fair (Messe), marked by the skyscraper with the pointy top, is a huge convention center—the size of 40 soccer fields. It sprawls behind the skyscraper that looks like a classical column sporting a visor-like capital. (The protruding lip of the capital is heated so that icicles don't form, break off, and impale people on the street below.) Frankfurt's fair originated in 1240, when the emperor promised all participating merchants safe passage. The black twin towers of the Deutsche Bank in the foreground are typical of mid-1980s mirrored architecture.

5. West End and Good Living: The West End—with vast green spaces and the telecommunications tower—is Frankfurt's trendiest residential quarter. The city's most enjoyable zone cuts from the West End to the right. Stretching from the classic-looking **Opera House** are broad and people-filled boulevards made to order for eating and shopping. Your skyscraper spin-tour is over. Why don't you go join them?

Opera House, Gourmet Street, and Zeil—From the Opera House to pedestrian boulevards, this is Frankfurt's good-living spine. The Opera House was finished in 1880 to celebrate high German culture and the newly created nation. Mozart and Goethe flank the entrance, reminding everyone that this is a house of both music and theater. The original opera house was destroyed in World War II. Over the objections of a mayor nicknamed "Dynamite Rudy," the city rebuilt it in the original style (U-Bahn: Alte Oper). Facing the opera, turn right and walk down a restaurant-lined boulevard (Grosse Bockenheimer) nicknamed "Gourmet Street" (Fressgass'). (Frankfurt's version of Fifth Avenue, lined with top fashion shops, is the parallel Goethe Strasse.) Gourmet Street leads to Zeil, a lively, tree-lined festival-of-life pedestrian boulevard and department-store strip.

Near the Train Station

Jewish Museum (Jüdisches Museum)—Housed in the former Rothschild Palace (of the famous banking family), this worthwhile museum traces the history of Frankfurt's Jews since the 12th century. Rather than simply presenting artifacts, it tries to engage visitors in a dialogue about culture and society as a whole. The €7.80 English guidebook is unnecessary, since detailed English handouts are available on each floor (€4, €5 combo-ticket with Museum Judengasse—see next, Tue–Sun 10:00–17:00, Wed until 20:00, closed Mon, Untermainkai 14/15, tel. 069/2123-5000, www. juedischesmuseum.de). The museum is just across the road from the lovely riverside promenade, a perfect place to rest your feet and watch people and planes go by.

The museum also runs the smaller and less interesting **Museum Judengasse,** centering on the ruins of an ancient Jewish settlement. The exhibit consists of the medieval foundations of five houses, two ritual baths, and two wells (€2, €5 combo-ticket with Jewish Museum, same hours as Jewish Museum, just east of St. Bartholomew's Cathedral at Kurt-Schumacher-Strasse 10, tel. 069/297-7419).

▲Frankfurt's Red Light District—A browse through Frankfurt's sleazy red light district offers a fascinating way to kill time between trains. From the station, Taunusstrasse leads two blocks to Elbestrasse, where you'll find a zone of 20 "eros towers"—each a five-story-tall brothel filled with prostitutes. Climbing through a few of these may be one of the more memorable experiences of your European trip (€25, daily). While hiking through the towers feels safe, the aggressive women at the neighboring strip shows can be pretty unsettling. Ever since the Middle Ages, Frankfurt's thriving prostitution industry has gone hand-in-hand with its trade fairs. Today, it thrives with the Messe. Prostitutes note that business varies with the theme of the trade show—while the auto show is boom time, they complain that Frankfurt's massive book fair is a bust. Frankfurt's prostitutes are legal and taxed. Since they pay taxes, they are organizing to get the same benefits that any other taxed worker gets. This area can be dangerous if you're careless. If you take a wrong turn, you'll find creepy streets littered with drug addicts. In 1992, Frankfurt began offering "pump rooms" to its hard-drug users. These centers provide clean needles and a safe and caring place for addicts to go to maintain their habit and get counseling. More than a decade and a half later, while locals consider the program a success, wasted people congregate in neighborhoods like this one.

Across the River

The Schaumainkai riverside promenade (across the river, over the Eiserner Steg pedestrian bridge from Römerberg) is great for an evening stroll or people-watching on any sunny day. Keep your eyes peeled for nude sunbathers. On Saturdays, the museum strip street is closed off for a sprawling flea market.

Sachsenhausen District and Frankfurt's Culinary Specialties—Rather than beer-garden ambience, Frankfurt offers an apple-wine pub district. For a traditional eating-and-drinking zone with more than a hundred characteristic apple-wine pubs (and plenty of ethnic and other options), visit cobbled and cozy Sachsenhausen (wander to the east end of Schaumainkai, or from the train station take tram #16 to Schweizer Platz; also see "Eating," page 217). *Apfelwein*, drunk around here since Charlemagne's time 1,200 years ago, became more popular in the 16th century, when local grapes were diseased. It enjoyed another boost two centuries later, when a climate change meant that grapes grew poorly in the area. Apple wine is about the strength of beer (5.5 percent alcohol). It's served spiced and warm in winter, cold in summer. To complement your traditional drink with a traditional meal, order Frankfurt sausage or pork chops and kraut.

Frankfurt's Museum Embankment (Museumsufer)—The Museum Embankment features nine museums lining the Main River along Schaumainkai (mostly west of the Eiserner Steg pedestrian bridge). In the 1980s, Frankfurt decided that it wanted to buck its "Bankfurt" and "Krankfurt" (*krank* means "sick") image. It went on a culture kick and devoted 11 percent of the city budget to the arts and culture. The result: Frankfurt has become a city of art. Today, locals and tourists alike enjoy an impressive strip of museums housed in striking buildings. These nine museums (including architecture, film, world cultures, and great European masters—the Städel Collection) and a dozen others are all well described in the TI's *Museumsufer* brochure (all museums here are covered by the 2-day, €12 Museum Ticket sold at TI and participating museums—see page 204; most museums open Tue–Sun 10:00–17:00, Wed until 20:00, closed Mon; www.kultur.frankfurt.de).

SLEEPING

Avoid sleeping in Frankfurt, since the city's numerous trade fairs send hotel prices skyrocketing. In 2008, the busiest months for trade fairs are January, March, May, and June. July, August, and December have almost none, and the rest of the months fall somewhere in between (an average of eight days a month). Visit www.messefrankfurt.com (and select "Trade fairs and events") for an exact schedule.

Room prices in most Frankfurt hotels fluctuate €20 or more with demand. The price ranges listed here are only approximate, and may skew higher or lower. If you'll be overnighting in Frankfurt during a non-convention summer weekend, you can land a great place relatively cheaply—call around to several places to get the best deal.

Near the Train Station

Pleasant Rhine or Romantic Road towns are just a quick drive or train ride away. But if you must spend the night in Frankfurt, here are some places within a few blocks of the train station (and its fast and handy train to the airport; to sleep even nearer to the airport, see "Frankfurt's Airport," page 219). This isn't the safest neighborhood; don't wander into seedy-feeling streets, and be careful after dark.

For a rough idea of directions to hotels, stand with your back to the main entrance of the station: Hotel Manhattan is across the street at 10 o'clock, Hotel Victoria at 1 o'clock, Hotel Memphis at 2 o'clock, Colour Hotel at 4 o'clock, Hotel Paris at 5 o'clock, and Bristol Hotel and Hotel Hamburger Hof at 7 o'clock. The Ibis Hotel is on a nicer street two blocks beyond Hotel Paris.

Sleep Code

(€1 = about $1.30, country code: 49, area code: 069)
S = Single, **D** = Double/Twin, **T** = Triple, **Q** = Quad, **b** = bathroom, **s** = shower only. Unless otherwise noted, credit cards are accepted, English is spoken, and breakfast is included.

To help you sort easily through these listings, I've divided the rooms into three categories, based on the price for a standard double room with bath:

$$$ **Higher Priced**—Most rooms €100 or more.
$$ **Moderately Priced**—Most rooms between €70–100.
$ **Lower Priced**—Most rooms €70 or less.

$$$ Bristol Hotel is a swanky boutique hotel run by Michael Rosen. The Bristol reflects a new generation of train-station hotels, serving up style and flair, from its nod to Pacific Rim architecture to its teak-furnished patio café called Summer Lounge. Thirsty? Have a drink at the 24-hour bar downstairs. Just two blocks from the station, it's surprisingly quiet. If you're looking to splurge on your first or last night in Europe, this is the place (Sb-€55–90, larger Sb-€70–110, Db-€85–140, huge breakfast buffet, elevator, free Internet access, Ludwigstrasse 15, tel. 069/242-390, fax 069/251-539, www.bristol-hotel.de, info@bristol-hotel.de).

$$ Manhattan Hotel, with 60 late-1980s-chic rooms, is beautifully located across from the station. An unusual mix of a warm and accommodating staff with all the business-class comforts, it also includes a scrumptious breakfast buffet (Sb-€90, Db-€105, show this book to get a 10 percent break during non-convention times in 2008, further discount when really slow—including weekends, kids under 12 free, elevator, free Internet access, Düsseldorfer Strasse 10, tel. 069/269-5970, fax 069/2695-97777, www.manhattan -hotel.com, manhattan-hotel@t-online.de) The Manhattan is also run by Hotel Bristol's Michael Rosen. If these two are full, ask about Herr Rosen's reliably good other hotels, including the Gerbermühle and the Pure.

$$ Hotel Victoria, midway between the station and Römerberg on the grand Kaiserstrasse, is friendly and has 75 rooms (Sb-€65–85, Db-€75–95, suite-€105–120, prices can triple during conventions, Kaiserstrasse 59, entrance on Elbestrasse, tel. 069/273-060, fax 069/2730-6100, www.victoriahotel.de, victoria -hotel@t-online.de).

$$ Hotel Hamburger Hof, directly across from the train station, has a shiny lobby and 66 elegantly simple, spacious rooms. The side facing the station is cheerfully sunny, and rooms on the other side are quieter (Sb-€55–70, Db-€75–90, Tb-€90, non-smoking floors, elevator, free Internet access, Poststrasse 10–12, tel. 069/2713-9690, fax 069/235-802, www.hamburgerhof.com, hamburgerhof@t-online.de).

$$ Memphis Hotel, three long blocks from the station on a busy street in the colorful Turkish district, is another stylish business hotel that's affordable when there's no convention in town (Sb-€55–85, Db-€70–90, prices soft—call for exact rates, ask for a room on the quiet side—*ruhige Seite*, Münchener Strasse 15, tel. 069/242-6090, fax 069/2426-0999, www.memphis-hotel.de, memphis-hotel@t-online.de).

$$ Ibis Hotel Frankfurt Friedensbrücke, a reliable chain hotel, is a good value, with 233 identical rooms on a quiet riverside street away from the station riffraff (Sb/Db-€59–76, or €159 during fairs, Tb-€79–96, lower prices are for weekends, breakfast-€9.50

per person, non-smoking rooms, elevator, parking-€10/day; exit station to right and follow Baseler Strasse 3 blocks, before river turn right on Speicherstrasse to #4; tel. 069/273-030, fax 069/237-024, www.ibishotel.com, h1445@accor.com).

$ Hotel Paris has 30 fine but small rooms and a nice staff, making this a great value (Sb-€45, or €90 during conventions; Db-€60, or €110 during conventions; Tb-€70, Karlsruher Strasse 8, tel. 069/273-9963, fax 069/2739-9651, www.hotelparis.de, reservation@hotelparis.de).

$ Colour Hotel is a funky, minimalist, primary-colors type of place across from the station. It has a bustling bar in the lobby and kind management, and it feels safe (S-€49, Sb-€59, D-€59, Db-€69, Tb-€79, Qb-€89, prices soft, breakfast-€7, free Internet access, Baseler Strasse 52, tel. 069/3650-7580, fax 069/252-845, www.colourhotel.de, info@colourhotel.de).

Away from the Station

Hotel Neue Kräme is near Römerberg, Hotel Maingau is in the Sachsenhausen District (see page 213), and the hostel is a bus ride away.

$$$ Hotel Neue Kräme is a quiet little oasis tucked away above the center of Frankfurt's downtown action, just steps from Römerberg and the restaurant-filled Fressgass'. Friendly Hermann, who lived in the US and loves to revive his English, welcomes guests in this bright and cheerful little blue-and-white place. If you are just here for one night, stay near the station—but if you're in town for a few days and want a central base, you'll enjoy this location (Sb-€70–85, Db-€85–105, prices much higher during conventions, non-smoking rooms, elevator, parking-€27/day, Neue Kräme 23, tel. 069/284-046, fax 069/296-288, www.hotel-neuekraeme.de, hotel.neuekraeme@t-online.de).

$$ Hotel Maingau, located across the river in the museum- and pub-friendly Sachsenhausen District, is in a quiet, residential neighborhood facing a park. The hotel hallways are dark, but the rooms are bright. If you're looking for a little tranquility away from the station, stay here (Sb-€60–75, Db-€75–95, Tb-€100–110, prices soft—lower prices are for weekends and in summer; fancy dinners at adjacent Maingau restaurant—see "Eating"; Schiffer Strasse 38–40, tel. 069/609-140, fax 069/620-790, www.maingau.de, hotel@maingau.de).

$ *Hostel:* The **Haus der Jugend** hostel, with 440 beds, is open to guests of any age (€20–24 per bed in 8- and 10-bed dorms, €24–28 in 3- to 4-bed dorms, Sb-€38–43, Db-€66–76, higher prices are for guests age 27 or older; price includes daily hostel membership fee, sheets, and breakfast; €4.80 for lunch or dinner, Internet access, laundry, 2:00 curfew; take bus #46 (direction: Mühlberg)—goes

2/hr from station to Frankensteiner Platz, Deutschherrnufer 12; tel. 069/610-0150, fax 069/6100-1599, www.jugendherberge-frankfurt .de, jugendherberge_frankfurt@t-online.de).

EATING

The Sachsenhausen District, an easy walk from Schweizer Platz, abounds with traditional apple-wine pubs (see page 213). All the ones I've listed have both indoor and outdoor seating in a woodsy, rustic setting. Not just for tourists, these characteristic places are popular with Frankfurters, too. If you are craving *Leiterchen* ("mini-ladders," or spare ribs—surprisingly meaty and salty), these are your best bet. Here are two more local specialties, available at most apple-wine bars, for the adventurous to try: boiled eggs (or beef) and potatoes topped with a green sauce of seven herbs, called *Grüne Sosse;* or an aged, cylindrical, ricotta-like cheese served with onions and vinegar, called *Handkäse mit Musik* ("hand cheese with music").

Fichtekränzi offers the typical specialties (and some lighter fare) both in its cozy bench-filled beer hall, and outside under the trees. The staff is friendly and the atmosphere relaxed—expect to share a table and make some new friends (€7–12 entrées, daily from 17:00, Wall Strasse 5, tel. 069/612-778).

Adolf Wagner is a traditional joint that serves a local con-stituency. It tends to get a little smoky, so try to score a table in the outside courtyard area (€7–13 entrées, daily 11:00–24:00, Schweizer Strasse 71, tel. 069/612-565).

Klaane Sachshäuser, owned by the same family for five gen-erations, is popular with German tour groups and locals alike, and prides itself on its *Leiterchen* (€7–15 entrées, Mon–Sat from 16:00, closed Sun, Neuer Wall 11, tel. 069/615-983).

Zum Gemalten Haus, named for the wall murals that adorn its facade, serves German cuisine and is deceptively mellow—it's rumored to get a little wild on the weekends (€5–12 entrées, Tue–Sun 10:00–24:00, closed Mon, Schweizer Strasse 67, tel. 069/614-559).

Pub Crawl: Irish pubs and salsa bars clutter the pedestrian zone around Rittergasse and Klappergasse, just north of the Affentor. The cobblestone streets and medieval buildings feel like Epcot Center, rather than historic Frankfurt. But if you're looking for a place to do a pub crawl, this is it.

International Splurge: **Maingau** is *the* place for a break from traditional German food and pubs. Often hailed as one of the best restaurants in Frankfurt, it boasts an extensive wine list, fancy "tasting *menus,*" recommended wine pairings, and an inter-national lineup, including filet of venison and vegetarian options such as thyme-infused risotto. For less of an investment, indulge in a three-course lunch special. Don't be fooled by its modest exterior—this place is elegant inside (€15–26 entrées; fixed-price meals are €13–30 for lunch, €25–46 for dinner, more with wine pairings; Tue–Fri 11:30–15:00 & 17:00–22:30, Sat 18:00–22:30, Sun 11:30–15:00, closed Mon, call for reservations, tel. 069/610-752, Schiffer Strasse 38, www.maingau.de).

TRANSPORTATION CONNECTIONS

Frankfurt am Main

From Frankfurt by Train to: Rothenburg (hourly, 2.5–3 hrs, changes in Würzburg and Steinach; the tiny Steinach–Rothenburg train often leaves from track 5, shortly after the Würzburg train arrives), **Würzburg** (hourly, 1.5–2 hrs), **Nürnberg** (at least hourly, 2 hrs), **Munich** (hourly, 3.5 hrs, occasionally with 1 change), **Baden-Baden** (at least hourly, 1.5 hrs, transfer in Mannheim or Karlsruhe), **Bacharach** (hourly, 1.5 hrs, change in Mainz; first train to Bacharach departs at 6:00, last train at 20:45), **Freiburg** (hourly, 2 hrs, some require change in Mannheim), **Bonn** (2/hr, 1.5–2 hrs, most with change in Mainz or Köln), **Koblenz** (1–2/hr, 1.5–2 hrs direct, some with change in Mainz), **Köln** (2/hr, 1.25 hrs, many with change in Mainz or Frankfurt's airport), **Berlin** (2/hr, 4.5 hrs), **Amsterdam** (every 2 hrs, 4 hrs direct), **Bern** (hourly, 4 hrs, many with changes in Basel), **Brussels** (nearly hourly, 4–5 hrs, change in Köln), **Copenhagen** (4/day, 9 hrs, change in Hamburg), **London** (5/day, 7–8 hrs, 1–4 changes), **Milan** (hourly, 8–9 hrs, 1–2 changes), **Paris** (5/day, 4–6 hrs, 1–2 changes), **Vienna** (3/day direct, 2 more with change in Munich or Würzburg, 7.5 hrs). Train info: tel. 11861 (€0.60/min).

Romantic Road Bus: If you're taking this bus tour, you can either pay cash when you board, or buy your ticket at the Deutsche Touring office at the train station (Mon–Fri 7:00–19:00, Sat 7:00–14:00, Sun 7:00–13:00; entrance at Mannheimer Strasse 15—from inside the station, follow signs to *Südausgang,* bus stop is to the right under the white canopy marked with turquoise *Touring* sign, Deutsche Touring office is across the street from this stop; tel. 069/790-3230, www.romantic-road-coach.de). While the company claims you're 90 percent safe without a reservation, you can book a seat for free by calling 01805/790-303. The Frankfurt–Munich bus trip costs €99. Travelers with railpasses that cover Germany (German or Eurail) get a 60 percent discount (does not use up a flexipass day). The bus departs from in front of the Deutsche Touring office promptly at 8:00 (April–Oct; confirm time at TI, Deutsche Touring office, or www.euraide.de/ricksteves).

Frankfurt

Frankfurt's Airport

The airport *(Flughafen)* is user-friendly. There are two separate terminals (know your terminal—call the airline). All trains and subways operate out of Terminal 1 (but taxis serve both). A skyline train connects the two terminals.

The airport offers showers (€6), a baggage-check desk (daily 6:00–22:00, €3.50 per bag, per day), lockers (€3–5/24 hrs, depending on size), free Internet access (at the *e-lounge* by departures Terminal 1B), ATMs, fair banks with long hours, a grocery store (daily 6:30–21:30, Terminal 1, on level 0 between sectors A and B), a post office, a train station, a business lounge (Europe City Club—€16/4 hrs for anyone with a plane ticket, on departure level, daily 7:00–22:00), easy rental-car pickup, plenty of parking, an information booth, a pharmacy (7:00–21:30, Terminal 1B), a medical clinic (Terminal 1C), a casino, and even McBeer. McWelcome to Germany.

If you're meeting someone, each terminal has a hard-to-miss "meeting point" near where those arriving pop out.

Airport Info: For flight information in English, call 01805-372-4636 (www.airportcity-frankfurt.com) or contact the airlines directly during business hours (wait for an announcement in English): Lufthansa—tel. 01803-803-803 or 069/6969-4433, American Airlines—tel. 069/5098-5070, Delta—tel. 01803-337-880 or 069/6902-8751, Northwest/KLM—tel. 01805-214-201. Pick up the free brochure *Your Airport Guide* for a map and detailed information on airport services (available at the airport and at most Frankfurt hotels).

Getting Between the Airport and Downtown Frankfurt: The airport is a 12-minute train ride from Frankfurt's downtown train station (€3.55, 4/hr, ride included in €8 Frankfurt Card and €8.40 version of all-day *Tageskarte Frankfurt* transit pass, but not in €5.40 version of *Tageskarte Frankfurt*). Figure about €25 for a taxi from any of my recommended hotels.

From Frankfurt Airport by Train: The airport has its own train station (at Terminal 1). Train travelers can validate railpasses or buy tickets at this airport station. Connections include to **Rothenburg** (hourly, 3 hrs, with transfers in Würzburg and Steinach), **Würzburg** (1–2/hr, 1.5 hrs), **Nürnberg** (1–2/hr, 2.5 hrs), **Munich** (2/hr, 3.5 hrs, some with 1 change), **Baden-Baden** (roughly hourly, 1.5 hrs), **Köln** (1–3/hr, 1 hr), **Koblenz** (1–2/hr, 1.25 hrs, several require transfer in Mainz), **Bacharach** (hourly, 1–1.5 hrs, most change in Mainz or Bingen; first train to Bacharach departs at 3:49, then at 5:00 Mon–Fri or 6:00 Sat–Sun, last train at 21:00), and **international destinations** (such as Paris, London, Milan, Amsterdam, Vienna, and many more).

Flying Home from Frankfurt: Some of the trains from

the Rhine stop at the airport on their way into Frankfurt (1–1.5 hrs, e.g., hourly direct from Bonn; hourly from Bacharach with a change in Mainz; earliest train from Bacharach to Frankfurt leaves Mon–Fri at about 5:30, Sat at 6:30, Sun at 7:30; last train at 22:30). By car, head toward Frankfurt on the autobahn and follow the little airplane signs to the airport.

Sleeping at Frankfurt Airport: You can sleep at the airport, but you'll pay a premium and miss out on seeing Frankfurt. Considering the ease of the shuttle train from Frankfurt (4/hr, 12 min), I don't advise it. But if you must, the airport **$$$ Sheraton** has 1,000 international business-class rooms (rates vary wildly depending on season and conventions, but Db usually about €200–250, about 25 percent discount with major corporate ID—try anything, AAA and senior discounts, kids up to age 18 free in the room, includes big breakfast, non-smoking rooms, fitness club, Terminal 1, tel. 069/69770, fax 069/6977-2351, www .sheraton.com/frankfurt, reservationsfrankfurt@sheraton.com). The **$$ Ibis** has cheaper rooms in the same neighborhood, but it isn't as handy and the staff is impersonal (Db-€70–80, breakfast-€9.50, Internet access, Langer Kornweg 9a–11, Kelsterbach, tel. 06107/9870, fax 06107/987-444, www.ibishotel.com, h2203 @accor-hotels.com).

Route Tips for Drivers

Frankfurt to Rothenburg: The three-hour autobahn drive from the airport to Rothenburg is something even a jet-lagged zombie can handle. It's a 75-mile straight shot to Würzburg on A-3; just follow the blue autobahn signs to *Würzburg*. While you can carry on to Rothenburg by autobahn, for a scenic back-road approach, leave the freeway at the Heidingsfeld–Würzburg exit. If going directly to Rothenburg, follow signs south to *Stuttgart/ Ulm/Road 19,* then continue to Rothenburg via a scenic slice of the Romantic Road. If stopping at Würzburg, leave the freeway at the Heidingsfeld–Würzburg exit and follow *Stadtmitte,* then *Zentrum* and *Residenz* signs from the same freeway exit. From Würzburg, *Ulm/Road 19* signs lead to Bad Mergentheim and Rothenburg.

Frankfurt to the Rhine: Driving from Frankfurt to the Rhine or Mosel takes 90 minutes (follow blue autobahn signs from airport, major cities are signposted).

The Rhine to Frankfurt: From St. Goar or Bacharach, follow the river to Bingen, then autobahn signs to *Mainz,* then *Frankfurt,* then *Messe,* and finally the *Hauptbahnhof* (train station). The Hauptbahnhof garage (€22.50/day) is under the station, near most recommended hotels.

RHINE VALLEY

The Rhine Valley is storybook Germany, a fairy-tale world of legends and robber-baron castles. Cruise the most castle-studded stretch of the romantic Rhine as you listen for the song of the treacherous Loreley. For hands-on thrills, climb through the Rhineland's greatest castle, Rheinfels, above the town of St. Goar. Castle connoisseurs will also enjoy the fine interior of Marksburg Castle. Spend your nights in a castle-crowned village, either Bacharach or St. Goar. With more time, mosey through the neighboring Mosel Valley (see next chapter).

Planning Your Time

The Rhineland does not take much time to see. Both Bacharach and St. Goar are an easy 90-minute train ride from Frankfurt Airport, and make a good first or last stop for air travelers.

The blitziest tour of the area is an hour at Köln's cathedral (see Köln chapter, page 293) and an hour looking at the castles from your train window. But for a better look, cruise in, tour a castle or two, sleep in a medieval town, and take the train out. If you have limited time, cruise less and explore Rheinfels Castle.

Ideally, if you have only two nights to spend here, sleep in Bacharach, cruise the best hour of the river (from Bacharach to St. Goar), and tour the Rheinfels Castle. Those with more time can ride the riverside bike path. With another day, day-trip to the Mosel or Köln.

If you have all the time in the world, you could visit countless castles without leaving this region. But with limited time and energy, you need to be selective in your castle-going. Aside from Rheinfels Castle, my favorites are Burg Eltz (see page 267 in next chapter; medieval interior, well-preserved, lost in a romantic forest in the next valley over), Marksburg Castle (page 233; rebuilt medieval interior, commanding Rhine setting), and Rheinstein Castle (page 237; 19th-century duke's hunting palace overlooking the Rhine). Of these, Rheinfels is the only castle that's easy to reach by train. Though only in German, www.burgen-am-rhein .de is a handy website with photos and opening times of the main Rhine castles.

The Best of the Rhine

Ever since Roman times, when this was the empire's northern boundary, the Rhine has been one of the world's busiest shipping rivers. You'll see a steady flow of barges with 1,000- to 2,000-ton loads. Tourist-packed buses, hot train tracks, and highways line both banks.

Many of the castles were "robber-baron" castles, put there by petty rulers (there were 300 independent little countries in medieval Germany, a region about the size of Montana) to levy tolls on passing river traffic. A robber baron would put his castle on, or even in, the river. Then, often with the help of chains and a tower on the opposite bank, he'd stop each ship and get his toll. There were 10 customs stops in the 60-mile stretch between Mainz and Koblenz alone (no wonder merchants were early proponents of the creation of larger nation-states).

Some castles were built to control and protect settlements, and others were the residences of kings. As times changed, so did the lifestyles of the rich and feudal. Many castles were abandoned for more comfortable mansions in the towns.

Most Rhine castles date from the 11th, 12th, and 13th centuries. When the pope successfully asserted his power over the German emperor in 1076, local princes ran wild over the rule of their emperor. The castles saw military action in the 1300s and 1400s, as emperors began reasserting their control over Germany's many silly kingdoms.

The castles were also involved in the Reformation wars, in which Europe's Catholic and Protestant dynasties fought it out using a fragmented Germany as their battleground. The Thirty Years' War (1618–1648) devastated Germany. The outcome: Each ruler got the freedom to decide if his people would be Catholic or Protestant, and one-third of Germany was dead. (Production of Gummi bears ceased entirely.)

The French—who feared a strong Germany and felt the Rhine was the logical border between them and Germany—destroyed most of the castles prophylactically (Louis XIV in the 1680s, the

Rhine Overview

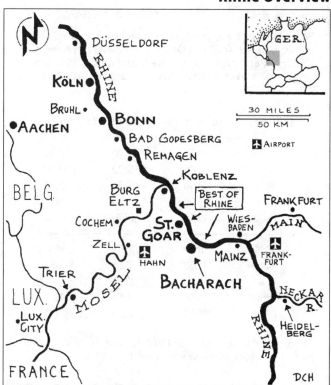

Revolutionary army in the 1790s, and Napoleon in 1806). Many were rebuilt in Neo-Gothic style in the Romantic Age—the late 1800s—and today are enjoyed as restaurants, hotels, hostels, and museums. These days, the Rhine Valley is in a bit of a rut. After the US military pulled out of the region, tourism took a hit, and jobs became scarce.

Getting Around the Rhine

While the Rhine flows north from Switzerland to Holland, the scenic stretch from Mainz to Koblenz hoards all the touristic charm. Studded with the crenellated cream of Germany's castles, it bustles with boats, trains, and highway traffic. Have fun exploring with a mix of big steamers, tiny ferries *(Fähre)*, trains, and bikes.

By Boat: While some travelers do the whole Mainz–Koblenz trip by boat (5.5 hours downstream, 8.5 hours up), I'd just focus on the most scenic hour—from St. Goar to Bacharach. Sit on the top deck with your handy Rhine map-guide (or the kilometer-keyed tour in this chapter) and enjoy the parade of castles, towns, boats,

K-D Line Rhine Cruise Schedule

Boats run May through September and on a reduced schedule for parts of April and October; no boats run November through March. These times are based on the 2007 schedule. Check www.k-d.com or www.euraide.de/ricksteves for changes.

Koblenz	Boppard	St. Goar	Bacharach
—	9:00	10:20	11:30
*9:00	*11:00	*12:20	*13:30
11:00	13:00	14:20	15:30
—	14:00	15:20	16:30
14:00	16:00	17:20	18:30
13:10	11:50	10:55	10:15
14:10	12:50	11:55	11:15
—	13:50	12:55	—
18:10	16:50	15:55	15:15
*20:10	*18:50	*17:55	*17:15

These sailings are on the 1913 steamer Goethe, *with working paddle wheel and viewable engine room.*

and vineyards.

Two boat companies take travelers along this stretch of the Rhine. Most travelers sail on the bigger, more expensive, and romantic Köln–Düsseldorfer (K-D) Line (free with a German railpass or any Eurailpass that covers Germany, but uses up a day of any flexipass; otherwise about €9 for the first hour, then progressively cheaper per hour; the recommended Bacharach–St. Goar trip costs €10 one-way, €12 round-trip; bikes cost €1.70; half-price days: Tue for bicyclists, Mon and Fri for seniors over 60; tel. 06741/1634 in St. Goar, tel. 06743/1322 in Bacharach, www.k-d.com). Boats run daily in both directions April through October, with no boats off-season (see the abridged schedule above). Complete, up-to-date schedules are posted in any Rhineland station, hotel, or TI; at www.k-d.com; and at www.euraide.de/ricksteves. Purchase tickets at the dock up to five minutes before departure. (Confirm times at your hotel the night before.) The boat is never full. Romantics will enjoy the old-time paddle-wheel *Goethe*, which sails each direction once a day (see "K-D Line Rhine Cruise Schedule" above; €1.50

extra, confirm time locally).

The smaller Bingen–Rüdesheimer Line is slightly cheaper than K-D (railpasses not valid, buy tickets on boat, tel. 06721/14140, www.bingen-ruedesheimer.com), with three two-hour round-trip St. Goar–Bacharach trips daily from mid-April to October (€9 one-way, €11 round-trip; departing St. Goar at 11:00, 14:10, and 16:10; departing Bacharach at 10:10, 12:00, and 15:00).

By Car: Drivers have these options: 1) skip the boat; 2) take a round-trip cruise from St. Goar or Bacharach; 3) draw pretzels and let the loser drive, prepare the picnic, and meet the boat; 4) rent a bike, bring it on the boat for free, and bike back; or 5) take the boat one-way and return by train. When exploring by car, don't hesitate to pop onto one of the many little ferries that shuttle across the bridgeless-around-here river (see below).

By Ferry: While there are no bridges between Koblenz and Mainz, you'll see car-and-passenger ferries (usually family-run for generations) about every three miles (pay on the boat). Bingen–Rüdesheim, Lorch–Niederheimbach, Engelsburg–Kaub, and St. Goar–St. Goarshausen are some of the most useful routes (times vary; St. Goar–St. Goarshausen ferry departs each side every 15–20 min, Mon–Sat 6:00–21:00, Sun 8:00–21:00, May–Sept until 23:00, one-way fares: adult-€1.30, car and driver-€3, www.faehre -loreley.de). For a fun little jaunt, take a quick round-trip with some time to explore the other side.

By Bike: You can bike on either side of the Rhine, but for a designated bike path, stay on the west side, where a 35-mile path runs between Koblenz and Bingen. The six-mile stretch between St. Goar and Bacharach is smooth and scenic, but mostly along the highway. The bit from Bacharach to Bingen hugs the riverside and is road-free. Either way, biking is a great way to explore the valley. Many hotels provide free or cheap bikes to guests; in Bacharach, anyone can rent bikes at Hotel Hillen (see page 245, €10/day for non-guests).

Consider biking one-way and taking the bike on the riverboat back, or designing a circular trip using the fun and frequent shuttle ferries. A good target might be Kaub (where a tiny boat shuttles sightseers to the better-from-a-distance castle on the island) or Rheinstein Castle.

By Train: Hourly milk-run trains down the Rhine hit every town (St. Goar–Bacharach, 12 min; Bacharach–Mainz, 60 min; Koblenz–Mainz, 90 min). Some train schedules list St. Goar but not Bacharach as a stop, but any schedule listing St. Goar also stops at Bacharach. Tiny stations are not staffed—buy tickets at the platform machines (user-friendly, takes paper money). Prices are cheap (for example, €2.90 between St. Goar and Bacharach); consider the Rhineland-Pfalz-Ticket, which covers travel on milk-run

Best of the Rhine

NOTE:
NUMBERS REFER
TO RIVERSIDE SIGNS
INDICATING KILOMETERS
NORTH OF THE RHINEFALLS

TO BONN & KÖLN

TO COCHEM & BURG ELTZ

EHRENBREITSTEIN

KOBLENZ 590

5 MILES
8 KM

STOLZENFELS

LAHNECK 585

MARKSBURG 580

BOPPARD 570

STERRENBERG & LIEBENSTEIN 567

MAUS 559

ST. GOARSHAUSEN

RHEINFELS

KATZ 556

ST. GOAR 557

LORELEY 554

KAUB

GUTENFELS 546

OBERWESEL 550

PFALZ

SCHÖNBURG

NIEDERWALD MONUMENT 528

LORCH 540

STAHLECK

ASSMANNS-HAUSEN

RÜDES-HEIM

BACHARACH 543

SOONECK 538

REICHENSTEIN 534

TO MAINZ

BINGEN

MÄUSETURM

RHEINSTEIN 533

EHRENFELS 530

DCH

🏰 CASTLE
■ OTHER MONUMENT
● TOWN
⋯ CAR FERRIES

trains to anywhere in this chapter—and the Mosel and Trier chapters—for up to five people (€25, not good before 9:00 on weekdays). Express trains speed past the small towns, taking only 50 minutes between Koblenz and Mainz.

SELF-GUIDED TOUR

▲▲▲Rhine Blitz Tour by Train or Boat

One of Europe's great train thrills is zipping along the Rhine enjoying this blitz tour. Or, even better, do it relaxing on the deck of a Rhine steamer, surrounded by the wonders of this romantic and historic gorge. This quick and easy tour (you can cut in any-where) skips the syrupy myths filling normal Rhine guides. You can follow along on a train, bike, car, or boat. By train or boat, sit on the left (river) side going south from Koblenz. While nearly all the castles listed are viewed from this side, train travelers need to clear a path to the right window for the times I yell, "Cross over!"

You'll notice large black-and-white kilometer markers along the riverbank. I erected these years ago to make this tour easier to follow. They tell the distance from the Rhinefalls, where the Rhine leaves Switzerland and becomes navigable. Now the river-barge pilots have accepted these as navigational aids as well. We're tackling just 36 miles (58 kilometers) of the 820-mile-long (1,320-kilometer) Rhine. Your Rhine Blitz Tour starts at Koblenz and heads upstream to Bingen. If you're going the other direction, it still works. Just hold the book upside-down.

Km 590—Koblenz: This Rhine blitz starts with Romantic Rhine thrills—at Koblenz. Koblenz is not a nice city (it was really hit hard in World War II), but its place as the historic *Deutsche Eck* (German corner)—the tip of land where the Mosel joins the Rhine—gives it a certain historic charm. Koblenz, from the Latin for "confluence," has Roman origins. Walk through the park, noticing the reconstructed memorial to the *Kaiser*. Across the river, the yellow Ehrenbreitstein Castle now houses a hostel. It's a 30-minute hike from the station to the Koblenz boat dock.

Km 585—Lahneck Castle (Burg Lahneck): Above the modern autobahn bridge over the Lahn River, this castle *(Burg)* was built in 1240 to defend local silver mines; the castle was ruined by the French in 1688 and rebuilt in the 1850s in Neo-Gothic style. Burg Lahneck faces another Romantic rebuild, the yellow Schloss Stolzenfels (out of view above the train, a 10-min climb from tiny parking lot, open for touring, closed Mon). Note that a *Burg* is a defensive fortress, while a *Schloss* is mainly a showy palace.

Km 580—Marksburg Castle: This castle (black and white, with the three modern chimneys behind it, just before town of Spay) is the best-looking of all the Rhine castles and the only surviving medieval castle on the Rhine. Because of its command-ing position, it was never attacked in the Middle Ages (though it was captured by the US Army in March 1945). It's now open as a museum with a medieval interior second only to the Mosel's Burg Eltz (see self-guided tour of Marksburg Castle, page 233; for all the details on Burg Eltz, see page 267). The three modern smoke-stacks vent Europe's biggest car-battery recycling plant just up the valley. (If you haven't read the sidebar on river traffic on page 228, now's a good time.)

Km 570—Boppard: Once a Roman town, Boppard has some impressive remains of fourth-century walls. Notice the Roman

Rhine River Trade and Barge-Watching

The Rhine is great for barge-watching. There's a constant parade of action, and each boat is different. Since ancient times, this has been a highway for trade. Today, the world's biggest port (Rotterdam) waits at the mouth of the river.

Barge workers are almost a subculture. Many own their own ships. The captain (and family) live in the stern. Workers live in the bow. The family car often decorates the bow like a shiny hood ornament. In the Rhine town of Kaub, there was once a boarding school for the children of the Rhine merchant marine—but today it's closed, since most captains are Dutch, Belgian, or Swiss. The flag of the boat's home country flies in the stern (Dutch—horizontal red, white, and blue; Belgian: vertical black, yellow, and red; Swiss—white cross on a red field; German—horizontal black, red, and yellow; or French—vertical red, white, and blue). Logically, imports go upstream (Japanese cars, coal, and oil) and exports go downstream (German cars, chemicals, and pharmaceuticals). A clever captain manages to ship goods in each direction. Recently, giant Dutch container ships (which transport five times the cargo) are driving many of the traditional barges out of business, presenting the German economy with another challenge.

Tugs can push a floating train of up to five barges at once. Upstream it gets steeper and they can push only one at a time. Before modern shipping, horses dragged boats upstream (the faint remains of towpaths survive at points along the river). From 1873 to 1900, they laid a chain from Bonn to Bingen, and boats with cogwheels and steam engines hoisted themselves

towers and the substantial chunk of Roman wall near the train station, just above the main square.

If you visit Boppard, head to the fascinating church below the main square. Find the carved Romanesque crazies at the doorway. Inside, to the right of the entrance, you'll see Christian symbols from Roman times. Also notice the painted arches and vaults. Originally most Romanesque churches were painted this way. Down by the river, look for the high-water *(Hochwasser)* marks on the arches from various flood years. (You'll find these flood marks throughout the Rhine and Mosel Valleys.)

Km 567—Sterrenberg Castle and Liebenstein Castle: These are the "Hostile Brothers" castles across from Bad Salzig. Take the wall between the castles (actually designed to improve the defenses of both castles), add two greedy and jealous brothers and a fair maiden, and create your own legend. Burg Liebenstein is now a fun, friendly, and affordable family-run hotel (9 rooms,

upstream. Today, 265 million tons travel each year along the 530 miles from Basel on the German–Swiss border to the Dutch city of Rotterdam on the Atlantic.

Riverside navigational aids are of vital interest to captains

who don't wish to meet the Loreley (see page 230). Boats pass on the right unless they clearly signal otherwise with a large blue sign. Since downstream ships can't stop or maneuver as freely, upstream boats are expected to do the tricky do-si-do work. Cameras monitor traffic all along and relay warnings of oncoming ships by posting large triangular signals before narrow and troublesome bends in the river. There may be two or three triangles per signpost, depending upon how many "sectors," or segments, of the river are covered. The lowest triangle indicates the nearest stretch of river. Each triangle tells whether there's a ship in that sector. When the bottom side of a triangle is lit, that sector is empty. When the left side is lit, an oncoming ship is in that sector.

The **Signal and Riverpilots Museum** (Wahrschauer- und Lotsenmuseum), located at the signal triangles at the upstream edge of St. Goar, explains how barges are safer, cleaner, and more fuel-efficient than trains or trucks (May–Sept Wed and Sat 14:00–17:00, outdoor exhibits always open).

Db-€110, suite-€135, giant king-and-the-family room-€210, easy parking, tel. 06773/308 or 06773/251, www.castle-liebenstein.com, hotel-burg-liebenstein@rhinecastles.com, Nickenig family).

Km 560: While you can see nothing from here, a 19th-century lead mine functioned on both sides of the river, with a shaft actually tunneling completely under the Rhine.

Km 559—Maus Castle (Burg Maus): The Maus (mouse) got its name because the next castle was owned by the Katzenelnbogen family. (*Katz* means "cat.") In the 1300s, it was considered a state-of-the-art fortification...until Napoleon had it blown up in 1806 with state-of-the-art explosives. It was rebuilt true to its original plans in about 1900. Today, the castle hosts a falconry show (€7, Tue–Sun at 11:00 and 14:30, also at 16:30 on Sun, closed Mon, 20-min walk up, tel. 06771/7669, www.burg-maus.de).

Km 557—St. Goar and Rheinfels Castle: Cross to the other side of the train. The pleasant town of St. Goar was named for a sixth-century hometown monk. It originated in Celtic times (really old) as a place where sailors would stop, catch their breath, send home a postcard, and give thanks after surviving the seductive and treacherous Loreley crossing. St. Goar is worth a stop to explore its mighty Rheinfels Castle. (For information, a guided castle tour, and accommodations, see page 249.)

Km 556—Katz Castle (Burg Katz): Burg Katz (Katzenelnbogen) faces St. Goar from across the river. Together, Burg Katz (built in 1371) and Rheinfels Castle had a clear view up and down the river, effectively controlling traffic. There was absolutely no duty-free shopping on the medieval Rhine. Katz got Napoleoned in 1806 and rebuilt in about 1900.

Today, the castle is shrouded by intrigue and controversy. In 1995, a wealthy and eccentric Japanese man bought it for about $4 million. His vision: to make the castle—so close to the Loreley that Japanese tourists are wild about—an exotic escape for his countrymen. But the town wouldn't allow his planned renovation of the historic (and therefore protected) building. Stymied, the frustrated investor just abandoned his plans. Today, Burg Katz sits empty...the Japanese ghost castle.

Below the castle, notice the derelict grape terraces—worked since the eighth century, but abandoned only in the last generation. The Rhine wine is particularly good because the local slate absorbs the heat of the sun and stays warm all night, resulting in sweeter grapes. Wine from the flat fields above the Rhine gorge is cheaper and good only as table wine. The wine from the steep side of the Rhine gorge—harder to grow and harvest—is tastier and more expensive.

About Km 555: A statue of the Loreley, the beautiful-but-deadly nymph (see next listing for legend), combs her hair at the end of a long spit—built to give barges protection from vicious ice floes that until recent years would rage down the river in the winter. The actual Loreley, a cliff (marked by the flags), is just ahead.

Km 554—The Loreley: Steep a big slate rock in centuries of legend and it becomes a tourist attraction—the ultimate Rhinestone. The Loreley (flags and visitors center on top, name painted near shoreline), rising 450 feet over the narrowest and deepest point of the Rhine, has long been important. It was a holy site in pre-Roman days. The fine echoes here—thought to be ghostly voices—fertilized legend-tellers' imaginations.

Because of the reefs just upstream (at kilometer 552), many ships never made it to St. Goar. Sailors (after days on the river) blamed their misfortune on a *wunderbares Fräulein* whose long blond hair almost covered her body. Heinrich Heine's *Song of Loreley* (the Cliffs Notes version is on local postcards) tells the story of a count who sent his men to kill or capture this siren after she distracted his horny son, causing him to drown. When the soldiers cornered the nymph in her cave, she called her father (Father Rhine) for help. Huge waves, the likes of which you'll never see today, rose from the river and carried Loreley to safety. And she has never been seen since.

But alas, when the moon shines brightly and the tour buses are parked, a soft, playful Rhine whine can still be heard from the Loreley. As you pass, listen carefully ("Sailors...sailors...over my bounding mane").

Km 552—The Seven Maidens: Killer reefs, marked by red-and-green buoys, are called the "Seven Maidens." Okay, one more goofy legend: The prince of Schönburg Castle (*über* Oberwesel—described below) had seven spoiled daughters who always dumped men because of their shortcomings. Fed up, he invited seven of his knights up to the castle and demanded that his daughters each choose one to marry. But they complained that each man had too big a nose, was too fat, too stupid, and so on. The rude and teasing girls escaped into a riverboat. Just downstream, God turned them into the seven rocks that form this reef. While this story probably isn't entirely true, there's a lesson in it for medieval children: Don't be hard-hearted.

Km 550—Oberwesel: Cross to the other side of the train. Oberwesel was a Celtic town in 400 B.C., then a Roman military station. It now boasts some of the best Roman-wall and medieval-tower remains on the Rhine, and the commanding Schönburg Castle. Notice how many of the train tunnels have entrances designed like medieval turrets—they were actually built in the Romantic 19th century. Okay, back to the river side.

Km 546—Gutenfels Castle and Pfalz Castle, the Classic Rhine View: Burg Gutenfels (see white-painted *Hotel* sign) and

the shipshape Pfalz Castle (built in the river in the 1300s) worked very effectively to tax medieval river traffic. The town of Kaub grew rich as Pfalz raised its chains when boats came, and lowered them only when the merchants had paid their duty. Those who didn't pay spent time touring its prison, on a raft at the bottom of its well. In 1504, a pope called for the destruction of Pfalz, but the locals withstood a six-week siege, and the castle still stands. Notice the overhanging outhouse (tiny white room—with faded medieval stains—between two wooden ones). Pfalz (also known as Pfalzgrafenstein) is tourable but bare and dull (€3 ferry from Kaub, €2.10 entry; March–Oct Tue–Sun 10:00–18:00, until 17:00

in March, closed Mon; Nov and Jan–Feb Sat–Sun 10:00–17:00, closed Mon–Fri; closed Dec; last entry 1 hour before closing, tel. 0172/262-2800).

In Kaub, on the riverfront directly below the castles, a green statue honors the German general Gebhard von Blücher. He was Napoleon's nemesis. In 1813, as Napoleon fought his way back to Paris after his disastrous Russian campaign, he stopped at Mainz—hoping to fend off the Germans and Russians pursuing him by controlling that strategic bridge. Blücher tricked Napoleon. By building the first major pontoon bridge of its kind here at the Pfalz Castle, he crossed the Rhine and outflanked the French. Two years later, Blücher and Wellington teamed up to defeat Napoleon once and for all at Waterloo.

Km 544—"The Raft Busters": Immediately before Bacharach, at the top of the island, buoys mark a gang of rocks notorious for busting up rafts. The Black Forest, upstream from here, was once poor, and wood was its best export. Black Foresters would ride log booms down the Rhine to the Ruhr (where their timber fortified coal-mine shafts) or to Holland (where logs were sold to shipbuilders). If they could navigate the sweeping bend just before Bacharach and then survive these "raft busters," they'd come home reckless and likely horny—the German folkloric equivalent of American cowboys after payday.

Km 543—Bacharach and Stahleck Castle (Burg Stahleck): Cross to the other side of the train. The town of Bacharach is a great stop (see details and accommodations on page 237). Some of the Rhine's best wine is from this town, whose name likely derives from "altar to Bacchus." Local vintners brag that the medieval Pope Pius II ordered Bacharach wine by the cartload. Perched above the town, the 13th-century Burg Stahleck is now a hostel.

Km 540—Lorch: This pathetic stub of a castle is barely visible from the road. Check out the hillside vineyards. These vineyards once blanketed four times as land as they do today, but modern economics have driven most of them out of business. The vineyards that do survive require government subsidies. Notice the small car ferry (3/hr, 10 min), one of several along the bridgeless stretch between Mainz and Koblenz.

Km 538—Sooneck Castle: Cross back to the other side of the train. Built in the 11th century, this castle was twice destroyed by people sick and tired of robber barons.

Km 534—Reichenstein Castle and **Km 533—Rheinstein Castle:** Stay on the other side of the train to see two of the first castles to be rebuilt in the Romantic era. Both are privately owned, tourable, and connected by a pleasant trail. See my listing for Rheinstein Castle on page 237.

Km 530—Ehrenfels Castle: Opposite Bingerbrück and the Bingen station, you'll see the ghostly Ehrenfels Castle (clobbered by the Swedes in 1636 and by the French in 1689). Since it had no view of the river traffic to the north, the owner built the cute little *Mäuseturm* (mouse tower) on an island (the yellow tower you'll see near the train station today). Rebuilt in the 1800s in Neo-Gothic style, it's now used as a Rhine navigation signal station.

Km 528—Niederwald Monument: Across from the Bingen station on a hilltop is the 120-foot-high Niederwald monument, a memorial built with 32 tons of bronze in 1877 to commemorate "the reestablishment of the German Empire." A lift takes tourists to this statue from the famous and extremely touristy wine town of Rüdesheim.

From here, the Romantic Rhine becomes the industrial Rhine, and our tour is over.

SIGHTS

The following sights—Marksburg Castle, the Loreley Visitors Center, and Rheinstein Castle—are listed in the order you'd see them on the Rhine Blitz Tour, above.

▲▲Marksburg Castle

Thanks to its formidable defenses, medieval invaders decided to give Marksburg a miss. This best-preserved castle on the Rhine can be toured only with a guide, and tours are generally in German only (4/hr in summer, 1/hr in winter). There are no explanations in English in the castle itself, but your ticket includes an English handout. Still, it's an awesome castle, and my self-guided walking tour (below) fits the 50-minute German-language tour.

Cost, Hours, Location: €5, family card-€13, daily April–Oct 10:00–18:00, Nov–March 11:00–17:00, last tour departs 1 hour before closing, tel. 02627/206, www.marksburg.de. Marksburg caps a hill above the Rhine town of Braubach (a short hike or shuttle train from the boat dock).

◐ Self Guided Tour: Our tour starts inside the castle's first gate.

1. Inside the First Gate: While the dramatic castles lining the Rhine are generally Romantic rebuilds, Marksburg is the real McCoy—nearly all original construction. It's littered with bits of its medieval past, like the big stone ball that was swung on a rope to be used as a battering ram. Ahead, notice how the inner gate—originally tall enough for knights on horseback to gallop through—was made smaller, and therefore safer from enemies on horseback. Climb the Knights' Stairway carved out of slate rock and pass under the murder hole—handy for pouring boiling pitch on invaders. (Germans still say someone with bad luck "has pitch on his head.")

2. Coats of Arms: Colorful coats of arms line the wall just inside the gate. These are from the noble families who have owned the castle since 1283. In that year, financial troubles drove the first family to sell to the powerful and wealthy Katzenelnbogen family (who made the castle into what you see today). When Napoleon took this region in 1803, an Austrian family who sided with the French got the keys. When Prussia took the region in 1866, control passed to a friend of the Prussians who had a passion for medieval things—typical of this Romantic period. Then it was sold to the German Castles Association in 1900. Its offices are in the main palace at the top of the stairs.

3. Romanesque Palace: White outlines mark where the larger original windows were located, before they were replaced by easier-to-defend smaller ones. On the far right, a bit of the original plaster survives. Slate, which is soft and vulnerable to the elements, needs to be covered—in this case, by plaster. Because this is a protected historic building, restorers can use only the traditional plaster methods...but no one knows how to make plaster that works as well as the 800-year-old surviving bits.

4. Cannons: The oldest cannon here—from 1500—was back-loaded. This was advantageous because many cartridges could be pre-loaded. But since the seal was leaky, it wasn't very powerful. The bigger, more modern cannons—from 1640—were one piece and therefore airtight, but had to be front-loaded. They could easily hit targets across the river from here. Stone balls were rough, so they let the explosive force leak out. The best cannonballs were stones covered in smooth lead—airtight and therefore more powerful and more accurate.

5. Gothic Garden: Walking along an outer wall, you'll see 160 plants from the Middle Ages—used for cooking, medicine, and witchcraft. The *Schierling* (hemlock, in the first corner) is the same poison that killed Socrates.

6. Inland Rampart: This most vulnerable part of the castle had a triangular construction to better deflect attacks. Notice the factory in the valley. In the 14th century, this was a lead, copper, and silver mine. Today's factory—Europe's largest car-battery recycling plant—uses the old mine shafts as vents (see the three modern smokestacks).

7. Wine Cellar: Since Roman times, wine has been the traditional Rhineland drink. Because castle water was impure, wine—less alcoholic than today's beer—was the way knights got their fluids. The pitchers on the wall were their daily allotment. The bellows were part of the barrel's filtering system.

Stairs lead to the...

8. Gothic Hall: This hall is set up as a kitchen, with an oven designed to roast an ox whole. The arms holding the pots have notches to control the heat. To this day, when Germans want someone to hurry up, they say, "give it one tooth more." Medieval windows were made of thin sheets of translucent alabaster or animal skins. A nearby wall is peeled away to show the wattle-and-daub construction (sticks, straw, clay, mud, then plaster) of a castle's inner walls. The iron plate to the left of the next door enabled servants to stoke the heater without being seen by the noble family.

9. Bedroom: This was the only heated room in the castle. The canopy kept in heat and kept out critters. In medieval times, it was impolite for a lady to argue with her lord in public. She would wait for him in bed to give him what Germans still call "a curtain lecture." The deep window seat caught maximum light for needlework and reading. Women would sit here and chat (or "spin a yarn") while working the spinning wheel.

10. Hall of the Knights: This was the dining hall. The long table is an unattached plank. After each course, servants could replace it with another pre-set plank. Even today, when a meal is over and Germans are ready for the action to begin, they say, "Let's lift up the table." The action back then consisted of traveling minstrels who sang and told of news gleaned from their travels.

Notice the outhouse—made of wood—hanging over thin air. When not in use, its door was locked from the outside (the castle side) to prevent any invaders from entering this weak point in the castle's defenses.

11. Chapel: This chapel is still painted in Gothic style with the castle's namesake, St. Mark, and his lion. Even the chapel was designed with defense in mind. The small doorway kept out heavily armed attackers. The staircase spirals clockwise, favoring the sword-wielding defender (assuming he was right-handed).

12. Linen Room: About the year 1800, the castle—with diminished military value—housed disabled soldiers. They'd earn a little extra money working raw flax into linen.

13. Two Thousand Years of Armor: Follow the evolution of armor since Celtic times. Because helmets covered the entire head, soldiers identified themselves as friendly by tipping their visor up with their right hand. This evolved into the military salute that is still used around the world today. Armor and the close-range weapons along the back were made obsolete by the invention of the rifle. Armor was replaced with breastplates—pointed (like the castle itself) to deflect enemy fire. This design was used as late as the start of World War I. A medieval lady's armor hangs over the door. While popular fiction has men locking their women up before heading off to battle, chastity belts were actually used by women as protection against rape when traveling.

14. The Keep: This served as an observation tower, a dungeon (with a 22-square-foot cell in the bottom), and a place of last refuge. When all was nearly lost, the defenders would bundle into the keep and burn the wooden bridge, hoping to outwait their enemies.

15. Horse Stable: The stable shows off bits of medieval crime and punishment. Cheaters were attached to stones or pillories. Shame masks punished gossipmongers. A mask with a heavy ball had its victim crawling around with his nose in the mud. The handcuffs with a neck hole were for the transport of prisoners. The pictures on the wall show various medieval capital punishments. Many times the accused was simply taken into a torture dungeon to see all these tools and, guilty or not, confessions spilled out of him. On that cheery note, your tour is over.

The Loreley Visitors Center (Besucherzentrum Loreley)

This lightweight exhibit reflects a little on Loreley, but focuses mainly on the landscape, culture, and people of the Rhine Valley. Though English explanations accompany most of the geological and cultural displays, the information about the famous mythical *Mädchen* is only given in German—making this place not worth its admission price. The 3-D movie is essentially a tourist brochure for the region, with scenes of the grape harvest over Bacharach that are as beautiful as the sword-fighting is lame (€2.50, March–Oct daily 10:00–18:00, closed Nov–Feb, tel. 06771/599-093, www.loreley-besucherzentrum.de). Far more exciting than the exhibit is the view from the cliffs themselves. A five-minute walk from the bus stop and visitors center takes you to the impressive viewpoint overlooking the Rhine Valley from atop the famous rock. From there, it's a steep 15-minute hike down to the riverbank.

Getting There: For a good two-hour **hike** from St. Goar up to the Loreley, catch the ferry across to the village of St. Goarshausen (€2.60 round-trip, every 15–20 min, Mon–Sat 6:00–21:00, Sun 8:00–21:00, May–Sept until 23:00). Then follow green *Burg Katz* (Katz Castle) signs up Burgstrasse under the train tracks to find steps on right *(Loreley über Burg Katz)* leading to the Katz Castle (privately owned) and beyond. Traverse the hillside, always bearing right toward the river. You'll pass through a residential area, hike down a 50-yard path through trees, then cross a wheat field until you reach the Loreley Visitors Center (shops and restaurants, see above) and rock-capping viewpoint.

From here, it's a steep 15-minute hike back down to the river, where the riverfront road takes you back to St. Goarshausen and the St. Goar ferry.

If you're not up for a hike, you can catch the hourly **bus** from St. Goarshausen up to the visitors center, and hike or bus back down again. From the St. Goarshausen ferry ramp, walk to your left along the river about 40 yards to get the bus (€2.20 each way; first bus at 10:15, then at :30 past each hour from 11:30–16:30; last bus down leaves at 16:42).

▲▲Rheinstein Castle (Schloss Burg Rheinstein)

This castle seems to rule its chunk of the Rhine from a com-

manding position. While its 13th-century exterior is medieval as can be, the interior is mostly a 19th-century duke's hunting palace. Visitors wander freely (with an English flier) among trophies, armor, and Romantic Age decor.

Cost and Hours: €3.80; mid-March–mid-Nov daily 9:30–17:30; off-season Mon–Thu 14:00–17:00, Sun 10:00–17:00, closed Fri–Sat; tel. 06721/6348, www.burg -rheinstein.de.

Getting There: This castle (at river kilometer marker #533, 2 kilometers upstream from Trechtingshausen on the main highway, B-9) is easy by **car** (small, free parking lot on B-9, steep 5-min hike from there), or **bike** (35 min upstream from Bacharach, stick to the great riverside path, after kilometer marker #534 look for small *Burg Rheinstein* sign and Rösler–Linie dock). It's less convenient by **boat** (no K-D stop nearby) or **train** (nearest stop in Trechtingshausen, 30-min walk away).

Bacharach

Once prosperous from the wine and wood trade, Bacharach (BAHKH-ah-rahkh, with a guttural *kh* sound) is now just a pleasant half-timbered village of a thousand people working hard to keep its tourists happy.

ORIENTATION

Tourist Information

The TI is on the main street in the Posthof courtyard next to the church. They store bags for day-trippers and provide ferry schedules (April–Oct Mon–Fri 9:00–17:00, Sat–Sun 10:00–15:00; Nov–March Mon–Fri 9:00–12:00, closed Sat–Sun; Oberstrasse 45, from train station turn right and walk 5 blocks down main street with castle high on your left, tel. 06743/919-303, www.bacharach .de or www.rhein-nahe-touristik.de, Herr Kuhn and his team).

Helpful Hints

Shopping: The **Jost** German gift store, across the main square from the church, carries most everything a souvenir-shopper could want (from beer steins to cuckoo clocks). The Josts offer a 10 percent discount to readers of this book who pay cash. They can also ship things to the US—even if you don't buy them at their shop (March–Oct Mon–Fri 8:30–18:00, Sat 8:30–17:00, Sun 10:00–17:00, shorter hours in winter and closed Sun, Blücherstrasse 4, tel. 06743/1224, www.phil-jost -germany.com, phil.jost@t-online.de).

Internet Access: The town's cheapest Internet terminals are a short walk past the Altes Haus (€1/hr, Mon–Tue and Thu–Fri 16:00–21:00, closed Sat–Sun and Wed, Koblenzer Strasse 10). The TI has a coin-op terminal (€0.50/15min).

Post Office: It's inside a shop, at Oberstrasse 37 between the train station and the TI (Mon–Fri 9:00–12:00 & 14:00–18:00, Sat 9:00–12:00, closed Sun).

Grocery Store: Across from the Altes Haus is a **Nahkauf,** a basic grocery store (Mon–Fri 8:00–12:30 & 14:00–18:00, Sat 8:00–15:00, closed Sun, Oberstrasse 46).

Bike Rental: While many hotels loan bikes to guests, the only real bike-rental business in the town center is run by Erich at Hotel Hillen (see listing on page 245). He rents 25 bikes daily from 9:00 until dark (€10/day for non-guests, €5/day for guests, Langstrasse 18, tel. 06743/1287).

Local Guides and Walking Tours: Get acquainted with Bacharach by taking a walking tour. Charming Herr Rolf Jung, retired headmaster of the Bacharach school, is a superb English-speaking guide who loves sharing his town's story with Americans (€30, 90 min, call to reserve, tel. 06743/1519). Manuela Maddes (tel. 06743/2759), Birgit Wessel (tel. 06743/937-514), and Aussie Joanne Augustine (tel. 06743/919-300, mobile 0179-231-1389) also give good tours. If none of the above is available, call the TI for advice, or take my self-guided walk (next). On Saturdays at 11:00

from May to October, the TI offers a 90-minute walking tour (€4) primarily in German—but if you ask for English, you'll get it as well.

SELF-GUIDED WALK

Welcome to Bacharach

• *Start at the Köln–Düsseldorfer ferry dock (next to a fine picnic park).*

View the town from the parking lot—a modern landfill. The Rhine used to lap against Bacharach's town wall, just over the present-day highway. Every few years the river floods, covering the highway with several feet of water. The **castle** on the hill is now a youth hostel. Two of the town's original 16 towers are visible from here (up to five if you look really hard). The huge roadside wine keg declares that this town was built on the wine trade.

Reefs farther upstream forced boats to unload upriver and reload here. Consequently, in the Middle Ages, Bacharach became the biggest wine trader on the Rhine. A riverfront crane hoisted huge kegs of prestigious "Bacharach" wine (which, in practice, was from anywhere in the region). The tour buses next to the dock and the flags of the biggest spenders along the highway remind you that today's economy is basically founded on tourism.

• *Before entering the town, walk upstream through the riverside park.*

This park was laid out in 1910 in the English style: Notice how the trees were planted to frame fine town views, highlighting the most picturesque bits of architecture. Until recently, stepping on the grass was *verboten*. The dark, sad-looking monument—its "eternal" flame long snuffed-out—is a war memorial. The German psyche is permanently scarred with memories of wars. Today, many Germans would rather avoid monuments like this, which revisit the dark periods before Germany became a nation of pacifists. Take a close look at the monument. Each panel honors sons of Bacharach who died for the Kaiser: in 1864 against Russia, in 1870 against France, in 1914 during World War I. The military Maltese cross—flanked by classic German helmets—has a *W* at its center, for Kaiser Wilhelm.

• *Continue to where the park meets the playground, and then cross the highway to the fortified riverside wall of the Catholic church—decorated with high-water marks recalling various floods.*

Check out the metal ring on the medieval slate wall. Before the 1910 reclamation project, the river extended out to here, and boats would use the ring to tie up. Upstream from here, there's a trailer park, and beyond that there's a campground. In Germany, trailer vacationers and campers are two distinct subcultures. Folks who travel in trailers, like many retirees in the US, are a nomadic bunch, hauling around the countryside in their mobile homes and

Bacharach

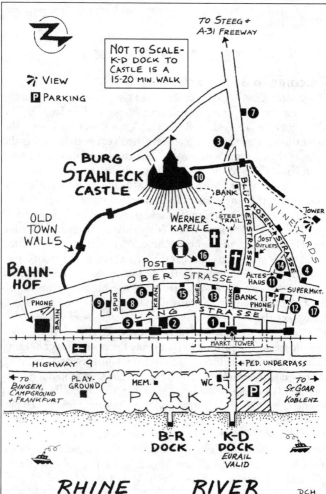

RHINE   RIVER

1. Rhein Hotel & Stüber Rest.
2. Hotel/Rest. Kranenturm
3. Pension im Malerwinkel
4. Pension Binz
5. Hotel Hillen & Bike Rental
6. Pension Lettie
7. Pension Winzerhaus
8. Ursula Orth B & B
9. Irmgard Orth B & B
10. Jugendherberge Stahleck Hostel
11. Altes Haus Restaurant
12. Kurpfälzische Münze Restaurant
13. Eis Café Italia
14. Bastian's Weingut zum Grüner Baum
15. Weingut Karl Heidrich
16. Old Posthof
17. Internet Café

paying about €6 a night to park. Campers, on the other hand, tend to set up camp—complete with comfortable lounge chairs and even TVs—and stay put for weeks, even months. They often come back to the same plot year after year, treating it like their own private estate. These camping devotees have made a science out of relaxing.

• *At the church, go under the 1858 train tracks and hook right past the yellow floodwater yardstick and up the stairs onto the town wall. Atop the wall, turn left and walk under the long arcade. After a few steps, notice a well on your left. This is one of 40 such wells that, until 1900, provided water to the townsfolk. You'll pass the Rhein Hotel (see listing on page 243; hotel is before the Markt tower, which marks one of the town's 15 original 14th-century gates), descend, pass another well, and follow Marktstrasse toward the town center, the two-tone church, and the town's main intersection.*

From here, Bacharach's main street (Oberstrasse) goes right to the half-timbered, red-and-white Altes Haus (from 1368, the oldest house in town) and left 400 yards to the train station. To the left (or south) of the church, a golden horn hangs over the old **Posthof** (home to the TI, free WC upstairs in courtyard). The post horn symbolizes the postal service throughout Europe. In olden days, when the postman blew this, traffic stopped and the mail sped through. This post station dates from 1724, when stagecoaches ran from Köln to Frankfurt and would change horses here, Pony Express–style.

Step past the old-oak doors into the courtyard—once a carriage house and inn that accommodated Bacharach's first VIP visitors. Notice the fascist eagle (from 1936, on the left as you enter; a swastika once filled its center) and the fine view of the church and a ruined chapel above. The Posthof is on a charming square. Spin around to enjoy the higgledy-piggledy building style.

Two hundred years ago, Bacharach's main drag was the only road along the Rhine. Napoleon widened it to fit his cannon wagons. The steps alongside the church lead to the castle. Return to the church, passing the Italian ice-cream café (Eis Café Italia), where friendly Mimo serves his special invention: Riesling wine–flavored gelato (see "Eating," page 247).

Inside the Protestant church (April–Oct daily 9:30–18:00, closed Nov–March, English info on table near door), you'll find Grotesque capitals, brightly painted in medieval style, and a mix of round Romanesque and pointed Gothic arches. Left of the altar, some medieval frescoes survive where an older Romanesque arch was cut by a pointed Gothic one.

• *Continue down Oberstrasse to the **Altes Haus**.*

Notice the 14th-century building style—the first floor is made of stone, while upper floors are half-timbered (in the ornate style common in the Rhine Valley). Some of its windows still look medieval, with small flattened circles as panes (small because that's all that glass-blowing technology of the time would allow), pieced together with molten lead. Frau Weber welcomes visitors to enjoy the fascinating ground floor of her Altes Haus, with its evocative old photos and etchings (consider eating here later—see "Eating," page 247).

• *Keep going down Oberstrasse to the* **old mint** *(Münze), marked by a crude coin in its sign.*

Across from the mint, the Bastian family's wine garden is the liveliest place in town after dark (see page 247). Above you in the vineyards stands a lonely white-and-red tower—your destination.

At the next street, look right and see the mint tower, painted in the medieval style (illustrating that the Dark Ages weren't really *that* dark), and then turn left. Wander 30 yards up Rosenstrasse to the **well.** Notice the sundial and the wall painting of 1632 Bacharach with its walls intact (the town is working to reconstruct the wall's missing sections—you may be able to walk the whole length of the wall in 2008). Climb the tiny-stepped lane behind the well up into the vineyard and to the tall, lonely tower. The slate steps lead to a small path through the vineyard that deposits you at a viewpoint atop the stubby remains of the old town wall. If the tower's open, hike to its top floor for the best view.

A grand medieval town spreads before you. For 300 years (1300–1600), Bacharach was big (population 4,000), rich, and politically powerful.

From this perch you can see the chapel ruins and six surviving **city towers.** Visually trace the wall to the castle. The castle was actually the capital of Germany for a couple of years in the 1200s. When Holy Roman Emperor Frederick Barbarossa went away to fight the Crusades, he left his brother (who lived here) in charge of his vast realm. Bacharach was home of one of seven electors who voted for the Holy Roman Emperor in 1275. To protect their

own power, these elector-princes did their best to choose the weakest guy on the ballot. The elector from Bacharach helped select a two-bit prince named Rudolf von Hapsburg (from a no-name castle in Switzerland). The underestimated Rudolf brutally silenced the robber barons along the Rhine and established the mightiest dynasty in European history. His family line, the Hapsburgs, ruled much of Central and Eastern Europe until 1918.

Plagues, fires, and the Thirty Years' War (1618–1648) finally did Bacharach in. The town, with a population of about a thousand, has slumbered for several centuries. Today, the castle houses commoners—40,000 overnights annually by youth hostelers.

In the mid-19th century, painters such as J. M. W. Turner and writers such as Victor Hugo were charmed by the Rhineland's romantic mix of past glory, present poverty, and rich legend. They put this part of the Rhine on the old Grand Tour map as the "Romantic Rhine." Victor Hugo pondered the ruined 15th-century chapel that you see under the castle. In his 1842 travel book, *Rhein Reise (Rhine Travels)*, he wrote, "No doors, no roof or windows, a magnificent skeleton puts its silhouette against the sky. Above it, the ivy-covered castle ruins provide a fitting crown. This is Bacharach, land of fairy tales, covered with legends and sagas." If you're enjoying the Romantic Rhine, thank Victor Hugo and company.

• *To get back into town, take the level path away from the river that leads along the once-mighty wall up the valley past the next tower. Then cross the street into the parking lot. Pass Pension—Malerwinkel on your right, being careful not to damage the old arch with your head. Follow the creek past a delightful little series of half-timbered homes and cheery gardens known as "Painters' Corner" (Malerwinkel). Resist looking into some pervert's peep show (on the right) and continue downhill back to the village center. Nice work.*

SLEEPING

(country code: 49, area code: 06743)
Ignore guest houses and restaurants posting *Recommended by Rick Steves* signs. If they're not listed in the current edition of this book, I do not recommend them. Parking in Bacharach is simple along the highway next to the tracks (3-hour daytime limit is generally not enforced) or in the boat parking lot. For locations, see the map on page 240.

$$$ Rhein Hotel, with 14 spacious and comfortable rooms, is classy, well-run, decorated with a modern flair, and overlooks the river. Since it's right on the train tracks, its river- and train-side rooms come with four-paned windows and air-conditioning. This place has been in the Stüber family for six generations (Sb-€55, Db-€90 with this book and direct reservation in 2008, cheaper for longer stays, half-board option, free loaner bikes for guests, directly inland from the K-D boat dock at Langstrasse 50, tel. 06743/1243, fax 06743/1413, www.rhein-hotel-bacharach.de, info @rhein-hotel-bacharach.de). For a culinary splurge, consider dining here (see "Eating," page 246).

$$ Hotel Kranenturm, offering castle ambience without the climb, combines hotel comfort with *Zimmer* coziness right downtown. Run by hardworking Kurt Engel and his intense but friendly

Sleep Code

(€1 = about $1.30)
S = Single, **D** = Double/Twin, **T** = Triple, **Q** = Quad, **b** = bathroom, **s** = shower only. All hotels speak some English. Breakfast is included and credit cards are accepted unless otherwise noted.

To help you sort easily through these listings, I've divided the rooms into three categories, based on the price for a standard double room with bath:

$$$ Higher Priced—Most rooms €70 or more.
 $$ Moderately Priced—Most rooms between €50–70.
  $ Lower Priced—Most rooms €50 or less.

The Rhine is an easy place for cheap sleeps. B&Bs and *Gasthäuser* with €25 beds abound (and normally discount their prices for longer stays). Rhine-area hostels offer €17 beds to travelers of any age. Each town's TI is eager to set you up, and finding a room should be easy any time of year (except for winefest weekends in Sept and Oct). Bacharach and St. Goar, the best towns for an overnight stop, are 10 miles apart, connected by milk-run trains, riverboats, and a riverside bike path. Bacharach is a much more interesting town, but St. Goar has the famous castle (for St. Goar recommendations, see page 248).

wife, Fatima, this hotel is actually part of the medieval fortification. Its former *Kran* (crane) towers are now round rooms. When the riverbank was higher, cranes on this tower loaded barrels of wine onto Rhine boats. While just 15 feet from the train tracks, a combination of medieval sturdiness, triple-paned windows, and included earplugs makes the riverside rooms sleepable (Sb-€39–45, small Db-€56–62, regular Db-€58–65, Db in huge tower rooms with castle and river views-€72–80, Tb-€83–95, honeymoon special-€90–105, lower price is for off-season or stays of at least 3 nights in high season, family deals, cash preferred, Rhine views come with train noise, back rooms are quiet, all rooms non-smoking, showers can be temperamental, kid-friendly, good breakfast, Internet access-€2/hr, laundry service-€12.80, Langstrasse 30, tel. 06743/1308, fax 06743/1021, www.kranenturm.com, hotel-kranenturm @t-online.de). Kurt, a good cook, serves €6–18 dinners.

$$ Pension im Malerwinkel sits like a grand gingerbread house that straddles the town wall in a quiet little neighborhood so charming it's called "Painters' Corner" *(Malerwinkel)*. The Vollmer family's 20-room place is super-quiet and comes with a

sunny garden on a brook, views of the vineyards, and easy parking (Sb-€38, Db-€62 for 1 night, €56 for 2 nights, €53 for 3 nights or more, cash only, some rooms have balconies, no train noise, bike rental-€6/day; from Oberstrasse, turn left at the church, and stay to the left of the babbling brook until you reach Blücherstrasse 41; tel. 06743/1239, fax 06743/93407, www.im-malerwinkel.de, pension@im-malerwinkel.de, Armin).

$$ Pension Binz offers four large, bright, plainly furnished rooms in a good location with no train noise (Sb-€35, Db-€55, third person-€18, slightly cheaper for 3 nights or more, apartment with kitchen but no breakfast and 2-night minimum-€65, Koblenzer Strasse 1, tel. 06743/1604, fax 06743/937-9916, pension .binz@freenet.de, warm Carla speaks a little English).

$ Hotel Hillen, a block south of the Hotel Kranenturm, has a little less charm and similar train noise (with the same ultra-thick windows). It offers spacious rooms, good food, and friendly owners (S-€25, Sb-€30, D-€35, Ds-€40, Db-€45, Tb-€60, Qb-€75, these special prices are for a 2-night minimum for those reserving directly with this book in 2008, €5 more for 1-night stays, closed mid-Nov–March, family rooms, Langstrasse 18, tel. 06743/1287, fax 06743/1037, hotel-hillen@web.de, kind Iris speaks some English). The Hillen also rents bikes (see page 238).

$ At Pension Lettie, effervescent and eager-to-please Lettie offers four bright rooms. Lettie speaks English (she worked for the US Army before they withdrew) and does laundry for €10.50 per load (Sb-€34, Db-€48, Tb-€65, Qb-€85, 5b-€100, these prices valid with this book in 2008 if you reserve direct rather than through TI, discount for 2-night stays, 10 percent more if paying with credit card, strictly non-smoking, buffet breakfast with waffles and eggs, no train noise, Internet access, a few doors inland from Hotel Kranenturm, Kranenstrasse 6, tel. 06743/2115, fax 06743/947564, pension.lettie@t-online.de).

$ Pension Winzerhaus, a 10-room place run by friendly Sybille and Stefan, is outside the town walls, 200 yards up the side-valley road from the town gate, directly under the vineyards. Though there's no train noise, the front rooms have a bit of street noise (ask for the back side). The rooms are simple, clean, and modern, and parking is easy (Sb-€30, Db-€49, Tb-€65, Qb-€75, 10 percent off with this book in 2008, cash only, non-smoking, free loaner bikes for guests, Blücherstrasse 60, tel. 06743/1294, winzerhaus@compuserve.de).

$ Orth *Zimmer*: Delightful sisters-in-law run two fine little B&Bs across the lane from each other (from station, walk down Oberstrasse, turn right on Spurgasse, and look for *Orth* sign). **Ursula Orth** rents five rooms and speaks a smidge of English (Sb-€22, Db-€35, Tb-€45, cash only, rooms 4 and 5 on ground floor, Spurgasse 3, tel. 06743/1557). **Irmgard Orth** rents two fresh rooms, one of which has a bathroom on the hall. She speaks even less English but is exuberantly cheery and serves homemade honey with breakfast (S-€20, D-€33, Db-€35, cash only, Spurgasse 2, look for beehive signs, tel. 06743/1553). Their excellent prices assume you're booking direct, instead of through the TI.

$ Jugendherberge Stahleck hostel is a 12th-century castle on the hilltop—500 steps above Bacharach—with a royal Rhine  view. Open to travelers of any age, this is a gem with 168 beds and a private modern shower and WC in most rooms. The steep 20-minute climb on the trail from the town church is worth it for the view, even if you're not sleeping there. The hostel serves hearty €6.50 all-you-can-eat buffet dinners, and its pub serves cheap local wine until midnight. To reach the hostel with luggage from the train station, call an €8 taxi at 06743/1653 or 06743/1418 (€17 dorm beds with breakfast and sheets, €3.10 extra for non-members, couples can share one of five €46 Db, no smoking in rooms, laundry-€5.50, dorm beds normally available but call and leave your name—they'll hold a bed until 18:00, tel. 06743/1266, fax 06743/2684, bacharach@diejugendherbergen.de). If driving, don't go in the driveway; park on the street and walk 200 yards.

EATING

Restaurants

You can easily find inexpensive (€10–15), atmospheric restaurants offering indoor and outdoor dining. There's also a cozy pizzeria and a *döner kebab* joint (daily until 23:00) on the main street.

The Rhein Hotel's **Stüber Restaurant** is Bacharach's best top-end choice. Chef Andreas Stüber is the sixth generation to prepare regional, seasonal plates, served on river- and track-side seating or indoors with a spacious wood-and-white-tablecloth elegance. Consider their William Turner pâté sampler plate, named after the British painter who liked Bacharach (€11–17 entrées, March–mid-Dec Wed–Mon 12:00–14:00 & 17:30–21:00, closed

Tue and mid-Dec–Feb, call to reserve an outdoor table, facing the K-D boat dock just below the center of town, Langstrasse 50, tel. 06743/1243).

Altes Haus, the oldest building in town (see page 241), serves reliably good food with Bacharach's most romantic atmosphere. Find the cozy little dining room with photos of the opera singer who sang about Bacharach, adding to its fame (€9–15 entrées, Easter–Nov Thu–Tue 12:00–15:30 & 18:00–23:00, last orders at 21:30, closed Wed and Dec–Easter, dead center by the church, tel. 06743/1209).

Kurpfälzische Münze, while more expensive than Altes Haus, is a popular standby for lunch or a drink on its sunny terrace or in its pubby candlelit interior (€7–15 entrées, daily 10:00–22:00, in the old mint, a half-block down from Altes Haus, tel. 06743/1375).

Hotel Kranenturm is another good value, with hearty dinners and good main-course salads. If you're a trainspotter, sit on their track-side terrace and trade travel stories with new friends over dinner, letting screaming trains punctuate your conversation. If you prefer charming old German decor, sit inside (see hotel listing on page 243; restaurant open daily 17:00–21:00). Kurt and Fatima are your hosts.

Eis Café Italia, on the main street and run by friendly Mimo Calabrese, is known for its refreshing, not-too-sweet Riesling-flavored gelato. Notice the big sundae bowls on the shelves. To enjoy your *Eis* German-style, sit down and order ice cream off the menu, or just stop by for a cone before an evening stroll (€0.60/scoop, no tastes offered, April–mid-Oct daily 10:00–22:00, closed off-season, opposite Posthof at Oberstrasse 48).

Wine-Tasting

Bacharach is proud of its wine. Two places in town—Bastian's rowdy and rustic Grüner Baum, and sophisticated Weingut Karl Heidrich—offer visitors an inexpensive chance to join in on the fun. Each place samples many varieties of wines in small glasses on spinning wine carousels.

At **Bastian's Weingut zum Grüner Baum,** groups of two to six people pay €13.50 for a wine carousel of 15 glasses—14 different white wines and one lonely rosé—and a basket of bread. Your mission: Team up with others who have this book to rendezvous here after dinner. Spin the Lazy Susan, share a common cup, and discuss the taste. Doris Bastian insists: "After each wine, you must talk to each other." They offer soup and cold cuts, and good ambience indoors and out (Mon–Wed and Fri from 13:00, Sat–Sun from 12:00, closed Thu and Feb–mid-March, just past Altes Haus, tel. 06743/1208). To make a meal of a carousel, consider the *Käse Teller* (7 different cheeses, including *Spundekäse,* the local soft cheese).

Weingut Karl Heidrich is a fun, family-run wine shop and *Stube* in the town center (at Oberstrasse 18, near Hotel Kranenturm), where Markus proudly shares his family's wine while passionately explaining its fine points to travelers. They offer a variety of wine carousels with six wines (€10), which are ideal for the more sophisticated wine-taster (April–Oct Thu–Tue 11:00–23:00, closed Wed and Nov–March, tel. 06743/93060).

St. Goar

St. Goar is a classic Rhine town. Its hulk of a castle overlooks a half-timbered shopping street and leafy riverside park, busy with sightseeing ships and contented strollers. Rheinfels Castle, once the mightiest on the Rhine, is the single best Rhineland ruin to explore. From the riverboat docks, the main drag—a dull pedestrian mall without history—cuts through town before ending at the road up to the castle.

While the town of St. Goar itself isn't much more than a few hotels and restaurants—and is less interesting than Bacharach—it still makes a good base for hiking or biking the region. A tiny car ferry will shuttle you back and forth across the busy Rhine from here. (One of my favorite pastimes in St. Goar is chatting with friendly Heike at the K-D boat kiosk.)

Tourist Information
The helpful St. Goar TI, which books rooms and offers a free baggage-check service, is on the pedestrian street, three blocks from the K-D boat dock and train station (May–Sept Mon–Fri 9:00–12:30 & 13:30–18:00, Sat 10:00–12:00, closed Sun; April and Oct Mon–Fri until 17:00, closed Sat–Sun; Nov–March Mon–Thu until 16:30, Fri 9:00–14:00, closed Sat–Sun; from train station, go downhill around church and turn left, Heerstrasse 86, tel. 06741/383, www.st-goar.de).

Helpful Hints

Picnics: St. Goar's waterfront park is hungry for a picnic. The small **Edeka supermarket** on the pedestrian street is great for picnic fixings. You can buy any quantity of produce—just push the photo or number on the scales (July–Sept Mon–Fri 8:00–18:00, Sat 8:00–16:00, closed Sun, shorter hours off-season, Heerstrasse 108).

Shopping: The friendly and helpful Montag family runs three shops (steins—Misha; Steiffs—Maria; and cuckoo clocks—Marion) and a hotel, all at the base of the castle hill road. The stein shop under the hotel has Rhine guides, fine steins, and copies of this year's *Rick Steves' Germany & Austria* guidebook. All three shops offer 10 percent off any of their souvenirs (including Hummels) for travelers with this book (€5 minimum purchase). On-the-spot VAT refunds cover about half of your shipping costs (if you're not shipping, they'll give you a VAT form to claim your refund at airport).

Internet Access: Hotel Montag offers expensive coin-op access (€6/hr, 5 terminals, disc-burning service, Heerstrasse 128, tel. 06741/1629).

Bike Rental: Try **Hotel zur Loreley,** and call ahead if possible (€8/day, Heerstrasse 87, tel. 06741/1614).

SIGHTS

St. Goar's Rheinfels Castle

Sitting like a dead pit bull above St. Goar, this mightiest of Rhine castles rumbles with ghosts from its hard-fought past. Burg

Rheinfels *was* huge—once the biggest castle on the Rhine (built in 1245). It withstood a siege of 28,000 French troops in 1692. But in 1797, the French Revolutionary army destroyed it. The castle was used for ages as a source of building stone, and today—while still mighty—it's only a small fraction of its original size. This hollow but interesting shell offers your single best hands-on ruined-castle experience on the river.

Cost and Hours: €4, family card-€10; mid-March–Oct daily 9:00–18:00, last entry at 17:00; Nov–mid-March only open Sat–Sun 11:00–17:00, last entry at 16:00—weather permitting.

Tours and Information: Call in advance or gather 10 English-speaking tourists and beg to get an English tour—perhaps from Günther, the "last knight of Rheinfels" (tel. 06741/7753).

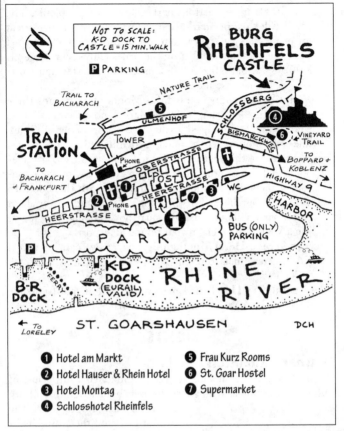

- ❶ Hotel am Markt
- ❷ Hotel Hauser & Rhein Hotel
- ❸ Hotel Montag
- ❹ Schlosshotel Rheinfels
- ❺ Frau Kurz Rooms
- ❻ St. Goar Hostel
- ❼ Supermarket

Otherwise, follow my self-guided tour (below). The castle map is mediocre; the €2 English booklet is better, with history and illustrations. If it's damp, be careful of slippery stones. A handy WC is immediately across from the ticket booth (check out the guillotine urinals—stand back when you pull to flush).

Let There Be Light: If planning to explore the mine tunnels, bring a flashlight, or do it by candlelight (museum sells candles with matches, €0.50).

Getting to the Castle by Taxi or Mini-Train: A taxi up from town costs €5 (tel. 06741/7011). Or take the kitschy "tschu-tschu" tourist train (€2 one-way, €3 round-trip, 7 min to the top, daily 10:00–17:00 but sometimes unpredictable, 2/hr, runs from square between station and dock, also stops by beer-stein shop, complete with lusty music, mobile 0171-496-3762).

Hiking Up to the Castle: Two steep but scenic paths take you up to the castle from the town (allow 15–20 minutes up). You can also simply follow the main road up through the railroad underpass at the top end of the pedestrian street, but it's not as much fun.

To take the **vineyard trail,** start at the beer-stein shop at the end of the pedestrian street, walk uphill through the underpass, make an immediate right on Bismarcksweg along the railroad tracks following the *Fussweg Burg Rheinfels* and yellow *Zur Burg* signs, pass the youth hostel, and then follow the yellow *Zur Burg* signs up the hill through the vineyard. The last couple hundred yards are along the road.

To take the **nature trail,** start at the St. Goar train station. Take the underpass under the tracks at the north end of the station, climb the stairs uphill, and turn right (following *Burg Rheinfels* signs) along the path just above the old city wall, which takes you to the castle in 10 minutes.

◆ **Self-Guided Tour:** Rather than wander aimlessly, visit the castle by following this tour: From the ticket gate, walk straight. Pass *Grosser Keller* on the left (where we'll end this tour) and walk through an internal gate past the *zu den gedeckten Wehrgängen* sign on the right (where we'll pass later) uphill to the museum (daily 10:00–12:30 & 13:00–17:30, included in castle entry) in the only finished room of the castle. The museum is pleasant, with good English descriptions, but it's not as important as seeing the castle itself—skip the museum if you're short on time.

❶ **Museum and Castle Model:** The seven-foot-tall carved stone immediately inside the door (marked *Keltische Säule von Pfalzfeld*)—a tombstone from a nearby Celtic grave—is from 400 years before Christ. There were people here long before the Romans...and this castle. Find the old wooden library chair near the tombstone. If you smile sweetly, the man behind the desk may demonstrate—pull the chair's back forward and it becomes stairs for accessing the highest shelves.

The sweeping castle history exhibit in the center of the room is well-described in English. The massive fortification was the only Rhineland castle to withstand Louis XIV's assault during the 17th century. At the far end of the room is a model reconstruction of the castle (not the one with the toy soldiers) showing how much bigger it was before French Revolutionary troops destroyed it in the 18th century. Study this. Find where you are (hint: look for the tall tower). This was the living quarters of the original castle, which was only the smallest ring of buildings around the tiny central courtyard (13th century). The ramparts were added in the 14th century. By 1650, the fortress was largely complete. Ever since its destruction by the French in the late 18th century, it's had no military value. While no WWII bombs were wasted on this ruin, it served St. Goar as a stone quarry for generations. The basement of

St. Goar

St. Goar's Rheinfels Castle

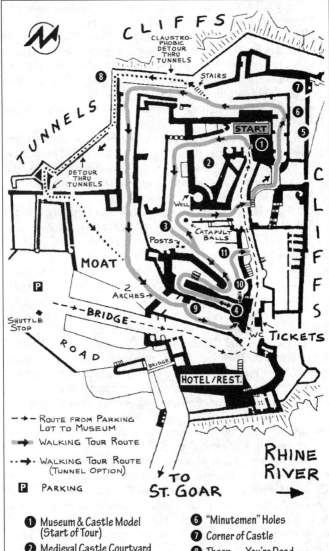

CLIFFS

CLAUSTRO-PHOBIC DETOUR THRU TUNNELS

STAIRS

START

① ②

DETOUR THRU TUNNELS

TUNNELS

WELL

③ POSTS

CATAPULT BALLS

⑪

⑦

⑥

⑤

MOAT

P

2 ARCHES

⑩ ⑨ ④

SHUTTLE STOP

BRIDGE

ROAD

BRIDGE

WC TICKETS

CLIFFS

HOTEL/REST.

- → ROUTE FROM PARKING LOT TO MUSEUM
➡ WALKING TOUR ROUTE
⋯→ WALKING TOUR ROUTE (TUNNEL OPTION)
P PARKING

RHINE RIVER →

↓ TO ST. GOAR

① Museum & Castle Model (Start of Tour)
② Medieval Castle Courtyard
③ Castle Garden
④ Highest Castle Tower Lookout
⑤ Covered Defense Galleries
⑥ "Minutemen" Holes
⑦ Corner of Castle
⑧ Thoop . . . You're Dead
⑨ Prison
⑩ Slaughterhouse (Below)
⑪ Big Cellar (Below)

the museum shows the castle pharmacy and an exhibit of Rhine-region odds and ends, including tools and an 1830 loom. Don't miss the photos of ice-breaking on the Rhine. While once routine, ice-breaking hasn't been necessary here since 1963.

• *Exit the museum and walk 30 yards directly out, slightly uphill into the castle courtyard.*

❷ **Medieval Castle Courtyard:** Five hundred years ago, the entire castle circled this courtyard. The place was self-sufficient and ready for a siege with a bakery, pharmacy, herb garden, brewery, well (top of yard), and livestock. During peacetime, 300 to 600 people lived here; during a siege, there would be as many as 4,000. The walls were plastered and painted  white. Bits of the original 13th-century plaster survive.

• *Continue through the courtyard and out Erste Schildmauer, turn left into the next courtyard, and walk straight to the two old, wooden, upright posts. Find the pyramid of stone catapult balls on your left.*

❸ **Castle Garden:** Catapult balls like these were too expensive not to recycle—they'd be retrieved after any battle. Across from the balls is a well—essential for any castle during the age of sieges. Look in. Spit. The old posts are for the ceremonial baptizing of new members of the local trading league. While this guild goes back centuries, it's now a social club that fills this court with a huge wine party the third weekend of each September.

• *If weary, skip to #5; otherwise, climb the cobbled path up to the castle's best viewpoint—up where the German flag waves.*

❹ **Highest Castle Tower Lookout:** Enjoy a great view of the river, the castle, and the forest. Remember, the fortress once covered five times the land it does today. Notice how the other castles (across the river) don't poke above the top of the Rhine canyon. That would make them easy for invading armies to see.

• *Return to the catapult balls, walk down the road, go through the tunnel, veer left through the arch marked* zu den gedeckten Wehrgängen *("to the covered defense galleries"), go down two flights of stairs, and turn left into the dark, covered passageway. From here, we will begin a rectangular walk taking us completely around (counterclockwise) the perimeter of the castle.*

❺ & ❻ **Covered Defense Galleries with "Minutemen" Holes:** Soldiers—the castle's "minutemen"—had a short commute: defensive positions on the outside, home in the holes below on the left. Even though these living quarters were padded with straw, life was unpleasant. A peasant was lucky to live beyond age 45.

• *Continue straight through the dark gallery and to the corner of the castle, where you'll see a white painted arrow at eye level. Stand with your back to the arrow on the wall.*

❼ **Corner of Castle:** Look up. A three-story, half-timbered building originally rose beyond the highest stone fortification. The two stone tongues near the top just around the corner supported the toilet. (Insert your own joke here.) Turn around and face the wall. The crossbow slits below the white arrow were once steeper. The bigger hole on the riverside was for hot pitch.

• *Follow that white arrow along the outside to the next corner. Midway you'll pass stairs on the right leading down* zu den Minengängen *(sign on upper left). Adventurers with flashlights can detour here (see "Optional Detour—Into the Mine Tunnels"). You may come out around the next corner. Otherwise, stay with me, walking level to the corner. At the corner, turn left.*

❽ **Thoop...You're Dead:** Look ahead at the smartly placed crossbow slit. While you're lying there, notice the stonework. The little round holes were for scaffolds used as they built up. They indicate this stonework is original. Notice also the fine stonework on the chutes. More boiling pitch...now you're toast, too.

• *Continue along the castle wall around the corner. At the gray railing, look up the valley and uphill where the sprawling fort stretched. Below, just outside the wall, is land where attackers would gather. The mine tunnels are under there, waiting to blow up any attackers (read below).*

Keep going along the perimeter, jog left, go down five steps and into an open field, and walk toward the wooden bridge. You may detour here into the passageway (on right) marked 13 Halsgraben. *The "old" wooden bridge is actually modern. Angle left through two arches (before the bridge) and through the rough entry to the* Verliess *(prison) on the left.*

❾ **Prison:** This is one of six dungeons. You just walked through an entrance prisoners only dreamed of 400 years ago. They came and went through the little square hole in the ceiling. The holes in the walls supported timbers that thoughtfully gave as many as 15 residents something to sit on to keep them out of the filthy slop that gathered on the floor. Twice a day, they were given bread and water. Some prisoners actually survived longer than two years in here. While the town could torture and execute, the castle only had permission to imprison criminals in these dungeons. Consider this: According to town records, the two men who spent the most time down here—2.5 years each—died within three weeks of regaining their freedom. Perhaps after a diet of bread and water, feasting on meat and wine was simply too much.

• *Continue through the next arch, under the white arrow, then turn left and walk 30 yards to the* Schlachthaus.

❿ **Slaughterhouse:** Any proper castle was prepared to survive a six-month siege. With 4,000 people, that's a lot of provisions. The cattle that lived within the walls were slaughtered in this room. The castle's mortar was congealed here (by packing all the organic waste from the kitchen into kegs and sealing it). Notice the drainage gutters. "Running water" came through from drains built into the walls (to keep the mortar dry and therefore strong... and less smelly).

• *Back outside, climb the modern stairs to the left. A skinny, dark passage (yes, that's the one) leads you into the...*

⓫ **Big Cellar:** This *Grosser Keller* was a big pantry. When the castle was smaller, this was the original moat—you can see the rough lower parts of the wall. The original floor was 13 feet deeper. The drawbridge rested upon the stone nubs on the left. When the castle expanded, the moat became this cellar. Halfway up the walls on the entrance side of the room, square holes mark spots where timbers made a storage loft, perhaps filled with grain. In the back, an arch leads to the wine cellar (sometimes blocked off) where finer wine was kept. Part of a soldier's pay was wine... table wine. This wine was kept in a single 180,000-liter stone barrel (that's 47,550 gallons), which generally lasted about 18 months.

The count owned the surrounding farmland. Farmers got to keep 20 percent of their production. Later, in more liberal feudal times, the nobility let them keep 40 percent. Today, the German government leaves the workers with 60 percent...and provides a few more services.

• *You're free. Climb out, turn right, and leave. For coffee on a terrace with a great view, visit Schlosshotel Rheinfels, opposite the entrance (WC at base of steps).*

Optional Detour—Into the Mine Tunnels: In about 1600, to protect their castle, the Rheinfellers cleverly booby-trapped the land just outside their walls by building tunnels topped with thin slate roofs and packed with explosives. By detonating the explosives when under attack, they could kill hundreds of invaders. In 1626, a handful of underground Protestant Germans blew 300 Catholic Spaniards to—they figured—hell. You're welcome to wander through a set of never-blown-up tunnels. But be warned: It's 600 feet long, assuming you make no wrong turns; it's pitch-dark, muddy, and claustrophobic, with confusing dead-ends; and you'll never get higher than a deep crouch. It cannot be done without a light (candles available at entrance—see above). At stop #6 of the above tour, follow the stairs on the right leading down *zu den Minengängen* (sign on upper left).

The *Fuchsloch* sign welcomes you to the foxhole. Walk level (take no stairs) past the first steel railing (where you hope to emerge later) to the second steel railing. Climb down. The "highway" in this foxhole is three feet high. The ceiling may be painted with a white line indicating the correct path. Don't venture into the narrower side aisles. These were once filled with the gunpowder. After a small decline, take the second right. At the T-intersection, go right (uphill). After about 10 feet, go left. Take the next right and look for a light at the end of the tunnel. Head up a rocky incline under the narrowest part of the tunnel and you'll emerge at that first steel railing. The stairs on the right lead to freedom. Cross the field, walk under the bigger archway, and continue uphill toward the old wooden bridge. Angle left through two arches (before the bridge) and through the rough entry to the *Verliess* (prison) on the left. Rejoin the tour here at stop #8.

SLEEPING

(country code: 49, area code: 06741)
Parking in St. Goar is tight; ask at your hotel.

$$$ Schlosshotel Rheinfels ("Rheinfels Castle Hotel") is the town splurge. Part of the castle, but in a purpose-built new building, this luxurious 60-room place is good for those with money and a car (Db-€145–185 depending on river views and balconies, extra adult bed-€57, extra bed for kids ages 12–18 costs €37, extra bed for kids ages 7–11 costs €25, kids under age 7 free, elevator, indoor pool and sauna, dressy restaurant, free parking, Schlossberg 47, tel. 06741/8020, fax 06741/802-802, www.schlosshotel-rheinfels.de, info@burgrheinfels.de).

$$$ Hotel Montag, with 28 rooms, is on the castle end of the pedestrian street just across the street from the world's largest free-hanging cuckoo clock. Manfred and Maria Montag and their son Mike speak New Yorkish. As this place is overpriced and packed with tour groups, I'd consider it a last resort (Sb-€35–45, Db-€70–80, Tb-€90–100, 10 percent discount with this book in 2008, pricey coin-op Internet access-€6/hr, disk-burning service, Heerstrasse 128, tel. 06741/1629, fax 06741/2086, hotelmontag @freenet.de). Check out their adjacent crafts shop (heavy on beer steins).

$$ Hotel am Markt, well-run by Herr and Frau Velich, is rustic and a good deal, with all the modern comforts. It features a hint of antler with a pastel flair, 18 bright rooms, Wi-Fi, and a good restaurant where the son, Gil, is a fine chef (see "Eating"). It's a good value and a stone's throw from the boat dock and train station (S-€35, Sb-€45, standard Db-€62, bigger riverview Db-€75, cheaper March–mid–April and Oct–mid-Nov, closed mid-Nov–Feb, Am Markt 1, tel. 06741/1689, fax 06741/1721, www.hotel-am-markt-sankt-goar.de, hotel.am.markt@gmx.de). They also rent 10 rooms of equal quality (for the same price) in the smaller riverside

Rhein Hotel a block away.

\$\$ Hotel Hauser, facing the boat dock, is another good deal, warmly run by another Frau Velich. Its 12 simple rooms sit over a fine restaurant (S-€22, D-€45, Db-€52, great Db with Rhine-view balconies-€58, these prices promised with this book and cash through 2008, cash preferred, à la carte half-pension-€12, Heerstrasse 77, tel. 06741/333, fax 06741/1464, www.hotelhauser .de, hotelhauser@t-online.de).

\$ Frau Kurz offers St. Goar's best B&B, renting three delight-ful rooms with refrigerators, a breakfast terrace, garden, fine view,

and homemade marmalade (S-€25, D-€46, 2-night minimum, cash only, non-smoking, free and easy parking, honor your reservation or call to cancel, Ulmenhof 11, tel. & fax 06741/459, www.gaestehaus -kurz.de, jeanette.kurz@t-online .de). It's a memorably steep five-minute hike from the train station (exit left from station, take immedi-ate left at the yellow phone booth, pass under tracks to paved path, go up stairs and follow zigzag path, turning right through archway onto Ulmenhof; #11 is just past tower).

\$ St. Goar Hostel, the big beige building down the hill from the castle, rents 18 doubles and piles of beds in 4- to 10-bed dorms. It has a well-run, strong, institutional atmosphere with a 22:30 curfew (but you can borrow the key) and hearty €5 dinners (dorm beds-€14, D-€35, includes breakfast, non-members pay €3.10 extra, all ages welcome, open all day, Bismarckweg 17, tel. 06741/388, fax 06741/2869, st-goar@diejugendherbergen.de). It's a fairly level 10-minute walk from the train station: Veer left and go all the way down narrow redbrick Oberstrasse, then turn left through the underpass and make an immediate right on Bismarcksweg, follow-ing the red *Jugendherberge* signs.

EATING

Hotel am Markt serves tasty traditional meals with plenty of game and fish (try Chef Gil's specialties: marinated roast beef and homemade cheesecake) at fair prices with good atmosphere and service (€8–16 daily specials, March–mid-Nov daily 11:00–21:00, closed mid-Nov–Feb, Am Markt 1, tel. 06741/1689).

Schlosshotel Rheinfels is your Rhine splurge, with an incredible view terrace in an elegant, dressy setting. As it's at the hilltop castle, you'll have to hike, taxi, or drive up (€17–25 main dishes, daily 12:00–14:00 & 18:00–21:00, reserve a table by the window, cheaper €7–12 main dishes without view in downstairs cellar restaurant, tel. 06741/8020; see also hotel listing).

Other Options: There are a couple of Italian places in town and plenty of ways to gather a picnic to enjoy on the riverside park. For more options, take the quick train to Bacharach, leaving and returning hourly until very late (see below).

TRANSPORTATION CONNECTIONS

Milk-run trains stop at Rhine towns each hour starting as early as 6:00, connecting at Mainz and Koblenz to trains farther afield. Trains between St. Goar and Bacharach depart at about :20 after the hour in each direction (€2.90, buy tickets from the machine in the unstaffed stations). The timings listed below are calculated from Bacharach; for St. Goar, the difference is only 12 minutes. Train info: tel. 11861 (€0.60/min).

From Bacharach by Train to: St. Goar (hourly, 12 min), **Cochem** (hourly, 1.5 hrs, change in Koblenz), **Trier** (hourly, 2.5 hrs, change in Koblenz), **Köln** (hourly, 1.75 hrs, change in Koblenz), **Frankfurt Airport** (hourly, 1.5 hrs, most change in Mainz or Bingen, first train Mon–Fri at 5:30, Sat at 6:30, Sun at 7:30), **Frankfurt** (hourly, 1.5 hrs, change in Mainz), **Rothenburg ob der Tauber** (almost hourly, 4.5 hrs, 3–4 changes), **Munich** (hourly, 5 hrs, change in Mainz and Mannheim), **Berlin** (hourly, 6.5–7 hrs, 2 changes), **Amsterdam** (7/day, 5 hrs, change in Koblenz and Köln).

MOSEL VALLEY

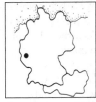

The misty Mosel is what some visitors hope the Rhine will be—peaceful, sleepy, romantic villages slipped between impossibly steep vineyards and the river; fine wine; a sprinkling of castles (Burg Eltz is tops); and lots of friendly B&Bs. Boat, train, and car traffic here is a trickle compared to the roaring Rhine. While the swan-speckled Mosel moseys 300 miles from France's Vosges mountains to Koblenz (where it dumps into the Rhine), the most scenic piece of the valley lies between the towns of Bernkastel-Kues and Cochem. I'd savor only this section. Cochem and Trier (see next chapter) are easy day trips from each other (1 hour by train, 55 miles by car). Cochem is the handiest home base unless you want the peace of Beilstein.

Throughout the region on summer weekends and during the fall harvest, wine festivals with oompah bands, dancing, and

colorful costumes are powered by good food and wine. You'll find a wine festival in some nearby village any weekend, June through September. The tourist season lasts from April through October. Things close down tight through the winter.

Look for the booklet *The Castles of the Moselle* (€3.80, at local TIs), with information on castles from Koblenz to Trier (including Burg Eltz, Cochem, and Metternich in Beilstein). The booklet not only has historical and structural information, but also some drawings of what the now-ruined castles looked like originally.

Getting Around the Mosel Valley

By Train and Bus: Fast trains zip you between Koblenz, Cochem, Bullay, and Trier in a snap. Other destinations require changing to a slow train or bus. Zell is a 10-minute bus ride from Bullay; Beilstein is a 20-minute ride on bus #716 from Cochem (hourly, no buses after 19:00 and fewer buses on weekends, €3). Burg Eltz is a scenic 90-minute hike from the tiny Moselkern train station (see "Transportation Connections," page 267). Pick up bus schedules at train stations or TIs, or visit Germany's excellent online train timetable at http://bahn.hafas.de/bin/query.exe/en.

By Boat: The Kolb Line has the most frequent departures and allows you to cruise the most scenic stretch of the Mosel between Cochem, Beilstein, and Zell (tel. 02673/1515, www.moselfahrplan.de). A simple and fun outing is the one-hour cruise between **Cochem** and **Beilstein,** passing through the Fankel lock (4–5/day in each direction May–Oct, no boats off-season, first departure from Cochem about 10:30, last departure from Beilstein about 17:30, €10 one-way, €12 round-trip). You can also sail between **Zell** and **Beilstein** (2 hrs) or **Cochem** (3 hrs), but check the schedules in advance—these boats don't run as often, so you may need to take the bus or train one way if planning a round-trip (1–2/day May–Oct, but none on Fri and Mon May–June; Zell–Beilstein: €13 one-way, €18 round-trip; Zell–Cochem: €15 one-way, €22 round-trip). Another option is the boat in the other direction (downstream) from **Cochem** to **Treis-Karden** (3/day mid-July–Aug, Wed and Sat–Sun only May–mid-July and Sept–Oct, 45 min, €8 one-way, €10 round-trip). From Treis-Karden, you can get to Burg Eltz via a long hike (2 steep hours) or a taxi ride, but it's much easier to reach Burg Eltz from the Moselkern train station (see "Getting to Burg Eltz," page 269). Kolb also runs one-hour **sightseeing cruises** and two-hour **dancing cruises** from Cochem (sightseeing cruises 5/day April–Oct; dancing cruises with live music daily at 20:15 mid-July–Aug; May–mid-July and Sept–Oct Tue and Sat only).

The KD (Köln–Düsseldorfer) line sails the lower Mosel, between **Cochem** and **Koblenz,** but only once a day in each direction (€23.40 one-way, mid-June–Sept daily, May–mid-June Fri–Mon only, none in winter, Koblenz to Cochem 9:45–15:00, Cochem to Koblenz 15:40–20:00; free with a German railpass or any Eurailpass that covers Germany, but uses up a day of a flexipass; tel. in Cochem 02671/980-023, www.k-d.com).

In early to mid-June, the Mosel locks close for 10 days of annual maintenance, and none of the boats listed here run. With all the locks, Mosel cruises feel more like a canal-boat ride than the cruises on the mighty Rhine.

By Car: The easygoing Mosel Wine Route turns anyone into a relaxed Sunday driver. Pick up a local map at a TI or service

Mosel Valley

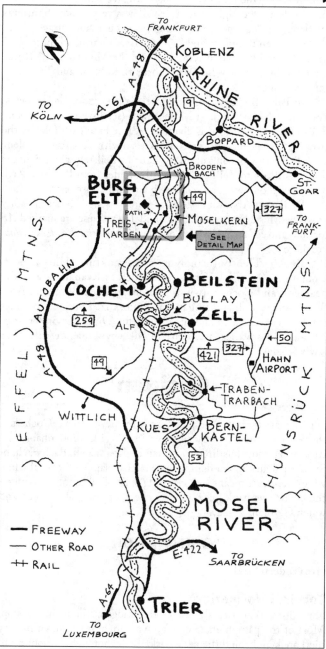

station. Two-lane roads run along both riverbanks. While river-side roads are a delight, the river valley is very windy. Shortcuts overland can "cut the corners" and save you serious time—especially between Burg Eltz and Beilstein (see "Getting to Burg Eltz," page 269) and if you're driving between the Mosel and the Rhine (note the Brodenbach–Boppard shortcut). Koblenz and Trier have car-rental agencies.

By Bike: Biking along the Mosel is the rage among Germans. You can rent bikes in most Mosel towns (see listings for Cochem, Beilstein, and Zell in this chapter). A fine bike path follows the river (with some bits still sharing the road with cars) from Koblenz to Zell. From Cochem, allow an hour to Beilstein and 2.5 hours for the full trip to Zell, and about 10 minutes from Bullay to Zell. Many pedal one-way and relax with a return cruise or train ride.

By Ferry: About a dozen car-and-passenger ferries *(Fähre)* cross the Mosel between Koblenz and Trier. These are marked *AF* for auto and *PF* for pedestrian on the *Moselle Wine Road/Mosellauf* brochure.

By Air: The confusingly named Frankfurt-Hahn airport, a popular hub for low-fare airlines such as Ryanair, is actually near Zell and Cochem (www.hahn-airport.de). Buses run from the airport to Zell and Bullay, and a subsidized taxi service takes you between Cochem and the airport for €9 per person (arrange 24 hours in advance, tel. 02671/4500, www.vuag.de/rufbus or www.5c5.de).

Cochem

With a majestic castle and picturesque medieval streets, Cochem is the very touristic hub of the middle Mosel. With 6,000 inhabitants, it's a larger, more bustling town than Beilstein, Zell, Bacharach, or St. Goar. Duck into a damp wine cellar to sample the local white wine (*Weinprobe* means "wine-tasting"). Stroll pleasant paths along the idyllic riverbank, play life-size chess, or just grab a bench and watch Germany at play.

ORIENTATION

(area code: 02671)

Tourist Information

The information-packed TI is by the bridge at the main bus stop. Most of the pamphlets (free map with town walk, town history flier) are kept behind the desk—ask. Their thorough 24-hour room listing in the window comes with a free phone connection. The TI

also has information on special events, wine-tastings held by local vintners, public transportation to Burg Eltz, area hikes, and the informative €3 *Mosellauf* brochure or the cartoony €1 *Moselle Wine Road* map (May–Oct Mon–Fri 9:00–17:00, Sat 9:00–15:00, closed Sun; July–Oct also Sat until 17:00 and Sun 10:00–12:00; off-season closed weekends and at lunch; tel. 02671/60040, www.cochem.de).

Arrival in Cochem

By Train: Cochem's train station has no lockers, but you can leave your bags at the Taxi-Zentrale storefront (€1.50/day, daily 9:00–18:00, to the right as you exit the station at Bahnhofsvorplatz 3). Make a hard right out of the station and walk about 10 minutes to the TI and bus station (both on your left, before the bridge). To get to the main square (Markt) and colorful medieval town center, continue under the bridge (€0.30 WC), then angle right and follow Bernstrasse.

By Car: Drivers can park in the multi-story garage just up Endertstrasse from the bridge, or in a lot behind the train station (€1.50/day, reach it by circling around on Ravenéstrasse and Pinnerstrasse).

Helpful Hints

Internet Access: Try the very pleasant **Espresso I-O** (€1/15 min, €3.50/hr, also has Wi-Fi, Mon–Fri 7:00–18:00, Sat 10:00–18:00, Sun 13:00–18:00, between TI and train station at Ravenéstrasse 18–20) or the more expensive **COCbit-Kommunikation,** on the street facing the river, across from the boat ticket booths (€1/15 min, Mon–Fri 10:00–12:00 & 14:00–18:00, Sat 10:00–13:00, closed Sun, Moselpromenade 7, tel. 02671/211). After 18:00, try the **Log-In Netzwerk Café** at Brückenstrasse 4, just before the railroad underpass (€4/hr, daily 10:00–24:00, ages 16 and over only).

Bike Rental: The **K-D boat kiosk** at the dock rents bikes (€8/24 hrs, May–Oct daily 9:30–18:00, closed Nov–April, small selection, tel. 02671/980-023). **Radsport Schrauth,** a bike shop run by serious cyclists, has a better selection and helpful service (€5/half-day, €7/day, €10/day for mountain bikes, Mon–Fri 9:30–18:00, Sat 9:00–13:00, Sun only May–Oct 10:00–12:00, arrange weekend drop-off time, leave driver's license for deposit, Endertstrasse 41, right across from chairlift, tel. 02671/7974). Consider taking a bike on the boat or train and riding back.

Festival: Cochem's biggest wine festival is held the last weekend in August (Aug 28–Sept 1 in 2008). High season for wine aficionados lasts from August through October.

SIGHTS AND ACTIVITIES

Cochem Castle (Reichsburg Cochem)—This pretty, pointy castle on a hill above town is the work of overly imaginative 19th-century restorers (€4.50; follow one of the frequent 40-min German-language tours while reading English explanation sheets, or gather 12 English speakers and call a day ahead to schedule an English tour; mid-March–mid-Nov daily 9:00–17:00, closed off-season, tel. 02671/255, www.reichsburg-cochem.de). Below the entrance, the resident falconer  frequently shows off his flock; check the notice at the gate to see if the birds are in fine feather (€3.50, 40-min show, Tue–Sun at 11:00, 13:00, 14:30, 16:00, no shows Mon, look for *Falknerei* sign).

Getting There: From the old town's main square (Markt), the castle is a very scenic 25-minute walk up a mostly gentle slope: Look for the red "A" hanging over Herrenstrasse and head down it until it veers left to meet Burgfrieden street, marked by the helpful man pointing to the castle; from there, the path is easy to follow. If you've already *probe*d a little *Wein* and would rather ride up, consider the shuttle bus that runs from the bus station (next to the TI) to the castle—but you still have to walk the last 10 minutes uphill (€2 one-way, 1–2/hr, May–Oct only, first bus up 10:30, last bus down 17:48, look for *Reichsburg Shuttle-Bus* sign at bus station).

Chairlift and Hikes—For great views, you could ride the *Sesselbahn* chairlift, which ascends the hill on the opposite side of town from the castle (€4.50 one-way, €5.80 round-trip, mid-March–mid-Nov 10:00–18:00, closed off-season, tel. 02671/989-065, www.cochemer-sesselbahn.de). You can scramble up the narrow path under the lift for 20 minutes of heart-pounding, aerobic excitement. Or take the trail up to the same point from behind the train station (find trailhead behind station parking lot). For the best of all worlds, take the lift up, take in the view from the restaurant, then follow the path to the station *(Bahnhof)*, down through the forest and then the vineyards to a wine-tasting at Weingut Rademacher (see below).

Wine-Tasting—At Weingut Rademacher, behind the train station, you can taste four local wines for €1.90. There's no charge for tasting if you buy at least three bottles (normally open Mon–Sat 9:00–20:00, Sun 9:00–13:00, different hours during festivals, call ahead to confirm, tel. 02671/4164, www.weingut-rademacher .de; see "Sleeping," for directions). Other wine cellars in town also offer tastings. For a unique treat, look for the Roter-Weinbergs-Pfirsich Likör—a local cordial made from the small, tart "red peaches" that are unique to the Mosel Valley.

Swimming, Tennis, and Golf—Cochem's Moselbad and Freizeit Zentrum offers an array of family-friendly activities: an indoor wave pool, an outdoor pool, a sauna, tennis courts, and mini-golf. The downside: it's 30 minutes on foot from the center of town (€7.70/3 hrs for pools, extra for tennis and mini-golf, Tue–Fri 10:00–22:00, Sat–Sun 10:00–19:00, closed Mon, 10 min beyond youth hostel at Moritzburger Strasse 1, tel. 02671/97990, www .moselbad.de).

Cruise—The Kolb Line offers one-hour sightseeing cruises and schmaltzy two-hour "Tanz Party" dancing cruises with live music (see "Getting Around the Mosel Valley," page 260).

Sightseeing Train—A little yellow **tourist train** leaves from under the bridge at the TI and does a 25-minute sightseeing loop through town. Since the commentary is only in German (ask for English flier), and Cochem is such a pedestrian-friendly town any-way, this is worth it only if you're bored and lazy (€4.70, includes a glass of wine, 2/hr, Easter–Oct daily 10:00–17:00, doesn't run Nov–Easter).

SLEEPING

(country code: 49, area code: 02671)
August is very tight, with various festivals and generally inflated prices.

$$$ Hotel Lohspeicher, an upscale-rustic hotel just off the main square on a street with tiny steps, is for those willing to pay a bit extra for quality lodgings in the thick of things. Its nine high-ceilinged rooms have modern comforts (Sb-€55, Db-€80–110, includes big breakfast in a fine stone-and-timber room, elevator, fancy restaurant, parking-€5/day, closed Feb, Obergasse 1, tel. 02671/3976, fax 02671/1772, www.lohspeicher.de, service @lohspeicher.de, Ingo).

$$$ Hotel am Hafen, across the bridge from the TI, offers views over the river to Cochem, and some of the 20 rooms have balconies (Sb-€60–75, Db-€75, slightly nicer Db-€90, deluxe Db-€110, all rooms €10 more for 1-night stays, Internet access, Uferstrasse 3, tel. 02671/97720, fax 02671/977-227, www.hotel-am -hafen.de, hotel-am-hafen.cochem@t-online.de).

Sleep Code

(€1 = about $1.30)
S = Single, **D** = Double/Twin, **T** = Triple, **Q** = Quad, **b** = bathroom,
s = shower only. Unless otherwise noted, credit cards are
accepted, English is spoken, and breakfast is included.

To help you sort easily through these listings, I've divided
the rooms into three categories based on the price for a standard double room with bath:

$$$ **Higher Priced**—Most rooms €70 or more.
 $$ **Moderately Priced**—Most rooms between €50–70.
  $ **Lower Priced**—Most rooms €50 or less.

$$ Weingut Rademacher rents six beautiful ground-floor
rooms, which share a TV room with a fridge and microwave.
Wedged between vineyards and train tracks, with a pleasant gar-
den, it's a great value. Charming hostess Andrea and her husband
Hermann own the vineyards behind the house and will happily
show you the wine cellar after breakfast (Sb-€27.50, Db on train
side-€48, Db on vineyard side-€54, cheaper for 3 nights, fam-
ily deals, non-smoking, free parking; go right from station on
Ravenéstrasse, turn right on Pinnerstrasse, walk under tracks and
curve right to Pinnerstrasse 10; tel. 02671/4164, fax 02671/91341,
www.weingut-rademacher.de, webmaster@weingut-rademacher
.de). This place also offers wine-tastings to guests and non-guests
alike (described previously in "Sights and Activities").

$ Haus Andreas has 10 clean rooms at fair prices (Sb-€25,
Db-€38–42, Tb-€60–62, prices vary by length of stay, cash only,
free parking, Schlossstrasse 9, reception is often across the street
in shop at #16, tel. 02671/1370 or 02671/5155, fax 02671/1370,
kind Frau Pellny speaks a little English). From the main square,
take Herrenstrasse; after a block, angle right up the steep hill on
Schlossstrasse.

$ *Hostel:* Cochem's hostel, opened in 2003, is a huge, family-
friendly complex just across the river from the train station, with
146 beds, picnic tables, grill pit, playground, game room, bar, res-
taurant, and a sundeck over the Mosel (dorm bed-€18.50, Db-€48,
€3.10 more for non-members, includes sheets and breakfast, half-
and full-board options available at extra cost, fills up—reserve
in advance, Klottener Strasse 9, tel. 02671/8633, fax 02671/8568,
www.diejugendherbergen.de, cochem@diejugendherbergen.de).
From the train station, walk straight down to the river, turn left,
and use the stairway to cross the modern bridge to the hostel.

EATING

Zum Stüffje, in the old town, is a traditional half-timbered *Weinstube* with €8–18 main dishes and veggie options (Wed–Mon 11:30–14:00 & 17:30–21:00, closed Tue, Oberbachstrasse 14, enter on side street, tel. 02671/7260).

Gaststätte Noss, with fine food served inside or out along the riverside promenade, is open later than most other restaurants. Don't confuse it with the hotel of the same name (€8–15 entrées; June–Oct daily 10:00–22:00; Nov–May Fri–Wed 10:00–15:00 & 17:30–22:00, closed Thu; Moselpromenade 4, tel. 02671/7067).

Alte Gutschänke, better known as "Arthur's place," is where locals go for a glass of wine in a cozy cellar seated at long, wooden get-to-know-your-neighbor tables (extensive wine list and basic pub food, Easter–Oct Tue–Fri from 18:00, Sat–Sun from 14:00, closed Mon and in winter, just uphill from the old town's Markt square at Schlossstrasse 6, tel. 02671/8950).

Picnics: The **Frischemarkt Diewald supermarket** is on Ravenéstrasse, between the train station and TI, across the street from the post office; enter from the side lane (Mon–Fri 7:00–18:30, Sat 8:00–16:00, closed Sun).

TRANSPORTATION CONNECTIONS

From Cochem by Train to: Bullay (where you catch the bus to Zell; 2/hr, 10 min), **Moselkern** (for hike to Burg Eltz; hourly, 20 min), **Trier** (2/hr, 1 hr), **Frankfurt** and **Frankfurt Airport** (hourly, 2.5 hrs, change in Koblenz and sometimes Mainz), **Köln** (hourly, 1.75–2 hrs, most with transfer in Koblenz), **Bacharach** (hourly, 1.5 hrs, change in Koblenz), **Rothenburg** (every 2 hours, 5 hrs, 3 changes), **Berlin** (nearly hourly, 6 hrs, all change in Köln and some also in Koblenz), **Paris** (7/day, 4–5 hrs, 1–2 changes). Train info: tel. 11861 (€0.60/min). Bus info: tel. 02671/8976.

Burg Eltz

My favorite castle in all of Europe—worth ▲▲▲—lurks in a mysterious forest. It's been left intact for 700 years and is furnished throughout as it was 500 years ago. Thanks to smart diplomacy and clever marriages, Burg Eltz was never destroyed. (It survived one five-year siege.) It's been in the Eltz family for 850 years. The scenic, 90-minute walk up the Elz Valley to the castle makes a great half-day outing if you're staying anywhere along the Mosel—and a fun day trip if you're staying on the Rhine.

Elz is the name of a stream that runs past the castle through a deep valley before emptying into the Mosel. The first record of a *Burg* (castle) on the Elz is from 1157. By 1472, the castle looked like it does today, with the homes of three big landlord families gathered around a tiny courtyard within one formidable fortification. Today, the excellent 45-minute tour winds you through two of those homes, while the third remains the fortified quarters of the Eltz family. The elderly countess of Eltz—whose family goes back 33 generations here (you'll see a photo of her family)—enjoys

flowers. Each week for 40 years, she's had grand arrangements adorn the public castle rooms.

It was a comfortable castle for its day: 80 rooms made cozy by 40 fireplaces and wall-hanging tapestries. Its 20 toilets were automatically flushed by a rain drain. The delightful chapel is on a lower floor. Even though "no one should live above God," this chapel's placement was acceptable because it fills a bay window, which floods the delicate Gothic space with light. The three families met—working out common problems as if sharing a condo—in the large "conference room." A carved jester and a rose look down on the big table, reminding those who gathered that they were free to discuss anything ("fool's freedom"—jesters could say anything to the king), but nothing discussed could leave the room (the "rose of silence"). In the bedroom, have fun with the suggestive decor: the jousting relief carved into the canopy, and the fertile and phallic figures hiding in the lusty green wall paintings.

Near the exit, the €3 treasury fills the four higgledy-piggledy floors of a cellar with the precious, eccentric, and historic mementos of this family that once helped elect the Holy Roman Emperor and, later, owned a sizable chunk of Croatia (Hapsburg favors).

Cost and Hours: €6 castle entry, €3 for treasury, €8 combo-ticket for both, April–Oct daily from 9:30, last tour departs at 17:30, closed Nov–March, tel. 02672/950-500, www.burg-eltz.de.

Tours: The only way to see the castle is with a 45-minute tour (included in entry price). German tours go constantly (with helpful English fact sheets, €0.50). Guides speak English and thoughtfully collect English-speakers into their own tours—well worth waiting for (never more than 20 min). It doesn't hurt to call ahead to see if an English tour is scheduled—or organize your own by corralling 20 English-speakers in the inner courtyard, then push the red button on the white porch and politely beg for an English-speaking guide.

Getting to Burg Eltz

While the castle isn't served by public transportation, it's a pleasant walk from the nearest train station. The 90-minute walk along the footpath to Burg Eltz from the little village of Moselkern is not difficult, and it's the most fun and scenic way to visit the castle. If the weather is poor or you'd prefer not to walk, take a taxi. Cars (and taxis) park in a lot near, but not quite at, Burg Eltz. From

the lot, hike 10 minutes downhill to the castle or wait (10 minutes at most) for the red castle shuttle bus (€1.50 each way).

Hiking from Moselkern: The hike between Moselkern train station and Burg Eltz runs through a magical pine forest, where sparrows carry crossbows, and maidens, disguised as falling leaves, whisper "watch out." You can do the hike in 70 minutes at a steady clip, but allow 90 minutes to enjoy the scenery. A few uneven parts are slippery when wet, and a steep flight of stairs leads up to the castle at the end, but the trail is mostly gentle, and the rise from the river to the castle is less than 400 feet.

To start the hike, take the slow milk-run train (hourly) to Moselkern from Cochem (20 min) or Koblenz (30 min). The Moselkern train station is not staffed and has no lockers, phones, or taxis. The path up to the castle begins at the other end of Moselkern village. To reach this path, turn right from the station along Oberstrasse. Cross the intersection with Weinbergsstrasse and continue straight along narrow Oberstrasse, passing the village church on your right after about five minutes. Keep going straight a few houses past the church; then, as the street ends, turn right through the underpass. On your left is the Elzbach stream that you'll follow all the way up to the castle. Follow the road straight along the stream through a mostly residential neighborhood. Where the road crosses the stream on a stone bridge, you can take either the footpath (stay right) or the bridge.

About 30 minutes from the train station, the road ends at the parking lot of the Hotel Ringelsteiner Mühle. Stay to the right of the hotel and continue upstream along the poorly marked trail—which starts out paved but soon changes to dirt—for another 45–60 minutes to the castle.

Variation: You can also hike between the castle and the Treis-Karden railway station, toward Cochem from Moselkern. This hike is longer (two hours), steeper, and less shady. The only reason to go through Treis-Karden rather than Moselkern is for more varied scenery, or if you want to connect with a river cruise between Cochem and Treis-Karden (see "Getting Around the

Burg Eltz Area

Mosel Valley

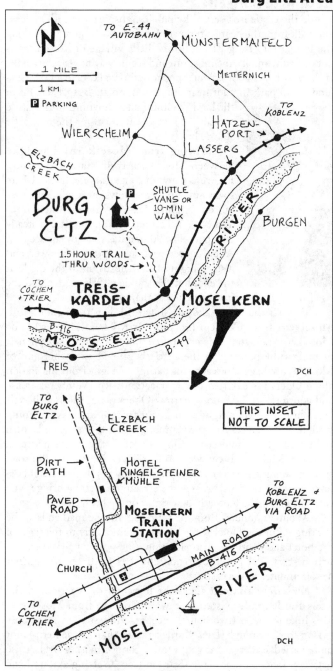

Mosel Valley," page 260).

By Taxi: You can taxi to the castle from Cochem (30 min, €50–60 one-way for up to 4 people, Cochem taxi tel. 02671/8080) or Moselkern (€18–20, taxi tel. 02672/1407 or 02625/2022). Even with a taxi, you still have a 10-minute walk from the parking lot to the castle. If you're planning to taxi from Moselkern, call ahead and ask the taxi to meet your train at Moselkern station. If you're in a hurry, consider taxiing up to Burg Eltz and then enjoying the hike downhill back to the train station in Moselkern.

If you have luggage, or want to combine visiting Burg Eltz with the Mosel cruise between Cochem and Treis-Karden, you could taxi up from Treis-Karden instead of Moselkern. If you have luggage, this works best if you eat at the elegant **Schloss-Hotel Petry,** a fine restaurant serving traditional food across from the Treis-Karden station (lunch daily 11:30–14:15, St. Castorstrasse 80, tel. 02672/9340, www.schloss-hotel-petry.de). They're normally happy to store your bags if you're eating at the restaurant. Ask the taxi to pick you up in Treis-Karden (same phone numbers as for taxis from Moselkern, about €5 more expensive).

By Car: From Koblenz, leave the river at Hatzenport, following the white *Burg Eltz* signs through the towns of Münstermaifeld and Wierschem. From Cochem, follow the *Münstermaifeld* signs from Moselkern. (Note that the *Eltz* signs at Moselkern lead to Hotel Ringelsteiner Mühle and the trailhead for the hour-long hike to the castle. To drive directly to the castle, ignore the *Eltz* signs until you reach Münstermaifeld.) The castle parking lot (€1.50/day, daily 9:00–18:00) is just over a mile past Wierschem.

Variation: If you're traveling by car but would enjoy the path up to the castle, you can drive to Moselkern, follow the *Burg Eltz* signs up the Elz Valley, park at the Hotel Ringelsteiner Mühle (€2), and enjoy the 45–60-minute hike up to the castle from there (described above).

If driving from Burg Eltz to Beilstein or Zell, you'll save 30 minutes with this **shortcut:** Cross the river at Treis-Karden, go through town, and bear right at the swimming pool (direction: Bruttig–Fankel). This overland route deposits you in Bruttig, a scenic three-mile riverside drive from Beilstein (21 miles from Zell).

Beilstein

Upstream from Cochem is the quaintest of all Mosel towns. Cozy Beilstein (BILE-shtine) is Cinderella-land—touristy but tranquil, except for its territorial swans. Beilstein has no food shop, one bus stop, one mailbox, and 180 residents who run about 30 guest houses and eateries.

Getting to Beilstein

Beilstein has no train station, but it's easy to reach from Cochem—either by **bus** (#716, hourly, no buses after 19:00 and fewer buses on weekends, 20 min, €3), by **taxi** (€25), or by **river cruise** (4–5/day in each direction May–Oct, no boats off-season, first departure from Cochem at about 10:30, last departure from Beilstein at about 17:30, €10 one-way, €12 round-trip). The best way to get between Zell and Beilstein is by riverboat (1–2/day May–Oct, 2 hrs, €13

one-way, €18 round-trip); by bus or train from Zell, you'll need to change at least twice (in Bullay, Cochem, and/or Ellenz Fähre). If **driving,** you can park for free in any space you find along the riverside road.

ORIENTATION

Beilstein has no **TI,** but the town provides a telephone information service (tel. 02673/1840), and cafés and guest houses can give you town info.

Herr Nahlen rents **bikes** for pleasant riverside rides (€6/day, Bachstrasse 47, reservations smart for groups, tel. 02673/1840, www.fahrradverleih-in-beilstein.de, info@fewo-nahlen.de).

SELF-GUIDED WALK

Welcome to Beilstein

Explore the narrow lanes, ancient wine cellar, resident swans, and ruined castle by following this short walk.

• *Stand where the village hits the river.*

Beilstein's Riverfront: In 1963, the big road and the Mosel locks were built, making the river peaceful today. Before then, access to Beilstein was limited to a tiny one-way lane and the small ferry. The cables that tether the ferry once allowed the motorless craft to go back and forth powered only by the current and an angled rudder. Today, it shuttles people (€1.30), bikes, and cars constantly (Easter–Oct daily 9:00–18:00, no ferries off-season). The campground across the river is typical of German campgrounds—80 percent of its customers set up their trailers and tents at Easter and use them as summer homes until October, when the regular floods chase them away for the winter. If you stood where you are now through the winter, you'd have cold water up to your crotch five times. Look inland. The Earl of Beilstein—who ruled from his castle above town—built the Altes Zollhaus in 1634 to levy tolls from river traffic. Today, the castle is a ruin, the once-mighty monastery (see the big church high on the left) is down to one monk, and the town's economy is based only on wine and tourists.

Beilstein's tranquility is a result of Germany's WWI loss. This war cost Germany the region of Alsace (now part of France). Before World War I, the Koblenz–Trier train line—which connects Alsace to Germany—was the busiest in Germany. It tunnels through the grape-laden hill across the river in what was the longest train tunnel in Germany. The construction of a supplemental line destined to follow the riverbank (like the lines that crank up the volume on the Rhine) was stopped in 1914 and, since Alsace went to France in 1918, the plans were scuttled.

Follow Bachstrasse into town. You'll notice blue plaques on the left marking the high-water *(Hochwasser)* points of historic floods.

At the first corner, Fürst-Metternich-Strasse leads left to the monastery (to get there, climb stairs marked *Klostertreppe*). While its population is down to one Carmelite, Rome maintains a handsome but oversized-for-this-little-town Catholic church that runs a restaurant with a great view.

Bachstrasse ("Creek Street") continues straight through Beilstein, covering up the brook that once flowed through town providing a handy disposal service 24/7. Today, Bachstrasse is lined by wine cellars. The only way for a small local vintner to make any decent money these days is to sell his wine directly to customers in inviting little places like these.

• *Your first right leads to the...*

Market Square (Marktplatz): For centuries, neighboring farmers sold their goods on Marktplatz. The *Zehnthaus* (tithe house) was the village IRS, where locals would pay one-tenth *(Zehnte)* of their produce to their landlord (either the Church or the earl). Pop into the Zehnthauskeller. Stuffed with peasants' offerings 400 years ago, it's now packed with vaulted medieval ambience. It's fun at night for candlelit wine-tasting, soup and cold cuts, and schmaltzy music (often live Fri and Sat). The Bürgerhaus (above the fountain) had nothing to do with medieval fast food. First the village church, then the *Bürger's* (like a mayor) residence, today it's *the* place for a town party or wedding. Haus Lipmann (on the riverside, now a recommended hotel and restaurant—see "Sleeping") dates from 1727. It was built by the earl's family as a residence after the French destroyed his castle. Haus Lipmann's main dining hall was once the knights' hall.

• *The stepped lane leads uphill (past the Zehnthaus, follow signs for* Burgruine Metternich) *to...*

Beilstein's Castle: Beilstein once rivaled Cochem as the most powerful town on this part of the Mosel. Its castle (officially named Burg Metternich) is a sorry ruin today, but those who make the steep 10-minute climb are rewarded with a postcard Mosel view and a chance to hike even higher to the top of its lone surviving tower (€2.50, April–Oct daily 9:00–18:30, closed Nov–March, view café/restaurant, tel. 02673/936-39).

For more exercise and an even better view, exit through the turnstile at the rear of the castle and continue uphill 100 yards, where you'll find the ultimate "castle–river bend–carpets of vineyards" photo stop. The der-elict roadside vineyard is a sign of recent times—the younger gen-eration is abandoning the family plots, opting out of all that hard winemaking work.

From this viewpoint, a sur-prising sight—a small but evoca-tive Jewish cemetery *(Jüdische Friedhof)*—is 200 yards farther up the road. During the 700 years leading up to 1942, Beilstein hosted a Jewish community. As in the rest of Europe, wealthy Jews could buy citizenship and enjoy all the protections afforded to residents. These *Schutzjuden,* or "protected Jews," were shielded from the often crude and brutal "justice" of the Middle Ages. In 1840, 25 percent of Beilstein's 300 inhabitants were Jewish. But no payment could shield this community from Hitler—so there are no Jews in today's Beilstein. (A small Jewish community in Koblenz main-tains this lovely cemetery.)

To reach the viewpoint and the cemetery without going through the castle, continue up the road past the castle entrance, then follow the signs for *Jüdische Friedhof.*

• *From here, you can return to the castle gate, ring the bell* (Klingel), *and show your ticket to get back in and retrace your steps; or continue on the road, which curves and leads downhill (a gravel path at the next bend on the left leads back into town).*

SLEEPING

(country code: 49, area code: 02673)

Many of Beilstein's hotels shut down from mid-November through March.

$$$ Hotel Haus Lipmann is your chance to live in a medi-eval mansion with hot showers and TVs. A prizewinner for atmo-sphere, it's been in the Lipmann family for 200 years. The creaky wooden staircase and the elegant dining hall, with long wooden tables surrounded by antlers, chandeliers, and feudal weapons, will get you in the mood for your castle sightseeing, but the riverside terrace may mace your momentum. Their new nearby annex offers larger rooms in an equally old house (12 rooms total, Sb-€75–90, Db-€85–100, Tb-€105–125, Qb-€125–150, price depends on length of stay and day of week, half-board deals, cash only, closed Nov–April, Marktplatz 3, tel. 02673/1573, fax 02673/1521, www .hotel-haus-lipmann.com, hotel.haus.lipmann@t-online.de). The entire Lipmann family—Marion and Jonas, their hardworking son David, and his wife Anja—hustle for their guests.

Marion's brother Joachim Lipmann runs two hotels of his own: **$$$ Hotel Lipmann Am Klosterberg** is a big, modern place with 16 comfortable rooms at the extremely quiet top of town (Db-€60– 80, closed Nov–March, Auf dem Teich 8, up the main street 200 yards inland, tel. 02673/1850, fax 02673/1287, www.hotel-lipmann .de, lipmann@t-online.de). The half-timbered, riverfront **$$ Altes Zollhaus Gästezimmer** packs all the comforts into eight tight, bright rooms (Sb-€45, Db-€60, deluxe Db-€80, elevator, closed Nov–March, same contact info as Hotel Lipmann Am Klosterberg; adjoining restaurant Alte Stadtmauer is open daily 10:30–22:00, closed Nov–March).

$$ Hotel Gute Quelle offers half-timbers, a good restaurant (see "Eating"), and 13 inviting rooms, plus seven more in an annex across the street (Sb-€40, D-€60, Db-€64, less for longer stays, closed Dec–March, Marktplatz 34, tel. 02673/1437, fax 02673/1399, www.hotel-gute-quelle.de, info@hotel-gute-quelle .de, helpful Susan speaks Irish).

$ The welcoming **Gasthaus Winzerschenke an der Klostertreppe** is a great value, with five rooms right in the tiny heart of town at the bottom of the stairs to the cloister (Db-€50, bigger Db-€60, cash only, discount for 3-night stays, open weekends only Nov–Easter, go up main street and take second left onto Fürst-Metternich-Strasse, reception in restaurant, tel. 02673/1354, fax 02673/962-371, www.winzerschenke-beilstein.de, winzerschenke-beilstein@t-online.de, young and eager Stefanie and Christian Sausen).

EATING

You'll have no problem in Beilstein finding a characteristic dining room or a relaxing riverview terrace.

Restaurant Haus Lipmann serves good, fresh food with daily specials on a glorious leafy riverside terrace (€8–19 entrées, May–Oct daily 10:00–23:00, closed Nov–April).

The **Zehnthauskeller** on the Marktplatz is *the* place for wine-tasting with soup, cold plates, and lively *Schlager* music (kitschy

German folk-pop) while old locals on holiday sit under a dark medieval vault (Easter–Oct Tue–Sun 11:00–23:00, closed Mon and off-season).

The recommended **Hotel Gute Quelle** runs a popular restaurant (€9–19 entrées, daily 11:00–21:00, closed Dec–March, Marktplatz 34).

Zell

Peaceful, with a fine riverside promenade, a pedestrian bridge over the water, and plenty of *Zimmer*, Zell makes a good overnight stop. Zell has a long pedestrian zone filled with colorful shops, restaurants, and *Weinstuben* (wine bars). A fun oompah folk band plays on weekend evenings on the main square, making evenings here a delight.

Getting to Zell

Trains go every 30 minutes from Cochem or Trier to Bullay, where the bus takes you to little Zell (€1.50, hourly, usually at :20 past the hour, 15 min; bus stop is across street from Bullay train station, check yellow MB schedule for times, last bus at 20:20 Mon–Fri, at 18:20 Sat–Sun). The central Zell stop is called Lindenplatz.

ORIENTATION

Tourist Information

The TI is just off the pedestrian street, four blocks downriver from the pedestrian bridge; at the fountain with the cat statue, walk away from the river (Aug–Oct Mon–Fri 9:00–18:00, Sat 10:00–15:00, closed Sun except during festivals; Nov–March Mon–Thu 9:00–12:30 & 13:30–17:00, Fri 9:00–13:00, closed Sat–Sun; April Mon–Fri 9:00–17:00, closed Sat–Sun; May–July Mon–Fri 9:00–17:00, Sat 9:00–13:00, closed Sun; tel. 06542/96220, www.zellmosel.de).

Helpful Hints

Internet Access: Berliner Kaffekännchen offers two terminals (€1.50/15 min, €5/hr, Mon–Tue and Thu–Fri 8:00–18:30, Sat 8:00–18:00, Sun 14:00–18:00, closed Wed, across pedestrian bridge opposite bus stop at Balduinstrasse 107, tel. 06542/5450).

Bike Rental: Frau Klaus rents bikes (€6.50/day, pick up 8:30–13:00, arrange return time, 1.25 miles out of town, toward Bullay at Hauptstrasse 5, tel. 06542/41087, no English spoken).

Views: For a village view, walk up to the medieval wall's gatehouse and through the cemetery to the old munitions tower.

SIGHTS

Mosel Museum—The little Wein und Heimatmuseum features Mosel history (only open May–Oct Wed and Sun 14:00–17:00, in same building as TI).

Winery Tour—Locals know Zell for its Schwarze Katze ("Black Cat") wine. Peter Weis, who runs the **F. J. Weis winery,** gives a clever, entertaining, and free tour of his 40,000-bottle-per-year wine cellar. Tour times and length vary—it's important to call ahead to reserve (open April–Nov daily 10:30–19:00, closed at lunchtime and Dec–March but call and they might fit you in for a tasting, he also rents apartments—see below, tel. 06542/41398, f.j.weis@t-online.de). Buy a bottle or two to keep this fine tour going. A blue flag marks his *Weinkeller* south of town, 200 yards past the bridge toward Bernkastel, riverside at Notenau 30.

SLEEPING

(country code: 49, area code: 06542)
Zell's hotels are a disappointment, but its private homes are a fine value. The owners speak almost no English and discount their rates if you stay more than one night. They don't take reservations long in advance for one-night stays; just call a day ahead.

$$$ **Hotel zum Grünen Kranz,** with 29 rooms, is the place if you're looking for room service, a sauna, a pool, and an elevator (Sb-€45–60, Db-€90–130, price depends on season and day of week, non-smoking rooms, Balduinstrasse 13, tel. 06542/98610, fax 06542/986-180, www.zum-gruenen-kranz.de, info @zumgruenenkranz.de). In the annex across the street, they rent 10 immense rooms (prices on request).

$$$ **Hotel Ratskeller,** just off the main square on a pedestrian street, rents 14 sharp rooms with tile flooring and fair rates (Sb-€45, Db-€72, cheaper Nov–mid-April, Internet access, above a pizzeria, Balduinstrasse 36, tel. 06542/98620, fax 06542/986-244, ratskeller-zellmosel@web.de, Gardi).

$$$ **Hotel Weinhaus Mayer** has 16 rooms with riverview balconies and top comforts (Db-€88, Balduinstrasse 5–7, tel. 06542/61169, fax 06542/61160, www.hotel-weinhaus-mayer.de, info@hotel-weinhaus-mayer.de).

$$$ **Weinhaus Mayer,** an old pension with 10 rooms, is perfectly central and has Mosel views. It's managed by the non-English-speaking parents of the daughter who runs the hotel

listed directly above (Db-€72, cash only, Balduinstrasse 15, tel. 06542/4530, fax 06542/61160, info@hotel-weinhaus-mayer.de).

$$ Peter Weis Apartments, of the F. J. Weis winery (recommended above), rents two luxurious apartments (Db-€60, less for 2 or more nights, extra person-€10, breakfast-€6.50, important to call in advance, 200 yards beyond bridge on Bernkastel road, riverside at Notenau 30, tel. 06542/41398, fax 06542/961-178, www.weingut-fjweis.de, f.j.weis@t-online.de).

$ Gasthaus Gertrud Thiesen is classy, with a TV/living/breakfast room and a river view. The Thiesen house has four big, bright rooms and is on the town's first corner, overlooking the Mosel from a great terrace (D-€40, Db-€45, cash only, closed Nov–Feb, Balduinstrasse 1, tel. 06542/4453).

TRIER

Germany's oldest city lies at the head of the scenic Mosel Valley, near the border with Luxembourg. An ancient Roman capital, Trier brags that it was inhabited by Celts for 1,300 years before Rome even existed. Today, Trier is thriving and feels very young. A short stop here offers you a look at Germany's oldest Christian church, one of its most enjoyable market squares, and its best Roman ruins.

Founded by Augustus in 16 B.C., Trier served as the Roman town Augusta Treverorum for 400 years. When Emperor Diocletian (who ruled A.D. 285–305) divided his overextended Roman Empire into four sectors, he made Trier the capital of the west: roughly modern-day Germany, France, Spain, and England. For most of the fourth century, this city of 80,000—with a four-mile wall, four great gates, and 47 round towers—was the favored residence of Roman emperors. Emperor Constantine used the town as the capital of his fading Western Roman Empire. Many of the Roman buildings were constructed under Constantine before he left for Constantinople. In 480, Trier fell to the Franks.

Today, Trier's Roman sights include the huge city gate (Porta Nigra), basilica, baths, and amphitheater. Trier's main draw is the chance to experience Germany's Roman and early Christian history. If you're more interested in wine-tasting and scenery, stay elsewhere on the Mosel River (see previous chapter).

ORIENTATION

(area code: 0651)

Tourist Information

Trier's cramped and busy TI is just through the Porta Nigra. You can pay €1.50 for an easily readable map, but cheapskates can squint at the free and sufficient small-print map. The TI also sells a useful little guide to the city called *Trier: History and Monuments* (€4) and hands out the *Holiday Region Trier* brochure (free, lists opening hours of Trier's sights, info on city tours, Mosel boat excursions, events, leisure activities, and more). Also consider the booklet *Walking Tours Through Trier* (€3), which has little information on sights but a great map and proposed walking routes (Roman, medieval, Jewish, rainy day). The TI also offers tours (see "Tours") and a free room-booking service (May–Oct Mon–Thu 9:00–18:00, Fri–Sat 9:00–19:00, Sun 10:00–17:00; Nov–Dec and March–April Mon–Sat 9:00–18:00, Sun 10:00–15:00; Jan–Feb Mon–Sat 9:00–17:00, Sun 10:00–13:00; tel. 0651/978-080, www.trier.de).

Discount Deals: The **Trier Card** allows free use of city buses and discounts on city tours, museums, and Roman sights (€9, family-€15, valid for 3 days, sold at TI). Since the town is small and walkable, this is only a good deal if you'll be here for two or three days and plan to visit lots of sights. If you're visiting at least three Roman sights (including the Porta Nigra, baths, and amphitheater, but not the Archaeological Museum), buy the **Roman sights combo-ticket** instead (a.k.a. "combination admission ticket," €6.20, family ticket-€14.80, each sight costs €2.10 individually—do the math and decide, available at participating sights).

Arrival in Trier

By Train: The *Reisezentrum* at the train station can answer your train-schedule questions and book tickets for you (Mon–Fri 6:50–19:15, Sat 8:30–17:15, Sun 10:30–18:15). The station also has lockers (€1.50–2.50), a WC (€0.50), and bike rental (see "Helpful Hints"). To reach the town center from the train station, walk 10 boring minutes and four blocks up Theodor-Heuss-Allee to the big black Roman gate (Porta Nigra), and turn left under the gate to find the TI. From here, the main pedestrian mall (Simeonstrasse) leads into the town's charm: Market Square and the cathedral (a five-minute walk) and basilica (five more minutes).

By Car: Drivers get off at Trier Verteilerkreis and follow signs to *Zentrum*. There's parking near the gate and TI.

Helpful Hints

Laundry: A well-maintained, self-service launderette is just beyond Karl Marx's House (€5–9, daily 8:00–22:00, Brückenstrasse 19).

Internet Access: Arcor, across the busy intersection from the Porta Nigra, charges a low hourly rate (€1.50/hr, Mon–Fri 9:00–22:30, Sat–Sun 12:00–23:00, US keyboards, Porta Nigra Platz 4).

Bike Rental: A local citizens' group called **Bürgerservice** rents bikes for reasonable daily rates. Find them just off track 11 at the train station (€8/24 hrs, €2 extra for mountain bikes, leave €30 and ID as deposit; mid-April–Oct daily 9:00–19:00; Nov–mid-April Mon–Fri 10:00–18:00, closed Sat–Sun; tel. 0651/148-856, www.bues-trier.de).

TOURS

Walking Tours—The TI offers a €7 two-hour walking tour in English on Saturdays at 13:30 (May–Oct only), and €80 private two-hour tours (tel. 0651/978-080).

Bus Tours—For a live guide and a big, air-conditioned bus, take the one-hour tour offered by the TI (€7, May–Oct daily at 13:00 in English, at 11:00 and 12:00 in German, no tours Nov–April).

Tourist Train—If you're tired and want a city overview, consider riding the hokey little red-and-yellow tourist train, the Römer-Express, for its

35-minute loop of Trier's major old-town sights (€6, daily April–Oct 2/hr 10:00–18:00, daily March and Nov–Dec hourly 10:00–17:00, Jan–Feb may run Sat–Sun hourly 11:00–16:00—weather permitting, recorded narration in English, departs from TI, buy tickets from driver or at TI, tel. 0651/9935-9525, www.roemer -express.de).

SELF-GUIDED WALK

Welcome to Trier

This fun walk, offering a taste of Trier old, new, and in-between, will take you to the historic city's top sights.

• *Start at the...*

▲Porta Nigra

Roman Trier was built as a capital. Its architecture mirrored the grandeur of the empire. Of the four-mile town wall's four huge gates, only this north gate sur-  vives. This most impressive Roman fortification in Germany was built without mortar—only iron pegs hold the sandstone blocks together. While the other three gates were destroyed by medieval metal and stone scavengers, this "black gate" (originally red sandstone, but darkened by time) survived because it became a church. St. Simeon—a pious Greek recluse—lived inside the gate for seven years. After his death in 1035, the St. Simeon monastery was established, and the gate was made into a two-story church—lay church on the bottom, monastery church on top. Napoleon wanted everything non-Roman about the structure destroyed in 1803, but the 12th-century Romanesque apse—the round part at the east end—survived. You can climb around the gate, but there's little to see aside from a fine town view. Just inside the entrance, look for pictures of how the gate looked during various eras, including its church phase (€2.10, daily April–Sept 9:00–18:00, March and Oct 9:00–17:00, Nov–Feb 9:00–16:00).

Trier's main pedestrian drag, which leads away from the gate, is named for St. Simeon. The arcaded courtyard and buildings of the monastery of St. Simeon remain, and are now home to the TI and a slick new **City Museum** (Stadtmuseum Simeonstift). The museum's collection seems to be largely made up of anything old that turned up in townspeople's basements, and most of the items on display are only mildly interesting. However, the third floor holds a fascinating model—painstakingly constructed over 19 years—of Trier as it looked in 1800, which might just make this museum worth the admission price (€5, includes audioguide, Tue–Sun 10:00–18:00, closed Mon, tel. 0651/718-1459).

• *As you walk to Market Square, you'll glimpse, about halfway down Simeonstrasse on your left at #19, the...*

House of the Three Magi (Dreikönigshaus)

Now a restaurant, this colorful Venetian-style building was constructed in the 13th century as a keep. Look for the floating door a story above the present-day entrance. A wooden staircase to this door was once the only way in or out. If the town was in danger, the staircase could be burned or torn down, in order to fend off enemies and protect inhabitants. (Look for another medieval keep

Trier

① Hotel/Rest. zum Christophel
② Hotel Römischer Kaiser
③ Hotel/Rest. Frankenturm
④ Warsberger Hof Hotel/Rest.
⑤ Hotel Pieper
⑥ Hotel Monopol
⑦ To Hotel Petrisberg Trier
⑧ Krim Restaurant
⑨ Zum Domstein Rest.
⑩ Launderette
⑪ Internet Café
⑫ Church of St. Gangolf

with a floating door—the Frankenturm—just off Market Square, near the recommended hotel of the same name.)

• *Continue down the pedestrian street until you reach the...*

▲▲Market Square (Hauptmarkt)

Trier's Hauptmarkt square is a people-filled swirl of fruit stands, flowers, painted facades, and fountains (with a handy public WC). This is one of Germany's most in-love-with-life marketplaces.

For an orientation to the sights, go to the square's centerpiece, a market cross, and stand on the side of the cross closest to the big stone **cathedral** a block away. This cathedral was the seat of the archbishop. In medieval times, the cathedral was its own walled city, and the archbishop of Trier was one of the seven German electors who chose the Holy Roman Emperor. This gave the arch-

bishop tremendous political, as well as spiritual, power (for more on the cathedral, see the next entry).

The pink-and-white building (now an H&M department store) on the corner of the lane leading to the cathedral was a **palace** for the archbishop. Notice the seal above the door: a crown flanked by a crosier, representing the bishop's ecclesiastical power, and a sword, demonstrating his political might. This did not sit well with the townspeople of Trier. The square you're standing in was the symbolic battlefield of a centuries-long conflict between Trier's citizens and its bishop.

The stone market **cross** (a replica of the A.D. 958 original, now in the City Museum) was the archbishop's way of bragging about the trading rights granted to him by King Otto the Great. This was a slap in the face to Trier's townspeople. They'd wanted Trier to be designated a "free imperial city," with full trading rights and beholden only to the king, not controlled by a local prince or bishop.

Look across the square from the lane to the cathedral, to the 15th-century **Town Hall** (Steipe). The people of Trier wanted a Town Hall, but the bishop wouldn't allow it—so they built this "assembly hall" instead, with a knight on each second-story corner. The knight on the left, facing Market Square, has his mask up, watching over his people. The other knight, facing the cathedral and the bishop, has his mask down and his hand on his sword, ready for battle.

Tensions mounted 30 years later. Look to the left, at the tall white steeple with yellow trim. This is the Gothic tower of the **Church of St. Gangolf,** the medieval townspeople's church and fire watchman's post. (From medieval times until the present day, a bell has rung nightly at 22:00, reminding local drunks to go home. When the automatic bell-ringer broke a few years back,

concerned locals flooded the mayor with calls.) In 1507, Trier's mayor built this new Gothic tower to make the people's church higher than the cathedral. A Bible verse in Latin adorns the top in gold letters: "Stay awake and pray." In retaliation, the bishop raised one tower of his cathedral (all he could afford). He topped it with a threatening message of his own, continuing the Town Hall's verse: "For you never know the hour when the Lord will come."

Look farther to the left, to the Renaissance **St. Peter's Fountain** (1595). This fountain symbolizes thoughtful city government, with allegorical statues of justice (sword and scale), fortitude (broken column), temperance (wine and water), and prudence (a snake and, formerly, a mirror—but since the mirror was stolen long ago, she's now empty-handed). The ladies represent idealized cardinal virtues—but notice the rude monkeys hiding on the column behind them, showing the way things are really done. The recommended **Zum Domstein** restaurant is next to the fountain (see "Eating").

The rest of the square is a textbook of architectural styles. Notice the half-timbered houses at the north end of the square (toward the Porta Nigra), marking Trier's 14th-century Jewish ghetto. Nearby, look for the Art Deco hotel that now houses a McDonald's (the locals have dubbed its famous arches "the golden horn").

• *When you're finished on the square, head down Sternstrasse to the...*

▲▲Cathedral (Dom)

This is the oldest Christian church in Germany. St. Helena was the mother of Emperor Constantine (who legalized Christianity

in the Roman Empire in A.D. 312) and an important figure in early Christian history. She allowed part of her palace to be used as the first church on this spot. In A.D. 326, to celebrate the 20th anniversary of his reign, Constantine began the construction of St. Peter's in Rome and this huge cathedral in Trier—also called St. Peter's. The Dom information center is on the courtyard across from the cathedral; ask if any excavations from the very first part of Constantine's cathedral are open for public viewing.

Begin your visit in the large front courtyard of the cathedral. As you face the cathedral, look in the corner behind you and to your left (near the pink palace); you'll see a large patch of light-colored bricks in an L shape in the ground. The original Roman cathedral was more than four times its present size; these light-colored bricks mark one corner of this massive "double cathedral." (The opposite corner was at the back of the smaller Liebfrau church, waaay across the courtyard.) The plaque by the corner shows the floor plan of the original Roman cathedral.

Enter the cathedral (free, €0.10 English info flyer, daily April–Oct 6:30–18:00, Nov–March 6:30–17:30, www.trierer-dom .de). You'll see many altars lining the nave, dedicated not to saints, but to bishops. These ornate funeral altars were a fashionable way for the powerful archbishop-electors to memorialize themselves. Even the elaborate black-and-white altar at the back of the church (where you entered) is not a religious shrine, but a memorial for a single rich bishop.

The "pilgrim's walk" (the stairway to the right of the altar) leads to the chapel holding the cathedral's most important relic: the Holy Robe of Christ, found by St. Helena on a pilgrimage to Jerusalem (rarely on view, but you can see its reliquary; look for photos of the actual robe after the first flight of stairs). Also up this stairway is the entrance to the **treasury** (Schatzkammer), displaying huge bishops' rings, the sandal of St. Andrew (in a box topped with a golden foot), and a holy nail supposedly from the Crucifixion (€1.50; April–Oct Mon–Sat 10:00–16:45, Sun 14:00–16:45; Nov–March Mon–Sat 11:00–15:45, Sun 14:00–15:45). From the treasury, you can fight the crowds up the last few stairs to the chapel (same hours as treasury). Back down the stairs, the door on your left leads to the peaceful Domkreuzgang **cloister** between the Dom and the Liebfrau church.

From inside the cathedral, enter the adjoining **Liebfrau Church,** which claims to be the oldest Gothic church in Germany (it dates from 1235). This church was built when Gothic was in vogue, so French architects were brought in—and paid with money borrowed from the bishop of Köln when funds ran dry. It's now filled with colorful, modern stained glass (daily April–Oct 7:30–18:00, Nov–March 7:30–17:30).

Returning to the cathedral and leaving the way you came in, notice the controversial modern (1972) paintings at the back of the church, representing the Alpha (Paradise/Creation, to the left) and the Omega (the Last Judgment, to the right).

If you want to visit the Bishop's Museum (described next), go right as you exit the cathedral's main door and turn down the first street on your right (Windstrasse). As you walk with the cathedral on your right, you'll be able to see the different eras of its construction. The big red cube that makes up the back half of the present-day cathedral is all that remains of the enormous, original fourth-century Roman construction (at one time twice as tall as what you see here). Arched bricks in the facade show the original position of Roman windows and doors. Around this Roman nucleus, chunks were grafted on over a millennium and a half of architectural styles: the front half of the cathedral facing the big courtyard, added in the 11th century; the choir on the back, from the 12th century; and the transept and round Baroque shrine on the far back, from the 18th century.

If you look at the original Roman construction squarely, you'll see that it's not perfectly vertical. Locks were built along the Mosel River in the 1960s, depleting groundwater—which was the only thing preserving the church's original wooden foundation. The foundation disintegrated, and the walls began to sag. Architects competed to find a way to prevent the cathedral from collapsing, and the winner—a huge steel bracket above the main nave, holding the walls up with cables—seems to be working.

• *Just past the cathedral on Windstrasse to the left is the...*

▲Bishop's Museum (Bischöfliches Diözesanmuseum)

This museum offers exhibits on the history of the cathedral. Inside and to the right, find the small model of the original Roman church, and the bigger model showing some of the present-day excavations of its various pieces. Don't miss the pieced-together remains of fine ceiling frescoes (dating from A.D. 310–320) from a Roman palace. The palace was destroyed in about 325, and the cathedral was built on top of it. The 50,000 pieces of the frescoes were discovered while cleaning up from WWII bombs. The vivid reds, greens, and blues of the restored works depict frolicking cupids, bejeweled women, and a philosopher clutching his scroll (all described in German). A good €3.60 English book clearly explains the palace ceiling's elaborate structure and the fresco restoration process. Elsewhere in the museum, the stone capitals, gold chalices, vestments, and icons are meaningless to most, unless you can read German (€2; April–Oct Mon–Sat 9:00–17:00, Sun 13:00–17:00; Nov–March Tue–Sat 9:00–17:00, Sun 13:00–17:00, closed Mon; Windstrasse 6, tel. 0651/710-5255, www.museum .bistum-trier.de).

• *Return to the front of the cathedral and head two blocks south (away from Market Square) to the 200-foot-by-100-foot...*

▲▲Basilica/Imperial Throne Room (Konstantin Basilica)

This building is the largest intact Roman structure outside of Rome. It's best known as a basilica, but it actually started as a throne room. Go inside and look up: Each of the squares in the ceiling above you is 10 feet by 10 feet—as big as your hotel room. Picture this throne room in ancient times, decorated with golden mosaics, rich marble, colorful stucco, and busts of Constantine and his family filling the seven niches. The emperor sat in majesty

under a canopy on his altar-like throne. The windows in the apse around him were smaller than the ones along the side walls, making his throne seem even bigger.

The last emperor moved out in A.D. 395, and petty kings set up camp in the building throughout the Middle Ages. By the 12th century, the bishops had taken it over and converted it to a five-story palace. The building became a Lutheran church in 1856, and it remains the only Lutheran church in Trier. It was badly damaged by WWII bombs, and later partially restored. A good €1 English booklet brings the near-empty shell to life (free; April–Oct Mon–Sat 10:00–18:00, Sun 12:00–18:00; Nov–March Tue–Sat 11:00–12:00 & 15:00–16:00, Sun 12:00–13:00, closed Mon; tel. 0651/72468).

A Rococo wing, the Elector's Palace, was added to the basilica in the 18th century to house the archbishop-elector; today, it houses local government offices (closed to the public).

• *The Rococo wing faces a fragrant, picnic-riffic garden, which leads to three sights: an interesting archaeological museum, the remains of a Roman bath, and a 25,000-seat amphitheater. We'll check out all three. Follow the path that cuts across the lawn to the left, where the archway near the pink atrium café leads to the...*

▲Archaeological Museum (Rheinisches Landesmuseum)

This is not only a great museum, but also an active research center. Since the museum was recently reorganized to display a temporary exhibit, expect changes from this description: Upstairs, in the back and to the right, is a huge model of Roman Trier (try to pick out the buildings that you're visiting today: cathedral, basilica, baths). Downstairs, explore the huge funerary monuments. Once these were all painted like the replica in the courtyard; today, they tell archaeologists volumes about daily life in Roman times. Find the woman visiting a beauty salon. (Hint: She's on the tallest monument.) The mosaics room is a highlight. On the wall, find the mosaic of four horses surrounding the superstar charioteer Polydus (mosaic floors were the *Sports Illustrated* covers of the Roman world), discovered intact at the Imperial Baths (cost and hours flexible, likely €5, daily 10:30–17:00, few English descriptions but good audioguide free with entry, tel. 0651/97740, www.landesmuseum-trier.de).

• *Exit the Archaeological Museum to the right, follow the path around the building to the archway in the wall, then go toward the red ruins of the...*

Imperial Baths (Kaiserthermen)

Built by Constantine, these were the biggest of Trier's three Roman baths, and the most intricate bath of the Roman world. Trier's cold northern climate, the size of the complex, and the enormity of Constantine's ego meant that these Imperial Baths required a two-story subterranean complex of pipes, furnaces, and slave galleys to keep the water at a perfect 47 degrees Celsius (120 degrees Fahrenheit). Explore the underground tunnels (almost a mile's worth), noticing the chest-high holes in the walls for the beams that used to hold the floor (slaves above, pipes below). It's an impressive complex—too bad the baths never quite worked right, and were left unfinished after Constantine left (€2.10, daily April–Sept 9:00–18:00, March and Oct 9:00–17:00, Nov–Feb 9:00–16:00, €2.50 English booklet, tel. 0651/436-2550).

• *For the unexceptional **amphitheater** (same price and hours as other Roman sights, tel. 0651/73010), follow the signs through the pedestrian underpass, then follow Hermesstrasse another half-mile as it curves up the hill and then turn left on Olewigerstrasse.*

Otherwise, consider heading back to town via another (less interesting) Roman bath: Leaving the Imperial Baths, take a left through the parking lot, cross the street to the Fischers Maathes restaurant, then follow Wechselstrasse two blocks. At Neustrasse, veer right to find Viehmarktstrasse, which leads to an open square (Viehmarktplatz). To your right is a modern glass box covering the bath excavations in the...

Viehmarkt Museum

Locals grouse that these ruins sat in the rain for years before their tax money was used to build this expensive new house. The red bricks in the square outside show the intersection of the original Roman roads, laid out as a grid (€2.10, Tue–Sun 9:00–17:00, closed Mon, last entry 30 min before closing, €1.50 English brochure, tel. 0651/994-1057). To get here from Market Square, walk down Brotstrasse, and head right on Fahrstrasse—past a cool fountain showing Trier craftsmen at work—to the museum entrance.

• *Our walk is over. From here, you can amble back to Market Square for more food, flowers, fountains, and people-watching; or, if Market Square's capitalism makes you see red, you can walk a few yards toward town on Stresemannstrasse, and make a hard left on Brückenstrasse for...*

Karl Marx's House

Communists can lick their wounds at Karl Marx's birthplace, where early manuscripts, letters, and photographs of the influential

economist/philosopher fill several rooms. The exhibition was beautifully redone in 2005, but the information is only in German. Oblivious to their slide out of a shrinking middle class, some people still sneer (€3, includes free brochure; April–Oct daily 10:00–18:00; Nov–March Tue–Sun 10:00–13:00 & 14:00–17:00, Mon 14:00–17:00; tel. 0651/970-680, www.fes.de/Karl-Marx-Haus). From Market Square, it's a 10-minute walk down Fleischstrasse—which becomes Brückenstrasse—to the house at Brückenstrasse 10.

SLEEPING

For locations, see the map on page 283.

Near the Porta Nigra

$$$ Hotel zum Christophel offers top comfort in its 11 classy rooms, above a fine restaurant and with a kind owner. It's an easy roll from the train station with your luggage (Sb-€60–65, Db-€90–95, elevator, Am Porta Nigra Platz/Simeonstrasse 1, tel. 0651/979-4200, fax 0651/74732, www.zumchristophel.de, info @zumchristophel.de).

$$$ Hotel Römischer Kaiser, next door, is also nice, but a lesser value—charging more for a polished lobby and 43 comparable rooms (Sb-€70–80, Db-€100–120, more during festivals, elevator, Wi-Fi in lobby, free parking, Am Porta Nigra Platz 6, tel. 0651/977-0010, fax 0651/9770-1999, www.hotels-trier.de, rezeption@hotels-trier.de).

Near Market Square

$$$ Hotel Frankenturm, decked out in modern style with track lighting and cheery color schemes, has 12 rooms above a lively saloon and next to a medieval keep of the same name. The six rooms with private baths are on the first floor up; the other six rooms are two floors up, with a shared bath (S-€45, Sb-€65, D-€55, Db-€85, T-€65, Tb-€95, no elevator, Dietrichstrasse 3, tel. 0651/978-240, fax 0651/978-2449, www.hotel-frankenturm.de, frankenturm@t-online.de).

$ Warsberger Hof, run by a local citizens' league, is a clean, simple hostel and budget hotel two blocks from Market Square, with 150 beds and an inexpensive restaurant. This is your best value for cheap sleeps in town (€19 per bed in 3- to 6-bed dorms,

---

Sleep Code

(€1 = about $1.30, country code: 49, area code: 0651)
S = Single, **D** = Double/Twin, **T** = Triple, **Q** = Quad, **b** = bathroom,
s = shower only. Unless otherwise noted, credit cards are
accepted, English is spoken, and breakfast is included.

To help you sort easily through these listings, I've divided
the rooms into three categories, based on the price for a standard double room with bath:

$$$ Higher Priced—Most rooms €85 or more.
$$ Moderately Priced—Most rooms between €50–85.
$ Lower Priced—Most rooms €50 or less.

---

sheets-€3, S-€23–27, D-€45, T-€65, Q-€82, showers down the
hall, breakfast-€5, Dietrichstrasse 42, tel. 0651/975-250, fax
0651/975-2540, www.warsberger-hof.de, info@warsberger-hof.de).

Near the Train Station

$$ Hotel Pieper is run by the friendly Becker family (he cooks and
she keeps the books). They rent 20 comfortable rooms furnished
with dark wood over a pleasant neighborhood restaurant (Sb-€48,
Db-€75, Tb-€96, Wi-Fi, 8-min walk from station, 2 blocks off
main drag, Thebärstrasse 39, tel. 0651/23008, fax 0651/12839,
www.hotel-pieper-trier.de, info@hotel-pieper-trier.de). From the
station, follow Theodor-Heuss-Allee (toward Porta Nigra) to the
second big intersection, angle right onto Göbenstrasse, and con-
tinue as the road curves and becomes Thebärstrasse.

$$ Hotel Monopol, at the train station, has 35 older but
clean rooms. It's dark but handy (S-€31–34, Sb-€39–47, D-€52–57,
Db-€62–77, Tb-€99, Qb-€120, elevator, Bahnhofsplatz 7, tel.
0651/714-090, fax 0651/714-0910, www.hotel-monopol-trier.de,
bernd.glatzel@hotel-monopol-trier.de).

Outside the Center

$$$ Hotel Petrisberg Trier, near the amphitheater, is top-quality
and ideal if you have a car. It's on a hillside overlooking the city,
exuding old-school elegance without being stuffy. The Pantenburg
family takes great care to spoil all their guests; Helmut whips up
tasty egg breakfasts, while his niece Christina—the 2001 Trier
Wine Queen—works reception. A pleasant footpath brings you
downhill to the cathedral in 20 minutes (Sb-€65, Db-€95, Internet
access and Wi-Fi, Sickingenstrasse 11–13, tel. 0651/4640, fax
0651/46450, www.hotel-petrisberg.de, info@hotel-petrisberg.de).

EATING

Good eateries abound on the side streets leading away from the pedestrian drag (Simeonstrasse) and from Market Square. Most of the recommended hotels have good-value restaurants.

Hotel Frankenturm, a few doors down Dietrichstrasse from Market Square, offers German cuisine with a twist of Asian and Mediterranean in a modern pub-style atmosphere (€8–16 main dishes, €4–8 weekday lunch specials, Mon–Sat 8:00–24:00, Sun 17:00–24:00, Dietrichstrasse 3).

Warsberger Hof Eateries: A few doors farther down Dietrichstrasse, in the big yellow pastel building on the right, the recommended **Warsberger Hof hostel** runs three inexpensive eateries: the **Leonardy** pub and cafe (daily 10:00–24:00), the **Rautenstrauch** restaurant (€12.50 main dishes, nice enclosed terrace, kid-friendly, daily 11:00–23:00), and a **self-service cafeteria** serving cheap lunches (Mon–Fri 11:30–14:15, closed Sat–Sun).

At **Krim,** also just off Market Square, young locals enjoy trendy Mediterranean cuisine (€9–16 main dishes, daily 9:00–24:00, breakfast until 18:00, Glockenstrasse 7, tel. 0651/73943).

Zum Domstein, right on Market Square, serves standard German fare and also has a special, pricier menu of entrées based on ancient Roman recipes. The Roman menu was inspired during renovations, when the owner discovered a Roman column in her cellar. (In Trier, you can't put a rec room in your basement without tripping over Roman ruins.) The finished dining room incorporates the column, plus a mini-museum of Roman crockery (€10–20 main dishes, open daily, Roman dishes downstairs 12:00–14:00 & 18:00–21:00, rest of café open 11:30–22:00, Am Hauptmarkt 5, tel. 0651/74490).

The recommended **Hotel zum Christophel** also has a reasonably priced restaurant with a view of the Porta Nigra (daily 11:00–23:00, Simeonstrasse 1).

TRANSPORTATION CONNECTIONS

From Trier by Train to: **Cochem** (2/hr, 45–65 min), **Bullay** (where you can transfer to a bus to **Zell;** hourly, 40 min), **Koblenz** (2/hr, 90 min), **Köln** (hourly, 2.5–3 hrs, some change in Koblenz), **St. Goar/Bacharach** (hourly, 2.5 hrs, change in Koblenz), **Frankfurt Airport** (1–2/hr, 3 hrs, 1–2 changes). Train info: tel. 11861 (€0.60/min).

KÖLN
AND THE UNROMANTIC RHINE

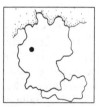

Romance isn't everything. Köln is an urban Jacuzzi that keeps the Rhine churning. It's home to Germany's greatest Gothic cathedral and its best collection of Roman artifacts, a world-class art museum, and a healthy dose of German urban playfulness.

Peaceful Bonn, which offers good people-watching and fun pedestrian streets, used to be the capital of West Germany. The small town of Remagen had a bridge that helped defeat Hitler in World War II, and unassuming Aachen, near the Belgian border, was once the capital of Europe.

Köln

Germany's fourth-largest city, Köln ("Cologne" in English) has a compact, lively center. The Rhine was the northern boundary

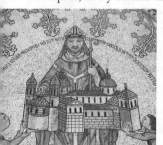

of the Roman Empire and, 1,700 years ago, Constantine—the first Christian emperor—made Colonia the seat of a bishopric. Five hundred years later, under Charlemagne, Köln became the seat of an archbishopric. With 40,000 people within its walls, it was the largest German city and an important cultural and religious center throughout the Middle Ages. Today, the city is most famous for its toilet water: Eau de Cologne was first made here by an Italian chemist in 1709.

Even though WWII bombs destroyed 95 percent of Köln

(population down from 800,000 to 40,000), it has become, after a remarkable recovery, a bustling commercial and cultural center, all the while keeping its traditions intact.

Planning Your Time

Köln makes an ideal on-the-way stop; it's situated on a major rail line and its top sights are clustered near the train station. With an hour or two, you can toss your bag in a locker, zip through the cathedral, and head out of town. If you're making that quick of a stop, make sure you'll be here when the whole church is open (see page 297 for times). More time (or an overnight) allows you to delve into a few of the city's fine museums and take in an old-time beer pub.

ORIENTATION

(area code: 0221)
Köln's old-town core, bombed out then rebuilt quaint, is traffic-free and includes a park and bike path along the river. From the cathedral/TI/train station, it's a short walk to Frankenwerft, the waterfront park, where the city's famously relaxed attitude is on display. From the park, look back at the Hohenzollernbrücke, which crosses the Rhine at the cathedral and is the busiest railway bridge in the world (30 trains per hour all day long). The old town's quaint medieval streets connect the riverside to Hohe Strasse, the main shopping street.

Tourist Information

Köln's energetic TI, opposite the cathedral entrance, has a basic €0.20 city map and several brochures (Mon–Sat 9:00–20:00, Sun 10:00–17:00, Unter Fettenhennen 19, tel. 0221/2213-0400, www.koelntourismus.de). They also offer a range of private guided tours, covering such topics as architecture, medieval Köln, and Romanesque churches (call TI to reserve).

Arrival in Köln

Köln couldn't be easier to visit—its three important sights cluster within two blocks of the TI and train station. This super pedestrian zone is a constant carnival of people.

Köln's busy **train station** has everything you need: a drugstore, food court, juice bar, shopping mall with grocery store, pricey WC (€1), travel center (*Reisezentrum*, Mon–Fri 6:00–22:00, Sat–Sun 7:00–21:00), and high-tech lockers (€4/24 hrs, accepts coins and €5 and €10 bills, put money in and wait 30 seconds for door to open, your luggage—up to 4 pieces—is transferred to storage via an underground conveyor belt and retrieved when you re-insert

Köln

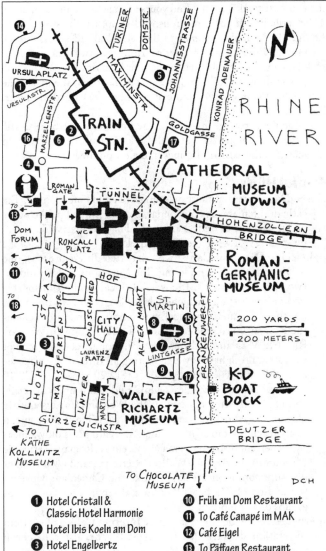

1. Hotel Cristall & Classic Hotel Harmonie
2. Hotel Ibis Koeln am Dom
3. Hotel Engelbertz
4. Central Hotel am Dom
5. Hotel Müller
6. Station Hostel
7. Gaffel Haus Restaurant
8. Papa Joe's Klimperkasten Pub
9. Papa Joe's Jazzlokal
10. Früh am Dom Restaurant
11. To Café Canapé im MAK
12. Café Eigel
13. To Päffgen Restaurant
14. Schreckenskammer Rest.
15. Frankenwerft Bars & Eateries
16. Internet Café
17. Bike Rentals (2)
18. To Kolumba Diocesan Museum

your ticket; next to *Reisezentrum*). Exiting the front of the station (the end near track 1), you'll find yourself smack-dab in the shadow of the cathedral. If your jaw drops, pick it up. Up the steps and to the right is the main entrance to the cathedral (TI across street). For Hotel Müller, leave the station from the back (the end near track 11; construction site may make it hard to find).

If you **drive** to Köln, follow signs to *Zentrum,* then continue to the huge Parkhaus am Dom pay lot under the cathedral (€2/hr, €18/day).

If you're arriving on a K-D Line **boat,** exit the boat to the right, then walk along the waterside park until just before the train bridge, when the cathedral comes into view on the left.

Helpful Hints

Closed Day: Note that most museums are closed on Monday. The cathedral remains open Monday, but has limited public hours on Sunday due to frequent services. For information on Köln's museums, visit www.museenkoeln.de.

Sightseeing Discount Cards: Köln has two different cards, one of which is worth considering. The **MuseumCard** is valid for two consecutive days. It covers all local public transportation on the first day (which includes local trains to Bonn, but not the slick InterCity and Express trains), and also includes the Roman-Germanic Museum, Museum Ludwig, Wallraf-Richartz Museum, and a few other minor attractions (but not the cathedral sights). If you're visiting all three of these museums, this card will save you money (€12.20/person, or €20.40 for a family pass—includes 2 adults and 2 kids up to 18, available at participating museums). The **WelcomeCard** is a waste of money—while it covers the city's transit system, you can easily reach the top sights on foot. The card gives only a measly 20 percent discount on major museums (Roman-Germanic Museum, Ludwig, and Wallraf-Richartz), and even smaller discounts on other attractions like the Chocolate Museum (€9/24 hrs, €14/48 hrs, €19/72 hrs; discounts for families or groups of 3 or more).

Internet Access: Consider **Via Phone Internet Café,** a block from the station at Marzellenstrasse 3–5 (€2/hr, also sells cheap phone cards, daily 9:00–24:00, tel. 0221/1399-6200).

Baggage Storage: The station's luggage service is the most convenient (see previous section, "Arrival in Köln"), but cheapskates can save a few euros by using Museum Ludwig's €0.50 lockers. From the station's underground passage, take the escalator to Platform 1, do a U-turn at the top, and walk past Section A, all the way down to where the platform joins the street—look straight ahead for the museum's large sign.

Bike Rental: Convenient rental is available at friendly **Radstation,** tucked under the train-track arcade (€5/3 hrs, €10/day, Mon–Fri 5:30–22:30, Sat 6:30–20:00, Sun 8:00–20:00, exit station to Breslauer Platz and turn right, tel. 0221/139-7190). You can also rent bikes from the riverside **Kölner Fahrradverleih,** a 10-minute walk from the station (€2/hr, €10/day, daily 10:00–18:00, ask about recommended route, just across promenade from K-D Line docks on Markmannsgasse, mobile 0171-629-8796). Consider biking the path along the Rhine River up past the convention center *(Messe)* to the Rheinpark for a picnic. Or consider a guided bike tour (described under "Tours").

Gadget Supply: You can pick up a new memory card or whatever high-tech gizmo you're lacking for a fair price at **Media Markt,** conveniently located two blocks from the cathedral (Mon–Thu 10:00–20:00, Fri–Sat 10:00–21:00, closed Sun, corner of Hohe Strasse and Minoritenstrasse).

Ticket Office: To get tickets to concerts, the opera, or the theater, stop by **KölnMusik Ticket** next to the Roman-Germanic Museum (Mon–Fri 10:00–19:00, Sat 10:00–16:00, closed Sun, tel. 0221/280-280, can book ahead at www.koelnticket.de).

Festival: Köln's Lichter Festival lights up the sky on July 12, with fireworks, music, and lots of boats on the river (get details from TI or at www.koelner-lichter.de).

TOURS

Bike Tours—Kölner Fahrradverleih (listed under "Bike Rental," above) offers German/English guided bike tours of the city (€15, 3 hrs, daily April–Oct at 13:30, rain poncho provided just in case, 10-person maximum, reservations recommended, mobile 0171-629-8796).

SIGHTS

▲▲▲Köln's Cathedral (Dom)

The Neo-Gothic Dom—Germany's most exciting church—looms immediately up from the train station.

Cost and Hours: Free, open daily 6:00–19:30; no tourist visits during church services daily 6:30–10:00 and at 18:30, Sun also at 12:00, 17:00, and 18:30 (get schedule at Domforum office or www.koelner-dom.de).

Tours: The one-hour English-only tours are reliably excellent (€6, Mon–Sat at 10:30 and 14:30, Sun at 14:30, meet inside front door of Dom, tel. 0221/9258-4730). Your tour ticket also gives you free entry to the English-language 20-minute video in the Domforum

Köln Cathedral

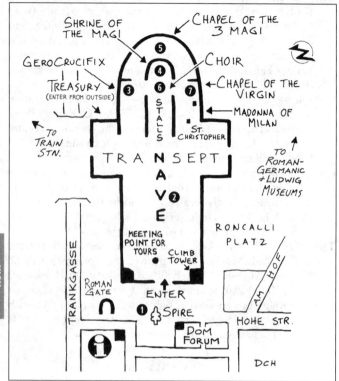

directly following the tour (see "Domforum," page 302).

● Self-Guided Tour: If you don't take the guided tour, follow this seven-stop walk (note that stops 3–7 are closed off during confession Sat 14:00–18:00, and anytime services are underway).

● Roman Gate and Cathedral Exterior: The square in front

of the cathedral has been a busy civic meeting place since ancient times. A Roman temple stood where the cathedral stands today. The north gate of the Roman city, from A.D. 50, marks the start of Köln's 2,000-year-old main street.

Look for the life-size replica tip of a spire. The real thing is 515 feet above you. The cathedral facade, finished according to the original 13th-century plan, is "Neo-Gothic" from the 19th century.

Postcards show the church after the 1945 bombing. The Roman-Germanic Museum lies beyond the facade to the right, and the modern-art Museum Ludwig sits behind that (both described below).

• *Step inside the church. Grab a pew in the center of the nave.*

❷ **Nave:** If you feel small, you're supposed to. The 140-foot-tall ceiling reminds us of our place in the vast scheme of things. Lots of stained glass—enough to cover three football fields—fills the church with light, representing God.

The church was begun in 1248. The choir—the lofty area from the center altar to the far end ahead of you—was finished in 1322. Later, with the discovery of America and routes to the Indies by sea, trade shifted away from inland ports like Köln. Funds dried up and eventually construction stopped. For 300 years, the finished end of the church was walled off and functioned as a church, while the unfinished torso (where you now sit) waited. For centuries, the symbol of Köln's skyline was a huge crane that sat atop the unfinished west spire.

With the rise of German patriotism in the early 1800s, Köln became a symbol of German unity. And the Prussians—the movers and shakers behind German unity—mistakenly considered Gothic a German style. They initiated a national tax that funded the speedy completion of this gloriously Gothic German church. Nearly 700 workers (compared to 100 in the 14th century) finished the church in just 38 years (1842–1880). The great train station was built in the shadow of the cathedral's towering spire.

The glass windows in the front of the church are medieval. The glass surrounding you in the nave is not as old, but it's precious nevertheless. The glass on the left is Renaissance. Notice the many coats of arms, which depict the lineage of the donors. One of these windows would have cost as much as two large townhouses. The glass on the right—a gift from Ludwig I, grandfather of the "Mad" King Ludwig who built the fairy-tale castles—is 19th-century Bavarian. Compare both the colors and the realism of the faces between the windows to see how techniques advanced over the centuries.

While 95 percent of Köln was destroyed by WWII bombs, the structure of the cathedral survived fairly well. In anticipation of the bombing, the glass and art treasures were taken to shelters and saved. The new "swallow's nest" organ above you was installed to celebrate the cathedral's 750th birthday in 1998. Attaching it to the wall would have compromised the cathedral's architectural integrity, so the organ is actually suspended from precarious-looking steel wires. Relics (mostly skulls) fill cupboards on each side of the nave. The guys in the red robes are cathedral cops, called *Schweizer* (after the Swiss guard at the Vatican); if a service is getting ready to start, they hustle tourists out (but you can stay for the service if you like).

• *Leave the nave by stepping through the gate on the left, into the oldest part of the church. As you enter, look down.*

This ninth-century mosaic shows a saint holding the Carolingian Cathedral, which stood on this spot for several centuries before this one was built.

❸ **Gero-Crucifix:** Ahead of you on the left, the Chapel of the Cross features the oldest surviving monumental crucifix from

north of the Alps. Carved in 976 with a sensitivity that was 300 years ahead of its time, it shows Jesus not suffering and not triumphant—but with eyes closed...dead. He paid the price for our sins. It's quite a two-fer: great art and powerful theology in one. The cathedral has three big pilgrim stops: this crucifix, the Shrine of the Magi, and the *Madonna of Milan* (both coming up).

• *Continue to the front end of the church, stopping to look at the big golden reliquary in the glass case behind the high altar.*

❹ **Shrine of the Magi:** Relics were a big deal in the Middle Ages. Köln's acquisition of the bones of the Three Kings in the 12th century put it on the pilgrimage map and brought in enough money to justify the construction of this magnificent place. By some stretch of medieval Christian logic, these relics also justified the secular power of the local king. This reliquary, made in about 1200, is the biggest and most splendid I've seen. It's seven feet of gilded silver, jewels, and enamel. Old Testament prophets line the bottom, and 12 New Testament apostles—with a wingless angel in the center—line the top.

Inside sit the bones of the Magi...three skulls with golden crowns. So what's the big deal about these three kings (of Christmas-carol fame)? They were the first to recognize Jesus as the Savior and the first to come as pilgrims to worship him. They inspired medieval pilgrims and countless pilgrims since. For a thousand years, a theme of this cathedral has been that life is a pilgrimage...a search for God.

❺ **Chapel of the Three Magi:** The center chapel, at the far end, is the oldest. It also features the church's oldest window (center, from 1265). The design is typical: a strip of Old Testament scenes on the left with a theologically and visually parallel strip of New Testament scenes on the right (such as, on bottom panels: to the left, the birth of Eve; to the right, the birth of Mary with her mother Anne on the bed).

Later glass windows (which you saw lining the nave) were made from panes of clear glass that were painted and glazed. This medieval window, however, is actually colored glass, which is assembled like a mosaic. It was very expensive. The size was limited to what pilgrim donations could support. Notice the plain, budget design higher up.

• *Peek into the center zone between the high altar and the carved wooden central stalls. (You can usually only get inside if you take the tour.)*

❻ **Choir:** The choir is surrounded by 13th- and 14th-century art: carved oak stalls, frescoed walls, statues painted as they would have been, and original stained glass high above. Study the fanciful oak carvings. The woman cutting the man's hair is a Samson-and-Delilah warning to the sexist men of the early Church.

• *The nearby chapel holds one of the most precious paintings of the important Gothic School of Köln.*

❼ **Chapel of the Virgin:** *The Patron Saints of Köln* was painted in 1442 by Stefan Lochner. Notice the photographic realism and

believable depth. There are literally dozens of identifiable herbs in the grassy foreground. During the 19th century, the city fought to move it to a museum. The Church went to court to keep it. The judge ruled that it could stay in the cathedral only as long as a Mass was said before it every day. For more than a hundred years, that happened at 18:30. Now, 21st-century comfort has trumped 19th-century law—in winter, services take place in the warmer Sacraments Chapel instead. (For more on the School of Köln art style, see "Wallraf-Richartz Museum," page 304.)

Overlooking the same chapel, the *Madonna of Milan* sculpture (1290), associated with miracles, was a focus of pilgrims for centuries. Its colors, scepter, and crown were likely added during a restoration in 1900.

The reclining medieval knight in the cage at the back of the chapel (just before the gate) was a wealthy but childless patron who donated his entire county to the cathedral. Worried that his angry brother and cousin would avenge this snub, his grave was covered to protect his body—an honor usually reserved for priests.

As you head for the exit, look into the transept on your left. The stained-glass windows above you are mostly clear. The local artist Gerhard Richter is designing new windows to create a "harmony of colors." Before leaving, find the statue of St. Christopher (with Jesus on his shoulder and the pilgrim's staff). Since 1470, pilgrims and travelers have looked up at him and taken solace in the hope that their patron saint is looking out for them.

• *Go in peace.*

More Cathedral Sights

Church Spire Climb—For 509 steps and €2, you can enjoy a fine city view from the cathedral's south tower (€5 combo-ticket also includes treasury, daily May–Sept 9:00–18:00, March–April and Oct until 17:00, Nov–Feb until 16:00). From the *Glockenstube* (only 400 steps up), you can see the Dom's nine huge bells, including *Dicke Peter* (24-ton Fat Peter), claimed to be the largest free-swinging church bell in the world.

Treasury—The treasury sits outside the cathedral's left transept (when you exit through the front door, turn right and continue right around the building to the gold pillar marked *Schatzkammer*). The six dim, hushed rooms are housed in the cathedral's 13th-century stone cellar vaults (€4, €5 combo-ticket also includes spire climb, daily 10:00–18:00, last entry 30 min before closing, lockers at entry with €1 coin deposit, tel. 0221/1794-0530).

Spotlights shine on black cases filled with gilded chalices and crosses, medieval reliquaries (bits of chain, bone, cross, and cloth in gold-crusted glass capsules), and plenty of fancy bishop garb: intricately embroidered miters and vestments, rings with fat gemstones, and six-foot gold crosiers. Displays come with brief English descriptions, but the little €4 book sold inside the cathedral shop provides extra information.

Domforum—This helpful visitors center, across from the entrance of the cathedral, is a good place to support the Vatican Bank (notice the Pax Bank ATM just outside the entrance), or just take a break (Mon–Fri 10:00–18:30, Sat 10:00–17:00, Sun 13:00–17:00, plenty of info, welcoming lounge with €1 coffee and juice, clean WC downstairs—free but donation requested, tel. 0221/9258-4720, www.domforum.de). They offer an English-language "multi-vision" video on the history of the church daily at 11:30 and 15:30 (starts slow but gets a little better, 20 min, €2 or included with church tour).

Kolumba Diocesan Museum—This museum contains some of the cathedral's finest art. In the fall of 2007, the museum opened in its new home at the corner of Kolumba and Brückenstrasse (a few blocks southwest of the cathedral; walking down Hohe Strasse from the cathedral, turn right on Minoritenstrasse, then left two blocks later). Built around the Madonna in the Ruins church, the museum is conceived as a place of reflection (€5, Wed–Mon 12:00–17:00, closed Tue, tel. 0221/257-7672, www.kolumba.de).

Near the Cathedral

▲▲**Roman-Germanic Museum (Römisch-Germanisches Museum)**—Germany's best Roman museum offers minimal English among its elegant and fascinating display of Roman artifacts: glassware, jewelry, and mosaics. All these pieces are evidence of Köln's status as an important site of civilization long before the cathedral was ever imagined. The permanent collection is downstairs and upstairs; temporary exhibits are on the ground floor.

Budget travelers can view the museum's prize piece, a fine mosaic floor, free from the big window facing the square. Once the dining-room floor of a rich Roman merchant, this is actually its original position (the museum was built around it). It shows scenes from the life of Dionysus...wine and good times, Roman-style. The tall monument over the Dionysus mosaic is the mausoleum of a first-century Roman army officer. Upstairs, you'll see a reassembled, arched original gate to the Roman city with the Roman initials for the town, CCAA, still legible, and incredible glassware that Roman Köln was famous for producing (€5, Tue–Sun 10:00–17:00, closed Mon, Roncalliplatz 4, tel. 0221/2212-4590, www.museenkoeln.de/rgm). The gift shop's €0.50 brochure provides too little information, and the €12 book too much (detailed descriptions for this museum, and about Roman artifacts displayed in other German cities).

▲▲**Museum Ludwig** —Next door and more enjoyable, this museum—in a slick and modern building—offers a stimulating trip through the art of the last century, including American Pop and post-WWII art. Displays include German and Russian Expressionists, Picasso, and works from the Blaue Reiter (Blue Rider) school (which is better represented at the Lenbachhaus in Munich—see page 57). The floor plan is a mess. Just enjoy the art (€7.50, often more because of special exhibitions, Tue–Sun 10:00–18:00, closed Mon, last entry 30 min before closing, €0.50 lockers mandatory for big bags, free WC, exhibits are fairly well described in English; classy but pricey cafeteria—€5–9 salads, pastas, sandwiches, and soups; Bischofsgartenstrasse 1, tel. 0221/2212-4802, www.museum-ludwig.de).

Hohe Strasse—The Roman arch in front of the cathedral reminds us that even in Roman times, this was an important trading street and a main road through Köln. In the Middle Ages, when Köln was a major player in the heavyweight Hanseatic League of northern European merchant towns, two major trading routes crossed here. This high street thrived. Following its complete destruction in World War II, Hohe Strasse emerged once again as an active trading street—the first pedestrian shopping mall in Germany.

Farther from the Cathedral

These museums are several blocks south of the cathedral.

▲▲**Wallraf-Richartz Museum**—Housed in a cinderblock of a building near the City Hall, this minimalist museum features a world-class collection of old masters, from medieval to northern Baroque and Impressionist. You'll see the best collection anywhere of Gothic School of Köln paintings (1300–1550), offering an intimate peek into those times. Included are German, Dutch, Flemish, and French works by masters such as Albrecht Dürer, Peter Paul Rubens, Rembrandt, Frans Hals, Jan Steen, Vincent van Gogh, Pierre-Auguste Renoir, Claude Monet, Edvard Munch, and Paul Cézanne (€5.80, often more due to special exhibitions, Tue 10:00–20:00, Wed–Fri 10:00–18:00, Sat–Sun 11:00–18:00, closed Mon, English descriptions and good €2.50 audioguide for permanent exhibit, Martin Strasse 39, tel. 0221/2212-1119, www .museenkoeln.de/wrm).

Imhoff-Stollwerck Chocolate Museum (Schokoladen-museum)—Chocoholics love this place, cleverly billed as the "MMMuseum." You'll take a tour—well described in English—

that follows the origin of the cocoa bean to the finished product. You can see displays on the culture of chocolate and watch the treats trundle down the conveyor belt in the functioning chocolate factory, the museum's highlight. The top-floor exhibit of chocolate advertising is fun. Sample sweets from the chocolate fountain, or take some home from the fragrant, choc-full gift shop (€6.50, Tue–Fri 10:00–18:00, Sat–Sun 11:00–19:00, closed Mon, last entry 1 hour before closing, Rheinauhafen 1a, tel. 0221/931-8880, www.schokoladenmuseum.de).

Getting There: The museum is a pleasant 10-minute walk south on the riverfront, between the Deutzer and Severins bridges. Or take the handy Schoko-Express tourist train from Roncalliplatz (€2 each way, 2/hr—or 1/hr if it's raining, pick-up point changes depending on events on the church square—either by TI or by the ticket office, confirm location at TI).

Käthe Kollwitz Museum—This contains the largest collection of the artist's powerful Expressionist art, welling from her experiences living in Berlin during the tumultuous first half of the last century (€3, Tue–Fri 10:00–18:00, Sat–Sun 11:00–18:00, closed Mon, Neumarkt 18–24, tel. 0221/227-2899, www.kollwitz.de).

Getting There: From Hohe Strasse, go west on Schildergasse for about 10 minutes; go past Neumarkt Gallerie to Neumarkt

Passage, enter Neumarkt Passage, and walk to the glass-domed center courtyard. Take the glass elevator to the fifth floor.

SLEEPING

Köln is *the* convention town in Germany. Consequently, the town is either jam-packed with hotels in the €180 range, or empty and hungry. Unless otherwise noted, prices listed are the non-convention weekday rates. You'll find that prices are much higher during conventions, but soft on weekends (always ask) and for slow-time drop-ins. Outside of convention times, the TI can always get you a discounted room in a business-class hotel (for a €3 fee).

In 2008, conventions are scheduled for these dates: Jan 14–20, Jan 27–30, Feb 9–11, Feb 15–24, Feb 28–March 1, March 9–12, April 2–6, April 16–20, May 7–9, May 27–29, June 4–15, July 12 (Köln's Lichter Festival), Aug 5–7, Aug 31–Sept 2, Sept 8–9, Sept 11–14, Sept 16–21, Sept 23–28, Oct 8–12, Oct 21–25, Oct 29–Nov 2, Nov 5–9, Nov 11–13, and Nov 28–30. For updates and additional conventions, visit www.koelnmesse.de. Unlisted smaller conventions can lead to small price increases. Big conventions in nearby Düsseldorf can also fill up rooms and raise rates in Köln.

Classy Hotels on Ursulaplatz

Two good business-class splurge hotels stand side-by-side a five-minute walk northwest of the station (exit straight out, near track 1, then turn right on Marzellenstrasse, up to Ursulaplatz). These can be pricey but are an excellent value on non-convention weekends.

$$$ Classic Hotel Harmonie is all class, striking a perfect balance between modern and classic. Its 72 rooms include some luxurious "superior" rooms (with hardwoods and swanky bathrooms, including a foot-warming floor). Rates are plenty pricey during

---

Sleep Code

(€1 = about \$1.30, country code: 49, area code: 0221)
S = Single, **D** = Double/Twin, **T** = Triple, **Q** = Quad, **b** = bathroom, **s** = shower only. Unless otherwise noted, credit cards are accepted, English is spoken, and breakfast is included.

To help you sort easily through these listings, I've divided the rooms into three categories, based on the price for a standard double room with bath:

$$$ Higher Priced—Most rooms €90 or more.
$$ Moderately Priced—Most rooms between €75–90.
$ Lower Priced—Most rooms €75 or less.

conventions, but become affordable on weekends and a downright steal when business is slow (it's important to ask—call ahead for prices). So *this* is how the other half lives (Sb-€50–85, Db-€75–120, some rooms have train noise so request quiet room, non-smoking rooms, some rooms with air-con, elevator, Ursulaplatz 13–19, tel. 0221/16570, fax 0221/165-7200, www.classic-hotel-harmonie.de, harmonie@cih-hotels.com, helpful staff).

$$$ Hotel Cristall is a modern "designer hotel" with 85 cleverly appointed rooms (enjoy the big easel paintings and play human chess on the carpet). The deeply hued breakfast room and lounge are so hip that German rock stars have photo shoots here (Sb-€65–79, Db-€96 but drops to €85 on weekends, rack rates can be higher, request quiet room to escape street and train noise, non-smoking rooms, air-con, elevator, limited parking-€6/day—reserve in advance, Ursulaplatz 9–11, tel. 0221/16300, fax 0221/163-0333, www.hotelcristall.de, info@hotelcristall.de).

Near the Pedestrian Zone

These moderately priced hotels, centrally located along the pedestrian zone, are more convenient than charming.

$$$ Hotel Ibis Koeln am Dom, a 71-room chain hotel, offers predictability, tidiness, and an extremely short walk from the train station—but no personality (Sb-€79, Db-€94; convention rate: Sb-€119, Db-€139; breakfast-€9.50, non-smoking rooms, air-con, elevator, Hauptbahnhof, entry across from station's *Reisezentrum,* tel. 0221/912-8580, fax 0221/9128-58199, www.ibishotel.com, h0739@accor.com).

$$ Hotel Engelbertz is a fine, family-run, 40-room place an eight-minute walk from the station and cathedral at the end of the pedestrian mall (specials for readers with this book in 2008 who request a discount during non-convention times: Sb-€52 and Db-€70 if you call to reserve on same day or day before, Sb-€65 and Db-€85 if you reserve in advance; regular rate Sb-€73 and Db-€104, convention rate Db-€190, elevator, just off Hohe Strasse at Obenmarspforten 1–3, tel. 0221/257-8994, fax 0221/257-8924, www.hotel-engelbertz.de, info@hotel-engelbertz.de).

$$ Central Hotel am Dom's location—just two blocks from the cathedral and one block from the station—and its clean, uncluttered rooms make it a good value (Sb-€59, Db-€80, can be cheaper in summer and is always more expensive during conventions, An den Dominikanern 3, tel. 0221/135-088, fax 0221/135-080, www.centralamdom.de, info@centralamdom.de).

Budget Options

Affordable, family-run hotels line Domstrasse and Brandenburger Strasse behind (northeast of) the train station in a quieter neighborhood. To reach Hotel Müller, exit the station away from the cathedral (the end near track 11). The hostel is on the other side of the station, between the cathedral and Ursulaplatz.

$ Hotel Müller, run with great pride by enthusiastic Frau Müller, has 15 recently renovated rooms offering three-star quality at two-star prices (because it doesn't have an elevator). Enjoy the grotto-like basement breakfast room/bar and the courtyard terrace (Sb-€60, Db-€75, prices can double during big conventions, Internet access; exit behind station to Breslauer Platz, walk 2 blocks up Johannisstrasse, then left on Brandenburger Strasse to #20; tel. 0221/912-8350, fax 0221/9128-3517, www.hotel-mueller -koeln.de, info@hotel-mueller.net).

$ Station Hostel, with 190 beds, is a two-minute walk from the train station and full of young travelers (dorm bed-€17–21, S-€30, Sb-€37, D-€45, Db-€52, Tb-€72, includes sheets, key deposit-€10, kitchen, small breakfast-€3, no curfew, free Internet access, laundry-€4, tel. 0221/912-5301, fax 0221/912-5303; exit station on Dom side, walk straight 1 block, turn right on Marzellenstrasse to #44–56; www.hostel-cologne.de, station@hostel-cologne.de).

EATING

Kölsch is three things: the dialect spoken here, the local cuisine, and the city's distinct type of beer (pale, hoppy, and highly fermented). You'll find plenty of places to enjoy all three in the streets around Alter Markt (2 blocks off the river, near City Hall), as well as along Lintgasse and the waterfront area called the Frankenwerft. Locals of all ages head to Friesenplatz for traditional eateries (such as Päffgen, below) and trendy cafés.

Gaffel Haus serves good local food. Look for the wall filled with coats of arms of Köln's old guilds *(Gaffeln)*—see how many crafts you can guess by their pictures (€10 meals, daily until 24:00, near Lintgasse at Alter Markt 20–22, tel. 0221/257-7692).

Papa Joe's Klimperkasten, in a dark pub packed with memorabilia and nightly live jazz (piano only, €4–9 meals, open daily for lunch and dinner, Alter Markt 50–52, tel. 0221/258-2132), and its rowdier sibling, **Papa Joe's Jazzlokal** (nightly from 20:30, Buttermarkt 37, tel. 0221/257-7931, www.papajoes.de for jazz schedule), win the atmosphere award.

Früh am Dom, closer to the cathedral and train station, offers three floors of touristy drinking and dining options. Head to the back wall to check out a painting of what the city looked like in 1534 (€7–16 meals, daily 8:00–24:00, Am Hof 12–14, tel. 0221/261-3211).

Café Canapé im MAK, with sophisticated locals enjoying light fare, is a good option for a non-*Bräuhaus* lunch. If you eat here on a Sunday morning, be sure to sit outside and enjoy a free organ concert *al fresco*—the courtyard abuts a church (€3–7 meals, Tue–Sun 11:00–17:00, closed Mon, just across Hohe Strasse from the cathedral in Museum of Applied Arts—Museum für Angewandte Kunst—at An der Rechtschule 1, inside front door and down the stairs, smoky inside, courtyard seating outside, tel. 0221/2212-6721).

Café Eigel, family-owned since 1851, is a good option for *Kaffee und Küchen* (afternoon cake and coffee) or for a light lunch of salads or omelets. It's been in the same location for 50 years, but was recently remodeled in a fresh, sleek, modern style. Enjoy delicious pastries in the airy atrium, and be sure to pick up some homemade chocolates (€7–10 plates, €3 slices of cake, Mon–Fri 9:00–19:00, Sat 9:00–18:00, Sun 14:00–18:00, Brückenstrasse 1–3, tel. 0221/257-5858).

Päffgen is where the *Köbes* (Köln's traditionally grumpy waiters) really live up to their reputation as they dish out traditional *Kölsch* food. Beers are served in delicate glasses (by Bavarian standards) and shuttled around in small, wreath-like trays *(Bierkranz)*. This is the place to satisfy your cravings for blood sausage *(Blutwurst)* and kidneys *(Nierchen)*...or, for something a little more mainstream, try the tasty *Rheinischer Sauerbraten* with *Klössen* (dumplings) and applesauce (€5–15 plates, daily 10:00–24:00, food served 11:30–23:00, can be smoky, Friesenstrasse 64–66, tel. 0911/135-461).

Schreckenskammer is a down-home joint just behind the St. Ursula church. The sand on the floor, swept out and replaced each morning, buffs the hardwood and also keeps it clean. The *kammer* is small and cozy, so be prepared to share a table and make new friends over a *Kölsch* or two. Most meals (choose from the *Tageskarte*, or daily specials) start with a complimentary cup of *Brühe* (broth). Don't mistake this as an act of hospitality—it only serves to make you thirstier. This eatery is really popular with locals, so arrive early or make a reservation (€6–14 plates, Mon–Fri 11:00–13:45 & 16:30–22:30, Sat 11:00–14:00, closed Sun, cash only, Ursulagartenstrasse 11–15, tel. 0221/132-581).

TRANSPORTATION CONNECTIONS

From Köln by Train to: Bonn (6/hr, 20 min), **Remagen** (3/hr, 30–50 min), **Aachen** (2/hr, 30–50 min), **Frankfurt** (2–3/hr, 1.25 hrs), **Frankfurt Airport** (at least hourly, 1 hr), **Bacharach** or **St. Goar** (1–2/hr, 1.75 hrs, transfer in Koblenz), **Cochem** (every 2 hrs direct, 1.75–2 hrs; most with transfer in Koblenz), **Trier** (at least hourly, 2.5 hrs), **Würzburg** (roughly hourly, 2.75 hrs), **Munich** (2/hr, 4–6 hrs), **Berlin** (hourly, 4.5 hrs), **Paris** (6/day direct, more with changes,

4–6 hrs, requires seat reservation on Thalys trains), **Amsterdam** (6/day direct, 2.5 hrs). Train info: tel. 11861 (€0.60/min).

The Unromantic Rhine

Highlights

▲Bonn—Bonn was chosen for its sleepy, cultured, and peaceful nature as a good place to plant West Germany's first post-Hitler government. Since the two Germanys became one again in 1989, Berlin has taken back its position as capital.

Today, Bonn is sleek, modern, and, by big-city standards, remarkably pleasant and easygoing. The pedestrian-only old town stretching out from the station will make you wonder why the US can't trade in its malls for real, people-friendly cities.

The market square and Münsterplatz—filled with street musicians—are a joy. People-watching doesn't get much better, though the actual sights are disappointing. There's a sparse exhibit at Beethoven's House (€5; April–Oct Mon–Sat 10:00–18:00, Sun 11:00–18:00; Nov–March Mon–Sat 10:00–17:00, Sun 11:00–17:00; last entry 30 min before closing, free English brochure,

The Unromantic Rhine

tel. 0228/981-7525, www.beethoven-haus-bonn.de). The **TI** is a five-minute walk from the station (Mon–Fri 9:00–18:30, Sat 9:00–16:00, Sun 10:00–14:00, €2 room-finding service, go straight on Windechstrasse, next to Karstadt department store, tel. 0228/775-000, www.bonn.de).

▲Remagen—Midway between Koblenz and Köln are the scant remains of the Bridge at Remagen, of WWII (and movie) fame. But the memorial and the bridge stubs are enough to stir the emotions of Americans who remember when it was the only bridge that remained, allowing the Allies to cross the Rhine and race to Berlin in 1945. A small museum tells the bridge's fascinating story in English. It was built during World War I to help supply the German forces on the Western Front. Ironically, one war later, Eisenhower said the bridge was worth its weight in gold for its service *against* Germany. Hitler executed four generals for their failure to blow it up. Ten days after US forces arrived, the bridge

Unrom. Rhine

did collapse, killing 28 American soldiers. Today you can pay your respects at the bridge and visit its "Peace Museum" (€3.50, March–mid-Nov daily 10:00–17:00, May–Oct until 18:00, closed mid-Nov–Feb; it's on the Rhine's west bank, south side of Remagen town, follow *Brücke von Remagen* signs; www.bruecke-remagen .de). Remagen **TI:** tel. 02642/20187.

▲**Aachen (Charlemagne's Capital)**—This city was the capital of Europe in A.D. 800, when Charles the Great (Charlemagne) called it Aix-la-Chapelle. The remains of his rule include an impressive Byzantine- and Ravenna–inspired church, with his sarcophagus and throne. Enjoy the town's charming historic pedestrian center and festive Christmas market. See the headliner newspaper museum and great fountains, including a clever arrange-'em-yourself version.

Lowlights

Heidelberg—This famous old university town attracts hordes of Americans. Any surviving charm is stained almost beyond recognition by commercialism. It doesn't make it into Germany's top three weeks.

Mainz, Wiesbaden, and Rüdesheim—These towns are all too big or too famous. They're not worth your time. Mainz's Gutenberg Museum is also a disappointment.

NÜRNBERG

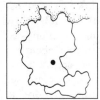

Nürnberg (sometimes spelled "Nuremberg" in English), Bavaria's second city, is packed with interesting sights. At one of Europe's most important medieval trading crossroads, and with a large imperial castle marking it as a stronghold of the Holy Roman Empire, Nürnberg was one of Europe's leading cities in about 1500. Today, the red-sandstone Gothic buildings in its charming old town make the city feel far smaller than its population of 500,000. Nürnberg is known for its glorious medieval architecture, its important Germanic history museum, its haunting Nazi past, its famous Christmas market (Germany's biggest), and its little bratwurst (Germany's tiniest).

Planning Your Time

Nürnberg is a handy stop between other German destinations, and an easy add-on to any itinerary that includes Munich, Würzburg, or Rothenburg (a several-times-hourly express train connects Nürnberg to Munich in under an hour). For the quickest visit to Nürnberg, toss your bag in a locker at the station and head directly to the Nazi Documentation Center. If you have the better part of a day, visit the Nazi sights, stroll through the old town from the train station up to the castle (following my self-guided walk, below), and—on the way back to the station (or your hotel)—tour the wonderful Germanic National Museum.

ORIENTATION

(area code: 0911)

Nürnberg's old town (containing all the non-Nazi sights) is surrounded by its three-mile-long wall and moat, and beyond that, a ring road. At the southeast corner of the ring is the train station; across the street, just inside the ring, is the medieval Frauentor gate. From the Frauentor, sights cluster along a straight line (Königstrasse) downhill to the small Pegnitz River, then back uphill through Market Square (Hauptmarkt) to the castle (Kaiserburg). The Nazi Documentation Center—at the former Nazi Rally Grounds—is southeast of the center (easily accessible by tram or S-Bahn; see page 325).

Tourist Information

Nürnberg's handy and helpful TI is in the modern building just inside the Frauentor (Mon–Sat 9:00–19:00, closed Sun, across ring road from station at Bahnhofplatz, tel. 0911/233-6132, www .tourismus.nuernberg.de). Pick up the free city map (with updated sight hours and prices on the back) and get information about bus and walking tours. The TI also offers free Internet access, books rooms (no fee), and sells transit passes and the Nürnberg Card (see below). The TI's second branch is at the Hauptmarkt (Mon–Sat 9:00–18:00, May–Oct and during Christmas Market also Sun 10:00–16:00, otherwise closed Sun).

Discount Deals: Nürnberg's city-run museums—including the Nazi Documentation Center, Albrecht Dürer House, Toy Museum, and the City Museum—are all covered by the same, amazingly cheap €5 **City Museums Combo-Ticket** (buy it at any participating sight). Because this is such a great value, I'd skip the two other available deals: the **"Take Five" Ticket** (€16, covers five entrances into your choice of seven different museums, shareable by multiple people, sold at participating sights and at Frauentor TI) and the **Nürnberg Card** (€19/2 days, free for kids 12 and under, sold at the TI and most hotels, covers all of your local transportation and admission to all of Nürnberg's museums, plus up to 25 percent off bus and walking tours and other discounts, only available to those spending at least one night in Nürnberg). Finally, a separate €12 **combo-ticket** covers the National Germanic Museum and Albrecht Dürer House, including a handheld computer guide with a walking tour connecting them.

Arrival in Nürnberg

Nürnberg's stately old Hauptbahnhof—with a shiny new interior—is conveniently located just outside the old city walls and ring road. The station has WCs, lockers, ATMs, and lots of shops.

Nürnberg

You can get train information and buy tickets at the *Reisezentrum* in the main hall (center of building, Mon–Fri 6:00–21:00, Sat–Sun 8:00–21:00).

To reach the Frauentor (the medieval city's southern gate)—which is near most recommended hotels and is also the starting point for exploring the old town—follow signs for *Ausgang/City* in the underpass, then signs to *Königstor/Frauentor* and *Altstadt*. When you emerge, the TI is on your right and the Frauentor tower is on your left.

To go directly to the Nazi Documentation Center from the station, follow the pink signs to *Tram* and catch tram #9 in the direction of Doku-Zentrum (leaves from in front of the Postbank Center every 10 min).

Getting Around Nürnberg

Most of Nürnberg's sights are in the strollable old town, but the Nazi sites are beyond easy walking distance. Nürnberg's public transportation network, run by VGN, has trams, buses, U-Bahns (subways), and S-Bahns (faster suburban trains). All work on the same tickets, which you can buy at the TI, vending machines *(Fahrausweise)* on the tram platform or before entering the U- or S-Bahns, or on board (buses only). A single ticket *(Einzelfahrkarte)* costs €1.80 (good for 90 min of travel in one direction, including transfers). A day ticket is €3.60 *(TagesTicket Solo,* good for one calendar day or Sat and Sun; the €6.30 *TagesTicket Plus* covers 2 adults and up to 4 children; www.vgn.de). While the day tickets come date-stamped, single tickets must be validated onboard (for the bus or tram) or before going down to the platform (for the subway).

TOURS

Walking Tours—Tours in English of Nürnberg's old town leave from the Hauptmarkt daily at 13:00 (May–Oct and Dec, €8 plus castle admission, kids under 14 free, 2.5 hrs, book in advance at TI or just show up and pay guide). This is the only way to see the sights in the castle interior with an English-speaking guide (see "Imperial Castle" on page 322).

Bus Tours—These tours, which include some walking, leave daily at 9:30 May through October from the Old Granary at Hallplatz, two blocks up from the Frauentor TI (€11, buy ticket on bus or at TI, 2.5 hrs, in German and English, tel. 0911/202-2910).

Tourist Train—A goofy little tourist train makes the rounds in the old town (€6, 40 min, recorded narration in German only, schedule posted at fountain, leaves Hauptmarkt about hourly 10:30–16:00).

Private Guide—For a good and charming local guide, call Doris Ritter (€95/3 hrs, tel. 0911/518-1719, mobile 0176-2421-5863, doris.ritter@nuernberg-tours.de).

SELF-GUIDED WALK

▲▲Welcome to Nürnberg's Old Town

Nürnberg's best sights are conveniently clustered along a straight-line thoroughfare connecting the Hauptbahnhof with Market Square (Hauptmarkt) and the castle (Kaiserburg). For a good orientation, take the following self-guided stroll. Plan on an hour, not including stops.

• *Begin at the Frauentor (where you emerge from the Hauptbahnhof underpass). Review the lay of the land on the 10-foot-tall city map posted in front of tunnel (find the four towers). This tour will take you from the red dot at the bottom to the* Burg *(castle) at the top.*

Frauentor: This tower guards one of the four medieval entrances to Nürnberg's old town. Nürnberg did not have abundant natural resources or a navigable waterway, so its people made their living through trade and crafts (such as making scientific instruments, weapons, and armor). The German emperors took note of this industrious little town, and granted it economic privileges by naming it a "free imperial city" in the 13th century (giving it the right to answer directly to the Holy Roman Emperor himself). The need to create a safe business environment led to the construction of these walls. Of the three miles of wall that once surrounded the city, 90 percent survives. Many Central European cities (such as Vienna) tore down their walls to make way for expansion in the 1800s, and Nürnberg nearly did the same. Now they're glad they didn't—it's better for tourism.

• *Between the walls just next to the gate, you'll see the entrance to the...*

Craftsmen's Courtyard (Handwerkerhof): This hokey collection of half-timbered houses was built in 1971 to celebrate craftsmanship and to honor the 500th birthday of Nürnberg's famous resident Albrecht Dürer. (Dürer, arguably Germany's best painter, was considered the ultimate craftsman.) The proud medieval tradition of craftsmanship continues today, as the city is home to some of Germany's top goldsmiths and glassblowers.

While a bit kitschy, this courtyard gives tourists a medieval vibe as they enter the old town from the station. The courtyard is packed with replicas of medieval shops, where artisans actually make—and, of course, sell—leather, pottery, and brass goods. In the Middle Ages, this area between the walls was not a medieval mall but *Passkontrolle*—a customs and security checkpoint zone where all visitors had to register before they could enter the town.

At the back of the courtyard, step through the old gate and

Central Nürnberg

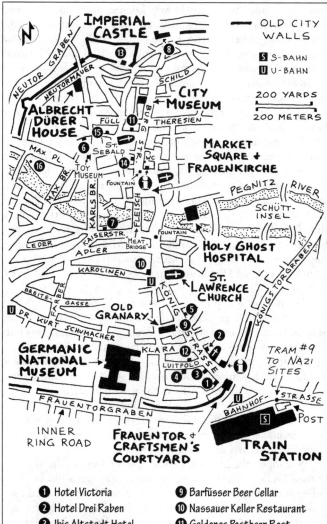

OLD CITY WALLS

S S-BAHN
U U-BAHN

200 YARDS
200 METERS

IMPERIAL CASTLE

NEUTOR GRABEN

NEUTORMAUER

ALBRECHT DÜRER HOUSE

MAX PL.

MAX BR.

TOY MUSEUM

KARLS BR.

FÜLL

ST. SEBALD

FOUNTAIN

KAISERSTR.

LEDER

ADLER

MEAT BRIDGE

FLEISCH

SCHILD

BURG

CITY MUSEUM

THERESIEN

WC

MARKET SQUARE + FRAUENKIRCHE

PEGNITZ RIVER

SCHÜTT-INSEL

FOUNTAIN

HOLY GHOST HOSPITAL

KAROLINEN

BREITE-GASSE

FÄRBER GASSE

DR. KURT SCHUMACHER

OLD GRANARY

KÖNIG STRASSE

ST. LAWRENCE CHURCH

KÖNIGSTORGRABEN

GERMANIC NATIONAL MUSEUM

KLARA

LUITPOLD

TRAM #9 TO NAZI SITES

FRAUENTORGRABEN

INNER RING ROAD

FRAUENTOR + CRAFTSMEN'S COURTYARD

BAHNHOFSTRASSE

TRAIN STATION

POST

Nürnberg

1. Hotel Victoria
2. Hotel Drei Raben
3. Ibis Altstadt Hotel
4. Hotels Probst & Keiml
5. City Hotel
6. Hotel Elch
7. Hotel Lucas
8. Nürnberg Youth Hostel
9. Barfüsser Beer Cellar
10. Nassauer Keller Restaurant
11. Goldenes Posthorn Rest.
12. Literaturhaus Nürnberg Rest.
13. Burgwächter Restaurant
14. Bratwursthäusle Rest.
15. Café Sebald
16. Kettensteg Biergarten

out onto a bridge over what was the moat. The bridge marks one of four entries into the medieval town. Look up at the mighty round tower. This was originally square, but was made round after the development of better cannons (so balls would glance off rather than hit it head-on). Imagine cannons lined up under the eaves of the tower, set to defend the city. When local kids look at the mighty train station, they remember that the first train in Germany choo-chooed from here in 1835.

• *When you're finished poking around the courtyard, head into town (with the train station at your back) on...*

Königstrasse: Though it had always been one of the four primary entrances to Nürnberg, this street became the city's main drag only after the train station was built in the early 20th century. It's lined with key sights, several recommended hotels and restaurants, and some wonderful Gothic and Neo-Gothic architecture.

Nürnberg hit its peak in the 14th century, when the Golden Bull law (1356) regularized the election of the Holy Roman Emperor. From then throughout the Middle Ages, German emperors were elected in Frankfurt, crowned in Aachen, and had their first Imperial Diet (a gathering of German nobles and VIPs) right here in Nürnberg.

Nürnberg's low point came during World War II. By the end of the war, 90 percent of the old town was destroyed—the only German city hit worse was Dresden. If a building was only damaged, it was repaired in the original Gothic style—check out the building with the Peschke Optik shop on the right. But some buildings were completely destroyed. Instead of rebuilding these exactly as they were, or replacing them with modern-style buildings, Nürnbergers compromised, creating a style that was at once modern and traditional. Look 50 yards down the street at #71. The design is modern, but it incorporates Gothic elements and uses the same distinctive red sandstone as older buildings.

Ahead, on the left, is the small **Clara Church** (Klarakirche). In the Middle Ages, Nürnberg had nine monasteries like this one. When the Reformation hit, Nürnberg turned Lutheran, and most of the monasteries were torn down. As they fell, so did Nürnberg's importance; the city was now Lutheran, but its emperors were still Catholic. The ever-important Imperial Diet—once Nürnberg's claim to fame—moved to more Catholic-friendly Regensburg. (Today, this church is an "ecumenical free church"—known because it's neither Lutheran nor Catholic and welcomes all stripes.)

Across the street from Clara Church, look for Mary on the second-story corner. Statues like this bless houses all over Nürnberg.

• *Continue down Königstrasse to Hallplatz and the Old Granary (where the pedestrian stretch begins). The minimalist metal arch (left) remembers the German refugees of World War II, and the hospitality of the Bavarians who took them in. If you want to visit the excellent Germanic National Museum (described on page 324) now, detour left at Hallplatz and walk 200 yards. Otherwise, check out the...*

Old Granary (Mauthalle): Medieval Nürnberg had 11 of these huge granaries to ensure that they'd have enough food in case of famine or siege. The grain was stored up above in the attic (behind all those little dormer windows). Today, the cellar is home to a lively beer hall, Barfüsser (see "Eating," page 332). On the back side of the building, the fun little **Vom Fass shop** sells all things liquid "from the tap" (as the name indicates). You choose a container and fill it with what you like, and write a gifty message right on the bottle (An der Mauthalle 2, Herr Eduard Stöber).

Continue down pedestrians-only Königstrasse. This drag used to have more cars and trams than any other street in town. But when the U-Bahn came in the 1970s, this part of the street became traffic-free.

• *After another two blocks, you'll see...*

St. Lawrence Church (Lorenzkirche): The church, a ▲▲ sight, is a massive house of worship, but it's not a cathedral—because Nürnberg never had a bishop (a fact locals were very proud of...a bishop would just order them around, and they prized their independence). The name of Königstrasse ("King's Street")—where you've been walking—is misleading. When most royals came to town, they actually preferred to come through the west gate, so they could approach this masterful facade head-on. Stand in front of the church's main door. Flip around and imagine the Holy Roman Emperor coming—right past Starbucks—down the "Imperial Way," which dead-ended at this magnificent Oz-like church.

Study the 260-foot-tall **facade** (completed c. 1360). Adam and Eve flank the doors (looking for a sweater). In the first row above the left door, you'll see two scenes: an intimate take on Jesus' birth on top, and the visit from the Magi on the bottom (with the starfish of Bethlehem shining from above). Over the right door, you'll see the slaughter of the innocents (with a baby skewered by a Roman sword—classic medieval subtlety), and below that, the presentation of Jesus in the temple and the flight to Egypt. Above those scenes is the Passion story (from lowest to highest: trial, scourging, carrying the cross, Crucifixion, deposition, entombment, Resurrection, and people coming out of their graves for Judgment Day). The saved (Peter—with his huge key—and company) are on the left, and the sorry chain gang of the damned (including kings and bishops) is shuttled off literally into the jaws of hell on the right. Above it all stands the triumphant resurrected Christ, with the sun and moon at his feet, flanked by angels tooting alphorns.

Step inside (enter around right side, €1 donation requested, €5 for a pass to take photos, Mon–Sat 9:00–17:00, Sun 12:00–16:00).

The **interior** wasn't completely furnished until more than a century after the church was built—just in time for the Reformation (so the Catholic decor adorned a now-Lutheran church). Most of the decorations inside were donated by wealthy Nürnbergers trying to cut down on their time in purgatory. Through the centuries, this art survived three separate threats: the iconoclasm of the Reformation, the whitewashing of the Baroque age, and the bombing of World War II. While Nürnberg was the first "Free Imperial City" to break with the Catholic Church and become Lutheran, locals didn't go wild (like Swiss Protestants did) in tearing down the rich, Mary-oriented decor of their fine churches. Luther told the iconoclasts, "Tear the idols out of your heart, and you'll understand that these statues are only pieces of wood."

Suspended over the altar, the woodcarving called *The Annunciation* is by a Nürnberg citizen who was one of medieval Germany's best woodcarvers, Veit Stoss. Carved in 1517, it shows the angel Gabriel telling Mary that she'll be giving birth to the Messiah. Startled, she drops her prayer book. This is quite Catholic (notice the rosary frame with beads, and a circle of roses—one for each Hail Mary, and with a medallion depicting the "Joys of Mary"). The dove sits on Mary's head, and God the Father—looking as powerful as a Holy Roman Emperor—looks down. The figures are carved from linden trees. This survived the Reformation covered in a sack, revealed only on special occasions. Around back, enjoy more details—Mary's cascading hair, and the sun and the moon. Nearby, the altar painting at the very front of the church (behind the altar) shows the city of Nürnberg in 1483 (before the city's square towers were made round).

To the left of the altar, the frilly **tabernacle** tower is the "house of sacraments" that stored the consecrated Communion wafer. After the Mass, leftovers needed a worthy—even heavenly—home...and this was it. The cupboard behind the gold grate was the appropriate receptacle for "the body of Christ." The theme of the carving is the Passion. The scenes ascend in chronological order: Last Supper, Judas' kiss, arrest, Crucifixion, and so on. Everything is carved of stone except for the risen Christ (way up high). He was living, and so was this...it's made of wood. The man holding the tabernacle on his shoulders is the artist who created

it, Adam Kraft. In the Middle Ages, artists were faceless artisans, no more important than a blacksmith or a stonemason. But in the 1490s, when this was made, the Renaissance was in the air, and artists like Kraft began putting themselves into their works. Kraft's contemporary, the painter Albrecht Dürer, actually signed his works—an incredible act in Germany at that time (see "Albrecht Dürer House," page 323). In anticipation of the Allied bombs of World War II, this precious work was encased in protective concrete except for the top 22 feet—which was the only part destroyed when the church was hit.

Adam Kraft is looking up at a **plaque** honoring the American philanthropist who donated nearly a million Deutschmarks in 1950 to help rebuild the church. Though the church was devastated by WWII bombs, everything movable was hidden away in bunkers, including the stained glass you see today. The plaque is in English, but it's hard to read, as it's written in the Gothic *Fraktur* font so popular back then. In the back of the church, a silent **video** (with dates in the upper corner) shows the preparations in anticipation of WWII bombs, the destruction, and the reconstruction.

As you leave, notice that the church has many **side chapels**—employing an innovative trick of expanding the nave out so the buttresses are actually inside the church.

From St. Lawrence Church to the River: Back outside, find the castle-like building on the corner across from the church facade. This is the only remaining **tower house** in Nürnberg. It was built in 1200, when there was no city wall, and the locals had to fend for themselves. It's basically a one-family castle. (In the basement, you'll find an appropriately medieval restaurant—complete with suits of armor—called the Nassauer Keller; see "Eating," page 332.)

Continue downhill to the river. American moralists might shield their eyes from the kinky **Fountain of the Seven Virtues.** Otherwise, play a game: Circle the sprightly fountain and try to identify the classic virtues by the symbolism: justice (on top), faith, love, hope (anchor), courage (lion), temperance (moderation), patience. Are any birds sipping?

• *Continue down the street. Caution: You'll pass Kaiserstrasse on your left—the most expensive shopping street in town (with a little shop filled with insanely expensive Steiff teddy bears). When you get to the bridge, look to the right.*

Holy Ghost Hospital (Heilig-Geist-Spital): This river-spanning hospital was donated to Nürnberg in the 14th century

by the city's richest resident, eager to do his part to help the poor... and hopefully skip purgatory altogether. (A statue of him hangs out on the second-story corner of the Spital Apotheke, the first building after the bridge.) He funded this very scenic hospital to care for ill, disabled, and elderly Nürnbergers. The wing over the river dates from the 16th century. The dove beneath the middle window under the turret represents the Holy Ghost, the hospital's namesake.

If you look in the distance to the right—beyond the hospital and the next two bridges—you'll see a half-timbered fragment of the town wall. The big white building to the right of that is Germany's biggest multiplex cinema, with 21 screens (most underground).

Cross to the other side of the bridge, and look at the next bridge over (the **"Meat Bridge"**). Look familiar? It's inspired by Venice's Rialto Bridge. This is the narrowest point of the river, and flooding was a big concern. Since this bridge doesn't have any piers, there's less chance of a collapse. When this was built in 1596, it was considered an engineering feat—the most high-tech bridge in Central Europe. The river once powered the town's medieval water mills.

Continue across the bridge, jogging left at the fork, and study the monument depicting characters from a 15th-century satire called *The Ship of Fools (Das Narrenschiff)*. It's adapted to follies that plague modern society—violence, technology, and apathy. Hey, how about the quiet, people-friendly ambience created by making this big city traffic-free in the center? Do a slow 360-degree spin and imagine this back home. (The ice-cream shop behind the fountain is popular for its 45 flavors.)

• Now enter the...

Market Square (Hauptmarkt): When Nürnberg boomed in the 13th century, it consisted of two distinct walled towns separated by the river. As the towns grew and it became obvious that the two should merge, the middle wall came down. This square (rated ▲▲), built by the Holy Roman Emperor Charles IV, became the center of the newly united city. Though Charles is more often associated with Prague (he's the namesake for the Charles Bridge and Charles University), he also loved Nürnberg—visiting 60 times during his reign.

The **Frauenkirche** church on the square is located on the site of a former synagogue (inside, there's a Star of David on the floor). When Nürnberg's towns were separate, Jewish residents were required to live in this swampy area close to the river and outside the walls. When the towns merged and the land occupied by the Jewish quarter became valuable, Charles IV allowed his subjects to force out the Jews—and 600 were killed in the process...a somber reminder that anti-Semitism predates the Nazis. Charles IV, the most powerful man in Europe in his time, oversees the square from a perch high on the church facade. He's waiting for noon, when the electors dance around him.

Year-round, Market Square is lively with fruit, flower, and souvenir stands. For a few weeks before Christmas, it hosts Germany's largest **Christmas market** (*Christkindlmarkt,* more than 2 million visitors annually, starts the Friday before the first Sunday in Advent).

• *Walk across the square to the pointy, gold...*

Beautiful Fountain (Schöner Brunnen): Medieval tanneries, slaughterhouses, and the hospital you just saw dumped their byproducts into the river. So this fountain brought clean drinking water into the square. Of course, it's packed with allegorical meaning. Step up to the iron railing. The outermost figures ringing the bottom represent the arts (such as philosophy, music, and astronomy). On the pillars just above them are the four church fathers and the four Evangelists, showing that religion is higher than the arts. On the column itself, the lowest figures are the seven electors of the Holy Roman Emperor and nine heroes—three Christian (including King Arthur and Charlemagne); three Jewish (such as King David); and three heathen (such as Julius Caesar). At the very top are eight prophets, hovering above—but granting legitimacy to—worldly power. On the side of the fountain facing the McDonalds, you'll probably see tourists fussing over a gold ring. If you believe in such silly tour-guide tales, spinning this ring three times brings good luck...okay, go ahead and spin it. The black ring opposite (nearest the stork bearing a baby—look for the rice on the ground) brings fertility. Civic marriage ceremonies that take place at the adjacent City Hall often end up here for photos.

• *Leave the square straight uphill from the fountain, heading for the castle. Along the way, you'll pass St. Sebald (Sebaldkirche), Nürnberg's second great Gothic church. About 100 yards farther up the hill, you'll see the...*

City Museum (Stadtmuseum Fembohaus): This museum is packed with fine artifacts, but explains nothing in English (they may have audioguides included in admission in 2008). The top-floor model of Nürnberg does come with an interesting audio sweep through the town's history (€5 for museum, €5 for film only—explained next, €7 for both, Tue–Fri 10:00–17:00, Sat–Sun 10:00–18:00, closed Mon, Burgstrasse 15, tel. 0911/231-2595). **Noricama Nürnberg Film** is a fascinating 50-minute video shown on the hour (in English with headphones) that gives a fun and thoughtful overview of the city, its story, and its great sights in a comfortable little theater.

• *Now huff the rest of the way up to the imperial castle. The cobbled path forks at the castle's base. The right fork leads to the garden and youth hostel, and the left leads to the castle courtyard (see big, round tower high above) and over the Burgwächter restaurant (see "Eating," page 322). If you want to head straight into the castle, take the left fork and skip to "Imperial Castle" (you'll circle counterclockwise, eventually returning to this spot). For a scenic detour, take the right fork, and go on a brief...*

Castle Garden (Burggarten) Walk: Before entering the main complex, pop behind the castle (to the right) into the Castle Garden for views of the north end of the town fortifications (16th-century bastions) and into the moat. From here you have access to the city walls, which lead down to the river (a 15-min walk along the park-like path past roses and other gardens).

• *After your walk, enter the castle courtyard, pausing under the tall tower for a superb city view.*

Imperial Castle (Kaiserburg): In the Middle Ages, Holy Roman Emperors stayed here when they were in town. This huge complex has 45 buildings. The part on the right, which housed the stables and stored grain, is now a youth hostel (see page 332).

The castle interior and museum are standard fare, and rated ▲. The most interesting bits here are the so-called Deep Well (which, at 165 feet, is...well, deep) and the Romanesque double-decker chapel (higher nobility in the upper chapel, lower nobility down below, plus a special balcony for the emperor). The tower climb offers only a higher city view and lots of exercise.

Unfortunately, you can only see these castle sights with a German tour (castle grounds free; entry to buildings only with German tours: €6 for 1-hr tour of museum, palace, and chapel, tour of well and climbing the tower on your own; €3 to climb tower on your own and join a German tour only for the well; tickets sold at top end of courtyard; daily April–Sept 9:00–18:00, Oct–March 10:00–16:00, tel. 0911/244-6590).

The only alternative is to go with the TI's English tour of the entire old town, which includes the castle (departs at 13:00, see "Tours," earlier in this chapter). Deep Well visits (about 4/hr), even with the German guide, are simple, quick, and fun: You'll see water poured way, waaay down—into an incredible hole dug

Nürnberg

in the 14th century. Then a small candle is lowered until it almost disappears into the water table.

• *After you leave the castle, consider a stroll to one of Nürnberg's oldest neighborhoods. Facing downhill, leave the castle to the right, then take the lower fork. In a couple of blocks, you'll reach Tiergärtnertorplatz. Near the top of the square, you'll see a huge rabbit. While it looks like roadkill with mice gnawing at it, it's actually a modern interpretation of one of the best-known paintings by medieval Nürnberg artist Albrecht Dürer,* The Hare *(the original painting is in Vienna).*

The rabbit faces a half-timbered building at the bottom of the square. That's the...

Albrecht Dürer House (Albrecht-Dürer-Haus): Nürnberg's most famous local lived in this house (rated ▲) for the last 20 years of his life. Albrecht Dürer (1471–1528) was a contemporary of Michelangelo who studied in Venice and brought the Renaissance to stodgy medieval Germany. He did things that were unthinkable to other northern European artists of his time—such as signing his works, or painting things like hares simply for study (not on commission).

Nothing in the museum is original (all of the paintings are replicas—the only Dürer originals in Nürnberg are in the Germanic National Museum, described next page). But it does a fine job of capturing the way that Dürer actually lived, including a replica of the workshop where he printed his woodcuts with a working printing press. A 17-minute movie plays continuously (in English on your headphones). The top floor is a gallery with copies of Dürer's most famous paintings and woodcuts. On Saturdays at 14:00, you can meet Dürer's wife, Agnes, who speaks English and takes you through their house (€5, includes Agnes-led audioguide, live Agnes tour-€2.50 extra, €1.50 English brochure also available, €12 combo-ticket with Germanic National Museum—described below, Tue–Sun 10:00–17:00, Thu until 20:00, closed Mon, Albrecht-Dürer-Strasse 39, tel. 0911/231-2568, www.albrecht-duerer-haus.de).

• *You've walked from the southern gate of Nürnberg to the northern gate, and your tour is over. If heading from here to the Nazi sites (see below), a taxi is your best bet. Or, for more old-town sightseeing on your way back to the Frauentor, consider a detour to two more museums, listed under "Sights."*

SIGHTS

In the Old Town

Toy Museum (Spielzeugmuseum)—Nürnberg is famous for woodworking. You can see some examples of this local craft—and lots more—at this entertaining, interactive collection of toys from across the ages. The chronological display starts on the ground floor and heads up through four more floors. Highlights are: for history buffs—the militarization of the 1930s and the rubble years through the 1950s section; for Nebraskans—the Omaha train station in miniature; and for kids—the top-floor play zone. The English coverage of the fine exhibit is mediocre. Ask about an audioguide, or consider the good little €3 booklet (€5 per adult, €10.50 for entire family, Tue–Fri 10:00–17:00, Sat–Sun 10:00–18:00, closed Mon, Karlstrasse 13–15, 0911/231-3164).

▲▲**Germanic National Museum (Germanisches National-museum)**—This sweeping museum is dedicated to the cultural history of the German-speaking world. Entering, you walk along the "Way of Human Rights." Designed by an Israeli artist, its pillars trumpet each right protected by the United Nations' Universal Declaration of Human Rights.

Since 1852, the nucleus of the collection consisted of its highly regarded Medieval Galleries, but recent expansions include an excellent **Pre- and Proto-History** exhibit tracing cultural evolution from the Stone Age to modern times (tools, burial rituals and weapons); a thought-provoking look at how 19th-century **bourgeois art** and culture shaped Germany's modern identity; and a textile collection, **Changes of Dress,** which traces 300 years of hoop skirts, corsets, and waistcoats to examine both the functionality and social status of clothing. English information is plentiful; pick up the excellent and free brochures in the individual galleries or ask at the ticket desk.

The museum also has a marvelous art collection that it arranges into various temporary exhibitions. Works by Dürer, Rembrandt, and Tilman Riemenschneider are usually the centerpiece of these exhibits. Other "must-sees" that are generally on display include an early globe (since it dates from 1492, the Americas are conspicuously missing), seven works by Dürer (the only originals in town), and the sumptuous *Nürnberg Madonna* (1515). More delicate and intimate than a Riemenschneider, this anonymous carving of the favorite hometown girl was the symbol of the city during the Romantic Age (19th century).

There's plenty to see in the rest of the museum. Entering the main section, you'll stand before a wall of street signs from East Berlin dating from the time when the main drag in many towns was called Strasse der Befreiung—"Street of the Liberation" (by the Soviets, from the Nazis and capitalism). You'll see an awesome collection of historical musical instruments, arms and armor, historic toys, stained glass, Bauhaus pottery, and 20th-century German art and culture. In room 219, don't miss the "approved Nazi art," a four-piece collection that promoted the ideals of Nazism (€6, free Wed 18:00–21:00, €12 combo-ticket includes entrance to Albrecht

Dürer House as well as a handheld computer tour of both museums and a connecting walking tour, worthwhile €1.50 audioguide, open Tue–Sun 10:00–18:00, Wed until 21:00, closed Mon, free English tours every other Sun at 14:00, mandatory bag check at €1 lockers, 2 blocks west of Königstrasse at Kartäusergasse 1, entrance on far side of building, tel. 0911/13310, www.gnm.de).

Nazi Sites

Today's Nürnberg is coming to terms with its Nazi past. Though the city tries to recast itself as the "City of Human Rights," its reputation as Hitler's favorite place for a really big rally will be hard to shake. For WWII-history buffs, Nürnberg offers an excellent museum—the Nazi Documentation Center—at the heart of the chilling remains of Hitler's vast Rally Grounds (now Luitpoldhain park).

Getting to the Nazi Documentation Center and Rally Grounds: The sprawling complex is near Dutzendteich, southeast of the old town. The handy tram #9 leaves from in front of the Postbank Center at the train station (Hauptbahnhof) every 10 minutes (direction: Doku-Zentrum, trip takes about 15 min, check return times upon arrival). From the Hauptmarkt or City Hall, you can also hop on the made-for-tourists bus #36. Both options cost the same (€1.80 one-way, covered by €3.60 transit day ticket).

▲▲▲Nazi Documentation Center (Dokumentationszentrum)—Visitors to Europe's Nazi and Holocaust sites inevitably ask the same haunting question: How could this happen? This superb museum does its best to provide an answer. It meticulously traces the evolution of the National Socialist (Nazi) movement, focusing on how it both energized and terrified the German people (the exhibit's official title is "Fascination and Terror"). Special attention is paid to Nürnberg's role in the Nazi movement, including the construction and use of the Rally Grounds, where Hitler's

largest demonstrations took place. This is not a World War II or Holocaust museum; those events are almost an afterthought. Instead, the Center frankly analyzes the Nazi phenomenon, to understand how it happened—and to prevent it from happening again.

The museum is housed in one small wing of Hitler's cavernous, unfinished Congress Hall—the largest surviving example of Nazi architecture. The building was planned to host the mammoth annual Nazi Party gatherings. Today, it's

Nazi Sites in Nürnberg

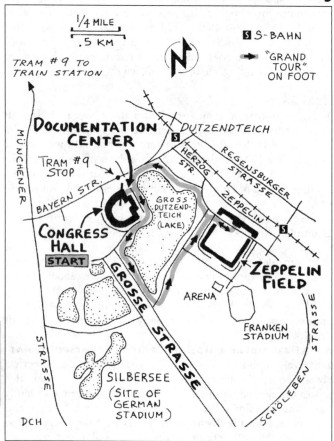

symbolically sliced open by its modern entryway to show the guts and brains of the Nazi movement.

The exhibit is a one-way walk. Allow two hours just for the fine videos you can see along the way. Nazi history buffs should allow an extra hour for the two movies that play continuously in the *Kino* at the start of the exhibit, offering excellent insights into the mass hypnosis of the German nation (interviews and old footage with English subtitles). Once you're in the exhibit, the included audioguide gives everything meaning and works well (turns on automatically at video presentations, you dial room numbers for overviews and specific numbers for details of displays—if rushed, listen to the overviews only). You'll see parts of Leni Riefenstahl's brilliant 1934 propaganda classic *Triumph of the Will*, and just before the end, footage of the Nürnberg Trials. The last stop (before the

Nazis in Nürnberg

It's no coincidence that Nürnberg appealed to Hitler. For one thing, it was convenient: Nürnberg is centrally located in Germany, making it a handy meeting point for Nazi supporters. Hitler also had a friend here, Julius Streicher (a.k.a. the "Franconian Führer"), who fanned the flames of Nazism and anti-Semitism though his inflammatory newspaper *Der Stürmer (The Storm Trooper)*.

But of far greater importance, Nürnberg was steeped in German history. Long before the rise of Nazism, the city—one-time home of Albrecht Dürer and the Holy Roman Emperor, and packed with buildings in the quintessential German Gothic style—was nicknamed the "most German of German cities." As one of the most important cities of medieval Europe, Nürnberg appealed to Hitler as a way to legitimize his Third Reich by invoking Germany's glorious past. Hitler loved the idea of staging his rallies within sight of the imposing Kaiserburg castle, a symbol of the "First Reich" (the Holy Roman Empire).

When Hitler took power in 1933, he made Nürnberg the site of his *Reichsparteitage*—**Nazi Party Rallies.** Increasingly elaborate celebrations of Nazi culture, ideology, and power took place here annually for the next six years. The chilling images from Leni Riefenstahl's documentary *Triumph of the Will* were filmed at the 1934 rallies. At the 1935 rallies, the Nazis devised the first laws—which came to be known as the **Nürnberg Laws**—that legally defined Jews as second-class citizens.

Hitler and his favorite architect, Albert Speer, designed staggeringly massive buildings (such as a stadium seating 400,000 spectators) to host the proceedings. The **Rally Grounds** were the ultimate example of Hitler's preferred architecture style: stark, huge, and Neoclassical. Only a few of the plans were completed before World War II broke out in 1939, forcing the construction budget to be reassigned to the war effort. Today, it's possible to walk around the still-unfinished remains of Hitler's megalomaniacal super-structures (see "Rally Grounds" on page 328).

As the war drew to a close, the world puzzled over what to do with the Nazi officers who had overseen some of the most gruesome atrocities in the history of humankind. It was finally decided that they should be tried as war criminals by an international tribunal (spearheaded by the US and based on the Anglo-American code of law). These trials took place right here, in the Nürnberg Trials Courtroom (see page 329). The **Nürnberg Trials**—the first ever such war-crimes tribunal—brought about a new concept of international law, which continues today in The Hague, Netherlands.

Nürnberg

long ramp back to the start) is a catwalk giving you a look into the core of what would have been a Congress Hall filled with 50,000 cheering Nazis (an artist's sketch is on a nearby wall).

Cost, Hours, Location: €5, includes audioguide, €6 combo-ticket includes Nürnberg Trials Courtroom (see next page), Mon–Fri 9:00–18:00, Sat–Sun 10:00–18:00, Bayernstrasse 110, tel. 0911/231-5666, www.museen.nuernberg.de. The €1 English guidebook is a must.

▲**Rally Grounds (Reichsparteitagsgelände)**—Albert Speer, Hitler's favorite architect, designed this immense complex of buildings (four square miles large) for the Nazi rallies. You'll get the best sense of the Rally Grounds simply from the exhibits inside the Documentation Center. Not many of Hitler's ambitious plans were completed, and to visit the surviving fragments, you'll have to make quite a hike. At a minimum, walk the 10 minutes from the Documentation Center to Zeppelin Field. For a more in-depth visit, the "Grand Tour" described later gives a sense of the mind-boggling scale of what Hitler and Speer planned (figure an hour round-trip from the Documentation Center—see map on page 326).

To get to Zeppelin Field directly from the Documentation Center, simply follow the lake for 10 minutes (with the lake on your right).

Zeppelin Field (Zeppelinwiese): This was the site of the Nazis' biggest rallies, including those famously filmed by Leni Riefenstahl. You can actually climb up on the grandstand and stand on the platform in front of the Zeppelin Tribune, where Hitler stood to survey the masses (up to 250,000 people at a time). The Tribune is based on the design of the ancient Greek Pergamon Altar (now in Berlin's Pergamon Museum); it was originally topped by a towering swastika, which was  blown up by the Allies soon after the end of the war. Clowning around on the speaking platform with any Nazi gestures is illegal and taken seriously by the police.

Grand Tour: To hike the entire area, begin at the Nazi Documentation Center, in the **Congress Hall** (Kongresshalle). This huge building—big enough for an audience of 50,000—was originally intended to be topped with a roof and skylight. At the hall's Nazi Documentation Center, pick up the free area plan *(Geländeplan);* the numbers on the map correspond to the information pillars that you'll find on-site. As you leave the Documentation Center, turn right and walk along the side of the building. Dip into the courtyard of the Congress Hall to appreciate its dimensions, then return to the main road. When you get to the end, turn right again and continue walking with the Congress Hall on your right. Continue past the end of the building, and then turn left (under the *Kommen Sie gut nach Hause* sign) onto the Great Road. The lights you see in the distance hover above the Franken Stadium (a soccer field before Hitler, then used for Nazi rallies, and most recently, for the 2006 World Cup soccer championship tournament).

As you walk along the **Great Road** (Grosse Strasse), with a lake on either side, consider the gigantic scale of this complex. At 200 feet wide, the Great Road was big enough to be used as a runway by the Allies after the war. The road points toward Nürnberg's imperial palace, Kaiserburg—Hitler's symbolic connection to the Holy Roman Empire (the "First Reich").

Near the end of the lake, ahead and to the right, was to be the site of the **German Stadium** (Deutsches Stadion)—the biggest in the world (with 400,000 seats). They got as far as digging a foundation before funding was redirected to the war effort. Today, the site of the stadium is a park surrounding the big lake, Silbersee—which was the hole for the never-built stadium's foundation.

If you'd like to detour to the German Stadium site, you can—but it's time-consuming, without much to see. Instead, walk down the first lakeside path on your left as you reach the end of the Great Road. Continue along the lake for a good 15 minutes until you dead-end into the parking lot. To your right is the huge Zeppelin Field (described earlier).

From Zeppelin Field, hike along the lake (with the lake on your left) back toward the Congress Hall. When you dead-end at the busy road, the S-Bahn station is to the right, and the tram stop is in front of the museum to your left.

Nürnberg Trials Courtroom (Nürnberger Prozesse)—In 1945, in courtroom *(Saal)* #600 of Nürnberg's Palace of Justice (Justizgebäude), 21 Nazi war criminals stood trial before an international tribunal of judges appointed by the four victorious countries. After a year of trials and deliberations, 12 Nazis were sentenced to death by hanging, three were acquitted, and the rest were sent to prison. One of the death sentences was for Hitler's right-hand man, Hermann Göring. He wanted to be shot by firing squad—a proper military execution—but his request was denied. Instead, two hours before his scheduled hanging, Göring committed suicide with poison he had smuggled into his cell, infuriating many who thought that this death was too easy for him.

While this historic courtroom is still in active use, you can tour it on weekends (€2.50, €6 combo-ticket includes Nazi Documentation Center, tours Sat–Sun 13:00–16:00 at the top of each hour, not all tours in English—call ahead to confirm schedule, west of center at Fürther Strasse 110, enter on Bärenschanzstrasse, take U-1 to Bärenschanze, it's just behind *Pit Stop* sign, tel. 0911/231-5666).

SLEEPING

Prices spike up during major conventions in the spring and fall, and in December—when the Christmas market brings visitors from around the world. July and August are generally low season and come with the lowest prices.

Near the Frauentor

These hotels cluster around the Frauentor, on or close to Königstrasse (within a 5-min walk of the train station). This handy neighborhood is convenient to the station and city sightseeing, just inside the old town walls. The small red light district on nearby Luitpoldstrasse—a sprinkling of strip clubs and sex shops—is harmless.

$$$ Hotel Victoria offers friendly staff and 65 fresh, new-feeling rooms behind its historic 1896 facade just inside the Frauentor. The standard rooms are a better value than the slightly bigger business rooms (standard rooms: S-€49, Sb-€78, Db-€99; business rooms: Sb-€88, Db-€109; discounts on slow summer weekends, non-smoking floor, elevator, parking garage-€11/day, Königstrasse 80, tel. 0911/24050, fax 0911/227-432, www .hotelvictoria.de, book@hotelvictoria.de).

$$$ Hotel Drei Raben is an artsy and fun splurge, with a super-stylish lobby, 25 comfortable rooms, a huge breakfast buffet (ask for eggs or a cappuccino), and lots of elegant touches. The standard rooms are plenty nice, but the "myth rooms" come with Franconian fairy tales on the walls. All guests get a free book of local folk tales (standard rooms: Sb-€80, Db-€120; myth rooms:

Sleep Code

(€1 = about $1.30, country code: 49, area code: 0911)
S = Single, **D** = Double/Twin, **T** = Triple, **Q** = Quad, **b** = bathroom, **s** = shower only. Unless otherwise noted, credit cards are accepted, English is spoken, and breakfast is included.

To help you sort easily through these listings, I've divided the rooms into three categories, based on the price for a standard double room with bath:

$$$ **Higher Priced**—Most rooms €95 or more.
  $$ **Moderately Priced**—Most rooms between €60–95.
    $ **Lower Priced**—Most rooms €60 or less.

Db-€150; spacious suites with freestanding bathtubs: Db-€185; ask for special summer discounts—especially on weekends, when myth rooms rent for standard prices or less; non-smoking rooms, elevator, free Wi-Fi, parking garage-€15/day, Königstrasse 63, tel. 0911/274-380, fax 0911/232-611, www.hotel-drei-raben.de, hotel-drei-raben@t-online.de).

$$ Ibis Altstadt Hotel, sandwiched between a bunch of fast-food joints, offers 53 good-value, cookie-cutter rooms in a convenient location (Sb/Db-€65 Mon–Thu, €59 Fri–Sun, €98 during conventions, breakfast-€9.50, elevator, Königstrasse 74, tel. 0911/232-000, fax 0911/209-684, www.ibis.com, h1069 @accor-hotels.com).

$$ Hotel Probst is run by the hardworking Probst family. They rent 34 clean, cheap rooms in a sterile, institutional, blocky apartment building. This place will do if you're watching your budget, but some guests complain about the thin walls (Ss-€40, Sb-€56, Db-€67–75, prices soft, elevator, Luitpoldstrasse 9, tel. 0911/203-433, fax 0911/205-9336, www.hotel-garni-probst.de, info@hotel-garni-probst.de).

$ Hotel Keiml is run by gracious Frau Keiml, who has been welcoming guests here since 1975. She rents 20 spacious, bright, and homey rooms up several flights of stairs (no elevator) in a sturdy former apartment building beautifully located on a pedestrian street just off Königstrasse. A nearby nightclub can be noisy on weekends, so request a quiet room (Ss-€30, Sb-€40, Ds-€45–50, Db-€60, these prices with this book and cash in 2008, Luitpoldstrasse 7, tel. 0911/226-240, fax 0911/241-760).

$ City Hotel, with 20 old, worn rooms in the pedestrian zone, has decent prices for the location and amenities (Sb-€40, Db-€55, elevator, Königstrasse 25–27, tel. 0911/232-645, fax 0911/203-999, Widtmann family).

In or near the Castle

These accommodations are in or near the castle at the far side of the old town. Getting here is a €8 taxi ride or a long hike from station. Or take the U-Bahn (line #1) to Lorenzkirche and exit toward Kaiserstrasse.

$$$ Hotel Elch, the oldest hotel in town (with 500-year-old exposed beams adding to its classic elk-friendly woodiness), is buried deep in the old town near the castle. It rents 12 charming and well-equipped rooms (Sb-€70, Db-€95, a bit cheaper Fri–Sun; prices plummet July–Aug: Sb-€46, Db-€77; kids under age 14 free, nearby parking garage-€10/day, behind St. Sebald Church at Irrerstrasse 9, tel. 0911/249-2980, fax 0911/2492-9844, www.hotel-elch.com, info@hotel-elch.com).

$$ Hotel Lucas, recently renovated, is in the heart of the old town just a short walk from Market Square. Because there are only 11 rooms, you can expect personalized care from Herr Singer and his team. Rooms are modern and cheerful, making this a great, non-smoking home base (Sb-€50–65, Db-€75–90, lower prices are for weekends; breakfast is simple, but ask for extras like eggs at no extra charge; attached restaurant, Kaiserstrasse 22, tel. 0911/227-845, fax 0911/244-9158, www.hotel-lucas.de, info@hotel-lucas.de).

$ *Hostel:* The **Nürnberg Youth Hostel** is romantically situated inside the castle (Kaiserburg) at the top of the old town. It's scenic, but can be crowded with school-age groups in the summer. Travelers over age 26 pay €4 more and are allowed only if traveling with a family or if there's space available (bed in 3- to 6-bed dorm-€21; limited singles and doubles: S-€38.50, D-€46; dorm dwellers pay less for longer stays, €3.10 more for non-members, includes breakfast and sheets, curfew at 1:00 in the morning, tel. 0911/230-9360, fax 0911/2309-3611, jhnuernberg@djh-bayern.de).

EATING

Nürnberg is famous for its pinkie-sized bratwurst (called, like local residents, *Nürnberger*). Nürnbergers—the people—insist that size doesn't matter; they maintain that *in der Kürze liegt die Würze* (in the shortness lies the tastiness). All over town, signs read *3 im Weckle,* meaning "three bratwurst in a little bun" (a good snack for about €2). Old-timers go for the mustard, while children like ketchup. Restaurant menus often offer them in 6-, 8-, or 10-weenie servings with *Beilagen,* which means your choice of a side dish (generally potato salad or kraut). Nürnberg is packed with atmospheric old places to try this or other regional specialties. For convenience, I've listed restaurants that are on (or near) Königstrasse, the main drag connecting the station to the castle. Only the last two places are away from this tourist zone—buried in the west end of the old town, and known only to locals.

Barfüsser Beer Cellar serves its own popular microbrew and fills the basement of the old grain storehouse *(Mauthalle)* with jovial Germans munching meat-on-the-bone (from pork knuckle to duck) and swilling beer. This is good, German fun. On hot nights, the cellar's empty and their tables spill out onto Königstrasse. Locals love the *Schäufele*—oven-roasted pork shoulder in home-brewed dark beer sauce; and the *Frankenschmaus*—a "greatest hits" platter of sausages, pork shoulder, kraut, and dumplings (€6–13 meals, daily 11:00–24:00, Hallplatz 2, tel. 0911/204-242).

Nassauer Keller is a snug and classy 13th-century vaulted cellar filled with suits of armor and diners enjoying the romantic atmosphere and traditional food. A small door leads down steep steps into a dressy dining room—popular for roast shoulder of pork and venison dishes. It's a little pricey but worth the extra euros. Avoid this place on hot days (€10–14 plates, Mon–Sat 12:00–15:00 & 18:00–24:00, kitchen closes at 14:00 & 22:00, closed Sun, reservations smart, across from St. Lawrence Church at Karolinenstrasse 2–4, tel. 0911/225-967).

Goldenes Posthorn is a venerable institution and—while no longer in its original historic location—once upon a time, Albrecht Dürer's favorite hangout. Come here to enjoy everything from Franconian specialties and bratwurst to daily fish and vegetarian plates, either in the light-wood, chalet-chic interior or on the patio in the shadow of St. Sebald Church (€6–10 meals, daily 11:00–23:00, daily specials, cash only, Glöckleingasse 2, tel. 0911/225-153, fax 0911/227-645).

Literaturhaus Nürnberg, run by the local book club, is popular for readings. It serves theme breakfasts (daily until 14:00) and creative international dishes for €5–11. Locals like to order several varied plates tapas-style, or just enjoy its booky café ambience for drinks and sweets (daily 9:00–24:00, 2 blocks from Frauentor just off Königstrasse at Luitpoldstrasse 6, tel. 0911/234-2658).

Burgwächter serves up German cuisine—either in its cozy restaurant, or on its covered patio, with big, rustic picnic tables. It's just under the castle, and therefore both touristy and practical (€5–10 plates, good salads, daily 11:00–24:00, Am Ölberg 10, tel. 0911/222-126).

Bratwursthäusle is a high-energy, woody-yet-mod place with a leafy terrace (enjoyable people-watching). Its cozy interior feels like a big farmhouse with tables gathered around an open grill. The menu is very limited, with little more than bratwurst and some nasty pickled animal parts. You come here for the best bratwurst in town—all made in-house by the *Häusle*'s own butcher, and dished up with efficient service. Chat up the owner, friendly Herr Behringer, and he'll be happy to tell you about Bratwurst Saints (Mon–Sat 10:00–22:00, closed Sun, midway between Market Square and the castle on the main drag, Rathausplatz 1, tel. 0911/227-695). For arguably the best local bratwurst to go, drop into Bratwursthäusle, pay €1.80 at the little door, take your receipt to the grill...and in seconds, you'll be on your way with Nürnberg's "Little Mac."

Café Sebald is a bratwurst-free bistro serving well-presented, Italian-inspired cuisine in a white-tablecloth, indoor/outdoor setting. They're friendly, stylish, and into smooth jazz. The local clientele appreciates their €8–15 daily blackboard specials (plates up to €22, daily 11:00–23:00, 2 blocks behind—west of—St. Sebald Church towards the wall at Weinmarkt 14, tel. 0911/381-303).

Kettensteg Biergarten is a hip jumble of picnic tables under trees overlooking the city's river and medieval wall. Its youthful energy and big flames give it a tribe-like ambience after dark. This is ideal on a balmy evening for leafy, cobbled outdoor dining surrounded by happy locals and in-the-know foreign students (€8–12 meals, strong German cuisine with a few modern and Asian surprises and decent salads, daily in summer 11:00–23:00, west of Market Square where the river hits the wall, Maxplatz 35, tel. 0911/221-081). If you just want a slow, hard drink, try their cool riverside bar overlooking Germany's first iron suspension bridge (the Kettensteg, 1825).

TRANSPORTATION CONNECTIONS

From Nürnberg by Train to: Rothenburg (hourly, 1–1.5 hrs, change in Ansbach and then Steinach), **Würzburg** (2–3/hr, 1 hr), **Munich** (2–3/hr, 1 hr), **Frankfurt** (at least hourly, 2 hrs), **Salzburg** (hourly with change in Munich, 3 hrs). Train info: tel. 11861 (€0.60/min).

DRESDEN

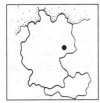

Dresden, the capital of Saxony, surprises visitors with fine Baroque architecture and impressive museums. It's historic, intriguing, and fun. While the city is packed with tourists, 90 percent of them are German or Russian. Until Americans rediscover Dresden's Baroque glory, you'll feel like you're in on a secret.

At the peak of its power in the 18th century, this capital of Saxony ruled most of present-day Poland and eastern Germany from the bank of the Elbe River. Dresden's "Louis XIV" was Augustus the Strong. As both prince elector of Saxony and king of Poland, he imported artists from all over Europe, peppering his city with stunning Baroque buildings and filling his treasury with lavish jewels and artwork. Dresden's grand architecture and dedication to the arts—along with the gently rolling hills surrounding the city—earned it the nickname "Florence on the Elbe."

Sadly, these days Dresden is better known for its destruction in World War II. American and British pilots firebombed the city on the night of February 13, 1945. More than 25,000 people were killed, and 75 percent of the historical center was destroyed. American Kurt Vonnegut, who was a POW in Dresden during the firebombing, later memorialized the event in his novel *Slaughterhouse-Five*.

When Germany was divvied up at the end of World War II, Dresden wound up in the Soviet sector. Forty years of communist rule left the city in an economic hole, from which it is just emerging. Some older Dresdeners feel nostalgia for the Red old days, when "everyone had a job." But in the almost two decades since the Berlin Wall fell, Dresden has made real progress in getting back on its feet—and most locals are enjoying capitalism with gusto. Today's Dresden is a young and vibrant city, crawling with happy-go-lucky students who barely remember communism.

Under the communists, Dresden patched up some of its damaged buildings, left many others in ruins, and replaced even more with huge, modern, ugly sprawl. But today, Dresden seems all about rebuilding. Circa-1946 photos are on walls everywhere, and the city's most important and beautiful historic buildings in the Old Town have been restored. Across the river, the New Town was missed by the bombs. While well-worn, it retains its prewar character and has emerged as the city's fun and lively people zone. Most tourists never cross the bridge away from the famous Old Town museums...but a visit to Dresden isn't complete without a wander through the New Town.

Planning Your Time

Dresden, conveniently located halfway between Prague and Berlin, is well worth even a quick stop. If you're short on time, Dresden's top sights can be seen in a midday break from your Berlin–Prague train ride (each one is less than a 2.5-hour ride away). Catch the early train, throw your bag in a locker at the station (€2), follow my self-guided walk (page 339), and visit some museums before taking an evening train out. If possible, reserve far ahead to visit one of Dresden's top sights, the Historic Green Vault (for reservations details, see page 349).

If you have more time, Dresden merits an overnight stay. The city is a handy home base for getting back to nature at Saxon Switzerland National Park (see page 354), or side-tripping to the town of Görlitz for its intriguing mix of rich architecture and culture (see next chapter).

ORIENTATION

(area code: 0351)

Dresden is big, with half a million residents. Its city center hugs a curve on the Elbe River. Despite the city's size, most of its sights are within easy strolling distance along the south bank of the Elbe in the Old Town (Altstadt). South of the Old Town (a 5-min tram ride or 15-min walk away) is the main train station (Hauptbahnhof). North of the Old Town, across the river, you'll find the residential-feeling New Town (Neustadt). While the New Town boasts virtually no sights, it's lively, colorful, and fun to explore—especially at night—and has some recommended hotels and restaurants.

Dresden

N

TO BERLIN

NEUSTADT STATION

TO ⑦

LOUIS ENSTR.

GÖRLITZERSTR.

⑧

⑱

⑨

ROTH STR.

BAUTZ- NER STR.

⑥

④

ANTON STR.

THERES.

HAIN STR.

KÖNIG STR.

⑯

⑤

⑮

ALBERT-PLATZ

N E W   T O W N

HAUPTSTR.

ALBERT STR.

WIGARDSTR.

R I V E R

PALAIS PLATZ

MARIEN BRÜCKE

GR. MEISS STR.

THREE KINGS CHURCH

KÖPCKE STR.

CAROLA BRÜCKE

PATH

ELBE

HOF-KIRCHE

AUGUSTUS BRÜCKE

⑭

BOATS

BRÜHLSCHE TERRASSE

⑬

SYNA-GOGUE

SEMPER OPER

THEATER PLATZ

②

⑪

ALBERT-INUM

TO YENIDZE

OSTRA. ALLEE

ZWINGER

ⓘ

FRAUEN-KIRCHE

TO ⑰

⑫

ROYAL PALACE

WILSD. STR.

⑩

ALT-MARKT

OLD   TOWN

RATHAUS

SEE DETAIL MAP

WAISENHAUS STR.

🚋 KEY TRAM STOP

🏞 VIEW

REITBAHN STR.

PRAGER STRASSE

ST. PETERSBURGER STR.

③

ⓘ

200 YDS.

200 METERS

TRAM #8

MAIN STATION

① Hotel Kipping

② Münzgasse (Hilton Dresden, Apts. an der Frauenkirche & Eateries)

③ Hotels Bastei, Königstein & Lilienstein

④ Hotel Bayerischer Hof Dresden

⑤ Hotel Martha Hospiz

⑥ AHA Hotel

⑦ To Guest House Mezcalero

⑧ Hostel "Louise 20"

⑨ Hostel Mondpalast Dresden

⑩ Altmarkt Keller Restaurant

⑪ Grand Café Rest. Cosel Palais

⑫ Sophienkeller Restaurant

⑬ Radeberger Spezialausschank Café

BAYRISCHE.

① WINCK.

TO PRAGUE VIA E-55

⑭ Augustus Garten Rest.

⑮ Wenzel Prager Bierstuben

⑯ Good Friends Restaurant

⑰ To Hygiene Museum & VW Transparent Factory

⑱ Innere Neustadt Nightlife

Dresden

Tourist Information

Dresden has two TIs: one in the **Old Town** at Theaterplatz (in the Schinkelwache building, next to the Zwinger); and another one 300 yards from the **main train station,** in a freestanding kiosk on Prager Strasse (both open Mon–Fri 10:00–18:00, Sat 10:00–16:00, closed Sun, general TI tel. 0351/491-920, www.dresden-tourist .de). Both TIs book rooms (€3/person), sell the Dresden City Card museum pass (see next entry) and concert and theater tickets, and operate travel agencies. Get the handy, free one-page city map with a listing of key sights, hours, and prices on the back. For live entertainment and cultural events, skim the monthly *Theater Konzert Kunst* (free, in German only).

Discount Deals: The **Dresden City Card** offers you entry into all of Dresden's top museums (except the Historic Green Vault), discounts on some lesser museums, and unlimited use of the city's transit system (€19/48 hours, €29 for 72-hour regional version that includes outlying areas, the Family City Card covers two adults and up to four children for €42/48 hours, sold at TI). If you're only here for the day, skip it and buy a one-day *Tageskarte* museum pass instead (€12, covers all state museums except the Historic Green Vault, no transit, sold at participating museums but not the TI). The website for all Dresden state museums is www.skd-dresden.de.

Arrival in Dresden

Dresden has two major train stations: Hauptbahnhof and Neustadt. (Note that express trains from Berlin stop first at Neustadt, then at Hauptbahnhof.)

If you're coming for the day and want the easiest access to the sights, use the **Hauptbahnhof** (main train station). Exit the station following signs for the city, taxis, and trams. To take a **tram** into the center, cross the tram tracks at Wiener Platz. Veer right (through the five-story rounded glass building) to find tram #8 or #11 (departing to your left), which zips you to the historical center (Theaterplatz or Postplatz). The 15-minute **walk** to the Old Town offers an insightful glimpse of the communist era as you stroll down Prager Strasse (described on page 352; from the station, continue straight through Wiener Platz, under and past the towering Mercure Hotel).

The **Neustadt** station serves the New Town north of the river, near some recommended hotels. From this station, tram #11 runs to Am Zwingerteich, a park in the center of the Old Town right next to the sights.

Trains run between the Hauptbahnhof and Neustadt stations every 10 minutes (€1.80, 10-min ride, most trains stop at each station—ask; the stations are also connected by slower tram #3).

Helpful Hints

Sightseeing Strategies: Note that many of Dresden's top museums are closed either Monday or Tuesday. The incredible treasury—the Historic Green Vault—requires a reservation well in advance; if you don't get one, try to line up early to buy a same-day ticket, sold at 10:00 (for all the details, see page 349). Once you have your appointed Historic Green Vault visit time, plan the rest of your day around it (it's conveniently located right in the center of the Old Town). The Hofkirche hosts free pipe-organ concerts twice a week (Wed and Sat at 11:30).

Internet Access: To check your email in the main train station, find the Sidewalk Express computers in the **"Point Shop To Go"** (€2/hr, 1-hour minimum, open long hours daily).

Local Guides: Genteel **Maren Koban** (mobile 0176-2922-6374, tel. 0351/311-1315) and **Liane Lowe** (lianeloewe@gmx.de) each enjoy sharing the story of their hometown with visitors (€100/half-day).

Getting Around Dresden

Dresden's slick **trams** and **buses** work well for the visitor. The tram network is so slick, you might just spend the hour your €1.80 ticket gets you joyriding—marveling at huge investment this city is making as it rebuilds. Buy tickets at the machines on the platforms or in the trams (€1.80 for a single ticket, or *Einzelfahrkarte;* €4.50 for a 4-pack of *Kurzstrecke*—short-ride tickets; machines accept coins only). A day ticket (*Tageskarte,* €4.50 for one calendar day) works for sightseeing within the city. Validate your ticket by date-stamping it in the little boxes on train platforms and on board buses and trams (for the day ticket, stamp it only the first time you ride). Free use of public transit is included with the Dresden City Card (see page 338).

Taxis are reasonable, plentiful, and generally honest (€2.50 to start, then €1.20/kilometer).

SELF-GUIDED WALK

▲▲▲Do-It-Yourself Dresden Baroque Blitz Tour

Dresden's major sights are conveniently clustered along a delightfully strollable promenade next to the Elbe River. Get to know this sightseeing zone by taking this walk. Though the city has a long and colorful history, we'll focus on the four eras that have shaped it the most: Dresden's Golden Age in the mid-18th century under Augustus the Strong; the city's destruction by firebombs in World War II; the communist regime (1945–1989); and the current "reconstruction after reunification" era.

Central Dresden

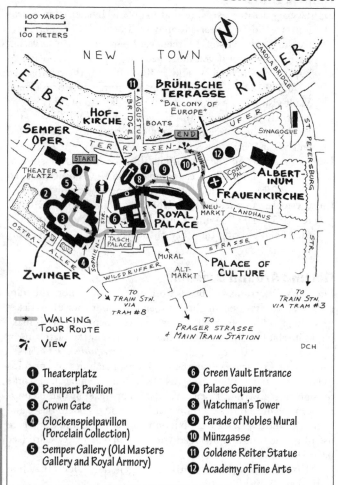

WALKING TOUR ROUTE

VIEW

DCH

1. Theaterplatz
2. Rampart Pavilion
3. Crown Gate
4. Glockenspielpavillon (Porcelain Collection)
5. Semper Gallery (Old Masters Gallery and Royal Armory)
6. Green Vault Entrance
7. Palace Square
8. Watchman's Tower
9. Parade of Nobles Mural
10. Münzgasse
11. Goldene Reiter Statue
12. Academy of Fine Arts

The following walk laces together Dresden's top sights in about an hour, not counting museum stops. It includes the three major sights (Zwinger, Royal Palace with Green Vault treasures, and Frauenkirche), each of which is described later in the chapter. Incorporating these visits into the walk will fill your day.

• Begin at Theaterplatz (a convenient drop-off point for tram #8 from the Hauptbahnhof).

Theaterplatz

Face the equestrian statue (King John, an unimportant mid-19th-century ruler) in the middle of the square. In front of you, behind the statue, is the Saxon State Opera House—nicknamed the **Semper Oper** after its architect, Gottfried Semper (visits only with a tour, see page 352).

As you face the Opera House, the nearest building on your left is the Neoclassical guardhouse called the Schinkelwache (housing the TI and opera box office). The big building behind it is the vast Zwinger palace complex (your next stop). Across the square from the Opera House is the Hofkirche, with its distinctive green-copper steeple, and to its right is the sprawling Royal Palace (with shiny new clock; both described later). All the buildings you see here—Dresden's Baroque treasures—are thoroughly reconstructed. The originals were destroyed in a single night by American and British bombs. For more than 60 years, Dresden has been rebuilding—and there's more work to do.

• *Walk through the passageway into the Zwinger courtyard, noticing the Crown Gate on the opposite side lowering majestically into view. Stop in the middle of the courtyard, where we'll survey all four wings.*

▲▲The Zwinger

This palace complex is a Baroque masterpiece—once the pride and joy of the Wettin dynasty, and today filled with fine museums.

The Wettins ruled Saxony for more than 800 years, right up until the end of the First World War (like so many of Europe's royal families). Saxony wasn't ruled by a king, but by a prince elector—one of a handful of nobles who elected the Holy Roman Emperor. The prince elector of Saxony was one of Germany's most powerful people. In the 18th century, the larger-than-life Augustus the Strong—who was both prince elector of Saxony and king of Poland—kicked off Saxony's Golden Age (see sidebar, page 343).

"Zwinger" means the no-man's-land running along the city wall. This empty space gradually evolved into the complex of buildings you see today. By Augustus' time, the Zwinger was used for celebrations of Saxon royalty. Imagine an over-the-top royal wedding in this complex. The courtyard served as an open-air palace, complete with orange trees in huge Chinese porcelain pots.

Let's get oriented. Face the north wing (with the Crown Gate on your left). You're looking at the **Rampart Pavilion** (Wallpavillon), the first wing of the palace—an orangerie capped with a sun pavilion built for Augustus' fruit trees and parties. Up top is Atlas (who happens to have Augustus' features) with the Earth on his back—a fitting symbol for Augustus the Strong. Stairs lead to a fine view from the terrace above. This wing of the Zwinger houses the fun **Mathematics-Physics Salon** (closed until 2009).

Turn to the left, facing the **Crown Gate** (Kronentor). The gate's golden crown is topped by four golden eagles supporting a smaller crown—symbolizing Polish royalty (since Augustus was also king of Poland).

Turn again to the left to see the **Glockenspielpavillon.** The glockenspiel near the top of the gate has 40 bells made of Meissen porcelain (bells chime every 15 minutes, and play a sweet three-minute melody at 10:15, 14:15, and 17:15). This wing of the Zwinger also houses Augustus the Strong's **Porcelain Collection** (see page 348).

Turn once more to the left (with the Crown Gate behind you) to see the **Semper Gallery.** This Zwinger wing was added to the original courtyard a hundred years later by Gottfried Semper (of Opera House fame). It houses Dresden's best painting collection, the **Old Masters Gallery,** as well as the **Royal Armory** (see page 348).

Throughout the city, you'll see the local sandstone looking really sooty. Locals claim that it's not pollution, but natural oxidation that turns the stone black in about 30 years. Once restored, the statues are given a silicon treatment that lets the stone breathe but keeps it from going black.

Take time to enjoy some of the Zwinger's excellent museums. Anticipating WWII bombs, Dresdeners preserved their town's art treasures by storing them in underground mines and cellars in the countryside. This saved these great works from Allied bombs... but not from the Russians. Nearly all of the city's artwork ended up in Moscow until after Stalin's death in 1953, when the art was returned by the communist regime to win over their East German subjects. Today, Russians invade only as tourists.

When you're finished with the museums, exit the Zwinger through the Glockenspielpavillon (south gate). Halfway through the corridor, look for the timelines telling the history of the

Augustus the Strong
(1670–1733)

Friedrich Augustus I of the Wettin family exemplified royal excess, and made Dresden one of Europe's most important cities of culture. Legends paint Augustus as a macho, womanizing, powerful, ambitious, properly Baroque man—a real Saxon superstar. A hundred years after his death, historians dubbed Augustus "the Strong." Today, tour guides love to impart silly legends about Augustus, who supposedly fathered 365 children and could break a horseshoe in half with his bare hands.

As prince elector of Saxony, Augustus wheeled and dealed—and converted from his Saxon Protestantism to a more Polish-friendly Catholicism—to become King Augustus II of Poland. Like most Wettins, Augustus the Strong was unlucky at war, but a clever diplomat and a lover of the arts.

The Polish people blame Augustus and his successors—who were far more concerned with wealth and opulence than with sensible governance—for Poland's precipitous decline after its own medieval Golden Age. According to Poles, the Saxon kings did nothing but "eat, drink, and loosen their belts" (it rhymes in Polish).

Whether you consider them the heroes of history, or the villains, Augustus and the rest of the Wettins—and the nobles who paid them taxes—are to thank for Dresden's rich architectural and artistic heritage.

Zwinger in German: to the right, its construction, and to the left, its destruction and reconstruction. Notice the Soviet spin: On May 8, 1945, the Soviet army liberated *(befreite)* Dresden from "fascist tyranny" *(faschistischen Tyrannei)*, and from 1945 to 1964, the Zwinger was rebuilt with the "power of the workers and peasants" *(Arbeiter- und Bauern-Macht)*.

• *As you exit the corridor, cross the street and the tram tracks and jog left, walking down the perpendicular Taschenberg Strasse with the yellow Taschenberg Palace on your right (ruined until 1990, today the city's finest five-star hotel). The yellow-windowed sky bridge ahead connects the Taschenberg, which was the crown prince's palace, with the prince electors'* **Royal Palace.** *This is where you can enter the spectacular* **Green Vault** *treasuries (described on page 349; entrance is before crossing under the sky bridge, through fancy gate on left). But if your Historic Green Vault reservation is for later today, you can continue this walk for now.*

Exiting the Royal Palace, go under the sky bridge. Ahead of you and to the right, the blocky modern building is the…

Palace of Culture (Kulturpalast)

Built by the communist government in 1969, this hall is still used for concerts today. Notice the mural depicting communist themes: workers; strong women; care for the elderly; teachers and students; and, of course, the red star and the seal of former East Germany. Little of this symbolism, which once inundated the lives of locals, survives in post-communist Germany.

• *Now turn left (with the Palace of Culture behind you). Walk along the palace wall toward the two copper spires, through a tunnel with (mostly Russian) musicians, until you emerge into the* **Palace Square.** *Ahead of you and to the left is the...*

Hofkirche (Cathedral)

Why does Dresden, a stronghold of local-boy Martin Luther's Protestant Reformation, boast such a beautiful Catholic cathedral? When Augustus the Strong died, his son wanted to continue as king of Poland, like his father. The pope would allow it only if Augustus Junior built a Catholic church in Dresden. Now, thanks to Junior's historical kissing-up, the mere 5 percent of locals who are Catholic get to enjoy this fine church. The elevated passageway connecting the church with the palace allowed the royal family to avoid walking in the street with commoners.

Step inside the cathedral (free, enter through side door facing palace, Mon–Thu 9:00–18:00, Fri 13:00–18:00, Sat–Sun 10:00–18:00, tel. 0351/484-4712, www.kathedrale-dresden.de). The fine Baroque pulpit—hidden in the countryside during World War II—is carved out of linden wood. The glorious 3,000-pipe organ filling the back of the nave is played for the public on Wednesdays and Saturdays at 11:30 (free).

The Memorial Chapel (facing the rear of the church, on the left) is dedicated to those who died in the WWII firebombing and to all victims of violence. Its evocative *pietà* altarpiece was made in 1973 of Meissen porcelain. Mary offers the faithful the crown of thorns, as if to remind us that Jesus—on her lap, head hanging lifeless on the left—died to save humankind. The altar (freestanding, in front) shows five flaming heads. It seems to symbolize how Dresdeners suffered...in the presence of their suffering savior. The dates on the high altar (30-1-33 and 13-2-45) mark the dark period between Hitler's rise to power and the night Dresden was destroyed.

The basement houses the royal crypt, including the heart of the still-virile Augustus the Strong—which, according to legend, still beats when a pretty woman comes near (crypt only open for one 45-min German tour each day).

• *As you leave the Hofkirche, you're facing the palace complex entry (with the* **Watchman's Tower** *above on the right—see page 350). To the* *left, next to the palace's main entrance, you'll see a long, yellow mural called the...*

▲▲Parade of Nobles (Fürstenzug)

This mural is painted on 24,000 tiles of Meissen porcelain. Longer than a football field, it illustrates 700 years of Saxon royalty. It was built to commemorate Saxon history and heritage after Saxony became a part of Germany in 1871. The artist carefully studied armor and clothing through the ages, allowing you to accurately trace the evolution of weaponry and fashions for seven centuries. (This is great for couples—try this for a switch: As you stroll, men watch the fashions, women the weaponry.)

The very last figure (or the first one you see, coming from this direction) is the artist himself, Wilhelm Walther. Then come com-

moners (miner, farmer, carpenter, teachers, students, artists), and then the royals, with 35 names and dates marking more than 700 years of Wettin rule. Stop at 1694. That's August II (Augustus the Strong), the most important of the Saxon kings. His horse stomps on the rose (symbol of Martin Luther, the Protestant movement, and the Lutheran church today) to gain the Polish crown. The first Saxon royal is Konrad der Grosse ("the Great"). And waaay up at the very front of the parade, an announcer with a band and 12th-century cheerleaders excitedly herald the arrival of this wondrous procession. The porcelain tiles, originals from 1907, survived the bombing. When created, they were fired three times at 2,400 degrees Fahrenheit...and then fired again during the 1945 firestorm, at only 1,800 degrees.

• *When you're finished looking at the mural, dogleg right and walk into the big square. Find a statue of Martin Luther.*

Neumarkt Square

This "New Market Square," once a town center ringed by rich merchants' homes, is being rebuilt and will soon be a lively people-and-café center. The statue of Martin Luther holds not just any Bible, but the Word of God he translated into German so that regular people could get their minds on it without Church control—basically what the Reformation was all about. Toppled in 1945, he's cleaned up and back on his feet again.

• *The big church looming over the square is the...*

▲▲▲Frauenkirche (Church of Our Lady)

This church is the heart and soul of Dresden. The people of

Dresden, jealous of the mighty Catholic domes of Venice and London, mobilized their Protestant pride to raise the money, and built this impressive Lutheran church. When completed in 1743, this was Germany's biggest Protestant church (310 feet high). Its unique central-stone-cupola design gave it the nickname "the handbell church." While it's a great church, this building garners the world's attention primarily because of its tragic history and phoenix-like resurrection: On the night of February 13, 1945, the firebombs came. When the smoke cleared the next morning, the Frauenkirche was smoldering but still standing. It burned for two days before finally collapsing. After the war, the Frauenkirche was kept in rubble as a peace monument. It was the site of many memorial vigils. In 2005, completely rebuilt, it reopened to the public. (For touring details and more information, see page 350.)

A big hunk of the bombed **rubble** stands in the square (near door E, river side of church) as a memorial. Notice the small relief of the dome that shows where this piece came from.

• *From here, stroll downhill through a busy little restaurant-lined street, Münzgasse, and up the stairs to Dresden's grand river-view balcony. Find a bulge in the promenade 30 yards to the right. Belly up to that banister.*

▲▲Brühlsche Terrasse

This so-called "Balcony of Europe," a delightful promenade, was once Dresden's defensive rampart. Look along the side of the terrace facing the Elbe River to see openings for cannons. By Baroque times, fortresses were no longer necessary, and this became one of Europe's most charming promenades, with a leafy canopy of linden trees.

Dresden claims to have the world's largest and oldest fleet of historic paddleboat steamers: nine riverboats from the 19th century. The hills in the distance (to the left) are home to Saxon vineyards, producing Germany's northernmost wine. Because only a small amount of the land is suitable for vineyards, Saxony's respected, expensive wine (mostly white) is consumed almost entirely by Saxons.

Below you to the left is the **Augustus Bridge** (Augustusbrücke), connecting Dresden's old and new towns. During the massive floods of August 2002, the water reached two-thirds of the way up the arches. At the far end of the Augustus Bridge, look for the golden equestrian statue, a symbol of Dresden. It's Augustus the Strong, the **Goldene Reiter** (Golden Rider), facing east to his

kingdom of Poland.

The area across the bridge is the **New Town** (Neustadt). While three-quarters of Dresden's Old Town was decimated by Allied firebombs, much of the New Town survived. The 18th-century apartment buildings here were restored—giving the area a Baroque look instead of the blocky Soviet style predominant on the Old Town side of the river. Today, the New Town is a trendy district, and well worth exploring (see page 353). The **Three Kings Church** (Dreikönigskirche, steeple visible above the Goldene Reiter) marks a neighborhood with some recommended restaurants (see page 359).

The interesting **mosque-shaped building** in the distance to the far left (marked *Yenidze*), originally a tobacco factory designed to advertise Turkish cigarettes, is now an office building with restaurants and nightclubs. A few steps to your left is the recommended **Radeberger Spezialausschank Café**—the best place for a drink or meal with a river view (see page 359).

Behind you on the right, you'll see the glass domes of the **Academy of Fine Arts,** capped by a trumpeting gold angel. (Locals call the big dome on the right "the lemon juicer.")

• *Your tour is over. Stairs at the end of the promenade lead back to Theaterplatz, where you began.*

SIGHTS

The Zwinger Museums

The museums around the Zwinger courtyard all have the same hours (Tue–Sun 10:00–18:00, closed Mon, tel. 0351/4914-2000, www.skd-dresden.de). These are all covered by the €12 *Tageskarte* museum pass (buy at any sight) or the Dresden City Card (which also includes transit), or you can pay individually for each museum (entry fees listed below).

▲▲▲**Old Masters Gallery (Gemäldegalerie Alte Meister)**— Dresden's best museum features works by Raphael, Titian, Rembrandt, Peter Paul Rubens, Jan Vermeer, and more. While it hangs 750 paintings at a time, it feels particularly enjoyable for its "quality, not quantity" approach to showing off great art. Locals remember the Old Masters Gallery as the first big public building reopened after the war, in 1956 (€6, includes Royal Armory entry, €2 audioguide, consider the good €13 English guidebook, in Zwinger's Semper Gallery).

Entering, you'll pass a small room with portraits of the Wettin kings who patronized the arts and founded this collection. The next room shows five cityscapes of Dresden, painted by Canaletto during the city's Golden Age. These paintings of mid-18th-century Dresden—showing the Hofkirche (still under construction) and the newly completed Frauenkirche—offer a great study of the city. Next, you enter a world of Rubens and Belgian Baroque. This high-powered Catholic art is followed by the humbler, quieter Protestant art of the Dutch Masters, including a fine collection of Rembrandts (don't miss his jaunty self-portrait—with Saskia on his lap and a glass of ale held aloft), and a pristine Vermeer *(Girl at a Window Reading a Letter)*. The German late-Gothic/early-Renaissance rooms include exquisite canvases by Lucas Cranach and Albrecht Dürer. Farther on, the Venetian masters include a sumptuous *Sleeping Venus* by Giorgione (1510). He died while still working on this, so Titian stepped in to finish it. Giorgione's idealized Venus sleeps soundly, at peace with the plush nature.

The collection's highlight: Raphael's masterful *Sistine Madonna*. The portrait features the Madonna and Child, two early Christian martyrs (Saints Sixtus and Barbara), and wispy angel faces in the clouds. Mary is in motion, offering the Savior to a needy world. But recently, the stars of this painting are the pair of whimsical angels in the foreground. These lovable tykes—of T-shirt and poster fame—are bored...just hanging out, oblivious to the exciting arrival of the Messiah just behind them. They connect the heavenly world of the painting with you and me.

Royal Armory (Rüstkammer)—One big room packed with swords and suits of armor, the armory is especially interesting for its tiny children's armor and the jousting exhibit in the back (€3 alone, or included with €6 ticket to Old Masters Gallery, across the entry passage from Old Masters Gallery).

Mathematics-Physics Salon (Mathematisch-Physikalischer Salon)—This fun collection features globes, lenses, and clocks from the 16th to the 19th centuries (north end of Zwinger courtyard, closed until 2009).

▲▲Porcelain Collection (Porzellansammlung)—Every self-respecting European king had a porcelain works, and the Wettins had the most famous: Meissen. The Saxon prince electors were pioneers in European porcelain production. They inspired other royal courts to get into the art form. They also collected other types—from France to Japan and China. Augustus the Strong was obsessed with the precious stuff...he liked to say he had "porcelain sickness." Here you can enjoy some of his symptoms, under chandeliers in elegant galleries (€5, good English descriptions, south end of Zwinger courtyard).

Royal Palace (Residenzschloss)

This Renaissance palace was once the residence of the Saxon prince elector. Formerly one of the finest Renaissance buildings in Germany, it's been rebuilt since its destruction in World War II. The grand state rooms of Augustus the Strong will open in 2009. For now, the prince's treasures are the big draw here: The New Green Vault is remarkable enough, but the Historic Green Vault (reservation required) is arguably the most impressive treasury in Europe. The entire complex has the same hours (Wed–Mon 10:00–18:00, closed Tue, Historic Green Vault until 19:00), but each attraction has its own entrance fee (Historic Green Vault-€10, not covered by €12 *Tageskarte;* New Green Vault-€8, Watchman's Tower-€3, both covered by *Tageskarte*).

▲▲▲**Historic Green Vault (Historisches Grünes Gewölbe)**— The famed, glittering Baroque treasury collection was begun by Augustus the Strong in the early 1700s. It evolved as the royal family's extravagant treasure-trove of ivory, silver, and gold knick-knacks. Your visit is thrilling in the Baroque style of wowing visitors—starting easy and crescendoing to a climax, taking a quick break, and finishing again with a flurry. Following the included (and essential) audioguide, you'll spend one hour progressing: the amber room, the ivory room, the silver room, the sumptuous crown jewels room, a soothing bronze room, and another jewels room. The incredible pieces in the crown jewels room (especially the Obeliscus Augustalis) are fine examples of *Gesamtkunstwerk*— a symphony of artistic creations. Your audioguide also describes treasures in the "pre-vault" (where you pick up and drop off the audioguide). In this room, don't miss photos of vaults before the war and Luther's signature ring.

Reservations: To protect this priceless collection and the extravagant rooms in which it's displayed, the number of visitors each day is carefully controlled. This means you have to reserve in advance (you'll be given a 15-minute entry window for your visit—once inside, you can stay as long as you like). You'll pass through a "dust sluice" as you enter to be sure you're free of irritants—a good feeling. To be assured entry, make a reservation far in advance (reserve at www.skd-dresden.de, email museum@dresden-tourist.de, or call 0351/4919-2285). While advance entry times can be booked months in advance, 200 tickets are saved for each day (the number of spots still available and entry times—*Freie Plätze*—are indicated at the ticket desk). These are sold starting at 10:00—line up early. When planning your visit, remember that the Historic Green Vault is closed Tuesday.

▲▲New Green Vault (Neues Grünes Gewölbe)—This collection shows off more of the treasure in a modern setting. Invest in the €2 audioguide, which beautifully describes the best 65 objects in 90 minutes.

Watchman's Tower (Hausmannsturm)—This palace tower is completely rebuilt (and feels entirely modern). For €3, you can climb past an underwhelming coin collection, see the rebuilt medieval clock mechanism from behind, peruse an extensive series of dome-damage photos, and earn a good city view after a long climb. In bad weather, the view terrace is closed, and you'll peer through small windows—a big disappointment. If climbing the Frauenkirche tower (which affords the best view in town but costs €8), skip this.

▲▲▲Frauenkirche (Church of Our Lady)

This landmark church was originally built by local donations—Protestant people-pride. Destroyed by the Allied firebombing in World War II, the church sat in ruins for decades. Finally, in 1992, the reconstruction of the church began. The restorers used these guidelines: rebuild true to the original design; use as much of the original material as possible; maximize modern technology in the procedure; and make it a lively venue for 21st-century-style wor-ship. After fitting it together like a giant jigsaw puzzle, about a third of the church is original stones (notice the dark ones, placed in their original spots). The reconstruction cost more than €100 million, 90 percent of which came from donors around the world.

Now open, the church is as worthwhile for its glorious interior as for its tragic, then uplifting recent history. Stepping inside, you're struck by the shape—not so wide (150 feet) but very tall (inner dome 120 feet, under a 225-foot main dome). The color scheme is pastel, in an effort to underline the joy of faith and enhance the festive ambience of the services and ceremonies held here. The curves create a community feeling. The seven entrances are perfectly equal (as people are, in the eyes of God). When the congregation exits, the seven exits point to all quarters—a reminder of "go ye,"

the Great Commission to spread the Word everywhere.

The Baroque sandstone altar shows Jesus praying on the Mount of Olives the night before his crucifixion. Soldiers, led by Judas, are on their way, but Christ is firmly in the presence of God and his angels. Eighty percent of today's altar is from original material—in the form of 2,000 individual fragments that were salvaged and pieced back together by restorers.

The Cross of Nails at the high altar is from Coventry, England—Dresden's sister city. Two fire-blackened nails found in the smoldering ruble of Coventry's bombed church are used as a symbol of peace and reconciliation. Coventry was bombed as thoroughly as Dresden (so thoroughly, it gave the giddy German Air Force a new word for "to bomb into smithereens"—to "coventrate"). From the destroyed town of Coventry was born the Community of the Cross of Nails, a worldwide network promoting peace and reconciliation through international understanding.

Near the exit stands the church's twisted old cross, which fell 300 feet and burned in the rubble. Lost until 1993, it was found relatively intact. A copy—a gift from British people in 2000 on the 55th anniversary of the bombing—crowns the new church. It was crafted by an English coppersmith whose father actually dropped bombs on the church on that fateful night. As they leave, visitors are invited to light a candle before this cross and enter a wish for peace in the guest book.

Cost, Hours, Location: Free but donation requested, enter through door D, Mon–Fri 10:00–12:00 & 13:00–18:00, open between services and concerts on Sat–Sun, €2.50 for 45-min audioguide, www.frauenkirche-dresden.de.

Climbing the Dome: Those feeling energetic can get a great view over the city by climbing the stairs to the top of the dome. After an elevator takes you a third of the way, you still have a long climb (€8—consider it a donation to the church, enter through door G, daily 10:00–13:00 & 14:00–18:00, follow signs to *Kuppelaufstieg*).

More Sights in Dresden

▲**Semper Opera**—This elegant opera house watches over Theaterplatz in the heart of town. Three opera houses have

stood in this spot: The first was destroyed by a fire in 1869, the second by firebombs in 1945. The rebuilt Semper Oper continues to be a world-class venue, and tickets for the Saxon State Orchestra (the world's oldest) are hard to come by (on sale a year in advance, box office in Schinkelwache TI across the square sells day-of tickets only, Mon–Fri 10:00–18:00, Sat 10:00–13:00, closed Sun, tel. 0351/491-1705, fax 0351/491-1700, www.semperoper.de).

The opulent opera house can only be visited with a tour. German-speaking tours (with an English handout) go regularly through the day. There is one daily English tour at 14:00 (€7, €2 to take photos, 1 hour, tour schedule depends on rehearsal schedule, enter on right side, tel. 0351/491-1496).

Albertinum—This historic building, at the end of the Brühlsche Terrasse, is closed for renovation until 2009. When it reopens, it may once again house two good museums: the Sculpture Collection (Skulpturensammlung) and the New Masters Gallery (Gemäldegalerie Neue Meister). In the meantime, these collections are likely on display at the Zwinger (ask at the TI or other museums). If you can find the New Masters Gallery, you'll enjoy paintings and sculptures by 19th- and 20th-century greats such as Pierre-Auguste Renoir, Auguste Rodin, Vincent van Gogh, Edgar Degas, and Gustav Klimt. I especially enjoy Otto Dix's moving triptych *War* (painted between the World Wars), Klimt's *Buchenwald*, and one of Rodin's *Thinkers*.

Prager Strasse—This communist-built pedestrian mall, connecting the train station and the historic center, was in ruins until the

1960s. Even today, "Prague Street" reflects Soviet ideals: big, blocky, functional buildings without extraneous ornamentation. As you stroll down Prager Strasse, imagine these buildings without any of the color or advertising. (Stores "advertised" with black-and-white signs reading *Milk*, *Bread*, or simply *Products*.) Today, the street is filled with corporate logos, shoppers with lots of choices, and a fun summertime food circus. When all the construction is finished, this will be an impressive people zone.

▲**New Town (Neustadt)**—A big sign across the river from the old center declares, "Dresden continues here." This seems directed at tourists who visit the city and stay exclusively in the Old Town. Don't be one of them—make a point to explore Dresden's New Town, too. While there are no famous sights in the New Town, it's the only part of Dresden that predates World War II. Today, it's thriving with cafés, shops, clubs, and—most important—just regular people. I've listed several hotels and restaurants worth considering in the neighborhood (see "Sleeping" and "Eating").

Hygiene Museum (Deutsches Hygiene Museum)—This museum is a highly conceptual compilation of vaguely health-related exhibits. The exterior fresco—by German Expressionist painter Otto Dix—sets the tone for the unsettling interior. The museum was founded in 1911, and the current location opened its doors in 1930, when its administration still embraced the idea of eugenics (genetic engineering). Since then, the museum has produced and collected models from the 16th century to the present, including little wooden anatomical figures with removable parts (complete with strategically placed fig leaves), X-ray machines from the 1930s, and graphic wax models of venereal diseases. The exhibit is divided into weirdly themed sections (Life and Death, Disease, Physiology, Reproduction, and Grooming). There are some English explanations, or you can rent the €1 audioguide, but most of the exhibits speak (or shriek) for themselves. Perhaps a reflection of the typically German pragmatism toward sexuality, this place is usually filled with school groups or families with young kids. People who enjoyed the Dieter sketches on *Saturday Night Live* will get a kick out of this highly interactive museum, but those easily disturbed should stay away (€6, Tue–Sun 10:00–18:00, closed Mon; take tram #1, #2, or #4 from Postplatz to the Deutsches Hygiene Museum stop; tel. 0351/484-6670, www.dhmd.de).

Volkswagen Transparent Factory (Gläserne Manufaktur)— Car buffs will make a pilgrimage to this new VW factory on the southeastern edge of town. Two floors of this fascinating, transparent building are open to visitors interested in the assembly of one of VW's high-end cars. You don't have to custom-order a luxury-model Phaeton to see how they're manufactured. (But if you do buy a car, you can bring a folding chair, park yourself on the platform, and follow it through every moment of the 36-hour "birth" process.) The parts are delivered to the logistics plant just on the edge of town, then transported to this manufacturing plant by "cargo trams" (which are used to avoid adding to traffic congestion in town). While you're basically paying to experience a VW ad, it is interesting to see the wild building, peek at the assembly

Dresden

line, and play with the informative, high-tech, English-language touchscreen displays (€4, daily 8:00–20:00, Lennestrasse 1 tel. 01805-896-268, www.glaesernemanufaktur.de). Take tram #1, #2, or #4 from Theaterplatz or Prager Strasse, or tram #10 from the train station, to Strassburgerplatz, from where it's a 100-yard walk.

Near Dresden: Saxon Switzerland National Park

Consider a break from big-city sightseeing to spend a half-day taking a *wunderbar* hike through this scenic national park.

Twenty miles southeast of Dresden (an easy 45-min S-Bahn ride away), the Elbe River cuts a scenic swath through the beech forests and steep cliffs of Saxon Switzerland (Sächsische Schweiz) National Park. You'll share the trails with serious rock climbers and equally serious Saxon grandmothers. Allow five hours (including lunch) to enjoy this day trip.

Take the S-Bahn line 1 from either the Hauptbahnhof or the Neustadt station (direction Schandau, departs hourly; an €11 *Verbundraum Tageskarte*—regional day ticket—covers the whole trip). Get off at the Kurort Rathen stop, follow the road downhill five minutes through town to the dock, and take the ferry across the Elbe (€1.30 round-trip, pay on board, crossing takes 2 min, runs continuously). When the ferry docks on the far (north) side of the river, turn your back on the river and walk 100 yards through town, with the little creek on your right. Turn left after the Sonniges Eck Restaurant (tasty lunch option, check out the 2002 flood photos in their front dining room) and walk up the lane. The trail begins with stairs on your left just past Hotel Amselgrundschlösschen (follow *Bastei* signs).

A 45-minute walk uphill through the woods leads you to the Bastei Bridge and stunning views of gray sandstone sentries rising several hundred feet above forest ridges. Elbe Valley sandstone was used to build Dresden's finest buildings (including the Frauenkirche and Zwinger), as well as Berlin's famous Brandenburg Gate. The multiple-arch bridge looks straight out of Oz—built in 1851 specifically for Romantic Age tourists, and scenic enough to be the subject of the  first landscape photos ever taken in Germany. Take the time to explore the short 50-yard spur trails that reward you with classic views down on the Elbe 900 feet below. Watch the slow-motion paddleboat steamers leave V-shaped wakes as they chug upstream toward the Czech Republic, just around the next river bend. If you're not afraid of heights, explore the maze of catwalks through the scant remains of the Neue Felsenberg, a 13th-century Saxon fort perched precariously on the bald stony spires (€1.50, entrance 50 yards before Bastei Bridge).

Just a five-minute uphill hike beyond the bridge is the Berg Hotel Panorama Bastei, with a fine restaurant, a quick snack bar, and memorable views. Return back down to the Elbe ferry via the same trail.

NIGHTLIFE

To really connect with Dresden as it unfolds, you need to go to the **Innere Neustadt** ("Inner New Town," a 10-min walk from Neustadt train station). This area was not bombed in World War II, and after 1989 it sprouted the first entrepreneurial cafés and bistros. While eateries are open long hours, the action picks up after 22:00. The clientele is young, hip, pierced, and tattooed.

Rather than seek out particular places in this continuously evolving scene, I'd just get to the epicenter (corner of Görlitzer Strasse and Louisenstrasse) and wander. Pop through the Kunsthofpassage, a Hundertwasser-type apartment block with some fun spots (Görlitzer Strasse 23). At Böhmischestrasse 34 (a half-block off Lutherplatz), the Russian-flavored Kneipe Raskolnikoff has an imported beach, giving it a Moscow/Maui ambience. The Carte Blanche Transvestite Bar is a hoot for some (€25, most nights from 20:00, Priessnitzstrasse 10, tel. 0351/204-720).

For more sedate entertainment, stroll along the New Town's riverbank after dark for fine floodlit views of the Old Town.

SLEEPING

Dresden is packed with big, conference-style hotels. Characteristic, family-run places are harder to come by. (The communists didn't do "quaint" very well.) Peak season for the big business-class hotels is May, June, September, and October. Peak season for hostels is July and August (especially weekends). For hotel locations, see the map on page 337.

In or near the Old Town

$$$ Hilton Dresden has 330 luxurious rooms (some with views of the Frauenkirche) in the heart of the Old Town, one block from the river. Complete with porters, fitness club, pool, and several restaurants, it's everything you'd expect from a four-star chain hotel (Sb-€155–190, Db-€170–205, breakfast-€22, parking €12–17/day, An der Frauenkirche 5, tel. 0351/86420, fax 0351/864-2725, www .hilton.de, info.dresden@hilton.com).

Sleep Code

(€1 = about $1.30, country code: 49, area code: 0351)
S = Single, **D** = Double/Twin, **T** = Triple, **Q** = Quad, **b** = bathroom,
s = shower only. All of these places speak English and accept
credit cards. Unless otherwise noted, breakfast is included.

To help you sort easily through these listings, I've divided
the rooms into three categories, based on the price for a standard double room with bath:

$$$ **Higher Priced**—Most rooms €120 or more.
$$ **Moderately Priced**—Most rooms between €80–120.
$ **Lower Priced**—Most rooms €80 or less.

$$ Hotel Kipping, with 20 tidy rooms a hundred yards
behind the Hauptbahnhof, is professionally run by the friendly
and proper Kipping brothers (Rainer and Peter). The building was
one of few in this area to survive the firebombing—in fact, people
took shelter here during the attack (Sb-€75–105, Db-€90–120, 1-
person suite-€115–130, 2-person suite-€130–145, child's bed-€20;
higher prices are for weekends, May–June, and Sept–Oct; elevator,
free parking, exit the station following signs to *Bayerische Strasse*
near track 6, it's at Winckelmannstrasse 6, tram #8 whisks you
to the Old Town, tel. 0351/478-500, fax 0351/478-5090, www
.hotel-kipping.de, reception@hotel-kipping.de). Their restaurant
serves international cuisine and Saxon specialties (€9–12 entrées,
Mon–Sat 18:00–22:30, closed Sun).

$$ Apartments an der Frauenkirche rents 50 new units
just above all the restaurant action on Münzgasse. Designed for
longer stays but also welcoming two-nighters (minimum), these
modern, comfortable apartments come with kitchens and the
lived-in works (Db-€75–115, extra bed-€15, breakfast-€10, cheaper
for longer stays and off-season, parking at
nearby garage-€10/day, Münzgasse 10, tel.
0351/438-1111, www.dresden-tourismus.de,
info@dresden-tourismus.de).

$ Hotels Bastei, Königstein, and
Lilienstein are cookie-cutter members of
the Ibis chain, goose-stepping single-file
up Prager Strasse (listed in order from the
station to the center). Each is practically
identical, with 360 rooms. Though utterly
lacking in charm, they are an excellent
value in a convenient location between the
Hauptbahnhof and the Old Town (Sb-€65,

Db-€80, apartment-€85 for a family of 3–4, breakfast-€10, parking-€6.50/day, reservations for all: tel. 0351/4856-2000; individual receptions: tel. 0351/4856-5445, tel. 0351/4856-6445, and tel. 0351/4856-7445, respectively; www.ibis-dresden.de).

In the New Town

The first two hotels are fancy splurges in a tidy residential neighborhood surrounding the Neustadt train station. The rest are cheap and funky, buried in the trendy, newly happening café-and-club zone called the Innere Neustadt ("Inner New Town," about a 10-min walk from Neustadt station—see page 355).

$$ Hotel Bayerischer Hof Dresden, a hundred yards toward the river from the Neustadt train station, offers 50 rooms and elegant and inviting public spaces in a grand old building (Sb-€85–95, Db-€110–130, pricier suites, non-smoking rooms, elevator, free parking, Antonstrasse 33–35, yellow building across from station, tel. 0351/829-370, fax 0351/801-4860, www.bayerischer-hof-dresden.de, info@bayerischer-hof-dresden.de).

$$ Hotel Martha Hospiz, with 50 rooms near the recommended restaurants on Königstrasse, is bright and cheery. The two old buildings that make up the hotel have been smartly renovated and connected in back with a glassed-in winter garden and an outdoor breakfast terrace in a charming garden. It's a 10-minute walk to the historical center, and a five-minute walk to the Neustadt station (S-€54, Sb-€77–84, Db-€110–118, extra bed-€26, elevator; leaving Neustadt station, turn right on Hainstrasse, left on Theresenstrasse, and then right on Nieritzstrasse to #11; tel. 0351/81760, fax 0351/8176-222, www.vch.de/marthahospiz.dresden, marthahospiz.dresden@t-online.de).

$ AHA Hotel, on a big, noisy street, has a homey and welcoming ambience. The 29 simple but neat apartments all come with kitchens; most (except the top floor) have balconies. It's a bit farther from the center—10 minutes by foot east of Albertplatz, a 20-minute walk or a quick ride on tram #11 from the Old Town—but its friendliness, coziness, and good value make it a winner (Sb-€60–65, Db-€70–90, small Db about €10 cheaper, breakfast-€8, request quieter back side, non-smoking rooms, elevator, Bautzner Strasse 53, tel. 0351/800-850, fax 0351/8008-5114, www.ahahotel-dresden.de, kontakt@ahahotel-dresden.de).

$ Guest House Mezcalero, decorated Mexican from top to bottom, is a 22-room place a 10-minute walk from the Neustadt station at the edge of the lively Innere Neustadt zone. It feels classy and comfy, with an adobe ambience (S-€33, Sb-€50, D-€54, Db-€64, dorm bed-€20, breakfast-€6, from either station catch tram #7 to Bischofsweg, Königsbrücker Strasse 64, tel. 0351/810-770, fax 0351/810-7711, www.mezcalero.de, info@mezcalero.de).

$ Hostel "Louise 20" rents 83 beds in the heart of the Innere Neustadt. Though located in the wild-and-edgy nightlife district, it feels safe, solid, clean, and comfy. The newly furnished rooms, guests' kitchen, cozy common room, and friendly staff make it the best place in town for cheap beds (S-€30, D-€42, small dorm-€18/bed, 20-bed dorm-€12.50/bed, €2.50 less if you have sheets, breakfast extra, no lockers, generally booked on summer weekends, Louisenstrasse 20, tel. 0351/8894-894, www.louise20.de, info@louise20.de).

$ Hostel Mondpalast Dresden is young and hip, in the heart of the Innere Neustadt above a cool bar. It's good for backpackers with little money and an appetite for late-night fun (S-€34, Sb-€44, D-€40, Db-€50, dorm bed-€14, one-time €2 fee for sheets, breakfast-€5, lockers, kitchen, lots of facilities, tram #7 from Hauptbahnhof or #11 from Neustadt station, near Kamenzer Strasse at Louisenstrasse 77, tel. 0351/563-4050, fax 0351/563-4055, www.mondpalast.de, info@mondpalast.de).

EATING

Dresden's ancient beer halls were destroyed in the firebombing and not replaced by the communists. As the city comes back to life, nearly every restaurant seems bright, shiny, and modern. While Old Town restaurants are touristy, the prices are reasonable, and it's easy to eat for €10 to €15 just about anywhere. For cheaper prices and authentic local character, leave the famous center, cross the river, and wander through the New Town.

The special local dessert sold all over town is *Dresdner Eierschecke,* an eggy cheesecake with vanilla pudding, raisins, and almond shavings.

In the Old Town

Münzgasse, the busy and touristy lane that connects the Brühlsche Terrasse promenade and the Frauenkirche, is the liveliest street in the Old Town, with a fun selection of eateries. Choose from tapas, Aussie, goulash, crêpes, and even antiques (Kunst Café Antik scatters its tables among a royal estate sale of fancy furniture and objets d'art—around the corner, riverside). Service is a necessary evil, the clientele is international, and the action spills out onto the cobbled pedestrian lane on balmy evenings.

Altmarkt Keller, a few blocks farther from the river on Altmarkt square, is a festive beer cellar that serves nicely presented Saxon and Bohemian food (from separate menus) and has good Czech beer on tap. The lively crowd, cheesy music (live Sat only), and jolly murals add to the fun. While the on-square seating is fine, the vast-but-stout air-conditioned cellar offers your best memories. The giant mural inside the entryway—representing the friendship between Dresden and Prague—reads, "The sunshine of life is drinking and being happy" (€8–13 entrées, daily 11:00–24:00, Altmarkt 4, to the right of McDonald's, tel. 0351/481-8130).

Grand Café Restaurant Cosel Palais serves Saxon and French cuisine in the shadow of the newly rebuilt Frauenkirche. This is a Baroque, chandeliered dining experience with fine if touristy courtyard seating—great for an elegant meal or tea and pastries (€10–17 meals, daily specials, daily 10:00–24:00, An der Frauenkirche 12, tel. 0351/496-2444).

Erlebnisgastronomie *("Experience Gastronomy"):* All the rage among Dresdeners (and German tourists in Dresden) is *Erlebnisgastronomie.* Elaborately decorated theme restaurants have sprouted next to the biggest-name sights around town, with over-the-top, theme-park decor and historically costumed waitstaff. These can offer a fun change of pace and aren't the bad value you might suspect. The best is **Sophienkeller,** which does its best to take you to the 18th century and the world of Augustus the Strong. The king himself, along with his countess, musicians, and magicians, stroll and entertain, while court maidens serve traditional Saxon food from a "ye olde" menu. Read their colorful brochure to better understand the place. It's big (400 seats), and it even has a rotating carousel table with suspended swing-chairs that you sit in while you eat. Before choosing a seat, survey the two big and distinct zones—one bright and wide open, the other more intimate and cellar-like (€10–15 plates, daily 11:00–24:00, under the five-star Taschenberg Palace Hotel, Taschenberg 3, tel. 0351/497-260, www.sophienkeller-dresden.de).

With a River View: **Radeberger Spezialausschank Café** is dramatically situated on the Brühlsche Terrasse promenade with a rampart-hanging view terrace and three levels taking you down to river level. For river views from the "Balcony of Europe," this is your spot. The inviting-yet-simple menu includes daily Saxon specials and cheap wurst and kraut. The cool river-level bar comes with big copper brewery vats and good beer (daily 11:00–24:00, reservations smart for view terrace, Terrassenufer 1, tel. 0351/484-8660).

In the Main Train Station: For a quick bite at the Hauptbahnhof, the healthy market-style **Marché Cafeteria** is fast and reasonable (daily 5:30–21:00).

In the New Town

Venture to these eateries—across Augustus Bridge from the Old Town—for lower prices and a more local scene. I've listed them nearest to farthest from the Old Town.

Just Across Augustus Bridge

Augustus Garten is a lazy, crude-yet-inviting beer garden with super-cheap self-service food (pork knuckle, kraut, cheap beer, and lots of mustard). You'll eat among big bellies—and no tourists—with a fun city-skyline-over-the-river view. While enjoyable in balmy weather, this place is dead when it's cool (€3–8.50 plates, €2–5 beers, €2 refundable deposit on beer glasses, daily 11:00–24:00, closed in bad weather, Wiesentorstrasse 2, tel. 0351/404-5854). As you walk across the bridge from the Old Town, it's on your immediate right.

On Königstrasse

For trendy elegance without tourists, have dinner on Königstrasse. After crossing the Augustus Bridge, hike five minutes up the communist-built main drag of the New Town, then turn left to find this charming Baroque street. As this is a fast-changing area, you might survey the other options on and near Königstrasse (be sure to tuck in to a few courtyards) before settling down.

Wenzel Prager Bierstuben serves country Bohemian cuisine in a woodsy bar that spills out into an airy, glassed-in gallery—made doubly big by its vast mirror. Stepping inside, you immediately feel this is a winner. They offer a fun Bohemian menu with great Czech beer on tap (€7 dinner-with-beer specials on Tue–Thu, €8–10 entrées, open daily 11:00–24:00, Königstrasse 1, tel. 0315/804-2010).

Good Friends is a favorite for Thai and Vietnamese food, and a welcome relief from pork and potatoes (€6–12 plates, Mon–Fri 11:30–15:00 & 17:30–23:00, Sat–Sun 12:00–23:00, An der Dreifaltigkeitskirche 9, tel. 0351/646-5814). Walk down Königstrasse to the towering Three Kings Church. It's under the steeple.

TRANSPORTATION CONNECTIONS

From Dresden by Train to: Görlitz (hourly, 1.5 hrs), **Bautzen** (about hourly, 30–45 min; Bautzen-bound trains continue on to Görlitz), **Zittau** (better from Neustadt, hourly, 1.5–2 hrs), **Berlin** (every 2 hrs, 2.25 hrs), **Prague** (every 2 hrs, 2.25–2.5 hrs), **Frankfurt** (hourly, 4.75 hrs), **Nürnberg** (hourly, 4.5 hrs, transfer in Leipzig), **Munich** (about hourly, 5.75–6.25 hrs, transfer in Leipzig or Nürnberg; plus 1 night train/day, 7.5 hrs), **Vienna** (2/day, 7 hrs; plus 1 night train/day, 9 hrs), **Budapest** (1/day, 9 hrs). There are overnight trains from Dresden to Zürich, Vienna, the Rhineland, and Munich. Train info: tel. 11861 (€0.60/min).

GÖRLITZ

Tucked away in Germany's easternmost corner, the surprisingly beautiful town of Görlitz is a treasure-trove of architecture and one of this country's best-kept secrets.

During the Middle Ages, Görlitz was a major European crossroads, at the intersection of trade routes from Moscow to Barcelona and from the Baltic Sea to Venice. Trade in cloth and beer made the city flourish. Görlitz's rich cultural tapestry was gradually enhanced as the centuries passed, leaving it a delightful collage of architectural styles. The town escaped most of World War II's bombs, but soon after was split down the middle along its river—with half of the town in Germany, the other half in Poland. Görlitz's historic buildings were preserved by the East German government, saving it from the unsightly communist-era blemishes that mark most former East German towns.

Since the Wall fell, Görlitz has sprung back to life and is busily polishing its gorgeous facades. The town offers a unique opportunity to venture to the eastern fringes of Germany, sample Silesian culture and cuisine, and appreciate some breathtaking architecture and stay-a-while squares. Best of all, although German tourists fill Görlitz on weekends during the summer, it's virtually undiscovered by foreign tourists—making it a real Back Door experience.

Planning Your Time

Although Görlitz is an ideal day trip from Dresden (hourly 1.5-hour trains), the city's subtle charm warrants an overnight stay. Görlitz opens up on long summer nights, as pubs and cafés spill out into the cobbles. Get lost and wander the back streets and alleys.

ORIENTATION

(area code: 03581)

With a population of about 66,000, Görlitz is the largest city in what's left of German Silesia. While Görlitz lost a third of its population to Poland in 1945, the historic center and most sights of interest to travelers remain in Germany. The compact Old Town (Altstadt), and almost everything to see and do, is an easy stroll, roughly between Marienplatz and the western bank of the Neisse River. The focal point of the Old Town are the twin market squares, Upper (Obermarkt) and Lower (Untermarkt).

Tourist Information

The TI, called Görlitzinformation, sells €1 maps and can book you a room for free. Information in English is sparse, but there are a few English guidebooks available, and people seem genuinely helpful and welcoming (Mon–Fri 9:00–20:00, Sat–Sun 9:00–19:00, between Obermarkt and Untermarkt at Brüderstrasse 1, tel. 03581/475-723, www.europastadt-goerlitz.de). Pick up the €6.90 *Görlitz Town Guide*, a small but informative do-it-yourself walking tour, but skip the €3 map. The *Architectural Guide Through the Old Town of Görlitz* (€7) is overkill for most visitors but indispensable for architecture buffs, but it does describe almost every building in the Old Town in a convenient flip-out format. To arrange for a guided tour in English, call 03581/47570.

Arrival in Görlitz

By Train: Görlitz's train station, about a half-mile southwest of the city center, is a sight in itself. Built in 1901, the main hall is a pearl of Prussian *Jugendstil,* while the building itself is Neoclassical. Its opening hours are shorter than those at larger stations, and it's virtually deserted after 21:00. Lockers are in the passage between the tracks and the main hall (€1–2). You'll also find handy WCs (€0.50, deposit coin, then wait for buzzer) and a *Reisezentrum* for train information and tickets (Mon and Thu–Fri 6:30–18:30, Tue–Wed 7:30–13:00 & 13:45–17:00, Sat 7:30–13:00, Sun 12:30–18:00).

To get into town (a 15-min walk), exit straight out the front entrance and follow Berliner Strasse. At the first large square *(Postplatz),* the road veers left, and you'll see the Karstadt department store (marking Marienplatz and the start of my self-guided walking tour). You can also take tram #2 or #3 to Demianiplatz (departs from the platform on your right as you exit the station; €1.20, 5 min).

Görlitz: A Silesian Brew

Görlitz is a city with an identity crisis, much like the entire region of Silesia. Silesia, which has never been a "nation" of its own, encompasses parts of Germany (where it's called "Schlesien"), Poland ("Śląsk"), and the Czech Republic ("Slezsko"). Silesians are proud of this diversity, and of their pragmatic ability to work and live peacefully with each other despite the borders that separate them. Just like the Silesians themselves, their cuisine, folk art, and customs are a mishmash of German, Polish, and Czech.

After Slavic Sorbs founded Gorelec in 1071, the village—renamed Görlitz—came under the German sphere of cultural influence in the 12th century, and has been predominantly German ever since. For most of its early existence, the city technically belonged to Bohemia, but was ceded to Saxony after the Peace of Prague in 1635. In 1815, Görlitz fell into Prussian hands at the Congress of Vienna and became the largest city in the province of Lower Silesia.

The city's unusual experience in World War II made it the unique place it is today: While Görlitz almost miraculously escaped destruction (only its bridge was bombed), it was split in two by the Potsdam Agreement in 1945. This treaty determined the Neisse River—which runs through the center of Görlitz—to be the border between Germany and Poland. The following year, Poland expelled all Germans from its country, which included booting them out of Silesia and, therefore, out of the Polish side of Görlitz.

This expulsion created two ethnically distinct halves: the German town of Görlitz on the west side of the river, and the Polish town of Zgorzelec, which is still part of Poland on the east. Although most German Silesians have long since abandoned any hope of re-establishing their lost homeland, they have gone to great efforts to stress the unity between Silesians of all ethnic backgrounds—Germans, Poles, and Czechs—by re-establishing cultural connections across the rivers and mountains. Czechs and Poles are strong participants at all city festivals. After German, the most common languages you'll hear spoken in the streets and see on signs in Görlitz are Polish and Czech.

German Görlitz and Polish Zgorzelec recently completed the reconstruction of the bridge across the Neisse, destroyed during World War II. Locals like to think this largely symbolic gesture makes Görlitz the most European city in Europe.

Getting Around Görlitz

The communists left little Görlitz with a highly developed and efficient public-transportation system (€1.20 per ride, *Einzelfahrt Normal;* €3 day pass, *Tageskarte Normal;* €6.50 pass for up to 5 people, *Kleingruppenkarte*). Tickets are valid on both trams and buses. Buy your tickets from bus drivers or the machines on the platforms and trams (coins only), and validate tickets in the little blue box on board. All buses and trams converge at Demianiplatz. The Old Town is compact, so unless you're planning to visit the Holy Sepulcher or go out to the Landskrone mountain, you'll probably only use public transit to get from the train station into the city center.

SELF-GUIDED WALK

Welcome to Görlitz

The joy of Görlitz is simply wandering the Old Town and appreciating the architecture. Begin this orientation walk at Marienplatz, the small square right outside the former city walls.

Marienplatz: The unique *Jugendstil* department store **Karstadt** (completed in 1911) has a richly decorated facade concealing an ornate glass-domed interior with intricate staircases and galleries (Mon–Fri 9:30–18:30, Sat 9:30–16:00, closed Sun).

Behind Karstadt is the **Church of our Lady** (Frauenkirche), a 15th-century, late-Gothic church built near the hospital and poorhouse outside the city walls. Although this church seems unremarkable, take a moment to step inside (free, Mon–Sat 10:00–18:00, Sun 11:00–18:00; Mon–Fri try to catch the *Mittagsrast* prayer and organ music at 12:00). Imagine being here in the fall of 1989, shortly before the Berlin Wall came down. This church served as a forum for discussions and peace prayers *(Friedensgebete).* A poster announcing the first prayer meeting was placed in the glass cabinet on the front of the church. Soon, like-minded shopkeepers began to follow suit, and 580 people attended the first meeting. Just two weeks later, 1,300 people showed up, and subsequent meetings swelled to 5,000—so large that they spilled over into other churches. The meetings became a forum for discussing impending political changes, civil rights, and environmental issues. As each participant came forward and voiced their concerns, a candle was blown out until the church was dark. Then, as those who had a hopeful or positive experience came forward, a candle was lit until the church was illuminated once again. The German secret police, the *Stasi*, stationed plainclothes police in the buildings across the street to document who was participating in these "acts of civil disobedience." Many people lost their jobs or were punished. But the hope for democracy and self-determination had already caught on,

Görlitz

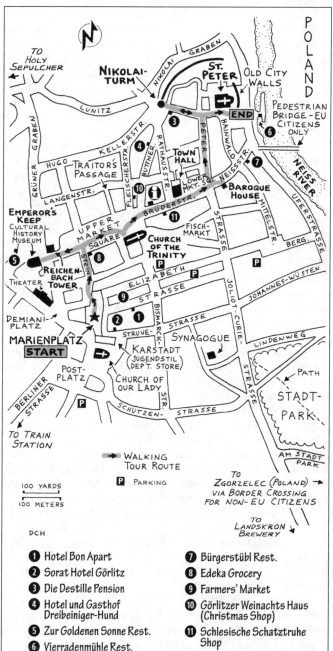

TO HOLY SEPULCHER

NIKOLAI-TURM

GRABEN

NIKOLAI

ST. PETER

OLD CITY WALLS

POLAND

LUNITZ

KELLERSTR.

RATHAUSSTR.

FLEISCHERSTR.

BUTTNER

PETER

HAINWALD

END

PEDESTRIAN BRIDGE – EU CITIZENS ONLY

NEISSSTR.

NEISSE RIVER

GRÜNER GRABEN

HUGO

TRAITOR'S PASSAGE

LANGENSTR.

TOWN HALL

LOWER MKT. SQ.

BRÜDERSTR.

BAROQUE HOUSE

MITTELSTR.

UFERSTRASSE

BERG.

EMPEROR'S KEEP CULTURAL HISTORY MUSEUM

UPPER MARKET SQUARE

STEIN

CHURCH OF THE TRINITY

FISCH-MARKT

STRASSE

REICHEN-BACH TOWER

THEATER

ELIZABETH STRASSE

BISMARCK-

STRUVE-

JOLIOT-CURIE-

JOHANNES-WÜSTEN

DEMIANI-PLATZ

MARIENPLATZ START

POST-PLATZ

KARSTADT (JUGENDSTIL) DEP.T STORE)

SYNAGOGUE

STRASSE

LINDENWEG

PATH

STADT-PARK

BERLINER STRASSE

CHURCH OF OUR LADY

STR.

SCHÜTZEN-   STRASSE

TO TRAIN STATION

AM STADT PARK

→ WALKING TOUR ROUTE

P PARKING

TO ZGORZELEC (POLAND) → VIA BORDER CROSSING FOR NON-EU CITIZENS

100 YARDS

100 METERS

TO LANDSKRON BREWERY

DCH

❶ Hotel Bon Apart
❷ Sorat Hotel Görlitz
❸ Die Destille Pension
❹ Hotel und Gasthof Dreibeiniger-Hund
❺ Zur Goldenen Sonne Rest.
❻ Vierradenmühle Rest.

❼ Bürgerstübl Rest.
❽ Edeka Grocery
❾ Farmers' Market
❿ Görlitzer Weinachts Haus (Christmas Shop)
⓫ Schlesische Schatztruhe Shop

and today, this church stands as a symbol of peace and solidarity.

To the north, the **Fat Tower** (Dicker Turm) is the second-oldest tower in the city's defensive network. Although the tower itself is Gothic (from 1270), it's topped by a copper Renaissance cupola. The tower was attached to the so-called Women's Gate (Frauen Tor) in 1477. It's decorated with a sandstone relief of the Görlitz city coat of arms, featuring a Bohemian lion and a Silesian black eagle—representing Görlitz as an independent and free city.

· *Walk down the street to the left of the tower (Steinstrasse) and onto the...*

Upper Market Square (Obermarkt): This square dates from the 13th century, and is lined with mainly Baroque houses. The

Reichenbach Tower dominates the western end of the square. The tower formed the western city wall and dates from the 13th century, although the cylindrical portion was added in 1485 and is topped with a Baroque cupola from 1782. The tower housed city guards and watchmen—who among other things kept a lookout for fires—until the last "tower family" moved out in 1904. Inside is an impressive collection of armaments, early 20th-century photographs, and an interesting exhibit on the daily lives of the tower's occupants (€1.50, May–Oct Tue–Sun 10:00–17:00, closed Mon and Nov–April, Platz des 17 Juni, tel. 03581/671-355). The view from the top is worth the 165 steps.

In 1490, Görlitz strengthened its city fortifications by building a circular bastion outside Reichenbach Tower. The structure came to be known as the **Emperor's Keep** (Kaisertruz) when the Swedish troops made their last stand against the Imperial Saxon army during the Thirty Years' War. Since then, the Emperor's Keep has been used as an archive, and today houses the Cultural History Museum, which is currently being renovated.

In 1245, Franciscan monks consecrated the **Church of the Trinity** (Dreifaltigkeitskirche) at the southeast side of Obermarkt. Although originally a Romanesque structure, renovations in 1380 gave the church its current late-Gothic appearance. When the Reformation took hold in Silesia in 1563, the monks were forced to surrender the keys to the church.

Go inside (free, daily 9:00–18:00, tel. 03581/311-311). The interior seems austere, but upon careful inspection, reveals delightful little details. As you enter, go immediately to your left. This is the oldest part of the church. Pillars from the original 13th-century Romanesque chapel are integrated into the walls. The fancy balcony

---

Görlitz Architecture

Although no bombs fell on Görlitz itself during World War II (only on its bridge), the city didn't escape partial destruction during the Thirty Years' War or the ravages of three great city fires. Each wave of devastation allowed Görlitz to rebuild in the architectural style of the time. The results are an astonishing collection of exemplary buildings from every architectural era: Gothic, Renaissance, Baroque, *Gründerzeit* (late 19th century), and *Jugendstil*. The East German government placed the entire city under a protection order, rescuing it from the bleak communist aesthetic of the late 20th century. More than 3,700 buildings are registered historical monuments. This, combined with energetic reconstruction, makes Görlitz the gem that it is today.

---

is where the nobility sat. If you've been to Dresden, the high altar will look familiar, as it was built by artists brought from Dresden, and resembles the crown gate of the Zwinger. The swirly clouds identify this as Rococo. The missing crucifix on the left wall (now in Warsaw) is a reminder of the artifacts that were pillaged from this church during various wars, but the choir stalls, carved in the 1430s, are original. As you follow signs to the *Marienaltar*, look up at the vaulted ceiling, and notice how complex it gets as you walk into newer parts of the church.

The church's trophy is the beautiful 15th-century carved triptych, the *Marienaltar*. The simple side was used on regular worship days, while the gilded side was reserved for high feast days. Today, you can usually see it open, and can admire the closed panels via the display on the bench to the right of the altar. It's an eyeful—rich with action and symbolism. The symmetry and order of the checked tablecloth is replaced in the other panels by lots of action and purposefully conflicting lines that create energy and tension. Notice the symbolism—there's a turban-wearing Ottoman (archenemy of the time) and Jesus wearing a Franciscan frock (a nod to the church's Franciscan heritage). Behind you, an exhausted Jesus, reminiscent of Auguste Rodin's *The Thinker*, ponders the fate of man. This statue, from 1910, used to sit on the grass outside of the Holy Sepulcher (see page 371)—notice the rotting wood at the base.

This is an active church, still very much alive; during a recent

Görlitz

celebration based on the theme, "Christ carries you—have no fear," parish kids rappelled down from the balconies.

The church's **tower** is unusually thin (the locals call it the *Mönch,* or "Monk"). The clock doesn't keep very good time, thanks to one in a series of Cloth-Maker Rebellions. In the Middle Ages, Görlitz was run by the powerful guilds of the cloth trade and the brewers, who neglected the rights of their workers and forbade non-members from practicing their trades. Finally, in the early 16th century, the workers rose up against the corrupt city council, which allowed the guilds to continue their unfair practices. The rebels ended their meetings punctually at midnight to avoid the night watchmen, who would be on the other side of town at that hour. But the city council was one step ahead: They ordered the church bell to chime seven minutes before midnight to fool the conspirators out onto the street and into the waiting arms of the guard. Fourteen of the conspirators were executed, and 25 more banished from the city. To this day, the bell chimes seven minutes early.

Across the square is the **Traitor's Passage** (Verrätergasse), a dark, sinister passageway used by the instigators of the rebellion to sneak in and out of the main marketplace.

• *To leave Obermarkt, walk down...*

Brüderstrasse: This street, connecting Obermarkt and Untermarkt, is home to one of the finest collections of Renaissance houses in Europe. The orange-and-gray house at the end of Brüderstrasse (#8) claims to be Germany's oldest Renaissance civic building (from 1526) and now houses the **Silesian Museum of Görlitz** (Schlesisches Museum zu Görlitz), a state museum featuring Silesian culture (€3, Tue–Sun 10:00–17:00, closed Mon, Brüderstrasse 8, tel. 03581/87910, www.schlesisches-museum.de). As you pass Schwarzestrasse, look left. The street's flying buttresses are typical of Görlitz's Old Town—these two are remnants of a series of brick barriers used to keep insurgents out of the inner city during the Cloth-Maker Rebellions.

• *At the end of Brüderstrasse, you'll reach...*

Lower Market Square (Untermarkt): The remarkably well-preserved Untermarkt is typical of Central European squares: It's built up in the middle to make maximum use of this prime real estate. The square shows just how prosperous the cloth trade made Görlitz.

• *Untermarkt is dominated by the tall Gothic tower (on your left) of the...*

Town Hall: Görlitz had no town hall until 1350, when the city purchased this building from a prominent citizen. The tower was extended to 195 feet in 1368. A lightning strike blew the top off the tower on July 9, 1742, prompting the addition of the current Baroque turret. The tower houses two clocks: The upper clock measures day, month, and phase of the moon, while the lower clock tells the time. The warrior's head used to stick out his tongue every hour, but now just seems to open his mouth. The date inscribed on the clock, 1584, commemorates the year when Bartholomäus Sculteus, an astronomer and mathematician, first divided the clock into 12 points. Sculteus also helped develop the Gregorian calendar. The city honored Sculteus, a Görlitz native, by being the first city in Germany to adopt both the new calendar and the clock. The Town Hall stairs represent the height of Görlitz Renaissance sculpture, and lead from the street level to the building's then–main entrance. Local officials used the balcony to make public announcements and decrees. If you look closely at the statue of Justice (1591), she's not blindfolded—in other words, the city is the highest authority.

The building at #14 (east end of the square) housed the city **scales** and was one of the most important commercial buildings since, at its peak, more than 1,000 wagons per day entered Görlitz. Everything had to be weighed and duties paid here. The late-Gothic ground floor, which housed the scales, is topped off with three Renaissance levels. The column-topping busts are a virtual Who's Who of the town's masons and scale-masters.

Around the corner from the scales, on the northern edge of the square, the city established a **commodity exchange** at the beginning of the 18th century. The building was also a kind of department store used to drive simple street vendors away from the financial center. With the rabble banished, the Baroque building with its adorning portal was a favored place for merchants to meet and deal.

• *For evidence that Görlitz is definitely a Protestant town, head down Neissstrasse to #29. There you'll find the...*

Biblical House: Since the Church banned religious depictions on secular buildings, the carvings on the Biblical House made it clear that the Reformation had come to stay. The houses in the Neissstrasse had all burned to the ground in 1526. Hanz Heinz, a cloth trader, purchased this house and rebuilt it completely in the Renaissance style. The house is named after the sandstone reliefs decorating the facade between the first and second floor parapets. The top level represents the New Testament, with (from left to right) the Annunciation, birth of Jesus, Jesus' baptism, the Last Supper, and the Crucifixion. The bottom row depicts the creation of Eve, the Fall of Man, Isaac's sacrifice, Moses receiving the Ten

Commandments, and Moses banishing serpents.

• *Next door, step into the...*

Baroque House (Barockhaus): This museum offers a peek at life in the 17th and 18th centuries. There's also an exhibit honoring Görlitz's favorite son (the philosopher Jacob Böhme, who lived here from 1575–1624), and a fascinating library, which is only accessible with a docent (request a viewing when you buy your ticket). This amazing library is still functioning today—for a €2.50 annual fee, you can have access to any of the books three days a week... anyone interested in tax records from 1475? The rest of the exhibit includes elaborately painted farm furniture, formal 18th-century apartments, a glass exhibit, and a unique lab of electrophysical instruments that belonged to a local contemporary of scientist (and "volt" namesake) Alessandro Volta. The natural sciences library holds geological samples, topographic models, and a first edition of a book by Benjamin Franklin—it's in the last room of books, on the shelf to your right by the window, fifth shelf from the bottom (€3.50, Tue–Sun 10:00–17:00, Fri until 20:00 but library only until 13:00, closed Mon, little English information but ask for the free explanatory fliers, tel. 03581/671-355, www.museum-goerlitz.de).

• *Backtrack to Untermarkt and hang a right onto...*

Peterstrasse: On the corner of Peterstrasse is the **City Apothecary** (Ratsapotheke). The owner attempted to transform a Gothic building into a Renaissance masterpiece, but ended up only combining the two styles. The two sundials on the southern facade were added in 1550. The left dial (Solarium) displays the time using the Arabic, local, Roman, and Babylonian clocks. The dial on the right (*Arachne*, "spider" in Greek) displays the position of the planets and the signs of the zodiac. The City Apothecary houses one of the city's best cafés, Kretschmer Ratscafé.

Peterstrasse is yet another impressive street. Look inside #14—the staircase seems to hang in mid-air. The house at #6 is a perfect example of renovations gone wrong: The building is Renaissance, with Gothic doors and windows, Ionic columns, and Baroque decorations—the mishmash doesn't really work, does it?

At the end of Peterstrasse, you can turn either right or left. Left leads to the **Nikolaiturm** (open to the public only on rare occasions), the oldest of Görlitz's towers, which marks the site of the original village of Gorelec. The Nikolaiturm, like all of the city-wall towers, got a facelift in the 18th century that replaced its pointy top with its current round dome. The city walls and gates were destroyed in 1848—

the stones were used to build the Jägerkaserne, a barracks off in the distance to the left of the Nikolaiturm. The only remaining section of the city wall is now a pleasant park that curves around from the base of the Nikolaiturm to the back of the Church of St. Peter. Alternatively, to the right of the park entrance, a small alleyway (Karpfengurnd) snakes its way back to the Peterstrasse.

• *If you turn right at the end of Peterstrasse, you'll reach the...*

Church of St. Peter (Peterskirche): The church was completed—after many setbacks, landslides, and Hussite invasions—in 1457, and renovated after fire destroyed the interior in 1691. The spires were added in 1890. The facade looks like a thousand other Gothic churches, but it's what's inside that counts: The Silesian-Italian Eugenio Casparini's **Sun Organ** (Sonnenorgel) is a spectacular, one-of-a-kind musical instrument and the center of Görlitz's musical life since 1701. The organ gets its name not from the golden sun at the center (which spins when air is pushed through the pipe), but for the circularly arranged pipes that shoot out like the sun's rays. Take in a free concert Thursday or Sunday at noon (Nov–March Sun only). The colorful baptistery, from 1617, is also worth a look.

• *Your walk is finished. Consider visiting some of Görlitz's other sights (described next), or relax with a local Landskron beer.*

SIGHTS

In Görlitz

▲Holy Sepulcher (Heiliges Grab)—One of Görlitz's most unusual and interesting sights, this is the only complete and

relatively accurate replica of the garden of Gethsemane and the holy places in Jerusalem, as they appeared in the 15th century. It takes a bit longer to visit than other sights in Görlitz, but pilgrims find it well worth ▲▲▲.

After making a pilgrimage to Jerusalem, Georg Emmerich commissioned this site as an offering to those who could not make such a journey themselves (built 1480–1503). The first building is the two-story Chapel of the Holy Cross. Reflecting the traditional belief that Christ was crucified on the site of Adam's grave, the crypt represents the tomb of Adam with the Golgotha Chapel above. Next door is the Salbhaus, a tiny chapel with a statue of Mary anointing Jesus' dead body. Finally, the Church of the Holy Sepulcher is a much smaller version of the original, but nonetheless is an interesting fusion of Middle

Eastern and European architecture. This version actually predates the restored Jerusalem site, which was damaged by fire in the 16th century. Medieval pilgrims to this site purchased a *Görlitzer Scheckel*—gold, silver, or pewter, according to their means—as payment to the church and a symbol of their pilgrimage (€1.50, daily April–Sept 10:00–18:00, Oct–March 10:00–16:00, English handout, Heilige-Grab-Strasse 79, tram #1, #2, or #3 to Heilige Grab, www.heiligesgrab-goerlitz.de).

▲▲**Landskron Brewery**—Beer has been brewed in Görlitz since the 12th century. The last remaining (and best) brewery is Landskron. The brewery offers tours in German, but the staff tries to be accommodating to English-speakers. In the end, it's all about the taste samples anyway. There are two versions: the ".33l Tour" (€5, 1.5 hours) or the ".5l Tour" (€8, 2.5 hours). Contact the brewery in advance to check the tour schedule and reserve (An der Landskronbrauerei 116, tel. 03581/4650, www.landskron.de, besichtigung@landskron.de). In the summer, the brewery hosts myriad concerts and other events.

▲**Landskrone**—On the outskirts of the city is a dormant volcano that stretches 1,376 feet above sea level. The city of Görlitz purchased the Landskrone from the aristocracy and incorporated it into the city in 1440. The mountainside provided wood for building (especially for rebuilding the town after fire) and basalt for cobblestones, and gave the city a commanding view over the area to defend against marauding robber-barons. The observation tower on top came in the 18th century, and a small restaurant in 1844 (although the current version was rebuilt in 1951). The entire area is a park, ideal for short hikes to the top. To get here, take tram #2 to the stop Biesnitz/Landskrone.

Near Görlitz

Three Silesian towns near Görlitz offer an interesting and diverse glimpse into this unique cultural crossroads.

▲▲▲**Zgorzelec**—When everything east of the Neisse River (and, farther north, the Oder River) became a part of Poland, Görlitz lost its eastern suburb. By 1946, Poles transplanted from Belarus and Ukraine eliminated all traces of the German past and created the city of Zgorzelec. On both sides of the river, government and citizenry are making great strides to glue the city back together (at least culturally) in a united Europe. A walk across the bridge into Poland is an interesting experience and offers a stark contrast to wonderfully restored Görlitz. Zgorzelec is obviously the less wealthy part of the city, but offers a fine collection of patrician and burgher houses (along ulica Warszawska), although in desperate need of repair. Once across the bridge, turn to the right and go up the hill to reach the Upper Lusatian Memorial Hall (nowadays the

Dom Kultury, or Civic House of Culture), a memorial to Kaiser Wilhelm I.

Important Note: The bridge near the end of the Neissstrasse is only for citizens of the European Union. Everybody else has to cross farther south, down the river, at the main bridge-crossing point. This is better for you anyway, since the main part of Zgorzelec is closer to that border. Americans and Canadians need a passport, but no visa, to cross into Poland.

Zittau and Oybin Castle (Burg Oybin)—Although Zittau is a splendid city in its own right, with pretty squares and a town hall by Karl Friedrich Schinkel, the real reason to come here is to take the narrow-gauge railroad to the castle ruins at Oybin. Bohemian Emperor Charles IV built the fortress and monastery Burg Oybin in the 14th century. The structure fell into disuse by the 16th century, and was repeatedly struck by lightning in the 18th and 19th centuries. The ruins are huge and fun to poke around, and the views of the unique geological formations of the Zittau Mountains are grand (castle entry-€3.50, daily April–Oct 9:00–18:00, Nov–March 10:00–16:00, www.burgundkloster-oybin.de).

Bautzen/Budyšin—This town, about halfway between Dresden and Görlitz, is the cultural capital of the Sorbs (or "Wends," as they are known in the US). The Sorbs—not to be confused with the Serbs of the former Yugoslavia, much farther south—are of Slavic descent, and still speak a distinct language that's a hybrid of Polish and Czech. About 20,000 Sorbs live in Germany, making up the country's only indigenous ethnic minority.

Bautzen's dual-language signs and slightly Mediterranean feel of spacious squares and public fountains, combined with intact city walls and a tower that's more off-center than Pisa's, make this town a perfect stopover between Dresden and Görlitz. Bautzen is also home to Germany's only Simultaneous Church, a house of worship shared by Catholics on one side and Protestants on the other. Germany's best spicy mustard comes from Bautzen. For more information on the town, see www.bautzen.de.

SHOPPING

Görlitzer Weinachts Haus celebrates Christmas all year long. Stop here for good deals on traditional crafts such as nutcrackers, incense burners shaped like smoking men, and Nativity scenes. Big draws are traditional paper stars from Herrnhut, handblown Sorb glass eggs, and Thuringian glass (Mon–Fri 10:00–18:00, Sat 10:00–17:00, Sun 11:00–16:00 in summer only, otherwise closed Sun, Fleischerstrasse 19, just off Obermarkt—look for the huge nutcracker out front, tel. 03581/649-205).

Schlesische Schatztruhe is one-stop shopping for all your

Silesian souvenir needs: books, posters, maps, cookbooks, and more. This is the first place to stop for Silesian ceramics and "Polish pottery" from Bolesławiec (Bunzlau in German). Unfortunately, they don't ship pottery to the US—you'll have to ship or carry it yourself. Their *Streuselkuchen* pastry seems to stay fresh forever (Mon–Fri 9:00–18:00, Sat 10:00–19:00, Sun 10:00–18:00, Brüderstrasse 13, tel. 03581/410-956, www.schlesien-heute.de).

SLEEPING

$$ Hotel Bon Apart is a comfortable hotel with an eclectic interior design that can only be described as "Gothic meets Baroque." It's a great value, with the best breakfast buffet in town. The rooms and suites have kitchens, and they brew their own beer (Sb-€60–90, Db-€70–90, 1-person suite-€110, 2-person suite-€130, family suites-€170–225, Elisabethstrasse 41, tel. & fax 03581/48080, www.bon-apart.de, hotel@bon-apart.de). Also contact owner François about his new hotel **Am Stadtpark,** which has renovated rooms in a gorgeous old building a little farther from the center, but a good budget option.

$$ Sorat Hotel Görlitz offers good, basic, business-style rooms for a fair price in a *Jugendstil* villa built in 1901 (Sb-€66–76, Db-€88–98, includes champagne breakfast buffet, Struvestrasse 1, near Marienplatz behind Karstadt department store, tel. 03581/406-577, fax 03581/406-579, www.sorat-hotels.com).

$ Die Destille ("The Distillery") is a clean, friendly, family-run pension with well-apportioned rooms near the Nikolaiturm. A good breakfast is left in the refrigerator near your room, so you can have breakfast whenever you want. During renovation of the building in the 1990, workers discovered a *mikveh* (ritual Jewish bath) in the basement (Sb-€50, Db-€65, cash only, Nikolaistrasse 6, tel. & fax 03581/405-302, www.destille-goerlitz.de).

Sleep Code

(€1 = about $1.30, country code: 49, area code: 03581)
S = Single, **D** = Double/Twin, **T** = Triple, **Q** = Quad, **b** = bathroom, **s** = shower only. Unless otherwise noted, credit cards are accepted, English is spoken, and breakfast is included.

To help you sort easily through these listings, I've divided the rooms into two categories, based on the price for a standard double room with bath:

$$ Higher Priced—Most rooms €75 or more.
$ Lower Priced—Most rooms less than €75.

Görlitz

$ Hotel und Gasthof Dreibeiniger-Hund ("Three-Legged Dog"), down the street from Die Destille, is a small, meticulously restored pension offering 13 cozy and romantic rooms in a 14th-century shell (Sb-€55, Db-€72, cash only, book ahead in summer, Büttnerstrasse 13, tel. 03581/423-980, www.dreibeinigerhund.de).

EATING

Silesians are a hearty people, and their cooking combines German, Polish, and Czech elements into one of Germany's most interesting regional cuisines. The Silesian specialty is *Schlesisches Himmelreich* ("Silesian Heaven"), a mix of pork roast and ham with stewed fruit in a white sauce served with dumplings. For dessert, try Silesian *Streuselkuchen*, a yummy crumb cake available everywhere. Landskron is Görlitz's ubiquitous brew, and one of the best pilsners in Germany.

Die Destille (see "Sleeping"), literally in the shadow of the Nikolaiturm, is a delightful restaurant oozing comfortable country elegance, with a friendly staff to boot. They excel at extremely traditional Silesian dishes, including the best *Schlesisches Himmelreich* in Görlitz. It's small, so come early or be prepared to share a table (€7–12 plates, daily 12:00–15:00 & 17:30–22:00, Nikolaistrasse 6, tel. 03581/405-302).

The **Dreibeiniger-Hund** (see "Sleeping") has a personal and homey restaurant. Regional cuisine with fresh seasonal specialties makes the "Dog" a must. In summer, sit outside under the sprawling oak tree (€6–14 plates, daily 11:00–23:00, Büttnerstrasse 13, tel. 03581/423-980).

Zur Goldenen Sonne, a favorite among the artsy clientele from the neighboring theater, serves traditional Silesian cuisine as well as exotic meats such as ostrich, bison, and crocodile. Don't worry—you can get a steak or a schnitzel here, too. Or try one of the excellent *Pfannen* dishes, served in a cast-iron skillet. Housed in a former stable, the Sonne has a cozy ambience and reasonable prices, and offers a sunny Mediterranean break from dumplings (€6–18 plates, daily 12:00–14:30 & 17:00–22:00, closed Mon for lunch, Demianiplatz 54, tel. 03581/311-609).

Vierradenmühle, Germany's easternmost restaurant, is the perfect place to ponder the division and reunification of Europe. The restaurant sits on top of a water-filtration station and former power plant (with museum) in the Neisse River, so the eastern foundation wall is actually the German-Polish border. The food is fine, although slightly overpriced, but the location is great. This is the ideal spot to enjoy a cold beer—and it's one of the few places in Görlitz that has the rare, but out-of-this-world, Landskron Hefeweizen on tap. The two sides of the border are marked by wooden poles on either side in the colors of the respective country: white and red for Poland, and black, red, and yellow for Germany (Mon–Sat 11:00–24:00, Sun 10:00–22:00, at the end of Neissstrasse at Hotherstrasse 20, tel. 03581/406-661).

Near the Lower Market Square: Good eateries abound near the Untermarkt. The best are on Peterstrasse, between the market and the Church of St. Peter; and on Neissstrasse, stretching from Untermarkt to the river. Almost every building on Neissstrasse was once a brewery. The pick of the litter is the **Bürgerstübl,** which was recently renovated with the help of the Landskron brewery and has a secret *Biergarten* in the back (€7–10 plates, open daily from 18:00, Sat–Sun also 12:00–14:00, Neissstrasse 27, tel. 03581/879-579).

Picnic Supplies: The only grocery store in the city center is the **Edeka,** at the corner of Steinstrasse and Obermarkt (Mon–Fri 8:00–18:30, Sat 8:00–16:00, closed Sun). For fresh fruit and produce, try the **Farmer's Market,** on Elisabethstrasse across from Hotel Bon-Apart (Mon–Fri 6:00–18:00, Sat 6:00–12:00, closed Sun).

TRANSPORTATION CONNECTIONS

From Görlitz by Train to: Zittau (hourly, 45 min, not covered by railpass—see below), **Bautzen** (about hourly, 30–45 min; Bautzen-bound trains continue on to Dresden), **Dresden** (hourly, 1.5 hrs), **Berlin** (hourly, 2.5 hrs, transfer in Cottbus, not fully covered by railpass—see below). Train info: tel. 11861 (€0.60/min).

Important Note: If you have a railpass (such as a German Railpass, or a Eurailpass that includes Germany), it covers the trip from Görlitz to Bauten and on to Dresden. However, your railpass is *not* valid between Görlitz and Cottbus (where you transfer to Berlin), or between Görlitz and Zittau, as these blue-and-yellow trains are not part of the Deutsche Bahn system (you can buy tickets at the Deutsche Bahn ticket window, but it's easier just to get them on the train). If you are day-tripping from Görlitz to Zittau, your best bet is the **Tageskarte Lausitz** day pass—at the ticket machine, choose *Tageskarte Lausitz,* then *1* (€10); or *Kleingruppenkarte Lausitz,* then *1* (€20 for up to 5 adults).

BERLIN

No tour of Germany is complete without a look at its historic and reunited capital. Over the last decade, Berlin has been a construction zone. Standing over ripped-up tracks and under a canopy of cranes, visitors witnessed the rebirth of a great European capital. Today, as we enjoy the thrill of walking over what was the Wall and through the well-patched Brandenburg Gate, it's clear that history is not contained in some book, but an exciting story that we are a part of. Historians find Berlin exhilarating.

Berlin had a tumultuous 20th century. After the city was devastated in World War II, it was divided by the Allied powers: The American, British, and French sectors became West Berlin, and the Soviet sector, East Berlin. That division was set in stone in 1961 when the East Germans boxed in the East by building the Berlin Wall. The Wall lasted 28 years. In 1990, less than a year after the Wall fell, the two Germanys officially became one. When the dust settled, Berliners from both sides of the once-divided city faced the monumental challenge of reunification.

While the work is far from over, a new Berlin has emerged. Berliners joke that they don't need to go anywhere because their city's always changing. Spin a postcard rack to see what's new. A five-year-old guidebook on Berlin covers a different city.

Reunification has had its negative side, and locals are fond of saying, "The Wall survives in the minds of some people." Some "Ossies" (impolite slang for Easterners) miss their security. Some "Wessies" miss their easy ride (military deferrals, subsidized rent, and tax breaks). For free spirits, walled-in West Berlin was a citadel of freedom within the East.

The city government has been eager to charge forward with

little nostalgia for anything that was Eastern. Big corporations and the national government have moved in, and the dreary swath of land that was the Wall and its notorious "death strip" has been transformed. City planners have boldly made Berlin's reunification and the return of the national government a good opportunity to make Berlin a great capital once again.

Today, Berlin feels like the nuclear fuel rod of a great nation. It's so vibrant with youth, energy, and an anything-goes-and-anything's-possible buzz that Munich feels spent in comparison. Berlin is both extremely popular and surprisingly affordable. As a booming tourist attraction, the year 2007 was, by far, its best year yet. And 2008 promises to be even better.

Planning Your Time

Because of Berlin's inconvenient location, try to enter and/or leave by either night train or plane. On a three-week trip through Germany and Austria, I'd give Berlin at least two days and spend them this way:

Day 1: Begin your day getting oriented to this huge city: Either take the 10:00 "Discover Berlin" guided walking tour offered by Original Berlin Walks (see page 387) or follow my "Do-It-Yourself Orientation Tour" by bus to the Reichstag (page 391), then continue by foot down Unter den Linden (page 401). Focus on sights along Unter den Linden, including the Reichstag dome (most crowded 10:00–16:00; best to visit 8:00–9:00 or 21:00–22:00), the German History Museum, and Museum Island (with the Pergamon and Egyptian museums).

Day 2: Concentrate on the sights in central Berlin, and in eastern Berlin south of Unter den Linden. Here's a plan to do just that: Spend the morning with the paintings at the Gemäldegalerie. After lunch, hike via Potsdamer Platz to the Topography of Terror exhibit and along the surviving Zimmerstrasse stretch of Wall to the Museum of the Wall at Checkpoint Charlie. If you're not museum-ed out yet, swing by the magnificent Jewish Museum. Finish your day in the lively East—particularly the once glum, then edgy, now fun-loving and trendy Prenzlauer Berg district.

If you're maximizing your sightseeing, you could squeeze a hop-off, hop-on bus tour into Day 1. Remember that the Reichstag dome and the Museum of the Wall are open late.

Berlin merits additional time if you have it. There's much more in the city. And the concentration camp memorial at Sachsenhausen and the palace at Potsdam are both worthwhile side-trips.

Berlin Sightseeing Modules

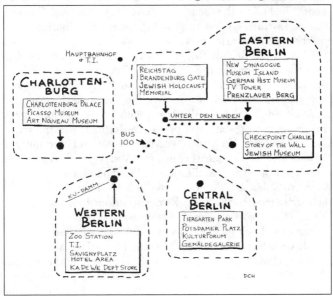

ORIENTATION

(area code: 030)

Berlin is huge, with 3.4 million people. But the tourist's Berlin can be broken into four digestible chunks:

1. Eastern Berlin: The former East Berlin has the highest concentration of notable sights and colorful neighborhoods, plus the new Hauptbahnhof (Main Station). Near the famous Brandenburg Gate, you'll find the Reichstag building, Pariser Platz, and the new Holocaust Memorial. From the Brandenburg Gate, the famous Unter den Linden boulevard runs east through eastern Berlin, passing the marvelous German History Museum and Museum Island (Pergamon Museum, Egyptian Museum, and Berlin Cathedral) on the way to Alexanderplatz (TV Tower). The intersection of Unter den Linden and Friedrichstrasse is emerging as the new center of the city. South of Unter den Linden, you'll find the delightful Gendarmenmarkt square, most Nazi sites (including the Topography of Terror exhibit), the Jewish Museum, the best Wall-related sights (Museum of the Wall at Checkpoint Charlie, and East Side Gallery), and the colorful Turkish neighborhood of Kreuzberg. North of Unter den Linden are these worth-a-wander neighborhoods: around Oranienburger Strasse (Jewish Quarter and New Synagogue), Hackescher Markt, and Prenzlauer Berg (several recommended hotels and a very lively restaurant/nightlife zone).

Berlin

2. Central Berlin: Potsdamer Platz, the Kulturforum museum cluster (including the Gemäldegalerie, New National Gallery, Musical Instruments Museum, and Philharmonic Concert Hall), and the giant Tiergarten park.

3. Western Berlin: This is the area around the Bahnhof Zoo (Zoo train station) and the grand Kurfürstendamm boulevard, nicknamed "Ku'damm" (transportation hub, tours, information, shopping, and recommended hotels). The East is all the rage. But the West, while staid, is still vibrant, with lots of big-name stores and destination restaurants that keep Berliners coming back. During the Cold War, this "Western Sector" was the hub for Western visitors. Capitalists visited the West, with a nervous side-trip behind the Wall into the grim and foreboding East. (Cubans, Russians, Poles, and Angolans stayed behind the Wall and did their sightseeing in the East.) Remnants of this Iron Curtain–era Western focus have left today's visitors with a stronger focus on the Ku'damm and Bahnhof Zoo than the district really deserves.

4. Charlottenburg Palace Area: The palace and nearby museums (Picasso, Art Nouveau, and Surrealist), on the western edge of the city center. This area is of least interest to a visitor on a tight schedule.

Tourist Information

Berlin's TIs are run by a for-profit agency working for the city's big hotels, which colors the information they provide. TI branches are appropriately called "infostores" (tel. 030/250-025, www.berlin -tourist-information.com). You'll find them at: the **Hauptbahnhof** train station (daily 8:00–22:00, by main entrance); **Ku'damm** (Kurfürstendamm 21, Mon–Sat 10:00–20:00, Sun 10:00–18:00, shorter hours in winter); the **Reichstag** (on Scheidemannstrasse, daily April–Oct 8:00–20:00, Nov–March 10:00–18:00); and the **Brandenburg Gate** (daily April–Oct 9:30–18:00, Nov–March 10:00–18:00).

The TIs sell a good city map (€1), the three-day Museumspass (and other passes, see below), and various local publications and entertainment guides (see below). They also offer a €3 room-finding service (but only to hotels that give them kickbacks—many don't). Most hotels have free city maps.

Museum Passes: The three-day **Museumspass** (Schaulust MuseenBerlin) gets you into 70 museums (including the national museums and most of the recommended biggies) on three consecutive days for €15. It covers more than you'd otherwise pay for, so with this pass you'll enjoy the ease of popping in and out of museums that you might not otherwise visit. As you'll routinely pay €5 to €8 per admission, this pays for itself in a hurry. Buy it at the TI or any participating museum. Note that if a museum is

closed on one of the days of your Museumspass, you have access
to that museum on a fourth day to make up for lost time. The
€12 **Museum Island Pass** (Standortkarte Museumsinsel) covers
all the museums on the island (otherwise €8 each) and is a fine
value—but for €3 more, the three-day Museumspass gives you
triple the days and many more entries. TIs also sell the **Welcome
Card,** a transportation pass that also gives some museum discounts (see page 384).

Local Publications: Various magazines can help make your
time in Berlin more productive (all available at the TI and most
at newsstands). *Berlin Programm* is a comprehensive German-
language monthly, especially strong in high culture, that lists
upcoming events and museum hours (€2, www.berlin-programm
.de). *Berlin To Go* is a sketchier German–English, TI-produced
bimonthly magazine offering timely features on Berlin and a partial calendar of events (€1). *Exberliner Magazine* is the only real
English-language monthly (published mostly for expat Americans,
but very helpful for curious travelers). It has an edgy, youthful
focus and gives a fascinating insider's look at this fast-changing
city (€2, www.exberliner.com). The free, informative magazines
that promote the upstart tour companies **New Berlin Walks** and
Insider Tours (both described on page 390) are also useful.

Arrival in Berlin

By Train
Berlin's newest and grandest train station, **Berlin Hauptbahnhof**

(Main Station, a.k.a. simply "der
Bahnhof"), opened in 2006.
Almost all long-distance trains
now arrive at Europe's biggest,
mostly underground train station.
Tracks 1 through 8 are underground, while tracks 11 through
16 are a floor above ground level
(along with the S-Bahn).

It's a "transfer station"—unique for its major lines coming in
at right angles—where the national train system meets the city's
train system (S-Bahn). It's also the home of 80 shops with long
hours—some locals call the station a "shopping mall with trains"
(daily 8:00–22:00, even Sunday). The Kaisers supermarket (above
track 2) is handy for assembling a picnic for the ride.

Baggage Storage and WCs: While the station has no lockers, the Gepäck Center is an efficient and secure deposit service
(€3/day per bag, daily 6:00–22:00, on level EG—ground floor—by
track 14). The WC Center (public toilets) is next to the Virgin
Megastore.

Train Information: The station has two DeutscheBahn *Reisezentrum* information counters (one upper level, one lower—just follow signs; both open daily 6:00–22:00). If you're staying in the West, keep in mind that the info center at the Bahnhof Zoo station is just as good and much less crowded.

EurAide is an English-speaking information desk with answers to your questions about train travel around Europe. It operates from a single counter in the lower-level *Reisezentrum* (labeled *-1,* not *+1,* follow signs to tracks 5–6). It's American-run, so communication is simple, and they have a knack for predicting your needs. This is an especially good place to make fast-train and *couchette* reservations for later in your trip. EurAide also gives out a helpful free city map and sells public-transit tickets and passes (daily 9:00–19:00 except Oct–March closed Sat–Sun, www.euraide.com).

Getting into Town: While taxis and buses await outside the station, the S-Bahn is probably your best means of connecting to your destination within Berlin. The cross-town express S-Bahn line connects the station in a few minutes with my recommended hotels. It's simple: All S-Bahn trains are on tracks 15 and 16 at the top of the station. All trains on track 15 go east (toward the Ostbahnhof and Hackescher Markt), and trains on track 16 go west (toward Bahnhof Zoo and Savignyplatz). Your train ticket or railpass into the station covers you on your connecting S-Bahn ride into town (and your ticket out includes the transfer via S-Bahn to the Hauptbahnhof). U-Bahn rides are not covered by tickets or railpasses.

If you're sleeping in the West, catch any train on track 16 to Savignyplatz, and you're a five-minute walk from your hotel (see map on page 435). Savignyplatz is one stop after Bahnhof Zoo (rhymes with "toe," a.k.a. Bahnhof Zoologischer Garten), the once-grand train hub now eclipsed by the Hauptbahnhof. Nowadays it's useful mainly for its shops, uncrowded train-information desk, and BVG transit office (outside the entrance, amid the traffic).

If you're sleeping in eastern Berlin, take any train on track 15 two stops to Hackescher Markt, then catch tram #M1 north (see map on page 437).

By Plane

For information on reaching the city center from Berlin's airports, see "Transportation Connections" at the end of this chapter.

Helpful Hints

Medical Help: "Call a Doc" is a non-profit referral service designed for tourists (tel. 01804-2255-2362, phone answered 24 hours a day, www.calladoc.com). Payment is arranged between you and the doctor, and is likely far more affordable than similar care in the US. The US Embassy also has a list of local English-speaking doctors (www.usembassy.de).

Museum Hours: Many major Berlin museums are closed on Monday. All national museums, including the Pergamon and Gemäldegalerie (plus others as noted in "Sights," page 393), are free for the last four hours on Thursdays (for example, if it closes at 18:00, it's free from 14:00 on; www.museen-berlin.de).

Monday Activities: Since many museums close on Monday, save the day for Berlin Wall sights, the Reichstag dome, my "Do-It-Yourself Orientation Tour" and strolling Unter den Linden, walking/bus tours, the Jewish Museum, churches, the zoo, or shopping (the Kaufhaus des Westens—KaDeWe—department store is a sight in itself). Be aware that when Monday is a holiday—as it is several times a year—museums are open then and closed Tuesday.

Addresses: Many Berlin streets are numbered with odd and even numbers on the same side of the street, often with no connection to the other side (for example, Ku'damm #212 can be across the street from #14). To save steps, check the white street signs on curb corners; many list the street numbers covered on that side of the block.

Internet Access: You'll find Internet access in most hotels and hostels, as well as at small Internet cafés all over the city. The **easyInternetcafé** outlets, generally paired with Dunkin' Donuts (daily 6:00–23:00), have handy locations, including Hardenbergplatz 2 (across from Bahnhof Zoo, next to McDonald's), Ku'damm 224 (10-min walk from Bahnhof Zoo, near several recommended hotels), and Rathaus-Passagen (on Alexanderplatz). Buy a ticket at the self-service machines and follow the English instructions. Unused time can be used at any branch in Berlin for up to a week.

Bookstore: Berlin Story, a big, fun bookshop, has the best selection anywhere in town of English-language books on Berlin. They also have a fascinating, free little museum in the back with a model of Unter den Linden from 1930 and a room showing a good 25-minute Berlin history video (in English). The shop has a knowledgeable staff and stocks an amusing mix of knickknacks and East Berlin nostalgia souvenirs (daily 10:00–19:00, Unter den Linden 40, tel. 030/2045-3842, www .berlinstory.de).

Laundry: Schnell und Sauber Waschcenter is a handy launderette near my recommended western Berlin hotels (€5–9 wash and dry, daily 6:00–23:00, Leibnizstrasse 72, 4 blocks west of Savignyplatz, near intersection with Kantstrasse). Near my recommended hotels in Prenzlauer Berg, try **Holly's Wasch-Theke** (€5–9 wash and dry, includes detergent, daily

8:00–22:00, self- or full-serve, attached café, Kollwitzstrasse 93, tel. 030/443-9210).

Travel Agency: Last Minute Flugbörse can help you find a flight in a hurry (discount flights, no train tickets, in Europa Center near Bahnhof Zoo, Mon–Sat 10:00–20:00, closed Sun, tel. 030/2655-1050, www.lastminuteflugboerse.de). **American Express** is a few blocks off Unter den Linden at Friedrichstrasse 172 (sells train tickets for €4 service fee, Mon–Fri 9:00–19:00, Sat 10:00–14:00, closed Sun, tel. 030/201-7400).

Getting Around Berlin

Berlin's sights spread far and wide. Right from the start, commit yourself to the city's fine public-transit system.

By Subway and Bus: The U-Bahn (*Untergrund-Bahn*, Berlin's subway), S-Bahn (*Schnell-Bahn*, or "fast train," mostly above ground and with fewer stops), *Strassenbahn* (streetcars, called "trams" by locals), and all buses are consolidated into one system, the BVG, that uses the same tickets. *Erwachsener* means "adult"—anyone 14 or older. Here are your options:

• A basic ticket *(Einzelfahrschein)* for two hours of travel in one direction on buses or subways—€2.10. It's easy to make this ticket stretch to cover several rides...as long as they're all in the same direction.

• A cheap short-ride ticket *(Kurzstrecke)* for a single short ride of six bus stops or three subway stations, with one underground transfer—€1.20.

• A day pass *(Tageskarte)* covering zones A and B, the city proper—€6.10 (good until 3:00 the morning after). To get out to Potsdam, you need a ticket covering zone C—€6.30. (For longer stays, a 7-day *Tageskarte* is also available—€26, or €32 including zone C; or buy 2 WelcomeCards, described next.) The *Kleingruppenkarte* lets groups of up to five travel all day for €16.

• The Berlin/Potsdam **WelcomeCard** gives you transportation in zones A, B, and C, and 25-percent discounts on lots of minor and a few major museums (including Checkpoint Charlie), sightseeing tours (including 25 percent off the recommended Original Berlin Walks), and music and theater events (€16/48 hrs, €22/72 hrs; valid for an adult and up to three kids younger than 14). If you plan to cover a lot of ground using public transportation during a two- or three-day visit, this is usually the best transit deal. There are two versions: Berlin (zones A and B) and Berlin with Potsdam (zones A, B, C).

Buy your U- or S-Bahn tickets from machines at stations. (They are also sold at BVG pavilions at train stations and airports, the TI, and EurAide.) Don't be afraid of the automated machines: First select the type of ticket you want, then load in the coins or

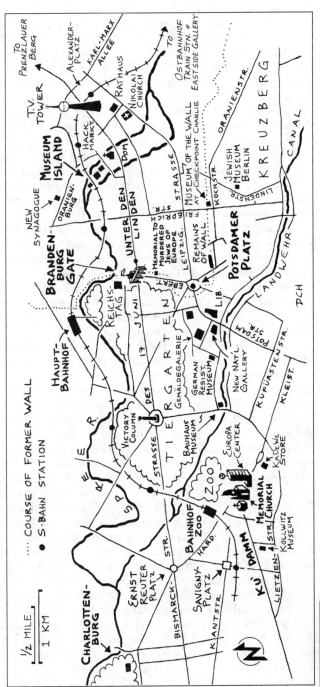

Berlin

paper bills. As you board the bus or tram, or enter the subway system, punch your ticket in a red or yellow clock machine to validate it (or risk a €40 fine; for an all-day or multi-day pass, only validate it the first time you ride). Within Berlin, Eurailpasses are only good on S-Bahn connections to the station when you're arriving and departing.

The S-Bahn crosstown express is a river of public transit through the heart of the city, in which many lines converge on one basic highway. Get used to this and you'll leap within a few minutes between: Savignyplatz (hotels), Bahnhof Zoo (Ku'damm, bus #100, tour meeting spot), the Hauptbahnhof (all major trains in and out of Berlin), Friedrichstrasse (Unter den Linden), Hackescher Markt (Museum Island, hotels, restaurants, nightlife), and Alexanderplatz (eastern end of Unter den Linden walk).

Sections of the U- or S-Bahn sometimes close temporarily for repairs. In this situation, a bus route often replaces the train (*Ersatzverkehr*, or "replacement transportation"). Bus schedules are available on the helpful BVG website, www.bvg.de.

By Taxi: Taxis are easy to flag down, and taxi stands are common. A typical ride within town costs €8–10, and a crosstown trip (for example, Bahnhof Zoo to Alexanderplatz) will run you about €15. A taxi to either airport costs about €20.

Money-Saving Taxi Tip: For any ride of less than 2 kilometers (about a mile), you can save several euros if you take advantage of the *Kurzstrecke* (short-stretch) rate. To get this rate, it's important that you flag the cab down on the street—not at or even near a taxi stand. Also, you must ask for the *Kurzstrecke* rate as soon as you hop in: Confidently say *"Kurzstrecke, bitte"* (KOORT-streck-uh BIT-uh), and your driver will flip the meter to a fixed €3.50 rate.

By Bike: Be careful—in Berlin, motorists don't brake for bicyclists (and bicyclists don't brake for pedestrians). Fortunately, some roads and sidewalks have special red-painted bike lanes. Just don't ride on the regular sidewalk—it's *nicht erlaubt* (not allowed).

In western Berlin, you can rent good bikes at the **Bahnhof Zoo** left-luggage counter, next to the lockers at the back of the station (€10/day, €23/3 days, €35/7 days; bikes come with lock, air pump, and mounted basket; daily 7:00–21:00, there's a limited supply of bikes and they've been known to run out). In the east, **Fahrradstation** near the Friedrichstrasse S-Bahn station has a huge number of bikes (€15/day; April–Oct daily 8:00–20:00; Nov–March Mon–Fri 10:00–19:00, Sat 10:00–16:00, closed Sun; leave the S-Bahn station via Friedrichstrasse exit, turn left on Dorotheenstrasse and walk 500 yards, and you'll find it at the entrance to the parking garage at Dorotheenstrasse 30; tel. 030/2045-4500).

TOURS

▲▲▲Walking Tours

Berlin is an ideal city to get to know with a walking tour. The city is a battle zone of extremely competitive and creative walking tour companies, all offering employment to American and British expats and students and cheap, informative tours to visiting travelers. The Original Berlin Walks was, as its name implies, the original. Smelling a business opportunity, some of its former guides and others spliced guerilla business tactics into O.B.W.'s established model and started their own walking tour companies. All give variations on the same themes: general introductory walk, Hitler and Nazi sites walk, communism walk, and day trips to Potsdam and the Sachsenhausen Concentration Camp Memorial. The youth-oriented outfits also do nightly pub crawls. For details, see the various websites. Here's my take on the current situation.

Original Berlin Walks—This is the most established operation, with tours aiming at a clientele that's curious about the city's history. They don't offer "free tours" or pub crawls, and their guides are professionals. I've enjoyed the help of O.B.W.'s high-quality, high-energy guides for many years, and routinely hire them when my tour groups are in town. I'm always impressed with founder Nick Gay's ability to assemble guides of such high caliber. Tours generally cost €12 (€9 with WelcomeCard, or €10 if you're under 26). Readers of this book get a €1 discount (off the adult or youth price) per tour in 2008.

There's no need to reserve ahead—just show up. All tours meet at the taxi stand in front of the Bahnhof Zoo, and start at 10:00 unless otherwise noted. The Discover Berlin and Jewish Life tours have a second departure point 30 minutes later in eastern Berlin's Hackescher Markt S-Bahn station, outside Häagen-Dazs; if you're staying in the East, save time by showing up here.

Discover Berlin, their flagship introductory walk, covers the birthplace of the city, Museum Island, then heads up Unter den Linden, stops at the Reichstag, and then goes on to Checkpoint Charlie (no interior visits, 4 hours, English only, daily year-round, meet at 10:00 at Bahnhof Zoo, April–Oct also daily at 14:30). Other tours include: **Infamous Third Reich Sites** (May–Sept Wed at 10:00, Sat at 14:30, Sun at 10:00; runs less often Oct–April—check their website or pick up a flier for the schedule); **Jewish Life in Berlin** (May–Sept Mon at 10:00 at Bahnhof Zoo); **Potsdam** (€15, see page 429); and the newest itinerary, **Nest of Spies** (May–Sept only, Tue and Sat at 12:30). Many of the Third Reich and Jewish history sights are difficult to pin down without these excellent walks.

Their six-hour trip to the **Sachsenhausen Concentration**

Berlin at a Glance

▲▲▲**Reichstag** Germany's historic Parliament building, topped with a striking dome you can climb. **Hours:** Daily 8:00–24:00, last entry 22:00. Long lines—go very early (8:00) or late (after 21:00). See page 393.

▲▲▲**Museum of the Wall at Checkpoint Charlie** Moving museum near the former site of the famous border checkpoint between the American and Soviet sectors, with stories of brave escapes during the Cold War and the gleeful days when the Wall fell. **Hours:** Daily 9:00–22:00. See page 413.

▲▲▲**Jewish Museum Berlin** User-friendly museum celebrating Jewish culture, in a highly conceptual building. **Hours:** Daily 10:00–20:00, Mon until 22:00. See page 415.

▲▲▲**German History Museum** The ultimate swing through the tumultuous history of this country. **Hours:** Daily 10:00–18:00. See page 406.

▲▲▲**Gemäldegalerie** Germany's top collection of 13th-through 18th-century European paintings, featuring Dürer, van Eyck, Rubens, Titian, Raphael, Caravaggio, and more. **Hours:** Tue–Sun 10:00–18:00, Thu until 22:00, Sun until 20:00, closed Mon. See page 424.

▲▲**Berlin Wall** Mostly gone, but parts of the Wall are still visible—including the East Side Gallery, the Documentation Center on Bernauer Strasse, and a chunk near the Topography of Terror (former SS and Gestapo headquarters). **Hours:** Always open.

▲▲**Brandenburg Gate** One of Berlin's most famous landmarks, a multi-arched gateway, at the former border of East and West. **Hours:** Always open. See page 398.

▲▲**Memorial to the Murdered Jews of Europe** New Holocaust memorial with almost 3,000 symbolic pillars, plus an exhibition about Hitler's Jewish victims. **Hours:** Memorial always open; exhibition open Tue–Sun 10:00–20:00, closed Mon. See page 400.

▲▲**Unter den Linden** Leafy boulevard through the heart of former East Berlin, lined with some of the city's top sights. **Hours:** Always open. See page 401.

▲▲**Pergamon Museum** World-class museum of classical antiquities on Museum Island (just off Unter den Linden), featuring the fantastic second-century B.C. Greek Pergamon Altar. **Hours:** Daily 10:00–18:00, Thu until 22:00. See page 407.

▲▲**Egyptian Museum/Altes Museum** Proud home (on Museum Island) of the exquisite 3,000-year-old bust of Queen Nefertiti. **Hours:** Daily 10:00–18:00, Thu until 22:00. See page 408.

▲▲**Gendarmenmarkt** Inviting square bounded by twin churches (one with a fine German history exhibit), a chocolate shop, and a concert hall. **Hours:** Always open. See page 411.

▲▲**Deutsche Kinemathek Film and TV Museum** An entertaining look at German film and TV from *Metropolis* to Dietrich, from Hitler through the Communist days. **Hours:** Tue–Sun 10:00–18:00, Thu until 20:00, closed Mon. See page 423.

▲**New Synagogue** Largest prewar synagogue in Berlin, destroyed in WWII, with a facade that has since been rebuilt. **Hours:** Generally Sun–Fri 10:00–17:00 or later, closed Sat. See page 416.

▲**Prenzlauer Berg** One of Berlin's most colorful and lively neighborhoods, worth exploring. **Hours:** Always bustling. See page 418.

▲**Potsdamer Platz** The "Times Square" of old Berlin, long a postwar wasteland, now rebuilt with huge glass skyscrapers, an underground train station, and—covered with a huge canopy—the Sony Center mall with eateries. **Hours:** Always open. See page 421.

▲**Kaiser Wilhelm Memorial Church** Evocative destroyed church in the heart of the former West Berlin, with a modern annex. **Hours:** Church open Mon–Sat 10:00–16:00, closed Sun, annex open daily 9:00–19:00. See page 425.

▲**Käthe Kollwitz Museum** The black-and-white art of the Berlin artist who conveyed the suffering of her city's stormiest century. **Hours:** Wed–Mon 11:00–18:00, closed Tue. See page 426.

▲**Kaufhaus des Westens (KaDeWe)** The "Department Store of the West"—the biggest on the Continent—where East Berliners flocked when the Wall came down. **Hours:** Mon–Fri 10:00–20:00, Sat 9:30–20:00, closed Sun. See page 426.

Camp Memorial intends to "provide a challenging history lesson with universal applications" (€15, May–Sept Tue and Thu–Sun at 10:15 from Bahnhof Zoo meeting point, also from Hackescher Markt meeting point at 9:50, runs less off-season—check website or flier for details).

You can confirm these starting times at EurAide or by phone with Nick or his wife and business partner, Serena (tel. 030/301-9194, www.berlinwalks.de, info@berlinwalks.de). They can also arrange private guides (€150/3 hrs).

Insider Tours and New Berlin Walks—Unlike many other European cities, Berlin has no regulations controlling who can give tours. Lots of upstart companies come and go, but these two feisty and aggressive newcomers are well-established. They target a younger crowd and offer free introductory tours. Their guides make their money off of tips, cross-selling their specialty tours, and the hugely successful pub crawls (with profit supplemented by featured bars). Each company publishes a practical, free Berlin guide magazine (distributed all over town and worth grabbing for the sightseeing information even if you're not taking their walks). They offer essentially the same itineraries as Original Berlin Walks and roughly this formula: You take their introductory walk for free, then choose—if you wish—to take any of their other walks (€10–12 each). For all the details, see their magazines or visit www.insidertour.com or www.newberlintours.com. For example, basic introductory city walks leave daily at 11:00, 13:00, and 16:00 (free, 3.5 hrs, meet at Starbucks at Brandenburg Gate/Pariser Platz, just show up). Their wildly popular €12 **pub crawls** occur nightly (for details see "Nightlife," on page 432).

Brewer's Berlin Tours—For a more exhaustive (or, for some, exhausting) walking tour of Berlin, consider Brewer's Berlin Tours. These are run by Terry (retired from the British diplomatic service—he worked at the embassy in East Berlin) and his well-trained and engaging staff (all native English speakers). Their All-Day Berlin tours are legendary for their length, and best for those with a long attention span and a serious interest in Berlin (€12, tour lasts 8 hours or more and covers the entire old center, departs daily at 10:30 year-round from Bandy Brooks ice cream shop at Friedrichstrasse U- and S-Bahn station, tel. 030/2248-7435, mobile 0177-388-1537, www.brewersberlintours.com). Just show up. They also do all-day Potsdam tours (May–Oct Wed and Sun; see "Near Berlin: Potsdam's Palaces" on page 429 for details).

Bus Tours

Full-blown Bus Tours—Severin & Kühn offers a long list of bus tours in and around Berlin; their three-hour "Big Berlin Tour" is a good introduction (€22, daily at 10:00 and 14:00, two stops:

Checkpoint Charlie and Brandenburg Gate, live guides in two languages, departs from Ku'damm 216, buy ticket at bus, tel. 030/880-4190, www.severin-kuehn-berlin.de).

Hop-on, Hop-off City Circle Tours—Several companies cooperate so that you can make a circuit of the city with unlimited hop-on, hop-off privileges (about 14 stops) on buses with boring recorded commentary (€20, 4/hr, daily 10:00–18:00, last bus leaves all stops at 16:00, 2-hour loop). Just hop on where you like and pay the driver. On a sunny day when some double-decker buses are convertible and go topless, these are a photographer's delight, cruising slowly by just about every major sight in town. In the winter (Nov–March), the buses come only twice an hour and the last departure is at 15:00.

Bike Tours

Berlin is a flat, bike-friendly city. **Fat Tire Bike Tours** offers three different four-hour, six-mile tours (€20; City Tour—daily March–Nov at 11:00, June–Aug also at 16:00; Berlin Wall Tour—mid-May–Sept Mon, Thu, and Sat at 10:30; Third Reich Tour—mid-May–Sept Wed, Fri, and Sun at 10:30; meet at TV Tower at Alexanderplatz, no need to reserve for the Wall or for the Third Reich tours, tel. 030/2404-7991, fax 030/2404-8837, www.fattirebiketoursberlin.com, info@fattirebiketoursberlin.com).

SELF-GUIDED TOUR

Do-It-Yourself Orientation Tour: Bus #100 from Bahnhof Zoo to the Reichstag

This tour narrates the route of convenient bus #100, which connects my recommended hotel neighborhood in western Berlin with the sights in eastern Berlin. If you have the €20 and two hours for a hop-on, hop-off bus tour (described earlier), take that instead. But this short €2.10 bus ride provides a fine city introduction. Bus #100 is a sightseer's dream, stopping at Bahnhof Zoo, the Berlin Zoo, Victory Column (Siegessäule), Reichstag, Brandenburg Gate, Unter den Linden, Pergamon Museum, and Alexanderplatz. While you could ride it to the end, it's more fun to get out at the Reichstag and walk down Unter den Linden at your own pace (using my commentary on page 401). When combined with the self-guided walk down Unter den Linden, this tour merits ▲▲▲. Before you take this bus into eastern Berlin, consider checking out the sights in western Berlin (see page 425).

The Tour Begins: Buses start from Hardenbergplatz in front of Bahnhof Zoo. Buses come every 10 minutes, and single tickets are good for two hours—so take advantage of hop-on-and-off privileges. Climb aboard, stamp your ticket (giving it a time), and grab a seat on top. This is about a 15-minute ride. The upcoming stop will light up on the reader board inside the bus.

➲ On your left and then straight ahead, before descending into the tunnel, you'll see the bombed-out hulk of the **Kaiser Wilhelm Memorial Church,** with its postwar sister church (described on page 425) and the **Europa Center.** This is the "West End" shopping district, a bustling people zone with big department stores nearby. When the Wall came down, East Berliners flocked to this area's department stores (especially KaDeWe, described on page 426). Soon after, the biggest, swankiest new stores were built in the East. Now the West is trying to win those shoppers back by building even bigger and better shopping centers around the Europa Center.

➲ At the stop in front of Hotel Palace: On the left, the elephant gates mark the entrance to the **Berlin Zoo** and its aquarium (described on page 427).

➲ Driving down Kurfürstenstrasse, you'll pass several Asian restaurants—a reminder that, for most, the best food in Berlin is not German. Turning left, with the huge Tiergarten park in the distance ahead, you'll cross a canal and see the famous **Bauhaus Archive** (hard to see—it's the off-white, blocky building with scoopy roof ducts) behind the trees on the right. The Bauhaus movement ushered in a new age of modern architecture that emphasized function over beauty, giving rise to blocky steel-and-glass skyscrapers in big cities around the world. On the left is Berlin's new embassy row. The big turquoise wall marks the communal home of all five Nordic embassies. This building is perfectly "green," run entirely by solar power.

➲ The bus enters a 400-acre park called the **Tiergarten,** packed with cycling paths, joggers, and—on hot days—nude sunbathers. Straight ahead, the **Victory Column** (Siegessäule, with the gilded angel, described on page 419) towers above this vast city park that was once a royal hunting grounds, now nicknamed the "green lungs of Berlin."

➲ On the left, a block after leaving the Victory Column is the 18th-century, late-Rococo **Bellevue Palace.** Formerly a Nazi VIP guest house, it's now the residence of the federal president (whose power is mostly ceremonial). If the flag's out, he's in.

➲ Driving along the Spree River, look left for the next sights: This park area was a residential district before World War II. Now it's filled with the buildings of the **national government.** The huge brick "brown snake" complex was built to house government workers—but it didn't sell, so now its apartments are available to anyone. A metal Henry Moore sculpture entitled *Butterfly* floats in front of the slope-roofed House of World Cultures (Berliners have nicknamed this building "the pregnant oyster"). The modern tower (next on left) is a carillon with 68 bells (from 1987).

❷ Leap out at the Platz der Republik stop. (While you could continue on bus #100, it's better on foot from here.) Through the trees on the left you'll see Germany's new and sprawling **Chancellory.** Started during the more imperial rule of Helmut Kohl, it's now considered overly grand. The big open space is the **Platz der Republik,** where the Victory Column stood until Hitler moved it. The Hauptbahnhof (Berlin's vast new train station, marked by its tall tower with the *DB* sign) is across the field between the Chancellory and the Reichstag. Watch your step—excavators found a 250-pound, undetonated American bomb here.

❷ Just down the street stands an old building with a new dome...the **Reichstag.**

SIGHTS

Eastern Berlin
I've arranged the following sights in the order of a convenient self-guided orientation walk, picking up where my "Do-It-Yourself Orientation Tour" (previous section) leaves off. Allow a comfortable hour for this walk from the Reichstag to Alexanderplatz, including time for lingering (but not museum stops).

Near the Brandenburg Gate
▲▲▲**Reichstag Building**—The parliament building—the heart of German democracy—has a short but complicated and emotional

history. When it was inaugurated in the 1890s, the last emperor, Kaiser Wilhelm II, disdainfully called it the "house for chatting." It was from here that the German Republic was proclaimed in 1918. In 1933, this symbol of democracy nearly burned down. While the Nazis blamed a Communist plot, some believe that Hitler himself (who needed what we'd call today a "new Pearl Harbor") planned the fire, using it as a handy excuse to frame the Communists and grab power. As World War II drew to a close, Stalin ordered his troops to take the Reichstag from the Nazis by May 1 (the workers' holiday). More than 1,500 Nazis made their last stand here—extending World War II by two days. On April 30, 1945, it fell to the Allies. It was hardly used from 1933 to 1999. For the building's 101st birthday in 1995, the Bulgarian-American artist Christo wrapped it in silvery-gold cloth. It was then wrapped again—in scaffolding, rebuilt by British architect Lord Norman Foster,

Eastern Berlin

- - - FORMER COURSE OF THE WALL

400 YARDS
400 METERS

BERLIN WALL
DOCUMENTATION
CENTER

Eberswalder
Strasse
PANZIGER.

BERNAUER STRASSE

PRENZLAUER
BERG

Bernauer
Str.

Nordbahnhof

Zinn.-
Str.

NATURAL HIST.
MUSEUM

INVALIDEN-

Senefelder-
platz

Rosenthaler
Platz

Rosa-Lux.-
Platz

Weinmeister

TOR- STRASSE

TO
HAUPT BAHNHOF
& BAHNHOF ZOO

Oranienburger
Tor

Oranienburger
Str.

REIN-
HARDT.

New
SYNAGOGUE

MUSEUM
ISLAND

Hack.
Markt

ALEXANDER-
PLATZ

Alexander-
platz

KARL-
MARX-
ALLEE

Friedrichstrasse

SPREE

MITTE

KARL LIEB.-STR.

REICHSTAG

Unter den
Linden

UNTER DEN
LINDEN

STR. DES
17 JUNI

RATHAUS-

GERTRAUD.

STRAL.

RIVER

Jann.
brücke

BRANDENBURG
GATE

FRANZ.
STR.

Franz.str.

GENDARMENMARKT

Mark.
Museum

EASTSIDE
GALLERY

MEMORIAL TO
MURDERED
JEWS OF
EUROPE

Mohren-
Str.

Stadtmitte

LEIPZIGER

Spittel-
markt

KÖPEN.

Heinrich-
Heine-Str.

POTSDAMER

Potsdamer
Platz

ZIMMERSTR.

MUSEUM OF THE WALL
AT CHECKPOINT CHARLIE

JAKOBI-

POTSDAMER
PLATZ

TOPOGRAPHY
OF TERROR

KOCH-

Kochstr.

ALTE

RITTER -

ORANIENSTR.

Moritzpl.

SCHÖNE-
BERG

Anhalter
Bahnhof

STRESSE

STRASSE

JEWISH
MUSEUM
BERLIN

HEINE-

STR.

LANDWEHR

CANAL

GITSCHINER - STRASSE

Prinzenstr.

KREUZBERG

Kottbusser
Tor

U U-BAHN STN.
S S-BAHN STN.

DCH

and turned into the new parliamentary home of the Bundestag (Germany's lower house). To many Germans, the proud resurrection of the Reichstag symbolizes the end of a terrible chapter in German history.

The **glass cupola** rises 155 feet above the ground. Its two sloped ramps spiral 755 feet to the top for a grand view. Inside the dome, a cone of 360 mirrors reflects natural light into the legislative chamber below. Lit from inside at night, this gives Berlin a memorable nightlight. The environmentally friendly cone also helps with air circulation, drawing hot air out of the legislative chamber and pulling in cool air from below.

Cost, Hours, Location: Free, daily 8:00–24:00, last entry at 22:00, most crowded 10:00–16:00 (wait in line to go up—good street musicians, metal detectors, no big luggage allowed, some hour-long English tours when parliament is not sitting). Platz der Republik 1, S- or U-Bahn: Friedrichstrasse or Unter den Linden, tel. 030/2273-2152, www.bundestag.de.

Crowd-Beating Tips: Berlin is now Germany's biggest tourist attraction. Lines at the Reichstag can be terrible. If possible, visit before 9:00 or after 21:00. Pick up the English-language flier just before the security checkpoint to have something to read as you wait. The skip-the-line entrance is under the grand front porch on the right. If you're here with a child (younger than 8 years old) or a frail person, or have reservations for the Dachgarten rooftop restaurant, you can get in here without a wait. To reserve at the restaurant, call 030/2262-9933 (€58 three-course meals, lunch from €15, dinner from €20, daily 9:30–16:30 & 18:30–24:00).

❷ Self-Guided Tour: As you approach the building, look above the door, surrounded by stone patches from WWII bomb damage, to see the motto and promise: *Dem Deutschen Volke* ("To the German People"). The open, airy lobby towers 100 feet high, with 65-foot-tall colors of the German flag. See-through glass doors show the **central legislative chamber.** The message: There will be no secrets in government. Look inside. The seats are "Reichstag blue," a lilac-blue color designed by the architect to brighten the otherwise gray interior. The German eagle (a.k.a. the "fat hen") spreads his wings behind the podium. Notice the doors marked "Yes," "No," and "Abstain"...the Bundestag's traditional "sheep jump" way of counting votes (for critical and close votes, all 669 members leave and vote by walking through the door of their choice).

Ride the elevator to the base of the glass **dome.** Take time to study the photos and read the circle of captions—an excellent

exhibit telling the Reichstag story. Then study the surrounding architecture: a broken collage of new on old, like Germany's history. Notice the dome's giant and unobtrusive sunscreen that moves as necessary with the sun. Peer down through the skylight to look over the shoulders of the elected representatives at work. For Germans, the best view from here is down—keeping a close eye on their government.

Start at the ramp nearest the elevator

and wind up to the top of the **double ramp.** Take a 360-degree survey of the city as you hike: First, the big park is the **Tiergarten,** the "green lungs of Berlin." Beyond that is the **Teufelsberg,** or "Devil's Hill" (built of rubble from the destroyed city in the late 1940s, and famous during the Cold War as a powerful ear of the West—notice the telecommunications tower on top). Knowing the bombed-out and bulldozed story of their city, locals say, "You have to be suspicious when you see the nice, green park." Find the **Victory Column** (Siegessäule, moved by Hitler in the 1930s from in front of the Reichstag to its present position in the Tiergarten). Next, scenes of the new Berlin spiral into your view—**Potsdamer Platz,** marked by the conical glass tower that houses Sony's European headquarters. The yellow building to the right is the Berlin Philharmonic Concert Hall, marking the museums at the Kulturforum. Continue circling left, and find the green chariot atop the **Brandenburg Gate.** The new **Memorial to the Murdered Jews of Europe** stretches south of the Brandenburg Gate. Next, you'll see **former East Berlin** and the city's next huge construction zone, with a forest of 300-foot-tall skyscrapers in the works. Notice the TV Tower (featuring the Pope's Revenge—explained on page 410), the Berlin Cathedral's massive dome, the red tower of the City Hall, the golden dome of the New Synagogue, and the Reichstag's **Dachgarten Restaurant** (see "Crowd-Beating Tips," previous page).

Follow the train tracks in the distance to the left toward Berlin's huge, new central train station, the **Hauptbahnhof.** Just in front of it, alone in a field, is the Swiss Embassy. It used to be surrounded by buildings, but now it's the only one left. Complete your spin-tour with the blocky **Chancellory,** nicknamed by Berliners "the washing machine." It may look like a pharaoh's tomb, but it's the office and home of Germany's most powerful person, the chancellor (currently Angela Merkel).

Memorial to Politicians Who Opposed Hitler—As you leave the Reichstag, look for the row of slate slabs imbedded in the ground by the park across from the main entry (looks like a fancy slate bicycle rack). This is a memorial to the 96 politicians (the equivalent of our congressmen) who were murdered and persecuted because their politics didn't agree with Chancellor Hitler's. They were part of the weak and ill-fated attempt at post-WWI democracy in Germany, the Weimar Republic. These were the people who could have stopped Hitler... so they became his first victims. Each slate slab remembers one man—his name, party (mostly

The Berlin Wall

The 100-mile "Anti-Fascist Protective Rampart," as it was called by the East German government, was erected almost overnight in 1961 to stop the outward flow of people (three million leaked out between 1949 and 1961). The 13-foot-high Wall *(Mauer)* had a 16-foot tank ditch, a no-man's-land (or "death strip") that was 30 to 160 feet wide, and 300 sentry towers. During its 28 years, border guards fired 1,693 times and made 3,221 arrests, and there were 5,043 documented successful escapes (565 of these were East German guards).

The carnival atmosphere of those first years after the Wall fell is gone, but hawkers still sell "authentic" pieces of the Wall, flags of the DDR (East Germany), and military paraphernalia to gawking tourists. When it fell, the Wall was literally carried away by the euphoria. What managed to survive has been nearly devoured by a decade of persistent "Wall-peckers."

Americans—the Cold War victors—have the biggest appetite for Wall-related sights, and a few bits and pieces remain for us to seek out. Berlin's single best Wall-related sight is the Museum of the Wall at Checkpoint Charlie (see page 413). Actual stretches of the Wall still standing include the short section at Zimmerstrasse/Wilhelmstrasse (near the Topography of Terror exhibit; see page 414), the longer East Side Gallery (near the Ostbahnhof; see page 416), and at the Berlin Wall Documentation Center along Bernauer Strasse (near S-Bahn: Nordbahnhof; see page 419).

KPD—Communists, and SPD—Social Democrats), and date and location of death—generally in concentration camps. (*KZ* stands for "concentration camp.") They are honored here because it's in front of the building in which they worked.

To the Brandenburg Gate: Let's continue our walk and cross what was the Berlin Wall. Leaving the Reichstag, return to the busy road and walk around the building. At the rear of the building (across the street, at the edge of the park) is a small memorial to some of the East Berliners who died trying to cross the Wall. Look at the faces of these exceptionally free spirits. The Wall was built on August 13, 1961. Of these people—many of whom died within months of the wall's construction—most died trying to swim the river to freedom. In the park just behind this memorial,

Berlin

another memorial is planned. It will remember the Roma (Gypsy) victims of the Holocaust. (The Roma, as disdained by the Nazis as the Jews were, lost the same percentage of their population to Hitler.)

The Brandenburg Gate is ahead. Stay on the park side of the street for a better view of the gate. The new road construction is an American taxpayer–funded project. Because the US Embassy needs a buffer zone from traffic for security concerns, the road was moved back, and was replaced by a bigger pedestrian zone.

As you cross at the light, notice the double row of **cobblestones**—it goes around the city, marking where the Wall used to stand. (You could go directly to the Jewish memorial from here, but we'll go through the Brandenburg Gate first, then reach the memorial through Pariser Platz.)

▲▲**Brandenburg Gate (Brandenburger Tor)**—The historic Brandenburg Gate (1791) was the grandest, and is the last survivor, of 14 gates in Berlin's old city wall (this one led to the neighboring region of Brandenburg). The gate was the symbol of Prussian Berlin...and later the symbol of a divided Berlin. It's crowned by a majestic four-horse chariot with the Goddess of Peace at the reins. Napoleon took this statue to the Louvre in Paris in 1806. After the Prussians defeated Napoleon and got it back (1813), she was renamed the Goddess of Victory.

The gate sat unused, part of a sad circle dance called the Wall, for more than 25 years. Now postcards all over town show the ecstatic day—November 9, 1989—when the world enjoyed the sight of happy Berliners jamming the gate like flowers on a parade float. Pause a minute and think about struggles for freedom—past and present. (There's actually a special room built into the gate for this purpose—see the sidebar.) Around the gate, look at the information boards with pictures of how much this area changed throughout the 20th century. The latest chapter: The shiny white gate was completely restored in 2002 (but you can still see faint patches marking war damage). The TI within the gate is open daily (April–Oct 9:30–18:00, Nov–March 10:00–18:00, S-Bahn: Unter den Linden).

The Brandenburg Gate, the center of old Berlin, sits on a major boulevard running east to west through Berlin. The western segment, called Strasse des 17 Juni (named for a workers' uprising against the DDR government in 1953), stretches for four miles from the Brandenburg Gate and Victory Column to the Olympic

The Brandenburg Gate, Arch of Peace

Two hundred years ago, the Brandenburg Gate was designed as an arch of peace, crowned by the Goddess of Peace and showing Mars sheathing his sword. The Nazis misused it as a gate of triumph and aggression. Today a Room of Silence is dedicated to the peaceful message of the original Brandenburg Gate (daily 11:00–18:00). As you consider the history of Berlin in this room—which is carefully not dedicated to any particular religion—you may be inspired to read the prayer of the United Nations:

"Oh Lord, our planet Earth is only a small star in space. It is our duty to transform it into a planet whose creatures are no longer tormented by war, hunger, and fear, no longer senselessly divided by race, color, and ideology. Give us courage and strength to begin this task today so that our children and our children's children shall one day carry the name of man with pride."

Stadium. But we'll follow this city axis in the opposite direction, east, walking along what is known as Unter den Linden—into the core of old imperial Berlin and past what was once the palace of the Hohenzollern family who ruled Prussia and then Germany. The palace—the reason for just about all you'll see—is a phantom sight, long gone (though the facade—which we'll see later on this walk—is now being rebuilt). Alexanderplatz, which marks the end of this walk, is near the base of the giant TV Tower hovering in the distance.

Ponder the fact that you're standing in what was the so-called "death strip." Now cross through the gate, into...

▲**Pariser Platz**—"Paris Square," so named after the Prussians defeated Napoleon in 1813, was once filled with important government buildings—all bombed to smithereens in World War II. For decades, it was an unrecognizable, deserted no-man's-land. But now, sparkling new banks, embassies (the French Embassy rebuilt where it was before WWII), a palace of coffee (Starbucks), the small Kennedys Museum (described later), and a swanky hotel have filled in the void. The winners of World War II got prime real estate: The American, French, British, and Soviet (now Russian) embassies are all on or near this square.

Face the gate and look to your left. The **US Embassy** is slated to move back here when this building is completed in 2008. This new embassy has been controversial: For safety's sake, Uncle Sam wanted it away from other buildings, but the Germans preferred it in its original location. A compromise was reached, building the embassy by the gate—but routing roads farther from it (at the expense of American taxpayers) to reduce the security risk. Throughout the world, American embassies are the most fortified buildings in town. Taking security one step further, plans are for the US Embassy in Berlin to be reached by a tunnel that visitors will enter from the park across the big street opposite the Brandenburg Gate.

Just to the left, the **DZ Bank building** is by Frank Gehry, the unconventional American architect famous for Bilbao's organic Guggenheim Museum, Prague's Dancing House, Seattle's Experience Music Project, Chicago's Millennium Park, and Los Angeles' Walt Disney Concert Hall. Gehry fans might be surprised at the DZ Bank building's low profile. Structures on Pariser Platz are expected to be bland so as not to draw attention away from the Brandenburg Gate. (The glassy facade of the Academy of Arts, next to Gehry's building, is controversial for that very reason.) For your fix of the good old Gehry, step into the lobby and check out its undulating interior. It's a fish—and you feel like you're both inside and outside of it. Gehry's vision is explained on a nearby plaque.

The **Academy of Arts** (Akademie der Kunst), with its notorious glass facade, is next door. Its doors lead to a mall (daily 10:00–22:00), which leads directly to the vast...

▲▲**Memorial to the Murdered Jews of Europe (Denkmal für die Ermordeten Juden Europas)**—The new Holocaust memorial, consisting of 2,711 gravestone-like pillars and completed in 2005,

is an essential stop for any visit to Berlin. This is the first formal German government-sponsored Holocaust memorial. Jewish-American architect Peter Eisenman won the competition for the commission (and built it on time and on budget—€27 million). It's controversial for the focus—just Jews. The government promises to make memorials to the other groups targeted by Hitler.

The pillars are made of hollow concrete, each chemically coated for easy removal of graffiti. The number of pillars, symbolic of nothing, is simply how many fit on the provided land.

Is it a labyrinth...symbolic cemetery...intentionally disorienting? The meaning is entirely up to the visitor to derive. The idea is for you to spend time pondering this horrible chapter in human history.

The pondering takes place under the sky. For the learning, you go under the field of concrete pillars to the state-of-the-art information center (there may be a short line because visitors must go through a security check). This studies the Nazi system of extermination, humanizes the victims, traces stories of individual families and collects vivid personal accounts, and lists 200 different places of genocide (all well-explained in English, free, Tue–Sun 10:00–20:00, closed Mon, last entry 45 min before closing, S-Bahn: Unter den Linden or Potsdamer Platz, tel. 030/2639-4336, www.stiftung-denkmal.de). The €3 audioguide augments the experience.

The location—where the Wall once stood—is coincidental. It's just a place where lots of people will experience it. Nazi propagandist Joseph Goebbels' bunker was discovered during the work and left buried under the northeast corner of the memorial. Hitler's bunker is just 200 yards away, under a nondescript parking lot. Such Nazi sites are intentionally left hidden to discourage neo-Nazi elements from creating a shrine.

Now backtrack to Pariser Platz (through the yellow building). Across the square, consider dropping into...

Kennedys Museum—This crisp new private enterprise facing the Brandenburg Gate recalls Kennedy's Germany trip in 1963, with great photos and video clips as well as a photographic shrine to the Kennedy clan in America. It's a small, overpriced, yet delightful experience with interesting mementos—such as JFK's notes with the phonetic "ish bin ein Bear lee ner." Jacqueline Kennedy commented on how strange it was that this was her husband's most quotable quote (€7, €3.50 to a broad array of visitors—dream up a discount and ask for it, daily 10:00–18:00, Pariser Platz 4a, tel. 030/2065-3570).

Leave Pariser Platz and begin strolling...

▲▲Along Unter den Linden

Unter den Linden is the heart of former East Berlin. In Berlin's good old days, Unter den Linden was one of Europe's grand boulevards. In the 15th century, this carriageway led from the palace to the hunting grounds (today's big Tiergarten). In the 17th century, Hohenzollern princes and princesses moved in and built their palaces here so they could be near the Prussian emperor.

Named centuries ago for its thousand linden trees, this was the most elegant street of Prussian Berlin before Hitler's time, and the main drag of East Berlin after his reign. Hitler replaced the venerable trees—many 250 years old—with Nazi flags. Popular discontent actually drove him to replant linden trees. Today, Unter den Linden is no longer a depressing Cold War cul-de-sac, and its pre-Hitler strolling café ambience is returning.

As you walk toward the giant TV Tower, the big building you see jutting out into the street on your right is the **Hotel Adlon.**

Berlin

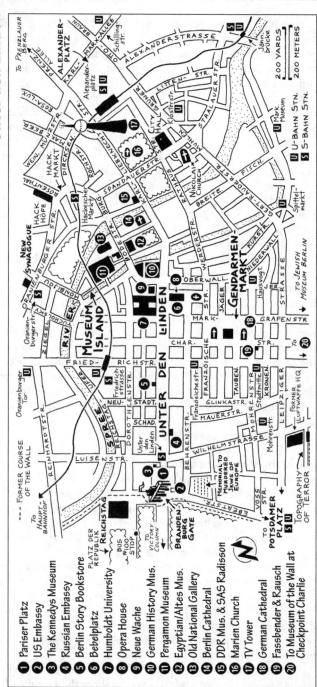

Unter den Linden

1 Pariser Platz
2 US Embassy
3 The Kennedys Museum
4 Russian Embassy
5 Berlin Story Bookstore
6 Bebelplatz
7 Humboldt University
8 Opera House
9 Neue Wache
10 German History Mus.
11 Pergamon Museum
12 Egyptian/Altes Mus.
13 Old National Gallery
14 Berlin Cathedral
15 DDR Mus. & SAS Radisson
16 Marien Church
17 TV Tower
18 German Cathedral
19 Fassbender & Rausch
20 To Museum of the Wall at
   Checkpoint Charlie

Berlin

It hosted such notables as Charlie Chaplin, Albert Einstein, and Greta Garbo. This was where Garbo said, "I want to be alone," during the filming of *Grand Hotel*. And, perhaps fresher in your memory, this is where Michael Jackson shocked millions by dangling his little baby over the railing (second balcony up, center of facade). Destroyed by Russians just after World War II, the grand Adlon was rebuilt in 1996. See how far you can get inside.

Descend into the Unter den Linden S-Bahn station ahead of you. It's one of Berlin's former **ghost subway stations.** During the Cold War, most underground train tunnels were simply blocked at the border. But a few Western lines looped through the East. To make a little hard Western cash, the Eastern government rented the use of these tracks to the West, but the stations (which happened to be in East Berlin) were strictly off-limits. For 28 years, the stations were unused, as Western trains slowly passed through, seeing only eerie DDR (East German) guards and lots of cobwebs. Literally within days of the fall of the Wall, these stations were reopened, and today they are a time warp (looking essentially as they did when built in 1931, with dreary old green tiles and original signage). Walk along the track (the walls are lined with historic photos of the Reichstag through the ages) and exit on the other side, following signs to *Russische Botschaft*...the Russian Embassy.

The **Russian Embassy** was the first big postwar building project in East Berlin. It's built in the powerful, simplified, Neoclassical style Stalin liked. While not as important now as it was a few years ago, it's immense as ever. It flies the Russian white, blue, and red. Find the hammer-and-sickle motif decorating the window frames—a reminder of the days when this was the USSR embassy.

Continuing past the Aeroflot airline offices, look across Glinkastrasse to the right to see the back of the **Komische Oper** (Comic Opera; program and view of ornate interior posted in window). While the exterior is ugly, the fine old theater interior—amazingly missed by WWII bombs—survives.

Across from Aeroflot is **Neustadtische Kirchstrasse.** This street is a commercial wasteland—the fate of any street

unlucky enough to host the US Embassy. While cars are *verboten*, pedestrians are welcome to wander through. When the US Ambassador moves into his impressive new digs by the Brandenburg Gate in 2008, this street will spring back to life.

Back on the main drag, next to Einstein Café (at #40),

is a great bookstore, **Berlin Story.** In addition to a wide range of English-language books, this shop has a free museum (with a model of 1930s Unter den Linden) and a 25-minute English film about the history of Berlin (daily 10:00–19:00; for more details, see page 383). This is also a good opportunity to pick up some nostalgic knickknacks from the Cold War. The West lost no time in consuming the East; consequently, some are feeling a wave of nostalgia—or *Ostalgie*—for the old days of East Berlin. In recent local elections, nearly half of East Berlin's voters—and 6 percent of West Berliners—voted for the old Communist Party.

One symbol of that era has been given a reprieve. As you continue to Friedrichstrasse, look at the DDR-style pedestrian lights, and you'll realize that someone had a sense of humor back then. The perky red and green men—*Ampelmännchen*—were under threat of replacement by the far less jaunty Western signs. Fortunately, the DDR signals will be kept after all.

At **Friedrichstrasse,** look right. Before the war, the Unter den Linden/Friedrichstrasse intersection was the heart of Berlin. In the 1920s, Berlin was famous for its anything-goes love of life. This was the cabaret drag, a springboard to stardom for young and vampy entertainers like Marlene Dietrich. (Born in 1901, Dietrich starred in the first German "talkie" and then headed straight to Hollywood.) Over the last few years, this boulevard—lined with super department stores (such as Galeries Lafayette) and big-time hotels (such as the Hilton and Regent)—has slowly begun to replace Ku'damm as the grand commerce and café boulevard of Berlin. (More recently, the West is retaliating with some new stores of its own.) Across from Galeries Lafayette is American Express (handy for any train-ticket needs—see page 384). Consider detouring to Galeries Lafayette, with its cool marble and glass waste-of-space interior (Mon–Sat 9:30–20:00, closed Sun; belly up to its amazing ground-floor viewpoint, or have lunch in its basement cafeteria—see page 442).

If you continued down Friedrichstrasse, you'd wind up at the sights listed in "South of Unter den Linden," on page 411—including the Museum of the Wall at Checkpoint Charlie (a 10-min walk from here). But for now, continue along Unter den Linden. You'll notice big, colorful **water pipes** around here, and throughout Berlin. As long as the city remains a big construction zone, it will be laced with these drainage pipes—key to any building project. Berlin's high water table means any new basement comes with lots of pumping out. The VW Automobil Forum shows off the latest models from the many car companies owned by VW (free, corner of Friedrichstrasse and Unter den Linden, VW art gallery in the basement).

Continue down Unter den Linden a few more blocks, past the

large equestrian statue of Frederick II ("the Great"), and turn right into the square called **Bebelplatz.** Stand on the glass window in the center.

Frederick the Great—who ruled from 1740 to 1786—established Prussia as a military power. This square was the center of the "new Rome" Frederick envisioned. His grand palace was just down the street (explained below).

Look down through the glass you're standing on (center of Bebelplatz): The room of empty bookshelves is a memorial to the notorious Nazi **book burning.** It was on this square in 1933 that staff and students from the university threw 20,000 newly forbidden books (like Einstein's) into a huge bonfire on the orders of the Nazi propaganda minister Joseph Goebbels. A memorial plaque nearby reminds us of the prophetic quote by the German Jewish poet Heinrich Heine. In 1820, he said, "When you start by burning books, you'll end by burning people." A century later, his books were among those that went up in flames on this spot.

Bebelplatz is bounded by great buildings. Survey it counterclockwise:

Humboldt University, across Unter den Linden, was one of Europe's greatest. Marx and Lenin (not the brothers or the sisters) studied here, as did the Grimms (both brothers) and more than two dozen Nobel Prize winners. Einstein, who was Jewish, taught here until taking a spot at Princeton in 1932 (smart guy).

The former **state library** is where Vladimir Lenin studied during much of his exile from Russia. If you climb to the second floor of the library and go through the door opposite the stairs, you'll see a 1968 vintage stained-glass window depicting Lenin's life's work with almost biblical reverence. On the ground floor is Tim's Canadian Deli, a great little café with light food, student prices, and garden seating (€2 plates, Mon–Sat 7:00–20:00, closed Sun, easy WC).

The **German State Opera** was bombed in 1941, rebuilt to bolster morale and to celebrate its centennial in 1943, and bombed again in 1945.

The round, Catholic **St. Hedwig's Church**—nicknamed the "upside-down teacup"—was built to placate the subjects of Catholic lands Frederick added to his empire. (Step inside to see the cheesy DDR government renovation.)

Continue down Unter den Linden. The next square on your right holds the **Opera House.** The Opernpalais, preening with fancy prewar elegance, hosts the pricey Operncafé. With the best desserts and the longest dessert bar in Europe, it's popular with Berliners for their *Kaffee und Kuchen* (see page 441).

On the university side, the Greek temple-like building set in the small, chestnut tree–filled park is the **Neue Wache** (the

emperor's "New Guardhouse," from 1816). When the Wall fell, this memorial to the victims of fascism was transformed into a new national memorial. Look inside, where a replica of the Käthe Kollwitz statue, *Mother with Her Dead Son,* is surrounded by thought-provoking silence. This marks the tombs of Germany's unknown soldier and the unknown concentration camp victim. The inscription in front reads, "To the victims of war and tyranny." Read the entire statement in English (on wall, left of entrance). The memorial, open to the sky, incorporates the elements—sunshine, rain, snow—falling on this modern-day *pietà*.

After the Neue Wache, the next building you'll see is Berlin's pink-yet-formidable Zeughaus, or arsenal. Dating from 1695, it's considered the oldest building on the boulevard and now houses the...

▲▲▲**German History Museum (Deutsches Historisches Museum)**—This fantastic museum is a two-part affair: the pink former Prussian arsenal building, and the I. M. Pei–designed annex. The main building (fronting Unter den Linden) houses the permanent collection. Two huge rectangular floors are packed with more than 8,000 artifacts telling the story of Germany—making this the top history museum in town. Historical objects, photographs, and models are intermingled with multimedia stations to help put everything in context. The first floor traces German history from 1 B.C. to 1918, with exhibits on early cultures, the Middle Ages, Reformation, Thirty Years' War, German Empire, and First World War. Exhibits on the ground floor continue with the Weimar Republic, Nazism, World War II, Allied occupation, and a divided Germany, wrapping up with reunification and a quick look at Germany today (€5, daily 10:00–18:00, excellent €3 audio-guide has six hours of info for you to choose from, tel. 030/2030-4751, www.dhm.de).

For architects, the big attraction is the Pei annex behind the history museum, which complements the museum with often-fascinating temporary history exhibits. From the old building (with the Pei glass canopy over its courtyard), take a tunnel to the new wing, emerging under a striking glass spiral staircase that unites four floors with surprising views and lots of light. It's here that you'll experience why Pei—famous for his glass pyramid at Paris' Louvre—is called the "perfector of classical modernism," "master of light," and a magician of uniting historical buildings with new ones. (If the museum is closed, or you don't have a ticket, venture down the street—Hinter dem Giesshaus—to the left of the museum to see the Pei annex from the outside.)

Back on Unter den Linden, head toward the **Spree River.** Just before the bridge, wander left along the canal through a tiny but colorful arts-and-crafts market (weekends only; a larger flea market is just outside the Pergamon Museum). Canal tour boats leave from here (€7, 1 hour, departures on the half-hour, tour in German only but so lame it hardly matters). Continue up the riverbank two blocks and cross the Spree at the footbridge, which takes you to...

Museum Island (Museumsinsel)

This island, home of Berlin's first museum, is undergoing a formidable renovation. The grand vision is to integrate the city's major museums with a grand entry and tunnels that will lace the complex together (intended completion date: 2015). The complex was originally built in about 1871, when Germany was newly unified as one nation—and when Berlin was calling itself the "Athens on the Spree River." Today, its imposing Neoclassical buildings host four grand museums—the Pergamon (classical antiquities), the Altes Museum (housing the Egyptian Museum, with the bust of Queen Nefertiti), the Old National Gallery (19th-century German Romantic painting), and the Bode Museum (European statuary through the ages, coins, and Byzantine art). The museums function as one with the same prices, phone number, and a €12 combo-ticket that's far better than buying individual €8 entries (all are also included in the city's €15 Museumspass; Pergamon and Altes Museums open daily 10:00–18:00, Thu until 22:00, free on Thu after 18:00; Old National Gallery and Bode Museum open same hours except closed Mon, tel. 030/2090-5577, www.museumsinsel -berlin.de) The nearest S-Bahn station is Hackescher Markt.

Consider visiting any of these museums, and other Museum Island attractions (mentioned later), before continuing our walk. Once you're finished, skip over to "Museum Island to Alexanderplatz," page 409, to resume the self-guided tour.

▲▲**Pergamon Museum**—This world-class museum, part of Berlin's Collection of Classical Antiquities (Antikensammlung), stars the fantastic Pergamon Altar. From a second-century B.C. Greek temple, the altar shows the Greeks under Zeus and Athena beating the giants in a dramatic pig pile of mythological mayhem. Check out the action spilling onto the stairs. The Babylonian Ishtar Gate (glazed blue tiles from the sixth century B.C.) and many ancient Greek and Mesopotamian treasures are also impressive. The superb audioguide (free with admission, but €4 during free Thu extended hours) covers the museum's highlights and broadens your experience by introducing you to wonders you might not otherwise notice.

▲▲**Egyptian Museum (Ägyptisches Museum)/Altes Museum**—
Showing off one of the world's top collections of Egyptian art, this
wonderfully presented new museum fills the second floor of Berlin's
Altes Museum (Old Museum), facing the grassy Lustgarten park.

The curator welcomes you on the included audioguide and
encourages a broader approach to the museum than just seeing its
claim to fame, the bust of Queen Nefertiti (described next). The
fine audioguide celebrates new knowledge about ancient Egyptian
civilization and offers fascinating insights into workaday Egyptian
life as it describes the vivid papyrus collection, slice-of-life artifacts, and dreamy wax portraits decorating mummy cases.

But let's face it: The main reason to visit is to enjoy one of the
great thrills in art appreciation—gazing into the still-young-and-

beautiful face of 3,000-year-old Queen
Nefertiti, the wife of King Akhenaton.
This bust of Queen Nefertiti (c. 1340
B.C.) is the most famous piece of
Egyptian art in Europe. Discovered in
1912, Nefertiti—with all the right beauty
marks: long neck, symmetrical face,
and just the right makeup—is called
"Berlin's most beautiful woman." The
bust never left its studio, but served as
a master model for all other portraits of
the queen. (That's probably why the left
eye was never inlaid.) Buried for more
than 3,000 years, she was found in the early 1900s by a German
team who, by agreement with the Egyptian government, got to
take home any workshop models they found. Although this bust
is not particularly representative of Egyptian art in general, it has
become a symbol for Egyptian art by popular acclaim. (Note that
the Egyptian Museum is destined to move in a few years to the
island's fifth museum, the New Museum.)

Old National Gallery (Alte Nationalgalerie)—This gallery,
behind the Egyptian Museum/Altes Museum, designed to look
like a Greek temple, shows mostly paintings—three floors with
French and German Impressionists on the second, and Romantic
German paintings (which I find most interesting) on the top
(audioguide is free).

Lustgarten—For 300 years, the island's big central square has
flip-flopped between being a military parade ground and a people-
friendly park, depending upon the political tenor of the time. In
1999, it was made into a park again (read the history posted in
corner opposite church). On a sunny day, it's packed with relaxing
locals and is one of Berlin's most enjoyable public spaces.

Berlin Cathedral (Berliner Dom)—This century-old church towers over Museum Island (€5 includes access to dome gallery,  not covered by Museum Island ticket, Mon–Sat 9:00–20:00, Sun 12:00–20:00, until 19:00 in winter, www.berliner-dom.de; many organ concerts—generally Sat at 20:00, tickets about €10 always available at the door, tel. 030/2026-9136). Inside, the great reformers (Luther, Calvin, and company) stand around the brilliantly restored dome like stern saints guarding their theology. Frederick I rests in an ornate tomb (right transept, near entrance to dome). The 270-step climb to the outdoor dome gallery is tough, but offers pleasant, breezy views of the city at the finish line (last entry 45 min before closing). The crypt downstairs is not worth a look.

Across Unter den Linden is a construction site that once held the decrepit **Palace of the Republic**—formerly East Berlin's parliament building/futuristic entertainment complex, and a symbol of the communist days. Much of Frederick the Great's earlier palace actually survived World War II, but was replaced by the communists with this blocky Soviet-style building. The landmark building fell into disrepair after reunification, and was eventually dismantled in 2007. After long debate, the German Parliament decided to construct a building which will have the rebuilt facade of the old palace. Investing a huge sum, they will create a huge new public venue to be filled with museums, shops, galleries, and concert halls.

Museum Island to Alexanderplatz

Continue walking down Unter den Linden. Before crossing the bridge (and leaving Museum Island), look right. The pointy twin spires of the 13th-century Nikolai Church mark the center of medieval Berlin. This Nikolaiviertel (*Viertel* means "quarter" or "district") was restored by the DDR and was trendy in the last years of socialism. Today, it's a lively-at-night riverside restaurant district.

As you cross the bridge, look left in the distance to see the gilded **New Synagogue dome,** rebuilt after WWII bombing (see page 416). Across the river to the left of the bridge is the giant SAS Radisson Hotel and shopping center, with a huge aquarium in the center. The elevator goes right through the middle of an undersea world (you can see it from the unforgettable Radisson hotel lobby—tuck in your shirt and walk past the guards with the confidence of a guest who's sleeping there). Here in the center of the old communist capital, it seems that capitalism has settled in with a spirited vengeance.

At the river side of the SAS Radisson Hotel, the little **DDR Museum** offers an interesting peek at a humbler life before capitalism took hold. You'll crawl through a Trabant car, see a DDR kitchen, and be surrounded by former DDR residents reminiscing about the bad old days (€5 admission steep for what it is, daily 10:00–22:00, Karl-Liebknecht Strasse 1, tel. 030/847-123-731).

In the park immediately across the street (a big jaywalk from the Radisson) are grandfatherly statues of Marx and Engels (nicknamed by locals "the old pensioners"). Surrounding them are stainless-steel monoliths with evocative photos that show the struggles of the workers of the world.

Walk toward **Marien Church** (from 1270, an artist's rendering helps you follow the interesting but very faded old Dance of Death mural which wraps around the narthex inside the door), just left of the base of the TV Tower. The big, redbrick building past the trees on the right is the **City Hall,** built after the revolution of 1848 and arguably the first democratic building in the city.

The 1,200-foot-tall **TV Tower** (Fernsehturm) offers a fine view from halfway up (€8.50, daily March–Oct 9:00–24:00, Nov–Feb 10:00–24:00). The tower offers a handy city orientation and an interesting view of the flat, red-roofed sprawl of Berlin—including a peek inside the city's many courtyards *(Höfe)*. Consider a kitschy trip to the observation deck for the view and lunch in its revolving restaurant (mediocre food, €12 plates, horrible lounge music, reservations smart for dinner, tel. 030/242-3333). It's very retro and somewhat trendy these days, so expect a line for the elevator. Built (with Swedish know-how) in 1969, the tower was meant to show the power of the atheistic state at a time when DDR leaders were having the crosses removed from church domes and spires. But when the sun shined on their tower—the greatest spire in East Berlin—a huge cross was reflected on the mirrored ball. Cynics called it "The Pope's Revenge." East Berliners dubbed the tower the "Big Asparagus." They joked that if it fell over, they'd have an elevator to the West.

Farther east, pass under the train tracks into **Alexanderplatz.** This area—especially the Kaufhof department store—was the commercial pride and joy of East Berlin. Today, it's still a landmark, with a major U- and S-Bahn station.

Our orientation stroll is finished. For a ride through workaday eastern Berlin, with its Lego-hell apartments (dreary even with their new facelifts), hop back on bus #100 from here. It loops five minutes to the end of the line and then, after a couple minutes' break, heads on back. (This bus retraces your route, finishing at Bahnhof Zoo.) Or consider extending this foray into eastern Berlin to...

Karl-Marx-Allee

The buildings along Karl-Marx-Allee in East Berlin (just beyond Alexanderplatz) were completely leveled by the Red Army in 1945. As an expression of their adoration to the "great Socialist Father" (the "cult of Stalin" was in full gear), the DDR government decided to rebuild the street better than ever (the USSR provided generous subsidies). They named it Stalinallee. Today, this street, done in the bold "Stalin Gothic" style so common in Moscow in the 1950s, has been restored, renamed after Karl Marx, and lined with "workers' palaces"—providing a rare look at Berlin's communist days. Distances are a bit long for convenient walking, but you can cruise Karl-Marx-Allee by taxi, or ride the U-Bahn to Strausberger Platz and walk to Frankfurter Tor (good information posts along the way). Notice the Social Realist reliefs on the buildings and the lampposts, which incorporate the wings of a phoenix (rising from the ashes) in their design.

The **Café Sibylle,** just beyond the Strausberger Platz U-Bahn station, is a fun spot for a coffee, traditional DDR ice-cream treats, and a look at its free, informal museum that tells the story of the most destroyed street in Berlin. While the humble exhibit is nearly all in German, it's fun to see the ear and half a moustache from what was the largest statue of Stalin in Germany (the centerpiece of the street until 1961) and a few intimate insights into apartment life in a DDR flat. The café is known for its good coffee and *Schwedeneisbecher mit Eierlikor*—an ice-cream sundae with a shot of liquor, popular among those nostalgic for communism (daily 10:00–20:00, Karl-Marx-Allee 72, at intersection with Koppenstrasse, a block from U-Bahn: Strausberger Platz, tel. 030/2935-2203).

Heading out to Karl-Marx-Allee (just beyond the TV Tower), you're likely to notice a giant colorful **mural** decorating a blocky communist-era skyscraper. This was the Ministry of Education, and the mural is a tile mosaic trumpeting the accomplishments of the DDR's version of "No Child Left Behind."

South of Unter den Linden

The following sights—heavy on Nazi and Wall history—are listed roughly north to south (as you reach them from Unter den Linden).

▲▲**Gendarmenmarkt**—This delightful and historic square is bounded by twin churches, a tasty chocolate shop, and the Berlin Symphony's concert hall (designed by Karl Friedrich Schinkel, the man who put the Neoclassical stamp on Berlin). In summer, it hosts a few outdoor cafés, *Biergarten*s, and sometimes concerts. Wonderfully symmetrical, the square is considered by Berliners to be the finest in town. The name of the square—part French and part German—reminds us that in the 17th century, a fifth of all Berliners were French émigrés, Protestant Huguenots fleeing Catholic France. Back then, tolerant Berlin was a magnet for the persecuted. The émigrés vitalized the city with new ideas and know-how.

The German Cathedral (described next) on the square has an exhibit worthwhile for history buffs. The French Cathedral (Französischer Dom) offers a humble museum on the Huguenots (€2, Tue–Sun 12:00–17:00, closed Mon, U-Bahn: Französische Strasse or Stadtmitte). Fun fact: Neither of these churches are true cathedrals, as they never contained a bishop's throne; their German title of *Dom* (cathedral) is actually a mistranslation from the French word *dôme* (cupola).

▲**German Cathedral (Deutscher Dom)**—This cathedral, bombed flat in the war and rebuilt only in the 1980s, houses the thought-provoking *Milestones, Setbacks, Sidetracks (Wege, Irrwege, Umwege)* exhibit, which traces the history of the German parliamentary system. The parliament-funded exhibit—while light on actual historical artifacts—is well done and more interesting than it sounds. It takes you quickly from the revolutionary days of 1848 to the 1920s, and then more deeply through the tumultuous 20th century. There are no English descriptions, but you can follow the essential, excellent, and free 90-minute English-language audioguide or buy the wonderfully detailed €10 guidebook. If this museum seems to be an attempt by the German government to develop a more sophisticated and educated electorate in the interest of stronger democracy, you're exactly right. Germany knows (from its own troubled history) that a dumbed-down electorate, manipulated by clever spin-meisters and sound-bite media blitzes, is a dangerous thing (free; May–Sept Tue–Sun 10:00–19:00, Oct–April Tue–Sun 10:00–18:00, closed Mon year-round, on Gendarmenmarkt just off Friedrichstrasse, tel. 030/2273-0431).

Fassbender & Rausch, on the corner near the German Cathedral, claims to be Europe's biggest chocolate store. After 150 years of chocolate-making, this family-owned business proudly displays its sweet delights—250 different kinds—on a 55-foot-long buffet. Truffles are sold for about €0.60 each—it's fun to compose a fancy little eight-piece box of your own for about €5 (daily 10:00–20:00, corner of Mohrenstrasse at Charlottenstrasse 60, tel. 030/2045-8440). Upstairs is an elegant hot chocolate café with fine views.

Gendarmenmarkt is buried in what has recently emerged as

Berlin's new "Fifth Avenue" shopping district. For the ultimate in top-end shops, find the corner of Jägerstrasse and Französische Strasse and wander through the Quartier 206 (Mon–Fri 10:30–19:30, Sat 10:00–18:00, closed Sun, www.quartier206.com).

▲▲▲**Museum of the Wall at Checkpoint Charlie (Mauermuseum Haus am Checkpoint Charlie)**—While the famous border checkpoint between the American and Soviet sectors is long gone, its memory is preserved by one of Europe's most interesting, though cluttered, museums. During the Cold War, the House at Checkpoint Charlie stood defiantly—spitting distance from the border guards—showing off all the clever escapes over, under, and through the Wall. Today, while the drama is over and hunks of the Wall stand like victory scalps at its door, the museum still tells a gripping history of the Wall, recounts the many ingenious escape attempts (early years—with a cruder wall—saw more escapes), and includes plenty of video coverage of those heady days when people-power tore down the Wall (€9.50, assemble 10 tourists and get in for €5.50 each, €3 audioguide, discount with WelcomeCard but not covered by Museumspass, cash only, daily 9:00–22:00, U-6 to Kochstrasse or—better from Zoo—U-2 to Stadtmitte, Friedrichstrasse 43–45, tel. 030/253-7250, www.mauermuseum .de). If you're pressed for time, this is a good after-dinner sight. With extra time, consider the "Hear We Go" audioguide about the Wall that takes you outside the museum (€7, 90 min, leave ID as deposit).

▲▲**Checkpoint Charlie Street Scene**—Where Checkpoint Charlie once stood, notice the thought-provoking post with larger-than-life posters of a young American soldier facing east and a young Soviet soldier facing west. The area has become a Cold War freak show. The rebuilt guard station now hosts two actors playing American guards who pose for photos. Across the street is Snack Point Charlie. The old checkpoint was not named for a person, but because it was checkpoint number three—as in Alpha (at the East–West German border, a hundred miles west of here), Bravo (as you enter Berlin proper), and Charlie (the most famous because it was where most of the foreigners would pass). A fine photo exhibit stretches down the street with great English descriptions telling the story of the Wall. While you could get this information from a book, it's poignant to stand here in person and ponder the gripping history of this place. A few yards away (on Zimmerstrasse), a glass panel describes the former checkpoint. From there, a double row of cobbles in Zimmerstrasse traces the former path of the Wall.

Berlin

Hitler and Third Reich Sites

While many come to Berlin to see Hitler sites, these are essentially invisible. The German Resistance Museum is in German only and difficult for the tourist to appreciate (see page 421). The Topography of Terror (SS and Gestapo headquarters) is a fascinating exhibit but—again—only in German, and all that remains of the building is its foundation (see below). (Both museums have helpful audioguides in English.) Hitler's bunker is completely gone (near Potsdamer Platz). Your best bet for "Hitler sites" is to take the Infamous Third Reich Sites walking tour offered by Original Berlin Walks (see "Tours," page 387).

These innocuous cobbles run throughout the city, even through some modern buildings. Follow the cobbles one very long block to Wilhelmstrasse, a surviving stretch of Wall, and the...

Topography of Terror (Topographie des Terrors)—The park behind the Zimmerstrasse/Wilhelmstrasse bit of Wall marks the site of the command center of Hitler's Gestapo and SS. Because of the horrible things planned here, the rubble of these buildings will always be left as rubble. The SS, Hitler's personal bodyguards, grew to become a state-within-a-state, with its talons in every corner of German society. Along an excavated foundation of the building, an exhibit tells the story of National Socialism and its victims in Berlin (free, info booth open daily May–Sept 10:00–20:00, Oct–April 10:00–18:00 or until dark, tel. 030/2548-6703, www.topographie.de). All of the posted information is in German, so the free English-language audioguide is essential (available only until 18:45 in summer).

Across the street (facing the Wall) is the **German Finance Ministry** (Bundesministerium der Finanzen). Formerly the head-quarters of the Nazi Luftwaffe (Air Force), this is the only major Hitler-era government building that survived the war's bombs. The communists used it to house their—no joke—Ministry of Ministries. Walk up Wilhelmstrasse (to the north) to see an entry gate (on your left) that looks much like it did when  Germany occupied nearly all of Europe. On the north side of the building (farther up Wilhelmstrasse, at corner with Leipziger Strasse) is a wonderful example of communist art. The mural, from the 1950s, is classic Social Realism, showing the entire society—

industrial laborers, farm workers, women, and children—all happily singing the same patriotic song. This was the communist ideal. For the reality, look at the ground in the courtyard in front of the mural to see an enlarged photograph from a 1953 uprising here against the communists—quite a contrast.

▲▲▲**Jewish Museum Berlin (Jüdisches Museum Berlin)**—This museum is one of Europe's best Jewish sights. The highly concep-

tual building is a sight in itself, and the museum inside—an overview of the rich culture and history of Europe's Jewish community—is excellent. The Holocaust is appropriately remembered, but it doesn't overwhelm this celebration of Jewish life.

Designed by American architect Daniel Libeskind (who is redeveloping New York City's World Trade Center site), the zinc-walled building's zigzag shape is pierced by voids symbolic of the irreplaceable cultural loss caused by the Holocaust. Enter through the 18th-century Baroque

building next door, then go through an underground tunnel to reach the museum interior.

Before you get to the exhibit, your visit starts with three memorial spaces. Underground, follow the Axis of Exile to a

disorienting slanted garden with 49 pillars. Then the Axis of Holocaust leads to an eerily empty tower shut off from the outside world. A detour near the bottom of the long stairway leads to the "Memory Void," a thought-provoking space of "fallen leaves": heavy metal

faces that you walk on, making un-human noises with each step.

Finally, climb the stairs to the top of the museum, from where you stroll chronologically through the 2,000-year story of Judaism in Germany. The exhibit, on two floors, is engaging. Interactive bits (for example, spell your name in Hebrew) make it lively for kids. English explanations interpret both the exhibits and the design of the very symbolic building. Even though the museum is in a nondescript residential neighborhood (a 10-min walk from the Hallesches Tor U-Bahn station or the Checkpoint Charlie museum), it's well worth the trip (€5, covered by Museumspass, discount with WelcomeCard, daily 10:00–20:00, Mon until 22:00, last entry 1 hour before closing, closed on Jewish holidays, tight security includes bag check and metal detectors; U-Bahn line 1, 6, or 15 to Hallesches Tor, take exit marked *Jüdisches Museum*, exit straight ahead, then turn right on Franz-Klühs-Strasse, museum is 5 min ahead on your left at Lindenstrasse 9; tel. 030/2599-3300, www.jmberlin.de). The museum has a good café/restaurant (€9 daily specials, lunch 12:00–16:00, snacks at other times, tel. 030/2593-9760).

East Side Gallery—The biggest remaining stretch of the Wall is now "the world's longest outdoor art gallery." It stretches for nearly a mile and is covered with murals painted by artists from around the world. The murals are routinely whitewashed so new ones can be painted. This segment of the Wall makes another poignant walk. For a quick look, take the S-Bahn to the Ostbahnhof station (follow signs to *Stralauerplatz* exit; once outside, TV Tower will be to your right; go left and at next corner look to your right—the Wall is across the busy street). The gallery is slowly being consumed by developers. If you walk the entire length of the East Side Gallery, you'll find a small Wall souvenir shop at the end and a bridge crossing the river to a subway station at Schlesisches Tor (in Kreuzberg). The bridge, a fine example of Brandenburg Neo-Gothic brickwork, has a fun neon "rock, paper, scissors" installment poking fun at the futility of the Cold War.

Kreuzberg—This district—once abutting the dreary Wall and inhabited mostly by poor Turkish guest laborers and their families—is still run-down, with graffiti-riddled buildings and plenty of student and Turkish street life. It offers a gritty look at melting-pot Berlin, in a city where original Berliners are as rare as old buildings. Berlin is the fourth-largest Turkish city in the world, and Kreuzberg is its "downtown." But to call it a "little Istanbul" insults the big one. You'll see *Döner Kebab* stands, shops decorated with spray paint, and mothers wrapped in colorful scarves looking like they just got off a donkey in Anatolia. But lately, an influx of immigrants from many other countries has diluted the Turkishness of Kreuzberg. Berliners come here for fun ethnic eateries. For a dose of Kreuzberg without getting your fingers dirty, joyride on bus #129 (catch it near Jewish Museum). For a colorful stroll, take the U-Bahn to Kottbusser Tor and wander—ideally on Tuesday and Friday between 12:00 and 18:00, when the Turkish Market sprawls along the Maybachufer riverbank.

North of Unter den Linden

While there are few major sights to the north of Unter den Linden, this area has some of Berlin's trendiest, most interesting neighborhoods.

▲New Synagogue (Neue Synagogue)—A shiny gilded dome marks the New Synagogue, now a museum and cultural center on Oranienburger Strasse. Only the dome and facade have been restored—a window overlooks the vacant field marking what used to be the synagogue. The largest and finest synagogue in Berlin before World War II, it was desecrated by Nazis on "Crystal Night" (Kristallnacht) in 1938, bombed in 1943, and partially rebuilt in 1990. Inside, past tight security, there's a small but moving exhibit on the Berlin Jewish community through the centuries with some good English descriptions (ground floor and first floor). On its facade, the *Vergesst es nie* message—added by East Berlin Jews in 1966—means "Never forget." East Berlin had only a few hundred Jews, but now that the city is united, the Jewish community numbers about 12,000 (€3; March–Oct Sun–Mon 10:00–20:00, Tue–Thu 10:00–18:00, Fri 10:00–17:00, closed Sat; Nov–Feb Sun–Thu 10:00–18:00, Fri 10:00–14:00, closed Sat; Oranienburger Strasse 28/30, U-Bahn: Oranienburger Tor, tel. 030/8802-8300 and press 1, www.cjudaicum.de).

Cheer things up 50 yards away with every local kid's favorite traditional candy shop—**Bonbonmacherei**—where you can see candy being made the old-fashioned way (at Oranienburger Strasse 32, in another example of a classic Berlin courtyard).

A block from the synagogue, walk 50 yards down Grosse Hamburger Strasse to a little park. This street was known for 200 years as the "street of tolerance" because the Jewish community donated land to Protestants so that they could build a church. Hitler turned it into the "street of death" *(Todes Strasse)*, bulldozing 12,000 graves of the city's oldest Jewish cemetery and turning a Jewish nursing home into a deportation center. With the small but persistent neo-Nazi element still a problem in Berlin, a plain-clothes police officer keeps watch over this park and the Jewish high school nearby.

▲**Oranienburger Strasse**—Berlin is developing so fast, it's impossible to predict what will be "in" next year. The area around Oranienburger Strasse is definitely trendy (but is being challenged by hip Friedrichshain, farther east, and Prenzlauer Berg, described later). While the area immediately around the synagogue is dull, 100 yards away things get colorful. The streets behind Grosse Hamburger Strasse flicker with atmospheric cafés, *Kneipen* (pubs), and art galleries. At night (from about 20:00), techno-prostitutes line Oranienburger Strasse. Prostitution is legal here, but there's a big debate about taxation. Since they don't get unemployment insurance, why should they pay taxes?

Hackescher Markt—This area, in front of the S-Bahn station by the same name, is a great people scene day and night. The brick trestle supporting the train track is another classic example of the city's Brandenburg Neo-Gothic brick work. Most of the brick archways are now filled with hip shops, which have official—and newly

Stolpersteine (Stumbling Stones)

As you wander through the Hackesche Höfe and Oranienburger Strasse neighborhoods—and throughout Germany—
you might stumble over small brass plaques in the sidewalk
called *Stolpersteine*. *Stolpern* literally means "to stumble,"
which is what you are meant to do. These plaques are placed
in front of former homes of Jewish residents who were killed
during World War II. The *Stolpersteine* serve not only to honor
the victims, but also to stimulate thought and discussion on a
daily basis (rather than only during visits to memorial sites).

More than 7,500 of these plaques have been installed
across Germany. They're made of brass so they stay polished
as you walk over them, instead of fading into the sidewalk.
On each plaque is the name of the person who lived in that
spot, and how and where they died. While some Holocaust
memorials formerly used neutral terminology like "perished,"
now they use words like "murdered"—part of the very honest
way in which today's Germans are dealing with their country's
past. Installation of a *Stolperstein* can be sponsored for €95 and
has become popular in schools, where the students research
the memorialized person's life as a class project.

trendy—addresses such as "S-Bahn Arch #9, Hackescher Markt."
Within 100 yards of the S-Bahn station, you'll find Hackesche
Höfe (see below), recommended Turkish and Bavarian restaurants,
walking-tour and pub-crawl departure points, and tram #M1 to
Prenzlauer Berg.

Hackesche Höfe (a block in front of the Hackescher Markt
S-Bahn station) is a series of eight courtyards bunny-hopping
through a wonderfully restored 1907 *Jugendstil* building. Berlin's
apartments are organized like this—courtyard after courtyard
leading off the main roads. This complex is full of trendy restaurants (including a good Turkish place, Hasir—see page 442),
theaters, and cinema (playing movies in their original languages).
This is a wonderful example of how to make huge city blocks livable. Two decades after the Cold War, this area has reached the
final evolution of East Berlin's urban restoration—this is where
Prenzlauer Berg is heading. (These courtyards also serve a useful lesson for visitors: Much of Berlin's charm hides off the street
front.)

▲**Prenzlauer Berg**—Young, in-the-know locals agree that
"Prenzl'berg" is one of Berlin's most colorful neighborhoods
(roughly between Helmholtzplatz and Kollwitzplatz and along
Kastanienallee, U-Bahn: Senefelderplatz and Eberswalder Strasse;
or take the S-Bahn to Hackescher Markt and catch tram #M1

Berlin

north). This part of the city was largely untouched during World War II, but its buildings slowly rotted away under the communists. Since the Wall fell, it's been overrun with laid-back hipsters, energetic young families, and clever entrepreneurs who are breathing life back into its classic old apartment blocks, deserted factories, and long-forgotten breweries. While it's no longer "up-and-coming," but on the road to gentrification, Prenzlauer Berg is a celebration of life and a joy to stroll through. The area feels strangely wholesome and family-friendly, as former ruffians with tattoos, piercings, and an appetite for the cutting-edge life are now responsible young parents. Though it's a few blocks farther out than the neighborhoods described earlier, it's a fun area to explore and have a meal (see page 443) or spend the night (see page 436).

Natural History Museum (Museum für Naturkunde)—This museum is worth a visit just to see the largest dinosaur skeleton ever assembled. While you're there, meet "Bobby" the stuffed ape (€4, Tue–Fri 9:30–17:00, Sat–Sun 10:00–18:00, closed Mon, last entry 30 min before closing, U-Bahn line 6 to Zinnowitzer Strasse, Invalidenstrasse 43, tel. 030/2093-8591, www.museum.hu-berlin.de).

Berlin Wall Documentation Center (Dokumentationszentrum Berliner Mauer)—The last surviving complete "Wall system" (with both sides of its Wall and its no-man's-land, or "death strip," all still intact) is now part of a sober little memorial and "Doku-Center." While it's really directed at German-speakers and far from other sights, it's handy enough to the S-Bahn that any Wall aficionado will find it worth a quick visit. The Documentation Center has a photo gallery and rooftop viewpoint (accessible by elevator), from which you can view the "Wall system." It's poignantly located where a church was destroyed to make way for the Wall; today, a memorial chapel has been built where the church once stood (free, April–Oct Tue–Sun 10:00–18:00, Nov–March until 17:00, closed Mon year-round, Bernauer Strasse 111, tel. 030/464-1030, www.berliner-mauer-dokumentationszentrum.de). Take the S-Bahn to Nordbahnhof and walk 200 yards along Bernauer Strasse, which is still lined with a long chunk of Wall.

Central Berlin

Tiergarten Park and Nearby

Berlin's "Central Park" stretches two miles from Bahnhof Zoo to the Brandenburg Gate.

Victory Column (Siegessäule)—The Tiergarten's centerpiece, the Victory Column, was built to commemorate the Prussian defeat of France in 1870. The pointy-helmeted Germans rubbed it in, decorating the tower with French cannons and paying for it all with francs received as war reparations. The three lower rings

Berlin

Central Berlin

TO ALEXANDER-PLATZ

BRANDENBURG GATE

UNTER DEN LINDEN

Französische Strasse

FRANZÖSISCHE STRASSE

GENDARMEN-MARKT

MOHREN STR.

Unter den Linden

BEHREN STR.

MEMORIAL TO MURDERED JEWS OF EUROPE

WILHELM STR.

Mohrenstr.

Voss STR.

LEIPZIGER STR.

Former LUFTWAFFE HQ

Potsdamer Platz

POTSDAMER PLATZ

MUSEUM OF THE WALL AT CHECKPOINT CHARLIE

ZIMMER. STR.

KOCHSTR.

Kochstr.

FRIEDRICH STR.

To JEWISH MUSEUM BERLIN

NIEDERKIRCHNER STR.

Topography of Terror

STRESEMANNSTR.

BERN. STR.

ANHALTER STR.

SCHÖNEBERGER STR.

Anhalter Bahnhof

TO REICHSTAG

STRASSE DES 17 JUNI

ENTLASTUNGS STR.

TIERGARTEN

MUSICAL INSTRUMENTS MUSEUM

Sony Center

EBERTSTR.

POTSDAMER STRASSE

Mend.-Bartholdy Park

LIBRARY

PIETERSCUFER

CANAL

LANDWEHR CANAL

PHILHARMONIC CONCERT HALL

ARTS + CRAFTS MUSEUM

TIERGARTENSTR.

SIGISMUND STR.

New Natl. Gallery

STAUFFEN. STR.

POTSDAMER STR.

LUTZOWUFER

GEMALDEGALERIE

GERMAN RESISTANCE MEMORIAL REICH-

To VICTORY COLUMN

STRASSE DES

400 YARDS
400 METERS

FORMER COURSE OF THE WALL

U U-BAHN STN.
S S-BAHN STN.
★ KULTURFORUM
--- FORMER COURSE OF THE WALL

commemorate Bismarck's victories. I imagine the statues of Moltke and other German military greats—which lurk in the trees nearby—goose-stepping around the floodlit angel at night. Originally standing at the Reichstag, the immense tower was moved to this position by Hitler in 1938 to complement his anticipated victory parades. Streets leading to the circle are flanked by surviving Nazi guardhouses—built in the bold style that fascists loved. At the memorial's first level, notice how WWII bullets chipped the fine marble columns. Climbing its 285 steps earns you a breathtaking Berlin-wide view and a close-up look at the gilded angel that starred in Wim Wenders' 1987 art-house classic *Wings of Desire* and in the video he directed for U2's *Stay (Faraway, so Close)* (€2.20; April–Sept Mon–Thu 9:30–18:30, Fri–Sun 9:30–19:00; Oct–March daily 9:30–17:30; closes in the rain, WCs for paying guests only, no elevator, bus #100, tel. 030/8639-8560). From the tower, the grand Strasse des 17 Juni leads east to the Brandenburg Gate.

Flea Market—A colorful flea market with great antiques, more than 200 stalls, collector-savvy merchants, and fun German fast-food stands thrives weekends beyond the Victory Column on Strasse des 17 Juni (Sat–Sun 6:00–16:00, S-Bahn: Tiergarten).

German Resistance Memorial (Gedenkstätte Deutscher Widerstand)—This memorial and museum, just south of the Tiergarten, tells the story of the German resistance to Hitler. The Bendlerblock was a military headquarters where an ill-fated attempt to assassinate Hitler was plotted (the actual attempt occurred in Rastenburg, eastern Prussia). Claus von Stauffenberg and his co-conspirators were shot here in the courtyard. While posted explanations are in German only and there are no real artifacts, the spirit that haunts the place is multilingual (free, Mon–Fri 9:00–18:00, Thu until 20:00, Sat–Sun 10:00–18:00, free and good English audioguide with passport, €3 printed English translation, no crowds, near Kulturforum at Stauffenbergstrasse 13, enter in courtyard, door on left, main exhibit is on third floor, bus #M29, tel. 030/2699-5000).

Potsdamer Platz

The "Times Square" of Berlin, and possibly the busiest square in Europe before World War II, Potsdamer Platz was cut in two by the Wall and left a deserted no-man's-land for 40 years. Today, this immense commercial/residential/entertainment center, sitting on a futuristic transportation hub, is home to the European corporate headquarters of several big-league companies.

The new Potsdamer Platz was a vision begun in 1991, when it was announced that Berlin would resume its position as capital of Germany. Sony, Daimler-Chrysler, and other major corporations have turned the square once again into a center of Berlin. Like great Christian churches were built upon pagan holy grounds, Potsdamer Platz—with its corporate logos flying high and shiny above what was the Wall—trumpets the triumph of capitalism.

While Potsdamer Platz tries to give Berlin a common center, the city has always been—and remains—a collection of towns. Locals recognize 28 distinct neighborhoods that may have grown together but still maintain their historic orientation. While Munich has the single dominant Marienplatz, Berlin will always have Charlottenburg, Savignyplatz, Kreuzberg, Prenzlauer Berg, and so on. In general, Berliners prefer these characteristic neighborhoods. They're unimpressed by the grandeur of Potsdamer Platz, and consider it simply a good place for movies, with overpriced, touristy restaurants.

While most of the complex just feels big (the arcade is like any huge, modern, American mall), the entrance to the complex and Sony Center are worth a visit, and German-film buffs will enjoy the Deutsche Kinemathek museum (described later).

For an overview of the new construction, and a scenic route to the Sony Center, start at the Bahnhof Potsdamer Platz (east end of Potsdamer Strasse, S- and U-Bahn: Potsdamer Platz, exit following *Leipziger Platz* signs to see the best view of skyscrapers as you emerge). Find the green hexagonal clock tower with the traffic lights on top. This is a replica of the first automatic traffic light in Europe, which once stood at the six-street intersection of Potsdamer Platz. On either side of Potsdamer Strasse, you'll see enormous cubical entrances to the new underground Potsdamer Platz train station. Near these entrances, notice the slanted glass cylinders sticking out of the ground. The mirrors on the tops of the tubes move with the sun to collect light and send it underground (saving piles of euros on energy). A line in the pavement indicates where the Berlin Wall once stood. Notice also the slabs of the Wall re-erected where the Wall once stood. Imagine when the first piece was cut out (see photo and history on nearby panel). These hang like scalps at the gate of Fort Capitalism...look up at the towering corporate headquarters: Market forces have won a clear victory. Now descend into one of the train station entrances and follow signs to *Sony Center*.

You'll come up the escalator into the **Sony Center** under a grand canopy (designed to evoke Mt. Fuji). At night, multicolored floodlights play on the underside of this tent. Office workers and tourists eat here by the fountain, enjoying the parade of people.

The modern Bavarian Lindenbräu beer hall—the Sony boss wanted a *Bräuhaus*—serves traditional food (€5–16, daily 11:00–24:00, big salads, three-foot-long taster boards of eight different beers, tel. 030/2575-1280). The adjacent Josty Bar is built around a surviving bit of a venerable hotel that was a meeting place for Berlin's rich and famous before the bombs (expensive, daily 10:00–24:00, tel. 030/2575-9702). CineStar is a rare cinema that plays mainstream movies in their original language (www.cinestar.de). Pop into the VW Startklar showroom (where the VW "my first car" exhibit prepares kids for the exciting day that they turn 18 and can get their license so that they, too, can enjoy Germany's beloved autobahns).

▲**Deutsche Kinemathek Film and TV Museum**—This exhibit is the most interesting place to visit in the Sony Center. Your admission ticket gets you into several floors of exhibits (third floor is permanent exhibits, first and fourth floor are temporary exhibits) made meaningful by the included (and essential) English audioguide. The film section takes you from the German film industry's beginnings, with emphasis on the Weimar Republic period in the 1920s, when Berlin rivaled Hollywood (*Metropolis* was a 1927 German production). Three rooms are dedicated to Marlene Dietrich, and another section features Nazi use of film as propaganda. The TV section tells the story of das Booben Tube from its infancy (when it was primarily used as a Nazi propaganda tool) to today. The 30-minute kaleidoscopic review—kind of a frantic fast-forward montage of greatest hits in German TV history—is great fun even if you don't understand a word of it (it plays all day long, with 10-minute breaks). Upstairs is a TV archive where you can dial through a wide range of new and classic German TV standards (€7.50, Tue–Sun 10:00–18:00, Thu until 20:00, closed Mon, tel. 030/2474-9888). The Kino Arsenal theater downstairs shows off-beat artistic films in their original language.

Across Potsdamer Strasse, you can ride what's billed as "the fastest elevator in Europe" to skyscraping rooftop views at the **Panaromapunkt.** You'll travel at nearly 30 feet per second to the top of the 300-foottall Kollhoff Tower. Its sheltered but open-air view deck provides a fun opportunity to survey Berlin's ongoing construction from above (€3.50, daily 11:00–20:00, last lift 19:30, closed Mon in winter, in red-brick building at Potsdamer Platz 1, tel. 030/2529-4372, www .panoramapunkt.de).

Kulturforum

Just west of Potsdamer Platz, with several top museums and Berlin's concert hall—home of the world-famous Berlin Philharmonic orchestra—is the city's cultural heart (admission to all Kulturforum sights covered by a single €8 "Standortkarte Kulturforum" combo-ticket or the €15 Museumspass; phone number for all museums: tel. 030/266-2951). Of its sprawling museums, only the Gemäldegalerie is a must (S- or U-Bahn to Potsdamer Platz, then walk along Potsdamer Platz, or from Bahnhof Zoo, take bus #200 to Kulturforum).

▲▲▲Gemäldegalerie—Germany's top collection of 13th-through 18th-century European paintings (more than 1,400 canvases) is beautifully displayed in a building that's a work of art in itself. Follow the excellent free audioguide. The North Wing starts with German paintings of the 13th to 16th centuries, including eight by Albrecht Dürer. Then come the Dutch and Flemish—Jan van Eyck, Pieter Brueghel, Peter Paul Rubens, Anthony van Dyck, Frans Hals, and Jan Vermeer. The wing finishes with German, English, and French 18th-century art, such as Thomas Gainsborough and Antoine Watteau. An octagonal hall at the end features an impressive stash of Rembrandts. The South Wing is saved for the Italians—Giotto, Botticelli, Titian, Raphael, and Caravaggio (€8 Kulturforum ticket or €15 Museumspass, free Thu after 18:00, open Tue–Sun 10:00–18:00, Thu until 22:00, closed Mon, clever little loaner stools, great salad bar in cafeteria upstairs, Matthäikirchplatz 4).

New National Gallery (Neue Nationalgalerie)—This features 20th-century art, with ever-changing special exhibits (€8 Kulturforum ticket or €15 Museumspass, Tue–Sun 10:00–18:00, Thu–Sat 10:00–22:00, Sun 10:00–20:00, closed Mon, café downstairs, Potsdamer Strasse 50).

Museum of Arts and Crafts (Kunstgewerbemuseum)—Wander through a thousand years of applied arts—porcelain, fine *Jugendstil* furniture, Art Deco, and reliquaries. There are no English descriptions and no crowds—especially in 2008, when it will be closed for renovation (Herbert-von-Karajan-Strasse 10).

▲**Musical Instruments Museum (Musikinstrumenten Museum)**—This impressive hall is filled with 600 exhibits from the 16th century to modern times. Wander among old keyboard instruments and funny-looking tubas. There's no English, aside from a €0.10 info sheet, but it's fascinating if you're into pianos

(€8 Kulturforum ticket or €15 Museumspass, Tue–Fri 9:00–17:00, Thu until 22:00, Sat–Sun 10:00–17:00, closed Mon, low-profile white building east of the big, yellow Philharmonic Concert Hall, tel. 030/254-810).

Poke into the lobby of Berlin's yellow **Philharmonic Concert Hall** and see if there are tickets available during your stay (ticket office open Mon–Fri 15:00–18:00, Sat–Sun 11:00–14:00, must purchase tickets in person, box office tel. 030/2548-8132). You can often get inexpensive and legitimate tickets sold on the street before the performance. Even from the outside, this is a remarkable building—notice how different it looks from every angle.

Western Berlin

Throughout the Cold War, Western travelers learned to think of Berlin's "West End" as the heart of the city. But it no longer is. With the huge changes the city has undergone since 1989, the real "city center" is now, once again, Berlin's historic center (the Mitte district, around Unter den Linden and Friedrichstrasse). While the West End has long had the best infrastructure to support your visit, and still works well as a home base, it's no longer the obvious base from which to explore Berlin. And after the new Hauptbahnhof essentially put the Bahnhof Zoo out of business in 2006, this change became even more pronounced. Having said all that, there still are a few interesting sights within an easy walk of the recommended West End hotels and Bahnhof Zoo.

For a detailed map of this area, see page 435.

▲**Kurfürstendamm**—West Berlin's main drag, Kurfürstendamm boulevard (nicknamed "Ku'damm"), starts at Kaiser Wilhelm Memorial Church and does a commercial cancan for two miles. In the 1850s, when Berlin became a wealthy and important capital, her new rich chose Kurfürstendamm as their street. Bismarck made it Berlin's Champs-Elysées. In the 1920s, it became a chic and fashionable drag of cafés and boutiques. During the Third Reich, as home to an international community of diplomats and journalists, it enjoyed more freedom than the rest of Berlin. Throughout the Cold War, economic subsidies from the West made sure that capitalism thrived on Ku'damm. And today, while much of the old charm has been hamburgerized, Ku'damm is still a fine place to enjoy elegant shops (around Fasanenstrasse), department stores, and people-watching.

▲**Kaiser Wilhelm Memorial Church (Gedächtniskirche)**—This church was originally a church dedicated to the first emperor of Germany. Reliefs and mosaics show great events in the life of Germany's favorite *Kaiser,* from his coronation in 1871 to his death in 1888. The church's bombed-out ruins have been left standing as a memorial to the destruction of Berlin in World War II.

Under a Neo-Romanesque mosaic ceiling, a small exhibit features interesting photos about the bombing and before-and-after models of the church (free, Mon–Sat 10:00–16:00, closed Sun, Breitscheidplatz, S-Bahn: Zoologischer Garten or U-Bahn: Wittenbergplatz, www.gedaechtniskirche .com).

After the war, some Berliners wanted to tear the church down and build it anew. Instead, it was decided to keep the ruin as a memorial, and stage a competition to design a modern add-on section. The winning selection—the short, modern building (1961) next to the church—offers a world of 11,000 little blue windows (free, daily 9:00–19:00). The blue glass was given to the church by the French as a reconciliation gift. For more information on both churches, pick up the English booklet (€2.60).

The lively square between the churches and the Europa Center (a once-impressive, shiny high-rise shopping center built as a showcase of Western capitalism during the Cold War) usually attracts street musicians.

The Story of Berlin—Filling most of what seems like a department store right on Ku'damm (at #207), this sprawling history exhibit is a business venture making money by telling the stormy 800-year story of Berlin in a creative way. While there are almost no real historic artifacts, the exhibit does a good job of cobbling together many dimensions of the life and tumultuous times of this great city. However, for similar information, the German History Museum on Unter den Linden is a far better use of your time and money (see page 406).

▲Käthe Kollwitz Museum—This local artist (1867–1945), who experienced much of Berlin's stormiest century, conveys some powerful and mostly sad feelings about motherhood, war, and suffering through the stark faces of her art. This small yet fine collection (the only one in town of Kollwitz's work) consists of three floors of charcoal drawings, topped by an attic with a handful of sculptures (€5, €1 pamphlet has necessary English explanations of a few major works, Wed–Mon 11:00–18:00, closed Tue, a block off Ku'damm at Fasanenstrasse 24, U-Bahn: Uhlandstrasse, tel. 030/882-5210, www.kaethe-kollwitz.de).

▲Kaufhaus des Westens (KaDeWe)—The "Department Store of the West" celebrated its 100th birthday in 2007. With a staff of 2,100 to help you sort through its vast selection of 380,000 items, KaDeWe claims to be the biggest department store on the Continent. You can get everything from a haircut and train ticket (basement) to souvenirs (third floor). The theater and concert box office on the sixth floor charges an 18 percent booking fee, but they know all your options (cash only). The sixth floor is a world of gourmet taste treats. The biggest selection of deli and exotic food in Germany offers plenty of classy opportunities to sit down and eat. Ride the glass elevator to the seventh floor's glass-domed Winter Garden self-service cafeteria—fun but pricey (Mon–Fri 10:00–20:00, Sat 9:30–20:00, closed Sun, S-Bahn: Zoologischer Garten or U-Bahn: Wittenbergplatz, tel. 030/21210, www.kadewe .de). The Wittenbergplatz U-Bahn station (in front of KaDeWe) is a unique opportunity to see an old-time station. Enjoy its interior.

Berlin Zoo (Zoologischer Garten Berlin)—More than 1,400 different kinds of animals call Berlin's famous zoo home—or so the zookeepers like to think. The recent big hit here is Knut, a young polar bear who first made headlines for being born in captivity, but quickly became an international star after he was abandoned by his mother and raised by zookeepers. Germans also enjoy seeing the pandas at play (straight in from the entrance). I enjoy seeing the Germans at play (€12 for zoo or world-class aquarium, €18 for both, children half-price, daily 9:00–18:30, Nov–Feb until 17:00, aquarium closes 30 min earlier; feeding times—*Fütterungszeiten*— posted on map just inside entrance, the best feeding show is the sea lions—generally at 15:30; enter near Europa Center in front of Hotel Palace or opposite Bahnhof Zoo on Hardenbergplatz, Budapester Strasse 34, tel. 030/254-010, www.zoo-berlin.de).

Erotic Art Museum—This offers two floors of graphic art (especially Oriental), old-time sex-toy knickknacks, and a special exhibit on the queen of German pornography, the late Beate Uhse. This amazing woman, a former test pilot for the Third Reich and groundbreaking purveyor of condoms and sex ed in the 1950s, was the female Hugh Hefner of Germany and CEO of a huge chain of porn shops (€6, Mon–Sat 9:00–24:00, Sun 13:00–24:00, last entry at 23:00, hard-to-beat gift shop, at corner of Kantstrasse and Joachimstalerstrasse, a block from Bahnhof Zoo, tel. 030/8862-6613). If you just want to see sex, you'll see much more for half the price in a private video booth next door.

Charlottenburg Palace Area

The Charlottenburg district—with a cluster of museums across the street from a grand palace—is a popular side-trip from downtown. But the palace isn't much to see, and in 2005 the Egyptian Museum (with the bust of Queen Nefertiti—see page 408) moved downtown and took with it the main reason I'd go all the way out to Charlottenburg. The building that housed the Egyptian Museum should reopen here in spring of 2008 as the **Scharf-Gerstenberg Museum,** which will feature more than 250 works of Surrealist

Charlottenburg Palace Area

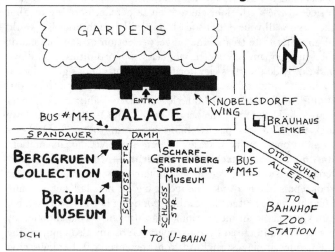

art (ask at any TI for opening times and prices, Schlossstrasse 70, 030/3435-7315). To get here, ride U-2 to Sophie-Charlotte Platz and walk 10 minutes up the tree-lined boulevard Schlossstrasse (following signs to *Schloss*), or—much faster—catch bus #M45 (direction Spandau) direct from Bahnhof Zoo.

For a Charlottenburg lunch, the **Bräuhaus Lemke** is a comfortable brewpub restaurant with a copper and woody atmosphere, good local microbeers (*dunkles* means "dark," *helles* is "light"), and traditional German grub (€5–8 meals, daily 9:00–24:00, fun for groups, across from palace at Luisenplatz 1, tel. 030/3087-8979).

▲**Charlottenburg Palace (Schloss Charlottenburg)**—If you've seen the great palaces of Europe, this Baroque Hohenzollern palace comes in at about number 10 (behind Potsdam, too). It's even more disappointing since the main rooms can be toured only with a German guide (€8 includes 50-min tour, €2 to see just upper floors without tour, €7 to see palace grounds excluding tour areas, cash only, Tue–Sun 10:00–17:00, closed Mon, last tour at 16:00, tel. 030/320-911, www.spsg.de).

The **Knobelsdorff Wing** features a few royal apartments. Go upstairs and take a substantial hike through restored-since-the-war, gold-crusted white rooms (€5 depending on special exhibitions, free English audioguide, Tue–Fri 10:00–18:00, Sat–Sun 11:00–18:00, closed Mon, last entry at 17:00, when facing the palace walk toward the right wing, tel. 030/3209-1442).

▲**Berggruen Collection: Picasso and His Time**—This tidy little museum is a pleasant surprise. Climb three floors through a fun and substantial collection of Picassos. Along the way, you'll see

Berlin

plenty of notable works by Henri Matisse. Enjoy a great chance to meet Paul Klee (€6, covered by Museumspass, free Thu after 14:00, open Tue–Sun 10:00–18:00, closed Mon, Schlossstrasse 1, tel. 030/326-9580).

▲**Bröhan Museum**—Wander through a dozen beautifully furnished *Jugendstil* and Art Deco living rooms, a curvy organic world of lamps, glass, silver, and posters. English descriptions are posted on the wall of each room on the main floor. While you're there, look for the fine collection of Impressionist paintings by Karl Hagemeister (€4–8 depending on special exhibits, covered by Museumspass excluding special exhibits, Tue–Sun 10:00–18:00, closed Mon, Schlossstrasse 1A, tel. 030/3269-0600, www.broehan-museum.de).

Near Berlin: Potsdam's Palaces

Featuring a lush park strewn with the extravagant whimsies of Frederick the Great, the sleepy town of Potsdam has long been Berlin's holiday retreat—it's worth ▲. Frederick's super-Rococo Sanssouci Palace is one of Germany's most dazzling. His equally extravagant New Palace, built to disprove rumors that Prussia was running out of money after the costly Seven Years' War, is on the other side of the park (it's a 30-minute walk between palaces). Potsdam's much-promoted Wannsee boat rides are exceedingly dull.

Getting to Potsdam: Potsdam is easy to reach from Berlin (17 min on direct Regional Express/RE trains from Hauptbahnhof, Bahnhof Zoo, or Friedrichstrasse every 30 min; round-trip covered by €6.30 transit day pass with zones A, B, and C; any train to Brandenburg or Magdeburg stops in Potsdam). Once in Potsdam, bus #695 runs from the Potsdam train station to the palaces, and is invariably packed (3/hr, 20 min, leaves from lane 4; April–Oct bus #X15 runs the same route at weekends). A less-crowded option is to take tram #91 to Luisenplatz (3/hr, 11 minutes, leaves from lane 1), then walk 20 minutes through the park and enjoy a classic view of Sanssouci Palace. The tram is also the better option if you're taking the Potsdam TI's tour (see "Tours at Potsdam," next page). Use the same bus #695 to shuttle between the sights in the park.

Orientation and Information: Unless you're planning on spending time exploring the town of Potsdam itself, skip the Potsdam **TI** (April–Oct Mon–Fri 9:30–18:00, Sat–Sun 9:30–16:00; Nov–March Mon–Fri 10:00–18:00, Sat–Sun 9:30–14:00; tel. 0331/275-580, Brandenburger Strasse 3, www.potsdamtourismus .de) and head straight to the **palace information office** (across the street from windmill near Sanssouci entrance, helpful English-speaking staff, daily April–Oct 8:30–17:00, Nov–March 9:00–16:00, tel. 0331/969-4202, www.spsg.de; clean WC in same

Greater Berlin

building, €0.30). To supplement the English tour handouts, consider picking up the gray "official guide" booklets (available for all of the sights, €3 each at palace information office and gift shop).

Combo-Ticket: If you plan on seeing several of the buildings, save money by getting a **Premium Day Ticket** (€15, only available at the Sanssouci ticket office—the regular day ticket does not include Sanssouci).

Tours at Potsdam: The Potsdam TI offers a bus tour of Potsdam sights, plus the interior of Sanssouci Palace. This normally wouldn't be worth the time...except that it's the only way to get into Sanssouci with an English-speaking guide (often with some German, too; €26 covers tour, palace, and park; Sun–Tue at 11:00, no tours Mon, 3.5 hrs, departs from TI at Luisenplatz, reserve by phone, in summer reserve at least 2 days in advance, tel. 0331/275-5850).

Tours from Berlin: Both Original Berlin Walks and Brewer's Tours offer inexpensive all-day tours from Berlin through Potsdam (small groups, English-language only, admissions and public transportation not included, doesn't actually go into the Sanssouci Palace). Given the frustration of trying to do this on your own, these tours can help you avoid a lot of stress and be an efficient use of time and money. Original Berlin Walks' tour leaves from Berlin's Bahnhof Zoo at 10:00 every Sunday, May through September (€15, meet at taxi stand at Bahnhof Zoo, tel. 030/301-9194). The guide takes you to Cecilienhof Palace (site of postwar Potsdam conference attended by Churchill, Stalin, and Truman), through pleasant green landscapes to the historic heart of Potsdam for lunch, and finishes outside Sanssouci Palace. The Brewer's tour is similar (€12, Wed and Sun, May–Oct only, leaves at 9:20 from Bandy Brooks ice cream shop at Friedrichstrasse U- and S-Bahn station, call to confirm and hold a spot, tel. 030/2248-7435, mobile 0177-388-1537, www.brewersberlintours.com).

Sanssouci Palace—Even though *sans souci* means "without a care," it can be a challenge for an English-speaker to have an enjoyable visit. The palaces of Vienna, Munich, and even Würzburg offer equal sightseeing thrills with fewer headaches. If you want to see inside the palace of Sanssouci itself, make sure you arrive early. In the summer, if you arrive by 9:00, you'll get right in. If you arrive after 10:00, plan on a wait. If you arrive after 12:00, you may not get in at all (€12, April–Oct Tue–Sun 9:00–17:00, Nov–March Tue–Sun 9:00–16:00, closed Mon year-round). Entry includes a 40-minute audioguide.

New Palace (Neues Palais)—This palace's apartments are underwhelming and frustrating for non-German speakers (€5, plus €1 for optional live tour in German; April–Oct Sat–Thu 9:00–17:00, Nov–May Sat–Thu 9:00–16:00, closed Fri year-round). If you also want to see the king's apartments, you must take a required 45-minute tour in German (€6, offered May–Oct daily at 11:00, 13:00, and 15:00). Off-season (Nov–April), the king's apartments are closed, and you can visit the rest of the New Palace only on a German tour (€5); it can take up to an hour for enough people to gather.

Cecilienhof—The former residence of Crown Prince William and the site of the 1945 Potsdam Conference is a short bus ride away (€5, April–Oct Tue–Sun 9:00–17:00, Nov–March Tue–Sun 9:00–16:00, closed Mon year-round; take bus #695 from Sanssouci Palace to Reiterweg, then transfer to bus #692; tel. 0331/969-4224).

NIGHTLIFE

Berlin is a happening place for nightlife—whether it's nightclubs, pubs, jazz music, cabaret, hokey-but-fun German variety shows, theater, or concerts.

Sources of Entertainment Info: *Berlin Programm* lists a non-stop parade of concerts, plays, exhibits, and cultural events (€2, in German, www.berlin-programm.de); *Exberliner Magazine* (€2, www.exberliner.com) and the TI-produced *Berlin To Go* (€1) have less information, but are in English (all sold at kiosks and TIs). For the young and determined sophisticate, *Zitty* and *Tip* are the top guides to alternative culture (in German, sold at kiosks). Also pick up the free schedules *Flyer* and *030* in bars and clubs. The free magazines by walking-tour companies such as New Berlin Walks

(www.newberlintours.com) and Insider Tour (www.insidertour
.com) are also good, providing the English-language inside scoop
on nightlife, cheap eats, and pub crawls (available all over town).

Visit KaDeWe's ticket office for your music and theater
options (sixth floor, 18 percent fee but access to all tickets; see page
426). Ask about "competitive improvisation" and variety shows.

West End Jazz—To enjoy live music near my recommended
Savignyplatz hotels in western Berlin, consider **A Trane Jazz Club**
(all jazz, great stage and intimate seating, €7–18 cover depending
on act, opens at 21:00, live music nightly 22:00–2:00 in the morning, Bleibtreustrasse 1, tel. 030/313-2550) and **Quasimodo Live**
(mix of jazz, rock, and blues, €5–12 cover, Tue–Sat from 22:00,
closed Sun–Mon, Kantstrasse 12A, under Delphi Cinema, tel.
030/312-8086, www.quasimodo.de).

Cabaret—Bar Jeder Vernunft offers modern-day cabaret a short
walk from the recommended hotels in western Berlin. This variety show—under a classic old tent perched atop a modern parking
lot—is a hit with German speakers, but can still be worthwhile for
those who don't speak the language (as some of the music shows are
in a sort of "Denglish"). Even some Americans perform here peri-
odically. Tickets are generally about €20, and shows change regularly (performances start Mon–Sat at 20:30, Sun at 20:00, Wed is
non-smoking, seating can be a bit cramped, south of Ku'damm at
Schaperstrasse 24, tel. 030/883-1582, www.bar-jeder-vernunft.de).

German Variety Show—To spend an evening enjoying Europe's
largest revue theater, consider Revue Berlin at the Friedrichstadt
Palast. This super-kitschy German Moulin Rouge–type show basically depicts the history of Berlin, and is choreographed in a funny
and musical way that's popular with the Lawrence Welk–type
German crowd (€17–61, Tue–Sat 20:00, Sat–Sun also at 16:00,
no shows Mon, U-Bahn: Oranienburger Tor, tel. 030/2326-2326,
www.friedrichstadtpalast.de).

Nightclubs and Pubs—Oranienburger Strasse's trendy scene
(page 417) is being eclipsed by the action at Friedrichshain (farther
east). To the north, you'll find the hip Prenzlauer Berg neighborhood, packed with everything from smoky pubs to small art bars
and dance clubs (best scene is around Helmholtsplatz, U-Bahn:
Eberswalder Strasse; see page 418).

Pub Crawls—Insider Tours and New Berlin Walks each offer €12
pub crawls (or, some would say, "pub brawls"). Insider Tours leaves
at 20:30 from Hackescher Markt; New Berlin Walks at 21:00 from
the Oranienburger Strasse S-Bahn station. Those who show up
early are treated to a warm-up keg. After a recent binge-drinking
death, police are enforcing the 18-year-old minimum. A new
marketing slogan for one organization: "Our mission: To show
you Berlin's great nightlife...not to hospitalize you." Both tours

generally visit four bars and two clubs, and provide a great way to get drunk with new English-speaking friends from around the world while getting a peek at Berlin's bar scene...or at least how its bars look when invaded by 50 loud tourists.

SLEEPING

When in Berlin, I sleep in the former West, on or near Savignyplatz. While Bahnhof Zoo and Ku'damm are no longer the center of Berlin, the trains, TI, and walking tours are all still handy to the Zoo. And the streets around the tree-lined Savignyplatz (a 10-min walk behind the station) have a neighborhood charm. While towering new hotels are being built in the new center, simple, small, friendly, good-value places abound here. My listings are generally located a couple of flights up in big, run-down buildings. Inside, they're clean, quiet, and spacious enough so that their well-worn character is actually charming. Rooms in back are on quiet courtyards.

For those interested in staying in a livelier, more colorful district, I've also listed some suggestions in eastern Berlin's youthful and increasingly popular Prenzlauer Berg neighborhood.

Berlin is packed and hotel prices go up on holidays, including Green Week in mid-January, Easter weekend, the first weekend in May, Ascension weekend in May, the Love Parade (mid-July), German Unification Day (Oct 3), Christmas, and New Year's.

Western Berlin

Near Savignyplatz and Bahnhof Zoo

These hotels and pensions are a 5- to 15-minute walk from Bahnhof Zoo (or take the S-Bahn to Savignyplatz). Asking for a quieter room in back gets you away from any street noise. The area has an artsy charm going back to the cabaret days in the 1920s, when it was the center of Berlin's gay scene. Of the accommodations listed in this area, Pension Peters offers the best value for budget travelers.

$$$ Hotel Askanischerhof is the oldest *Zimmer* in Berlin, posh as can be with 16 sprawling, antique-furnished living rooms you can call home. Photos on the walls brag of famous movie-star guests. Frau Glinicke offers Old World service and classic Berlin atmosphere (Sb-€95–110, Db-€117–145, extra bed-€25, elevator, free parking, Ku'damm 53, tel. 030/881-8033, fax 030/881-7206, www.askanischer-hof.de, info@askanischer-hof.de).

$$$ Hecker's Hotel is an ultramodern, four-star business hotel with 69 rooms and all the sterile Euro-comforts (Sb-€125, Db-€150, all rooms €200 during conferences but generally only €100 July–Aug, breakfast-€15, non-smoking rooms, elevator, parking-€9–12/day, between Savignyplatz and Ku'damm

---

Sleep Code

(€1 = about $1.30, country code: 49, area code: 030)
S = Single, **D** = Double/Twin, **T** = Triple, **Q** = Quad, **b** = bathroom, **s** = shower only. Unless otherwise noted, credit cards are accepted, English is spoken, and breakfast is included.

To help you sort easily through these listings, I've divided the rooms into three categories, based on the price for a standard double room with bath:

$$$ Higher Priced—Most rooms €125 or more.
  $$ Moderately Priced—Most rooms between €85–125.
   $ Lower Priced—Most rooms €85 or less.

---

at Grolmanstrasse 35, tel. 030/88900, fax 030/889-0260, www.heckers-hotel.com, info@heckers-hotel.com).

$$ Hotel Carmer 16, with 30 bright, airy (if a bit dated) rooms, is both business-like and homey, and has an inviting lounge and charming balconies (Db-€93, big Db-€99, ask for a Rick Steves discount, extra person-€20, some rooms have balconies, elevator and a few stairs, Carmerstrasse 16, tel. 030/3110-0500, fax 030/3110-0510, www.hotel-carmer16.de, info@hotel-carmer16.de).

$$ Hotel Astoria is a friendly, three-star, business-class hotel with 32 comfortably furnished rooms and affordable summer and weekend rates (high-season Db-€118; prices drop to Db-€94 during low season of July–Aug and Nov–Feb—check their website for deals; breakfast-€10 extra, non-smoking floors, elevator, Internet access, parking-€5/day, around corner from Bahnhof Zoo at Fasanenstrasse 2, tel. 030/312-4067, fax 030/312-5027, www.hotelastoria.de, info@hotelastoria.de).

$$ Hotel-Pension Funk, the former home of a 1920s silent-movie star, is delightfully quirky. Kind manager Herr Michael Pfundt offers 14 elegant old rooms with rich Art Nouveau furnishings (S-€34–57, Ss-€41–72, Sb-€52–82, D-€62–82, Ds-€72–93, Db-€90, extra person-€23, these prices guaranteed through 2008 with this book, cash preferred, a long block south of Ku'damm at Fasanenstrasse 69, tel. 030/882-7193, fax 030/883-3329, www.hotel-pensionfunk.de, berlin@hotel-pensionfunk.de).

$$ Hotel Bogota is a once-elegant old slumbermill renting 115 rooms in a sprawling old maze of a building that once housed the Nazi Chamber of Culture. Today, pieces of the owner's modern-art collection lurk around every corner (S-€44, Ss-€57, Sb-€72, D-€69, Ds-€77, Db-€98, extra bed-€22, children under 12 free, elevator, 10-min walk from Savignyplatz at Schlüterstrasse

Western Berlin

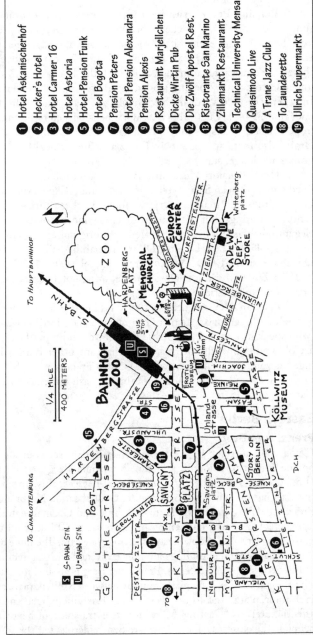

1. Hotel Askanischerhof
2. Hecker's Hotel
3. Hotel Carmer 16
4. Hotel Astoria
5. Hotel-Pension Funk
6. Hotel Bogota
7. Pension Peters
8. Hotel Pension Alexandra
9. Pension Alexis
10. Restaurant Marjellchen
11. Dicke Wirtin Pub
12. Die Zwölf Apostel Rest.
13. Ristorante San Marino
14. Zillemarkt Restaurant
15. Technical University Mensa
16. Quasimodo Live
17. A Trane Jazz Club
18. To Launderette
19. Ullrich Supermarkt

45, tel. 030/881-5001, fax 030/883-5887, www.hotelbogota.de, hotel-bogota@t-online.de).

$ Pension Peters, run by a German–Swedish couple, is sunny and central, with a cheery breakfast room. Decorated sleek Scandinavian, with each of its 37 rooms renovated, it's a winner (S-€36, Ss-€47, Sb-€55, D-€51, Ds-€68, Db-€75–78, extra bed-€10, these prices guaranteed through 2008 with this book, up to 2 kids under 13 free with 2 paying adults, family room, cash preferred, Internet access, 10 yards off Savignyplatz at Kantstrasse 146, tel. 030/3150-3944, fax 030/312-3519, www.pension-peters-berlin.de, info@pension-peters-berlin.de, Annika and Christoph). The same family also rents apartments in Prenzlauer Berg (ideal for small groups and longer stays).

$ Hotel Pension Alexandra has 11 pleasant rooms on a tree-lined street between Savignyplatz and Ku'damm. Expect the usual high ceilings and marble entryway found in these turn-of-the-century buildings, but with added touches—most rooms and the elegant breakfast room are decorated with original antique furniture (Ss-€45, Sb-€59, Ds-€69, Db with small bed-€70, standard Db-€85, extra bed-€30, Wielandstrasse 32, tel. 030/881-2107, fax 030/885-77818, www.hotelalexandra.de, info@hotelalexandra.de, Frau Kuhn and Mariane).

$ Pension Alexis is a classic Old World four-room pension in a stately 19th-century apartment run by Frau and Herr Schwarzer (who speak just enough English). The shower and toilet facilities are old and cramped, but this, more than any other Berlin listing, has you feeling at home with a faraway grandmother (S-€43, D-€67, T-€97, Q-€128, 2-night minimum, cash only, big rooms, Carmerstrasse 15, tel. 030/312-5144).

Eastern Berlin

Prenzlauer Berg

If you want to sleep in the former East Berlin, set your sights on the youthful, colorful, and fun Prenzlauer Berg district (or "Prenzl'berg" for short). After decades of neglect, this corner of the East has quickly come back to life. Gentrification has brought Prenzlauer Berg great hotels, tasty ethnic and German eateries (see page 443), and a happening nightlife scene. Think of all the graffiti as just some people's way of saying they care. The huge and impersonal concrete buildings are now enlivened with a street fair of fun little shops and eateries. Prenzlauer Berg is about a mile and a half north of Alexanderplatz, roughly between Kollwitzplatz and Helmholtzplatz, and to the west, along Kastanienallee (known affectionately as "Casting Alley" for its extra share of beautiful people). The closest U-Bahn stops are Senefelderplatz at the south end of the neighborhood and Eberswalder Strasse at the north end.

Prenzlauer Berg Neighborhood

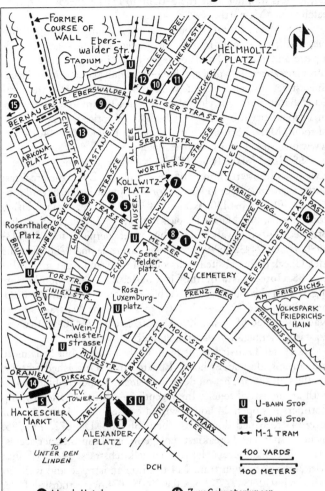

1. Myer's Hotel
2. Hotel Jurine
3. Hotel Kastanienhof
4. Hotel Transit Loft
5. EastSeven Hostel
6. Steiner Apartments
7. Gugelhof Restaurant
8. Metzer Eck
9. Prater Biergarten
10. Zum Schusterjungen Speisegaststätte
11. La Bodeguita del Medio Cuban Bar Restaurant
12. Knoppke's Imbiss
13. Kauf Dich Glücklich
14. Walking Tour & Pub Crawl Departure Point
15. To Berlin Wall Documentation Center, Nordbahnhof S-Bahn & Natural History Museum

U U-bahn Stop
S S-bahn Stop
M-1 tram

400 YARDS
400 METERS

Berlin

Or, for less walking, take the S-Bahn to Hackescher Markt, then catch tram #M1 north.

$$$ Myer's Hotel is a boutique-hotel splurge renting 52 simple, small, but elegant rooms. The gorgeous public spaces include a patio and garden. Details done right and impeccable service set this place apart. This peaceful hub—off a quiet courtyard and tree-lined street, just a five-minute walk from Kollwitzplatz or the nearest U-Bahn stop (Senefelderplatz)—makes it hard to believe you're in a capital city (Sb-€85–135, Db-€110–175, price depends on size of room, Metzer Strasse 26, tel. 030/440-140, fax 030/4401-4104, www.myershotel.de, info@myershotel.de).

$$ Hotel Jurine (yoo-REEN) is a pleasant 53-room business-style hotel whose friendly staff aims to please. Enjoy the breakfast buffet surrounded by modern art, or relax in the lush backyard (Sb-€75, Db-€100, Tb-€130, extra bed-€37, prices can zoom up during conventions, breakfast-€14, parking garage-€13/day, Schwedter Strasse 15, 10-min walk to U-Bahn: Senefelderplatz, tel. 030/443-2990, fax 030/4432-9999, www.hotel-jurine.de, mail@hotel-jurine.de). Check their website for discounts in July and August.

$$ Hotel Kastanienhof is a basic, less-classy hotel offering 35 sleepable but slightly overpriced rooms (Sb-€78, Db-€103, reception closed 22:00–6:30, 40 yards from the M1 tram stop at Kastanienallee 65, tel. 030/443-050, fax 030/4430-5111, www.kastanienhof.biz, info@kastanienhof.biz).

$ Hotel Transit Loft is technically a hostel, but feels more like an upscale budget hotel. Located in a refurbished factory, it offers clean, bright, modern, new-feeling, mostly-blue rooms with an industrial touch. The reception—staffed by friendly, hip Berliners—is open 24 hours, with a bar serving drinks all night long (4- to 6-bed dorms-€21/bed, Sb-€60, Db-€72, Tb-€93, includes sheets and breakfast, no age limit, cheap Internet access, fully wheelchair-accessible, Emmanuelkirchstrasse 14A, U-Bahn: Alexanderplatz then tram M4 to Hufelandstrasse and walk 50 yards, tel. 030/4849-3773, fax 030/4405-1074, www.transit-loft.de, loft@hotel-transit.de).

$ EastSeven Hostel rents the best cheap beds in Prenzlauer Berg. It's sleek and modern, with all the hostel services and more: 24-hour reception, inviting lounge, fully equipped guests' kitchen, lockers, garden, and bike rental. Children are welcome. While most hostels—especially in Prenzlauer Berg—are annoyingly youthful to people over 30, easygoing people of any age are comfortable here (S-€35, D-€48, T-€63, €17 for a bed in a 4-, 5-, or 6-bed dorm, bathrooms always down the hall, one-time €3 fee for sheets, free Internet access and Wi-Fi, 100 yards from U-Bahn: Senefelderplatz at Schwedter Strasse 7, tel. 030/9362-2240, www.eastseven.de, info@eastseven.de).

$ Steiner Apartments, run by Pension Peters, are nine well-located, modern, and comfortable apartments near Hackescher Markt (Sb-€50, Db-€70, Tb-€75, Qb-€80, cash only, up to 2 children under 13 sleep free with 2 paying adults, fully equipped as if you live there, Linienstrasse 60—enter on Gormannstrasse, 350 yards from S-Bahn: Hackescher Markt, even closer to U-Bahn: Rosenthaler Platz, www.pension-peters-berlin.de, info@pension-peters-berlin.de; to book, contact Pension Peters, described on page 436).

Hostels

Berlin is known among budget travelers for its fun, hip hostels. Here are three good bets—the first one is south of Bahnhof Zoo and the other two are in Prenzlauer Berg.

$ Studentenhotel Meininger 10 (€14/bed in 8-bed dorms, D-€46, includes sheets and breakfast, no curfew, elevator, free parking, near City Hall on JFK Platz, Meininger Strasse 10, a 200-yard walk from U-Bahn: Rathaus Schöneberg, tel. 030/7871-7414, www.meininger-hostels.de).

$ Mitte's Backpacker Hostel (€15/bed in 32-bed dorms, S-€30–35, D-€48–56, T-€63, Q-€80, sheets-€2.50, no breakfast, could be cleaner, no curfew, Internet access, English newspapers, laundry, bike rental, U-Bahn: Zinnowitzer Strasse, Chausseestrasse 102, tel. 030/2839-0965, fax 030/2839-0935, www.backpacker.de, reservation@backpacker.de).

$ Circus is a brightly colored, well-run place with 230 beds, a Dylanesque ambience, and a bar downstairs (€18/bed in 4- to 8-bed dorms, S-€33, Sb-€46, D-€50, Db-€62, T-€63, Q-€76, 2-person apartment with kitchen-€77, 4-person apartment-€134, sheets-€2, breakfast-€5, no curfew, Internet access; U-Bahn: Rosenthaler Platz, Weinbergsweg 1a; tel. 030/2839-1433, www.circus-berlin.de, info@circus-berlin.de).

EATING

Don't be too determined to eat "Berlin-style." The city is known only for its mildly spicy sausage. Still, there is a world of restaurants in this ever-changing city to choose from. Your best approach may be to select a neighborhood, rather than a particular restaurant.

For quick and easy meals, colorful pubs—called *Kneipen*—offer light meals and the fizzy local beer, *Berliner Weiss*. Ask for it *mit Schuss* for a shot of fruity syrup in your suds. Germans—especially Berliners—consider their food old-school; when they go out to eat, they're not usually looking for the "traditional local" fare many travelers are after. Nouveau German is California cuisine with scant memories of wurst, kraut, and pumpernickel.

If the kraut is getting the wurst of you, try one of the many Turkish, Italian, or Balkan restaurants. Eat cheap at *Imbiss* snack stands, bakeries (sandwiches), and falafel/kebab counters. Train stations have grocery stores, as well as bright and modern fruit-and-sandwich bars.

Western Berlin

Near Savignyplatz

Many good restaurants are on or within 100 yards of Savignyplatz, near my recommended western Berlin hotels. Take a walk and survey these; continue your stroll along Bleibtreustrasse to discover many trendier, more creative little eateries.

Restaurant Marjellchen is a trip to East Prussia. Dine in a soft, jazzy elegance in one of two six-table rooms. While it doesn't have to be expensive (€25 for two courses), plan to go the whole nine yards here, as this can be a great Prussian experience with a great and caring service. The menu is inviting and the Königsberg meatballs are the specialty. Reservations are smart (daily 17:00–23:30, family run, Mommsenstrasse 9, tel. 030/883-2676).

Dicke Wirtin is a smoky pub with traditional old-Berlin *Kneipe* atmosphere, six good beers on tap, and good, solid home cooking at reasonable prices—such as their famously cheap *Gulaschsuppe* (€3.40). Their interior is fun and pubby; their street-side tables are also inviting (€5 daily specials, open daily from 12:00 with dinner served from 18:00, just off Savignyplatz at Carmerstrasse 9, tel. 030/312-4952).

Die Zwölf Apostel ("The Twelve Apostles") is trendy for good Italian food. Choose between indoors with candlelit ambience, on a sun-dappled patio, or overlooking the parade on its pedestrian street. A dressy local crowd packs this restaurant for excellent €10 pizzas and €15–30 meals (open 24 hours daily, cash only, immediately across from Savignyplatz S-Bahn entrance, Bleibtreustrasse 49, tel. 030/312-1433).

Ristorante San Marino, on the square, is another good Italian eatery, serving cheaper pasta and pizza. It's more kid-friendly (€8 pizza or pasta, €8–12 plates, daily 11:00–24:00, Savignyplatz 12, tel. 030/313-6086).

Zillemarkt Restaurant, which feels like an old-time Berlin *Biergarten,* serves traditional Berlin specialties in the garden or in the rustic candlelit interior. Their *Berliner Allerlei* is a fun way to sample a bit of nearly everything (for a minimum of two people...but it can feed up to five). They have their own microbrew (€10 meals, daily 12:00–24:00, near the S-Bahn tracks at Bleibtreustrasse 48A, tel. 030/881-7040).

Technical University Mensa, a student cafeteria with impossibly cheap prices, puts you in a modern university scene with fine food and good indoor or streetside seating (€5 meals, Mon–Fri 11:00–15:30, closed Sat–Sun, general public entirely welcome, cheap coffee bar downstairs with Internet access, just north of Uhlandstrasse at Hardenbergstrasse 34).

Ullrich Supermarkt is the neighborhood grocery store (Mon–Sat 9:00–22:00, Sun 11:00–22:00, Kantstrasse 7, under the tracks near Bahnhof Zoo). There's plenty of fast food near Bahnhof Zoo and on Ku'damm.

Near Bahnhof Zoo

Self-Service Cafeterias: The top floor of the famous department store, **KaDeWe,** holds the Winter Garden Buffet view cafeteria, and its sixth-floor deli/food department is a picnicker's nirvana. Its arterials are clogged with more than 1,000 kinds of sausage and 1,500 types of cheese (Mon–Fri 10:00–20:00, Sat 9:30–20:00, closed Sun, U-Bahn: Wittenbergplatz). **Wertheim** department store, a half-block from Kaiser Wilhelm Memorial Church, has cheap food counters in the basement and a city view from its self-service cafeteria, Le Buffet, located up six banks of escalators (Mon–Sat 9:30–20:00, closed Sun, U-Bahn: Ku'damm). **Marche,** a chain that's popped up in big cities all over Germany, is another inexpensive, self-service cafeteria within a half-block of Kaiser Wilhelm Memorial Church (Mon–Thu 8:00–22:00, Fri–Sat 8:00–24:00, Sun 10:00–22:00, plenty of salads, fruit, made-to-order omelets, Ku'damm 14, tel. 030/882-7578).

Eastern Berlin

Along Unter den Linden

These eateries are listed as you'll reach them as you walk along Unter den Linden from west to east.

At the Opera House (Opernpalais): The **Operncafé** is perhaps the classiest coffee stop in Berlin, with a wide selection of 50—count 'em: 50—decadent desserts (daily 8:00–24:00, across from university and war memorial at Unter den Linden 5, tel. 030/202-683). The **Schinkel Klause Biergarten** serves good €9–14 meals on its shady terrace with a view of the Unter den Linden scene when sunny, or in its cellar otherwise (daily 11:30–24:00).

Near the Pergamon Museum: Georgenstrasse, a block behind the Pergamon Museum and under the S-Bahn tracks, is lined with fun eateries filling the arcade of the train trestle—close to the sightseeing action but in business mainly for students from nearby Humboldt University. **Deponie3** is a trendy Berlin *Kneipe* usually filled with students. Garden seating in the back is nice if you don't mind the noise of the S-Bahn passing directly above you. The interior is a cozy, wooden wonderland of a bar with several inviting spaces. They serve basic sandwiches, salads, traditional

Berlin dishes, and hearty daily specials (€3–7 breakfasts, €5–11 lunches and dinners, open daily from 9:00, sometimes live music, Georgenstrasse 5, tel. 030/2016-5740). A branch of Die Zwölf Apostel is nearby (daily until 24:00, described earlier under "Near Savignyplatz").

In the Heart of Old Berlin's Nikolai Quarter: During the Cold War, the Nikolai Quarter *(Nikolaiviertel)* was the cute, cobbled, and characteristic old town of East Berlin. Today, the district feels pretty soulless but is a popular restaurant zone at night. **Bräuhaus Georgbrau** is a thriving beer hall sitting on a picturesque courtyard overlooking the Spree River. Eat in the lively and woody but mod-feeling interior, or outdoors with fun riverside seating—thriving with German tourists (cheap plates, three-foot-long sampler board with a dozen small glasses of beer, daily 10:00–24:00, 2 blocks south of Berlin Cathedral and across the river at Spreeufer 4, tel. 030/242-4244).

South of Unter den Linden, near Gendarmenmarkt

The twin churches of Gendarmenmarkt seem to be surrounded by people in love with food. The lunch and dinner scene is thriving with upscale restaurants serving good cuisine at highly competitive prices to local professionals. If in need of a quick-yet-classy lunch, stroll around the square and along Charlottenstrasse.

Lutter & Wegner Restaurant is well-known for its Austrian cuisine (*Schnitzel* and *Sauerbraten*) and popular with business-people. It's dressy, with fun sidewalk seating or a dark and elegant interior (two-course lunch with wine-€15 Mon–Fri, €20 on Sat and Sun; fixed-price gourmet dinner-€34, daily 11:00–24:00, Charlottenstrasse 56, tel. 030/202-9540).

Maredo Argentine Steak Restaurant, a family-friendly chain restaurant, is generally a good value with a fine salad bar (€6.20) that can make a healthy and cheap meal (behind French Cathedral at Gendarmenmarkt, at Charlottenstrasse 57, tel. 030/2094-5230).

Galeries Lafayette Food Circus is a festival of fun eateries in the basement of the landmark department store (Mon–Sat 10:00–20:00, closed Sun, U-Bahn: Französische Strasse).

Turkish and Bavarian Cuisine at Hackescher Markt

Hasir Turkish Restaurant is your chance to dine with candles, hardwood floors, and happy Berliners as snappy Turkish waiters bring plates piled high with meaty Anatolian specialties. As Berlin is one of the world's largest Turkish cities, it's no wonder you can find some good Turkish restaurants here. But while most people think of Turkish food as fast and cheap, this is a dining experience. The restaurant, in a courtyard next to the Hackesche Höfe shopping complex (see page 418), offers indoor and outdoor tables filled with an enthusiastic local crowd. Their giant €32 mixed plate is an Anatolian feast for up to five people (€14 plates, huge and splittable portions, daily from 11:30 until late, a block from the Hackescher Markt S-Bahn station at Oranienburger Strasse 4, tel. 030/2804-1616).

Weihenstephaner Bavarian Restaurant serves up-market Bavarian traditional food for around €15 a plate, offers an atmospheric cellar and a busy people-watching street-side terrace, and, of course, has excellent beer (daily 11:00–24:00, Neue Promenade 5 at Hackescher Markt, tel. 030/2576-2871).

In Prenzlauer Berg

Prenzlauer Berg is packed with fine restaurants—German, ethnic, and everything in between. (For more on this district, see page 418.) Before making a choice, I'd spend half an hour strolling and browsing through this bohemian wonderland of creative eateries. **Kollwitzplatz** is an especially good area to prowl for dinner—this square, home of the DDR student resistance in 1980s, is now trendy and upscale. With its leafy playground park in the center, it's a good place for up-market restaurants. Walk the square and choose. Just about every option offers sidewalk seats in the summer—these are great on a balmy evening. Nearby **Helmholtzplatz** (especially Lychener Strasse) is a somewhat younger, hipper, and edgier place to eat and drink.

Gugelhof, right on Kollwitzplatz, is the Prenzlauer Berg stop for visiting dignitaries. It's an institution famous for its Alsatian German cuisine. You'll enjoy French quality with German proportions. It's highly regarded with a boisterous and enthusiastic local crowd filling its minimal, yet classy interior (3-course-meal-€25, daily from 16:00, reservations required during peak times, where Knaackstrasse meets Kollwitzplatz, tel. 030/442-9229).

Metzer Eck is a time-warp *Kneipe* with a family tradition dating to 1913 and a cozy charm. It serves cheap basic typical Berlin food with Czech Budvar beer on tap (€5–7 meals, daily from 18:00, Metzer Strasse 33, on the corner of Metzer Strasse and Strassburger Strasse, tel. 030/442-7656).

Prater Biergarten offers two great eating opportunities: a rustic restaurant indoors and a mellow, shady, super-cheap, and family-friendly beer garden outdoors—each proudly pouring its own microbrew. In the beer garden—Berlin's oldest—you step up to the counter and order (simple €3–5 plates and an intriguing selection of beer munchies). The restaurant serves serious traditional *Biergarten* cuisine and good salads (€8–14 plates, Mon–Sat 18:00–24:00, Sun 12:00–24:00, cash only, Kastanienallee 7, tel. 030/448-5688).

Zum Schusterjungen ("The Boot Boy") Speisegaststätte is a classic old-school, German-with-attitude eatery that retains its circa-1986 DDR decor. Famous for its schnitzel and filling €7–8 meals, it's a no-frills place with quality ingredients and a strong local following. It serves the eating needs of those Berliners lamenting the disappearance of solid traditional German cooking amid the flood of ethnic eateries (small 40-seat dining hall, daily 11:00–24:00, corner of Lychener Strasse and Danziger Strasse 9, tel. 030/442-7654).

La Bodeguita del Medio Cuban Bar Restaurant is purely fun-loving Cuba—Christmas lights, graffiti-caked walls, Che Guevara posters, animated staff, and an ambience that makes you want to dance. Come early to eat or late to drink. It seems the waiters know the regulars' drinks. Cuban ribs and salad for €7 is a hit (€4–10 tapas, struggle with a menu in German and Spanish, puff a Cuban cigar, daily from 17:00–24:00, 1 block from U-Bahn: Eberswalder Strasse at Lychener Strasse 6, tel. 030/4171-4276). This restaurant has been here for over a decade—and in fast-changing Prenzlauer Berg, that's an eternity.

Knoppke's Imbiss, a super-cheap German-style hot-dog stand, has been a Berlin institution for over 70 years—it was family-owned even during DDR times. Berliners say Knoppke's cooks up the best *Currywurst* (grilled hot dog with curry-infused ketchup, €2) in town. There are a few tables under a nearby tent for sit-down wurst-munching (Mon–Sat 6:00–20:00, closed Sun; Kastanienallee dead-ends at the elevated train tracks, and under them you'll find Knoppke's at Schönhauser Allee 44A). Don't be fooled by the Currystation at the foot of the stairs coming out of the station; Knoppke's is actually across the street, under the tracks.

For Dessert: **Kauf Dich Glücklich** makes a great capper to a Prenzlauer Berg dinner. It serves an enticing array of sweet Belgian waffles and ice cream in a candy-sprinkled, bohemian, retro setting under WWII bullet holes on a great Prenzlauer Berg street (daily until late, indoor and outdoor seating, Oderberger Strasse 44, tel. 030/4435-2182).

TRANSPORTATION CONNECTIONS

Berlin used to have several major train stations. But now, with the Hauptbahnhof emerging as the single, massive central station, all the others are wilting into glorified subway stations. Virtually every long-distance train passes through the Hauptbahnhof. Ignore the other stations.

EurAide is a godsend for train travelers, answering your questions in American English and selling high-speed- and overnight-train reservations (see "Arrival in Berlin" on page 381).

From Berlin by Train to: Dresden (every 2 hrs, 2.25 hrs, more with a transfer in Leipzig), **Frankfurt** (hourly, 4 hrs, more with a transfer in Hannover), **Nürnberg** (hourly, 4.5 hrs), **Munich** (hourly, 5.75–6.25 hrs), **Köln** (hourly, 4.5 hrs), **Amsterdam** (3/day direct, 3 more with change in Duisberg, 6.5 hrs), **Budapest** (3/day, 13 hrs; these go via Czech Republic and Slovakia, where Eurailpass is not valid, for an overnight you need to go to Vienna and then change), **Copenhagen** (5/day, 6.5 hrs, reservation required, change in Hamburg; also consider the direct overnight train-plus-ferry route to Malmö, Sweden, which is just 20 min from Copenhagen—covered by a railpass that includes Germany or Sweden), **London** (4/day, 11–12 hrs, but you're better off flying cheap on easyJet or Air Berlin—see below), **Paris** (7/day, 9 hrs, 1–2 changes, 1 direct 12-hr night train, most connections go via Belgium), **Zürich** (hourly, 8.5 hrs, 1 direct 12-hr night train), **Prague** (5/day, 5 hrs, no overnight trains), **Warsaw** (3/day, 6 hrs, 1 night train; reservations required on all Warsaw-bound trains), **Kraków** (2/day, 10 hrs, one night train), **Vienna** (12/day, 10 hrs, most via Czech Republic—for second-class ticket, Eurailers pay an extra €40; the Berlin–Vienna via Passau train avoids Czech Republic—nightly at 20:00). It's wise but not required to reserve in advance for trains to or from Amsterdam or Prague. Train info: tel. 11861 (€0.60/min). Before buying a ticket for any long train ride from Berlin (over 7 hours), consider taking a cheap flight (buy it well in advance to get a super fare).

Eurailpasses don't cover the Czech Republic, so if you're headed to Prague you need to buy a ticket for the Czech portion of the trip. You can either buy that in the station before leaving Berlin (€14), or save about €5 by buying it directly from the Czech conductor (German stations charge twice what Czechs do for Czech tickets; note that you can only buy tickets on board on long-distance trains—if you go to Prague indirectly via a milk-run train, you can be fined heavily for boarding without a ticket).

There are **night trains** from Berlin to these cities: Munich, Frankfurt, Köln, Brussels, Paris, Vienna, Budapest, Kraków, Warsaw, Malmö, Basel, and Zürich. There are no night trains from Berlin to anywhere in Italy or Spain. A *Liegeplatz,* or *couchette* berth (€13–36), is a great deal; inquire at EurAide at the Hauptbahnhof for details. Beds generally cost the same whether you have a first- or second-class ticket or railpass. Trains are often full, so reserve your *couchette* a few days in advance from any travel agency or major train station in Europe.

The **Berlin–Paris night train** goes through Belgium. If you're using a railpass, either the pass must include Benelux, or you'll have to pay extra for the Belgian segment of the trip (roughly €50 in second class).

Berlin

Berlin's Two Airports

Allow €20 for a taxi ride to or from either of Berlin's airports.
Tegel Airport handles most flights from the United States and
Western Europe (4 miles from center, no subway trains, catch
the faster bus #X9 to Bahnhof Zoo, or bus #109 to Ku'damm and
Bahnhof Zoo for €2.10; bus TXL goes between Tegel Airport and
the Hauptbahnhof and Alexanderplatz in eastern Berlin). Flights
from the east and discount airlines usually arrive at **Schönefeld
Airport** (12.5 miles from center, 3-min walk to S-Bahn station
where you catch the regional express train into the city—going
direct to Savignyplatz, Hauptbahnhof, and Hackescher Markt,
railpass valid). The central telephone number for both airports is
01805-000-186. For British Air, tel. 01805-266-522; Delta, tel.
01803-337-880; SAS, tel. 01805-117-002; or Lufthansa, tel. 01803-
803-803.

Berlin, the New Discount Airline Hub: Berlin's Schönefeld
Airport is now the Continental European hub for discount airlines
such as easyJet (with lots of flights to Spain, Italy, Eastern Europe,
the Baltics, and more—book long in advance to get the incredible
€30-and-less fares, www.easyjet.com). Ryanair (www.ryanair.com)
and Air Berlin (www.airberlin.com) are also making the London–
Berlin trip (and other routes) dirt cheap. Consequently, British
visitors to the city are now outnumbered only by Americans. For
more on cheap flights, see page 683.

AUSTRIA

AUSTRIA

Österreich

 During the grand old Hapsburg days, Austria was Europe's most powerful empire. Its royalty built a giant kingdom (*Österreich* means "Eastern Empire") of more than 60 million people by making love, not war—having lots of children and marrying them into the other royal houses of Europe.

Today, this small, landlocked country does more to cling to its elegant past than any other nation in Europe. The waltz is still the rage. Austrians are very sociable—it's important to greet people in the breakfast room and those you pass on the streets or meet in shops. The Austrian version of "Hi" is a cheerful *"Grüss Gott"* ("May God greet you"). You'll get the correct pronunciation after the first volley—listen and copy.

While they speak German and talked about unity with Germany long before Hitler ever said *"Anschluss,"* the Austrians cherish their distinct cultural and historical traditions. They are not Germans. Austria is mellow and relaxed compared to Deutschland. *Gemütlichkeit* is the word most often used to describe this special Austrian cozy-and-easy approach to life. It's good living—whether engulfed in mountain beauty or bathed in lavish high culture. The people stroll as if every day were Sunday, topping things off with a cheerful visit to a coffee or pastry shop.

It must be nice to be past your prime—no longer troubled by being powerful, able to kick back and celebrate life in the clean, untroubled mountain air. While the Austrians make less money than their neighbors, they enjoy a short workweek and a long life span.

Austria's capital city, Vienna, has enjoyed many progressive people-oriented programs that locals attribute to its socialistic city government. While Austria has gained recent notoriety for electing racist right-wingers, that attitude does not prevail everywhere. Large parts of the country may be conservative, but Vienna is extremely liberal. For 80 years (except for the Nazi occupation), Vienna has had a socialist government. Since the fall of the Soviet Union, the party changed its name to "Social Democrat"...but its people-oriented agenda is still the same.

Austria Almanac

Official Name: Republik Österreich ("Eastern Empire"), or simply Österreich.

Population: Austria's eight million people (similar to the state of Georgia) are 91 percent ethnic Austrian, plus 4 percent from the former Yugoslavia. Three out of four Austrians are Catholic; one in 20 is Muslim. German is the dominant language, but some provinces recognize other official languages for their Slavic- and Hungarian-descended citizens.

Latitude and Longitude: 47°N and 13°E. The latitude is the same as Minnesota or Washington state.

Area: With 32,700 square miles, Austria is similar in size to South Carolina or Maine.

Geography: The northeast is flat and well populated; the less-populated southwest is mountainous, with the Alps rising up to the 12,450-foot Grossglockner. The 1,770-mile-long Danube River meanders west-to-east through the upper part of the country, passing through Vienna.

Biggest Cities: One in five Austrians lives in the capital of Vienna (1.6 million in the city; 2.2 million in the greater metropolitan area). Graz has 250,000, and Linz has 189,000.

Economy: Located at the crossroads of Europe and bordered by eight countries, Austria is well-integrated into the EU economy. The Gross Domestic Product is $279 billion (similar to Washington state's). It has a GDP per capita of $35,500—among Europe's highest. One of its biggest moneymakers is tourism. Austria produces wood, paper products (nearly half the land is forested)...and Red Bull Energy Drink. The country faces an aging population that increasingly collects social security—a situation that will strain the national budget in years to come.

Government: Alfred Gusenbauer—head of a center-left coalition government—became chancellor in the fall of 2006, when his Social Democrat party edged out a right-leaning government. Two minority parties make news beyond their numbers—the liberal Greens (10 percent) and the conservative BZÖ, headed by "yuppie fascist" Jörg Haider. Austria has been officially neutral since 1955.

Flag: Three horizontal bands of red (top), white, and red.

The Average Austrian: A typical Austrian is 40 years old, has 1.36 children, and will live to be 79. He or she inhabits a 900-square-foot home, and spends the majority of his or her leisure time with a circle of a few close friends.

Austria

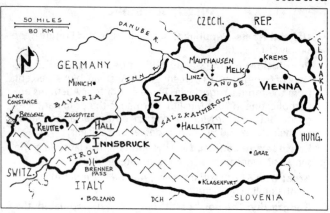

Austrians eat on about the same schedule we do. Treats include *Wiener Schnitzel* (breaded veal cutlet), *Knödel* (dumplings), *Apfelstrudel,* and fancy desserts like the *Sachertorte,* Vienna's famous chocolate cake. Bread on the table sometimes costs extra (if you eat it). Service is included in restaurant bills, but it's polite to leave a little extra (about 5 percent).

In Austria, all cars must have a **Vignette** toll sticker stuck to the inside of their windshield to legally drive on the freeways. These are sold at all border crossings (24 hours a day), big gas stations near borders, and car-rental agencies. Stickers cost €8 for 10 days (€22 for 2 months). Not having one earns you a stiff fine.

In the following chapters, I'll cover Austria's top destinations *except* for Reutte, in Tirol. For this book, Reutte has been annexed by Germany. You'll find it in the Bavaria and Tirol chapter.

VIENNA

Wien

Vienna is a head without a body. The capital of the once-grand Hapsburg Empire for 640 years, Vienna started and lost World War I, and with it its far-flung holdings. Culturally, historically, and from a sightseeing point of view, this city is the sum of its illustrious past. The home of Freud, Brahms, Maria Theresa's many children, a gaggle of Strausses, and a dynasty of Holy Roman Emperors ranks right up there with Paris, London, and Rome.

Vienna has always been the easternmost city of the West. In Roman times, it was Vindobona, on the Danube facing the Germanic barbarians. In the Middle Ages, Vienna was Europe's bastion against the Ottomans—a Christian breakwater against the riding tide of Islam (hordes of up to 200,000 Ottomans were repelled in 1529 and 1683). During this period, as the Ottomans dreamed of conquering what they called "the big apple" for their sultan, Vienna lived with a constant fear of invasion (and the Hapsburg court ruled from safer Prague). You'll notice none of Vienna's great palaces were built until after 1683, when the Turkish threat was finally over.

The Hapsburgs, who ruled the enormous Austrian Empire from 1273 to 1918, shaped Vienna. Some ad agency has convinced Vienna to make Elisabeth, wife of Emperor Franz Josef—with her narcissism and struggles with royal life—the darling of the local tourist scene. You'll see images of "Sisi" (SEE-see) all over town. But stay focused on the Hapsburgs who mattered: Maria Theresa (ruled 1740–1780, see page 490) and Franz Josef (ruled 1848–1916, see page 482).

After Napoleon's defeat and the Congress of Vienna in 1815 (which shaped 19th-century Europe), Vienna enjoyed its violin-filled belle époque, giving us our romantic image of the city: fine wine, chocolates, cafés, waltzes, and the good life.

In 1900, Vienna's 2.2 million inhabitants made it the world's fifth-largest city—after New York, London, Paris, and Berlin.

While Vienna's old walls had held out would-be invaders (including the Ottomans), they were no match for WWII bombs, which destroyed nearly a quarter of the city's buildings. In modern times, neutral Austria took a big bite out of the USSR's Warsaw Pact buffer zone. Today, Vienna is a springboard for the newly popular destinations in Eastern Europe.

Vienna's population has dropped to 1.6 million, with dogs being the preferred "child" and the average Viennese mother having only 1.3 children. Even with fewer residents, Vienna is still a grand and elegant capital containing one-fifth of Austria's population.

The truly Viennese person is not Austrian, but a second-generation Hapsburg cocktail, with grandparents from the distant corners of the old empire—Hungary, the Czech Republic, Slovakia, Poland, Slovenia, Croatia, Bosnia, Serbia, Romania, and Italy. Vienna is the melting-pot capital of a now-collapsed empire that, in its heyday, consisted of 60 million people—only eight million of whom were Austrian.

Planning Your Time

For a big city, Vienna is pleasant and laid-back. Packed with sights, it's worth two days and two nights on the speediest trip. To be grand-tour efficient, you could sleep in and sleep out on the train (Berlin, Kraków, Venice, Rome, the Swiss Alps, Paris, and the Rhine Valley are each handy night trains away). But then you'd miss the Danube and Melk. I'd come in from Salzburg via Hallstatt, Melk, and the Danube.

The Hofburg and Schönbrunn are both world-class palaces, but seeing both is redundant—with limited time or money, I'd choose just one. The Hofburg comes with the popular new Sisi Museum and is right in the town center, making for an easy visit. With more time, a visit to Schönbrunn—set outside town amid a grand and regal garden—is also a great experience. (For efficient sightseeing, drivers should note that Schönbrunn Palace is conveniently on the way out of town toward Salzburg.)

If you have two days for Vienna, here's a great way to spend them:

Day 1

9:00   Circle the Ringstrasse by tram, following my self-guided tram tour (page 461).

10:00   Drop by the TI for any planning and ticket needs,

then see the sights in Vienna's old center (using my self-guided commentary): Monument Against War and Fascism, Kaisergruft crypt, Kärntner Strasse, St. Stephen's Cathedral (nave closed 11:30–13:30), and the Graben pedestrian zone.

12:00   Lunch of finger sandwiches at Buffet Trzesniewski.

13:00   Tour the Hofburg Palace and Treasury.

16:00   Hit one more museum, or shop, browse, and people-watch.

19:30   Choose classical music (concert or opera), Haus der Musik, *Heuriger* wine garden, or any sight listed under "Sightseeing After Dark."

Day 2

Morning   Choose between Schönbrunn Palace (which could be redundant if you've seen the Hofburg Palace yesterday) or the Lipizzaner stallions. If you choose Schönbrunn Palace, arrive by 9:00 and return to central Vienna by noon. The Lipizzaner stallions' practice starts at 10:00 (about Feb–June and Sept–Oct Tue–Sat 10:00–12:00, no practice Sun–Mon or July–Aug).

12:00   Have lunch at Naschmarkt.

13:00   Tour the Opera (check red sign on door for today's schedule).

14:00   Visit the Kunsthistorisches Museum.

16:00   Choose from the many sights left to see in Vienna.

Evening   See Day 1 evening options.

Sightseeing After Dark

Several of Vienna's sights are open late one or more evenings a week.

Haus der Musik: Nightly until 22:00.

KunstHausWien: Nightly until 19:00.

Mozart Haus Museum: Nightly until 19:00.

Museum of Applied Art (MAK): Tue until 24:00.

Albertina Museum: Wed until 21:00.

Natural History Museum: Wed until 21:00.

Kunsthistorisches Museum: Thu until 21:00.

The Secession: Thu until 20:00.

Other late-night activities include: going to an opera (see page 473), a concert (see page 518), or a free, open-air cultural event on the Rathausplatz (see page 525). Also remember that Vienna's coffee shops (see page 521) and wine gardens (see page 522) are generally open late.

Greater Vienna

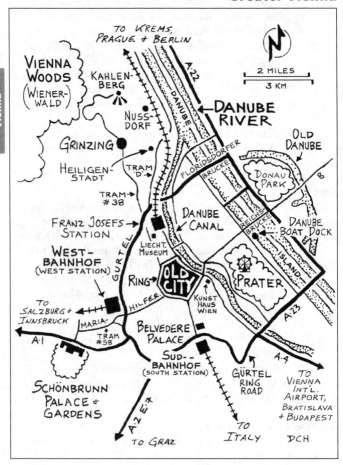

ORIENTATION

(area code: 01)

Vienna—*Wien* in German (pronounced "veen")—sits between the Vienna Woods (Wienerwald) and the Danube (Donau). To the southeast is industrial sprawl. The Alps, which arc across Europe from Marseille, end at Vienna's wooded hills, providing a popular playground for walking and sipping new wine. This greenery's momentum carries on into the city. More than half of Vienna is parkland, filled with ponds, gardens, trees, and statue-maker memories of Austria's glory days.

Think of the city map as a target with concentric sections: The bull's-eye is St. Stephen's Cathedral, the towering cathedral south of the Danube; the first circle is the Ringstrasse; and the second is the Gürtel outerbelt. The old town—snuggling around St. Stephen's—is bound tightly by the Ringstrasse, marking what used to be the city wall. The Gürtel, a broader ring road, contains the rest of downtown.

Addresses start with the district, or *Bezirk,* followed by street and building number. The Ringstrasse (a.k.a. the Ring) circles the first *Bezirk.* Any address higher than the ninth *Bezirk* is beyond the Gürtel, far from the center. The middle two digits of Vienna's postal codes show the *Bezirk.* The address "7, Lindengasse 4" is in the seventh district, #4 on Linden street. Its postal code would be 1070.

Nearly all your sightseeing will be done in the core first district or along the Ringstrasse. As a tourist, concern yourself only with this compact old center. When you do, sprawling Vienna suddenly becomes manageable.

Tourist Information

Vienna's one real tourist office is a block behind the Opera at Albertinaplatz (daily 9:00–19:00, tel. 01/24555, press 2 for English info, www.vienna.info).

Confirm your sightseeing plans and pick up the free and essential city map with a list of museums and hours (also available at most hotels), the monthly program of concerts (called *Wien-Programm*—details below), the *Vienna from A to Z* booklet (details below), the biannual city guide *(Vienna Journal),* and the youth guide *(Vienna Hype).* If you're visiting in summer, pick up the *KlangBogen* brochure, which lists the summer symphony schedule (runs June–Sept; see page 518). The TI also books rooms for a €2.90 fee. While hotel and ticket-booking agencies at the train stations and airport can answer questions and give out maps and brochures, I'd rely on the official TI if possible.

The *Wien-Programm* monthly entertainment guide is particularly important in Europe's music capital. It includes a daily calendar and information on the contemporary cultural scene, including live music, jazz, walks, expositions, and evening museum options. First you see the month's events, then guided walks offered (*E* means in English), then the opera schedule, followed by other theaters and concert halls (with phone numbers to call direct to check seat availability, and to save the 20 percent booking fees that you'll pay for buying tickets through an agency). Last is the calendar section (with codes for venues that are all listed—with their phone numbers—on the first page of the section).

Consider the TI's handy €3.60 *Vienna from A to Z* booklet. Every important building sports a numbered flag banner that keys into this guidebook. *A to Z* numbers are keyed into the TI's city map. When lost, find one of the "famous-building flags" and match its number to your map. If you're at a famous building, check the map to see what other key numbers are nearby, then check the *A to Z* book description to see if you want to go in. This system is especially helpful for those just wandering aimlessly among Vienna's historic charms.

The much-promoted €18.50 **Vienna Card** might save the busy sightseer a few euros. It gives you a 72-hour transit pass (worth €13.60) and discounts of 10 to 50 percent at the city's museums. For most, this is not worth the mental overhead. (Seniors and students will do better with their own discounts.)

Arrival in Vienna

By Train

At the Westbahnhof (West Station): Trains from Munich, Salzburg, and Melka arrive at the Westbahnhof. The *Verkersbüro* desk has maps, books hotels (for a pricey €5.50 fee), sells the Vienna Card (described earlier), and answers questions (daily 8:00–21:00, follow *Reisebüro am Bahnhof* signs). In the same area is a train info desk (daily 7:30–21:00). The Westbahnhof also has a grocery store (daily 5:30–23:00), ATMs, Internet access (including a modern Speednet at the Starbucks-like coffee shop), change offices, a post office, and storage facilities. Airport buses and taxis wait in front of the station.

To get to the city center (and most likely, your hotel), take the U-Bahn (subway) on the U-3 line (buy your ticket or transit pass—described under "Getting Around Vienna," later—from a *Tabak* shop in the station or from a machine). *U-3* signs lead down to the tracks (for Mariahilfer Strasse hotels or the center, direction: Simmering). If your hotel is along Mariahilfer Strasse, your stop is on this line (see page 530). If you're sleeping in the center or just sightseeing, ride five stops to Stephansplatz, escalate in the exit (direction: Stephansplatz), and you'll hit St. Stephen's Cathedral. From the cathedral, the TI is a five-minute stroll down the busy Kärntner Strasse pedestrian street.

At the Südbahnhof (South Station): Those traveling from Italy, Prague, and most of Eastern Europe will probably arrive here. The Südbahnhof has all the services, including left luggage, a post office, and a TI (daily 9:00–19:00).

To reach Vienna's center, tram D goes to the Ring (departs every five minutes, stops right at the Opera). Bus #13A goes to Mariahilfer Strasse. (You can also take the S- or U-Bahn, but the tram or bus is much easier.)

At Franz Josefs Bahnhof: If you're coming from Krems (in the Danube Valley), you'll arrive at Vienna's Franz Josefs station, which has no U-Bahn connections to the center of town. While you can take tram D into town from the station, you could instead get off your train one stop early at Spittelau, and use its handy U-Bahn station to get into town.

By Plane

Vienna International Airport: The airport (tel. 01/700-722-233, www.viennaairport.com), 12 miles from the center, is connected to the central Wien-Mitte Bahnhof by S-Bahn (S-7 yellow, €3, price includes any bus or S- or U-Bahn transfers, 2/hr, 24 min) and the newer City Airport Train (CAT, follow green signs, €8, 2/hr, usually departs at :05 and :35, 16 min, www.cityairporttrain.com).

Express airport buses (parked immediately in front of the arrival hall, €6, 2/hr, 30 min, buy ticket from driver, note time to destination on curbside TV monitors) go conveniently to the Schwedenplatz U-Bahn station (for city-center hotels), Westbahnhof (for Mariahilfer Strasse hotels), and Südbahnhof, where it's easy to continue by taxi or public transportation (see above).

Taxis into town cost about €35 (including the €11 airport surcharge); taxis also wait at the downtown terminus of each airport transit service. Hotels arrange for fixed-rate car service to the airport (€30, 30-min ride).

Bratislava Airport: Some budget carriers—especially SkyEurope—fly into Bratislava Airport (Letisko Bratislava, airport code: BTS, www.letiskobratislava.sk). This airport is marketed as "Vienna–Bratislava," thanks to its proximity to both capitals (it's six miles northeast of downtown Bratislava). To reach Vienna, there are several buses coordinated to meet SkyEurope flights (€10–15, trip takes about 90 min), or you can take a taxi (figure €60–90, depending on whether you use a less expensive Slovak cab or pricier Austrian cab). SkyEurope's website has more details (www.skyeurope.com).

Helpful Hints

Money: ATMs are everywhere. Banks are open weekdays roughly from 8:00 to 15:00 (until 17:30 on Thu). After hours, you can change money at train stations, the airport, post offices, or the American Express office (Mon–Fri 9:00–17:30, Sat 9:00–12:00, closed Sun, Kärntner Strasse 21–23, tel. 01/5124-0040).

Internet Access: The TI has a list of Internet cafés. **BigNet** is the dominant outfit (www.bignet.at), with lots of stations at Hoher Markt 8–9 (daily 9:00–23:00). **Surfland Internet Café** is near the Opera (daily 10:00–23:00, Krugerstrasse 10, tel. 01/512-7701).

Post Offices: Choose from the main post office (Postgasse in center, daily 6:00–22:00, handy metered phones), Westbahnhof

(Mon–Fri 7:00–22:00, Sat–Sun 9:00–20:00), Südbahnhof (daily 7:00–22:00), near the Opera (Mon–Fri 7:00–19:00, closed Sat–Sun, Krugerstrasse 13), and many other locations scattered around town.

English Bookstores: Consider the **British Bookshop** (Mon–Fri 9:30–18:30, Sat 9:30–18:00, closed Sun, at corner of Weihburggasse and Seilerstätte, tel. 01/512-1945; same hours at branch at Mariahilfer Strasse 4, tel. 01/522-6730) or **Shakespeare & Co.** (Mon–Sat 9:00–19:00, closed Sun, north of Hoher Markt, Sterngasse 2, tel. 01/535-5053).

Keeping Up with the News: Don't buy newspapers. Read them for free in Vienna's marvelous coffee houses. It's much classier.

Travel Agency: Intropa is convenient, with good service for flights and train tickets (Mon–Fri 9:00–18:00, Sat 10:00–13:00, closed Sun, Spiegelgasse 15, tel. 01/513-4000). Train tickets come with a €7 service charge when purchased from an agency rather than at the station—but, for many, the convenience is worth it.

Getting Around Vienna

By Public Transportation: Take full advantage of Vienna's simple, cheap, and super-efficient transit system, which includes trams, buses, U-Bahn (subway), and S-Bahn (faster suburban trains). I use the tram mostly to zip around the Ring (tram #1 or #2) and take the U-Bahn to outlying sights or hotels. Numbered lines (such as #38) are trams, and numbers followed by an *A* (such as #38A) are buses. The smooth, modern trams are Porsche-designed, with "backpack technology" locating the engines and mechanical hardware on the roofs for a lower ride and easier entry. Lines that begin with U (e.g., U-3) are U-Bahn lines (directions are designated by the end-of-the-line stops). Blue lines are the speedier S-Bahns. Take a moment to study the eye-friendly city-center map on station walls to internalize how the transit system can help you. The free tourist map has essentially all the lines marked, making the too-big €1.50 transit map unnecessary (info tel. 01/790-9105).

Trams, buses, the U-Bahn, and the S-Bahn all use the same tickets. Buy your tickets from *Tabak* shops, station machines, marked *Vorverkauf* offices in the station, or on board (just on trams, single tickets only, more expensive). You have lots of choices:

- Single tickets (€1.70, €2.20 if bought on tram, good for one journey with necessary transfers);
- 24-hour transit pass (€5.70);
- 72-hour transit pass (€13.60);
- 7-day transit pass (*Wochenkarte*, €14, pass always starts on Mon); or
- 8-day card *(Acht Tage Karte)*, covering eight full days of free

transportation for €27.20 (can be shared—for example, 4 people for 2 days each). With a per-person cost of €3.50/day (compared to €5.70/day for a 24-hour pass), this can be a real saver for groups. Kids under 15 travel free on Sundays and holidays.

Stamp a time on your ticket as you enter the Metro system, tram, or bus (stamp it only the first time for a multiple-use pass). Cheaters pay a stiff €50 fine if caught—and then they make you buy a ticket. Rookies miss stops because they fail to open the door. Push buttons, pull latches—do whatever it takes. Study the excellent wall-mounted street map before you exit the U-Bahn station. Choosing the right exit—signposted from the moment you step off the train—saves lots of walking.

Cute little electric buses wind through the tangled old center (bus #1A is best for a joy ride—hop on and see where it takes you).

By Taxi: Vienna's comfortable, civilized, and easy-to-flag-down taxis start at €2.50. You'll pay about €10 to go from the Opera to the Westbahnhof. Pay only what's on the meter—any surcharges (other than the €2 fee added to fares when you telephone them, or €10 for the airport) are just crude cabbie rip-offs.

By Car with Driver: Consider the luxury of having your own car and driver. Johann (a.k.a. John) Lichtl is a kind, honest, English-speaking cabbie who can take up to four passengers in his car (€25/1 hr, €20/hr for 2 or more hours, €23 to or from airport, mobile 0676-670-6750). Consider hiring gentle Johann for a day trip to the Danube Valley (see next chapter, €130, up to 8 hours), or to drive you to Salzburg with Danube sightseeing en route (€300, up to 14 hours; other trips by negotiation). These special prices are valid with this book in 2008.

By Bike: Vienna is a great city for biking—*if* you own a bike. The bike path along the Ring is wonderfully entertaining. But bike rental is a hassle (get list at TI). Your best biking is likely up and down the traffic-free and people-filled Donauinsel (Danube Island). Weather permitting from March through October, you can rent a bike all day (about 9:30 until dusk) from one of two shops near these bridges: **Floridsdörferbrücke** (€3.60/hr, €18/day, near tram #31 stop, tel. 01/278-8698) and **Reichsbrücke** (€5.40/hr, €27/day, tel. 01/263-5242).

American Rick Watts runs **Pedal Power,** and will deliver your bike to your hotel and pick it up when you're done (€32/day including delivery, Ausstellungsstrasse 3, tel. 01/729-7234, www .pedalpower.at).

Crazy Chicken bike rental, a short tram ride from the Westbahnhof, is less convenient but a bit cheaper (€15/half-day, €22/day, daily 8:30–19:00, near recommended Pension Fünfhaus at Grangasse 8—see page 534 for directions, tel. 01/892-2134, mobile 0664-421-4789).

Citybikewien, which has bikes parked in public racks all over town, is a clever program that works fine for locals and technically works for tourists (but the complexity of the credit-card forms befuddled me). The bikes lock in their stalls (50 of which are scattered through the city center) and are released when you insert your credit card and log on. Figure it out, and you have a bike for €2 per hour (first hour free, fliers explain the process in English, www.citybikewien.at).

TOURS

Walking Tours—The TI's *Walks in Vienna* brochure describes Vienna's many guided walks. The basic 90-minute "Vienna First Glance" introductory walk is offered daily throughout the summer (€12, leaves at 14:00 from near the Opera, in English and German, tel. 01/894-5363, www.wienguide.at). Various specialized tours go once a week and are listed on their website.

Hop-On, Hop-Off Bus Tours—Vienna Sightseeing operates hop-on, hop-off tours (departures from the Opera at top of each hour 10:00–17:00, recorded commentary). The schedule is posted curbside (three different routes, €13 for one, €16 for two). You could pay much more to get 24 hours of hop-on and hop-off privileges, but given the city's excellent public transportation and this outfit's meager one-bus-per-hour frequency, I'd take this not to hop on and off, but only to get the narrated orientation drive through town.

City Bus Tour—Vienna Sightseeing offers a basic three-hour city tour, including a tour of Schönbrunn Palace (€35, 3/day, call 01/7124-6830 or go to www.viennasightseeingtours.com, which also lists their many other tours).

Horse and Buggy Tour—These traditional horse-and-buggies, called *Fiakers,* take rich romantics on clip-clop tours lasting 20 minutes (€40–old town), 40 minutes (€65–old town and the Ring), or one hour (€95–all of the above, but more thorough). You can share the ride and cost with up to five people. Because it's a kind of guided tour, before settling on a carriage, talk to a few drivers and pick one who's fun and speaks English.

Local Guides—The tourist board website (www.vienna.info) has a long list of local guides with their specialties and contact information. Lisa Zeiler is an excellent English-speaking guide (two-hour walks for €130—if she's booked up, she can set you up with another guide, tel. 01/402-3688, lisa.zeiler@gmx.at). Ursula Klaus—an art scholar specializing in turn-of-the-20th-century Vienna, music, art, and architecture—also offers two-hour tours for €130 (mobile 0676-421-4884, ursula.klaus@aon .at). Lisa and Ursula are both top-notch, bring art museums to life masterfully, and can tailor tours to your interests.

SELF-GUIDED TRAM TOUR

▲▲Around the Ringstrasse

In the 1860s, Emperor Franz Josef had the city's ingrown medieval wall torn down and replaced with a grand boulevard 190 feet wide. The road, arcing nearly three miles around the city's core, predates all the buildings that line it—so what you'll see is very "Neo": Neoclassical, Neo-Gothic, and Neo-Renaissance. One of Europe's great streets, the Ringstrasse is lined with many of the city's top sights. Trams #1 and #2 and an excellent bike path circle the whole route—and so should you.

This self-guided tram tour gives you a fun orientation and a

ridiculously quick glimpse of the major sights as you glide by (€1.70, €2.20 if bought on tram, 30-min circular tour). Tram #1 goes clockwise; tram #2, counterclockwise. Most sights are on the outside, so use tram #2 (sit on the right, ideally in the front seat of the front car). Start immediately across the street from the Opera. You can (and should) jump on and off as you go

(trams come every 5 min). Read ahead and pay attention—these sights can fly by. While this works best in the daylight, this tram ride is still worthwhile after dark, when nearly every sight on the route is well-lit. Let's go:

❍ Immediately on the left: The city's main pedestrian drag, Kärntner Strasse, leads to the zigzag-mosaic roof of **St. Stephen's Cathedral.** This tram tour makes a 360-degree circle around the cathedral, staying about this same distance from it.

❍ At first bend (before first stop): Look right, toward the tall fountain and the guy on a horse. Schwarzenberg Platz shows off its **equestrian statue** of Prince Charles Schwarzenberg, who fought Napoleon. Behind that is the Russian monument (behind the fountain with the Soviet soldier holding a flag), which was built in 1945 as a forced thank-you to the Soviets for liberating Austria from the Nazis. Formerly a sore point, now it's just ignored. Beyond that (out of sight, on tram D route) is Belvedere Palace (see page 510).

❍ Going down Schubertring, you reach the huge **Stadtpark** (City Park) on the right, which honors many great Viennese musicians and composers with statues. At the beginning of the park, the gold-and-cream concert hall behind the trees is the **Kursalon,** opened in 1867 by the Strauss brothers, who directed many waltzes here. The touristy Strauss concerts are held in this building (see "Music Scene," page 518). If you'd like, hop off here for a stroll in the park.

Vienna

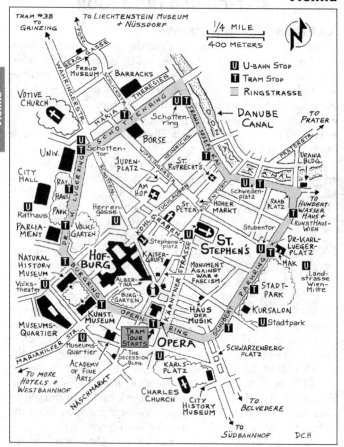

➜ Immediately after the next stop, look right: In the same park, the gilded statue of "Waltz King" **Johann Strauss** holds a violin as he did when he conducted his orchestra, whipping his fans into a three-quarter-time frenzy.

➜ Just after the next stop, at end of park: On the left, a green statue of **Dr. Karl Lueger** honors the popular man who was mayor of Vienna until 1910. Coming up, on the right, the big red-brick building is the **Museum of Applied Art** (MAK, showing furniture and design through the ages; described on page 515).

➜ At next bend: On the right, the quaint white building with military helmets decorating the windows was the **Austrian Ministry of War**—back when that was a big operation. Field Marshal Radetzky, a military big shot in the 19th century under Franz Josef, still sits on his high horse. He's pointing toward the

Post Office Savings Bank, the only Art Nouveau building facing the Ring.

The architecture along the Ring is known as **"historicism"** because it's all Neo-this and Neo-that—generally fitting the purpose of the particular building. For example, farther along the Ring, we'll see a Neoclassical parliament building—celebrating ancient Greek notions of democracy; the Neo-Gothic City Hall—recalling when medieval burghers ran the city government in Gothic days; Neo-Renaissance museums—celebrating learning; and the Neo-Baroque National Theater—recalling the age when opera and theater flourished.

❯ At next corner: The white-domed building over your right shoulder as you turn is the **Urania,** Franz Josef's 1910 observatory. Lean forward and look behind it for a peek at the huge red cars of the giant 100-year-old Ferris wheel in Vienna's Prater Park (fun for families, described on page 516).

❯ Now you're rolling along the **Danube Canal.** This "Baby Danube" is one of the many small arms of the river that once made up the Danube at this location. The rest have been gathered together in a mightier modern-day Danube, farther away. This neighborhood was thoroughly bombed in World War II. The buildings across the canal are typical of postwar architecture (1960s). They were built on the cheap, and are now being replaced by sleek, futuristic buildings. On your left was the site of the original Roman town, Vindobona.

In three long blocks, on the left (opposite the BP station, be ready—it passes fast), you'll see the ivy-covered walls and round Romanesque arches of **St. Ruprecht's** (Ruprechtskirche), the oldest church in Vienna (built in the 11th century on a bit of Roman ruins). Remember, medieval Vienna was defined by that long-gone wall that you're tracing on this tour. Across the river is an OPEC headquarters, where oil ministers often meet to set prices. Relax for a few stops (or marvel at the public-transit infrastructure Vienna enjoys) until the corner.

❯ Leaving the canal, turning left up Schottenring, at first corner: A block down on the right, you can see a huge red-brick **castle**—actually high-profile barracks built here at the command of a nervous Emperor Franz Josef (who found himself on the throne as an 18-year-old in 1848, the same year people's revolts against autocracy were sweeping across Europe).

❯ At next stop: On the left, the orange-and-white, Neo-Renaissance temple of money—the **Börse**—is Vienna's stock exchange.

❯ Next stop, at corner: The huge, frilly, Neo-Gothic church on the right is a **"votive church,"** a type of church built to fulfill a vow in thanks for God's help—in this case, when an 1853

Vienna at a Glance

▲▲▲Opera Dazzling, world-famous opera house. **Hours:** Visit the Opera by guided 35-minute tour only, daily in English; generally July–Aug at 11:00, 13:00, 14:00, 15:00, and often at 10:00 and 16:00; Sept–June fewer tours, afternoon only; call ahead to confirm tour times or check out daily schedule in red on door. Opera Museum open Tue–Sun 10:00–18:00, closed Mon. See page 473.

▲▲▲Hofburg Palace's Imperial Apartments Lavish main residence of the Hapsburgs. **Hours:** Daily 9:00–17:00, July–Aug until 17:30. See page 479.

▲▲▲Hofburg Palace's Treasury The Hapsburgs' collection of jewels, crowns, and other valuables—the best on the Continent. **Hours:** Wed–Mon 10:00–18:00, closed Tue. See page 484.

▲▲▲Kunsthistorisches Museum World-class exhibit of the Hapsburgs' art collection, including Raphael, Titian, Caravaggio, Bosch, and Brueghel. **Hours:** Tue–Sun 10:00–18:00, Thu until 21:00, closed Mon. See page 491.

▲▲▲Schönbrunn Palace Spectacular summer residence of the Hapsburgs, similar in grandeur to Versailles. **Hours:** Daily July–Aug 8:30–18:00, April–June and Sept–Oct 8:30–17:00, Nov–March 8:30–16:30, reservations recommended. See page 513.

▲▲St. Stephen's Cathedral Enormous, historic Gothic cathedral in the center of Vienna. **Hours:** Church doors open Mon–Sat 6:00–22:00, Sun 7:00–22:00; nave open for tourists only Mon–Sat 9:00–11:30 & 13:30–16:30, Sun 13:00–16:30. Tower open July–Aug 8:30–18:00, April–June and Sept–Oct 8:30–17:30, Nov–March 8:30–17:00. See page 475.

▲▲Hofburg's New Palace Museums Uncrowded collection of armor, musical instruments, and ancient Greek statues, in the elegant halls of a Hapsburg palace. **Hours:** Wed–Mon 10:00–18:00, closed Tue. See page 485.

▲▲Albertina Museum Hapsburg residence with decent apartments and world-class temporary exhibits. **Hours:** Daily 10:00–18:00, Wed until 21:00. See page 489.

▲▲Kaisergruft Crypt for the Hapsburg royalty. **Hours:** Daily 10:00–18:00. See page 489.

▲▲Haus der Musik Modern museum with interactive exhibits on Vienna's favorite pastime. **Hours:** Daily 10:00–22:00. See page 503.

▲▲Belvedere Palace Elegant palace of Prince Eugene of Savoy, with a collection of 19th- and 20th-century Austrian art (including Klimt). **Hours:** Daily 10:00–18:00. See page 510.

▲Monument Against War and Fascism Powerful four-part statue remembering victims of the Nazis. **Hours:** Always open. See page 467.

▲Lipizzaner Museum Displays dedicated to the regal Lipizzaner stallions; horse-lovers should check out their practice sessions. **Hours:** Museum open daily 9:00–18:00; stallions practice across the street roughly Feb–June and Sept–Oct Tue–Sat 10:00–12:00 when the horses are in town—call to confirm. See page 487.

▲Imperial Furniture Collection Eclectic collection of Hapsburg furniture. **Hours:** Tue–Sun 10:00–18:00, closed Mon. See page 491.

▲Natural History Museum Big building facing Kunsthistorisches Museum, featuring the ancient *Venus of Willendorf*. **Hours:** Wed–Mon 9:00–18:30, Wed until 21:00, closed Tue. See page 502.

▲Academy of Fine Arts Small but exciting collection with works by Bosch, Botticelli, Rubens, Guardi, and van Dyck. **Hours:** Tue–Sun 10:00–18:00, closed Mon. See page 506.

▲The Secession A great chance to see Klimt *in situ*. **Hours:** Tue–Sun 10:00–18:00, Thu until 20:00, closed Mon. See page 507.

▲Naschmarkt Sprawling, lively, people-filled outdoor market. **Hours:** Mon–Fri 6:00–18:30, Sat 6:00–17:00, closed Sun, closes earlier in winter. See page 508.

▲Liechtenstein Museum Impressive Baroque collection. **Hours:** Fri–Mon 10:00–17:00, closed Tue–Thu. See page 509.

▲KunstHausWien Modern art museum dedicated to zany local artist/environmentalist Hundertwasser. **Hours:** Daily 10:00–19:00. See page 509.

assassination attempt on Emperor Franz Josef failed. Ahead on the right (in front of tram stop) is the **Vienna University** building (Universität, established in 1365, it has no real campus as the buildings are scattered around town). It faces (on the left, behind a gilded angel across the Ring) a chunk of the old **city wall.** Beethoven lived and composed in the building just above the piece of wall.

➲ At next stop, on right: Flying the flag of Europe, the Neo-Gothic **City Hall** (Rathaus) towers over Rathausplatz. This square is a festive site in summer, with a huge screen showing outdoor movies, operas, and concerts and a thriving food circus (see page 541—or, if you're hungry and it's thriving, hop off now). In the winter, the City Hall becomes a huge Advent calendar, with 24 windows opening—one each day—as Christmas approaches.

Immediately across the street (on left) is the **Burgtheater,** Austria's national theater. Behind that is the Landtmann Café (the only café built with the Ringstrasse buildings, and one of the city's finest).

➲ At next stop, on right: The Neo-Greek temple of democracy houses the **Austrian Parliament.** The lady with the golden helmet is Athena, goddess of wisdom. Across the street (on left) is the imperial park called the **Volksgarten,** with a fine rose garden (free and open to the public).

➲ After the next stop on the right is the **Natural History Museum** (Naturhistorisches Museum), the first of Vienna's huge twin museums. It faces the **Kunsthistorisches Museum,** containing the city's greatest collection of paintings (see page 491). The **MuseumsQuartier** behind them completes the ensemble with a collection of mostly modern art museums (see page 502). A hefty statue of Empress Maria Theresa squats between the museums, facing the grand gate to the **Hofburg,** the emperor's palace (on left, across the Ring, described on page 477). Of the five arches, only the center one was used by the emperor. (Your tour is essentially finished. If you want to jump out here, you're at many of Vienna's top sights.)

➲ Fifty yards after the next stop, on the left through a gate in the black-iron fence, is a statue of Mozart. It's one of many charms in the **Burggarten,** which until 1918 was the private garden of the emperor. Vienna had more than its share of intellectual and creative geniuses. A hundred yards farther (on left, just out of the park), the German philosopher Goethe sits in a big, thought-provoking chair playing trivia with German poet Schiller (across the street on your right). Behind the statue of Schiller is the **Academy of Fine Arts** (see listing on page 506; and next to it is the Burg Kino, which plays the movie *The Third Man* three times a week in English—see page 526).

⊃ Hey, there's the **Opera** again. Jump off the tram and see the rest of the city.

SELF-GUIDED WALK

Welcome to Vienna

This walk connects the top three sights in Vienna's old center: the Opera, St. Stephen's Cathedral, and the Hofburg Palace. Along the way, you'll get a glimpse of Vienna past and present. The total trip takes about an hour, not counting sightseeing stops (which could be lengthy).

• *Begin by standing on the square in front of Vienna's landmark Opera.*

Opera

This is regarded by music-lovers as one of the planet's premier houses of music. If you're a fan, consider taking a guided tour of the Opera, or spring for a performance (standing-room tickets are surprisingly cheap; for information on all your Opera options, see page 473). The U-Bahn station in front of the Opera is actually a huge underground shopping mall with fast food, newsstands, lots of pickpockets, and even an Opera Toilet Vienna experience (€0.60, *mit Musik*).

• *Walk behind the Opera to find the famous...*

Sacher Café

This is the home of every chocoholic's fantasy, the *Sachertorte*. While locals complain that the cakes have gone downhill (and many tourists are surprised by how dry they are), coffee and a slice of cake here can be €8 well invested. For maximum elegance, sit inside (daily 8:00–23:30, Philharmoniker Strasse 4, tel. 01/51456). While the café itself is grotesquely touristy, the adjacent Sacher Stube has ambience and natives to spare.

• *Near the Sacher Café (turn right as you exit) is a square called Albertinaplatz, where you'll find the **TI**, as well as the evocative...*

▲Monument Against War and Fascism

This is a powerful, thought-provoking, four-part statue. The split white monument, *The Gates of Violence*, remembers victims of all wars and violence, including the 1938–1945 Nazi rule of Austria. Standing directly in front of it, you're at the gates of a concentration camp. Step into a montage of wartime images: clubs and WWI gas masks, a dying woman birthing a future soldier, and chained slave laborers sitting on a pedestal of granite cut from the infamous quarry at Mauthausen Concentration Camp (see page 556). The hunched-over figure on the ground behind is a Jew forced to scrub anti-Nazi graffiti off a street with a toothbrush. The statue with

Vienna

Vienna Self-Guided Walk

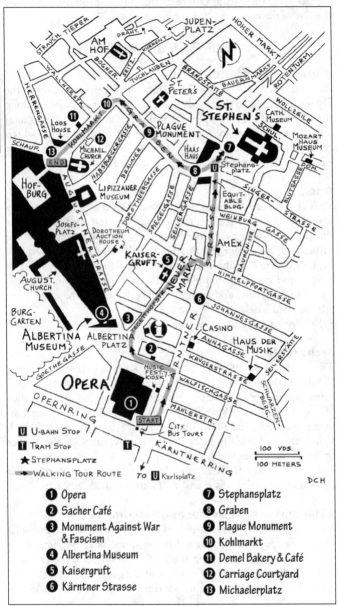

U U-Bahn Stop
T Tram Stop
★ Stephansplatz
➡ Walking Tour Route

100 YDS.
100 METERS

DCH

1 Opera
2 Sacher Café
3 Monument Against War & Fascism
4 Albertina Museum
5 Kaisergruft
6 Kärntner Strasse

7 Stephansplatz
8 Graben
9 Plague Monument
10 Kohlmarkt
11 Demel Bakery & Café
12 Carriage Courtyard
13 Michaelerplatz

its head buried in the stone (Orpheus entering the underworld) reminds Austrians (and the rest of us) of the consequences of not keeping their government on track. Behind that, the 1945 declaration of Austria's second republic—with human rights built into it—is cut into the stone. The experience gains emotional impact when you realize this monument stands on the spot where several hundred people were buried alive when the cellar they were hiding in was demolished during a WWII bombing attack (see photo to right of park, English description of memorial on the left).

Austria was pulled into World War II by Germany, which annexed the country in 1938, saying Austrians were wannabe Germans anyway. But Austrians are not Germans—never were, never will be. They're quick to tell you that while Austria was founded in the 10th century, Germany wasn't born until 1870. For seven years during World War II (1938–1945), there was no Austria. In 1955, after 10 years of joint occupation by the victorious Allies, Austria regained total independence on the condition that it would be forever neutral (and never join NATO or the Warsaw Pact). To this day, Austria is outside of NATO (and Germany).

• *Across the square from the TI is the...*

Albertina Museum

Overlooking Albertinaplatz is what looks like a big terrace. This was actually part of Vienna's original defensive rampart. Later, it was the home to Empress Maria Theresa's daughter Maria Christina. And today, it's topped by a sleek, controversial titanium canopy (called the "diving board" by critics) that welcomes visitors into a recently restored museum. For details on the Albertina Museum, see page 489.

• *Across Albertinaplatz from the Albertina Museum (beyond the memorial photo plaque) is the street called Tegetthoffstrasse. Walk down this street a block to the square called Neuer Markt. Fronting the square is the...*

Kaisergruft

This church has a crypt filled with the fancy coffins of the Hapsburgs. Before moving on, consider paying your respects here (described on page 489).

• *After visiting the Kaisergruft, cross to the center of the square.*

The **fountain,** with the "four rivers" of the Hapsburg Empire (only the Danube is famous), dates from the mid-1700s. The original nude statues were replaced with more modest versions by Maria Teresa (originals are in the Lower Belvedere Palace). The buildings all around you were rebuilt after World War II, when half of the first district was intentionally destroyed by Churchill to demoralize the Viennese, who were disconcertingly enthusiastic about the Nazis.

Vienna

Adolf Loos
(1870–1933)

"Decoration is a crime," wrote Adolf Loos, the turn-of-the-20th-century architect who was Vienna's answer to Frank Lloyd Wright. Foreshadowing the Modernist style of "less is more" and "form follows func-tion," Loos stripped buildings down to their structural skel-eton.

In his day, most buildings were plastered with fake Greek columns, frosted with Baroque balustrades, and studded with statues. Even the newer buildings featured flowery Art Nouveau additions. Loos' sparse, geometrical style stood out at the time—and it still does a century later. Loos was convinced that unnecessary ornamen-tation was a waste of workers' valuable time and energy, and was a symbol of an unevolved society. (He even went so far as to compare decoration on a facade with a lavatory wall smeared with excrement.) On this Self-Guided Walk through Vienna, you'll see four examples of his work:

American Bar (Kärntner Durchgang 10)**:** Built the same year that Loos published his famous essay *Ornament and Crime*, this tiny bar features Loos' specialties. The facade is cubical, with square columns and crossbeams (and no flowery capitals). The interior is elegant and understated, with rich marble and mirrors that appear to expand the small space.

Public WCs on the Graben: Yes, these modern loos are by Loos.

Manz Bookstore: The facade is a perfect cube, divided into other simple, rectangular shapes.

Loos House on Michaelerplatz: The facade is a per-fectly geometrical grid of square columns and windows. Compare it with the Hofburg's ornate, Neo-Rococo look (done only a few decades earlier) to see how revolutionary Loos was. An anti–Art Nouveau statement (inspired by Frank Lloyd Wright and considered Vienna's first "modern" building), this was actually considered shocking. The building's trapezoidal footprint makes no attempt to hide the awkward street corner it's placed on. This "house without eyebrows" features win-dows without the customary cornice framing the top. The 10 flower boxes beneath the windows (the "moustaches") were only added by Loos reluctantly, after citizens protested that the building was just too stark.

• *Atop the fountain is a statue of Providence. Her one bare breast points to Kärntner Strasse (50 yards away). Go there and turn left.*

Kärntner Strasse

This grand, mall-like street (traffic-free since 1974) is the people-watching delight of this in-love-with-life city. While it's mostly a crass commercial pedestrian mall with its famed elegant shops now long gone, locals know it's the same road Crusaders marched down as they headed off for the Holy Land in the 12th century. Its name indicates that it points south, in the direction of the region of Kärnten (Carinthia, a province that today is divided between Austria and Slovenia).

Along this drag, you'll find lots of action: shops, street music, the city casino (at #41), the venerable Lobmeyr Crystal shop (#26—climb up the classic Old World interior to the glass museum), and American Express (#21). Note the minimalism of the **American Bar,** designed by Modernist master Adolf Loos (see sidebar). It's dark, plush, and small, with great €8 cocktails (Kärntner Durchgang 10, tel. 01/512-3283). At the end of this street, you'll come to the cathedral. Where Kärntner Strasse hits Stephansplatz (at #3), the Equitable Building (filled with lawyers, bankers, and insurance men) is a fine example of historicism from the turn of the 20th century. Look up and imagine how slick Vienna must have felt in 1900.

Across the street on the corner, facing St. Stephen's, is the sleek concrete-and-glass **Haas Haus** by noted Austrian architect Hans Hollein (finished in 1990). The curved facade is supposed to echo the Roman fortress of Vindobona (whose ruins were found near here)...but the Viennese, who protested having this stark modern tower right next to their beloved cathedral, were not convinced. Since then, it's become a fixture of Vienna's main square. Notice how the smooth, rounded glass reflects St. Stephen's pointy Gothic architecture, providing a great photo opportunity. The café and pricey restaurant inside offer a nice perch, complete with a view of Stephansplatz below.

• *At the end of Kärntner Strasse, you'll wander into...*

Stephansplatz

Vienna's fun and colorful main square is also home to its cathedral, St. Stephen's. Now's the time to visit this massive church (see page 475).

• *When you're finished on Stephansplatz, head for the Hofburg. At the bottom of the square (near the start of Kärntner Strasse) is the street called...*

Graben

This was once a *Graben*, or ditch—originally the moat for the Roman military camp. In the middle of this pedestrian zone (at the intersection with Bräuner Strasse), top-notch street entertainers dance around an extravagant **plague monument,** officially called the Trinity Column (step back to notice the wonderful gilded "Father, Son, and Holy Ghost" at its top). In the Middle Ages, people didn't understand the causes of plagues, and figured

they were a punishment from God. It was common for survivors—and their rulers—to bribe or thank God with a monument like this one (c. 1690). One-third of Vienna died; this column is thanks from the other two-thirds. Find Emperor Leopold I, who ruled during the plague and ordered this statue created in gratitude. (Hint: The typical inbreeding of royal families left him with a gaping underbite.) Below Leopold, Faith (with the help of a disgusting little cupid) tosses an old naked woman—symbolizing the plague—into the abyss.

Just before the plague monument is Dorotheergasse, leading to the Dorotheum auction house (see page 503). Just beyond the monument, you'll pass a fine set of **public WCs.** In about 1900, a local chemical-maker needed a publicity stunt to prove that his chemicals really got things clean. He purchased two wine cellars under the Graben and had them turned into classy WCs in the Modernist style (designed by Loos, see sidebar page 470), complete with chandeliers and finely crafted mahogany. The restrooms remain clean to this day—in fact, they're so inviting that they're used for poetry readings. Locals and tourists happily pay €0.50 for a quick visit.

• *The Graben dead-ends at the aristocratic supermarket Julius Meinl am Graben (see page 539). At the end of the Graben, turn left onto...*

Kohlmarkt

This is Vienna's most elegant shopping street (except for "American Catalog Shopping" at #5, second floor), with the emperor's palace at the end. Strolling Kohlmarkt, daydream about the edible window displays at **Demel** (#14, daily 10:00–19:00). Demel is the ultimate Viennese chocolate shop. The room is filled with Art Nouveau boxes of Empress Sisi's choco-dreams come true: *Kandierte Veilchen* (candied violet petals), *Katzenzungen* (cats' tongues), and so on. The cakes here are moist (compared to the dry *Sachertortes*). The delectable window displays change monthly, reflecting current happenings in Vienna. Inside, an impressive cancan of cakes is displayed to tempt visitors into springing for the €10 cake-and-coffee deal (point to the cake you want). You can sit inside, with a view of the cake-making, or outside, with the street action. (Upstairs is less crowded.) Shops like this boast "K.u.K."—good enough for the *König und Kaiser* (king and emperor—same guy).

Next to Demel, the **Manz Bookstore** has a Loos-designed facade (see sidebar on page 470). Just beyond Demel and across the street, at #1152, you can pop in to a charming little Baroque **carriage courtyard,** with the surviving original carriage garages.

• *Kohlmarkt ends at...*

Michaelerplatz

In the center of this square, a scant bit of Roman Vienna lies exposed. On the left are the fancy Loden Plankl shop, with traditional formal wear, and the stables of the Spanish Riding School. Study the grand entry facade to the Hofburg Palace—it's Neo-Baroque from about 1900. The four heroic giants illustrate Hercules wrestling with his great challenges (much like the Hapsburgs, I'm sure). Opposite the facade, notice the modern **Loos House** (now a bank, described in sidebar on page 470); it was built at about the same time.

• *You've made it to the Hofburg Palace. To get to the sights inside, simply walk through the gate, under the dome, and into the first square (In der Burg). For details on all the sights here, see page 477.*

SIGHTS

For a self-guided walk connecting these first three landmark sights, see page 467.

▲▲▲Opera (Staatsoper)

The Opera, facing the Ring and near the TI, is a central point for any visitor. While the critical reception of the building 130 years ago led the architect to commit suicide, and though it's been rebuilt since its destruction by WWII bombs, it's still a sumptuous place.

Tours: Unless you're attending a performance, you can enter the Opera only with a guided 50-minute tour, offered daily in English (€6.50; generally July–Aug at 11:00, 13:00, 14:00, 15:00, and often at 10:00 and 16:00; Sept–June fewer tours, afternoons only, tel. 01/514-442-606). Tour times are often changed or cancelled due to rehearsals and performances. The opera posts a monthly schedule (blue, on the wall), but the more accurate schedule is the daily listing (red, posted on the door on the Operngasse side of building, farthest from St. Stephen's Cathedral). Tour tickets include the tiny and disappointing Opera Museum (across the street toward the Hofburg), except on Monday, when the museum is closed.

Opera Museum: New and included in your opera tour ticket (whether you like it or not), the Opera Museum is a let-down, with descriptions only in German and rotating six-month-long special exhibits (€3, or included in the €6.50 tour ticket, Tue–Sun 10:00–18:00, closed Mon, a block away from the Opera, near Albertina Museum, tel. 01/514-442-100).

Performances: The Vienna State Opera—with musicians provided by the Vienna Philharmonic Orchestra in the pit—is one of the world's top opera houses. There are 300 performances a year, but in July and August the singers rest their voices (or go on tour). Since there are different operas nearly nightly, you'll see big trucks out back and constant action backstage—all the sets need to be switched each day. Even though the expensive seats normally sell out long in advance, the opera is perpetually in the red and subsidized by the state.

Opera Tickets: To buy tickets in advance, call 01/513-1513 (phone answered daily 10:00–21:00, www.wiener-staatsoper.at). The theater's box office is open from 9:00 until two hours before each performance. Unless Placido Domingo is in town, it's easy to get one of 567 **standing-room tickets** (*Stehplätze*, €2.50 at the top or €3.50 downstairs). While the front doors open one hour before the show starts, a side door (middle of building, on the Operngasse side) opens 80 minutes before curtain time, giving those in the know an early grab at standing-room tickets. Just walk in straight, then head right until you see the ticket booth marked *Stehplätze* (tel. 01/514-442-419). If fewer than 567 people are in line, there's no need to line up early. If you're one of the first 160 in line, try for the "Parterre" section and you'll end up directly under the Emperor's Box. You can even buy standing-room tickets after the show has started—in case you want only a little taste of opera. Dress is casual (but do your best) at the standing-room bar. Locals save their spot along the rail by tying a scarf to it.

Rick's Crude Tips: For me, three hours is a lot of opera. But just to see and hear the Opera in action for half an hour is a treat. You can buy a standing-room spot and just drop in for part of the show. Ushers don't mind letting tourists with standing-room tickets in for a short look. Ending time is posted in the lobby—you could stop by for just the finale. If you go at the start or finish, you'll see Vienna dressed up. Of the 567 people with cheap standing-room tickets, invariably many will not stand through the entire performance. You can drop by at about 21:30, ask for standing-room tickets, and if none are available, just wait for tourists to leave and bum their tickets off them. Guards don't care. Even those with standing-room tickets are considered "ticket-holders," and are welcome to explore the building. As you leave, wander around the first floor (fun if leaving early, when halls are empty) to enjoy the sumptuous halls (with prints of famous stage sets and performers) and the grand entry staircase. The last resort (and worst option) is to drop into the Opera Café and watch the opera live on TV screens (reasonable menu and drinks).

▲▲St. Stephen's Cathedral (Stephansdom)

This massive church is the Gothic needle around which Vienna spins. According to the medieval vision, it stands like a giant jeweled reliquary, offering praise to God from the center of the city. It has survived Vienna's many wars and today symbolizes the city's freedom.

Cost: Entering the church is free (except July–mid-Oct, when it's €3 to get past the rear of the nave). Going up the towers costs €3 (by stairs, south tower) or €4 (by elevator, north tower). For more information, see "Towers," page 477.

Hours: The church doors are open Mon–Sat 6:00–22:00, Sun 7:00–22:00, but the nave is only open for tourists Mon–Sat 9:00–11:30 & 13:30–16:30, Sun 13:30–16:30. During services, you can't enter the main nave (unless you're attending Mass), but you can go into the back of the church to reach the north tower elevator (€4, daily July–Aug 8:30–18:00, April–June and Sept–Oct 8:30–17:30, Nov–March 8:30–16:30). The stairs up to the south tower (enter from outside) are open daily 9:00–17:30.

Tours: The €4 tours in English are entertaining (daily April–Oct at 15:45, check information board inside entry to confirm schedule). Audioguides may be available.

❷ Self-Guided Tour: This is the third church to stand on this spot. The church survived the bombs of World War II, but, in the last days of the war, fires from the ruins leapt to the rooftop. The original timbered Gothic rooftop burned, and the cathedral's huge bell crashed to the ground. With a financial outpouring of civic pride, the roof was rebuilt in its original splendor by 1952. The ceramic tiles are purely decorative (locals who contributed to the postwar reconstruction each "own" one for their donation). Dramatic photos show WWII damage (with bricks neatly stacked and ready).

The **grounds** around the church were a cemetery until Josef II emptied it as an "anti-plague" measure in 1780. All the tombs were removed, and the remains were dumped into mass graves outside of town (as was the case when Mozart died here in 1791). A few of the most important tombstones decorate the church walls (see west facade flanking entry). You can still see the footprint of the old cemetery church in the pavement, today ignored by the buskers and human statues. Remains of the earlier Virgil Chapel (dating from the 13th century) are immediately under this (actually on display underground, in the U-Bahn station).

Study the church's **main entrance** (west end). You can see the original Romanesque facade (c. 1240) with classical Roman statues embedded in it. Above are two stubby towers, nicknamed "pagan towers" because they're built with a few Roman stones (flipped over to hide the inscriptions and expose the smooth sides). The two 30-foot-tall columns flank the main entry. If you stand back and look at the tops, you'll see that they symbolize creation (one's a penis, the other's a vagina).

Stepping inside, you'll find a Gothic nave with a Baroque overlay. While the columns support the roof, they also tell a story. Richly populated with statues, the columns make a saintly parade leading to the high altar. Near the church's right rear, find the "Madonna with the Protective Mantle"—showing people of all walks of life seeking and finding refuge in the holy mother. The Tupperware-colored glass windows date from 1950. Before World War II, the entire church was lit with windows like the richly colored ones behind the altar. Those, along with the city's top art treasures, were hidden safely from the Nazis in cellars and mines. The altar painting of the stoning of St. Stephen is early Baroque, painted on copper.

St. Stephen's is proud to be Austria's national church. A **plaque** (10 feet up, three pillars in front of the main altar) explains how each region contributed to the rebuilding after World War II: windows from Tirol, furniture from Vorarlberg (westernmost Austrian state), the floor from Lower Austria, and so on.

The Gothic sandstone **pulpit** in the rear of the nave (on left) is a realistic masterpiece carved from three separate blocks (find the seams). A spiral stairway winds up to the lectern, surrounded and supported by the four Latin Church fathers: saints Ambrose, Jerome, Gregory, and Augustine. The railing leading up swarms with symbolism: lizards (animals of light) and toads (animals of darkness). The "Dog of the Lord" stands at the top, making sure none of those toads pollutes the sermon. Below the toads, wheels with three parts (the Trinity) roll up, while wheels with four parts (the four

seasons, symbolizing mortal life) roll down. This work, attributed by most scholars to Anton Pilgram, has all the elements of the Flamboyant Gothic style—in miniature. Gothic art was done for the glory of God. Artists were anonymous. But the year was about 1500, and the Renaissance was going strong in Italy. While Gothic persisted in the North, the Renaissance spirit had already arrived. In the more humanist Renaissance, humanity was allowed to shine—and artists became famous. So Pilgram included a rare self-portrait bust in his work (the guy with sculptor's tools, in the classic "artist observing the world from his window" pose under the stairs). A few steps farther ahead on the left wall, you'll see a similar self-portrait of Pilgram in color (symbolically supporting the heavy burden of being a master builder of this huge place).

Towers: You can ascend both towers—the south (outside right transept, by spiral staircase) and the north (via crowded elevator inside on the left). The 450-foot-high south tower, called St. Stephen's Tower, offers the far better view, but you'll earn it by hiking 343 tightly wound steps up the spiral staircase (€3, daily 9:00–17:30, this hike burns about one *Sachertorte* of calories). From the top, use your city map to locate the famous sights. The north tower elevator takes you to a mediocre view and a big bell: the 21-ton Pummerin, cast from the cannon captured from the Ottomans in 1683, and supposedly the second biggest bell in the world that rings by swinging (locals know it as the bell that rings in the Austrian New Year; elevator-€4, daily July–Aug 8:30–18:00, April–June and Sept–Oct 8:30–17:30, Nov–March 8:30–17:00).

Cathedral Museum (Dom Museum): This forlorn museum (outside left transept, past the horses) gives a close-up look at piles of religious paintings, statues, and a treasury (€7, Tue–Sat 10:00–17:00, closed Sun–Mon, Stephansplatz 6, tel. 01/515-523-689).

Hofburg Palace

The complex, confusing, and imposing Imperial Palace, with 640 years of architecture, demands your attention. This first Hapsburg residence grew with the family empire from the 13th century until 1913, when the last "new wing" opened. The winter residence of the Hapsburg rulers until 1918, it's still the home of the Spanish Riding School, the Vienna Boys' Choir, the Austrian president's office, 5,000 government workers, and several important museums.

Rather than lose yourself in its myriad halls and courtyards, focus on three sections: the Imperial Apartments, Treasury, and New Palace (Neue Burg). Note that Hapsburg sights not actually inside the Hofburg (including the Lipizzaner stallions, the Augustinian Church, and the Albertina Museum) are covered on page 488.

Vienna's Hofburg Palace

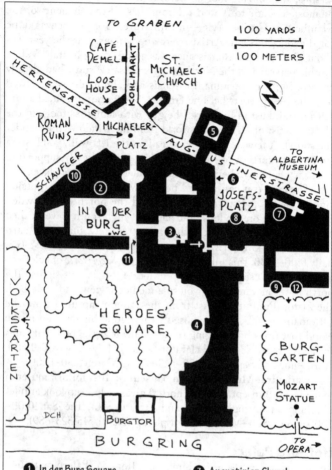

1. In der Burg Square
2. Imperial Apartments
3. Schweizerhof (Entrances to Treasury & Imperial Chapel)
4. New Palace Museums
5. Lipizzaner Museum
6. Lipizzaner Stallions Ticket Line
7. Augustinian Church
8. National Library
9. Butterfly Exhibit
10. Rest. zum Alten Hofkeller
11. Hofburg Stüberl (Snacks)
12. Café Rest. Palmenhaus

Orientation from In der Burg

Begin at the square called In der Burg (enter through the gate from Michaelerplatz). The statue is of Emperor Franz II, grandson of Maria Theresa, grandfather of Franz Josef, and father-in-law of Napoleon. Behind him is a tower with three kinds of clocks (the yellow disk shows the phase of the moon tonight). On the right, a door leads to the Imperial Apartments. Franz faces the oldest part of the palace. The colorful gate (behind you), which used to have a drawbridge, leads to the 13th-century Swiss Court (named for the Swiss mercenary guards once stationed here), the Treasury (Schatzkammer), and the Imperial Chapel (Hofburgkapelle, where the Boys' Choir sings the Mass—see page 518). For the Heroes' Square and the New Palace, continue opposite the way you entered In der Burg, passing through the left-most tunnel.

Eating at the Hofburg: Down the tunnel to Heroes' Square is a tiny but handy sandwich bar called **Hofburg Stüberl** (same €2 sandwich price whether you sit or go, Mon–Fri 7:00–18:00, Sat–Sun 10:00–16:00). For a cheap, quick meal, duck into **Restaurant zum Alten Hofkeller** in a cellar under the palace (€5 plates, Mon–Fri 11:00–13:30, closed Sat–Sun and in Aug, breakfast from 7:30, cafeteria-style, mod and efficient, Schauflergasse 7).

▲▲▲ Imperial Apartments (Kaiserappartements)

These lavish, Versailles-type, "wish-I-were-God" royal rooms are the downtown version of the grander Schönbrunn Palace. If you're rushed and have time for only one palace, do this. Palace visits are a one-way romp through 20 rooms. You'll find some helpful posted English information, and the included audioguide brings the exhibit to life. With those tools and the following description, you won't need the €8 *Imperial Apartments and Sisi* museum guidebook. Your ticket also gets you into the royal silver and porcelain collection *(Silberkammer)* near the turnstile. If touring the silver and porcelain, do it first to save walking.

Cost, Hours, Location: €10, daily July–Aug 9:00–17:30, Sept–June 9:00–17:00, last entry 30 min before closing, from courtyard through St. Michael's Gate—just off Michaelerplatz, tel. 01/533-7570, www.hofburg-wien.at.

◑ Self-Guided Tour: Get your ticket, tour the silver and porcelain collection, climb the stairs, go through the turnstile, consider the WC, and use the big model of the palace complex to understand the complex lay of the imperial land. Then head into the...

Sisi Museum: The first six rooms tell the life story of Empress Elisabeth's fancy world—her luxury homes and fairy-tale existence (see sidebar on page 480). While Sisi's life story is the perfect stuff of legends, the exhibit tries to keep things from getting too giddy,

Sisi
(1837–1898)

Empress Elisabeth—Franz Josef's mysterious, narcissistic, and beautiful wife—is in vogue. Sisi was mostly silent. Her main goals in life seem to have been preserving her reputation as a beautiful empress, maintaining her Barbie-doll figure, and tending to her fairy-tale, ankle-length hair. In spite of severe dieting and fanatic exercise, age took its toll. After turning 30, she allowed no more portraits to be painted and was generally seen in public with a delicate fan covering her face (and bad teeth).

Complex and influential, Sisi was adored by Franz Josef, whom she respected. Her personal mission and political cause was promoting Hungary's bid for nationalism. Her personal tragedy was the death of her son Rudolf, the crown prince, an apparent suicide (an incident often dramatized as "The Mayerling Affair," after the royal hunting lodge where it happened).

Disliking Vienna and the confines of the court, Sisi traveled more and more frequently. As years passed, the restless Sisi and her hardworking husband became estranged. In 1898, while visiting Geneva, Switzerland, she was murdered by an Italian anarchist.

Sisi has been compared to Princess Diana because of her beauty, bittersweet life, and tragic death. Her story is wonderfully told in the new Sisi Museum, now part of the Hofburg Imperial Apartments tour.

and doesn't add to the sugary, kitschy image that's been created. The exhibit starts with her assassination (see her death mask) and traces the development of her legend, analyzing how her fabulous but tragic life could create a 19th-century Princess Diana from a rocky start (when she was disdained for abandoning Vienna and her husband, the venerable Emperor Franz Josef). You'll read bits of her poetic writing, see exact copies of her now-lost jewelry, and learn about her escapes, dieting mania, and chocolate bills. Admire Sisi's hard-earned thin waist (20 inches at age 16, 21 inches at age 50...after giving birth to four children). The black statue in the dark room represents the empress after the suicide of her son—aloof, thin, in black, with her back to the world. At the end, ponder the crude knife that killed Sisi.

A special exhibit opened in August 2006 to celebrate the 50th anniversary of the films that made Sisi a household name (at least in Austria): *Sisi* (1955); *Sisi: The Young Empress* (1956); *Sisi: Fateful Years of an Empress* (1957); and the condensed English version,

Forever My Love (1962). The exhibition showcases the furniture borrowed from the palace for the movies, along with photographs and props from the filming.

After the Sisi Museum, a one-way route takes you through a series of royal rooms. The first room—as if to make clear that there was more to the Hapsburgs than Sisi—shows a family tree tracing the Hapsburgs from 1273 to their messy WWI demise. From here, you enter the private apartments of the royal family (Franz Josef's first, then Sisi's).

Waiting Room for the Audience Room: A map and mannequins from the many corners of the Hapsburg realm illustrate the multiethnicity of the vast empire. Every citizen had the right to meet privately with the emperor. Three huge paintings entertained guests while they waited. They were propaganda, showing crowds of commoners enthusiastic about their Hapsburg rulers.

On the right: an 1809 scene of the emperor returning to Vienna, celebrating news that Napoleon had begun his retreat.

Left: the return of the emperor from the 1814 Peace of Paris, the treaty that ended the Napoleonic wars. The 1815 Congress of Vienna that followed was the greatest assembly of diplomats in European history. Its goal: to establish peace through a "balance of power" among nations. While rulers ignored nationalism in favor of continued dynastic rule, it worked for about a century, until a colossal war—World War I—wiped out the Hapsburgs and the rest of Europe's royal families.

Center: Less important, the emperor makes his first public appearance to adoring crowds after recovering from a life-threatening illness (1826). The chandelier—considered the best in the palace—is Baroque, made of Bohemian crystal.

Audience Room: Suddenly, you were face-to-face with the emp himself. The portrait on the easel shows Franz Josef in 1915, when he was more than 80 years old. Famously energetic, he lived a spartan life dedicated to duty. He'd stand at the high table here to meet with commoners, who came to show gratitude or make a request. (Standing kept things moving.) On the table, you can read a partial list of 56 appointments he had on January 3, 1910 (three columns: family name, meeting topic, and *Anmerkung*—the emperor's "action log").

Conference Room: The emperor presided here over the equivalent of cabinet meetings. After 1867, he granted Hungary some authority over his sprawling and suddenly unruly lands (creating the "Austro-Hungarian Empire")—so Hungarians also attended these meetings. The paintings on the wall show the military defeat of a popular Hungarian uprising...subtle.

Emperor Franz Josef's Study: This room evokes how seriously the emperor took his responsibilities as the top official of a

Emperor Franz Josef
(1830–1916)

Franz Josef I—who ruled for 68 years (1848–1916)—was the embodiment of the Hapsburg Empire as it finished its six-century-long ride. Born in 1830, Franz Josef had a stern upbringing that instilled in him a powerful sense of duty and—like so many men of power—a love of things military.

His uncle, Ferdinand I, was a dimwit. As the revolutions of 1848 were rattling royal families throughout Europe, the Hapsburgs replaced Ferdinand, putting 18-year old Franz Josef on the throne. FJ put down the revolt with bloody harshness and spent the first part of his long reign understandably paranoid as social discontent simmered.

FJ was very conservative. But worse, he figured wrongly that he was a talented military tactician, leading Austria into catastrophic battles against Italy (which was fighting for its unification and independence) in the 1860s. As his army endured severe, avoidable casualties, it became clear: FJ was a disaster as a general.

Wearing his uniform to the end, he never saw what a dinosaur his monarchy was becoming, and never thought it strange that the majority of his subjects didn't even speak German. He had no interest in democracy and pointedly never set foot in Austria's parliament building. But, like his contemporary Queen Victoria, he was the embodiment of his empire—old-fashioned but sacrosanct. His passion for low-grade paperwork earned him the nickname "Joe Bureaucrat." Mired in these petty details, he missed the big picture. In 1914, he helped start a Great War that ultimately ended the age of monarchs. The year 1918 marked the end of Europe's big royal families: Hohenzollerns (Prussia), Romanovs (Russia), and Hapsburgs (Austria).

vast empire. The desk was originally between the windows. Franz Josef could look up from his work and see his lovely, long-haired, tiny-waisted Empress Elisabeth's reflection in the mirror. Notice the trompe l'oeil paintings above each door, giving the believable illusion of marble relief. Notice also all the family photos—the perfect gift for the dad/uncle/hubby who has it all.

The walls between the rooms are wide enough to hide servants' corridors (the hidden door to his valet's room is in the back left corner). The emperor lived with a personal staff of 14: "three valets, four lackeys, two doormen, two manservants, and three chambermaids."

Emperor's Bedroom: Franz Josef famously slept on this no-frills iron bed, and used the portable washstand until 1880 (when the palace got running water). While he had a typical emperor's share of mistresses, his dresser was always well-stocked with photos of Sisi. Franz Josef lived here after his estrangement from Sisi. An etching shows the empress—a fine rider and avid hunter—sitting sidesaddle while jumping a hedge.

Large Salon: This room was for royal family gatherings, and went unused after Sisi's death. The big, ornate stove in the corner was fed from behind. Through the 19th century, this was a standard form of heating.

Small Salon: This room is dedicated to the memory of the assassinated Emperor Maximilian of Mexico (bearded portrait, Franz Josef's brother, killed in 1867). It was also a smoking room—necessary in the early 19th century, when smoking was newly fashionable (but only for men—never done in the presence of women). Left of the door is a small button the emperor had to buzz before entering his estranged wife's quarters. You, however, can go right in.

Empress' Bedroom and Drawing Room: This was Sisi's, refurbished in the Neo-Rococo style in 1854. She lived here—the bed was rolled in and out daily—until her death in 1898.

Sisi's Dressing/Exercise Room: Servants worked two hours a day on Sisi's famous hair here. She'd exercise on the wooden structure. You can psychoanalyze Sisi from the people and photos she hung on her walls. It's mostly her favorite dogs, her Bavarian family, and several portraits of the romantic and anti-monarchist poet Heinrich Heine. Her infatuation with the liberal Heine caused a stir in royal circles.

Sisi's Bathroom: Detour into the behind-the-scenes palace. In the narrow passageway, you'll walk by Sisi's hand-painted-porcelain, dolphin-head WC (on the right). In the main bathroom, you'll see her huge copper tub (with the original wall coverings behind it). Sisi was the first Hapsburg to have running water in her bathroom (notice the hot and cold faucets). You're walking on the first linoleum ever used in Vienna (c. 1880).

Servants' Quarters: Next, enter the servants' quarters, with tropical scenes painted by Bergl in 1766. Take time to enjoy Bergl's playful details. As you leave these rooms and re-enter the imperial world, look back to the room on the left.

Empress' Great Salon: The room is painted with Mediterranean escapes, the 19th-century equivalent of travel posters. The statue is of Elisa, Napoleon's oldest sister (by the Neoclassical master Antonio Canova). A print shows how the emperor and Sisi would share breakfast in this room. Turn the corner and pass through the anterooms of Alexander's apartments.

Small Salon: The portrait is of Crown Prince Rudolf, Franz Josef and Sisi's son, who supposedly committed suicide at age 30. The mysterious circumstances around his death at Mayerling hunting lodge have been dramatized in numerous movies, plays, opera—and even a ballet.

Red Salon: The Gobelin wall hangings were a 1776 gift from Marie-Antoinette and Louis XVI in Paris to their Viennese counterparts.

Dining Room: It's dinnertime, and Franz Josef has called his extended family together. The settings are modest...just silver. Gold was saved for formal state dinners. Next to each name card was a menu with the chef responsible for each dish. (Talk about pressure.) While the Hofburg had tableware for 4,000, feeding 3,000 was a typical day. The cellar was stocked with 60,000 bottles of wine. The kitchen was huge—50 birds could be roasted on the hand-driven spits at once. (Drop off your audioguide in this room.)

Zip through the shop, go down the stairs, and you're back on the street. Two quick lefts take you back to the palace square (In der Burg), where the Treasury awaits just past the black, red, and gold gate on the far side.

▲▲▲Treasury (Weltliche und Geistliche Schatzkammer)

This "Secular and Religious Treasure Room" contains the best jewels on the Continent. Slip through the vault doors and reflect on the glitter of 21 rooms filled with scepters, swords, crowns, orbs, weighty robes, double-headed eagles, gowns, gem-studded bangles, and a unicorn horn.

Cost, Hours, Information: €10, Wed–Mon 10:00–18:00, closed Tue, follow *Schatzkammer* signs to the Schweizerhof, tel. 01/525-243-410, www.hofburg-wien.at. While no English descriptions are provided within the Treasury, the well-produced, €3 audioguide provides a wealth of information and is worth renting.

❷ Self-Guided Tour: Here's a basic rundown of the highlights (the audioguide is much more complete).

Room 2: The personal crown of Rudolf II has survived since 1602—it was considered too well-crafted to cannibalize for other crowns. It's a big deal because it's the adopted crown of the Austrian Empire, established in 1806 after Napoleon dissolved the Holy Roman Empire (an alliance of Germanic kingdoms so named because it wanted to be considered the continuation of the Roman Empire). Pressured by Napoleon, the Austrian Francis II—who had been Holy Roman Emperor—became Francis I, Emperor of Austria. Francis I/II (the stern guy on the wall, near where you entered) ruled from 1792 to 1835. Look at the crown. Its design symbolically merges the typical medieval king's crown and a bishop's miter.

Rooms 3 and 4: These contain some of the coronation vestments and regalia needed for the new Austrian emperor.

Room 5: Ponder the Throne Cradle. Napoleon's son was born in 1811 and made king of Rome. The little eagle at the foot is symbolically not yet able to fly, but glory-bound. Glory is symbolized by the star, with dad's big *N* raised high.

Room 8: The eight-foot-tall, 500-year-old unicorn horn (possibly a narwhal tusk), was considered incredibly powerful in the old days, giving its owner the grace of God. This was owned by the Holy Roman Emperor—clearly a divine monarch.

Room 11: The collection's highlight is the 10th-century crown of the Holy Roman Emperor (HRE). The imperial crown swirls with symbolism "proving" that the emperor was both holy and Roman. The jeweled arch over the top is reminiscent of the parade helmet of ancient Roman emperors whose successors the HRE claimed to be. The cross on top says the HRE ruled as Christ's representative on earth. King Solomon's portrait (on the crown, right of cross) is Old Testament proof that kings can be wise and good. King David (next panel) is similar proof that they can be just. The crown's eight sides represent the celestial city of Jerusalem's eight gates. The jewels on the front panel symbolize the 12 apostles.

The nearby 11th-century Imperial Cross preceded the emperor in ceremonies. Encrusted with jewels, it carried a substantial chunk of *the* cross and *the* holy lance (supposedly used to pierce the side of Jesus while on the cross; both items displayed in the same glass case). This must be the actual holy lance, as Holy Roman Emperors actually carried this into battle in the 10th century. Look behind the cross to see how it was a box that could be clipped open and shut, used for holding holy relics. You can see bits of the "true cross" anywhere, but this is a prime piece—with the actual nail hole.

The other case has jewels from the reign of Karl der Grosse (Charlemagne), the greatest ruler of medieval Europe. Notice Charlemagne modeling the crown (which was made a hundred years after he died) in the tall painting adjacent.

Room 12: The painting shows the coronation of Maria Theresa's son Josef II in 1764. In a room filled with the literal big wigs of the day, Josef is wearing the same crown and royal garb that you've just seen.

Room 16: Most tourists walk right by perhaps the most exquisite workmanship in the entire Treasury, the royal vestments (15th century). Look closely—they're painted with gold and silver threads.

▲New Palace (Neue Burg)

This last grand addition to the palace, from the early 20th century, was built for the Hapsburg heir Franz Ferdinand (it was tradition for rulers not to move into their predecessor's quarters). But—while he was waiting politely for his long-lived uncle, Emperor Franz Josef, to die so he could move into his new digs—Franz Ferdinand was assassinated in Sarajevo in 1914, sparking the beginning of World War I.

The palace's grand facade arches around **Heroes' Square** (Heldenplatz). Notice statues of two great Austrian heroes on horseback: Prince Eugene of Savoy (who defeated the Ottomans that had earlier threatened Vienna) and Archduke Charles (first to beat Napoleon in a battle, breaking Nappy's image of invincibility and heralding the end of the Napoleonic age). The frilly spires of Vienna's Neo-Gothic City Hall break the horizon, and a line of horse-drawn carriages await customers.

▲▲New Palace Museums: Armor, Music, and Ancient Greek Statues—The New Palace (Neue Burg)—technically part of the Kunsthistorisches Museum across the way—houses three fine museums (same ticket): an armory (with a killer collection of medieval weapons), historical musical instruments, and classical statuary from ancient Ephesus. The included audioguide brings the exhibits to life and lets you actually hear the collection's fascinating old instruments being played. An added bonus is the chance to wander all alone among those royal Hapsburg halls, stairways, and painted ceilings (€10, Wed–Mon 10:00–18:00, closed Tue, almost no tourists, tel. 01/525-243-430).

More Hapsburg Sights near the Hofburg

Central Vienna has plenty more sights associated with the Hapsburgs. With the exception of the last one (on Mariahilfer Strasse), these are all near the Hofburg. Remember that the biggest Hapsburg sight of all, Schönbrunn Palace, makes a great half-day trip (four miles from the center—see page 513).

Palace Garden (Burggarten)

This greenbelt, once the backyard of the Hofburg and now a people's park, welcomes people to loiter on the grass. On nice days, it's lively with office workers enjoying a break. The statue of Mozart facing the Ringstrasse is popular. The iron-and-glass pavilion now houses the recommended Café Restaurant Palmenhaus (see page 540) and a small but fluttery butterfly exhibit (€5; April–Oct Mon–Fri 10:00–16:45, Sat–Sun 10:00–18:15; Nov–March daily 10:00–15:45). The butterfly zone is delightfully muggy on a brisk off-season day, but trippy any time of year. If you tour it, notice the butterflies hanging out on the trays with rotting slices of banana. They lick the fermented banana juice as it beads, and then just hang out there in a stupor... or fly giddy loop-de-loops.

▲Lipizzaner Museum

While the famous court horses of the Hapsburg emperors were originally from Spain, by the 16th century they were moved closer to Vienna (to the Slovenian town of Lipica, then part of the Hapsburg Empire). For four centuries, the "Lipizzaner stallions" have been bred, raised, and trained in Lipica. They actually have "surnames" that can be traced to the original six 16th-century stallions that made the trip from Spain. A must for horse-lovers, this tidy museum in the Renaissance Stallburg Palace shows (and tells in English) the 400-year history of the famous "Spanish Riding School" and the Lipizzaner stallions.

Cost, Hours, Location: €5, €15 combo-ticket includes training sessions (described later), daily 9:00–18:00, between Josefsplatz and Michaelerplatz at Reitschulgasse 2, tel. 01/525-243-450, www.lipizzaner.at. Ask about the next English showing of the film, which plays in the basement.

⊙ Self-Guided Tour: This commentary will make your visit more meaningful.

First Room: One horse's family tree—Conversano Toscana (born 1984)—is shown, tracing his father's line (Conversano) back to 1767. Paintings show how horses were bred for small heads and legs, but massive bodies. The three-minute video is quite graphic, starting with a horse worked up and ready to "joust," followed by a horse giving birth, then a wobbly baby—just minutes old—taking its first steps.

Downstairs: Videos clearly illustrate how the traditional moves so appreciated today evolved. After horses were antiquated on the battlefield, dressage morphed from no-nonsense military moves to court entertainment. The "dancing" originated as battle moves: *pirouette* (quick turns for surviving in the thick of battle) and *courbette* (on hind legs, to make a living shield for the knight). The *capriole* is a strong back-kick that could floor any enemy.

Theater: A 45-minute movie with great horse footage runs constantly (showings alternate between German and English).

Back Upstairs: Here an exhibit retells the dramatic WWII Lipizzaner rescue story. Lipizzaner fans have a warm spot in their hearts for General Patton, who, at the end of World War II—knowing that the Soviets were about to take control of

Vienna—ordered a raid on the stable to save the horses and ensure the survival of their fine old bloodlines.

If all this horse information gets you fired up for more, consider...

Seeing the Lipizzaner Stallions—Seats for performances by Vienna's prestigious Spanish Riding School book up months in advance, but standing room is often available the same day (tickets-€45–160, standing room-€28, Feb–June and Sept–Oct Sun at 11:00, sometimes also Fri at 18:00, no shows July–Aug, fewer Nov–Jan, tel. 01/533-9031, www.srs.at). Luckily for the masses, training sessions with music in a chandeliered Baroque hall are open to the public (€12 at the door, roughly Feb–June and Sept–Oct Tue–Sat 10:00–12:00—but only when the horses are in town).

Tourists line up early at Josefsplatz, gate 2. Save money and avoid the wait by buying the €15 combo-ticket that covers both the museum and the training session (and lets you avoid that ticket line). If you want to hang out with Japanese tour groups, get there early and wait for the doors to open at 10:00. Better yet, simply show up late. Almost no one stays for the full two hours—except for the horses. As people leave, new tickets are printed continuously, so you can just waltz in with no wait at all. Don't have high expectations, as the horses often do little more than trot and warm up.

With the riding school enduring financial problems, other ways to see the horses and their stables are now possible (pricey, but for some a good value, details online at www.lipizzaner.at).

▲Augustinian Church (Augustinerkirche)

This is the Gothic and Neo-Gothic church where the Hapsburgs latched, then buried, their hearts (weddings took place here, and the royal hearts are in the vault). Don't miss the exquisite, tomb-like Canova memorial (Neoclassical, 1805) to Maria Theresa's favorite daughter, Maria Christina, with its incredibly sad white-marble procession. The church's 11:00 Sunday Mass is a hit with music-lovers—both a Mass and a concert, often with an orchestra accompanying the choir. To pay, contribute to the offering plate and buy a CD afterwards. Programs are available at the table by the entry all week (church open long hours daily, Augustinerstrasse 3).

The church faces Josefsplatz, with its statue of the great reform emperor Josef II. Next to the Augustinian Church, the **National Library** and its State Hall are impressive (€5, Tue–Sun 10:00–18:00, Thu until 21:00, closed Mon).

▲▲Albertina Museum

This building, at the southern tip of the Hofburg complex (near the Opera), was the residence of Maria Teresa's favorite daughter: Maria Christina, who was the only one allowed to marry for love rather than political strategy. Her many sisters were jealous. (Marie-Antoinette had to marry the French king...and lost her head over it.) Maria Christina's husband, Albert of Saxony, was a great collector of original drawings. He amassed an enormous assortment of works by Dürer, Rembrandt, Rubens, and others. Today, the Albertina allows visitors to tour its elegant state rooms, which hold reproductions of some of these works, and presents temporary exhibits of other artists.

First, head up the central staircase and stroll through the Hapsburg staterooms *(Prunkräume)*, decorated in the French Classicist style—lots of white marble. Top-quality facsimiles of the collection's greatest pieces hang in these rooms. Then browse the modern gallery, featuring special exhibitions well-described in English.

Cost, Hours, Location: €9.50, price can vary based on special exhibits, audioguide-€4, daily 10:00–18:00, Wed until 21:00, overlooking Albertinaplatz across from the TI and Opera, tel. 01/534-830, www.albertina.at.

▲▲Kaisergruft, the Remains of the Hapsburgs

Visiting the imperial remains is not as easy as you might imagine. These original organ donors left their bodies—about 150 in all—in the unassuming Kaisergruft (Capuchin Crypt), their hearts in the Augustinian Church (described earlier; church open long hours daily, but to see the goods you'll have to talk to a priest), and their entrails in the crypt below St. Stephen's Cathedral. Don't tripe.

Cost, Hours, Location: €4, daily 10:00–18:00, last entry at 17:40, behind the Opera on Neuer Markt, tel. 01/512-685-316. Upon entering the Kaisergruft, buy the €0.50 map with a Hapsburg family tree and a chart locating each coffin.

Highlights: The double coffin of **Maria Theresa** (1717–1780) and her husband, **Franz I** (1708–1765), is worth a close look for its artwork. Maria Theresa outlived her husband by 15 years—which she spent in mourning. Old and fat, she installed a special lift enabling her to get down into the crypt to be with her dear, departed Franz (even though he had been far from faithful). The couple recline—Etruscan-style—atop their fancy lead coffin. At each corner are the crowns of the Hapsburgs—the Holy Roman Empire, Hungary, Bohemia, and Jerusalem. Notice the contrast between the Rococo splendor of Maria Theresa's tomb and the simple box holding her more modest son, **Josef II** (at his parents' feet; for more on Maria Theresa and Joe II, see the sidebar, next page).

Empress Maria Theresa (1717–1780) and Her Son, Emperor Josef II (1741–1790)

Maria Theresa was the only woman to officially rule the Hapsburg Empire in that family's 640-year reign. She was a strong and effective empress (r. 1740–1780). People are quick to remember Maria Theresa as the mother of 16 children (10 survived). Imagine that the most powerful woman in Europe either was pregnant or had a newborn for most of her reign. Maria Theresa ruled after the Austrian defeat of the Ottomans, when Europe recognized Austria as a great power. (Her rival, the Prussian emperor, said, "When at last the Hapsburgs get a great man, it's a woman.")

The last of the Baroque imperial rulers, and the first of the modern rulers of the Age of Enlightenment, Maria Theresa marked the end of the feudal system and the beginning of the era of the grand state. She was a great social reformer. During her reign, she avoided wars and expanded her empire by skillfully marrying her children into the right families. For instance, after daughter Marie-Antoinette's marriage into the French Bourbon family (to Louis XVI), a country that had been an enemy became an ally. (Unfortunately for Marie-Antoinette, Maria Theresa's timing was off.)

Maria Theresa was a great reformer and in tune with her age. She taxed the Church and the nobility, provided six years of obligatory education to all children, and granted free health care to all in her realm. Maria Theresa also welcomed the boy genius Mozart into her court.

The empress' legacy lived on in her son, Josef II, who ruled as emperor himself for a decade (1780–1790). He was an even more avid reformer, building on his mother's accomplishments. An enlightened monarch, Josef mothballed the too-extravagant Schönbrunn Palace, secularized the monasteries, established religious tolerance within his realm, freed the serfs, made possible the founding of Austria's first general hospital, and promoted relatively enlightened treatment of the mentally ill. Josef was a model of practicality (for example, reusable coffins à la *Amadeus,* and no more than six candles at funerals)—and very unpopular with other royals. But his policies succeeded in preempting the revolutionary anger of the age, enabling Austria to avoid the turmoil that shook so much of the rest of Europe.

Franz Josef (1830–1916; see sidebar on page 482) is nearby, in an appropriately austere military tomb. Flanking Franz Josef are

the tombs of his son, the archduke **Rudolf,** and Empress Elisabeth. Rudolf and his teenage mistress supposedly committed suicide together in 1889 at Mayerling hunting lodge and—since the Church figured he forced her and was therefore a murderer—it took considerable legal hair-splitting to win Rudolf this spot (after examining his brain, it was determined that he was mentally disabled and therefore incapable of knowingly killing himself and his girl). *Kaiserin* Elisabeth (1837–1898), a.k.a. **Sisi,** always gets the "Most Flowers" award (see sidebar on page 480).

In front of those three is the most recent Hapsburg tomb. **Empress Zita** was buried in 1989. Her burial procession was probably the last such Old Regime event in European history. The monarchy died hard in Austria.

While it's fun to chase down all these body parts, remember that the real legacy of the Hapsburgs is the magnificence of this city. Step outside. Pan up. Watch the clouds glide by the ornate gables of Vienna.

▲Imperial Furniture Collection (Kaiserliches Hofmobiliendepot)

Bizarre, sensuous, eccentric, or precious, this collection is your peek at the Hapsburgs' furniture—from grandma's wheelchair to the emperor's spittoon—all thoughtfully described in English. The Hapsburgs had many palaces, but only the Hofburg was permanently furnished. The rest were furnished on the fly—set up and taken down by a gang of royal roadies called the "Depot of Court Movables" (Hofmobiliendepot). When the monarchy was dissolved in 1918, the state of Austria took possession of the Hofmobiliendepot's inventory—165,000 items. Now this royal storehouse is open to the public in a fine and sprawling museum. Don't go here for the *Jugendstil* furnishings. The older Baroque, Rococo, and Biedermeier pieces are the most impressive and tied most intimately to the royals. Combine a visit to this museum with a stroll down the lively shopping boulevard, Mariahilfer Strasse.

Cost, Hours, Location: €7, Tue–Sun 10:00–18:00, closed Mon, Mariahilfer Strasse 88, U-3: Zieglergasse, tel. 01/5243-3570.

▲▲▲Kunsthistorisches Museum

This exciting museum, across the Ring from the Hofburg Palace, showcases the grandeur and opulence of the Hapsburgs' collected artwork in a grand building (built as a museum in 1888). There are European masterpieces galore, all well-hung on one glorious floor, plus a fine display of Egyptian, classical, and applied arts.

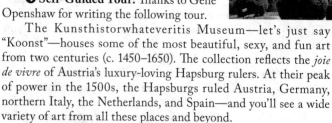

Cost, Hours, Location: €10, audioguide-€3, Tue–Sun 10:00–18:00, Thu until 21:00, closed Mon, on the Ringstrasse at Maria-Theresien-Platz, U-2 or U-3: Volkstheater/Museumsplatz, tel. 01/525-240, www.khm.at.

❷ **Self-Guided Tour:** Thanks to Gene Openshaw for writing the following tour.

The Kunsthistorwhateveritis Museum—let's just say "Koonst"—houses some of the most beautiful, sexy, and fun art from two centuries (c. 1450–1650). The collection reflects the *joie de vivre* of Austria's luxury-loving Hapsburg rulers. At their peak of power in the 1500s, the Hapsburgs ruled Austria, Germany, northern Italy, the Netherlands, and Spain—and you'll see a wide variety of art from all these places and beyond.

Of the museum's many exhibits, we'll tour only the Painting Gallery (Gemäldegalerie) on the first floor. Climb the main staircase, featuring Antonio Canova's statue of *Theseus Clubbing the Centaur.* Italian Art is in the right half of the building (as you face Theseus), and Northern Art to the left. Notice that the museum labels the largest rooms with Roman numerals (Saal I, II, III), and the smaller rooms around the perimeter with Arabic (Rooms 1, 2, 3).

• *Enter Saal I and walk right into the High Renaissance.*

Venetian Renaissance (1500–1600)—Titian, Veronese, Tintoretto: About the year 1500, Italy had a Renaissance, or "rebirth," of interest in the art and learning of ancient Greece and Rome. In painting, that meant that ordinary humans and Greek gods joined saints and angels as popular subjects.

Saal I spans the long career of **Titian** the Venetian (it rhymes)—who seemed particularly intimate with the pre-Christian gods and their antics. In *Mars, Venus, and Amor,* a busy cupid oversees the goddess of love, making her case that war is not the answer. Mars—his weapons blissfully discarded—sees her point.

Danae with Nursemaid (also usually in Saal I, but may be out for renovation in 2008) features more pre-Christian mythology. Zeus, the king of the gods, was always zooming to earth in the form of some creature or other to fool around with mortal women. Here, he descends as a shower of gold to consort with the willing Danae. You can almost see the human form of Zeus within the cloud. Danae is helpless with rapture, opening her legs to receive him, while her servant tries to catch the heavenly spurt with a

Kunsthistorisches Museum

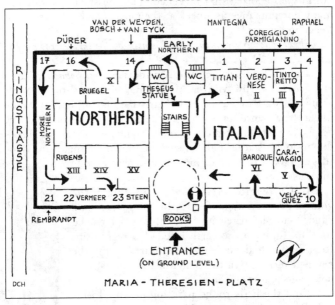

towel. Danae's rich, luminous flesh on the left of the canvas is set off by the dark servant at right and the threatening sky above. The white sheets beneath her make her glow even more. This is more than a classic nude—it's a Renaissance Miss August. How could ultra-conservative Catholic emperors have tolerated such a downright pagan and erotic painting? Apparently, without a problem.

In *Ecce Homo* (just to the right), Titian tackles a Christian theme. A crowd mills about, when suddenly there's a commotion. They nudge each other and start to point. Follow their gaze diagonally up the stairs to a battered figure entering way up in the corner. "Ecce Homo!" says Pilate. "Behold the man." And he presents Jesus to the mob. For us, as for the unsympathetic crowd, the humiliated Son of God is not the center of the scene, but almost an afterthought.

In the next large galleries (Saal II and Saal III), the colorful

works by Paolo Veronese and Tintoretto reflect the wealth of Venice, the funnel where luxury goods from the exotic East flowed into northern Europe. In Veronese's *Adoration of the Magi (Anbetung der Könige)*, these-Three-Kings-from-Orient are dressed not in biblical costume, but in the imported silks of Venetian businessmen. Tintoretto's many portraits give us a peek at the movers and shakers of the Venetian Empire.

• *Find the following paintings in Rooms 1–4, the smaller rooms that adjoin Saals I, II, and III.*

Italian Renaissance and Mannerism: *St. Sebastian (Der Hl. Sebastian)*, by **Andrea Mantegna,** is shot through with arrows. Sebastian was an early Christian martyr, but he stands like a Renaissance statue—on a pedestal, his weight on one foot, displaying his Greek-god anatomy. Mantegna places the three-dimensional "statue" in a three-dimensional setting, using floor tiles and roads that recede into the distance to create the illusion of depth.

In **Correggio**'s *Jupiter and Io,* the king of the gods appears in a cloud—see his foggy face and hands?—to get a date with a beautiful nymph named Io. ("Io, Io, it's off to earth I go.") Correggio tips Renaissance "balance"—the enraptured Io may be perched vertically in the center of the canvas right now, but she won't be for long.

Find the little round painting nearby. In his *Self-Portrait in a Convex Mirror (Selbstbildnis im Konvexspiegel),* 21-year-old **Parmigianino** (like the cheese) gazes into a convex mirror and perfectly reproduces the curved reflection on a convex piece of wood. Amazing.

The 22-year-old **Raphael** (roff-eye-EL) captured the spirit of

the High Renaissance, combining symmetry, grace, beauty and emotion. His *Madonna of the Meadow (Die Madonna im Grünen)* is a mountain of motherly love—Mary's head is the summit and her flowing robe is the base—enfolding baby Jesus and John the Baptist. The geometric perfection, serene landscape, and Mary's adorable face make this a masterpiece of sheer grace...but then you get smacked by an ironic fist: The cross the little tykes play with foreshadows their gruesome deaths.

• *Find Caravaggio in Saal V.*

Caravaggio: Caravaggio (karra-VAH-jee-oh) shocked the art world with brutally honest reality. Compared with Raphael's super-sweet *Madonna of the Meadow,* Caravaggio's *Madonna of the Rosary (Die Rosenkranzmadonna,* the biggest canvas in the room) looks perfectly ordinary, and the saints kneeling around her have dirty feet.

In *David with the Head of Goliath (David mit dem Haupt des Goliath)*—in the corner near the window—Caravaggio turns a third-degree-interrogation light on a familiar Bible story. David shoves the dripping head of the slain giant right in our noses. The painting, bled of color, is virtually a black-and-white crime-scene photo—slightly overexposed. Out of the deep darkness shine only a few crucial details.

This David is not a heroic Renaissance Man like Michelangelo's famous statue, but a homeless teen that Caravaggio paid to portray God's servant. And the severed head of Goliath is none other than Caravaggio himself, an in-your-face self-portrait.

• *Find Room 10, in the corner of the museum.*

Velázquez: When the Hapsburgs ruled both Austria and Spain, cousins kept in touch through portraits of themselves and their kids. Diego Velázquez (veh-LOSS-kehs) was the greatest of Spain's "photo-journalist" painters: heavily influenced by Caravaggio's realism, capturing his subjects without passing judgment, flattering, or glorifying them.

Watch little Margarita Hapsburg grow up in three different *Portraits of Margarita Theresa (Die Infantin Margarita Teresa),* from age two to age nine. Margarita was destined from birth to marry her Austrian cousin, the future Emperor Leopold I. Pictures like these, sent from Spain every few years, let her pen-pal/fiancé get to know her. Also see a portrait of Margarita's little brother, *Philip Prosper,* looking like a tiny priest. The kids' oh-so-serious faces, regal poses, and royal trappings are contradicted by their cuteness. No wonder Velázquez was so popular.

• *Complete the Italian Art wing by passing through several rooms of Baroque art, featuring large, colorful canvases showcasing over-the-top emotions and the surefire mark of Baroque art—pudgy, winged babies. If you don't have time to get out to Schönbrunn Palace on this visit, you can get a good look at it here—find Canaletto's* Schloss Schönbrunn, *which also shows the Viennese skyline in the distance. Then head to the east wing, opposite the Titian Room, to see some...*

Early Northern Art: The "Northern Renaissance," brought on by the economic boom of Dutch and Flemish trading, was more secular and Protestant than Catholic-funded Italian art. We'll see fewer Madonnas, saints, and Greek gods and more peasants, landscapes, and food. Paintings are smaller and darker, full of down-to-earth objects. Northern artists sweated the details, encouraging the patient viewer to appreciate the beauty in everyday things.

In the three sections of Room 14 are three early northern painters. **Rogier van der Weyden**'s *Triptych: The Crucifixion (Kreuzigungsaltar)* strips the Crucifixion down to the essential characters, set in a sparse landscape. The agony is understated, seen in just a few solemn faces

and dramatically creased robes. Just to the left, in the painstakingly detailed *Portrait of Cardinal Niccolò Albergati*, **Jan van Eyck** refuses to airbrush out the jowls and wrinkles, showcasing the quiet dignity of an ordinary man. And in the freestanding case, **Hieronymus Bosch**'s *Christ Carrying the Cross (Kreuztragung Christi)* is crammed with puny humans, not supermen.

• *Saal X contains the largest collection of Bruegels in captivity. Linger. If you like it, linger longer.*

Pieter Bruegel (c. 1525–1569)— Norman Rockwell of the 16th Century: The undisputed master of the slice-of-life village scene was Pieter Bruegel the Elder. (His name is pronounced "BROY-gull," and is sometimes spelled *Brueghel*. Don't confuse Pieter Bruegel the Elder with his sons, Pieter Brueghel the Younger and Jan Brueghel, who added luster and an "h" to the family name.) Despite his many rural paintings, Bruegel was actually an urban metrosexual who liked to wear peasants' clothing to observe country folk at play (a trans-fest-ite?). He celebrated their simple life, but he also skewered their weaknesses—not to single them out as hicks, but as universal examples of human folly.

The Peasant Wedding (Bauernhochzeit), Bruegel's most famous work, is less about the wedding than the food. It's a farmers' feed-

ing frenzy as the barnful of wedding guests scramble to get their share of free eats. Two men bring in the next course, a tray of fresh pudding. The bagpiper pauses to check it out. A guy grabs bowls and passes them down the table, taking our attention with them. Everyone's going at it, including a kid in an oversize red cap who licks the bowl with his fingers. In the middle of it all, look who's been completely forgotten—the demure bride sitting in front of the blue-green cloth. (One thing: The guy carrying the front end of the food tray—is he stepping forward with his right leg, or with his left, or with...all three?)

Speaking of two left feet, Bruegel's *Peasant Dance (Bauerntanz)* shows peasants happily clogging to the tune of a lone bagpiper who wails away while his pit crew keeps him lubed with wine. The three Bruegel landscape paintings are part of an

original series of six "calendar" paintings, depicting the seasons of the year. *The Gloomy Day (Der düstere Tag)* opens the cycle, as winter turns to spring...slowly. The snow has melted, flooding the distant river, the trees are still leafless, and the villagers stir, cutting wood and mending fences. We skip ahead to autumn *(The Return of the Herd)*—still sunny, but winter's storms are

fast approaching. We see the scene from above, emphasizing the landscape as much as the people. Finally, in *Hunters in Snow (Jäger im Schnee)* it's the dead of winter, and three dog-tired hunters with their tired dogs trudge along with only a single fox to show for their efforts. As they crest the hill, the grove of bare trees opens

up to a breathtaking view—they're almost home, where they can join their mates playing hockey. Birds soar like the hunters' rising spirits—emerging from winter's work and looking ahead to a new year.

• *Linger among the Breugels, then head for the nearby Room 16.*

Albrecht Dürer: As the son of a goldsmith and having traveled to Italy, Dürer (DEW-rer) combined meticulous Northern detail with Renaissance symmetry.

So his *Landauer Altarpiece of the Trinity (Allerheiligenbild)* may initially look like a complex pig-pile of saints and angels, but it's perfectly geometrical. The crucified Christ forms a triangle in the center, framed by triangular clouds and flanked by three-sided crowds of people—appropriate for a painting about the Trinity. Dürer practically invented the self-portrait as an art form, and he included himself, the lone earthling in this heavenly vision (bottom right), with a plaque announcing that he, Albrecht Dürer, painted this in 1511.

• *Locate these paintings scattered through Rooms 17–21.*

More Northern Art: Contrast Dürer's powerful Renaissance Christ with **Lucas Cranach**'s all-too-human *Crucifixion (Die Kreuzigung)*—twisted, bleeding, scarred, and vomiting blood, as the storm clouds roll in.

Albrecht Altdorfer's garish *Resurrection (Die Auferstehung Christi*—see photo on right) looks like a poster for a bad horror film: "Easter Sunday III. He's back from the dead...and he's ticked!" A burning Christ ignites the dark cave, tingeing the dazed guards.

Hans Holbein painted *Jane Seymour*, wife number III of the VI wives of Henry VIII. The former lady in waiting—timid and modest—poses stiffly (see photo on left), trying very hard to look the part of Henry's queen. Next.

Giuseppe Arcimboldo's *Summer*—a.k.a "Fruit Face"—is one of four paintings the Hapsburg court painter did showing the seasons (and elements) as people. With a pickle nose, pear chin, and corn-husk ears, this guy literally is what he eats.

In *Flowers in a Wooden Vessel (Der Grosse Blumenstrauss)*, **Jan Brueghel,** the son of the famous Bruegel, puts meticulously painted flowers from different seasons together in one artfully arranged vase.

• *Leaving the simplicity of Northern Art—small canvases, small themes, attention to detail—reenter the big-canvas, bright-colored world of Baroque in Saal XIII.*

Peter Paul Rubens: Stand in front of Rubens' *Self-Portrait (Selbstbildnis)* and admire the darling of Catholic-dominated Flanders (Belgium) in his prime: famous, wealthy, well-traveled, the friend of kings and princes, an artist, diplomat, man about town, and—obviously—confident. Rubens' work runs the gamut, from realistic portraits to lounging nudes, Greek myths to altarpieces, from pious devotion to violent sex. But, can we be sure it's Baroque? Ah yes, I'm sure you'll find a pudgy, winged baby somewhere.

The 53-year-old Rubens married Hélène Fourment, this dimpled girl of 16. She pulls the fur around her ample flesh, simultaneously covering herself and exalting her charms. Rubens called both this painting and his young bride "The Little Fur" *(Das Pelzchen)*. Hmm. Hélène's sweet cellulite was surely an inspiration to Rubens—many of his female figures have Helene's gentle face and dimpled proportions.

In the large *Ildefonso Altarpiece,* a glorious Mary appears (with her entourage of p.w.b.'s) to reward the grateful Spanish saint with a chasuble (priest's smock).

• *Saal XIV features more big Rubens canvases.*

How could Rubens paint all these enormous canvases in one lifetime? He didn't. He kept a workshop of assistants busy painting backgrounds and minor figures, working from Rubens' small sketches (often displayed in Room 14 or nearby). Then the master stepped in to add the finishing touches.

• *From there, find Room 23.*

Jan Steen: In *The World Upside-Down (Die Verkehrte Welt),* Steen (1626–1679) gives us an intimate look into Dutch life. Not everyone could afford a masterpiece, but even the poorer people wanted works of art for their own homes (like a landscape from

Sears to hang over the sofa). Steen painted humorous scenes from the lives of the lower classes. As a tavern owner, he observed society firsthand. In this scene, everything's going wrong.

• *In the adjoining Room 22:*

Jan Vermeer: In his small canvases, the Dutch painter Jan Vermeer quiets the world down to where we can hear our own heartbeat, letting us appreciate the beauty in common things.

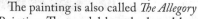

The curtain opens and we see *The Art of Painting (Die Malkunst),* a behind-the-scenes look at Vermeer at work. He's painting a model dressed in blue, starting with her laurel-leaf headdress. The studio is its own little dollhouse world framed by a chair in the foreground and the wall in back. Then Vermeer fills this space with the few gems he wants us to focus on—the chandelier, the map, the painter's costume. Everything is lit by a crystal-clear light, letting us see these everyday items with fresh eyes.

The painting is also called *The Allegory of Painting.* The model has the laurel leaves, trumpet, and book that symbolize fame. The artist—his back to the public—earnestly tries to capture fleeting fame with a small sheet of canvas.

• *Finish your tour in the corner room.*

Rembrandt van Rijn: Rembrandt got wealthy painting portraits of Holland's upwardly mobile businessmen, but his greatest subject was himself. In the *Large Self-Portrait (Grosses Selbstbildnis)* we see the hands-on-hips, defiant, open-stance determination of a man who will do what he wants, and if they don't like it, tough.

In typical Rembrandt style, most of the canvas is a dark, smudgy brown, with only the side of his face glowing from the darkness. (Remember Caravaggio? Rembrandt did.) Unfortunately, the year this was painted, Rembrandt's fortunes changed. Looking at the *Small Self-Portrait (Kleines Selbstbildnis)* from 1657, consider Rembrandt's last years. His wife died, his children died young, and commissions for paintings dried up as his style veered from the common path. He had to auction off paintings to pay his debts, and he died a poor man. Rembrandt's numerous self-portraits painted from youth until old age show a man

The Case of the *Salt Cellar* Stealer

In the middle of the night of May 11, 2003, someone broke into the Kunsthistorisches Museum, smashed the glass case containing Cellini's *Salt Cellar (Saliera)*, and set off the alarm. The thief grabbed the $60 million, gold-plated salt bowl and ran, scrambling through a second-story window and down some construction scaffolding. The security guard, assuming it was a false alarm, simply turned it off and went back to sleep.

For the next two years, the Kunsthistorisches' prize possession vanished from sight. Police looked everywhere—including a foray into Italy, chasing a tip from a prankster—but came up empty. Meanwhile, the 10-inch-high masterpiece lay hidden right nearby, tucked under a bed in a Vienna apartment.

Then, in October of 2005, a ransom note arrived at the insurance company: Pay $12 million and the statue will be returned. The thief even sent proof he really had it, enclosing the tiny pickle-fork trident held by Neptune. An exchange was arranged, but on the appointed day, the thief suddenly got suspicious. He called it off by sending a text message from his mobile phone. Crafty police traced the call, and located the Vienna store where the phone had been purchased. They pored over the store's security camera footage until they found who had bought it. When they published the images in the media, the thief turned himself in. He was an otherwise ordinary security-alarm salesman who'd almost pulled off the art crime of the century.

Police found the salt cellar carefully wrapped, boxed, and buried in the woods near Vienna, with only a few scratches on it. The 1,000-day ordeal was over, and Cellini's one-of-a-kind masterpiece was home.

always changing—from wide-eyed youth to successful portraitist to this disillusioned, but still defiant, old man.

The Rest of the Kunst: We've seen only the *Kunst* (art) half of the Kunsthistorisches (history) Museum. The collections on the ground floor are among Europe's best, filled with ancient treasures and medieval curios. Highlights include a statue of the Egyptian pharaoh Thutmosis III, and the Gemma Augustea, a Roman cameo kept by Julius Caesar on his private desk. Happily, one of the glittering jewels in the museum's crown is now back, after being stolen several years ago (see sidebar). The *Salt Cellar*, a divine golden salt bowl by Renaissance sculptor Benvenuto Cellini, will be the centerpiece of a new "Kunstkammer"—a section dedicated to Hapsburg medieval and Renaissance jeweled wonders.

Near the Kunsthistorisches Museum

▲**Natural History Museum**—In the twin building facing the Kunsthistorisches Museum, you'll find moon rocks, dinosaur stuff, and a copy of the fist-size *Venus of Willendorf*—at 25,000 years old, the world's oldest sex symbol, found in the Danube Valley (the original is in the museum's vault). This museum is a hit with children (€8, Wed–Mon 9:00–18:30, Wed until 21:00, closed Tue, tel. 01/521-770).

MuseumsQuartier—The vast grounds of the former imperial stables now corral several impressive, cutting-edge museums.

Walk into the complex from the Hofburg side, where the main entrance (with visitors center) leads to a big courtyard with cafés, fountains, and ever-changing "installation lounge furniture," all surrounded by the quarter's various museums (behind Kunsthistorisches Museum, U-2 or U-3: Volkstheater/Museumsplatz).

Various combo-tickets are available for those interested in more than just the Leopold and Modern Art museums (visit www.mqw.at).

The **Leopold Museum** features several temporary exhibits of modern Austrian art, and a top floor that holds the largest collection of works by Egon Schiele (1890–1918; many Americans are offended by Schiele's relaxed comfort with human nudity) and a few paintings by Gustav Klimt and Oskar Kokoschka (€9, €2.50 audioguide—worth it only for enthusiasts, daily 10:00–18:00, Thu until 21:00, tel. 01/525-700, www.leopoldmuseum.org). Note that for these three artists, you'll do better in the Belvedere Palace (described on page 510).

The **Museum of Modern Art** (Museum Moderner Kunst Stiftung Ludwig, a.k.a. "MUMOK") is Austria's leading modern-art gallery. It's the striking lava-paneled building—three stories tall and four stories deep, offering seven floors of far-out art that's hard for most visitors to appreciate. This huge, state-of-the-art museum displays revolving exhibits showing off art of the last generation—including Paul Klee, Pablo Picasso, and Pop artists (€9, €2 audioguide has more than you probably want to hear, Tue–Sun 10:00–18:00, Thu until 21:00, closed Mon, tel. 01/52500, www.mumok.at).

Rounding out the sprawling MuseumsQuartier are an architecture museum, Transeuropa, Electronic Avenue, children's museum, and the Kunsthalle Wien—an exhibition center for contemporary art (€7.50, Thu–Tue 10:00–19:00, Thu until 22:00, closed Wed, tel. 01/521-8933, www.kunsthallewien.at).

Central Vienna, Inside the Ring

▲▲**Haus der Musik**—Vienna's "House of Music" has a small first-floor exhibit on the Vienna Philharmonic, and upstairs you'll enjoy fine audiovisual exhibits on each of the famous hometown boys (Haydn, Mozart, Beethoven, Strauss, and Mahler). But the museum is unique for its effective use of interactive touch-screen computers and headphones to actually explore the physics of sound. You can twist, dissect, and bend sounds to make your own musical language, merging your voice with a duck's quack or a city's traffic roar. Wander through the "sonosphere" and marvel at the amazing acoustics—I could actually hear what I thought only a piano tuner could hear. Pick up a virtual baton to conduct the Vienna Philharmonic Orchestra (each time you screw up, the musicians put their instruments down and ridicule you). Really experiencing the place takes time. It's open late and makes a good evening activity (€10, €15 combo-ticket with Mozart Haus Museum, daily 10:00–22:00, last entry 1 hour before closing, 2 blocks from the Opera at Seilerstätte 30, tel. 01/51648, www.hdm.at).

Mozart Haus Museum—Opened in 2006 to commemorate Wolfgang's 250th birthday, this museum is easy to get excited about, but it disappoints. Exhibits fill the only surviving Mozart residence in Vienna, where he lived from 1784 to 1787, when he had lots of money. You'll learn his life story, with an emphasis on his most creative years...when he lived here. Included is a rundown on the Vienna music scene during the Mozart years, a quirky look at his gambling habits and his interest in crudely erotic peep shows, and a four-minute montage of his most famous arias in a minitheater. Unfortunately, visiting the museum is like reading a book standing up—rather than turning pages, you climb stairs. There are almost no real artifacts. Wolfie would have found the audioguide dreadful. While the museum might be worth the time and money for Mozart enthusiasts, both Mozart sights in Salzburg (the Birthplace and the Residence—see Salzburg chapter) are more gratifying. In Vienna, I enjoy the Haus der Musik (described previously) much more (€9, €15 combo-ticket with Haus der Musik, daily 10:00–19:00, a block behind the cathedral, go through arcade at #5 and walk 50 yards to Domgasse 5, tel. 01/512-1791, www .mozarthausvienna.at).

▲**Vienna's Auction House, the Dorotheum**—For an aristocrat's flea market, drop by Austria's answer to Sotheby's, the Dorotheum. Its five floors of antique furniture and fancy knickknacks have been put up either for immediate sale or auction, often by people who inherited old things they don't have room for. Wandering through here, you feel like you're touring a museum with exhibits you can buy (Mon–Fri 10:00–18:00, Sat 9:00–17:00, closed Sun, classy little café on second floor, between the Graben and Hofburg at Dorotheergasse 17, tel. 01/51560, www.dorotheum.com). The info desk at the ground floor has a building map and schedule of upcoming auctions. Labels on each item predict the auction value. Continue your hunt for the perfect curio on the streets around the Dorotheum, lined with many fine antique shops.

Judenplatz Memorial and Museum—The square called Judenplatz marks the location of Vienna's 15th-century Jewish community, one of Europe's largest at the time. The square, once filled with a long-gone synagogue, is now dominated by a blocky memorial to the 65,000 Austrian Jews killed by the Nazis. The memorial—a library turned inside out—symbolizes Jews as "people of the book" and causes viewers to ponder the huge loss of culture, knowledge, and humanity that took place between 1938 and 1945.

The Judenplatz Museum, while sparse, has displays on medieval Jewish life and a well-done video recreating community scenes from five centuries ago. Wander the scant remains of the medieval synagogue below street level—discovered during the construction of the Holocaust memorial. This was the scene of a medieval massacre. Since Christians weren't allowed to lend money, Jews were Europe's moneylenders. As so often happened in Europe, when Viennese Christians fell too deeply into debt, they found a convenient excuse to wipe out the local ghetto—and their debts at the same time. In 1421, 200 of Vienna's Jews were burned at the stake. Others who refused a forced conversion committed mass suicide in the synagogue (€4, €10 combo-ticket includes synagogue and Jewish Museum of the City of Vienna—see page 516, Sun–Thu 10:00–18:00, Fri 10:00–14:00, closed Sat, Judenplatz 8, tel. 01/535-0431, www.jmw.at).

Near Karlsplatz

These sights cluster around Karlsplatz, just southeast of the Ringstrasse (U-1, U-2, or U-4: Karlsplatz).

Karlsplatz—This picnic-friendly square, with its Henry Moore sculpture in the pond, is ringed with sights. The Art Nouveau station pavilions—from the late 19th-century municipal train system *(Stadtbahn)*—are textbook *Jugendstil* by Otto Wagner, with iron frames, decorative marble slabs, and painted gold ornaments. One of Europe's first subway systems, this precursor to today's U-Bahn was built with a military purpose in mind: to move troops quickly in time of civil unrest—specifically, out to Schönbrunn Palace. One of the pavilions is open as an exhibit on Otto Wagner

(€2, June–Oct Tue–Sun 9:00–18:00, closed Mon and Nov–May).

Charles Church (Karlskirche)—Charles Borromeo, a 16th-century bishop from Milan, was an inspiration during plague times. This "votive church" was dedicated to him in 1713, when an epidemic spared Vienna. The church offers the best Baroque in Vienna, with a unique combination of columns (showing scenes from the life of Charles Borromeo, à la Trajan's Column in Rome), a classic pediment, and an elliptical dome. But this church is especially worthwhile for the chance (probably through 2008) to see restoration work in progress and up close (€6 includes a skippable one-room museum, audioguide, and visit to renovation site; Mon–Sat 9:00–12:30 & 13:00–18:00, Sun 13:00–17:45, last entry 30 min before closing). The entry fee may seem steep, but remember that it funds the restoration.

Visitors ride the industrial lift to a platform at the base of the

dome. (Consider that the church was built and decorated with a scaffolding system essentially the same as this one.) Once up there, you'll climb stairs to the steamy lantern at the extreme top of the church. At that dizzying height, you're in the clouds with cupids and angels. Many details that appear smooth and beautiful from ground level—such as gold leaf, rudimentary paintings, and fake marble—look rough and sloppy up close. It's surreal to observe the 3-D figures from an unintended angle. Faith, Hope, Charity, and Borromeo triumph and inspire—while Protestants and their stinkin' books are trashed. Borromeo lobbies heaven for plague relief. At the very top, you'll see the tiny dove representing the Holy Ghost, surrounded by a cheering squad of nipple-lipped cupids.

Historical Museum of the City of Vienna (Wien Museum Karlsplatz)—This underappreciated museum walks you through the history of Vienna with fine historic artifacts. You'll work your way up, chronologically: The ground floor exhibits Roman artifacts and original statues from St. Stephen's Cathedral (c. 1350), with various Hapsburgs showing off the slinky hip-hugging fashion of the day. The first floor features old city maps, booty from a Turkish siege, and an 1850 city model showing the town just before the wall was replaced by the Ring. Finally, the second floor displays a city model from 1898 (with the new Ringstrasse), sentimental Biedermeier paintings and objets d'art, and early 20th-century paintings (including some by Gustav Klimt). The museum is worth the €6 admission (free Sun and Fri morning, open Tue–Sun 9:00–18:00, closed Mon, www.wienmuseum.at).

Vienna

Art Nouveau (a.k.a. *Jugendstil* or the Vienna Secession), c. 1896–1914

As Europe approached the dawn of a new *(nouveau)* century, it embraced a new art: Art Nouveau.

On the one hand, it was very forward-looking and modern, embracing the new technology of iron and glass. But Art Nouveau was also a reaction against the sheer ugliness of the mass-produced, boxy, rigidly geometrical art of the Industrial Age. Art Nouveau artists returned to nature (which abhors a straight line), and were inspired by the curves of plants. And as in nature, no two objects are exactly the same, leaving the artist free to make his work unique.

Art Nouveau street lamps twist and bend like flower stems. Ironwork fountains sprout buds that squirt water. Dining rooms are paneled with leafy garlands of carved wood. Advertising posters feature flowery typefaces and beautiful young women rendered in pure, curving lines. A hit with interior decorators, Art Nouveau was a total "look" that could be applied to furniture, jewelry, paintings, and the building itself.

Though the Art Nouveau movement began in Paris and Belgium, each country gave it its own spin. In German-speaking lands (including Austria), Art Nouveau was called *Jugendstil* (meaning "youth style").

The innovators in Vienna called their particular *Jugendstil* movement The Secession, named for the daring artists who "seceded" from tradition. They turned their backs on Vienna's centuries-long love affair with Baroque, Rococo, and Neoclassical styles. They preferred buildings that were simple and geometrically pure, which they then decorated with a few unadulterated Art Nouveau touches. Various artists were part of this movement. Architects, painters, and poets had no single unifying style, except a commitment to what was new. The Secessionist motto was: "To each age its art, and to art its liberty."

▲**Academy of Fine Arts (Akademie der Bildenden Künste)**— This small but exciting collection includes works by Bosch, Botticelli, and Rubens (quick, sketchy cartoons used to create his giant canvases); a Venice series by Guardi; and a self-portrait by a 15-year-old van Dyck. It's all magnificently lit and well-described by the €2 audioguide, and comes with comfy chairs.

The fact that this is a working art academy gives it a certain realness. As you wander the halls of the academy, ponder how history might have been different if Hitler—who applied to study architecture here but was rejected—had been accepted as a student. Before leaving, peek into the ground floor's central hall—textbook historicism, the Ringstrasse style of the late 1800s.

The TI has a brochure laying out Vienna's 20th-century architecture. Here are some of the best of Vienna's scattered *Jugendstil* sights:

The Secession: This clean-lined building at the Ring end of the Naschmarkt (see below) was the headquarters of the group of artists calling themselves The Secession. It's nicknamed the "golden cabbage" for its bushy gilded rooftop designed by the painter Gustav Klimt. It was here that young artists first exhibited their "youth-style" art in 1897. In the basement is Klimt's *Beethoven Frieze* (see below).

Belvedere Palace: This museum's collection includes work by Secessionist leader and poster boy Gustav Klimt (1862–1917). He gained fame painting slender young women entwined together in florid embrace, exploring the highly charged erotic terrain of his contemporary, Sigmund Freud. Klimt took the decorative element of Art Nouveau to extremes. In many of his paintings, only the face and bits of body show through gilded ornamental friezes. The two lovers of *The Kiss* are wrapped up in the colorful gold-and-jeweled cloak of bliss (for more about the palace, see page 510).

The Anchor Clock on Hoher Markt: This mosaic-decorated clock (1911–1917) spans two buildings and does a musical act at noon. The clock honors 12 great figures from Vienna's history, from Marcus Aurelius to Joseph Haydn. While each gets his own top-of-the-hour moment, all parade by at high noon. A plaque on the left names each figure. Notice the novel way to mark the time.

Karlsplatz: Otto Wagner (1841–1918), Vienna's premier *Jugendstil* architect, designed several structures for Vienna's subway system, including the original arched entrances (see page 504).

Cost, Hours, Location: €7, Tue–Sun 10:00–18:00, closed Mon, 3 blocks from the Opera at Schillerplatz 3, tel. 01/5881-6225, www.akademiegalerie.at.

▲**The Secession**—This little building, behind the Academy of Fine Arts, was created by the Vienna Secession movement, a group of non-conformist artists led by Gustav Klimt, Otto Wagner, and friends. (For more on the art movement, see the sidebar above.)

The young trees carved into the walls and its bushy "golden cabbage" rooftop (see photo, next page) are symbolic of a renewal cycle. Today, the Secession continues to showcase cutting-edge art, as well as one of Gustav Klimt's most famous works, the *Beethoven Frieze*.

Vienna

While the staff hopes you take a look at the temporary exhibits (and the ticket includes this price whether you like it or not), most tourists head directly for the basement, home to a small exhibit about the history of the building and the museum's highlight: Klimt's classic *Beethoven Frieze* (a.k.a. the "Searching Souls").

One of the masterpieces of Viennese Art Nouveau, this 105-foot-long fresco was a centerpiece of a 1902 "homage to Beethoven" exhibition. Sit down and read the free flier, which explains Klimt's still-powerful work. The theme, inspired by Beethoven's *Ninth Symphony*, features floating female figures "yearning for happiness." They drift and weave and search—like most of us do—through internal and external temptations and forces, falling victim to base and ungodly temptations, and losing their faith. Then, finally, they become fulfilled by poetry, music, and art as they reach the "Ideal Kingdom" where "True Happiness, Pure Bliss, and Absolute Love" are found in a climactic embrace.

Glass cases show sketches Klimt did in preparation for this work. The adjacent room tells the history of this masterpiece, and how the building was damaged in World War II.

Cost, Hours, Location: €6, Tue–Sun 10:00–18:00, Thu until 20:00, closed Mon, Friedrichstrasse 12, tel. 01/587-5307, www.secession.at.

▲**Naschmarkt**—In 1898, the city decided to cover up its Vienna River. The long, wide square they created was filled with a lively

produce market that still bustles most days (closed Sun). It's long been known as *the* place to get exotic faraway foods. In fact, locals say, "From here start the Balkans."

From near the Opera, the Naschmarkt (roughly, "Munchies Market") stretches along Wienzeile street. This "Belly of Vienna" comes with two parallel lanes—one lined with fun and reasonable eateries, and the other featuring the town's top-end produce and gourmet goodies. This is where top chefs like to get their ingredients. At the gourmet vinegar stall, you sample the vinegar like perfume—with a drop on your wrist (see photo). Farther from the center, the Naschmarkt becomes likeably seedy and surrounded by sausage stands, Turkish *döner kebab* stalls, cafés, and theaters. At the market's far end is a line of buildings with fine

Art Nouveau facades. Each Saturday, the Naschmarkt is infested by a huge flea market where, in olden days, locals would come to hire a monkey to pick little critters out of their hair (Mon–Fri 6:00–18:30, Sat 6:00–17:00, closed Sun, closes earlier in winter, U-4: Kettenbruckengasse). For a picnic in the park, pick up your grub here and walk over to Karlsplatz (described on page 504).

Beyond the Ring

▲Liechtenstein Museum

The noble Liechtenstein family (who own only a tiny country, but whose friendship with the Hapsburgs goes back generations) amassed an incredible private art collection. Their palace was long a treasure for Vienna art lovers. Then, in 1938—knowing Hitler was intent on plundering artwork to create an immense "Führer Museum"—the family fled to their tiny homeland with their best art. Since the museum reopened in 2004, attendance has been disappointing, and each year the museum cuts back its hours. The problem is its location...not its worthiness.

The Liechtensteins' "world of Baroque pleasures" includes the family's rare French Rococo carriage (which was used for their grand entry into Paris; it had to be carted to the edge of town and assembled, as nearly all such carriages were destroyed in the French Revolution), a plush Baroque library, an inviting English Garden, and an impressive collection of paintings including a complete cycle of early Rembrandts.

Cost, Hours, Location: €10, audioguide-€1, Fri–Mon 10:00–17:00, closed Tue–Thu, tram D to Bauernfeldplatz, Fürstengasse 1, tel. 01/319-5767-252, www.liechtensteinmuseum.at.

▲KunstHausWien: Hundertwasser Museum

This "make yourself at home" museum and nearby apartment complex is a hit with lovers of modern art. It mixes the work and philosophy of local painter/environmentalist Friedensreich Hundertwasser (1928–2000). Stand in front of the colorful checkerboard building and consider Hundertwasser's style. He was against "window racism": Neighboring houses allow only one kind of window, but $100H_2O$'s windows are each different—and he encouraged residents in the Hundertwasserhaus (a 5–10 minute walk away, see below) to personalize them. He recognized "tree tenants" as well as human tenants. His buildings are spritzed with a forest and topped with dirt and

grassy little parks—close to nature and good for the soul.

Floors and sidewalks are irregular—to "stimulate the brain" (although current residents complain it just causes wobbly furniture and sprained ankles). Thus $100H_2O$ waged a one-man fight—during the 1950s and 1960s, when concrete and glass ruled—to save the human soul from the city. (Hundertwasser claimed that "straight lines are godless.")

Inside the museum, start with his interesting biography. His fun paintings are half *Jugendstil* and half just kids' stuff. Notice the photographs from his 1950s days as part of Vienna's bohemian scene. Throughout the museum, keep an eye out for the fun philosophical quotes from an artist who believed, "If man is creative, he comes nearer to his creator."

Cost, Hours, Location: €9 for Hundertwasser Museum, €12 combo-ticket includes special exhibitions, half-price on Mon, open daily 10:00–19:00, extremely fragrant and colorful garden café, Weissgerberstrasse 13, U-3: Landstrasse, tel. 01/712-0491, www.kunsthauswien.com.

Hundertwasserhaus: The KunstHausWien provides by far the best look at Hundertwasser, but for an actual lived-in apartment complex by the green master, walk five minutes to the one-with-nature Hundertwasserhaus (free, at Löwengasse and Kegelgasse). This complex of 50 apartments, subsidized by the government to provide affordable housing, was built in the 1980s as a breath of architectural fresh air in a city of boring, blocky apartment complexes. While not open to visitors, it's worth visiting for its fun and colorful patchwork exterior and the Hundertwasser festival of shops across the street. Don't miss the view from Kegelgasse to see the "tree tenants" and the internal winter garden that residents enjoy.

Hundertwasser detractors—of which there are many—remind visitors that $100H_2O$ was a painter, not an architect. They describe the Hundertwasserhaus as a "1950s house built in the 1980s," and colorfully painted with no real concern about the environment, communal living, or even practical comfort. Almost all of the original inhabitants got fed up with the novelty and moved out.

▲▲Belvedere Palace

This is the elegant palace of Prince Eugène of Savoy (1663–1736), the still-much-appreciated conqueror of the Ottomans. Eugène, a Frenchman considered too short and too ugly to be in the service of Louis XIV, offered his services to the Hapsburgs. While he was indeed short and ugly, he became the greatest military genius of his age. When you conquer cities, as Eugène did, you get really rich. He had no heirs, so the state got his property and Emperor Josef II established the Belvedere as Austria's first great public art

Restitution of Art Stolen by Nazis

The Austrian government has worked diligently to fairly reimburse victims of the Nazis, whose buildings, businesses, personal belongings, and art were taken after the 1938 *Anschluss* (when Germany annexed Austria).

A fund of more than $200 million was established by both the Austrian government and corporations who profited through their collaboration with the Nazis. Surviving locals (mostly Jews) who paid a *Reichsfluchtsteuer* ("tax for fleeing the country") were located and given some money. Former slave laborers were also tracked down and given €5,000 each. (Imagine what an amazing windfall that would be for an 80-year-old Romanian peasant woman.)

Most significantly for sightseers, great art was returned to its rightful owners. The big news for the Vienna art world was the return of several Gustav Klimt paintings, most notably his *Golden Adele,* from Vienna's Belvedere Palace collection to a Jewish woman in California. In 2006, *The Golden Adele* was auctioned off for $135 million, the highest price ever paid for a painting. While the Austrian government wanted to buy it back, it figured she was asking too much for the art and refused to get into a bidding war. Fortunately for art-lovers, the most famous Klimt *(The Kiss)* was not involved in the restitution and remains in Vienna's Belvedere Palace.

gallery. Today, his palace boasts sweeping views and houses the Austrian gallery of 19th- and 20th-century art.

The palace is actually two grand buildings separated by a fine garden. For our purposes, the **Upper Belvedere Palace** is what matters. The Upper Palace was Eugène's party house. Today, like the Louvre in Paris (but much easier to enjoy), this palace contains a fine collection of paintings. The collection is arranged chronologically: On the first floor, you'll find Historicism, Romanticism, Impressionism, Realism, tired tourism, Expressionism, Art Nouveau, and early Modernism. Each room tries to pair Austrian works from that period with much better-known European works. It's fun to see the original work of artists like Vincent van Gogh, Edvard Munch, and Claude Monet hang with their lesser-known Austrian contemporaries. Austria became a leader in art in about 1900, and so the collection from this era gets stronger, with fine works by late-19th-century Romantics Gustav Klimt and Egon Schiele.

In the two rooms full of sumptuous paintings by Klimt (facing the city center, on the far right) you can get caught up in his fascination with the beauty and danger he saw in women. To Klimt, all art was erotic art. He painted during the turn-of-the-century, when Vienna was a splendid laboratory of hedonism. For Klimt, Eve was the prototypical woman; her body, not the apple, provided the seduction. Frustrated by the censorship of his age, Klimt refused every form of state support. While he couldn't paint nudes, he managed to paint a fully clothed yet bewitching eroticism in a world full of pollen and pistils.

The famous painting of Judith shows no biblical heroine—Klimt paints her as a high-society Vienna woman with an ostentatious dog-collar necklace. With half-closed eyes and slightly parted lips, she's dismissive...yet mysterious and bewitching. Holding the head of her biblical victim, she's the modern femme fatale.

In what is perhaps his most well-known painting, *The Kiss,* Klimt's woman is no longer dominating, but submissive, abandoning herself to her man in a fertile field and a vast universe. In a glow emanating from a radiance of desire, the body she presses against is a self-portrait of the artist himself.

Don't miss the poignant Schiele family portrait from 1918—his wife died while he was still working on it. (Schiele and his child were soon taken by the influenza epidemic that swept through Europe after World War I.)

The upper floor shows off early 19th-century Biedermeier paintings (hypersensitive, super-sweet, uniquely Viennese Romanticism—the poor are happy, things are lit impossibly well, and folk life is idealized). Your ticket also includes the Austrian Baroque and Gothic art in the Lower Belvedere Palace. Prince Eugène lived in that palace, but he's long gone, and I wouldn't bother to visit.

Cost, Hours, Location: €9.50 for Upper Belvedere Palace only, €12 for Upper and Lower Palaces—not worth it, audioguide-€3, daily 10:00–18:00, entrance at Prinz-Eugen-Strasse 27, tel. 01/7955-7134, www.belvedere.at. To get here from the center, catch tram D at the Opera (direction Südbahnhof, it stops at the palace gate).

View: *Belvedere* means "beautiful view." Sit at the top palace and look over the Baroque gardens, the mysterious sphinxes (which symbolized solving riddles and the finely educated mind of your host, Eugène), the lower palace, and the city. The spire of St. Stephen's Cathedral is 400 feet tall, and no other tall buildings are allowed inside the Ringstrasse. The hills—covered with vineyards—are where the Viennese love to go to sample the new wine. You can see Kahlenberg, from where you can walk down to several recommended *Heurigen* (wine gardens) beyond the spire (see page 522). These are the first of the Alps, which stretch from here all the way to Marseilles, France. The square you're overlooking was filled with people on May 15, 1955, as local leaders stood on the balcony of the Upper Palace (behind you) and proclaimed

Austrian independence following a decade-long Allied occupation after World War II.

▲▲▲Schönbrunn Palace (Schloss Schönbrunn)

Among Europe's palaces, only Schönbrunn rivals Versailles. This former summer residence of the Hapsburgs, located four miles  from the center, is big, with 1,441 rooms. But don't worry—only 40 rooms are shown to the public. (Today the families of 260 civil servants rent simple apartments in the rest of the palace, enjoying rent control and governmental protections so they can't be evicted.)

Getting There: Take U-4 to Schönbrunn and walk 400 yards (just follow the crowds). The main entrance is in the left side of the palace as you face it.

Royal Apartments

While the exterior is Baroque, the interior was finished under Maria Theresa in let-them-eat-cake Rococo. The chandeliers are either of Bohemian crystal or of hand-carved wood with gold-leaf gilding. Thick walls hid the servants as they ran around stoking the ceramic stoves from the back, and attending to other behind-the-scenes matters. Most of the public rooms are decorated in Neo-Baroque, as they were under Franz Josef (r. 1848–1916). When WWII bombs rained on the city and the palace grounds, the palace itself took only one direct hit. Thankfully, that bomb, which crashed through three floors—including the sumptuous central ballroom—was a dud.

Cost: The admission price is based on which route you select (each one includes an audioguide): the 22-room **Imperial Tour** (€9.50, 45 min, Grand Palace rooms plus apartments of Franz Josef and Elisabeth—mostly 19th-century and therefore least interesting) or the 40-room **Grand Tour** (€13, 60 min, includes Imperial tour plus Maria Theresa's apartments—18th-century Rococo). A combo-ticket called the **Schönbrunn Pass Classic** includes the Grand Tour, as well as other sights on the grounds: the Gloriette viewing terrace, maze, privy garden, and court bakery—complete with *Apfelstrudel* demo and tasting (€17, available April–Oct only). I'd go for the Grand Tour.

Hours: Daily July–Aug 8:30–18:00, April–June and Sept–Oct 8:30–17:00, Nov–March 8:30–16:30. Information: www .schoenbrunn.at.

Crowd-Beating Tips: Schönbrunn suffers from crowds. It can be a jam-packed sauna in the summer. It's busiest from 9:30

to 11:30, especially on weekends and in July and August; it's least crowded from 12:00 to 14:00 and after 16:00, when there are no groups. To avoid the long delays in summer, make a reservation by telephone (tel. 01/8111-3239, answered daily 8:00–17:00, wait through the long message for the operator). You'll get an appointment time and a ticket number. Check in at least 30 minutes early. Upon arrival, go to the "Group and Reservations" desk (immediately inside the gate on the left at the gate house—long before the actual palace), give your number, pick up your ticket, and jump in ahead of the masses. If you show up in peak season without calling first, you deserve the frustration. (In this case, you'll have to wait in line, buy your ticket, and wait until the listed time to enter—which could be tomorrow.) If you have any time to kill, spend it exploring the gardens or Coach Museum.

Palace Gardens

If you've visited the Kaisergruft and strolled by the Hapsburgs (tucked neatly into their crypts), enjoy a walk with the commoners, just to mix things up. This emperor's garden is a celebration of the evolution of civilization from autocracy into real democracy. As a civilization, we're doing well.

Most of the park itself is free, as it has been since the 1700s (open daily sunrise to dusk, entrance on either side of the palace). The small side gardens are the most elaborate. The Kammergarten on the left was a fancy private garden for the Hapsburgs (now restored and with a fee). The so-called Sisi Gardens on the right are free. Inside are several other sights, including a **palm house** (€4, daily May–Sept 9:30–18:00, Oct–April 9:30–17:00); Europe's oldest **zoo,** or *Tiergarten,* built by Maria Theresa's husband for the entertainment and education of the court in 1752 (€12, May–Sept daily 9:00–18:30, less off-season, tel. 01/8779-2940); and—at the end of the gardens—the **Gloriette,** a purely decorative monument celebrating an obscure Austrian military victory and offering a fine city view (viewing terrace–€2, included in €17 Schönbrunn Pass Classic, daily April–Sept 9:00–18:00, July–Aug until 19:00, Oct 9:00–17:00, closed Nov–March). A touristy choo-choo train makes the rounds all day, connecting Schönbrunn's many attractions.

Coach Museum Wagenburg

The Schönbrunn coach museum is a 19th-century traffic jam of 50 impressive royal carriages and sleighs. Highlights include silly sedan chairs, the death-black hearse carriage (used for Franz Josef in 1916, and most recently for Empress Zita in 1989), and an extravagantly gilded imperial carriage pulled by eight Cinderella horses. This was rarely used other than for the coronation of Holy Roman Emperors, when it was disassembled and taken to

Frankfurt for the big event (€4.50; April–Oct daily 9:00–18:00; Nov–March Tue–Sun 10:00–16:00, closed Mon; last entry 30 min before closing, 200 yards from palace, walk through right arch as you face palace, tel. 01/525-240).

"Honorable Mentions": More Vienna Museums

These museums, scattered around the city, are worth a peek if you have a special interest.

Museum of Applied Art—The Österreichisches Museum für Angewandte Kunst, or MAK, is Vienna's answer to London's Victoria and Albert Museum. It shows off the fancies of local aristocratic society, including a fine *Jugendstil* collection.

The MAK is more than just another grand building on the Ringstrasse. It was built to provide models of historic design for Ringstrasse architects, and is a delightful space in itself (many locals stop in to enjoy a coffee on the plush couches in the main lobby). Each wing is dedicated to a different era. Exhibits, well-described in English, come with a playful modern flair—notable modern designers were assigned various spaces.

Cost, Hours, Location: €8, €10 includes a big English guidebook, free on Sat, open Tue–Sun 10:00–18:00, Tue until 24:00, closed Mon, Stubenring 5, tel. 01/711-360, www.mak.at.

The associated **Restaurant Österreicher im MAK** is named for a chef renowned for his classic and modern Viennese cuisine. Classy and mod, it's trendy for locals (open daily, reserve for evening, €10–15 plates).

Sigmund Freud Museum—Freud enthusiasts travel to Vienna just to see this humble apartment and workplace of the man who fundamentally changed our understanding of the human psyche. Freud established his practice here in 1891, and it was here that he wrote his work on the interpretation of dreams. Freud, who was Jewish, fled with the rise of Nazism, and took most of his furniture with him. You won't see "the couch," but you will see his waiting room, along with three rooms packed with papers, photos, mementos, and documents. These, along with a family video from the 1930s, give an intimate peek at Freud's life. The old-fashioned exhibit is tediously described in a three-ring info binder loaned to visitors, which complements the more general audioguide.

Cost, Hours, Location: €7, daily 9:00–18:00, cool shop, half a block from a tram D stop at Berggasse 19, tel. 01/319-1596, www.freud-museum.at.

More Museums—There's much, much more. The city map lists everything. If you're into Esperanto, undertakers, tobacco, clowns, firefighting, or the homes of dead composers, you'll find them all in Vienna.

These good museums try very hard but are submerged in

the greatness of Vienna: **Jewish Museum of the City of Vienna** (€6.50, or €10 combo-ticket includes synagogue and Judenplatz Memorial and Museum—described on page 504, Sun–Fri 10:00–18:00, closed Sat, Dorotheergasse 11, tel. 01/535-0431, www .jmw.at), **Folkloric Museum of Austria** (Tue–Sun 10:00–17:00, closed Mon, Laudongasse 15, tel. 01/406-8905), and **Museum of Military History,** one of Europe's best if you like swords and shields (Heeresgeschichtliches Museum, €5.10, includes audio-guide, Sat–Thu 9:00–17:00, closed Fri, Arsenal district, Objekt 18, tel. 01/795-610).

ACTIVITIES

People-Watching and Strolling

These activities allow you to take it easy and enjoy the Viennese good life.

▲**Stadtpark (City Park)**—Vienna's major park is a waltzing world of gardens, memorials to local musicians, ponds, peacocks, music in bandstands, and Viennese escaping the city. Notice the *Jugendstil* entrance at the Stadtpark U-Bahn station. The Kursalon, where Strauss was the violin-toting master of waltzing ceremonies, hosts daily touristy concerts in three-quarter time.

▲**Prater**—Since the 1780s, when the reformist Emperor Josef II gave his hunting grounds to the people of Vienna as a public park, this place has been Vienna's playground. While tired and a bit rundown these days, Vienna's sprawling amusement park still tempts visitors with its huge 220-foot-tall, famous, and lazy Ferris wheel *(Riesenrad)*, roller coaster, bumper cars, Lilliputian rail-road, and endless eateries. Especially if you're traveling with kids, this is a fun, goofy place to share the evening with thousands of Viennese (daily 9:00–24:00 in summer, but quiet after 22:00, U-1: Praterstern). For a local-style family dinner, eat at Schweizerhaus (good food, great Czech Budvar—the original "Budweiser"—beer, classic conviviality).

Donauinsel (Danube Island)—In the 1970s, the city dug a canal parallel to the mighty Danube River, creating both a flood bar-rier and a much-loved island escape from the city (easy U-Bahn access on U-1 to Donauinsel). This skinny, 12-mile long island provides a natural wonderland. All along the traffic-free, grassy park you'll find locals—both Viennese, and especially immigrants and those who can't afford their own cabin or fancy vacation—at play. The swimming comes tough, though, with rocky entries rather than sand. The best activity here is a bike ride (see "Getting Around Vienna—By Bike," page 459). Be careful—if you venture too far from the crowds, you're likely to encounter nudists on Rollerblades.

A Walk in the Vienna Woods (Wienerwald)—For a quick side-trip into the woods and out of the city, catch the U-4 to Heiligenstadt, then bus #38A to Kahlenberg, where you'll enjoy great views and a café overlooking the city. From there, it's a peaceful 45-minute downhill hike to the *Heurigen* of Nussdorf or Grinzing to enjoy some new wine (see "Vienna's Wine Gardens," page 522). Your free TI-produced city map can be helpful...just go downhill. For the very best views, stay on bus #38A to Leopoldsberg, where you'll find a lovely Baroque church, a breezy *Weinstube* (wine pub), and shady tables with expansive panoramas of the city and the Danube. While it seems like a long way to go for a big view, buses are cheap (or free with a transit pass) and go twice an hour until 22:00.

Naschmarkt—Vienna's busy produce market is a great place for people-watching (see page 508).

Shopping

For Traditional Austrian Clothing—Two famous shops are fun to visit if you're interested in picking up a classy felt suit or dirndl. Most central is the fancy **Loden Plankl** shop (across from the Hofburg, at Michaelerplatz 6). But the **Tostmann Trachten** shop is the ultimate for serious shopping. Mrs. Tostmann powered the resurgence of this style. Her place is like a shrine to traditional Austrian and folk clothing—handmade and very expensive (Schottengasse 3A, 3-min walk from Am Hof, tel. 01/533-5331, www.tostmann.at).

Day-Tripping to Slovakia

Fast Boat to Bratislava—The generally overlooked (I've long thought for good reason) capital of Slovakia is suddenly on the radar screen for Vienna travelers for three reasons: its newly lively economy (thanks to its recent EU membership and intense foreign investment); its popular discount airport (see page 457); and the new, fast, catamaran day trip. The DDSG line offers several daily boat trips from Schwedenplatz (where Vienna's old town hits the canal) to Bratislava in 75 minutes with good views (€25 each way, cheaper at less convenient times). For a fine day trip, you can depart at 8:30, arrive at 9:45 in Bratislava's Old Town, explore Bratislava, and return to Vienna at 14:30 or 18:15 (departures daily June–Oct only, tel. 01/58880, www.ddsg-blue-danube.at). The train makes the trip a bit faster and much cheaper (2–3/hr, 1-hour trip).

If you visit Bratislava, you'll find a charming, increasingly rejuvenated Old Town (Staré Mesto) with cobbles upon cobbles of trendy cafés and restaurants. The Old Town is watched over by a drab hilltop fortress (worth climbing for the view, but not for the museums inside) and surrounded by ugly communist sprawl. The intensely dreary suburb of Petržalka, across the river, is an endless sea of concrete, communist-era apartment blocks. Bratislava has few worthwhile museums—especially compared to the world-class gems in Vienna—but the Old Town's relaxed café-culture ambience is nearly Mediterranean. Frankly, this trip isn't quite as exciting as it sounds. But Bratislava offers a Slavic flavor that's completely different from anything else in this book, and its much smaller size can be a nice break from the big-city intensity of Vienna. If you're not making the trek to Prague (or elsewhere in the East), this is your most convenient dip into Eastern Europe.

EXPERIENCES

Music Scene

As far back as the 12th century, Vienna was a mecca for musicians—both sacred and secular (troubadours). The Hapsburg emperors of the 17th and 18th centuries were not only generous supporters of music, but fine musicians and composers themselves. (Maria Theresa played a mean double bass.) Composers like Haydn, Mozart, Beethoven, Schubert, Brahms, and Mahler gravitated to this music-friendly environment. They taught each other, jammed together, and spent a lot of time in Hapsburg palaces. Beethoven was a famous figure, walking—lost in musical thought—through Vienna's woods. In the city's 19th-century belle époque, "Waltz King" Johann Strauss and his brothers kept Vienna's 300 ballrooms spinning.

This musical tradition continues into modern times, leaving some prestigious Viennese institutions for today's tourists to enjoy: the Opera (see page 473), the Boys' Choir, and the great Baroque halls and churches, all busy with classical and waltz concerts. As you poke into churches and palaces, you may hear groups practicing. You're welcome to sit and listen.

Vienna is Europe's music capital. It's music *con brio* (with brilliance) from October through June, reaching a symphonic climax during the Vienna Festival each May and June. Sadly, in July and August, the Boys' Choir, the Opera, and many more music companies are—like you—on vacation. But Vienna hums year-round with live classical music. Except for the Boys' Choir, the musical events listed below are offered in summer.

Vienna Boys' Choir—The boys sing (from a high balcony, where they are heard but not seen) at the 9:15 Sunday Mass from September through March in the Hofburg's Imperial Chapel (Hofburgkapelle; entrance at Schweizerhof, from Josefsplatz go through tunnel). Reserved seats must be booked two months in advance (€5–29; reserve by fax, email, or mail: fax from the US 011-431-533-992-775, whmk@chello.at, or write Hofmusikkapelle,

Hofburg-Schweizerhof, 1010 Wien; call 01/533-9927 for information only—they can't book tickets at this number). Much easier, standing room inside is free and open to the first 60 who line up. Even better, rather than line up early, you can simply swing by and stand in the narthex just outside, where you can hear the boys and see the Mass on a TV monitor. Boys' Choir concerts (on stage at the Musikverein) are also given Fridays at 16:00 in May, June, September, and October (€35–48, standing room goes on sale at 15:30 for €15, Karlsplatz 6; U-1, U-2, or U-4: Karlsplatz; tel. 01/5880-4141). They're talented kids, but, for my taste, not worth all the commotion. Remember, many churches have great music during Sunday Mass. Just 200 yards from the Boys' Choir chapel, Augustinian Church has a glorious 11:00 service each Sunday (see page 488).

Touristy Mozart and Strauss Concerts—If the music comes to you, it's touristy—designed for flash-in-the-pan Mozart fans.

Powdered-wig orchestra performances are given almost nightly in grand traditional settings (€25–50). Pesky wigged-and-powdered Mozarts peddle tickets in the streets. They rave about the quality of the musicians, but you'll get second-rate chamber orchestras, clad in historic costumes, performing the greatest hits of Mozart and Strauss. These are casual, easygoing concerts with lots of tour groups. While there's not a Viennese person in the audience, the tourists generally enjoy the evening. To sort through all your options, check with the ticket office in the TI (same price as on the street, but with all venues to choose from). Savvy locals suggest getting the cheapest tickets, as no one seems to care if cheapskates move up to fill unsold pricier seats. Critics explain that the musicians are actually very good (often Hungarians, Poles, and Russians working a season here to fund an entire year of music studies back home), but that they haven't performed much together so aren't "tight." Of the many fine venues, the Mozarthaus is a small room richly decorated in Venetian Renaissance style with intimate chamber-music concerts (€35–42, almost nightly at 19:30, Sat at 18:00, near St. Stephen's Cathedral at Singerstrasse 7, tel. 01/911-9077).

Strauss Concerts in the Kursalon—For years, Strauss concerts have been held in the Kursalon, where the "Waltz King" himself directed wildly popular concerts 100 years ago (€38–54, concerts nightly generally at 20:15, tel. 01/512-5790 to reserve). Shows last 1.75 hours and are a mix of ballet, waltzes, and a 15-piece orchestra. It's touristy—tour guides holding up banners with group numbers wait out front after the show. Even so, the performance is playful, visually fun, fine quality for most, and with a tried-and-tested, crowd-pleasing format. The conductor welcomes the crowd in German (with a wink) and English; after that...it's English only.

Serious Concerts—These events, including the Opera, are listed in the monthly *Wien-Programm* (available at TI, described on page 455). Tickets run from €36 to €75 (plus a stiff 22 percent booking fee when booked in advance or through a box office like the one at the TI). While it's easy to book tickets online long in advance, spontaneity is also workable, as there are invariably people selling their extra tickets at face value or less outside the door before concert time. If you call a concert hall directly, they can advise you on the availability of (cheaper) tickets at the door. Vienna takes care of its starving artists (and tourists) by offering cheap standing-room tickets to top-notch music and opera (generally an hour before each performance).

Theater an der Wien—Considered the oldest theater in Vienna, this venue was designed in 1801 for Mozart operas—intimate, with just a thousand seats. Reopened in 2006 for Mozart's 250th birthday, it treats Vienna's music lovers to a different opera every month—generally Mozart with a contemporary setting and modern interpretation—with the top-notch Vienna Radio Orchestra in the pit. With the reopening of Theater an der Wien, Vienna now supports three opera companies. This one is the only company playing through the summer (facing the Naschmarkt at Linke Wienzeile 6, tel. 01/5818-1110 for information, tickets available at www.theater-wien.at).

Summer of Music Festival (a.k.a. "KlangBogen")—This annual festival assures that even from June through September, you'll find lots of great concerts, choirs, and symphonies (special *KlangBogen* brochure at TI; get tickets at Wien Ticket pavilion off Kärntner Strasse next to the Opera, or go directly to location of particular event; Summer of Music tel. 01/42717, www.klangbogen.at).

Musicals—The Wien Ticket pavilion sells tickets to contemporary American and British musicals done in the German language (€10–95, €2.50 standing room), and offers these tickets at half price from 14:00 until 17:00 the day of the show. Or you can reserve (full-price) tickets for the musicals by phone (call combined office for the three big theaters at tel. 01/58885).

Films of Concerts—To see free films of great concerts in a lively, outdoor setting near City Hall, check "Nightlife," page 525.

Dance Evening—If you'd like to actually dance (waltz and ball-room), or watch people who are really good at it, consider the Dance Evening at the Tanz Café in the Volksgarten (€5–6, May–Sept Sat from 19:00 and Sun from 18:00, www.volksgarten.at).

Classical Music to Go—To bring home Beethoven, Strauss, or the Wiener Philharmonic on a top-quality CD, shop at Gramola on the Graben or EMI on Kärntner Strasse.

Vienna's Cafés

In Vienna, the living room is down the street at the neighborhood coffee house. This tradition is just another example of Viennese expertise in good living. Each of Vienna's many long-established (and sometimes even legendary) coffee houses has its individual character (and characters). These classic cafés are a bit tired, with a shabby patina and famously grumpy waiters who treat you like an uninvited guest invading their living room. Still, it's a welcoming place. They offer newspapers, pastries, sofas, quick and light workers' lunches, elegance, smoky ambience, and "take all the time you want" charm for the price of a cup of coffee. Order it *melange* (like a cappuccino), *brauner* (strong coffee with a little milk), or *schwarzer* (black). Americans who ask for a latte are mistaken for Italians and given a cup of hot milk. Rather than buy the *International Herald Tribune* ahead of time, spend the money on a cup of coffee and read the paper for free, Vienna-style, in a café.

These are my favorites:

Café Hawelka has a dark, "brooding Trotsky" atmosphere, paintings by struggling artists who couldn't pay for coffee, a saloon-wood flavor, chalkboard menu, smoked velvet couches, an international selection of newspapers, and a phone that rings for regulars. Mrs. Hawelka died just a couple weeks after Pope John Paul II. Locals suspect the pontiff wanted her much-loved *Buchteln* (marmalade-filled doughnuts) in heaven. Mr. Hawelka, now alone and understandably a bit forlorn, still oversees the action (Wed–Mon 8:00–2:00 in the morning, Sun from 10:00, closed Tue, just off the Graben, Dorotheergasse 6).

Café Sperl dates from 1880, and is still furnished identically to the day it opened—from the coat tree to the chairs (Mon–Sat 7:00–23:00, Sun 11:00–20:00 except closed Sun July–Aug, just off Naschmarkt near Mariahilfer Strasse, Gumpendorfer 11, tel. 01/586-4158).

Café Braunerhof, between the Hofburg and the Graben, offers a classic ambience with no tourists and live music on weekends (light classics, no cover, Sat–Sun 15:00–18:00), and a practical menu with daily specials (open long hours daily, Stallburggasse 2).

Other Classics in the Old Center: All of these places are open

Viennese Coffee: From Ottomans to Starbucks

The story of coffee in Vienna is steeped in legend. In the 17th century, the Ottomans (invaders from the Turkish Empire) were laying siege to Vienna. A spy working for the Austrians who infiltrated the Ottoman ranks got to know the Turkish lifestyle...including their passion for a drug called coffee. After the Austrians persevered, the ecstatic Hapsburg emperor offered the spy anything he wanted. The spy asked for the Ottomans' spilled coffee beans, which he gathered up to start the first coffee shop in town. (It's a nice story. But actually, there was already an Armenian in town running a coffee house.)

In the 18th century, coffee boomed as an aristocratic drink. In the 19th-century Industrial Age, people were expected to work 12-hour shifts, and coffee became a hit with the working class, too. By the 20th century, the Vienna coffee scene became so refined that old-timers remember when waiters brought a sheet with various shades of brown (like paint samples) so a customer could make clear exactly how milky she wanted her coffee.

In 2003, Vienna's first Starbucks boldly opened next to the Opera—across the street from the ultimate Old World coffee house, the Sacher Café. The locals like the easy-chair ambience and quality of Starbucks coffee, but think it's over-priced. Viennese coffee connoisseurs aren't impressed by quantity, can't relate to flavored coffee, and think drinking out of a paper cup is really trashy. The consensus: For the same price, you can have an elegant and traditional experience in a top Vienna-style coffee shop instead. While the "coffee to-go" trend has been picked up by many bakeries and other joints, the Starbucks invasion has stalled, with nowhere near as many outlets as the Seattle-based coffee empire had planned.

long hours daily: **Café Pruckel** (at Dr.-Karl-Lueger-Platz, across from Stadtpark at Stubenring 24); **Café Tirolerhof** (2 blocks from the Opera, behind the TI on Tegetthoffstrasse, at Führichgasse 8); and **Landtmann Café** (directly across from the City Hall on the Ringstrasse at Dr.-Karl-Lueger-Ring 4). The Landtmann is unique, as it's the only grand café built along the Ring with all the other grand buildings.

Vienna's Wine Gardens (Heurigen)

The *Heuriger* (HOY-rih-gur; plural is *Heurigen*, HOY-rih-gehn) is a uniquely Viennese institution. When the Hapsburgs let Vienna's vintners sell their own new wine (called *Sturm*) tax-free, several hundred families opened *Heurigen* (wine-garden restaurants clustered around the edge of town)—and a tradition was born. Today, they do their best to maintain the old-village atmosphere, serving the homemade new wine (the last vintage, until November 11, when a new vintage year begins) with light meals and strolling musicians. Most *Heurigen* are decorated with enormous antique presses from their vineyards. Wine gardens might be closed on any given day; always call ahead to confirm, if you have your heart set on a particular place. (For a near-*Heuriger* experience right downtown, drop by Gigerl Stadtheuriger—see page 535.)

At any *Heuriger,* fill your plate at a self-serve cold cut buffet (€6–9 for dinner). Food is sold by the *"10 dag"* unit. (A *dag* is a decigram, so *10 dag* is 100 grams...about a quarter-pound.) Dishes to look for...or look out for: *Stelze* (grilled knuckle of pork), *Fleischlaberln* (fried ground-meat patties), *Schinkenfleckerln* (pasta with cheese and ham), *Schmalz* (a spread made with pig fat), *Blunzen* (black pudding...sausage made from blood), *Presskopf* (jellied brains and innards), *Liptauer* (spicy cheese spread), *Kornspitz* (whole-meal bread roll), and *Kummelbraten* (crispy roast pork with caraway). Waitresses will then take your wine order (€2.20 per quarter-liter, about 8 oz). Many locals claim it takes several years of practice to distinguish between the *Sturm* wine and vinegar.

There are more than 1,700 acres of vineyards within Vienna's city limits, and countless *Heuriger* taverns. For a *Heuriger* evening, rather than go to a particular place, take a tram to the wine-garden district of your choice and wander around, choosing the place with the best ambience.

Getting to the *Heurigen:* You have three options: a 15-minute taxi ride, trams and buses, or a goofy tourist train.

Trams make a trip to the Vienna Woods quick and affordable. The fastest way is to ride U-4 to its last stop, Heiligenstadt, where trams and buses in front of the station fan out to the various neighborhoods. Ride tram D to its end point for Nussdorf. Ride bus #38A for Grinzing and on to the Kahlenberg viewpoint—#38A's end station. (Note that tram #38—different from bus #38A—starts at the Ring and finishes at Grinzing.) To get to Neustift am Walde, ride U-6 to Nussdorfer Strasse and catch bus #35A. Connect Grinzing and Nussdorf with bus #38A and tram D (transfer at Grinzinger Strasse).

The **Heurigen Express** tourist train is tacky but handy and relaxing, chugging you on a hop-on, hop-off circle from Nussdorf through Grinzing and around the Vienna Woods with light narration (€7.50, buy ticket from driver, 1 hour, daily April–Oct 12:00–18:00, departs from end station of tram D in Nussdorf at the top of the hour, tel. 01/479-2808).

Here are a couple of good *Heuriger* neighborhoods:

Grinzing—Of the many *Heuriger* suburbs, Grinzing is the most famous, lively…and touristy. Many people precede their visit to Grinzing by riding tram #38 from Schottentor (on the Ring) to its end (up to Kahlenberg for a grand Vienna view), and then ride 20 minutes back into the *Heuriger* action. From the Grinzing tram stop, follow Himmelgasse uphill toward the onion-top dome. You'll pass plenty of wine gardens—and tour buses—on your way up. Just past the dome, you'll find the heart of the *Heurigen.*

Heiligenstadt (Pfarrplatz)—Between Grinzing and Nussdorf, this area features several decent spots, including the famous and touristy Mayer am Pfarrplatz (a.k.a **Beethovenhaus,** Mon–Sat 16:00–24:00, Sun 11:00–23:00, bus #38A stop: Fernsprechamt/Heiligenstadt, walk 5 min uphill on Dübling Nestelbachgasse to Pfarrplatz 2, tel. 01/370-1287). This place has a charming inner courtyard with an accordion player and a sprawling backyard with a big children's play zone. Beethoven lived—and composed his *Sixth Symphony*—here in 1817. He hoped the local spa would cure his worsening deafness. **Weingut and Heuriger Werner Welser,** a block uphill from Beethoven's place, is lots of fun, with music nightly from 19:00 (open daily 15:30–24:00, Probusgasse 12, tel. 01/318-9797).

Nussdorf—A less-touristy district, characteristic and popular with the Viennese, Nussdorf has plenty of *Heuriger* ambience. Right at the end station of tram D, you'll find three long and skinny places side by side: **Schübel-Auer Heuriger** (Tue–Sat 16:00–24:00, closed Sun–Mon, Kahlenberger Strasse 22, tel. 01/370-2222) is my favorite. Also consider **Heuriger Kierlinger** (daily 15:30–24:00, Kahlenberger Strasse 20, tel. 01/370-2264) and **Steinschaden** (daily 15:00–24:00, Kahlenberger Strasse 18, tel. 01/370-1375). Walk through any of these and you pop out on Kahlenberger Strasse, where a walk 20 yards uphill takes you to some more eating and drinking fun: **Bamkraxler** ("Tree Jumper"), the only *Biergarten* amid all these vineyards. It's a fun-loving, youthful place with fine keg beer and a regular menu—traditional, ribs, veggie, kids' menu—rather than the *Heuriger* cafeteria line (€6–10 meals, kids' playground, Tue–Sat 16:00–24:00, Sun 11:00–24:00, closed Mon, Kahlenberger Strasse 17, tel. 01/318-8800).

Sirbu Weinbau *Heuriger*—This option is actually in the vineyards, high above Vienna with great city and countryside views, a top-notch buffet, a glass veranda, and a traditional interior for cool weather. It's a bit more touristy, and dinner reservations are often required, since it's more upmarket and famous as "the ultimate setting" (April–Oct from 15:00, closed Sun, big children's play zone, Kahlenberger Strasse 210, tel. 01/320-5928). It's high above regular transit service, but fun to incorporate into a little walking. Ideally, ride bus #38A to the end at Kahlenberg, and ask directions to the *Heuriger* (a 20-min walk downhill; if you prefer an uphill walk, take tram D from the Ring to Nussdorf Platz and walk up Kahlenberger Strasse for 25 min).

NIGHTLIFE

If old music and new wine aren't your thing, Vienna has plenty of alternatives. For an up-to-date rundown on fun after dark, get the TI's free *Vienna Hype* booklet.

Open-Air Classical Music Cinema and Food Circus—A thriving people scene erupts each evening in July and August at the park in front of City Hall (Rathaus, on the Ringstrasse). Thousands

of people keep a food circus of 24 simple stalls busy. There's not a plastic cup anywhere, just real plates and glasses—Vienna wants the quality of eating to be as high as the music that's about to begin. About 3,000 folding chairs face a 60-foot-wide screen up against the City Hall's Neo-Gothic facade. When darkness falls, an announcer explains the program, and then the music starts. The program is different every night—mostly movies of opera and classical concerts, with some films. The schedule is at the TI (programs generally last about two hours, starting when it's dark—between 21:30 in July and 20:30 in August).

Since 1991, the city has paid for 60 of these summer event nights each year. Why? To promote culture. Officials know that the City Hall Music Festival is mostly a "meat market" where young people come to hook up. But they believe many of these people will develop a little appreciation of classical music and high culture on the side.

Bermuda Triangle (Bermuda Dreieck)—The area known as the "Bermuda Triangle"—north of St. Stephen's Cathedral, between Rotenturmstrasse and Judengasse—is the hot local nightspot. You'll find lots of music clubs and classy pubs, or *Beisl* (such as Krah Krah, Salzamt, Bermuda Bräu, and First Floor—for cocktails with live fish). The serious-looking guards have nothing to do with the bar scene—they're guarding the synagogue nearby.

Gürtel—The Gürtel is Vienna's outer ring road. The arches of a lumbering viaduct (which carries a train track) are now filled with trendy bars, sports bars, dance clubs, strip clubs, antique shops, and restaurants. To experience—or simply see—the latest scene in town, head out here. The people-watching—the trendiest kids on the block—makes the trip fun even if you're looking for exercise rather than a drink. Ride U-6 to Nussdorfer Strasse or Thaliastrasse and hike along the viaduct.

English Cinema—Two great theaters offer three or four screens of English movies nightly (€6–9): **English Cinema Haydn,** near my recommended hotels on Mariahilfer Strasse (Mariahilfer Strasse 57, tel. 01/587-2262, www.haydnkino.at); and **Artis International Cinema,** right in the town center a few minutes from the cathedral (Schultergasse 5, tel. 01/535-6570).

The Third Man at Burg Kino—This movie, voted the best British film ever by the British Film Institute, takes place in 1949 Vienna—when it was divided, like Berlin, between the four victorious Allies. With a dramatic Vienna cemetery scene, coffee-house culture surviving amid the rubble, and Orson Welles being chased through the sewers, the tale of a divided city about to fall under Soviet rule and rife with smuggling is an enjoyable two-hour experience while in Vienna (€8, in English with German subtitles; three or four showings weekly: Fri at 22:45, Tue and Sun afternoons depending on other film times; Opernring 19, tel. 01/587-8406, www.burgkino.at).

SLEEPING

As you move out from the center, hotel prices drop. My listings are in the old center (figure at least €100 for a decent double), along the likeable Mariahilfer Strasse (about €90), and near the Westbahnhof (about €70). While few accommodations in Vienna are air-conditioned (they are troubled by the fact that, per person, Las Vegas expends more energy keeping people cool than arctic Norway does to keep people warm), you can generally get fans on request. Places with elevators often have a few stairs to climb, too.

Sleep Code

(€1 = about $1.30, country code: 43, area code: 01)
S = Single, **D** = Double/Twin, **T** = Triple, **Q** = Quad, **b** = bathroom, **s** = shower only. English is spoken at each place. Unless otherwise noted, credit cards are accepted, rooms have no air conditioning, and breakfast is included.

To help you sort easily through these listings, I've divided the rooms into three categories, based on the price for a standard double room with bath:

$$$ Higher Priced—Most rooms €120 or more.
  $$ Moderately Priced—Most rooms between €75–120.
   $ Lower Priced—Most rooms €75 or less.

In June 2008, the European soccer championships come to town, driving up hotel prices for most of the month. Since some places will raise their rates much more than others, it's worth calling around.

These hotels lose big and you pay more if you find a room through Internet booking sites. Book direct by phone, fax, or email and save. The city has deliberately created an expensive hell for cars in the center. Don't even try. If you must bring a car into Vienna, leave it at an expensive garage.

Vienna

Within the Ring, in the Old City Center

You'll pay extra to sleep in the atmospheric old center, but if you can afford it, staying here gives you the best classy Vienna experience.

$$$ Hotel am Stephansplatz is a four-star business hotel with 56 rooms. It's plush but not over-the-top, and reasonably priced for its incredible location—literally facing the cathedral—and sleek comfort. Every detail is modern and quality; breakfast is superb, with a view of the city waking up around the cathedral; and the staff is always ready with a friendly welcome (Db-€210–250, Tb-€250, €20 less July–Aug and in winter, €15 less Fri–Sun, children free or very cheap, air-con, free Internet access, Wi-Fi in lobby, sauna, elevator, Stephansplatz 9, U-1 or U-3: Stephansplatz, tel. 01/534-050, fax 01/5340-5710, www.hotelamstephansplatz.at, office@hotelamstephansplatz.at).

$$$ Pension Pertschy, circling an old courtyard, is bigger and more hotelesque than the following listings. Its 50 rooms are huge, but well-worn and a bit musty. Those on the courtyard are quietest (Sb-€93, Db-€134–167 depending on room size, €20–30 cheaper off-season, extra bed-€34, non-smoking rooms, elevator, Habsburgergasse 5, U-1 or U-3: Stephansplatz, tel. 01/534-490, fax 01/534-4949, www.pertschy.com, pertschy@pertschy.com).

$$$ Pension Aviano is another peaceful place, with 17 comfortable rooms on the fourth floor above lots of old-center action (Sb-€99, Db-€144–165 depending on size, cheaper in July–Aug and Nov–March, extra bed-€33, non-smoking rooms, fans, elevator, between Neuer Markt and Kärntner Strasse at Marco d'Avianogasse 1, tel. 01/512-8330, fax 01/5128-3306, www.secrethomes.at, aviano@secrethomes.at).

$$$ Hotel Schweizerhof is classy, with 55 big rooms, all the comforts, shiny public spaces, and a more formal ambience. It's centrally located midway between St. Stephen's Cathedral and the Danube Canal (Sb-€84–95, Db-€113–140, extra bed-€32, low prices are for July–Aug and slow times, with cash and this book get your best price and then claim a 10 percent discount in 2008, Wi-Fi, elevator, Bauernmarkt 22, U-1 or U-3: Stephansplatz, tel. 01/533-1931, fax 01/533-0214, www.schweizerhof.at,

Hotels in Central Vienna

1. Hotel am Stephansplatz
2. Pension Pertschy
3. Pension Aviano
4. Hotel Schweizerhof
5. Hotel zur Wiener Staatsoper
6. Pension Nossek
7. Pension Suzanne
8. Pension Neuer Markt
9. To Schweizer Pension
10. To Pension Dr. Geissler

office@schweizerhof.at). Since this is in the "Bermuda Triangle" nightclub area (see page 525), it can be noisy on weekends. Ask for a quiet room when you reserve.

$$$ Hotel zur Wiener Staatsoper, the Schweizerhof's sister hotel, is quiet, with a more traditional elegance. Its 22 tidy rooms come with high ceilings, chandeliers, and fancy carpets on parquet floors (tiny Sb-€79–86, Db-€113–128, Tb-€135–150, extra bed-€22, cheaper prices are for July–Aug and Dec–March, rooms €30 more than high season rates during soccer championship in June 2008, fans on request, elevator, a block from the Opera at Krugerstrasse 11, U-1, U-2, or U-4: Karlsplatz, tel. 01/513-1274, fax 01/513-127-415, www.zurwienerstaatsoper.at, office @zurwienerstaatsoper.at, manager Claudia).

$$ At Pension Nossek, an elevator takes you above any street noise into Frau Bernad's and Frau Gundolf's world, where the children seem to be placed among the lace and flowers by an interior designer. With 30 rooms right on the wonderful Graben, this is a particularly good value (S-€50–58, Ss-€60, Sb-€73–77, Db-€115, prices won't go up during June 2008 soccer championship, €28 extra for sprawling suites, extra bed-€35, cash only, elevator, Graben 17, U-1 or U-3: Stephansplatz, tel. 01/5337-0410, fax 01/535-3646, www .pension-nossek.at, reservation@pension-nossek.at).

$$ Pension Suzanne, as Baroque and doily as you'll find in this price range, is wonderfully located a few yards from the Opera. It's small, but run with the class of a bigger hotel. The 25 rooms are packed with properly Viennese antique furnishings (Sb-€79, Db-€100–121 depending on size, 4 percent discount with this 2008 book if you pay cash, prices won't go up during June 2008 soccer championship, extra bed-€20–25, spacious apartment for up to 6 also available, discounts in winter, fans on request, elevator, free Internet access, Walfischgasse 4, U-1, U-2, or U-4: Karlsplatz and follow signs for Opera exit, tel. 01/513-2507, fax 01/513-2500, www .pension-suzanne.at, info@pension-suzanne.at, manager Michael).

$$ Pension Neuer Markt is family-run, with 37 quiet, comfy rooms in a perfectly central locale. Its hallways have the ambience of a cheap cruise ship (Ss-€60–77, Sb-€90–130, smaller Ds-€80–96, Db-€110–135, prices vary with season and room size, extra bed-€19–22, request a quiet room when you reserve, fans, elevator, Seilergasse 9, tel. 01/512-2316, fax 01/513-9105, www.hotelpension .at/neuermarkt, neuermarkt@hotelpension.at).

$$ Schweizer Pension has been family-owned for three generations. The current owners, Anita and Gerhard, run an extremely tight ship, offering 11 homey rooms for a great price, with parquet floors and lots of tourist info (S-€42–47, big Sb-€55–67, D-€58–68, Db-€78–92, Tb-€102–114, Qb-€126–131, prices depend on season and room size, cash only, entirely non-smoking, elevator, laundry-€16/load, Heinrichsgasse 2, U-2 or U-4: Schottenring, tel. 01/533-8156, fax 01/535-6469, www.schweizerpension.com, schweizer.pension@chello.at).

$$ Pension Dr. Geissler has 23 comfortable rooms on the eighth floor of a modern, nondescript apartment building about 10 blocks northeast of St. Stephen's, near the canal (S-€48, Ss-€68, Sb-€76, D-€65, Ds-€77, Db-€95, 20 percent less in winter, elevator, Postgasse 14, U-1 or U-4: Schwedenplatz, tel. 01/533-2803, fax 01/533-2635, www.hotelpension.at/dr-geissler, dr.geissler@hotelpension.at).

Hotels and Pensions Along Mariahilfer Strasse

Lively Mariahilfer Strasse connects the Westbahnhof (West Train Station) and the city center. The U-3 line, starting at the West-bahnhof, goes down Mariahilfer Strasse to the cathedral. This very Viennese street is a tourist-friendly and vibrant area filled with shopping malls, simpler storefronts, and cafés. Its smaller hotels and private rooms are generally run by people from the non-German-speaking part of the former Hapsburg Empire (i.e., Eastern Europe). Most hotels are within a few steps of a U-Bahn stop, just one or two stops from the Westbahnhof (direction from the station: Simmering). The nearest place to do laundry is **Schnell & Sauber Waschcenter** (wash-€4.50 for small load or €9 for large load, plus a few euros to dry, daily 6:00–23:00, a few blocks north of Westbahnhof on the east side of Urban-Loritz-Platz).

$$$ NH Hotels, a Spanish chain, runs two stern, passion-less business hotels a few blocks apart on Mariahilfer Strasse. Both rent ideal-for-families suites, each with a living room, two TVs, bathroom, desk, and kitchenette (rack rate: Db suite-€155, going rate usually closer to €110, plus €15 per person for optional breakfast, apartments for 2–3 adults, kids under 12 free, non-smoking rooms, elevator). The 78-room **NH Atterseehaus** is at Mariahilfer Strasse 78 (U-3: Zieglergasse, tel. 01/5245-6000, fax 01/524-560-015, nhatterseehaus@nh-hotels.com), and the slightly pricier **NH Wien** has 106 rooms at Mariahilfer Strasse 32 (U-3: Neubaugasse—follow *Stiftgasse* signs to exit and turn left from top of escalator; from Mariahilferstrasse, enter through shop passage-way between Nordsee and Edusco—or from Lindergasse 9, tel. 01/521-720, fax 01/521-7215, nhwien@nh-hotels.com). The website for both is www.nh-hotels.com.

$$ Pension Corvinus is bright, modern, and proudly and warmly run by a Hungarian family: Miklós, Judit, Anthony, and Zoltan. Its 12 comfortable rooms are spacious, and some are downright sumptuous (Sb-€55–65, Db-€89–99, Tb-€105–115, these prices promised with this book in 2008 except during soccer

Hotels and Restaurants Outside the Ring

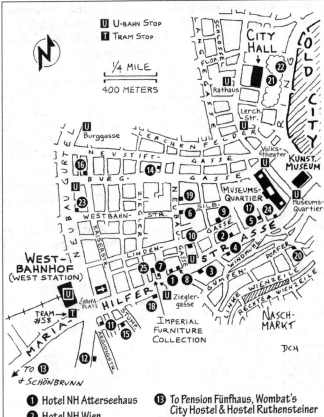

- **1** Hotel NH Atterseehaus
- **2** Hotel NH Wien
- **3** Pension Corvinus & Haydn Hotel
- **4** Pension Mariahilf
- **5** Hotel Admiral
- **6** Hotel Kugel
- **7** Pension Hargita
- **8** K&T Boardinghouse
- **9** Pension Lindenhof
- **10** Budai Ildiko Rooms
- **11** Hotel Mercure Wien Europaplatz
- **12** Hotel Ibis Wien
- **13** To Pension Fünfhaus, Wombat's City Hostel & Hostel Ruthensteiner
- **14** Jugendherberge Myrthengasse
- **15** Westend City Hostel
- **16** Lauria Rooms & Hostel
- **17** Spittelberg Quarter Eateries
- **18** Buffet Trzesniewski
- **19** Schnitzelwirt
- **20** Café Sperl
- **21** City Hall Food Circus
- **22** Landtmann Café
- **23** Launderette
- **24** British Bookshop
- **25** Imperial Furniture Collection

Vienna

championship in June, extra bed-€26, also has apartments with kitchens, most rooms non-smoking, air-con, elevator, free Internet access and Wi-Fi, parking garage-€11/day, on the third floor at Mariahilfer Strasse 57–59, U-3: Neubaugasse, tel. 01/587-7239, fax 01/587-723-920, www.corvinus.at, hotel@corvinus.at).

$$ Pension Mariahilf offers a clean, aristocratic air in an affordable and cozy pension package. Its 12 rooms are spacious but outmoded, with an Art Deco flair. Book direct and ask for a Rick Steves discount in 2008 (Sb-€60–70, twin Db €80–95, Db-€90–106, Tb-€105–134, five-person apartment with kitchen-€120–150, lower prices are for off-season or longer stays, elevator, Mariahilfer Strasse 49, U-3: Neubaugasse, tel. 01/586-1781, fax 01/586-178-122, www.mariahilf-hotel.at, office@mariahilf-hotel.at).

$$ Haydn Hotel is big and formal, with masculine public spaces and 50 spacious rooms (Sb-€80–90, Db-€110–120, suites and family apartments, extra bed-€30, ask for a 10 percent Rick Steves discount in 2008, all rooms non-smoking, air-con, elevator, Internet access, parking-€14/day, Mariahilfer Strasse 57–59, U-3: Neubaugasse, tel. 01/5874-4140, fax 01/586-1950, www.haydn -hotel.at, info@haydn-hotel.at, Nouri).

$$ Hotel Admiral is huge and practical, with 80 large, workable rooms (Sb-€68, Db-€92, extra bed-€23, manager Alexandra promises these prices with cash and this book in 2008, cheaper in winter, breakfast-€6 per person, free Internet access, limited free parking if you call to reserve it—otherwise €10/day, a block off Mariahilfer Strasse at Karl-Schweighofer-Gasse 7, U-2 or U-3: Volkstheater, tel. 01/521-410, fax 01/521-4116, www.admiral.co.at, hotel@admiral.co.at).

$$ Hotel Kugel is run with pride and attitude. "Simple quality and good value" is the motto of the hands-on owner, Johannes Roller. It's a big 34-room hotel with simple Old World charm, offering a fine value (S-€35, Sb-€55, D-€48, Db-€83, supreme Db with canopy beds-€100, prices about 10 percent higher during June 2008 soccer championship, Siebensterngasse 43, at corner with Neubaugasse, U-3: Neubaugasse, tel. 01/523-3355, fax 01/5233-3555, www.hotelkugel.at, office@hotelkugel.at). Herr Roller is happy to offer his cheaper rooms for backpackers.

$ Pension Hargita rents 24 generally small, bright, and tidy rooms (mostly twins) with Hungarian decor. This spick-and-span, well-located place is a good value (S-€38, Ss-€45, Sb-€55, D-€52, Ds-€58, Db-€66, Ts-€73, Tb-€80, Qb-€110, extra bed-€12, breakfast-€5, reserve with credit card but pay with cash to get these rates, corner of Mariahilfer Strasse and Andreasgasse, Andreasgasse 1, U-3: Zieglergasse, tel. 01/526-1928, fax 01/526-0492, www .hargita.at, pension@hargita.at, Erika and Tibor). While the pension is on a bustling street, its windows block noise well.

$ K&T Boardinghouse is a top value, renting four big, bright, airy, and comfortable rooms that face the bustling Mariahilfer

Strasse (Db-€69, Tb-€89, Qb-€109, €20–30 more in June 2008, 2-night minimum, no breakfast, air-con-€10/day, cash only, non-smoking, Internet access, coffee in rooms, 3 flights up, no elevator, Mariahilfer Strasse 72, U-3: Neubaugasse, tel. 01/523-2989, fax 01/522-0345, www.kaled.at, k.t @chello.at, Tina).

$ Pension Lindenhof rents 19 very basic, very worn but clean rooms. It's a dark and mysteriously dated time warp filled with plants; rooms have outrageously high ceilings and teeny bathrooms (S-€32, Sb-€40, D-€54, Db-€72, hall shower-€2, cash only, elevator, Lindengasse 4, U-3: Neubaugasse, tel. 01/523-0498, fax 01/523-7362, pensionlindenhof@yahoo.com, Gebrael family, Keram and his father speak English).

$ *Private Room:* If you're on a tight budget and wish you had a grandmother to visit in Vienna, stay with English-speaking **Budai Ildiko.** She rents high-ceilinged rooms with Old World furnishings out of her dark and homey apartment. Two cavernous rooms, which sleep two to four, and a skinny twin room all share one bathroom (S-€35–39, D-€46–49, T-€65–68, Q-€79, no breakfast but free coffee, cash only, lots of tourist information, classic old elevator, laundry-€4, Lindengasse 39, apartment #5, U-3: Neubaugasse, tel. 01/523-1058, tel. & fax 01/526-2595, www .wienwien.de, budai@hotmail.com).

Near the Westbahnhof (West Station)

$$$ Hotel Mercure Wien Europaplatz offers high-rise modern efficiency and comfort in 210 air-conditioned rooms, directly across from the Westbahnhof (Db-€130–170 depending on season, online deals as cheap as Db-€70 if you book well in advance, breakfast-€14, elevator, parking-€15/day, Matrosengasse 6, U-3: Westbahnhof, tel. 01/5990-1181, fax 01/597-6900, www.mercure .com, h1707@accor.com).

$$ Hotel Ibis Wien, a modern high-rise hotel with American charm, is ideal for anyone tired of quaint old Europe. Its 340 cookie-cutter rooms are bright, comfortable, and modern, with all the conveniences (Sb-€71, Db-€88, Tb-€103, €5 cheaper in July, €10–20 more during soccer championship in June 2008, breakfast-€9, non-smoking rooms, air-con, elevator, parking garage-€11/day; exit Westbahnhof to the right and walk 400 yards, Mariahilfer Gürtel 22–24, U-3: Westbahnhof; tel. 01/59998, fax 01/597-9090, www.ibishotel.com, h0796@accor.com).

$ Pension Fünfhaus is big, plain, clean, and stark—almost institutional. The neighborhood is rundown (with a few ladies loitering late at night) and the staff can be grouchy, but this 47-room pension offers the best doubles you'll find for about €50 (S-€34, Sb-€42, D-€47, Db-€57, T-€70, Tb-€85, 4-person apartment-€98, prices promised with this book in 2008, cash only, closed mid-Nov–Feb, Sperrgasse 12, U-3: Westbahnhof, tel. 01/892-3545 or 01/892-0286, fax 01/892-0460, www.pension5haus.at, pension5haus @tiscali.at, Frau Susi Tersch). Half the rooms are in the main building and half are in the annex, which has good rooms but is near the train tracks and a bit scary on the street at night. From the station, ride tram #52 or #58 two stops down Mariahilfer Strasse away from center, and ask for Sperrgasse. Crazy Chicken bike rental, listed on page 459, is just a block farther down Sperrgasse.

Cheap Dorms and Hostels near Mariahilfer Strasse

$ Jugendherberge Myrthengasse is your classic huge and well-run youth hostel, with 260 beds (€16–17 per person in 4- to 6-bed rooms, Db-€38–40, extra bed-€15, includes sheets and breakfast, non-members pay €3.50 extra, always open, no curfew, lockers and lots of facilities, Myrthengasse 7, tel. 01/523-6316, fax 01/523-5849, hostel@chello.at).

$ Westend City Hostel, just a block from the Westbahnhof and Mariahilfer Strasse, is well-run and well-located, with 180 beds in 4- to 12-bed dorms (€17–25 per person, depending on season and how many in the room—prices may go up during June 2008 soccer championship; includes sheets, breakfast, and locker; cash only, Internet access, laundry, Fügergasse 3, tel. 01/597-6729, fax 01/597-672-927, www.westendhostel.at, westendcityhostel @aon.at).

$ Lauria Rooms and Hostel is a creative little place run by friendly Gosha, with two 10-bed coed dorms with lockers for travelers ages 17 to 30 (€15/bed), plus several other rooms sleeping two to six each (any age, €24/bed, D-€48; Kaiserstrasse 77, tram #5 or a 10-min walk from Westbahnhof, tel. 01/522-2555, lauria_vienna @hotmail.com).

$ More Hostels: Other hostels with €17 beds and €40 doubles near Mariahilfer Strasse are **Wombat's City Hostel** (near tracks behind the station at Grangasse 6, tel. 01/897-2336, www.wombats-hostels.com, office@wombats-vienna .at) and **Hostel Ruthensteiner** (leave the Westbahnhof to the right and follow Mariahilfer Strasse behind the station, then left on Haidmannsgasse for a block, then turn right and find Robert-Hamerling-Gasse 24, tel. 01/893-4202, www.hostel ruthensteiner.com, info@hostelruthensteiner.com).

EATING

The Viennese appreciate the fine points of life, and right up there with waltzing is eating. The city has many atmospheric restaurants. As you ponder the Eastern European specialties on menus, remember that Vienna's diverse empire may be gone, but its flavor lingers.

While cuisines are routinely named for countries, Vienna claims to be the only *city* with a cuisine of its own: Vienna soups come with fillings (semolina dumpling, liver dumpling, or pancake slices). *Gulasch* is a beef ragout of Hungarian origin (spiced with onion and paprika). Of course, Viennese schnitzel *(Wiener Schnitzel)* is traditionally a breaded and fried veal cutlet (though pork is more common these days). Another meat specialty is boiled beef *(Tafelspitz)*. While you're sure to have *Apfelstrudel,* try the sweet cheese strudel, too (*Topfenstrudel*—wafer-thin strudel pastry filled with sweet cheese and raisins). The *dag* you see in some prices stands for "decigram" (10 grams). Therefore, *10 dag* is 100 grams, or about a quarter-pound.

On nearly every corner, you can find a colorful *Beisl* (BYE-zul). These uniquely Viennese taverns are a characteristic cross between an English pub and a French brasserie—filled with poetry teachers and their students, couples loving without touching, housewives on their way home from cello lessons, and waiters who enjoy serving hearty food and good drink at an affordable price. Ask at your hotel for a good *Beisl.*

Near St. Stephen's Cathedral

Each of these eateries is within about a five-minute walk of the cathedral.

Gigerl Stadtheuriger offers a friendly near-*Heuriger* experience (à la Grinzing—see "Vienna's Wine Gardens," page 522), often with accordion or live music, without leaving the city center. Just point to what looks good. Food is sold by the weight; 100 grams *(10 dag)* is about a quarter-pound (cheese and cold meats cost about €3 per 100 grams, salads are about €2 per 100 grams; price sheet is posted on the wall to right of buffet line). The *Karree* pork with herbs is particularly tasty and tender. They also have menu entrées, spinach strudel, quiche, *Apfelstrudel,* and, of course, casks of new and local wines (sold by the *Achtel*). Meals run €7 to €12 (daily 15:00–24:00, indoor/outdoor seating, behind cathedral, a block off Kärntner Strasse, a few cobbles off Rauhensteingasse on Blumenstock, tel. 01/513-4431).

Am Hof Eateries: The square called Am Hof (U-3: Herrengasse) is surrounded by a maze of atmospheric medieval lanes; the following eateries are all within a block of the square.

Restaurants in Central Vienna

1. Gigerl Stadtheuriger
2. Restaurant Ofenloch
3. Brezel-Gwölb
4. Beisl Zum Scherer
5. Esterhazykeller
6. To Melker Stiftskeller
7. To Zu den Drei Hacken
8. Zum Schwarzen Kameel
9. Wrenkh Restaurant & Bar
10. Buffet Trzesniewski
11. Julius Meinl am Graben Deli
12. Café Hawelka & Reinthaler's Beisl
13. Gyros
14. Cantinetta La Norma
15. To Plachutta Restaurant
16. Zanoni & Zanoni Gelateria
17. Café Rest. Palmenhaus
18. Rosenberger Markt Rest.
19. Ruckenbauer (in Underpass)
20. Kurkonditorei Oberlaa & Le Bol Patisserie Bistro
21. Danieli Ristorante
22. Sacher Café
23. Café Braunerhof
24. To Café Pruckel
25. Café Tirolerhof
26. American Bar

Restaurant Ofenloch serves good, old-fashioned Viennese cuisine with friendly service, both indoors and out. This 300-year-old eatery, with great traditional ambience, is dressy (with white tablecloths) but intimate and woodsy. It's central but not overrun with tourists (€12–19 main dishes, Mon–Sat 12:00–22:45, closed Sun, Kurrentgasse 8, tel. 01/533-8844). **Brezel-Gwölb,** a Tolkienesque wine cellar with outdoor dining on a quiet square, serves delicious light meals, fine *Krautsuppe* (cabbage soup), and old-fashioned Viennese dishes. It's ideal for a romantic late-night glass of wine (daily 11:30–23:30; leave Am Hof on Drahtgasse, then take first left to Ledererhof 9; tel. 01/533-8811). Around the corner, **Beisl zum Scherer** is untouristy and serves traditional plates for €10. Sitting outside, you'll face a stern Holocaust memorial. Inside comes with a soothing woody atmosphere and intriguing decor (Mon–Sat 11:30–22:00, closed Sun, Judenplatz 7, tel. 01/533-5164). Just below Am Hof, the ancient and popular **Esterhazykeller** has traditional fare deep underground. For a cheap and sloppy buffet, climb down to the lowest cellar. For table service on a pleasant square, sit outside (Mon–Sat 11:00–23:00, Sun 16:00–23:00, Haarhof 1, tel. 01/533-3482).

Wine Cellars: These wine cellars are fun and touristy but typical, in the old center, with reasonable prices and plenty of smoke: **Melker Stiftskeller,** less touristy, is a *Stadtheuriger* in a deep and rustic cellar with hearty, inexpensive meals and new wine (Tue–Sat 17:00–24:00, closed Sun–Mon and July–mid-Aug, between Am Hof and Schottentor U-Bahn stop at Schottengasse 3, tel. 01/533-5530). **Zu den Drei Hacken** is famous for its local specialties (€10 plates, Mon–Sat 11:00–23:00, closed Sun, indoor/outdoor seating, Singerstrasse 28, tel. 01/512-5895).

Zum Schwarzen Kameel ("The Black Camel") is popular for its two classy but very different scenes: a tiny, elegant restaurant and a trendy wine bar. The small, dark-wood, 12-table, Art Nouveau restaurant serves fine gourmet Viennese cuisine (three-course dinner-€45–60 plus pricey wine). The wine bar is filled with a professional local crowd enjoying small plates from the same kitchen at a better price. This is *the* place for horseradish and thin-sliced ham (*Beinschinken mit Kren,* €7 a plate, *Achtung*—the horseradish is *hot*). I'd order the *Vorspeistenteller* (a great antipasti dish that comes with ham and horseradish) and their *Tafelspitz* (boiled ham and vegetable, €15). Stand, grab a stool, or sit anywhere you can—it's customary to share tables in the wine-bar section. Fine Austrian wines are sold by the *Achtel* (eighth-liter glass) and listed on the board; Aussie bartender Karl can help you choose. They also have a buffet of tiny €1–2 sandwiches, warmly served by Mario, who calls himself the "best waiter in Vienna" (daily 8:30–22:00, Bognergasse 5, tel. 01/533-8125).

Austrian Wines

Austria's wine industry was scandalized in the 1980s when news broke of major vintners sweetening their wines with antifreeze. Already suffering from being characterized as "sweet and light," the local wine's reputation was scarred by this news. Austrians claim the practice was widespread in many countries, and believe Austria was just the scapegoat. Regardless, the local wine industry went into a tailspin.

Today, the Austrian wine industry no longer focuses on mass production, but instead specializes in fine boutique wines (generally not exported, and therefore not well-known). Locals order white or red Austrian wines expecting quality equal to French and Italian wines. When in Austria, I go for the better local wines when dining—well worth the cost (generally about €4 per small glass).

When sampling Austrian wine, some vocabulary helps. Try the *grüner Veltliner* (dry white wine), *Traubenmost* (a heavenly grape juice—alcohol-free but on the verge of wine), *Most* (the same thing but lightly alcoholic), and *Sturm* ("new wine," stronger than *Most*, autumn only—part of the *Heuriger* phenomenon, described on page 522). The local red wine (called *Portugieser*) is pretty good. Since the Austrian wine is often sweet, remember the word *trocken* (dry). You can order your wine by the *Viertel* (quarter-liter, 8 oz) or *Achtel* (eighth-liter, 4 oz). Beer comes in a *Krügel* (half-liter, 17 oz) or *Seidel* (third-liter, 10 oz).

Wrenkh Restaurant and Bar is well-liked for its vegetarian cuisine (though it does serve some meat dishes as well). Chef Wrenkh offers daily €8 lunch *menus* and €8 to €15 dinner plates in a bright, mod bar or in a dark, fancier restaurant (Mon–Fri 12:00–16:00 & 18:00–23:00, Sat 18:00–23:00, closed Sun, can be smoky, Bauernmarkt 10, tel. 01/533-1526).

Buffet Trzesniewski is an institution—justly famous for its elegant and cheap finger sandwiches and small beers (€1 each). Three different sandwiches and a *kleines Bier (Pfiff)* make a fun, light lunch. Point to whichever delights look tasty (or grab the English translation sheet and take time to study your 21 sandwich options). The classic favorites are *Geflügelleber* (chicken liver), *Matjes mit Zwiebel* (herring with onions), and *Speck mit Ei* (bacon and eggs). Pay for your sandwiches and a drink. Take your drink tokens to the lady on the right. Sit on the bench and scoot over to a tiny table when a spot opens up. Trzesniewski has been a Vienna favorite for a century...and many of its regulars seem to have been here for the grand opening (Mon–Fri 8:30–19:30, Sat 9:00–17:00,

---

Wieners in Wien

For hardcore Viennese cuisine, drop by a *Würstelstand*. The local hot-dog stand is a fixture on city squares throughout the old center, serving a variety of hot dogs and pickled side dishes with a warm corner-meeting-place atmosphere. The *Wiener* we know is named for Vienna, but the guy who invented the weenie studied in Frankfurt. Out of nostalgia for his school years, he named his fun fast food for that city... a Frankfurter. Only in Vienna are *Wieners* called *Frankfurters*. (Got that?)

Explore the fun menus. Be adventurous. The many varieties of hot dogs cost €2–3 each. *Kren* is horseradish. Check out the sausage primer on page 601. You'll find particularly good stands on Hoher Markt, the Graben, and in front of the Albertina Museum.

---

closed Sun; 50 yards off the Graben, nearly across from brooding Café Hawelka, Dorotheergasse 2; tel. 01/512-3291). In the fall, this is a good opportunity to try the fancy grape juices—*Most* or *Traubenmost* (described in "Austrian Wines" sidebar). Their other location, at Mariahilfer Strasse 95, serves the same sandwiches with the same menu in the same ambience, and is near many recommended hotels.

Reinthaler's Beisl is a time warp that serves simple, traditional *Beisl* fare all day. It's handy for its location (a block off the Graben, across the street from Buffet Trzesniewski) and because it's a rare restaurant in the center that's open on Sunday. Its fun, classic interior winds way back (use the handwritten daily menu rather than the printed English one, €6–10 plates, daily 11:00–22:30, at Dorotheergasse 4, tel. 01/513-1249).

Julius Meinl am Graben, a posh supermarket right on the Graben, has been famous since 1862 as a top-end delicatessen with all the gourmet fancies. Along with the picnic fixings on the shelves, there's a café with light meals and great outdoor seating, a stuffy and pricey restaurant upstairs, and a take-away counter (shop open Mon–Fri 8:30–19:30, Sat 9:00–18:00, closed Sun; restaurant open Mon–Sat until 24:00, closed Sun; Am Graben 19, tel. 01/532-3334).

Akakiko Sushi: If you're just schnitzeled out, this small chain of Japanese restaurants with an easy sushi menu may suit you. The €9 bento box meals are a tasty value. Three locations have no charm but are fast, reasonable, and convenient (€7–10 meals, all open daily 10:30–23:30): Singerstrasse 4 (a block off Kärntner Strasse near the cathedral), Heidenschuss 3 (near other recommended eateries just off Am Hof), and Mariahilfer Strasse 42–48 (fifth floor of

Kaufhaus Gerngross, near many recommended hotels).

Gyros is a humble little Greek/Turkish joint run by Yilmaz, a fun-loving Turk from Izmir. He simply loves to feed people—the food is great, the price is cheap, and you almost feel like you took a quick trip to Turkey (daily 10:00–21:30, a long block off Kärntner Strasse at corner of Fichtegasse and Seilerstätte, tel. 01/228-9551).

Cantinetta La Norma, a short walk from the cathedral, serves Italian dishes amid a cozy ambience that's both elegant and energetic. Even on weeknights the small dining area is abuzz with friendly chatter among its multinational, extremely loyal regulars. Owner Paco and his staff Hany and Novka will happily show you their snapshots of the notables who've dined here (€7–18 entrées, daily 11:00–24:00, Franziskaner Platz 3, tel. 01/512-8665).

Plachutta Restaurant, with a stylish green-and-crème, elegant-but-comfy interior and breezy covered terrace, is famous for the best beef in town. You'll find an enticing menu with all the classic Viennese beef dishes, fine deserts, attentive service, and an enthusiastic and sophisticated local clientele. They've developed the art of beef to the point of producing popular cookbooks. Their specialty is a page-long list of *Tafelspitz*—a traditional copper pot of boiled beef with broth and vegetables. Treat the broth as your soup course. A chart on the menu lets you choose your favorite cut. Make a reservation for this high-energy Vienna favorite (€16–21 per pot, daily 11:30–23:30, 10-min walk from St. Stephen's Cathedral to Wollzeile 38, U-3: Stubentor, tel. 01/512-1577).

Ice Cream!: **Zanoni & Zanoni** is a very Italian *gelateria* run by an Italian family. They're mobbed by happy Viennese hungry for their huge €2 cones to go. Or, to relax and watch the thriving people scene, lick your gelato in their fun outdoor area (daily 7:00–24:00, 2 blocks up Rotenturmstrasse from cathedral at Lugeck 7, tel. 01/512-7979).

Near the Opera

Café Restaurant Palmenhaus overlooks the Palace Garden (Burggarten—see page 486). Tucked away in a green and peaceful corner two blocks behind the Opera in the Hofburg's back yard, this is a world apart. If you want to eat modern Austrian cuisine surrounded by palm trees rather than tourists, this is it. And, since it's at the edge of a huge park, it's great for families. Their fresh fish with generous vegetables specials are on the board (€8 two-course lunches available Mon–Fri, €15–18 entrées, open daily 10:00–24:00, serious vegetarian dishes, fish, extensive wine list, indoors in greenhouse or outdoors, tel. 01/533-1033).

Rosenberger Markt Restaurant is mobbed with tour groups. Still, if you don't mind a freeway-cafeteria ambience in the center of the German-speaking world's classiest city, this self-service eatery is fast and easy. It's just a block toward the cathedral from the Opera. The best cheap meal here is a small salad or veggie plate stacked high (daily 10:30–23:00, lots of fruits, veggies, fresh-squeezed juices, addictive banana milk, ride the glass elevator downstairs, Maysedergasse 2, tel. 01/512-3458).

Ruckenbauer, a fast-food kiosk in a transit underpass (under the street in front of the Opera), is a favorite for a quick bite (Mon-Fri 6:00–20:00, Sat–Sun 9:00–20:00). Their €1.50 *Tramezzini* sandwiches and fine pastries make a classy, quick picnic lunch or dinner before the Opera (just 100 yards away).

Kurkonditorei Oberlaa may not have the royal and plush fame of Demel (see page 472), but this is where Viennese connoisseurs serious about the quality of their pastries go to get fat. With outdoor seating on Neuer Markt, it's particularly nice on a hot summer day (€10 daily three-course lunches, great selection of cakes, daily 8:00–20:00, Neuer Markt 16, tel. 01/5132-9360). Next door, **Le Bol Patisserie Bistro** satisfies your need for something French. The staff speaks to you in French, serving fine €8 salads, baguette sandwiches, and fresh croissants (daily 8:00–22:00, Neuer Markt 14).

Danieli Ristorante is your best classy Italian bet in the old center. White-tablecloth dressy, but not stuffy, it has reasonable prices (€8–13 pizza and pastas, fresh fish, open daily, 30 yards off Kärntner Strasse opposite Neuer Markt at Himmelpfortgasse 3, tel. 01/513-7913).

City Hall (Rathausplatz) Food Circus: During the summer, scores of outdoor food stands and hundreds of picnic tables are set up in the park in front of the City Hall. Local mobs enjoy mostly ethnic meals for decent-but-not-cheap prices. The fun thing here is the energy of the crowd, and a feeling that you're truly eating as the Viennese do...not schnitzel and quaint traditions, but trendy "world food" with young people out having fun in a fine Vienna park setting (July–Aug daily from 11:00 until late, in front of City Hall on the Ringstrasse).

Spittelberg Quarter

A charming cobbled grid of traffic-free lanes and Biedermeier apartments has become a favorite neighborhood for Viennese wanting a little dining charm between the MuseumsQuartier and Mariahilfer Strasse (handy to many recommended hotels; take Stiftgasse from Mariahilfer Strasse, or wander over here after you close down the Kunsthistorisches Museum). Tables tumble down sidewalks and into breezy courtyards filled with appreciative natives enjoying dinner or a relaxing drink. It's only worth the trip on a balmy summer evening, as it's dead in bad weather. Stroll Spittelberggasse, Schrankgasse, and Gutenberggasse and pick your favorite. Don't miss the vine-strewn wine garden at Schrankgasse 1.

Amerlingbeisl, with a casual atmosphere both on the cobbled street and in its vine-covered courtyard, is a great value (€7 plates, €6–8 daily specials, salads, veggie dishes, traditional specialties, daily 9:00–24:00, Stiftgasse 8, tel. 01/526-1660).

Plutzer Bräu, next door, is also good (ribs, burgers, traditional dishes, Tirolean beer from the keg, daily 11:00–2:00 in the morning, food until 22:30, Schrankgasse 4, tel. 01/526-1215).

Witwe Bolte is classier and a good choice for uninspired Viennese cuisine with tablecloths. Its tiny square has wonderful leafy ambience (daily 11:30–23:30, closed 15:00–17:30 in winter, Gutenberggasse 13, tel. 01/523-1450).

Zu Ebener Erde und Erster Stock is a charming little restaurant with a near-gourmet menu. The upstairs is Biedermeier-style, with violet tablecloths and seating for about 20. The downstairs is more casual and woody. Reservations are smart (modern Viennese seasonal fixed-price meal-€45, traditional three-course fixed-price meal-€34, Tue–Sat from 18:00, closed Sun–Mon, Burggasse 13, tel. 01/523-6254).

Near Mariahilfer Strasse

Mariahilfer Strasse is filled with reasonable cafés serving all types of cuisine. For a quick yet traditional bite, consider the venerable **Buffet Trzesniewski** sandwich bar at Mariahilfer Strasse 95 (see page 538).

Schnitzelwirt is an old classic with a 1950s patina and a clientele to match. In this smoky, working-class place, no one finishes their schnitzel ("to-go" for the dog is wrapped in newspaper, "to-go" for you is wrapped in foil). You'll find no tourists, just cheap €6 schnitzel meals (Mon–Sat 10:00–23:00, closed Sun, Neubaugasse 52, tel. 01/523-3771).

Naschmarkt (described on page 508) is Vienna's best Old World market, with plenty of fresh produce, cheap local-style eateries, cafés, *Döner Kebab* and sausage stands, and the best-value sushi in town (Mon–Fri 6:00–18:30, Sat 6:00–17:00, closed Sun, closes earlier in winter, U-4: Kettenbrückengasse). Survey the lane of eateries at the end of the market nearest the Opera. The circa-1900 pub is inviting. Picnickers can buy supplies at the market and eat on nearby Karlsplatz (plenty of chairs facing the Charles Church).

TRANSPORTATION CONNECTIONS

Vienna has two main train stations: the Westbahnhof (West Station), serving Munich, Salzburg, Melk, and Budapest; and the Südbahnhof (South Station), serving Budapest, Prague, Poland, Slovenia, Croatia, and usually Italy (though some Italy-bound trains go from the Westbahnhof). A third station, Franz Josefs, serves Krems and the Danube Valley (but Melk is served by the Westbahnhof). There are exceptions, so always confirm which station your train leaves from. Metro line U-3 connects the Westbahnhof with the center, tram D takes you from the Südbahnhof and the Franz Josefs station to downtown, and tram #18 connects Westbahnhof and Südbahnhof stations. Train info: tel. 051-717 (to get an operator, dial 2, then 2).

From Vienna by Train to: Melk (2/hr, 1.25 hrs, some with change in St. Pölten), **Krems** (hourly, 1 hr), **Salzburg** (1–2/hr, 3 hrs), **Innsbruck** (every 2 hrs, 5 hrs), **Bratislava** (2–3/hr, 1 hr; or try the new boat trip described on page 517), **Budapest** (6/day, 3 hrs), **Prague** (6/day, 4.5 hrs), **Český Krumlov** (5/day, 5–6 hrs, 1–2 changes, connections from all three Vienna stations depending on time of day), **Munich** (2/day direct, 4 hrs; otherwise about hourly, 4.75–5.75 hrs, transfer in Salzburg), **Berlin** (5/day, 9–9.5 hrs, longer on night train), **Dresden** (2/day, 7 hrs; plus 1 night train/day, 9 hrs), **Zürich** (3/day, 9 hrs, 1 with changes in Innsbruck and Feldkirch), **Ljubljana** (6/day, 6–7 hrs, convenient early-morning direct train, others change in Villach or Maribor), **Zagreb** (7/day, 6–8 hrs, 2 direct, others with up to 4 changes including Villach and Ljubljana), **Kraków** (4/day, 6.5–7.5 hrs, 2 direct including a night train departing at about 22:30, arriving at about 6:00), **Warsaw** (3/day, direct including 1 night train, 8–9 hrs), **Rome** (1/day, 13 hrs), **Venice** (2 direct/day, 7–8.5 hrs; plus 1 direct night train, 12 hrs), **Frankfurt** (3/day direct, 2 more with change in Munich or Würzburg, 7–8 hrs), **Amsterdam** (2/day, 11.5 hrs, 1–2 changes).

Excursions by Car with Driver: Those wishing they had wheels may consider hiring Johann (see page 459) for Danube excursions from Vienna or en route to Salzburg (particularly economic for groups of 3–4).

To Eastern Europe: Vienna is the springboard for a quick trip to Prague and Budapest—it's three hours by train to Budapest (€40 one-way; covered by any railpass that includes both Austria and Hungary) and four hours to Prague (€44 one-way, €88 round-trip). Americans and Canadians do not need visas to enter the Czech Republic or Hungary. Purchase tickets at the station or at most travel agencies.

Route Tips for Drivers

Driving in and out of Vienna: Navigating in Vienna isn't bad. Study the map. As you approach from Krems, you'll cross the North Bridge and land on the Gürtel, or outer ring. You can continue along the Danube Canal to the inner ring, called the Ringstrasse (clockwise traffic only). Circle around either thoroughfare until you reach the "spoke" street you need.

From Vienna west to Munich, Salzburg, and Hall in Tirol: To leave Vienna, from the Ringstrasse circle clockwise until just past the Opera. Then follow the blue signs past the Westbahnhof to *Schloss Schönbrunn* (Schönbrunn Palace), which is directly on the way to the West A-1 autobahn to Linz. Leave the palace by 15:00 and you should beat rush hour.

DANUBE VALLEY

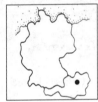

From the Black Forest in Germany to the Black Sea in Romania, the Danube flows 1,770 miles through a dozen countries. Western Europe's longest river (the Rhine is only half as long), it's also the only major river flowing west to east, making it invaluable for commercial transportation.

The Danube is at its romantic best just west of Vienna. Mix a cruise with a bike ride through the Danube's Wachau Valley, lined with ruined castles, beautiful abbeys, small towns, and vineyard upon vineyard. After touring the glorious Melk Abbey, douse your warm, fairy-tale glow with a bucket of Hitler at the Mauthausen concentration camp.

Planning Your Time

For a day trip from Vienna, catch the early train to Melk, tour the Abbey, eat lunch, and take an afternoon trip along the river from Melk to Krems. Note that the boat goes much faster downstream (eastbound, from Melk to Krems) than vice versa. From Krems, catch the train back to Vienna. Try a boat/bike combination or consider the Austrian railway's convenient Kombi-ticket. This special package includes the train trip from Vienna to Melk, entry to the Melk Abbey, a boat cruise to Krems, and the return train trip to Vienna for a total of €43 (buy at any train station). While this region is a logical day trip from Vienna, with good train connections to both Krems and Melk, spending a night in Melk is a convenient detour from the main Munich/Salzburg/Vienna train line (from Salzburg to Vienna, transfer in Amstetten or St. Pölten).

Mauthausen, farther away, should be seen en route to or from Vienna. On a three-week trip, I'd see only one concentration camp.

Mauthausen is more powerful than the more-convenient Dachau, and worthwhile if you have a car.

Cruising the Danube's Wachau Valley

By car, bike, or boat, the 24-mile stretch of the Danube between Krems and Melk is as pretty as they come. You'll cruise the Danube's wine road, passing wine gardens all along the river. Keep an eye out for wreaths of straw or greenery, hung out as an invitation to come in and taste. In local slang, someone who's feeling his wine is "blue." (Blue Danube?) Note that in German, Danube is *Donau* (DOE-now), as you'll see by the signs.

By Boat: Two different companies run boats between Melk and Krems: **DDSG** (3/day in each direction May–Sept, 1/day April and Oct, tel. 01/58880, www.ddsg -blue-danube.at) and **Brandner** (2/day in each direction May– Sept, 1/day weekdays and 2/day weekends late April and Oct, tel. 07433/259-021, www.brandner.at). Both charge the same amount: €18  one-way, €23 round-trip ticket allowing stopovers (bikes ride free); railpass-holders get a 20 percent discount with DDSG and a 10 percent discount with Brandner. In peak season (May–Sept), boats depart daily from Melk at 8:25, 11:00, 13:50 (two different boats), and 16:15 (100-min ride downstream). Boats depart from Krems at 10:10, 10:15, 13:00, 15:40, and 15:45 (because of the 6-knot flow of the Danube, the same ride upstream takes nearly twice as long—3 hours). The 16:15 departure from Melk and the 15:45 departure from Krems require an easy transfer in Spitz; the rest are direct. Confirm these times by calling the boat companies (see above), the Melk TI (see page 548), or the Krems TI (see page 553). For a longer cruise, consider the boats that start or end in Vienna.

By Bike: See the "Melk-to-Krems Danube Valley Bike Ride" described on page 552. Ask any local TI or your hotel for the latest on bike-rental options. Some hotels rent or loan bikes; in Melk, try Hotel zur Post (€7/half-day, €11/day, free for guests) or Gasthof Goldener Stern (€10/day for guests). Wachau Touristik Bernhardt has bike-rental depots at the Melk boat dock and by the train station at Spitz. For a €3 service fee, you can pick up your bike at one station and leave it at the other (€9 after 12:30, €12 for all day, June–Oct daily 10:00–16:30 at Melk, depot in Spitz is often unstaffed—call ahead and they'll meet you there in about 10 min, returns until 18:00, ID for deposit—they make a copy so you have the drop-off option, Melk tel. 0664/222-2070, Spitz tel. 02713/2222).

Danube Valley

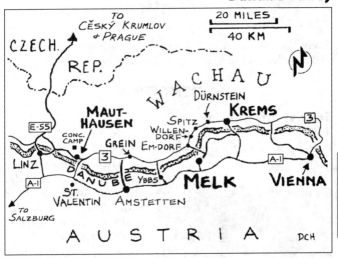

By Bus: The bus between Melk and Krems is a good budget or rainy-day alternative to the boat (€7, 60 min; Melk to Krems: Mon–Fri 4/day, Sat 2/day, Sun 1/day; Krems to Melk: Mon–Fri 3–5/day, Sat 2/day, none Sun; catch bus at train station, buy ticket on bus; for best views, sit on the driver's side from Melk to Krems or the non-driver's side from Krems to Melk, bus info tel. 02742/252-360). More connections are possible along the north side of the river if you catch the bus in Emmersdorf and change in Spitz.

By Train: Hourly trains connect Vienna with Krems and with Melk. Because they're on opposite sides of the river, trains to Krems and Melk run on different lines (trains to Melk depart from Vienna's Westbahnhof, and Krems-bound trains depart from Vienna's Franz Josefs Bahnhof). If you're starting or ending your visit to the Danube Valley with Krems, consider departing from or arriving at Vienna's Spittelau station (the train's first stop after the Franz Josefs Bahnhof) instead of Franz Josefs itself, because Spittelau has a U-Bahn station and Franz Josefs Bahnhof does not.

While tiny, one-car, milk-run trains chug along from village to village up the river, these trains don't stop at Melk (which affects bicyclists; see "Melk-to-Krems Danube Valley Bike Ride" on page 552).

By Car and Driver: Johann Lichtl, based in Vienna, can take you on a day tour of the Danube Valley (see page 459).

Melk

Sleepy and elegant under its huge abbey, which seems to police the Danube, the town of Melk offers a pleasant stop.

ORIENTATION

Tourist Information

The TI, run by helpful Manfred Baumgartner, is a block off the main square (look for green signs) and has info on nearby castles,

the latest on bike rental, specifics on bike rides along the river, a free town map with a self-guided walking tour, and a list of Melk hotels and *Zimmer* (July–Aug Mon–Sat 9:00–19:00, Sun 10:00–12:00 & 17:00–19:00; April–June and Sept Mon–Fri 9:00–12:00 & 14:00–18:00, Sat–Sun 10:00–12:00 & 16:00–18:00 except closed Sun in April; Oct Mon–Fri 9:00–12:00 & 14:00–17:00, Sat 10:00–12:00, closed Sun; closed Nov–March; good picnic garden with WC behind TI, Babenbergerstrasse 1, tel. 02752/5230-7410, www.niederoesterreich.at/melk).

Arrival in Melk

By Train: Walk straight out of the station (lockers-€2–3.50) and continue ahead for several blocks; at the curve, keep straight and go down the stairs, following the cobbled alley that dumps you into the center of the village. Access to Melk Abbey is up on your right (follow signs to *Zum Stift* or *Fussweg Stift Melk*), and the TI is a block off the end of the square to your right.

    By Boat: Turn right as you leave the boat dock and follow the canalside bike path toward the big yellow abbey (the village is beneath its far side). In about five minutes, you'll come to a flashing light (at intersection with bridge); turn left and you're steps from downtown.

    To reach the boat dock from Melk, leave the town toward the river, with the abbey on your right. Turn right when you get to the busy road and follow the canal (at the fork, it's quicker to jog left onto the bike path than to follow the main road). Follow signs for *Linienschifffahrt–Scheduled Trips–Wachau*.

SIGHTS AND ACTIVITIES

▲▲Melk Abbey (Benediktinerstift Melk)

Melk's newly restored abbey, beaming proudly over the Danube Valley, is one of Europe's great sights. Established as a fortified

Benedictine abbey in the 11th century, it was destroyed by fire. What you see today is 18th-century Baroque. Architect Jakob Prandtauer made the building one with nature. The abbey church, with its 200-foot-tall dome and symmetrical towers, dominates the complex—emphasizing its sacred purpose.

Freshly painted and gilded throughout, it's a Baroque dream, a lily alone. The grand restoration project—financed in part by the sale of the abbey's Gutenberg Bible to Harvard—was completed by 1996 to celebrate the 1,000th anniversary of the first reference to a country named Österreich (Austria).

Cost and Hours: €7.50, includes entrance to Abbey Park, daily May–Sept 9:00–17:30, mid-March–April and Oct 9:00–16:30, last entry 30 min before closing; Nov–mid-March the abbey is open only for tours in German with a little English at 11:00 and 14:00; tel. 02752/555-232, www.stiftmelk.at.

Tours: English tours of the abbey are offered daily (mid-March–Oct at 14:55, €9.30 ticket includes tour and admission). A private guide can be reserved at least one day in advance (€40 plus the €7.50 per-person entrance fee).

➲ **Self-Guided Tour:** Although you can take a guided tour, it's easiest just to wander through on your own. Each room is described in English.

• *Go through the first passageway and approach the grand entry to the...*

East Facade: Imagine the abbot on the balcony greeting you as he used to greet important guests. Flanking him are statues of Peter and Paul (leaders of the apostles and patron saints of the abbey church) and the monastery's coat of arms (crossed keys). High above are the Latin words "Glory only in the cross" and a huge copy of the Melk Cross (one of the abbey's greatest treasures—the original is hiding in the treasury and viewable only with special permission).

• *Pass into the main courtyard.*

Prelate's Courtyard: This is more than a museum. For 900 years, monks of St. Benedict have lived and worked here. Their task: bringing and maintaining Christianity and culture to the region. (Many of the monks live outside the abbey in the community.)

Melk

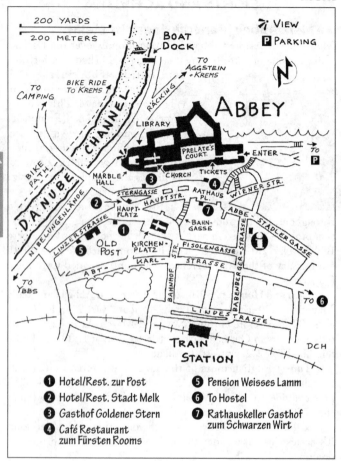

- **1** Hotel/Rest. zur Post
- **2** Hotel/Rest. Stadt Melk
- **3** Gasthof Goldener Stern
- **4** Café Restaurant zum Fürsten Rooms
- **5** Pension Weisses Lamm
- **6** To Hostel
- **7** Rathauskeller Gasthof zum Schwarzen Wirt

They run a high school with about 800 students, a small boarding school, and a busy retreat center.

There have been low points. During the Reformation (1500s), only eight monks held down the theological fort. Napoleon made his headquarters here in 1805 and 1809. And in 1938, when Hitler annexed Austria, the monastery was squeezed into one end of the complex and nearly dissolved. But today, the institution survives—that's the point of the four modern frescoes gracing the courtyard—funded by agriculture (historically, monasteries are big landowners) and your visit.

• *In the far left-hand corner, climb the stairs to the...*

Imperial Corridor and Abbey Museum: This 640-foot-long corridor, lined with paintings of Austrian royalty, is the spine of the Abbey Museum. Duck into the first room of the museum (on the left, near beginning of hall). Art treasures and a recently updated exhibit (with creepy sound-and-light effects and some English explanations) fill several rooms.

• *Continue through the museum—walking parallel to the corridor, passing through the trippy mirrored room and around a beautifully preserved Northern Renaissance altarpiece—and go through the room at the end, with the big rotating model of the abbey.*

Marble Hall: While the door frames are real marble, most of this large dining room/ballroom is stucco. The treasure here is the ceiling fresco (by Tirolean Paul Troger, 1731), best appreciated from the center of the room. Notice three themes: 1) The Hapsburgs liked to be portrayed as Hercules; 2) Athena, the goddess of wisdom, is included, because the Hapsburgs were smart as well as strong; and 3) The Hapsburgs were into art and culture. This is symbolized by angels figuratively reining in the forces of evil, darkness, and brutality. Through this wise moderation, goodness, beauty, art, and science can rule. Look up again as you leave the room to see how the columns were painted at an angle to give the illusion of a curved ceiling.

Balcony: Here, we enjoy dramatic views of the Danube Valley, the town of Melk, and the facade of the monastery church. The huge statue above everything shows the risen Christ, cross in hand and victorious over death—the central message of the entire place.

Library: For the Benedictine monks, the library was—except

for the church itself—the most important room in the abbey. Consider how much money they must have invested in its elaborate decor.

In the Middle Ages, monasteries controlled information and horded it in their libraries. At a time when most everyone else was illiterate, monks were Europe's educated elite, and had the power to dictate what was true...and what wasn't.

The inlaid bookshelves, matching bindings, and another fine Troger fresco combine harmoniously to create the Marble Hall's thematic counterpart. This room celebrates not wise politics, but faith. The ceiling shows a woman surrounded by the four cardinal virtues (wisdom, justice, fortitude, and recycling)—natural traits that lead to a supernatural faith. The statues flanking the doors represent the four traditional university faculties (law, medicine, philosophy, and theology).

There would be a Gutenberg Bible in this room...but it was sold to Harvard University to raise money to restore the library and glittering church.

Church: The finale is the church, with its architecture, ceiling frescoes, stucco marble, grand pipe organ, and sumptuous

chapels adorned with chubby cherubs (how many can you count?). All these elements combine in full Baroque style to make the theological point: A just battle leads to victory. The ceiling shows St. Benedict's triumphant entry into heaven (on a fancy carpet). In the front, below the huge papal crown, saints Peter and Paul shake hands before departing for their final battles, martyrdom, and ultimate victory. And, high above, the painting in the dome shows that victory: the Holy Trinity, surrounded by saints of particular importance to Melk, happily in heaven.

Other Abbey Sights: Near the entrance (and exit) to the abbey, you'll find the Abbey Park (included in abbey ticket, or €3 for just the park, May–Oct daily 9:00–18:00, closed Nov–April)—home to a picturesque Baroque pavilion housing some fine frescoes by Johann Wenzel Bergel and a café. Nearby, in the former orangerie, is the abbey's expensive restaurant.

Near Melk, in the Danube Valley

▲▲**Melk-to-Krems Danube Valley Bike Ride**—The three-hour pedal from Melk to Krems takes you through the Wachau Valley—steeped in tradition, blanketed with vineyards, and ornamented

with cute villages. Bicyclists rule here, and you'll find all the amenities that make this valley so popular with Austrians on two wheels. For bike-rental info in Melk, see page 546.

Bike routes are clearly marked with green *Donau–Radwanderweg* signs. The local

TIs give out a *Donauradweg* brochure with a helpful if basic route map. As you study it, note that the north bank has the best and most popular trail; it's paved all the way, winds through picturesque villages, and runs near, though not directly beside, the river. But consider the south bank, which has less car traffic. Although the bike trail merges with the actual road about half the time, it comes with better river views. (Note: The bike-in-a-red-border signs mean "no biking.")

Pedal downstream toward Krems to enjoy a gradual slope in your favor. While catching the boat back makes for a much longer day (it's slow upstream), cute one-car milk-run trains rattle up the valley stopping at most towns along the way (about hourly, 1 hour from Krems to Emmersdorf opposite Melk, bike rack at rear of train—carry bike up the stairs to reach rack). If you prefer, you can go half-and-half by cruising to Spitz—a good midway point—and then hopping on a bike (or vice versa). Spitz has a boat station and train station (the bike path between Spitz and Krems is more interesting than between Melk and Spitz). Little ferries shuttle bikers and vacation-goers regularly across the river at three points.

A good day-plan from Melk (though your times may vary depending on when you rent the bike): Depart Melk at 8:00, bike the valley, lunch in Krems or picnic on train, and catch the 13:00 train from Krems back to Emmersdorf (across the river and three miles from Melk). If you run out of steam or time, you can catch a train at most towns en route.

Krems—This is a gem of a town. From the boat dock, walk a few blocks north and east to the TI and pick up a town map (go inland past two roundabouts, veering slightly left, then turn right onto Steiner Landstrasse; the TI is on the left shortly after the overhead railroad tracks). Then stroll the traffic-free, shopper's-wonderland old town. If nothing else, it's a pleasant 20-minute walk from the dock to the train station (Krems–Vienna trains depart at least hourly, 1 hour). The local **TI** can usually find you a bed in a private home (D-€40, Db-€50, cheap rooms harder to come by in Sept–Oct) if you decide to side-trip into Vienna from this small-town alternative (TI open May–Oct Mon–Fri 9:00–18:00, Sat 11:00–17:00, Sun 11:00–16:00; Nov–April Mon–Fri 9:00–17:00, closed Sat–Sun; Undstrasse 6, tel. 02732/82676, kremstourismus @pegasus.at).

Sleeping in Krems: **$ Melanie Stasny's Gästezimmer** is a super place to stay—friendly, and with a proud vineyard and wine cellar (€23 per person in Db, Tb, or Qb, big Db-€50, 300 yards from dock at Steiner Landstrasse 22, tel. 02732/82843). When they're booked, they send travelers to their son's place down the street.

Dürnstein—This touristic flypaper lures hordes of tour bus and cruise ship visitors with its traffic-free quaintness and its one claim to fame (and fortune): Richard the Lionhearted was imprisoned here in 1193. You can probably sleep in his bedroom. Still, the town is a delight, and the ruined castle above can be reached by a good hike with great river views.

Willendorf—This is known among prehistorians as the town where the oldest piece of European art was found. There's a tiny museum in the village center (free, limited hours). A block farther uphill (follow the signs to *Venus*, just under tracks, follow stairs to right), you can see the monument where the well-endowed, 25,000-year-old fertility symbol, the *Venus of Willendorf*, was discovered. (The fist-sized original is now in Vienna's Natural History Museum—see page 502.)

SLEEPING

In Melk

Melk makes a fine overnight stop. Except during August, you shouldn't have any trouble finding a good room at a reasonable rate. The TI has a long list of people renting rooms for about €20 per person. Most of these are a few miles from the center.

$$$ Hotel zur Post is Melk's most modern-feeling hotel—professional and well-run by the Ebner family, with 28 comfy and tidy rooms over a good restaurant (Sb-€58–75, Db-€90–102 depending on size, suite for 2–5 people-€135–198, 8 percent discount with cash and this book in 2008, closed Jan–mid-Feb, elevator, sauna, Linzer Strasse 1, tel. 02752/52345, fax 02752/234-550, www.hotelpost-melk.at, info@hotelpost-melk.at). Hotel zur Post has free bikes for guests, and rents them to non-guests (€7/half-day, €11/day).

$$$ Hotel Stadt Melk, a block below the main square, has pink halls and drab, outmoded rooms. Melk's moderately priced options (listed next) offer better rooms for lower prices, but this will do in a pinch (Sb-€58–65, Db-€92, Hauptplatz 1, tel. 02752/524-750, fax 02752/524-7519, www.hotelstadtmelk.com, hotel.stadtmelk@netway.at).

$$ Gasthof Goldener Stern's 11 rooms have barn-flavored elegance and flowers on every pillow. The pricier canopy-bed

---

Sleep Code

(€1 = about $1.30, country code: 43, area code: 02752)
S = Single, **D** = Double/Twin, **T** = Triple, **Q** = Quad, **b** = bathroom, **s** = shower only. Breakfast is included and everyone speaks at least some English. Credit cards are accepted unless otherwise noted.

To help you sort easily through these listings, I've divided the rooms into three categories, based on the price for a standard double room with bath:

$$$ **Higher Priced**—Most rooms €75 or more.
$$ **Moderately Priced**—Most rooms between €50–75.
$ **Lower Priced**—Most rooms €50 or less.

rooms are very romantic. This lively place buzzes with locals eating in the atmospheric old restaurant—and with Regina and Kurt Schmidt's five children. It's on the small alley that veers off the main square above the twin turrets (D-€42–52, Db-€68, Db suite-€100, prices depend on room size, rooms for up to 6 also available, cash only, €10/day bike rental for guests, Sterngasse 17, they'll pick you up in Vienna if you've missed the last train, tel. 02752/52214, fax 02752/522-144, www.sternmelk.at, goldenerstern.melk @aon.at).

$$ Cafe Restaurant zum Fürsten rents 10 clean rooms over its creaky restaurant. Run by the Madar family, it's right on the traffic-free main square, with a fountain outside the door and the Melk Abbey hovering overhead (Sb-€39–45, small Db-€60, big Db with bathtub-€74, cash only, Rathausplatz 3–5, tel. 02752/52343, fax 02752/523-434, www.tiscover.at/cafe-madar, cafe.madar @netway.at).

$$ Gasthof zum Schwarzen Wirt offers classy, clean, basic rooms with nice floors and decor with a modern, African touch, right in the middle of town (Db-€63, Tb-€75, Qb-€90, cash only, Rathausplatz 13, tel. & fax 02752/52257, www.schwarzerwirt.at, addo@schwarzerwirt.at, Addo family). They also run a restaurant—see "Eating."

$ Pension Weisses Lamm has the cheapest beds in the center—and absentee management. All but two of the seven worn-but-clean rooms have bathrooms (Db-€50, Tb-€75, cash only, Linzer Strasse 7, look for namesake white lamb on sign, tel. 0664/231-5297, fax 02752/51224).

$ *Hostel:* The modern, institutional **youth hostel** is a 10-minute walk from the station; go straight out from the station down Bahnhofstrasse, then turn right at the next corner onto Abt-Karl-Strasse (24 4-bed rooms, one 8-bed room; beds-€17.90, Sb or Db-€10 extra, plus one-time €2 charge if staying less than 3 nights, includes sheets and breakfast, non-members-€3 extra, no curfew, reception open daily 8:00–12:00 & 16:00–21:00 with check-in only in evening, reception desk staffed intermittently Nov–March—call ahead, Abt-Karl-Strasse 42, tel. 02752/52681, fax 02752/526-815, http://melk.noejhw.at, melk@noejhw.at).

EATING

The recommended hotels **Gasthof Goldener Stern** and **Café Restaurant zum Fürsten** have restaurants with fine, inexpensive local cuisine (both open daily).

Hotel Restaurant zur Post, classier and pricier, is worth the few extra euros. Downstairs is a fun and atmospheric wine cellar, with both local and international wines (daily 11:30–21:30, closed

Jan–mid-Feb, good local dishes, courtyard and fine streetside seating with an abbey view, Linzer Strasse 1, tel. 02752/52345).

Hotel Restaurant Stadt Melk serves Melk's most elegant cuisine, with delicate nouvelle cuisine–type fixed-price meals (€75 for standard, €100 for 7-course blowout, €10–18 entrées, Thu–Tue 12:00–14:00 & 18:00–21:00, closed Wed, terrace seating, reservations smart, Hauptplatz 1, tel. 02752/524-7530).

Locals swear by the food at **Rathauskeller Gasthof zum Schwarzen Wirt,** with good Austrian and West African dishes. It's run by the Ghanaian-Austrian Addo family (€8–11 for most meals, lunch specials; May–Oct Mon–Sat usually 9:00–24:00, Sun 10:00–22:00; Nov–April closed midday 14:30–16:30, on Tue, and on Sun evenings; West African food in evening if you call ahead to order, Rathausplatz 13, tel. 02752/52257).

Supermarket: Pick up picnic supplies at the centrally located **Spar** (Mon–Fri 7:00–18:00, Sat 7:00–17:00, closed Sun, Rathausplatz 9).

TRANSPORTATION CONNECTIONS

Melk is on the autobahn and just off the Salzburg–Vienna train line.

From Melk by Train to: Vienna's Westbahnhof (2/hr, 1.25 hrs, some with transfer in St. Pölten), **Salzburg** (at least hourly, 2.5 hrs, transfer in Amstetten or St. Pölten), **Mauthausen** (hourly, 1.5 hrs, transfer in Amstetten and St. Valentin).

Mauthausen Concentration Camp

In the beautiful rolling hills flanking the Danube River, just upstream from Vienna, stands the notorious former concentration

camp at Mauthausen (MOWT-how-zehn). This slave-labor and death camp functioned from 1938 to 1945 for the exploitation and extermination of Hitler's opponents. More than half of its 206,000 quarry-working prisoners died here, mostly from starvation or exhaustion.

The Nazis' camps, scattered across much of Europe by the early 1940s, were of two types: extermination camps, where people were simply exterminated en masse (such as at Auschwitz), and concentration camps such as Mauthausen, where people were essentially worked to death. In these camps, your ability to endure forced labor amounted to a stay of execution.

Mauthausen, like many camps, was located at a quarry. Inmates generally labored for the German armaments industry or quarried stone for vast Nazi building projects. The long stairway that connected the quarry with the Mauthausen camp and its stone depot earned the name "stairway of death" for good reason.

With Nazi efficiency in mind, people were fed the bare minimum to continue working. If you couldn't carry slabs of rocks on your back up the stairway all day long—under the harshest of conditions and on this starvation diet—you were shot on the spot. Conditions were so harsh that most died within a year of their arrival.

Today the barracks of Mauthausen—which held as many as 80,000 slave-laborers at a time—tell the story of this camp. Outside the barracks is a park area where each home country of the camp's victims has erected a gripping memorial to their citizens who perished here. Many yellowed photos have fresh flowers to honor loved ones who are still not forgotten.

Allow two hours to tour the camp completely. You can borrow a free, 45-minute audioguide (leave ID as deposit). The barracks house a worthwhile museum at the far end of the camp on the right (no English, but the excellent €2.60 English guidebook has descriptions for every display case). The most emotionally moving rooms and the gas chamber are downstairs. The spirits of the victims of these horrors can still be felt.

Mauthausen rivals Dachau as the most powerful concentration-camp experience a traveler can have in Western Europe (€2, daily 9:00-17:30, last entry 1 hour before closing, some exhibits are at new visitors center near the car park—but tickets for the camp must be purchased inside camp at ticket booth, tel. 07238/2269, TI tel. 07238/3860, www.mauthausen-memorial.at; for directions, see "Transportation Connections"). A graphic 45-minute movie is shown at the top of each hour between 9:00 and 16:00. There are several film rooms—check in at the visitors center to request an English showing.

Back outside the camp, find the barbed-wire memorial overlooking the quarry and the "stairway of death" *(Todesstiege)*. Hike down and back up the sad stairway to ponder the vast quarry from its ground level; you'll be left with a lasting and poignant impression. (If you have a car and want to see the quarry but avoid the hike, turn right as you leave the main parking lot and park at the quarry.)

By visiting a concentration camp and putting ourselves through this emotional wringer, we heed and respect the fervent wish of the victims of this fascism—that we never forget. Many people forget by choosing not to know.

SLEEPING

Near Mauthausen
$$ Hotel zum Goldenen Schiff is a decent value, with 20 comfy rooms and a quaint location. It faces the delightful main square of Enns. This village, just off the autobahn—less than four miles southwest of Mauthausen and 62 miles west of Vienna—calls itself Austria's oldest town (Sb-€45, Db-€65, family rooms, free parking, Hauptplatz 23, tel. 07223/86086, fax 07223/860-8615, www.hotel-brunner.at, wolfgang.brunner@liwest.at).

EATING

Moststube Frellerhof, a farmhouse 50 yards below the Mauthausen parking lot, offers a refreshing, peaceful break after your visit. They serve *Most* (grape juice ready to become wine), homemade schnapps, and light, farm-fresh meals (May–mid-Sept daily from 13:00, April and mid-Sept–Oct Sat–Sun only, closed Nov–March, playground, tel. 07238/2789).

TRANSPORTATION CONNECTIONS

Getting to Mauthausen
Most trains stop at St. Valentin, midway between Salzburg and Vienna, where sporadic trains make the 15-minute ride to the Mauthausen station (get map from station attendant, camp is #9 on map). While there are no lockers at the station, the camp's information center will keep an eye on your bags during your visit.

Getting to Mauthausen Camp from Mauthausen Station: To cover the three miles between the camp and station, you can **hike** (1 hour, follow signs to *Ehemaliges KZ-Gedenkstätte Lager*), or **taxi** (minibus taxis available, about €10 one-way, ask taxi to pick you up in 2 hours, share the cost with other tourists, tel. 07238/2439). Train info: tel. 051-717 (to get an operator, dial 2 then 2).

From Vienna by Train to Mauthausen: You can reach Mauthausen direct from Vienna's Südbahnhof (once daily at about 7:00), or faster from the Westbahnhof with a transfer in St. Valentin (about hourly until 17:30, 2.5 hrs).

From Mauthausen by Train via St. Valentin to: **Salzburg** (hourly, 2 hrs, allow extra 20 min to get from camp memorial to station), **Vienna** (nearly hourly, 2 hrs).

Route Tips for Drivers

Hallstatt to Vienna, via Mauthausen, Melk, and Wachau Valley (210 miles): Leave Hallstatt early. Follow the scenic Route 145 through Gmunden to the autobahn and head east. After Linz, take exit #155, at Enns, and follow the signs for *Mauthausen* (five miles from freeway). Go through Mauthausen town and follow the *Ehemaliges KZ-Gedenkstätte Lager* signs. From Mauthausen, it's a speedy 60 minutes to Melk via the autobahn, but the curvy and scenic Route 3 along the river is worth the nausea. At Melk, signs to *Stift Melk* lead to the Benediktinerstift (Benedictine Abbey). Other *Melk* signs lead into the town.

The most scenic stretch of the Danube is the Wachau Valley between Melk and Krems. From Melk (get a Vienna map at the TI), cross the river again (signs to *Donaubrücke*) and stay on Route 3. After Krems, it hits the autobahn (A-22), and you'll barrel right into Vienna's traffic. (See "Route Tips for Drivers" in the Vienna chapter for details, page 544.)

Danube Valley

SALZBURG

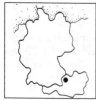

Salzburg is forever smiling to the tunes of Mozart and *The Sound of Music*. Thanks to its charmingly preserved old town, splendid gardens, Baroque churches, and Europe's largest intact medieval fortress, Salzburg feels made for tourism. It's a museum city with class. Vagabonds wish they had nicer clothes.

But even without Mozart and the von Trapps, Salzburg is steeped in history. In about A.D. 700, Bavaria gave Salzburg to Bishop Rupert for his promise to Christianize the area. Salzburg remained an independent state until Napoleon came (about 1800). Thanks in part to its formidable fortress, Salzburg managed to avoid the ravages of war for 1,200 years...until World War II. Much of the city was destroyed by WWII bombs (mostly around the train station), but the historic old town survived.

The year 2006 marked the 250th birthday of Salzburg's beloved and most marketable son, Wolfgang Amadeus Mozart. While that particular moneymaker may be history, you'll still notice how greedily the town exercises all its creative powers to milk the composer's legacy. Eight million tourists crawl Salzburg's cobbles each year. That's a lot of Mozart balls—and all that popularity has led to a glut of businesses hoping to catch the tourist dollar. Still, Salzburg is both a must and a joy.

Planning Your Time

While Vienna measures much higher on the Richter scale of sightseeing thrills, Salzburg is simply a touristy stroller's delight. If you're going into the nearby Salzkammergut lake country (see next chapter), skip the *Sound of Music* tour—if not, allow half a day for it. The *S.O.M.* tour kills a nest of sightseeing birds with one ticket (city overview, *S.O.M.* sights, and a fine drive through the lakes). You'll probably need two nights for Salzburg—nights are important for swilling beer in atmospheric local gardens and attending concerts in Baroque halls and chapels. Seriously consider one of Salzburg's many evening musical events (a few are free, some are as cheap as €12, and most average €30–40). While the sights are mediocre, the town itself is an enjoyable Baroque museum of cobbled streets and elegant buildings. And to get away from it all, bike down the river or hike across the Mönchsberg.

A day trip from Salzburg to Hallstatt (the highlight of the Salzkammergut Lake District—see next chapter) is doable, but involves about five hours of travel time and makes for a very long day. An overnight in Hallstatt is better.

ORIENTATION

(area code: 0662)

Salzburg, a city of 150,000 (Austria's fourth-largest), is divided into old and new. The old town, sitting between the Salzach River and its mini-mountain (Mönchsberg), holds nearly all the charm and most of the tourists. The new town, across the river, has its own share of sights and museums, plus some good accommodations.

Tourist Information

Salzburg has three helpful TIs (main tel. 0662/889-870, www.salzburg.info): at the **train station** (daily June–Sept 8:15–20:00,

often later July–Aug, Oct–May 8:45–19:00, tel. 0662/8898-7340), on **Mozartplatz** in the old center (daily 9:00–18:00, July–mid-Sept until 19:00, tel. 0662/8898-7330), and at the **Salzburg Süd park-and-ride** (generally open 10:00–18:00, often closed Mon–Tue, closed in winter, tel. 0662/8898-7360). At any TI, you can pick up a free city-center map (the €0.70 map has a broader coverage and more information on sights, but probably isn't necessary), the Salzburg Card brochure (listing sights with current hours and prices), and a bimonthly schedule of events. Book a concert upon arrival. The TIs also book rooms for a fee.

Salzburg Card: The TIs sell the Salzburg Card, which covers all your public transportation (including elevator and funicular) and admission to all the city sights (including Hellbrunn Castle and the river cruise). The card is pricey (€23/24 hrs, €31/48 hrs,

€36/72 hrs), but if you'd like to pop into all the sights without concern for the cost, this can save money and enhance your experience. To analyze your potential savings, here are the major sights and what you'd pay without the card: Hohensalzburg Fortress and funicular-€10; Mozart's Birthplace and Residence-€10; Hellbrunn Castle-€8.50; Salzburg Panorama 1829-€2; Salzach River cruise-€12; 24-hour transit pass-€3.40. Busy sightseers can save plenty. Get this card, feel the financial pain once, and the city will be all yours.

Arrival in Salzburg

By Train: The Salzburg station is user-friendly. The TI is at track 2A. Downstairs at street level, you can store your luggage, buy tickets, and get train information. Bike rental is nearby (see "Getting Around Salzburg"). City buses depart from the lot facing the station (monitors clearly show each bus' destination—any bus heading for *Zentrum* stops near the main bridge in the old town, including buses #1, #5, #6, and #25; get off at the first stop after you cross the river for most sights and city-center hotels, or just before the bridge for Linzergasse hotels). Figure €7 for a taxi to the center. To walk downtown (15 minutes), leave the station ticket hall to the left, and walk straight down Rainerstrasse, which leads under the tracks past Mirabellplatz, turning into Dreitaltigkeitsgasse. From here, you can turn left onto Linzergasse for many of the recommended hotels, or cross the Staatsbrücke bridge for the old town (and more hotels). For a more dramatic approach, leave the station the same way but follow the tracks to the river, turn left, and walk the riverside path toward the fortress.

By Car: Follow *Zentrum* signs to the center, and park short-term on the street (3-hour limit, pay at meter) or longer in the various garages (best under Mönchsberg mountain, €14/day). Ask at your hotel for suggestions. (For more driving and parking tips, see "Transportation Connections," page 603.)

Helpful Hints

Recommendations Skewed by Kickbacks: Salzburg is addicted to the tourist dollar, and it can never get enough. Virtually all hotels are on the take when it comes to concert and tour recommendations, influenced more by their potential kickback than by what's best for you. Take their advice with a grain of salt.

Internet Access: The Internet kiosk a few doors down from the TI is well-located, but too expensive (€2/10 min). Cheaper places around the old town aren't hard to find. Two Internet cafés at the bottom of the cliff, between Getreidegasse and the Mönchsberg lift, have good prices and hours (€2/hr, daily

10:00–22:00). Across the river, there's a big, handy Internet café on Theatergasse (near Mozart's Residence, €2/hr, daily 9:00–23:00), and plenty more near the station (including **Bubblepoint**, a modern launderette—see "Laundry"). Readers of this book can get online free at the Panorama Tours terminal on Mirabellplatz (daily 8:00–18:00).

Post Office: A full-service post office is located in the heart of town, in the new Residenz (Mon–Fri 7:00–18:30, Sat 8:00–10:00, closed Sun).

Laundry: The launderette at the corner of Paris-Lodron-Strasse and Wolf-Dietrich-Strasse, near my recommended Linzergasse hotels, is handy (€10 self-service, €15 same-day full-service, Mon–Fri 7:30–18:00, Sat 8:00–12:00, closed Sun, tel. 0662/876-381). To do your laundry and email at the same time, head to **Bubblepoint** (wash and dry for €7, six Internet terminals, daily 7:00–23:00, in CityCenter Mall opposite train station, Karl-Wurmb-Strasse 2, tel. 0664/471-1484).

American Express: AmEx has travel-agency services, but doesn't sell train tickets (Mon–Fri 9:00–17:30, closed Sat–Sun, Mozartplatz 5, tel. 0662/843-8400).

Lockers in the Old Town: The TI generously provides lockers right on Mozartplatz (€1/day, pick up key at the desk).

Getting Around Salzburg

By Bus: Single-ride tickets for central Salzburg *(Einzelkarte–Kernzone)* are sold on the bus for €1.80. At machines and *Tabak/Trafik* shops, you can buy €1.60 single-ride tickets or a €3.40 day pass *(Tageskarte,* good for 24 hours, €4.20 if you buy it on the bus). To signal the driver that you want to get off, press the buzzer on the pole. Bus info: tel. 0662/4480-1500.

By Bike: Salzburg is fun for cyclists. The following two bike-rental shops offer 20 percent off with a valid train ticket or Eurailpass—ask for it. **Top Bike** rents bikes from two outlets: at the river side of the train station (exit to the left and walk 50 yards), and on the river next to the Staatsbrücke (€6/2 hrs, €10/4 hrs, €15/24 hrs, usually daily April–June and Sept–Oct 10:00–17:00, July–Aug 9:00–19:00, closed Nov–March, tel. 06272/4656, mobile 0676-476-7259, www.topbike.at, Sabine). **Velo-Active** rents bikes on Mozartplatz, across from the American Express office in the old town (€4.50/1 hr, €7/2 hrs, €15/24 hrs; mountain bikes-€6/hr, €18/24 hrs; daily 9:00–18:00, until 19:00 July–Aug, but hours unreliable—you may have to call or let the Panorama Tours man nearby help you, shorter hours off-season and in bad weather, passport number for security deposit, tel. 0662/435-595, mobile 0676-435-5950).

By Funicular and Elevator: The old town is connected to the top of the Mönchsberg mountain (and great views) via funicular and elevator. The **funicular** *(Festungsbahn)* whisks you up to the imposing Hohensalzburg Fortress (included in castle admission, goes every few minutes—for details, see page 578). The **elevator** *(MönchsbergAufzug)* on the east side of the old town propels you to the recommended Gasthaus Stadtalm café and hostel, the Museum of Modern Art, wooded paths, and more great views (€2 one-way, €3 round-trip, Tue–Sun 8:00–1:00 in the morning, Mon 8:00–19:00, until 24:00 in Aug).

By Taxi: Meters start at about €3 (from train station to your hotel, allow about €7). As always, small groups can taxi for about the same price as riding the bus.

By Buggy: The horse buggies *(Fiaker)* that congregate at Residenzplatz charge €33 for a 25-minute trot around the old town (www.fiaker-salzburg.at).

TOURS

Walking Tours—On any day of the week, you can take a two-language, one-hour guided walk of the old town without a reservation—just show up at the TI on Mozartplatz and pay the guide. The tours are informative, but you'll be listening to a half-hour of German (€8, daily at 12:15 and 14:00, tel. 0662/8898-7330). To save money (and avoid all that German), you can easily do it on your own using my self-guided walk, page 568. There's also a *Sound of Music* walking tour (€8, 1 hour, English only, leaves from Mozartplatz TI at 11:00, tel. 0662/834-833).

Local Guides—**Christiana Schneeweiss** ("Snow White"), a hardworking young guide and art historian with a passion for fitting local history into the big picture, gives spirited private tours (€80/1 hr, €129/2 hrs, €150/3 hrs, tel. 0664/340-1757, www.kultur-tourismus.com, info@kultur-tourismus.com). Check her website for bike tours, private minibus tours, and more. **Bärbel Schalber,** one of Salzburg's senior guides, offers a two-hour walk packed with information and spicy opinions (€75 per family, €108 for a group of adults, tel. 0662/632-225, schalber.salzburg@aon.at). Salzburg has many other good guides (to book, call tel. 0662/840-406).

▲▲Sound of Music Tour—I took this tour skeptically (as part of my research) and liked it. It includes a quick but good general city tour, hits the *S.O.M.* spots (including the stately home, flirtatious gazebo, and grand wedding church), and shows you a lovely stretch of the Salzkammergut Lake District. This is worthwhile for *S.O.M.* fans and those who won't otherwise be going into the Salzkammergut. Warning: Many think rolling through the Austrian countryside with 30 Americans singing "Doe, a Deer" is pretty schmaltzy. Local Austrians don't understand all the

Salzburg

① Steingasse Stroll
② Top Bike (Bike Rental)
③ Salzach River Cruises
④ Alm River Canal Exhibit
⑤ Panorama Tours (Big-Bus S.O.M.)
⑥ Bob's Special Tours (Minibus S.O.M.)
⑦ Fräulein Maria Tours (Bike S.O.M.)
⑧ Salzburg Panorama 1829

commotion, and the audience is mostly native English speakers. For more on *S.O.M.*, see the "*Sound of Music* Debunked" sidebar on page 588.

Of the many companies doing the tour, consider Bob's Special Tours (usually uses a minibus) and Panorama Tours (more typical and professional, big 50-seat bus). Each one provides essentially the same tour (in English with a live guide, 4 hours, free hotel pick-up) for essentially the same price: €37 for Panorama,

Salzburg at a Glance

▲▲**Salzburg Cathedral** Glorious, harmonious, Baroque main church of Salzburg. **Hours:** Easter–Oct Mon–Sat 9:00–18:00, Sun 13:00–18:00; Nov–Easter Mon–Sat 10:00–17:00, Sun 13:00–17:00. See page 572.

▲▲**Getreidegasse** Picturesque old shopping lane with characteristic wrought-iron signs. **Hours:** Always open. See page 576.

▲▲**Hohensalzburg Fortress** Imposing castle capping the Mönchsberg mountain overlooking town, with tourable grounds, impressive interior, commanding views, and good evening concerts. **Hours:** Daily May–June 9:00–18:30, July–Aug 9:00–19:00, Sept 9:00–18:00, Oct–April 9:30–17:00. Concerts nearly nightly. See page 578.

▲▲**Mozart's Residence** Restored house where the composer lived, with the best Mozart exhibit in town. **Hours:** Daily 9:00–18:00, July–Aug until 19:00. See page 582.

▲▲*Sound of Music* **Tour** Cheesy but fun tour through the *S.O.M.* sights of Salzburg and the surrounding Salzkammergut Lake District, by minibus or big bus. **Hours:** Various options daily at 9:00, 9:30, and 14:00. See page 564.

▲**Salzburg Panorama 1829** A vivid peek at the city in 1829. **Hours:** Daily 9:00–17:00, Thu until 20:00. See page 571.

▲**Mozart's Birthplace** House where Mozart was born in 1756, featuring his instruments and other exhibits. **Hours:** Daily 9:00–18:00, July–Aug until 19:00. See page 577.

€40 for Bob's. You'll get a €5 discount from either in 2008 if you book direct, mention Rick Steves, and pay cash. Getting a spot is simple—just call and make a reservation (calling Bob's a week or two in advance is smart). Note: Your hotel will be eager to call to reserve for you—to get their commission—but if you let them do it, you're unlikely to get the discount I've negotiated.

Minibus Option: Most of **Bob's Special Tours** use an eight-seat minibus and therefore have good access to old-town sights, promote a more casual feel, and spend less time waiting to load and unload. Calling well in advance increases your chances of getting a seat (€40 for adults, or €35 with this book if you pay cash and book direct in 2008, €35 for kids and students with ID, €28 for kids

▲**Mönchsberg Walk** "The hills are alive" stroll you can enjoy right in downtown Salzburg. **Hours:** Doable anytime during daylight hours. See page 580.

▲**Mirabell Gardens and Palace** Beautiful palace complex with fine views, Salzburg's best concert venue, and *Sound of Music* memories. **Hours:** Gardens—always open; concerts—free in the park May–Aug Sun at 10:30 and Wed at 20:30, in the palace nearly nightly. See page 581.

▲**Steingasse** Historic cobbled lane with trendy pubs—a tranquil, tourist-free section of old Salzburg. **Hours:** Always open. See page 583.

▲**St. Sebastian Cemetery** Baroque cemetery with graves of Mozart's wife and father, and other Salzburg VIPs. **Hours:** Daily April–Oct 9:00–18:30, Nov–March 9:00–16:00. See page 584.

▲**Hellbrunn Castle** Palace on the outskirts of town featuring gardens with trick fountains. **Hours:** Daily May–Sept 9:00–17:30, July–Aug until 22:00, April and Oct 9:00–16:30, closed Nov–March. See page 584.

St. Peter's Cemetery Atmospheric old cemetery with minigardens overlooked by cliff face with monks' caves. **Hours:** Cemetery—daily April–Sept 6:30–19:00, Oct–March 6:30–18:00; caves—May–Sept Tue–Sun 10:30–17:00, closed Mon, shorter hours Oct–April. See page 574.

St. Peter's Church Romanesque church with Rococo decor. **Hours:** Open long hours daily. See page 574.

Salzburg

in car seats, daily at 9:00 and 14:00 year-round, buses leave from Bob's office along the river just east of Mozartplatz at Rudolfskai 38—or they'll pick you up at your hotel for the morning tour, tel. 0662/849-511, mobile 0664-541-7492, www.bobstours.com). Nearly all of Bob's tours stop for the luge ride when the weather is dry (mountain bobsled—€4 extra, confirm beforehand). Some travelers looking for Bob's tours at Mozartplatz have been hijacked by other companies...have Bob's pick you up at your hotel (morning only) or meet the bus at their office (see map on page 565). If you're unable to book with Bob's, and still want a minibus tour, try **Kultur Tourismus** (€50, tel. 0664/340-1757, www.kultur-tourismus .com, info@kultur-tourismus.com).

Big-Bus Option: Salzburg Panorama Tours depart from their smart kiosk at Mirabellplatz daily at 9:30 and 14:00 year-round (€37, or €32 with this book if you book direct and pay cash in 2008, book by calling 0662/874-029 or online at www .panoramatours.com). Many travelers appreciate their more businesslike feel, roomier buses, and slightly higher vantage point.

Bike Option: For some exercise with your tour, you can meet **Fräulein Maria** at the Mirabell Gardens (behind Hotel Bristol) for a *S.O.M.* bike tour. The main attractions that you'll pass during the seven-mile pedal include the Mirabell Gardens, the horse pond, St. Peter's Cemetery, Nonnberg Abbey, Leopoldskron Palace and, of course, the gazebo (€22 includes bike, €2 discount with this book in 2008, kids under 15 pay €15, daily at 9:30, allow 3.5 hours, May–Sept only, family-friendly, tel. 0650/342-6297, www .mariasbicycletours.com).

Walking Option (City Only): Those with a little less time or enthusiasm for the movie can take a one-hour *S.O.M.*-themed walking tour within the city (€8, leaves from Mozartplatz TI at 11:00, tel. 0662/834-833).

More Tours—Both Bob's and Panorama Tours also offer an extensive array of other day trips from Salzburg (Berchtesgaden/Eagle's Nest, salt mines, and Salzkammergut lakes and mountains are the most popular, with the same discount in 2008—€5 off with this book, book direct and pay cash). The tours are all explained in their brochures, which litter hotel lobbies all over town.

Salzach River Cruises runs a basic 40-minute round-trip cruise with recorded commentary (€12, 10/day July–Aug, 9/day in June, fewer in other months, no boats Nov–March). For a longer cruise, ride to Hellbrunn and return by bus (€15, 1–2/day April–Oct). Boats leave from the old-town side of the river just downstream of the Makartsteg bridge (tel. 0662/8257-6912). While views can be cramped, passengers are treated to a fun finale just before docking, when the captain twirls a fun "waltz."

SELF-GUIDED WALK

▲▲▲Salzburg's Old Town

I've linked the best sights in the old town into this handy self-guided orientation walk.

• *Begin in the heart of town, just up from the river, near the TI on...*

Mozartplatz

All the happy tourists around you probably wouldn't be here if not for the man honored by this statue—Wolfgang Amadeus Mozart (erected in 1842). Mozart spent much of his first 25 years (1756–1777) in Salzburg, the greatest Baroque city north of the

Salzburg's Old Town Walk

1. Mozartplatz
2. Residenzplatz
3. Neue Residenz & Glockenspiel
4. Salzburg Panorama 1829
5. Alte Residenz
6. Salzburg Cathedral
7. Kapitelplatz
8. St. Peter's Cemetery
9. St. Peter's Church
10. Toscanini Hof
11. Universitätsplatz
12. Getreidegasse
13. Mozart's Birthplace

Alps. But the city itself is much older: The Mozart statue actually sits on bits of Roman Salzburg. And the pink Church of St. Michael that overlooks the square dates from A.D. 800. The first Salzburgers settled right around here. Near you are the American Express office and the TI (with a concert box office). Just around the downhill corner is a pedestrian bridge leading over the Salzach River to the quiet and most medieval street in town, Steingasse (described on page 583).

• *Walk toward the cathedral and into the big square with the huge fountain.*

Residenzplatz

Important buildings ringed this square when it was the ancient Roman forum...and they still do. Salzburg's energetic Prince-Archbishop Wolf Dietrich (who ruled from 1587–1612) was raised in Rome, counted the Medicis as his buddies, and had grandiose Italian ambitions for Salzburg. After a convenient fire destroyed the cathedral, he set about building "the Rome of the North." This square, with his new cathedral and palace, was the centerpiece of his Baroque dream city. A series of interconnecting squares—like you'll see nowhere else—make a grand processional way, leading from here through the old town.

For centuries, Salzburg's leaders were both important church officials *and* princes of the Holy Roman Empire, hence the title "prince-archbishop"—mixing sacred and secular authority. But Wolf Dietrich misplayed his hand, losing power and spending his last five years imprisoned up in the Salzburg castle.

The fountain is as Italian as can be, with a Triton matching Bernini's famous Triton Fountain in Rome. Lying on a busy trade route to the south, Salzburg was well aware of the exciting things going on in Italy. Things Italian were respected (as in colonial America, when a bumpkin would "stick a feather in his cap and call it macaroni"). Local artists even Italianized their names in order to raise their rates.

• *Along the left side of Residenzplatz (as you face the cathedral) is the...*

New (Neue) Residenz

This former palace, long a government administration building, now houses the central post office, the Heimatwerk (a fine shop showing off all the best local handicrafts, Mon–Fri 9:00–18:00, Sat 9:00–17:00, closed Sun), the fascinating Salzburg Panorama 1829 exhibit (definitely worth the €2 and described later), and the new **Salzburg Museum**. The first floor of this museum shows off various influential Salzburgers. The second floor explores Salzburg's history, particularly its longstanding reputation as a fairy-tale "Alpine Arcadia." While it's impressively well-done and described in English, the museum is only enjoyable to the extent that you're fascinated with the city—so most will find this merely a good rainy-day option (€7, €8 combo-ticket with Salzburg Panorama, both tickets €2 cheaper on Sun, includes audioguide, Tue–Sun 9:00–17:00, Thu until 20:00, closed Mon except July–Aug and Dec—when it's open Mon 9:00–17:00, tel. 0662/6208-080).

• *Atop the new Residenz rings the famous...*

Glockenspiel

This bell tower has a carillon of 35 17th-century bells (cast in Antwerp) that chimes throughout the day and plays tunes (appropriate to the month) at 7:00, 11:00, and 18:00. There was a time when Salzburg could afford to take tourists to the top of the tower to actually see the big barrel with adjustable tabs turn (like a giant music-box mechanism)...pulling the right bells in the right rhythm. Notice the ornamental top: an upside-down heart in flames surrounding the solar system (symbolizing that God loves all of creation).

Look back, past Mozart's statue, to the 4,220-foot-high Gaisberg—the forested hill with the television tower. A road leads to the top for a commanding view. Its summit is a favorite destination for local nature-lovers and kids learning to ski.

• *Before continuing our walk, round the corner toward the back of the cathedral and drop into the...*

▲Salzburg Panorama 1829

In the early 19th century, 360-degree "panorama" paintings of great cities or events were popular. These creations were even taken on extended road trips. Salzburg, at a stagnant stage in its development, had this circular view painted by Johann Michael Sattler: the city as seen from the top of its castle. When complete, it spent 10 years touring the great cities of Europe, showing off Salzburg's breathtaking setting. Today, the exquisitely restored painting offers a fascinating look at the city in 1829. The river was slower and had beaches. The old town looks essentially as it does today, and Moosstrasse still leads into idyllic farm country. Paintings from that era of other great cities around the world are hung around the outside wall with numbers but without labels, as a kind of quiz game. A flier gives the cities names on one side, and keys them to the numbers. See how many 19th-century cities you can identify (€2, €8 combo-ticket with Salzburg Museum, combo-ticket is €2 cheaper on Sun, open daily 9:00–17:00, Thu until 20:00, Residenzplatz 9).

• *Backtrack into Residenzplatz and head to the opposite end from the new Residenz. This building is the...*

Old (Alte) Residenz

Opposite the new Residenz is Wolf Dietrich's skippable palace, the old Residenz, which is connected to the cathedral by a skyway. A series of ornately decorated rooms and an art gallery are open to visitors with time to kill (€6, Tue–Sun 10:00–17:00, closed Mon, tel. 0662/840-4510).

• *Walk under the prince-archbishop's skyway and step into Cathedral Square (Domplatz), where you'll find the...*

▲▲Salzburg Cathedral

This was one of the first Baroque buildings north of the Alps. It was consecrated in 1628, during the Thirty Years' War. (Pitting Roman Catholics against Protestants, this war devastated much of Europe and brought most grand construction projects to a halt.) Experts differ on what motivated the builders: to emphasize Salzburg's commitment to the Roman Catholic cause and the power of the Church here, or to show that there could be a peaceful alternative to the religious strife that was racking Europe at the time. Salzburg's archbishop was technically the top papal official north of the Alps, but the city managed to steer clear of the war. With its rich salt production, it had enough money to stay out of the conflict and carefully maintain its independence from the warring sides.

The dates on the iron gates refer to milestones in the church's history: In 774, the previous church (long since destroyed) was founded by St. Virgil, to be replaced in 1628 by the church you see today. In 1959, the reconstruction was completed after a WWII bomb blew through the dome.

Cathedral Square is surrounded by the prince-archbishop's secular administration buildings. The **statue of Mary** (1771) is looking away from the church, but if you stand in the rear of the square, immediately under the middle arch, you'll see that she's positioned to be crowned by the two angels on the church facade.

Step inside the cathedral (donation requested; Easter–Oct Mon–Sat 9:00–18:00, Sun 13:00–18:00; Nov–Easter Mon–Sat 10:00–17:00, Sun 13:00–17:00). Enter the cathedral as if part of a festival procession—drawn toward the resurrected Christ by the brightly lit area under the dome, and cheered on by ceiling paintings of the Passion. The stucco, by a Milanese artist, is exceptional. Sit under the dome—surrounded by the tombs of ten 17th-century archbishops—and imagine all four organs playing, each balcony filled

with musicians...glorious surround-sound. Mozart, who was the organist here for two years, would advise you that the acoustics are best in pews immediately under the dome. Study the symbolism of the decor all around you—intellectual, complex, and cohesive. Think of the altar in Baroque terms, as the center of a stage, with sunrays as spotlights in this dramatic and sacred theater. In the left transept, stairs lead down into the crypt *(Krypta),* where you can see foundations of the earlier church, more tombs, and a tourist-free chapel (reserved for prayer) directly under the dome.

Built in just 14 years (1614–1628), the church boasts harmonious architecture. When Pope John Paul II visited in 1998, 5,000 people filled the cathedral (330 feet long and 230 feet tall). The baptismal font (dark bronze, left of the entry) is from the previous cathedral (basin from about 1320, although the lid is modern). Mozart was baptized here ("Amadeus" means "beloved by God"). Concert and Mass schedules are posted at the entrance; the Sunday Mass at 10:00 is famous for its music.

The **Cathedral Museum** (Dom Museum) has a rich collection of church art (entry at portico, €5, mid-May–Oct Mon–Sat 10:00–17:00, Sun 11:00–18:00, closed Nov–mid-May, tel. 0662/844-189).
• *From the cathedral, exit left and walk toward the fortress into the next square...*

Kapitelplatz

Head past the free underground public WCs and the giant chessboard to the pond. This was a **horse bath,** the 18th-century equivalent of a car wash. Notice the puzzle above it—the artist wove the date of the structure into a phrase. It says, "Leopold the Prince Built Me," using the letters LLDVICMXVXI, which total 1732 (add it up...it works)—the year it was built. A small road (back by the chessboard) leads uphill to the fortress (and fortress lift). With your back to the cathedral, leave the square through a gate in the right corner that reads *zum Peterskeller.* It leads to a waterfall and St. Peter's Cemetery.

The **waterwheel** is part of a canal system that has brought water into Salzburg from Berchtesgaden, 16 miles away, since the 13th century. Climb uphill a few steps to feel the medieval water power. The stream, divided from here into smaller canals, was channeled through town to provide fire protection, to flush out the streets (Saturday morning was flood-the-streets day), and to power factories (there were more than 100 watermill-powered firms as late as the 19th century). Drop into the fragrant and traditional **bakery** at the waterfall. It's hard to beat their rocklike *Roggenbrot* (various fresh rolls for less than €1, Thu–Tue 7:00–17:30, Sat until 12:00, closed Wed). There's a good view of the funicular climbing up to the castle from here. For more on the canal system, check out

the free Alm River Canal exhibit nearby (described on page 580).
• *Now find the* Katakomben *sign and step into...*

St. Peter's Cemetery

This collection of lovingly tended mini-gardens abuts the Mönchberg's rock wall (free, silence is requested, daily April–Sept 6:30–19:00, Oct–March 6:30–18:00). Walk in about 50 yards to the intersection of lanes at the base of the cliff marked by a stone ball. (It's seemingly made-to-order for a little back-stretching break. Go ahead...I'll wait.) You're surrounded by three churches, each founded in the sixth century atop a pagan Celtic holy site. St. Peter's Church is closest to the stone ball. Notice the fine Romanesque stonework on the chapel nearest you, and the fancy rich guys' Renaissance-style tombs decorating its walls.

Wealthy as those guys were, they ran out of caring relatives. The graves surrounding you are tended by descendants of the deceased. In Austria, gravesites are rented, not owned. Rent bills are sent out every 10 years. If no one cares enough to make the payment, your remains are chucked. Iron crosses were much cheaper than tombstones. While the cemetery where the von Trapp family hid out in *The Sound of Music* was a Hollywood set, it was inspired by this one.

Look up the cliff. Legendary medieval hermit monks are said to have lived in the hillside—but "catacombs" they're not. For €1, you can climb lots of steps to see a few old caves, a chapel, and some fine views (May–Sept Tue–Sun 10:30–17:00, closed Mon; Oct–April Wed–Thu 10:30–15:30, Fri–Sun 10:30–16:00, closed Mon–Tue).

• *Continue downhill through the cemetery and out the opposite end. Just outside, hook right and drop into...*

St. Peter's Church

Just inside, enjoy a carved Romanesque welcome. Over the inner doorway, a fine tympanum shows Jesus on a rainbow flanked by Peter and Paul over a stylized Tree of Life and under a Latin inscription reading, "I am the door to life, and only through me can you find eternal life." Enter the nave and notice how the once purely Romanesque vaulting has since been iced with a sugary Rococo finish. Salzburg's only Rococo interior feels Bavarian (because it is—the fancy stucco work was done by Bavarian artists). Up the right side aisle is the tomb of St. Rupert, with a painting showing Salzburg in 1750 (one bridge, salt ships sailing the river, and angels hoisting barrels of salt to heaven as St. Rupert prays for his city). On pillars farther up the aisle are faded bits of 13th-century Romanesque frescos. Similar frescoes hide under Rococo whitewash throughout the church.

Leaving the church, notice the Stiftskeller St. Peter restaurant (on the left—described under "Eating," page 598, and for its Mozart Dinner Concert, page 588). Charlemagne ate here in A.D. 803—allowing locals to claim it's the oldest restaurant in Europe. Opposite where you entered the square (look through the arch), you'll see St. Rupert waving you into the next square (early-20th-century Bauhaus-style dorms for student monks), with a modern crucifix (1926) on the far wall. To the right of the crucifix (at #8), press the red button on the bronze door, enter, and see an unforgettable Expressionist-carved crucifix (also from the 1920s, free, open until 11:30 only).

• *Walk through the archway next to the crucifix into...*

Toscanini Hof

This square faces the 1925 Festival Hall. The hall's three theaters seat 5,000. This is where Captain von Trapp nervously waited before walking onstage (in the movie, he sang "Edelweiss"), just before he escaped with his family. On the left is the city's 1,500-space, inside-the-mountain parking lot; ahead, behind the *Felsenkeller* sign, is a tunnel (generally closed) leading to the actual concert hall; and to the right is the backstage of a smaller hall where carpenters are often building stage sets (door open on hot days). The stairway leads to the top of the cliff and eventually to the Stadtalm Café and hostel (more easily reached by elevator, see page 600).

• *Walk downhill through Max-Reinhardt-Platz, to the right of the church and past the public WC, into...*

Universitätsplatz

This square hosts an open-air produce market—Salzburg's liveliest (mornings Mon–Sat, best on Sat). Locals are happy to pay more here for the reliably fresh and top-quality produce. (These days, half of Austria's produce is grown organically.) The market really bustles on Saturday mornings, when the farmers are in town. Public marketplaces have fountains for washing fruit and vegetables. The fountain here—a part of the medieval water system—plummets down a hole and to the river. The sundial (over the water hole) is accurate (except for the daylight savings hour) and two-dimensional, showing both the time (obvious) and the date (less obvious). The fanciest facade overlooking the square (the yellow one) is the backside of Mozart's Birthplace (described next page).

• *Continue past the fountain to the end of the square, passing several characteristic and nicely arcaded medieval tunnels (on right) that connect the square to Getreidegasse. Cross the big road for a look at the giant horse troughs, adjacent to the prince's stables. Paintings show the various breeds and temperaments of horses in his stable. Like Vienna, Salzburg had a passion for the equestrian arts.*

Take two right turns and you're at the start of...

▲▲Getreidegasse

This street was old Salzburg's busy, colorful main drag. It's lined with *Schmuck* (jewelry) shops. Famous for its old wrought-iron

signs (best viewed from this end), the architecture on the street still looks much as it did in Mozart's day—though its former elegance is now mostly gone, replaced by chain outlets.

On the right at #39, **Sporer** serves up homemade spirits (€1.30 per shot). This has been a family-run show for a century—fun-loving, proud, and English-speaking. *Nuss* is nut, *Marille* is apricot (typical of this region), the *Kletzen* cocktail is like a super-thick Baileys with pear, and *Edle Brande* are

the stronger schnapps. The many homemade firewaters are in jugs at the end of the bar. Austrian spirits are sold by the *Achtel* (eighth of a liter).

Continue down Getreidegasse, noticing the old doorbells—

one per floor. At #40, **Eisgrotte** serves good ice cream. Across from Eisgrotte, a tunnel leads to **Bosna Grill,** the local choice for the very best sausage in town (see page 601). Farther along, you'll pass McDonald's (while required to keep its arches Baroque and low-key, it just couldn't hang anything less than the biggest sign on the street).

The knot of excited tourists and salesmen hawking goofy gimmicks marks the home of Salzburg's most famous resident. **Mozart's Birthplace** (Geburtshaus)—the house where Mozart was born, and where he composed many of his early works—is worth a visit for his true fans (described next). But for most, his Residence, across the river, is more interesting (described on page 582).

• *Our walk is finished. From here, you can head up to the Hohensalzburg Fortress on Mönchsberg mountain over the old town (see page 578); or continue to some of the sights across the river. To reach the sights across the river, head for the river, jog left (past the fast-food fish restaurant and free WCs), climb to the top of the Makartsteg pedestrian bridge, and turn to page 581.*

SIGHTS AND ACTIVITIES

▲Mozart's Birthplace (Geburtshaus)

Mozart was born here in 1756. It was in this building—the most popular Mozart sight in town—that he composed most of his boy-genius works. For fans, it's almost a pilgrimage. American artist Robert Wilson was recently hired to spiff up the exhibit, to make it feel more conceptual and less like a museum. But I was unimpressed. If you're tackling just one Mozart sight, skip this one. Instead, walk 10 minutes from here to Mozart's Residence (described on page 582), which provides a more informative visit. But if you want to max out on Mozart, a visit here is worthwhile.

Cost, Hours, Location: €6.50, or €10 for combo-ticket that includes Mozart's Residence, daily 9:00–18:00, July–Aug until 19:00, last entry 30 min before closing, Getreidegasse 9, tel. 0662/844-313.

❷ Self-Guided Tour: Here's what you'll see as you shuffle through with the herd:

Room 1: Around a baby crib showing an infant both old and young (Mozart's music is timeless...get it?) are walls heavy with historic etchings, portraits, and documents. Most important: an engraving of the family (lower right) and a fine "portrait with a bird's nest" of Mozart, painted from life when he was nine years old (upper left).

Room 2: The living room shows off authentic family portraits: Wolfgang's mom, dad, sister, and wife. Wolfgang composed his first pieces as a child on a clavichord (like the one in this room). A predecessor of the piano, it hit the strings with simple teeter-totter keys that played very softly...ideal for composers living in tight apartment quarters.

Room 3: The nursery is decorated like Mozart's music: light and free as a bird (hence the flying birds). Embedded in the walls are Mozart's personal possessions—his ring, silk wallet, and violin. He was born in this room, and the entire family slept here until Wolfgang was 14.

Room 4: Exactly what Mozart looked like is a bit of a mystery. Various portraits in this room give us something to go on.

Corridor: The neon phrase shows his juvenile sense of humor. It's a rhyme: *Madame Mutter, ich esse gerne Butter.* (Dear mother, I love to eat butter.) The next room is wallpapered with reproductions of actual circa-1840 photos of Mozart's wife and son (as an old man). More strange Wilson-designed rooms follow: Mozart loved to turn things upside-down—so the Salzburg cityscapes are that way, with stars on the floor. Downstairs, just before the shop, rooms dedicated to Mozart's operas play various video clips continuously.

Atop the Cliffs Above the Old Town

The main "sight" above town is the Hohensalzburg Fortress. But if you just want to enjoy the sweeping views over Salzburg, you have a couple of cheap options: Take the elevator up the cliffs of Mönchsberg (explained under "Getting Around Salzburg," page 563), head up to the castle grounds on foot, or visit the castle in the evening on a night when they're hosting a concert (about 300 nights a year). This is the only time you can buy a funicular ticket without paying for the castle entrance—since the castle museum is closed, but the funicular is still running to bring up concert-goers.

▲▲**Hohensalzburg Fortress (Festung)**—Built on a rock (called Festungsberg) 400 feet above the Salzach River, this fortress was never really used. That's the idea. It was a good investment—so foreboding, nobody attacked the town for a thousand years. The city was never taken by force, but when Napoleon stopped by, Salzburg wisely surrendered. After a stint as a military barracks, the fortress was opened to the public in the 1860s by Emperor Franz Josef. Today, it remains one of Europe's mightiest castles, dominating Salzburg's skyline and offering incredible views.

Cost: Your daytime ticket includes the price of the funicular up and down, as well as admission to the fortress grounds and all the museums inside—whether you want to see them or not (€10, €23.10 family ticket, €7 per person for museum entry if you hike to the castle without using the funicular). If you'd rather save money than see the museums, head up the hill in the evening (within 1 hour of the museum's closing time, it's €5.90 one-way/€7.20 round-trip for funicular and entry to castle grounds; after closing time, funicular is €3.40 round-trip).

Hours: The complex is open daily year-round (May–June 9:00–18:30, July–Aug 9:00–19:00, Sept 9:00–18:00, Oct–April 9:30–17:00, last entry 30 min before closing, tel. 0662/8424-3011). On nights when there's a concert, the castle grounds are free and open after the museum closes until 21:30.

Concerts: The fortress also serves as a venue for evening concerts (Festungskonzerte). For details, see the "Entertainment" section on page 587.

Café: The café between the funicular station and the castle entry is a great place to nibble on apple strudel while taking in the jaw-dropping view.

Orientation: The fortress visit has three parts: a relatively dull courtyard with some fine views from its various ramparts; the fortress itself (with a required and escorted 45-minute audio tour); and the palace museum (by far the best exhibit of the lot). At the bottom of the funicular, you'll pass through an interesting little exhibit on the town's canal system (free, described on page 580).

◗ **Self-Guided Tour:** Climb from the top of the funicular to the inner courtyard. Immediately inside, circling to the left (clockwise), you'll encounter cannons (still poised to defend Salzburg against a Turkish invasion), the marionette exhibit, the palace museum, the Kuenburg bastion, scant ruins of a Romanesque church, the courtyard (with path down for those walking), toilets, shops, a restaurant, and the fortress tour.

• *Begin at the...*

Marionette Exhibit: Several fun rooms show off this local tradition, with three videos playing continuously: two with peeks at Salzburg's ever-enchanting Marionette Theater performances of Mozart classics (see listing, page 587), and one with a behind-the-scenes look at the action. Give the hands-on marionette a whirl.

• *Hiking through the former palace, you'll find the site's best exhibits at the...*

Palace Museum (Festungsmuseum Carolino Augusteum): The second floor has exhibits on castle life, from music to torture. The top floor shows off fancy royal apartments, a sneak preview of the room used for the nightly fortress concerts, and the Rainier military museum, dedicated to the Salzburg regiments that fought in both World Wars.

Castle Courtyard: The courtyard was the main square of the castle residents, a community of a thousand—which could be self-sufficient when necessary. The square was ringed by the shops of craftsmen, blacksmiths, bakers, and so on. The well dipped into a rain-fed cistern. The church is dedicated to St. George, the protector of horses (logical for an army church) and decorated by fine red marble reliefs (c. 1502). Behind the church is the top of the old lift that helped supply the fortress. (From near here, steps lead back into the city, or to the mountaintop "Mönchsberg Walk," described later.) The scant remains of a Romanesque chapel are well-described.

• *Near the chapel, turn left into the Kuenburg Bastion (once a garden) for fine city and castle views.*

Kuenburg Bastion: Notice how the castle has three parts: the original castle inside the courtyard, the vast whitewashed walls (built when the castle was a residence), and the lower, beefed-up fortifications (added for extra defense against the expected Turkish

invasion). Survey Salzburg from here and think about fortifying an important city by using nature. Mönchsberg (the little mountain you're on) naturally cradles the old town, with just a small gate between the mountain and the river needed to bottle up the place. The new town across the river needed a bit of a wall arcing from the river to its hill. Back then, only one bridge crossed the Salzach into town, and it had a fortified gate.

• *Back inside the castle courtyard, continue your circle. The Round Tower (1497) helps you visualize the inner original castle.*

Fortress Interior: Tourists are allowed in this part of the fortified palace only with an escort. (They say that's for security, though while touring it, you wonder what they're protecting.) A crowd assembles at the turnstile, and every quarter-hour 40 people are issued their audioguides and let in for the escorted walk. You'll go one room at a time, listening to a 45-minute commentary. While the interior furnishings are mostly gone—taken by Napoleon—the rooms survived as well as they did because no one wanted to live here after 1500, so the building was never modernized. Your tour includes a room dedicated to the art of "excruciating questioning" ("softening up" prisoners, in current American military jargon)—filled with tools of that gruesome trade. The highlight is the commanding city view from the top of a tower.

• *After seeing the fortress, consider hiking down to the old town, or along the top of Mönchsberg (see "Mönchsberg Walk"). If you take the funicular down, keep an eye out for the...*

Alm River Canal Exhibit: At the base of the funicular, below the castle, is this fine little exhibit on how the river was broken into five smaller streams—powering the city until steam took up the energy-supply baton. Pretend it's the year 1200 and follow (by video) the flow of the water from the river through the canals, into the mills, and as it's finally dumped into the Salzach River (free, access from the bottom of the lift as you're leaving, or through Amber shop next door if you're not riding the funicular).

▲**Mönchsberg Walk**—For a great 30-minute hike, exit the fortress by taking the steep lane down from the castle courtyard. At the first intersection, right leads into the old town, and left leads across the Mönchsberg. The lane leads 20 minutes through the woods high above the city (stick to the high lanes, or you'll end up back in town), taking you to the Gasthaus Stadtalm café (light meals, cheap beds—see page 594 of "Sleeping," and page 600 of "Eating"). From the Stadtalm, pass under the medieval wall and walk left along the wall to a tableau showing how it once looked. Take the switchback to the right and follow the lane downhill to the Museum of Modern Art (described next), where the elevator zips you back into town (€2 one-way, €3 round-trip, Tue–Sun 8:00–1:00 in the morning, Mon 8:00–19:00, until 24:00 in Aug). If you stay on the lane past the elevator, you eventually pass the Augustine church that marks the rollicking Augustiner Bräustübl (see page 601).

In 1669, a huge Mönchsberg landslide killed more than 200

townspeople. Since then the cliffs have been carefully checked each spring and fall. Even today, you might see crews on the cliff, monitoring its stability.

Museum of Modern Art on Mönchsberg—The modern-art museum on top of Mönchsberg, built in 2004, houses Salzburg's Rupertinum Gallery, plus special exhibitions. While the collection is not worth climbing a mountain for, the M32 restaurant has some of the best views in town (€8, €9.70 including elevator ticket, Tue–Sun 10:00–18:00, Wed until 21:00, closed Mon; restaurant open Tue–Sat 9:00–24:00, Sun 9:00–18:00, closed Mon except during festival; both at top of Mönchsberg elevator, tel. 0662/842-220, www.museumdermoderne.at).

In the New Town, North of the River

The following sights are across the river from the old town. I've connected them with walking instructions.

• *Begin at the Makartsteg pedestrian bridge, where you can survey the...*

Salzach River—Salzburg's river is called "salt river" not because it's salty, but because of the precious cargo it once carried—the salt mines of Hallein are just nine miles upstream. Salt could be transported from here all the way to the Danube, and on to the Mediterranean via the Black Sea. The riverbanks and roads were built when the river was regulated in the 1850s. Before that, the Salzach was much wider and slower-moving. Houses opposite the old town fronted the river with docks and "garages" for boats. The grand buildings just past the bridge (with their elegant promenades and cafés) were built on reclaimed land in the late 19th century, in the historicist style of Vienna's Ringstrasse.

Scan the cityscape. Notice all the churches. Salzburg, nicknamed the "Rome of the North," has 38 Catholic churches (plus two Protestant churches and a synagogue). Find the five streams gushing into the river. These date from the 13th century, when the river was split into five canals running through the town to power its mills. Hotel Stein (upstream, just left of next bridge), described on page 584 has a popular roof-terrace café. Downstream, notice the Museum of Modern Art atop Mönchsberg, with a view restaurant and a faux castle (actually a water reservoir). The Romanesque bell tower with the copper dome in the distance is the Augustine church, site of the best beer hall in town (the Augustiner Bräustübl—see page 601).

• *Cross the bridge, pass the Café Bazar (a fine place for a drink—see page 602), walk two blocks inland, and take a left past the heroic statues into...*

▲Mirabell Gardens and Palace (Schloss)—The bubbly gardens laid out in 1730 for the prince-archbishop have been open to the public since 1850 (thanks to Emperor Franz Josef, who was rattled by the popular revolutions of 1848). The gardens are free and open until dusk. The palace is only open as a concert venue (explained later). The statues and the arbor (far left) were featured in *The Sound of Music*. Walk through the gardens to the palace. Look back, enjoy the garden/cathedral/castle view, and imagine how the prince-archbishop must have reveled in a vista that reminded him of all his secular and religious power. Then go around to the river side of the palace and find the horse.

The rearing **Pegasus statue** (rare and very well-balanced) is the site of a famous *Sound of Music* scene where the kids all danced before lining up on the stairs (with Maria 30 yards farther along). The steps lead to a small mound in the park (made of WWII rubble, and today a rendezvous point for Salzburg's gay community).

Nearest the horse, stairs lead between two lions to a pair of tough dwarfs (early volleyball players with spiked mittens) welcoming you to Salzburg's **Dwarf Park.** Cross the elevated walk (noticing the city's fortified walls) to meet statues of a dozen actual dwarfs who served the prince-archbishop—modeled after real people with real fashions in about 1600. This was Mannerist art, from the hyper-realistic age that followed the Renaissance.

There's plenty of **music,** both in the park and in the palace. A brass band plays free park concerts (May–Aug Sun at 10:30 and Wed at 20:30). To properly enjoy the lavish Mirabell Palace—once the prince-archbishop's summer palace, and now the seat of the mayor—get a ticket to a Schlosskonzerte (my favorite venue for a classical concert—see page 587).

• *To visit Salzburg's best Mozart sight, go a long block southeast to Makartplatz, where you'll find...*

▲▲Mozart's Residence (Wohnhaus)—This reconstruction of Mozart's second home (his family moved here when he was 17) is the most informative Mozart sight in town. The English-language audioguide (included with admission, 90 min) provides fascinating insight into Mozart's life and music, with the usual scores, old pianos, and an interesting 30-minute film (#17 on your audioguide for soundtrack) that runs continuously (€6.50, or €10 for combo-ticket that includes Mozart's Birthplace in the old town, daily 9:00–18:00, July–Aug until 19:00, last entry 1 hour before closing, allow at least 1 hour for visit, Makartplatz 8, tel. 0662/8742-2740).

In the main hall—used by the Mozarts to entertain Salzburg's high society—you can hear original instruments from Mozart's time. Mozart was proud to be the first in his family to compose a duet. Notice the family portrait (circa 1780) on the wall, showing Mozart with his sister Nannerl, their father, and their mother—who'd died two years earlier in Paris. Mozart also had silly crude bull's-eyes made for the pop-gun game popular at the time (licking an "arse," Wolfgang showed his disdain for the rigors of high society). Later rooms feature real artifacts that explore his loves, his intellectual pursuits, his travels, and more.

• *From here, you can walk a few blocks back to the main bridge (Staatsbrücke), where you'll find Platzl, a square once used as a hay market. Pause to enjoy the kid-pleasing little fountain. Near the fountain (with your back to the river), Steingasse leads darkly to the right.*

▲**Steingasse**—This street, a block in from the river, was the only street in the Middle Ages going south over the Alps to Venice (this was the first stop north of the Alps). Today, it's wonderfully tranquil and free of Salzburg's touristy crush.

At #9, a plaque (of questionable veracity) shows where Joseph Mohr, who wrote the words to "Silent Night," was born—poor and illegitimate—in 1792. There is no doubt, however, that the popular Christmas carol was composed and first sung in the village of Oberndorf, just outside of Salzburg, in 1818. Stairs lead from near here up to the monastery.

On the next corner, the wall is gouged out. This scar was left even after the building was restored, to remind locals of the American GI who tried to get a tank down this road during a visit to the town brothel—two blocks farther up Steingasse. Inviting cocktail bars along here come alive at night (described on page 602).

At #19, find the carvings on the old door. Some say these are notices from beggars to the begging community (more numerous after post-Reformation religious wars, which forced many people out of their homes and towns)—a kind of "hobo code" indicating whether the residents would give or not. Trace the wires of the old-fashioned doorbells to the highest floors.

Farther on, you'll find a commanding Salzburg view across the river. Notice the red dome marking the oldest nunnery in the German-speaking world (established in 712) under the fortress and to the left. The real Maria from *The Sound of Music* taught in this nunnery's school. In 1927, she and Captain von Trapp were married in the church you see here (not the church filmed in the movie). He was 47. She was 22. Hmmmm.

From here look back, above the arch you just passed through, at part of the town's medieval fortification. The coat of arms on the arch is of the prince-archbishop who paid Bavaria a huge ransom to stay out of the Thirty Years' War (smart move). He then built this fortification (in 1634) in anticipation of rampaging armies from both sides.

Today, this street is for making love, not war. The Maison de Plaisir (a few doors down, at #24) has for centuries been a Salzburg brothel. But the climax of this walk is more touristic.

• *For a grand view, head back to Platzl and the bridge, enter the Stein Hotel (left corner, overlooking the river), and ride the elevator to...*

Stein Terrasse—This café offers perhaps the best views in town (aside from the castle). Hidden from the tourist crush, it's a trendy, professional, local scene. You can discretely peek at the view, or enjoy a drink or light meal (€7 business lunch specials, indoor/outdoor seating, daily 9:00–24:00).

• *Back at Platzl and the bridge, you can head straight up Linzergasse (away from the river) into a neighborhood packed with recommended accommodations, as well as our final new-town sight...*

▲**St. Sebastian Cemetery**—Wander through this quiet place, so Baroque and so Italian (free, daily April–Oct 9:00–18:30, Nov–March 9:00–16:00, entry usually at Linzergasse 43). Mozart is buried in Vienna, his mom's in Paris, and his sister is in Salzburg's old town (St. Peter's)—but Wolfgang's wife Constantia and his father Leopold are buried here (from the black iron gate entrance on Linzergasse, walk 17 paces and look left). When Prince-Archbishop Wolf Dietrich had the cemetery moved from around the cathedral and put here, across the river, people didn't like it. To help popularize it, he had his own mausoleum built as its centerpiece. Continue straight past the Mozart tomb to this circular building (English description at door).

Near Salzburg

For information on Berchtesgaden—also near Salzburg—see the end of this chapter.

▲**Hellbrunn Castle**—About the year 1610, Prince-Archbishop Sittikus (after meditating on stewardship and Christ-like values) decided he needed a lavish palace with a vast and ornate garden purely for pleasure. He built this and just loved inviting his VIP guests out for a fun with his trick fountains. Today, the visit is worthwhile for the garden full of clever fountains...and the sadistic joy the tour guide gets from soaking tourists. (Hint: When you see a wet place, cover your camera.) After buying your ticket, you wait for the English tour, laugh and scramble through the entertaining 40-minute trick-water toy tour, and are then free to tour the forgettable palace with an included audioguide (€8.50, daily May–Sept 9:00–17:30, July–Aug until 22:00, April and Oct 9:00–16:30, closed Nov–March, tel. 0662/820-3720, www.hellbrunn.at).

Hellbrunn is nearly four miles south of Salzburg (bus #25 from station or from Staatsbrücke bridge, 2/hr, 20 min). While it can be fun—especially on a hot day or with kids—for many, it's a lot of trouble for a few water tricks. The Hellbrunn Baroque garden, one of the oldest in Europe, now features *S.O.M.*'s "Sixteen Going on Seventeen" gazebo.

Hellbrunn makes a good 30-minute bike excursion along the riverbank from Salzburg (described next).

Greater Salzburg

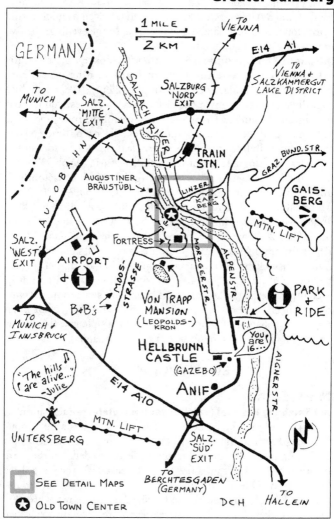

▲▲Riverside or Meadow Bike Ride—The Salzach River has smooth, flat, and scenic bike lanes along each side (thanks to medieval tow paths—cargo boats would float downstream and be dragged back up by horse). On a sunny day, I can think of no more shout-worthy escape from the city. The nearly four-mile path upstream to Hellbrunn Castle is easy, with a worthy destination (leave Salzburg on castle side). For a nine-mile ride, continue on to Hallein (where you can tour a salt mine—see next listing; the north, or new town, side of river is most scenic). Perhaps the most pristine, meadow-filled farm-country route is the four-mile Hellbrunner Allee from Akademiestrasse. Even a quickie ride across town is a great Salzburg experience. In the evening, the riverbanks are a world of floodlit spires.

▲**Hallein Bad Dürrnberg Salt Mine (Salzbergwerke)**—This salt-mine tour (above the town of Hallein, nine miles from Salzburg) is a popular excursion from Salzburg. Wearing white overalls and sliding down the sleek wooden chutes, you'll cross underground from Austria into Germany while learning about the old-time salt-mining process. The tour entails lots of time on your feet as you walk from cavern to cavern, learning the history of the mine by watching a series of video skits featuring Wolf Dietrich. The visit also includes a "Celtic Village" open-air museum (€17, allow 2.5 hours for the visit, daily April–Oct 9:00–17:00, Nov–March 10:00–15:00, these are last tour times, English-speaking guides—but let your linguistic needs be known loud and clear, tel. 06132/200-2400, www.salzwelten.at). The convenient *Salz Erlebnis* ticket from Salzburg's train station covers admission, train, and shuttle bus tickets, all in one money-saving round-trip ticket (€22, buy ticket at train station; 40-min trip with hourly departures in each direction at about :15 after the hour, with synchronized train-bus connection in Hallein—schedule posted in flier). Salt mine tours cost substantial time and money. One's plenty. This one is better than Hallstatt's (described in the next chapter).

ENTERTAINMENT

Music Scene

▲▲**Salzburg Festival (Salzburger Festspiele)**—Each summer, from late July to the end of August, Salzburg hosts its famous Salzburg Festival, founded in 1920 to employ Vienna's musicians in the summer. This fun and festive time is crowded, but there are plenty of beds (except for a few August weekends). There are three big halls: the Opera and Orchestra venues in the Festival House, and the Landes Theater, where German-language plays are performed. Tickets for the big festival events are generally expensive (€50–200) and sell out well in advance (bookable from Jan). Most tourists think they're "going to the Salzburg Festival" by seeing smaller non-festival events that go on during the festival weeks. For these lesser events, same-day tickets are normally available (the ticket office on Mozartplatz, in the TI, prints a daily list of concerts and charges a 30 percent fee to book them). For specifics on this year's festival schedule and tickets, visit www.salzburgfestival.at, or contact the Austrian National Tourist Office in the United States (P.O. Box 1142, New York, NY 10108-1142, tel. 212/944-6880, fax 212/730-4568, www.austria.info, travel@austria.info).

While I've never planned in advance, I've enjoyed great concerts with every visit.

▲▲**Musical Events Year-Round**—Salzburg is busy throughout the year, with 2,000 classical performances in its palaces and churches annually. Pick up the events calendar at the TI (free, bimonthly). Whenever you visit, you'll have a number of concerts (generally small chamber groups) to choose from. Here are some of the more accessible events:

Concerts at Hohensalzburg Fortress (Festungskonzerte): Nearly nightly concerts—Mozart's greatest hits for beginners—are held atop Festungsberg, in the "prince's chamber" of the fortress, featuring small chamber groups (open seating after the first six more expensive rows, €31 or €38 plus €3.40 for the funicular, at 19:30, 20:00, or 20:30, doors open 30 min early, tel. 0662/825-858 to reserve, pick up tickets at the door). The medieval-feeling chamber has windows overlooking the city, and the concert gives you a chance to enjoy the grand city view and a stroll through the castle courtyard. (The funicular ticket costs €3.40 within an hour of the show—ideal for people who just want to ascend for the view.) For €50, you can combine the concert with a four-course dinner (starts two hours before concert).

Concerts at the Mirabell Palace (Schlosskonzerte): The nearly nightly chamber music concerts at the Mirabell Palace are performed in a lavish Baroque setting. They come with more sophisticated programs and better musicians than the fortress concerts. Baroque music flying around a Baroque hall is a happy bird in the right cage (open seating after the first five pricier rows, €29, usually at 20:00—but check flyer for times, doors open 1 hour ahead, tel. 0662/848-586, www.salzburger-schlosskonzerte.at).

"Five O'Clock Concerts" (5-Uhr-Konzerte): These concerts—next to St. Peter's in the old town—are cheaper, since they feature young artists (€12, July–Sept Thu–Tue at 17:00, no concerts Wed or Oct–June, 45 min, tel. 0662/8445-7619, www.5-uhr-konzerte.com). While the series is formally named after the brother of Joseph Haydn, it offers music from various masters.

Mozart Piano Sonatas: St. Peter's Abbey hosts these concerts each weekend (€18, €9 for children, €45 for a family of four, Fri and Sat at 19:00 year-round, tel. 0662/423-5645). This short and inexpensive concert is ideal for families.

Marionette Theater: Salzburg's much-loved marionette theater offers operas with spellbinding marionettes and recorded music. Music-lovers are mesmerized by the little people on stage (€18–35, nearly nightly at 19:30 June–Sept except Sun, also 3–4/week in May, some matinees, box office open Mon–Sat 9:00–13:00 and 2 hours before shows, near the Mirabell Gardens and Mozart's Residence at Schwarzstrasse 24, tel. 0662/872-406,

Sound of Music **Debunked**

Rather than visit the real-life sights from the life of Maria von Trapp and family, most tourists want to see the places where Hollywood chose to film this fanciful story. Local guides are happy not to burst any *S.O.M.* pilgrim's bubble, but keep these points in mind:

- "Edelweiss" is not a cherished Austrian folk tune or national anthem. Like all the "Austrian" music in the *S.O.M.*, it was composed for Broadway by Rodgers and Hammerstein. It was, however, the last composition that the famed team wrote together, as Hammerstein died in 1960—nine months after the musical opened.
- The *S.O.M.* implies that Maria was devoutly religious throughout her life, but Maria's foster parents raised her as a socialist and atheist. Maria discovered her religious calling while studying to be a teacher. After completing school, she joined the convent not as a nun, but as a novitiate (that is, she hadn't taken her vows yet).
- Maria's position was not as governess to all the children, as portrayed in the musical, but specifically as governess and teacher for the Captain's second-oldest daughter, Maria, who was bedridden with rheumatic fever.
- The Captain didn't run a tight domestic ship. In fact, his seven children were as unruly as most. But he did use a whistle to call them—each kid was trained to respond to a certain pitch.
- Though the von Trapp family did have seven children, the show changed all their names and even their genders. Rupert, the eldest child, responded to the often-asked tourist question, "Which one are you?" with a simple, "I'm Liesl!"
- The family didn't escape by hiking to Switzerland (which

www.marionetten.at). For a sneak preview, check out the videos playing at the marionette exhibit up in the fortress.

Mozart Dinner Concert: For those who'd like some classical music but would rather not sit through a concert, Stiftskeller St. Peter offers a traditional candlelit meal with Mozart's greatest hits performed by a string quartet and singers in historic costumes gavotting among the tables. In this elegant Baroque setting, tourists clap between movements and get three courses of food (from Mozart-era recipes) mixed with three 20-minute courses of crowd-pleasing music (€48, Mozart-lovers with this guidebook receive a 20 percent discount if they book direct in 2008, almost nightly at 20:00, dress is "smart casual," call to reserve at 0662/828-6950, www.mozartdinnerconcert.com). When they run out of space, they book a second quartet to perform in the adjacent Haydn Zimmer.

is a five-hour drive away). Rather, they pretended to go on one of their frequent mountain hikes. With only the possessions in their backpacks, they "hiked" all the way to the train station (it was at the edge of their estate) and took a train to Italy. The movie scene showing them climbing into Switzerland was actually filmed near Berchtesgaden, Germany...home to Hitler's Eagle's Nest, and certainly not a smart place to flee to.

- The actual von Trapp family house exists...but it's not the one in the film. The mansion in the movie is actually two different buildings—one used for the front, the other for the back. The interiors were all filmed on Hollywood sets.
- For the film, Boris Levin designed a reproduction of the Nonnberg Abbey courtyard so faithful to the original (down to its cobblestones and stained-glass windows) that many still believe the cloister scenes were really shot at the abbey. And no matter what you hear in Salzburg, the graveyard scene (in which the von Trapps hide from the Nazis) was also filmed on the Fox lot.
- In 1956, a German film producer offered Maria $10,000 for the rights to her book. She asked for royalties, too, and a share of the profits. The agent explained that German law forbids film companies from paying royalties to foreigners (Maria had by then become a US citizen). She agreed to the contract and unknowingly signed away all film rights to her story. Only a few weeks later, he offered to pay immediately if she would accept $9,000 in cash. Because it was more money than the family had seen in all of their years of singing, she accepted the deal. Later, she discovered the agent had swindled them—no such law existed.

I find the ambience much nicer in the main Baroque Hall—when making the booking, get a promise that that's where you'll be seated. For more details, see page 598.

Sound of Salzburg Dinner Show: The show at the Sternbräu Inn (see page 600) is Broadway in a dirndl with tired food. But it's a good show, and *Sound of Music* fans leave with hands red from clapping. A piano player and a hardworking quartet of singers wearing historical costumes perform an entertaining mix of *S.O.M.* hits and traditional folk songs (€45 for dinner, begins at 19:30). You can also come by at 20:30, pay €29, skip the dinner, and get the show. Those who book direct (not through a hotel) and pay cash get a 10 percent discount with this book in 2008 (nightly mid-May–mid-Oct, Griesgasse 23, tel. 0662/826-617, www .soundofsalzburgshow.com).

Music at Mass: Each Sunday morning, three great churches offer a Mass generally with glorious music. The Salzburg Cathedral is likely your best bet for fine music to worship by (10:00). The Franciscan church (9:00) and St. Peter's Church (10:30) are also enthusiastic about their musical Masses. See the Salzburg events guide for details.

Free Brass Band Concert: A traditional brass band plays in the Mirabell Gardens (May–Aug Sun at 10:30 and Wed at 20:30).

SLEEPING

Finding a room in Salzburg, even during its music festival (mid-July–Aug), is usually easy. Rates rise significantly (20–30 percent) during the music festival, sometimes around Easter and Christmas, and throughout most of June 2008, when the European soccer championships are held here; these higher prices do not appear in the ranges I've listed. You'll often be charged 10 percent extra for a one-night stay.

In the New Town, North of the River

These listings, clustering around Linzergasse, are in a pleasant neighborhood (with easy parking) a 15-minute walk from the train station (for directions, see "Arrival in Salzburg," earlier in this chapter) and a 10-minute walk to the old town. If you're coming from the old town, simply cross the main bridge (Staatsbrücke) to the mostly traffic-free Linzergasse. If driving, exit the highway at Salzburg-Nord, follow Vogelweiderstrasse straight to its end, and turn right.

$$$ Altstadthotel Wolf-Dietrich, around the corner from Linzergasse on pedestrians-only Wolf-Dietrich-Strasse, is well-located (with half its rooms overlooking St. Sebastian Cemetery). With 27 tastefully plush rooms, it's the best value I could find for a big, stylish hotel (Sb-€82–97, Db-€119–164, price depends on size, family deals, €10–40 more during festival time, complex pricing but readers of this book get a 10 percent discount on prevailing price in 2008—insist on this discount deducted from whatever price is offered that day, elevator, pool with loaner suits, sauna, free DVD library, Wolf-Dietrich-Strasse 7, tel. 0662/871-275, fax 0662/871-2759, www.salzburg-hotel.at, office@salzburg-hotel.at). Their annex across the street has 14 equally comfortable rooms (but no elevator, and therefore slightly cheaper prices).

$$$ Hotel Trumer Stube, three blocks from the river just off Linzergasse, has 20 clean, cozy rooms and a friendly, can-do owner (Sb-€65, Db-€103, Tb-€125, Qb-€140, about €30 more during music festival, top-floor rooms have lower ceilings and are €7 less expensive, 10 percent discount if you book direct with this

Sleep Code

(€1 = about $1.30, country code: 43, area code: 0662)
S = Single, **D** = Double/Twin, **T** = Triple, **Q** = Quad, **b** = bathroom,
s = shower only. Unless otherwise noted, credit cards are
accepted and breakfast is included. All of these places speak
English.

To help you sort easily through these listings, I've divided
the rooms into three categories, based on the price for a standard double room with bath:

$$$ Higher Priced—Most rooms €90 or more.
 $$ Moderately Priced—Most rooms between €60–90.
  $ Lower Priced—Most rooms €60 or less.

book and pay cash in 2008—except during festival, entirely non-
smoking, elevator, Internet access, Bergstrasse 6, tel. 0662/874-
776, fax 0662/874-326, www.trumer-stube.at, info@trumer-stube
.at, pleasant Silvia).

$$$ Hotel Goldene Krone, about five blocks from the river,
is plain and basic, but a good value. Its 25 rooms are big, quiet,
creaky, and well-kept—it'll feel like home right away (Sb-€60, Db-
€95, Tb-€135, claim your 10 percent discount off these prices with
this book in 2008, dim lights, elevator, relaxing backyard garden,
Linzergasse 48, tel. 0662/872-300, fax 0662/8723-0066, www
.hotel-goldenekrone.com, office@hotel-goldenekrone.com, Claudia
and Günther Hausknost). Ask about Günther's tours (€10/person,
2 hrs, 5 people minimum).

$$ Institute St. Sebastian is in a somewhat sterile but very
clean historic building next to St. Sebastian Cemetery. From
October through June, the institute houses female students from
various Salzburg colleges, and also rents 40 beds for travelers (men
or women). From July through September, the students are gone
and they rent all 100 beds (including 20 doubles) to travelers. The
building has spacious public areas, a roof garden, a piano that
guests are welcome to play, and some of the best rooms and dorm
beds in town for the money. The immaculate doubles come with
modern baths and head-to-toe twin beds (S-€32, Sb-€39, D-€52,
Db-€63, Tb-€76, Qb-€92, includes breakfast, elevator, self-service laundry-€4/load; reception open daily July–Sept 7:30–12:00
& 13:00–21:30, Oct–June 8:00–12:00 & 16:00–21:00; Linzergasse
41, enter through arch at #37, tel. 0662/871-386, fax 0662/8713-
8685, www.st-sebastian-salzburg.at, office@st-sebastian-salzburg
.at). Students like the €19 bunks in 4- to 10-bed dorms (€2 less if
you have sheets, no lockout time, free lockers, free showers). You'll

Central Salzburg Hotels

1. Altstadthotel Wolf-Dietrich
2. Hotel Trumer Stube
3. Hotel Goldene Krone
4. To Bergland Hotel & Hotel-Pension Jedermann
5. Institute St. Sebastian
6. Hotel-Pension Chiemsee
7. Blaue Gans Arthotel
8. Hotel Weisse Taube
9. Gasthaus zur Goldenen Ente
10. Hotel am Dom
11. To Hotel Rosenvilla
12. Christkönig Pension
13. Gasthaus Stadtalm
14. To Jugendgästehaus Salzburg
15. To Haus Arenberg
16. To Moosstrasse Zimmer
17. Launderette

find self-service kitchens on each floor (fridge space is free; request a key).

Pensions on Rupertgasse: These two hotels are about five blocks farther from the river on Rupertgasse, a breeze for drivers but with more street noise than the places on Linzergasse. They're both modern and well-run—good values if you don't mind being a bit away from the old town. **$$$ Bergland Hotel** is charming and classy, with comfortable, neo-rustic rooms. It's a modern building, and therefore spacious and solid (Sb-€62–66, Db-€93–96, Tb-€114–117, Qb-€134–140, elevator, Internet access, English library, bike rental-€6/day, Rupertgasse 15, tel. 0662/872-318, fax 0662/872-3188, www.berglandhotel.at, kuhn@berglandhotel.at, Kuhn family). The similar, boutique-like **$$$ Hotel-Pension Jedermann,** a few doors down, is also tastefully done and comfortable, with an artsy painted-concrete ambience and a backyard garden (Sb-€65–75, Db-€90–130, Tb-€110–150, Qb-€150–180, much more during music festival, 5 percent discount with cash and 2-night stay, Internet access, Rupertgasse 25, tel. 0662/873-241, fax 0662/873-2419, www.hotel-jedermann.com, office@hotel-jedermann.com, Herr und Frau Gmachl).

In or Above the Old Town

Most of these hotels are near Residenzplatz. While this area is car-restricted, you're allowed to drive your car in to unload, pick up a map and parking instructions, and head for the €14-per-day garage in the mountain.

$$$ Blaue Gans Arthotel is ultra-modern, giving you a break from charming old Salzburg with artsy public spaces and 40 sleek but nothing-special rooms. It's beautifully located at the far end of Getreidegasse (Sb-€105–115, standard Db-€145, bigger superior Db-€175, fancier suites, free Internet access and Wi-Fi, elevator, Getreidegasse 41, tel. 0662/842-4910, fax 0662/842-4919, www.blauegans.at, office@blauegans.at).

$$$ Gasthaus zur Goldenen Ente is in a 600-year-old building with medieval stone arches and narrow stairs. Located above a good, smoke-free restaurant, it's as central as you can be on a pedestrian street in old Salzburg. The 17 rooms are modern and newly renovated (most of the year: Sb-€75, Db-€125; late July–Aug and Dec: Sb-€78, Db-€135; extra person-€29, non-smoking, elevator, free Internet access, Goldgasse 10, tel. 0662/845-622, fax 0662/845-6229, www.ente.at, hotel@ente.at). While this hotel's advertised rates are too high, travelers with this book get 10 percent off through 2008. Ulrika, Franziska, and Anita run a tight ship for the absentee owners.

$$$ Hotel Weisse Taube is a big, quiet, old-feeling, 30-room place with more comfort than character, well-located about a block

Salzburg

off Mozartplatz (Sb-€67–85, Db with shower-€98–132, bigger Db with bath-€116–158, 10 percent discount with this book and cash in 2008, elevator, Internet access, tel. 0662/842-404, fax 0662/841-783, Kaigasse 9, www.weissetaube.at, hotel@weissetaube.at).

$$$ Hotel am Dom is perfectly located—on Goldgasse a few steps from the cathedral. Its 14 rooms are big, old, and basic, but well-maintained and filled with hand-painted furniture (Db-€88–106 depending on season, extra bed-€36, non-smoking, Goldgasse 17, tel. 0662/842-765, fax 0662/8427-6555, www.amdom.at, bach @salzburg.co.at).

$$$ Hotel-Pension Chiemsee is a stony dollhouse nestled in a quiet lane just behind the cathedral. Hardworking Frau Höllbacher rents six big, beautifully renovated rooms and two suites (Sb-€48–58, Db-€88–98, Tb-€110–120, suite-€110 for 2 people, €28 each additional person up to 4; during music festival and Dec: Sb-€68, Db-€98–116, Tb-€120–130; these special Rick Steves prices available through 2008 if you book direct and pay cash, Chiemseegasse 5, tel. 0662/844-208, fax 0662/8442-0870, www.hotel-ami.de/hotel/chiemsee, hotel-chiemsee@aon.at).

$$ Christkönig Pension makes you feel like a guest of the bishop because, in a sense...you are. With 20 rooms in a 14th-century church building just under the castle and behind the cathedral, this is where the bishop's visitors stay. It's a charming, quiet, and unique way to sleep well and affordably in the old center (S-€35, Ss-€40, Sb-€45, Ds-€66, Db-€80, suite for 2–4 people roughly €45/person, twin beds only, €3/person extra for 1-night stays, cash only, Kapitelplatz 2a, tel. 0662/842627, www.christkoenig -kolleg.at, christkoenig-pension@salzburg.co.at). Heavenly Frau Anna Huemer will take excellent care of you.

Hostels

For another hostel (on the other side of the river), see "International Youth Hotel," next page.

$ Gasthaus Stadtalm (a.k.a. the Naturfreundehaus) is a local version of a mountaineer's hut and a great budget alternative. Snuggled in a forest on the remains of a 15th-century castle wall atop the little mountain overlooking Salzburg, it has magnificent town and mountain views. While the 26 beds are designed-for-backpackers rustic, the price and view are the best in town—with the right attitude, it's a fine experience (€15–18/person in 2-, 4-, and 6-bed dorms, includes breakfast, sheets, and shower; lockers, closed Jan–Feb, 2 minutes from top of €3 round-trip Mönchsberg elevator, Mönchsberg 19C, tel. & fax 0662/841-729, www.diestadtalm .com, ng.esterer@utanet.at, Peter and Roland). Once again, be warned: This is a rustic hostel on the mountaintop in a forest, an elevator ride above the city.

$ **Jugendgästehaus Salzburg** is just steps from the old town center, and yet removed from the bustle. While its dorm rooms are the standard crammed-with-beds variety, the doubles and family rooms are modern, roomy, and bright. The hallways will bring back high-school memories, but the recent renovation has made the public spaces quite pleasant (bed in 8-person dorm-€18–20, Db-€61–64, Qs-€90–96, higher prices are for May–Sept, €3 more for 1- or 2-night stays, non-members pay €3.50 extra, includes breakfast and sheets, free parking, just around the east side of the castle hill at Josef-Preis-Allee 18; from train station take bus #5 or #25 to the Justizgebäude stop, then turn right and walk down shady Josefs-Preis-Alle for a few minutes—it's the big renovated building on the right; tel. 0662/842-670, fax 0662/841-101, www.jfgh.at/salzburg.php, salzburg@jfgh.at). The new hotel at the back of the hostel isn't as cheap, but does offer more standard hotel amenities, such as TVs (Db-€82–96 depending on season, includes breakfast).

Near the Train Station

$$ **Pension Adlerhof,** a plain and decent old pension, is two blocks in front of the train station (left off Kaiserschutzenstrasse), but a 15-minute walk from the sightseeing action. It has a quirky staff, a boring location, and 30 stodgy-but-spacious rooms (Sb-€52–68, D-€58–72, Db-€74–86, Tb-€99–120, Qb-€100–148, cash only, elevator, Elisabethstrasse 25, tel. 0662/875-236, fax 0662/873-663, www.gosalzburg.com, adlerhof@pension-adlerhof.at).

$ **International Youth Hotel,** a.k.a. the "Yo-Ho," is the most lively, handy, and American of Salzburg's hostels. This easygoing place speaks English first; has cheap meals, 160 beds, lockers, Internet access, laundry, tour discounts, and no curfew; plays *The Sound of Music* free daily at 10:30; runs a lively bar; and welcomes anyone of any age. The noisy atmosphere and lack of a curfew can make it hard to sleep (€17–18 in 6- to 8-bed dorms, €21 in dorms with bathrooms, S-€29, D-€44, Ds-€50, T-€60, Ts-€69, Q-€76, Qs-€88, includes sheets, cheap breakfast, 6 blocks from station toward Linzergasse and 6 blocks from river at Paracelsusstrasse 9, tel. 0662/879-649, fax 0662/878-810, www.yoho.at, office@yoho.at).

Four-Star Hotels in Residential Neighborhoods away from the Center

Two plush, modern hotels in nondescript residential neighborhoods a 15-minute walk from the old town are a fine value for those wanting elegant, stylish furnishings, spacious public spaces, generous balconies, gardens, and free parking. While not ideal for train travelers, drivers in need of no-stress comfort for a home base should consider these.

$$$ **Hotel Rosenvilla,** closer to the river, offers 14 rooms with modern art, bright minimalist furnishings, and an organic closeness to nature (Sb-€79, Db-€128, bigger Db-€142, at least €30 more during music festival, Höfelgasse 4, tel. 0662/621-765, fax 0662/625-2308, www.rosenvilla.com, hotel@rosenvilla.com).

$$$ **Haus Arenberg,** higher up opposite the old town, rents 17 big, breezy rooms—most with generous balconies—in a quiet garden setting (Db-€123, €25 more during music festival, Blumensteinstrasse 8, tel. 0662/640-097, fax 0662/640-0973, www.arenberg-salzburg.at, info@arenberg-salzburg.at, family Leobacher).

Zimmer (Private Rooms)

These are generally roomy and comfortable, and come with a good breakfast, easy parking, and tourist information. Off-season, competition softens prices. While they are a bus ride from town, with a €3.40 transit day pass *(Tageskarte)* and the frequent service, this shouldn't keep you away. In fact, most will happily pick you up at the train station if you simply telephone them and ask. Most will also do laundry for a small fee for those staying at least two nights. I've listed prices for two nights or more—if staying only one night, expect a 10 percent surcharge. Most push tours and concerts to make money on the side. As they are earning a commission, if you go through them, you'll probably lose the discount I've negotiated for my readers who go direct.

Beyond the Train Station

$ **Brigitte Lenglachner** rents eight basic, well-cared-for rooms in her home in a quiet, suburban-feeling neighborhood that's a 25-minute walk, 10-minute bike ride, or easy bus ride away from the center. Frau Lenglachner serves breakfast in the garden (in good weather) and happily provides plenty of local information and advice (S-€25, D-€37, Db-€45, T-€51, Qb-€90, 5b-€105; apartment with kitchen-€36 for Sb, €56 for Db; bigger and newer apartment-€60 for Db, €90 for Tb, €120 for Qb; easy and free parking, Scheibenweg 8, tel. & fax 0662/438-044, bedandbreakfast4u @yahoo.de). It's a 10-minute walk from station: Head for the river, cross the pedestrian Pioneer Bridge (Pioniersteg), turn right, and walk along the river to the third street (Scheibenweg). Turn left, and it's halfway down on the right.

On Moosstrasse

The busy street called Moosstrasse, which runs southwest of Mönchsberg (behind the mountain and away from the old town center), is lined with *Zimmer*. Handy bus #21 connects Moosstrasse to the center frequently (Mon–Fri 4/hr until 17:00, evenings and weekends 2/hr). To get to these from the train station, take bus #1, #5, #6, or #25 to Makartplatz, where you'll change to #21. If you're coming from the old town, catch bus #21 from Hanuschplatz, just downstream of the Staatsbrücke bridge near the *Tabak* kiosk. Buy a €1.60 *Einzelkarte–Kernzone* ticket (for 1 trip) or a €3.40 *Tageskarte* (day pass, good for 24 hours) from the streetside machine and punch it when you board the bus. The bus stop you use for each *Zimmer* is included in the following listings. If you're driving from the center, go through the tunnel, continue straight on Neutorstrasse, and take the fourth left onto Moosstrasse. Drivers exit the autobahn at *Süd* and then head in the direction of *Grodig*.

$$ Pension Bloberger Hof, while more a hotel than a *Zimmer,* is comfortable and friendly, with a peaceful, rural location and 20 farmer-plush, good-value rooms. It's the farthest out, but reached by the same bus #21 from the center (Sb-€50–60, Db-€65, big new Db with balcony-€90, Db suite-€110, extra bed-€20, family apartment with kitchen, Inge und her daughter Sylvia offer those booking direct with this book and paying cash a 10 percent discount in 2008, non-smoking, free Internet access and Wi-Fi, restaurant for guests, free loaner bikes, free station pick-up if staying 3 nights, Hammerauer Strasse 4, bus stop: Hammerauer Strasse, tel. 0662/830-227, fax 0662/827-061, www.blobergerhof.at, office @blobergerhof.at).

$ Frau Ballwein offers four cozy, charming, and fresh rooms in two buildings, all with intoxicating view balconies (S-€25, Sb-€35, D-€48, Db-€50–55, Tb-€75, Qb-€80–85, family deals, cash only, farm-fresh breakfasts, non-smoking, small pool, free parking, Moosstrasse 69-A, bus stop: Gsengerweg, tel. & fax 0662/824-029, www.haus-ballwein.at, haus.ballwein@gmx.net).

$ Helga Bankhammer rents four nondescript rooms in a farmhouse, with a real dairy farm out back (D-€45, Db-€50, no surcharge for 1-night stays, family deals, non-smoking, laundry about €5 per load, Moosstrasse 77, bus stop: Marienbad, tel. & fax 0662/830-067, www.privatzimmer.at/helga.bankhammer, bankhammer@aon.at).

$ Haus Reichl, with three good rooms at the end of a long lane, feels the most remote (Db-€55, Tb-€66, Qb-€88, doubles and triples have balcony and view, non-smoking, between Ballwein and Bankhammer B&Bs, 200 yards down Reiterweg to #52, bus stop: Gsengerweg, tel. & fax 0662/826-248, www.privatzimmer .at/haus-reichl, haus.reichl@telering.at). Franziska offers free loaner bikes for guests (20-min pedal to the center).

EATING

In the Old Town

Salzburg boasts many inexpensive, fun, and atmospheric eateries. I'm a sucker for big cellars with their smoky, Old World atmosphere, heavy medieval arches, time-darkened paintings, antlers, hearty meals, and plump patrons. Most of these restaurants are centrally located in the old town, famous with visitors, but also enjoyed by the locals.

Gasthaus zum Wilden Mann is *the* place if the weather's bad and you're in the mood for *Hofbräu* atmosphere and a hearty, cheap meal at a shared table in one small, smoky, well-antlered room. Notice the 1999 flood photo on the wall. For a quick lunch, get the *Bauernschmaus*, a mountain of dumplings, kraut, and peasant's meats (€9.50). Owner Robert—who runs the restaurant with Schwarzenegger-like energy—enjoys fostering a convivial ambience (you'll share tables with strangers) and serving fresh traditional cuisine at great prices. I simply love this place (€7–11 daily specials, Mon–Sat 11:00–21:00, closed Sun, 2 min from Mozart's Birthplace, enter from Griesgasse 22, tel. 0662/841-787).

Stiftskeller St. Peter has been in business for more than 1,000 years—it was mentioned in the biography of Charlemagne. It's classy and central as can be, serving uninspired traditional Austrian cuisine (€10–25 meals, daily 11:30–22:30, indoor/outdoor seating, next to St. Peter's Church at foot of Mönchsberg, restaurant tel. 0662/841-268). They host the Mozart Dinner Concert described on page 588 (€48, nearly nightly at 20:00, call 0662/828-6950 to reserve, book direct with this guidebook for 20 percent off in 2008). Through the centuries, they've learned to charge for each piece of bread and not serve free tap water.

St. Paul's Stub'n Beer Garden is tucked secretly away under the castle with an ignore-the-tourists-attitude (menu in German only). The food is better than a beer hall, and a young, Bohemian-chic clientele fills its two smoky, troll-like rooms and its idyllic, tree-shaded garden. *Kasnock'n* is a tasty mountaineers' pasta with cheese served in an iron pan with a side salad for €8 (€6–9 daily specials, €7–15 plates, Mon–Sat 17:00–23:00, open later for drinks only, closed Sun, Herrengasse 16, tel. 0662/843-220).

Fisch Krieg Restaurant, on the river where the fishermen used to sell their catch, is a great value. They serve fast, fresh, and inexpensive fish in a casual dining room—where trees grow through the ceiling—as well as great riverside seating (€2 fish-wiches to go, self-serve €7 meals, salad bar, Mon–Fri 8:30–18:30, Sat 8:30–13:00, July–Aug until 14:00, closed Sun, Hanuschplatz 4, tel. 0662/843-732).

Central Salzburg Restaurants

① Gasthaus zum Wilden Mann
② Stiftskeller St. Peter Rest.
③ St. Paul's Stub'n Beer Garden
④ Fisch Krieg Rest.
⑤ Sternbräu Inn
⑥ Café Tomaselli
⑦ Saran Essbar
⑧ Bar Club Café Republic
⑨ To Afro Coffee
⑩ Gasthaus Stadtalm

⑪ Toskana Cafeteria Mensa
⑫ Bosna Grill
⑬ To Augustiner Bräustübl
⑭ Spicy Spices
⑮ Biergarten die Weisse
⑯ Café Bazar
⑰ Steingasse Pub Crawl
⑱ Sporer Schnapps Pub
⑲ Stein Terrasse

Sternbräu Inn, a sloppy, touristy Austrian food circus, is a sprawling complex of popular eateries (traditional, Italian, self-serve, and vegetarian) in a cheery garden setting. Explore both courtyards before choosing a seat (Bürgerstube is classic, most restaurants open daily 9:00–24:00, enter from Getreidegasse 34). One fancy, air-conditioned room hosts the Sound of Salzburg dinner show (see description on page 589).

Café Tomaselli (with its Kiosk annex across the way) has long been Salzburg's top place to see and be seen. While overpriced and often overcrowded, it is good for lingering and people-watching. Tomaselli serves light meals and lots of drinks, keeps long hours daily, and has fine seating on the square, a view terrace upstairs, and indoor tables. Despite its fancy inlaid wood paneling, 19th-century portraits, and chandeliers, it is surprisingly low-key (€3–7 entrées, daily 7:00–21:00, until 24:00 during music festival, Alter Markt 9, tel. 0662/844-488).

Saran Essbar is the product of hardworking Mr. Saran (from the Punjab), who cooks and serves with his heart. This delightful little eatery is rich orange under medieval vaults. Its fun menu is small (Mr. Saran is committed to both freshness and value), mixing Austrian (great schnitzel and strudel), Italian, Asian vegetarian, and salads (€9–12 meals, daily 11:00–22:00, often open later, a block off Mozartplatz at Judengasse 10, tel. 0662/846-628).

Bar Club Café Republic, a hip hangout for local young people near the end of Getreidegasse, feels like a theater lobby during intermission. It serves good food with smoky indoor and outdoor seating. It's ideal if you want something mod, untouristy, and un-wursty (trendy breakfasts 8:00–18:00, Asian and international menu, €7–12 plates, lots of hard drinks, daily until late, music with a DJ Fri and Sat from 23:00, salsa music on Tue night, no cover, Anton Neumayr Platz 2, tel. 0662/841-613).

Afro Coffee, between Getreidegasse and the Mönchsberg lift, is understandably popular with its student clientele. They serve tea, coffee, cocktails, and tasty food with a dose of '70s funk and a healthy sense of humor. The menu includes pan-African specialties—try the spicy chicken couscous—as well as standard soups and salads (€9–13 main dishes, Mon–Sat 9:00–24:00, closed Sun, between Getreidegasse and cliff face at Bürgerspitalplatz 5, tel. 0662/844-888).

On the Mountaintop Above the Old Town: **Gasthaus Stadtalm,** Salzburg's mountaineers' hut, sits high above the old town on the edge of the cliff with cheap prices, good food, and great views. If hiking across Mönchsberg, make this your goal (traditional food, salads, cliffside garden seating or cozy-mountain-hut indoor seating, an indoor view table booked for a decade of New Year's celebrations, 2 min from top of €3 round-trip Mönchsberg elevator, also reachable by stairs from Toscanini Hof, Mönchsberg 19C, tel. & fax 0662/841-729, Peter and Roland). While they're open daily from 10:00–24:00, they close in bad weather and in Jan–Feb.

Eating Cheaply in the Old Town

Toskana Cafeteria Mensa is the students' lunch canteen, fast and cheap—with indoor seating and a great courtyard for sitting outside with students and teachers instead of tourists. They serve a daily soup-and-main course special for €4 (Mon–Fri 9:00–15:00, hot meals served 11:00–13:30 only, closed Sat–Sun, behind the Residenz, in the courtyard opposite Sigmund-Haffnergasse 16).

Sausage stands serve the town's favorite "fast food." The best stands (like those on Universitätsplatz) use the same boiling water all day, which gives the weenies more flavor. Key words: *Weisswurst*—boiled white sausage; *Bosna*—with onions and curry; *Käsekrainer*—with melted cheese inside; *Debreziner*—spicy Hungarian; *Frankfurter*—our weenie; *frische*—fresh ("eat before the noon bells"); and *Senf*—mustard (ask for *süss*—sweet; or *scharf*—sharp). Only a tourist puts the sausage in a bun like a hot dog. Munch alternately between the meat and the bread ("that's why you have two hands"), and you'll look like a native. Generally, the darker the weenie, the spicier it is. The Salzburgers' favorite spicy sausage is sold at the 55-year-old **Bosna Grill,** run by chatty Frau Ebner (€2.70; survey the four spicy options—described in English—and choose a number; take-away only, steady and sturdy local crowd, Mon–Fri 11:00–19:00, May–Dec also Sat 11:00–17:00, July–Dec also Sun 16:00–20:00, hours vary according to demand, hiding down the tunnel at Getreidegasse 33 across from Eisgrotte).

Picnickers will appreciate the bustling morning **produce market** (daily except Sun) on Universitätsplatz, behind Mozart's house (see page 575).

Away from the Center

Augustiner Bräustübl, a huge 1,000-seat beer garden within the monk-run Augustiner brewery, is rustic and crude. Don't be fooled by second-rate gardens serving the same beer nearby. The

Augustiner is closed for lunch, but on busy nights, it's like a Munich beer hall with no music but the volume turned up. When it's cool, you'll enjoy a historic setting with beer-sloshed and smoke-stained halls. On balmy evenings, it's like a Monet painting—but with beer breath—under chestnut trees in the garden. Local students mix with tourists eating hearty slabs of schnitzel with their fingers or cold meals from the self-serve picnic counter, while children frolic on the playground kegs. For your beer: Pick up a half-liter or full-liter mug (*schank* means self-serve price, *bedienung* is the price with waiter service), pay the lady, wash your mug, give Mr. Keg your receipt and empty mug, and you will be made happy. Waiters don't bring food—instead, go up the stairs, survey the hallway of deli counters, and assemble your own meal (or, as long as you buy a drink, you can bring in a picnic). Classic pretzels from the bakery and spiraled, salty radishes make great beer even better. For dessert—after a visit to the strudel kiosk—enjoy the incomparable floodlit view of old Salzburg from the nearby Müllnersteg pedestrian bridge and a riverside stroll home (open daily 15:00–23:00, Augustinergasse 4, tel. 0662/431-246). It's about a 15-min walk along the river (with the river on your right) from the Staatsbrücke bridge. Head up Müllner Hauptstrasse northwest along the river and ask for "Müllnerbräu" (MEWL-ner-broy), its nickname.

North of the River, near Recommended Linzergasse Hotels

Spicy Spices is a trippy vegetarian-Indian restaurant where Suresh Syad serves tasty take-out curry and rice, samosas, organic salads, vegan soups, and fresh juices (€6 specials, Mon–Sat 10:00–22:00, Sun 12:00–21:00, Wolf-Dietrich-Strasse 1, tel. 0662/870-712).

Biergarten die Weisse, close to the hotels on Rupertgasse and away from the tourists, is a longtime hit with the natives. If a beer hall can be happening, this one—modern yet with antlers—is it. Their famously good beer is made right there; favorites include their fizzy wheat beer *(Weisse)* and their seasonal beers (on request). Enjoy the beer with their good, cheap traditional food in the great garden seating, or in the wide variety of indoor rooms—sports bar, young and noisy, or older and more elegant (daily specials, Mon–Sat 10:00–24:00, Sun 9:00–18:00, Rupertgasse 10, east of Bayerhamerstrasse, tel. 0662/872-246).

Café Bazar, overlooking the river between Mirabell Gardens and the Staatsbrücke bridge, is as close as you'll get to a Vienna coffee house in Salzburg. It's *the* venerable spot for a classy drink with an old-town-and-castle view (daily €7 plate and light meals, Mon–Sat 7:30–23:00, Sun 9:00–18:00, Schwarzstrasse 3, tel. 0662/874-278).

Steingasse Pub Crawl

For a fun post-concert activity, crawl through medieval Steingasse's trendy pubs (all open until the wee hours). This is a local and hip scene, but accessible to older tourists: dark bars filled with well-dressed Salzburgers lazily smoking cigarettes and talking philosophy, with avant-garde Euro-pop throbbing on the sound-track. Most of the pubs are in cellar-like caves...extremely atmospheric. (For more on Steingasse, see page 583.) These four pubs are all within about 100 yards of each other. Start at the Linzergasse end of Steingasse.

Pepe Cocktail Bar, with Mexican decor and Latin music, serves tostadas with fun toppings *con* cocktails (nightly 19:00–3:00 in the morning, live DJs Fri–Sat from 23:00, Steingasse 3, tel. 0662/873-662).

Shrimps, next door and less claustrophobic, is more a restaurant than a bar, serving creative international dishes (spicy shrimp sandwiches and salads, nightly 18:00–24:00, Steingasse 5, tel. 0662/874-484).

Saiten Sprung wins the "Best Atmosphere" award. The door is kept closed to keep out the crude and rowdy. Ring the bell and enter its hellish interior—lots of stone and red decor, with mountains of melted wax beneath age-old candlesticks and a classic soul music ambience. Stelios, who speaks English with Greek charm, serves cocktails, fine wine, and wine-friendly Italian antipasti (nightly 21:00–4:00 in the morning, Steingasse 11, tel. 0662/881-377).

Fridrich, a tiny place next door with lots of mirrors and a silver ceiling fan, specializes in wine. Bernd Fridrich is famous for his martinis, and passionate about Austrian wines and food (€5–12 small entrées, nightly from 18:00 in summer or 17:00 in winter, Steingasse 15, tel. 0662/876-218).

TRANSPORTATION CONNECTIONS

By train, Salzburg is the first stop over the German–Austrian border. This means that if Salzburg is your only stop in Austria, and you're using a Eurail Selectpass that does not include Austria, you do not have to pay extra or add Austria to your pass to get here.

From Salzburg by Train to: Berchtesgaden (hourly, 45–60 min; bus easier—hourly, 30 min, buses leave across from Salzburg train station), **Innsbruck** (direct every 2 hrs, 2 hrs), **Vienna** (hourly, 3 hrs), **Hallstatt** (hourly, 50 min to Attnang Puchheim, 20-min wait, then 90 min to Hallstatt), **Mauthausen** (hourly, 2 hrs, change in St. Valentin, allow extra 20 min to get from station to camp memorial), **Melk** (at least hourly, 2.5 hrs, transfer in Amstetten or St. Pölten), **Reutte** (hourly, 5 hrs, change either in Munich and Kempten, or in Innsbruck and Garmisch), **Munich** (2/hr, 1.5–2 hrs), **Nürnberg** (hourly with change in Munich, 3 hrs). Train info: tel. 051-717 (to get an operator, dial 2, then 2).

By Car: To leave town driving west, go through the Mönchsberg tunnel and follow blue *A-1* signs to Munich. It's 90 minutes from Salzburg to Innsbruck.

Route Tips for Drivers

From Munich (or the Autobahn) into Salzburg: After crossing the border, stay on the autobahn, taking the Salzburg Süd exit in the direction of Anif. First, you'll pass Schloss Hellbrunn (and zoo), then the Salzburg Süd TI and a park-and-ride service—a smart place to park for your time in Salzburg. Get sightseeing information and transit tickets from the TI (generally open 10:00–18:00, often closed Mon–Tue, closed in winter, tel. 0662/8898-7360). Park your car (€5) and catch the shuttle bus into town (€1.60 for a single ticket, or covered by €3.40 *Tageskarte* day pass, both sold at the TI, more expensive if you buy tickets on board, every 5 min, bus #3 or #8). Mozart never drove in the old town, and neither should you. If you don't believe in park-and-rides, the easiest, cheapest, most central parking lot is the 1,500-car Altstadt lot in the tunnel under the Mönchsberg (€14/day, note your slot number and which of the twin lots you're in, tel. 0662/846-434). Your hotel may provide discounted parking passes.

From Salzburg to Hallstatt (50 miles): Get on the Munich–Wien autobahn (blue *A-1* signs), head for Vienna, exit at Thalgau (#274), and follow signs to *Hof, Fuschl,* and *St. Gilgen.* The Salzburg–Hallstatt road passes two luge rides (see Hallstatt chapter), St. Gilgen (pleasant but touristy), and Bad Ischl (the center of the Salzkammergut with a spa, the emperor's villa if you need a Hapsburg history fix, and a good **TI**—Mon–Fri 8:00–18:00, Sat 9:00–15:00, Sun 10:00–13:00, tel. 06132/277-570).

Hallstatt is basically traffic-free. To park, try parking lot #1 in the tunnel above the town (free with guest card). Otherwise, try the lakeside lots (a pleasant 10–20-min walk from the town center) after the tunnel on the far side of town. If you're traveling off-season and staying downtown, you can drive in and park by the boat dock. (For more on parking in Hallstatt, see the next chapter.)

Near Salzburg: Berchtesgaden

This alpine ski town in the region of the same name (just across the border in Germany's southeastern tip, 12 miles south of Salzburg) is famous for its fjord-like lake and its mountaintop Nazi retreat. Long before its association with Hitler, it was one of the classic Romantic corners of Germany. In fact, Hitler's propagandists capitalized on the Führer's love of this region to establish the notion that the former Austrian was truly German at heart.

Getting There

From Salzburg, the bus is more scenic and direct than the train (bus runs hourly, 30 min, bus station across street from Salzburg's train station). You can also visit Berchtesgaden from Munich (at least hourly, 2.5–3 hrs, train to Salzburg or Freilassing, then train or—more frequently—bus to Berchtesgaden). From the Berchtesgaden station, bus #840 goes to the salt mines (a 20-min walk otherwise), bus #838 goes to the Nazi Documentation Center (Obersalzberg stop, plus a 5-min walk), and bus #841 goes to the Königsee.

Planning Your Time

Berchtesgaden's attractions include the **town** (a touristy mess); **salt mines** (similar to tours across the border in Austria); the romantic, pristine lake called **Königsee** (extremely popular with less-adventurous Germans); and Obersalzberg with **Hitler's Eagle's Nest** (fascinating if you're into Nazi history, and stunningly scenic from the top).

ORIENTATION

Berchtesgaden can be inundated with Germans on vacation. During peak season, you may find yourself in a traffic jam of tourists desperately trying to turn their money into fun. Still, its sights are impressive, connections from Salzburg (and Munich) are excellent, and its various attractions are quite handy by local bus from the train station.

Tourist Information: The TI is next to the train station (tel. 08652/656-500, from Austria tel. 00-49-8652/656-500, www .berchtesgadener-land.com).

Eagle's Nest Tours: For 20 years, David and Christine Harper—who rightly consider this visit more an educational opportunity than simple sightseeing—have organized thoughtful tours of the Hitler-related sites of Berchtesgaden. Their well-organized bus tours depart from the Visitors Center opposite the Berchtesgaden train station (€45, English only, daily at 13:30 mid-May–Oct, 4 hours, 25 people maximum, reservation required, tel. 08652/64971, www.eagles-nest-tours.com). While the price is €45, your actual cost for the guiding is only about €23, as the tour includes the (otherwise obligatory) bus connections and admissions. They also arrange private guides and *Sound of Music* excursions to Salzburg (see their website for details).

SIGHTS

▲**Salt Mines**—At the Berchtesgaden salt mines, you put on traditional miners' outfits, get on funny little trains, and zip deep into the mountain. For one hour, you'll cruise subterranean lakes; slide speedily down two long, slick, wooden banisters; and learn how they mined salt so long ago. Call for crowd-avoidance advice. When the weather gets bad, this place is mobbed. You can buy a ticket early and browse through the town until your appointed tour time. While tours are in German, English-speakers get audioguides (€14, daily May–Oct 9:00–17:00, Nov–April 11:30–15:00, German tel. 08652/600-220, from Austria tel. 00-49-8652/600-220).

▲**Königsee**—The idyllic Königsee stretches like a fjord through pristine mountain scenery from Berchtesgaden to the dramatically

situated Church of St. Bartholomew, and beyond. Most visitors simply glide scenically for 35 minutes on the silent, electronically propelled boat ride to the church, enjoy that peaceful setting, then glide back. Boats, going at a sedate Bavarian speed and filled with Germans chuckling at the captain's commentary, leave with demand—usually three per hour (€11 round-trip, bus #841 runs from train station to boat dock, parking-€3). At a rock cliff midway through the journey, your captain stops, and the first mate pulls out a trumpet to demonstrate the fine echo.

The remote red onion–domed **Church of St. Bartholomew** (once home of a monastery, then a hunting lodge of the Bavarian royal family) is surrounded by a fine beer garden, rustic fishermen's pub, and inviting lakeside trails. The family living next to St. Bartholomew's in the middle of this national park has a license to fish—so very fresh trout is the lunchtime favorite.

▲▲▲**Obersalzberg and Hitler's Eagle's Nest (Kehlsteinhaus)**—Early in his career as a wannabe tyrant, Adolf Hitler was inspired

by this dramatic corner of Bavaria, so steeped in legend and close to the soul of the German people. This place, partly Austrian and partly Bavarian, held a special appeal to the Austrian-German Hitler. In the 1920s, just out of prison, he checked into an alpine hut here to finish up work on his memoir and Nazi primer,

Mein Kampf. Because it was here that he claimed to be inspired and laid out his vision, some call Obersalzberg the "cradle of the Third Reich."

In the 1930s, as the German Führer, Hitler chose this place for his mountain retreat (and later, had it prepared for his last stand). His handlers crafted Hitler's image here—surrounded by nature, gently receiving alpine flowers from adoring little children, lounging around with farmers in lederhosen...no modern arms industry, no big-time industrialists, no ugly extermination camps. In reality, rather than an alpine chalet, it was a huge compound of 80 buildings—closed to the public after 1936—where the major decisions leading up to WWII were hatched. It was here that Hitler hosted world leaders, wowing them with the aesthetics and engineering of his mountain palace, the adoration of his people...and National Socialism.

Orientation: Visitors are often confused by the lay of the land. Your visit has three parts: the Obersalzberg complex and its small, modern **Nazi Documentation Center museum** (a short bus ride above Berchtesgaden, with free parking; also the terminus for the shuttle bus providing the only access to the Eagle's Nest high above; the vast and tourable remains of the **bunker system** (below the museum and included in that ticket); and the actual **Eagle's Nest** (a small yet mighty stone chalet capping the mountain high above).

Between 1945 and 1952, almost everything was destroyed by the victorious Allies (wanting to leave nothing as a magnet for future neo-Nazi pilgrims). If looking for actual pre-1945 artifacts, you'll only see this: the foundations of the Documentation Center (now mostly a modern building); the stripped-bare yet still evocative bunkers under it; the dramatic road to the Eagle's Nest; the stonework, elevator, and fireplace of the actual Eagle's Nest; and a very few papers and memorabilia in glass cases in the Documentation Center.

Nazi Documentation Center: This exhibit is built upon the remains of what was the second seat of Nazi administration. It's small—three floors of exhibits—with almost no actual artifacts,

but evocative for the setting. This center, with only German descriptions (rent the €2 English audioguide), is designed primarily for Germans to learn and understand their recent history. Only since the late 1990s has interest in Nazi history been considered healthy rather than taboo. Non-Germans, too, can learn from a thoughtful visit

(€3; April–Oct daily 9:00–17:00; Nov–March Tue–Sun 10:00–15:00, closed Mon; last entry 1 hour before closing, allow 90 min for visit, German tel. 08652/947-960, from Austria tel. 00-49-8652/947-960, www.obersalzberg.de). Buses depart from here to the Eagle's Nest.

Bunkers: From the Documentation Center, stairs lead into a complex and vast bunker system (same ticket and hours as Documentation Center). Construction began in 1943, after the Battle of Stalingrad ended the Nazi aura of invincibility. This is an incredibly engineered underground town with meeting rooms, offices, archives for the government, and lavish living quarters for Hitler—all connected by four miles of tunnels cut by slave labor through solid rock. It was stripped bare after the war. Today, you can wander among the concrete and marvel at megalomania gone mad.

Eagle's Nest: While many call the entire area "Hitler's Eagle's Nest," that name actually refers only to the mountaintop chalet given to the Führer for his 50th birthday in 1939. While a fortune was spent to build this perch, Hitler made only 14 official visits. Today, the chalet is basically a restaurant with a scenic terrace 100 yards below the summit of a mountain. The views are magnificent. Wander  into the fancy back dining room (the best-preserved from Hitler's time) where you can see the once-sleek marble fireplace chipped up by souvenir-seeking troops in 1945. From the bus stop, a finely crafted tunnel (which will have you humming the *Get Smart* TV theme song) leads to a polished brass elevator—one of the rare original elements of the complex. The site is open to visitors from mid-May through October. The round-trip bus ride up the private road and the lift to the top (a 2,000-foot altitude gain) together cost €19 from the Berchtesgaden train station, or €15 from the parking lot at the Documentation Center.

HALLSTATT
and the SALZKAMMERGUT

Commune with nature in Austria's Salzkammergut Lake District. "The hills are alive," and you're surrounded by the loveliness that has turned on everyone from Emperor Franz Josef to Julie Andrews. This is *Sound of Music* country. Idyllic and majestic, but not rugged, it's a gentle land of lakes, forested mountains, and storybook villages, rich in hiking opportunities and inexpensive lodging. Settle down in the postcard-pretty, lake-cuddling town of Hallstatt.

Planning Your Time

While there are plenty of lakes and charming villages in the Salzkammergut, Hallstatt is really the only one that matters. One night and a few hours to browse are all you'll need to fall in love. To relax or take a hike in the surroundings, give it two nights and a day. It's a relaxing break between Salzburg and Vienna. My best Austrian week: the two big cities (Salzburg and Vienna), a bike ride along the Danube, and a stay in Hallstatt.

ORIENTATION

(area code: 06134)

Lovable Hallstatt is a tiny town bullied onto a ledge between a selfish mountain and a swan-ruled lake, with a waterfall ripping furiously through its middle. It can be toured on foot in about 15 minutes. The town is one of Europe's oldest, going back centuries before Christ. The symbol of Hallstatt, which you'll see all over town, consists of two adjacent spirals—a design based on jewelry found in Bronze Age Celtic graves high in the nearby mountains.

The charms of Hallstatt are the village and its lakeside setting. Go there to relax, nibble, wander, and paddle. While tourist crowds can trample much of Hallstatt's charm in August, the place is almost dead in the off-season. The lake is famous for its good fishing and pure water.

Tourist Information

At the helpful TI, located on the main drag above the "Post Partner," Claudia and her staff can explain hikes and excursions, arrange private tours of Hallstatt (€75), and find you a room (July–Aug Mon–Fri 9:00–17:00, Sat 10:00–14:00, closed Sun; Sept–June Mon–Fri 9:00–12:00 & 14:00–17:00, closed Sat–Sun; a block from Market Square toward lakefront parking at Seestrasse 169, tel. 06134/8208, www.inneres-salzkammergut.at, hallstatt @inneres-salzkammergut.at).

In the summer, the TI offers 90-minute **walking tours** of the town in English and German (€4, May–Sept Sat at 10:00, July–Aug also Wed at 10:00, confirm schedule at TI).

Arrival in Hallstatt

By Train: Hallstatt's train station is a wide spot on the tracks across the lake. *Stefanie* (a boat) meets you at the station and glides scenically across the lake into town (€2, meets each train until about 18:30—don't arrive after that). The last departing boat-train connection leaves Hallstatt at about 18:00, and the first boat goes in the morning at 6:50 (9:20 on Sun). Once in Hallstatt, walk left from the boat dock for the TI and most hotels. Since there's no  train station in town, the TI can help you find schedule information, or check www.oebb.at.

By Car: The main road skirts Hallstatt via a long tunnel above the town. Parking is tight mid-June through mid-October. Hallstatt has several numbered parking areas outside the town center. Parking lot #1 is in the tunnel above the town (swing through to check for a spot, free with guest card, it's a laid-back system—just show your card later). Otherwise, several numbered lots are just after the tunnel. If you have a hotel reservation, the guard will let you drive into town to drop your bags (ask your hotel if it has any in-town parking when you book). It's a lovely 10- to 20-minute lakeside walk to the center of town from the lots. Without a guest card, you'll pay €4.20 per day for parking (less after 14:00). Off-season (Nov–April), parking in town is easy and free.

Hallstatt

NOT TO SCALE—
BUS STOP TO MARKET SQUARE
IS A 10-MINUTE WALK

B BOAT RENTAL
↗ VIEW
P PARKING

SALT MINE

CATHOLIC CHURCH + CEMETERY

RUDOLFS-TURM

TO ECHERNTAL VALLEY HIKE

TO BAD ISCHL + SALZBURG

SMALL UPPER PARKING LOT #1 IN TUNNEL

BONE CHAPEL

TUNNEL

FUNICULAR

TUNNEL

DR.-MORTON-WEG

MUSEUM

MARKET SQUARE

GOSAUMÜHL

GROC.

MAIN ROAD

BUS STOP, W.C. + PARKING LOT #2

LAHN DOCK

PROTESTANT CHURCH

MARKET DOCK

TO OBERTRAUN

BADE-INSEL

HALLSTÄTTERSEE

TO OBERTRAUN

TO HALLSTATT TRAIN STATION

❶ Hotel/Rest. Grüner Baum
❷ Gasthof Zauner
❸ Pension Hallberg-Tauchergasthof (Diver's Inn)
❹ Gasthof Simony
❺ Bräugasthof Hallstatt
❻ To Gasthof Pension Grüner Anger & Launderette
❼ Pension Sarstein

❽ Pension Seethaler
❾ Helga Lenz's Zimmer
❿ Haus Trausner
⓫ Herta Höll's Zimmer
⓬ Gasthaus zur Mühle Hostel & Pizza
⓭ Strand Café
⓮ Ruth Zimmermann Pub

Hallstatt

Helpful Hints

Internet Access: Try **Hallstatt Umbrella Bar** (€4/hr, summers only, weather permitting—since it's literally under a big umbrella, halfway between Lahn boat dock and Museum Square at Seestrasse 145). You can get online all year at **Hotel Grüner Baum** (expensive at €10/hr; on Market Square, see "Sleeping").

Laundry: A small full-service **launderette** is at the campground up from the town's man-made island, Bade-Insel, just off the main road (about €8/load, mid-April–mid-Oct daily 9:00–12:00 & 15:00–18:00, closed off-season, tel. 06134/83224). In the center, **Hotel Grüner Baum** does laundry for non-guests (€12/load, on Market Square, see "Sleeping").

Bike Rental: For prices and places to rent bikes, see page 618.

Parks and Swimming: Green and peaceful lakeside parks line the south end of Lake Hallstatt. If you walk 10 minutes south of town to Hallstatt-Lahn, you'll find a grassy public park, playground, mini-golf, and swimming area (*Badestrand*) with the fun Bade-Insel play-island.

Views: For a great view over Hallstatt, hike above Helga Lenz's *Zimmer* as far as you like (see page 623), or climb any path leading up the hill. The 40-minute steep hike down from the salt-mine tour gives the best views (see page 617). While most visitors stroll the lakeside drag between the old and new parts of town, make a point to do the trip once by taking the more higgledy-piggledy high lane called Dr.-Morton-Weg.

Evening Events: As Hallstatt is very touristy in the summer, check at the TI for evening entertainment. In July and August, the town stages concerts on most Tuesday evenings, and candlelit boat rides at 20:30 on Friday evenings.

SELF-GUIDED WALK

Welcome to Hallstatt

• *This short walk starts at the dock.*

Boat Landing: There was a Hallstatt before there was a Rome. In fact, because of the importance of salt mining here, an entire epoch—the Hallstatt Era, from 800 to 400 B.C.—is named for this important spot. Through the centuries, salt was traded and people came and went by boat. You'll still see the traditional *Fuhr* boats, designed to carry heavy loads in shallow water.

Towering above the town is the Catholic church. Its faded St. Christopher—patron saint of travelers, with his cane and baby Jesus on his shoulder—watched over those sailing in and out. Until 1875, the town was extremely remote...then came a real road and the train. The good ship *Stefanie* shuttles travelers back and forth from here to the Hallstatt train station, immediately across the lake. The *Bootverleih* sign advertises boat rentals. By the way, *Schmuck* is not an insult...it's jewelry.

Notice the one-lane road out of town (below the church). Until 1966, when a bigger tunnel was built above Hallstatt, all the traffic crept single-file right through the town.

Look down the shore at the huge homes. Several families lived in each of these houses back when Hallstatt's population was

about double its present 1,000. Today, the population continues to shrink, and many of these generally underused houses rent rooms to visitors.

Parking is tight here in the tourist season. Locals and hotels have cards getting them into the prime town-center lot. From November through April, the barricade is lifted and anyone can park here. Hallstatt gets about three months of snow each winter, but the lake hasn't frozen over since 1981.

See any swans? They've patrolled the lake like they own it since the 1860s, when Emperor Franz Josef and Empress Sisi—the Princess Diana of her day (see page 480)—made this region their annual holiday retreat. Sisi loved swans, so locals made sure she'd see them here. During this period, the Romantics discovered Hallstatt, many top painters worked here, and the town got its first hotel. Today, that hotel (the big, derelict Haus Kranz facing the square) has an absentee owner and a floor plan so tangled that it's too expensive to renovate, so it just sits, looking ugly in the heart of Hallstatt.

Tiny Hallstatt has two big churches—Protestant (bordering the square on the left, with a grassy lakeside playground) and Catholic up above (with its fascinating bone chapel—described under "Sights and Activities," page 615).

• *Walk over the town's stream, and pop into the...*

Protestant Church: In 1860, Emperor Franz Josef allowed non-Catholic Christians to build churches. Before that, they were allowed only to worship in low-key "houses of prayer." Back then, the Catholic Church was the church of royalty and the wealthy. The working class was more likely to be Protestant. As this was a mining town, it was quite Protestant. In 1863, the miners pooled their humble resources and built this fine church. Step inside (free and often open). It's very plain, emphasizing the pulpit and organ rather than fancy art and saints. Check out the portraits: Martin Luther (left of altar), the town in about 1865 with its new church (left wall), and a century of pastors.

• *Continue past the church to the...*

Market Square (Marktplatz): In 1750, a fire leveled this part of town. The buildings you see now are all late 18th-century and built of stone rather than flammable wood. The three big buildings on the left are government-subsidized housing (mostly for seniors and people with health problems). Take a close look at the two-dimensional, up-against-the-wall pear tree (it likes the sun-warmed wall). The statue features the Holy Trinity.

• *Continue a block past Gasthof Simony. At the first corner, just before the Gemeindeamt (City Hall), jog left across the little square and then right down the tiny lane marked* Am Hof, *which leads through an intimate bit of domestic town architecture, boat houses, lots of firewood, and maybe a couple of swans hanging out. The lane circles back to the main drag and the...*

Museum Square: Because 20th-century Hallstatt was of no industrial importance, it was untouched by World War II. But once upon a time, its salt was worth defending. High above, peeking out of the trees, is Rudolfsturm (Rudolf's Tower). Originally a 13th-century watchtower protecting the salt mines, and later the mansion of a salt-mine boss, it's now a restaurant with a great view. A zigzag trail connects the town with Rudolfsturm and the salt mines just beyond. The big, white houses by the waterfall were water-powered mills that once ground Hallstatt's grain. (If you hike up a few blocks, you'll see the river raging through town.)

Around you are the town's TI, post office, museum, City Hall, and Dachstein Sport Shop (described later). A statue recalls the mine manager who excavated prehistoric graves in about 1850. Much of the *Schmuck* sold locally is inspired by the jewelry found in the area's Bronze Age tombs.

The memorial wooden stairs in front of the museum are a copy of those found in Hallstatt's prehistoric mine—the original stairs are more than 2,500 years old. For thousands of years, people have been leaching salt out of this mountain. A brine spring sprung here, attracting Bronze Age people in about 1600 B.C. Later, they dug tunnels to mine the rock (which was 70 percent salt), dissolved it into a brine, and distilled out the salt—precious for preserving meat. For a look at early salt-mining implements and the town's story, visit the museum (described under "Sights and Activities").

Across from the TI, Pension Hallberg has a quirky hallway full of Nazi paraphernalia and other stuff found on the lake bed (€1). Only recently did local divers realize that, for centuries, the lake had been Hallstatt's garbage can. If something was *kaput*, locals would just toss it into the lake. In 1945, Nazi medals decorating German and Austrian war heroes suddenly became dangerous to own. Throughout the former Third Reich, hard-earned medals floated down to lonely lake beds, including Hallstatt's.

Under the TI is the "Post Partner"—a government-funded attempt to turn inefficient post offices into something more viable (selling souvenirs, renting bikes, and employing people with disabilities who otherwise wouldn't work). The *Fischerei* provides the town with its cherished fresh lake fish. The county allows two commercial fishermen on the lake. They spread their nets each morning and sell their catch here to town restaurants, or to any locals cooking up a special dinner (Mon–Fri 9:00–12:00, closed Sat–Sun).

• *Nearby, still on Museum Square, find the...*

Dachstein Sport Shop: During a renovation project, the builders dug down and hit a Celtic and ancient Roman settlement. Peek through the glass pavement on the covered porch to see where the Roman street level was. If the shop is open, pop in and go downstairs (free). You'll walk on Roman flagstones and see the small gutter that channeled water to power an ancient hammer mill (used to pound iron into usable shapes). In prehistoric times, people lived up by the mines. Romans were the first Hallstatt lakeside settlers. The store's owners are committed to sharing Hallstatt's fascinating history, and often display old town paintings and folk art.

• *From this square, the first right (after the bank) leads up a few stairs to...*

Dr.-Morton-Weg: House #26A dates from 1597. Follow the lane uphill to the left past more old houses. Until 1890, this was the town's main drag, and the lake lapped at the lower doors of these houses. Therefore, many main entrances were via the attic, from this level. Enjoy this back-street view of town. Just after the arch, near #133, check out the old tools hanging outside the workshop, and the piece of wooden piping. It's a section taken from the 25-mile wooden pipeline that carried salt brine from Hallstatt to Ebensee. This was in place from 1595 until the last generation, when the last stretch of wood was replaced by plastic piping. At the pipe, enjoy the lake view and climb down the stairs. From lake level, look back up at the striking traditional architecture (the fine woodwork on the left was recently rebuilt after a fire; parts of the old house on the right date to medieval times).

• *Your tour is finished. From here, you have boat rentals, the salt-mine tour, the town museum, and the Catholic church (with its bone chapel) all within a few minutes' walk.*

SIGHTS AND ACTIVITIES

▲▲**Catholic Church and Bone Chapel**—Hallstatt's Catholic church overlooks the town from above. From near the main boat dock, hike up the covered wooden stairway and follow the *Kath. Kirche* signs. The lovely church has twin altars. The one on the left was made by town artists in 1897. The one on the right is more historic—dedicated in 1515 to Mary, who's flanked by St. Barbara

(on right, patron of miners) and St. Catherine (on left, patron of foresters—a lot of wood was needed to fortify the many miles of tunnels, and to boil the brine to distill out the salt).

Behind the church, in the well-tended graveyard, is the 12th-century Chapel of St. Michael (even older than the church). Its bone chapel—or charnel house *(Beinhaus)*—contains more than 600 painted skulls. Each skull has been lovingly named, dated, and decorated (skulls with dark, thick garlands are oldest—18th century; those with flowers are more recent—19th century). Space was so limited in this cemetery that bones had only 12 peaceful, buried years here before making way for the freshly dead. Many of the dug-up bones and skulls ended up in this chapel. They stopped this practice in the 1960s, about the same time the Catholic

Church began permitting cremation. But one woman (who died in 1983) managed to sneak her skull in later (dated 1995, under the cross, with the gold tooth). The skulls on the books are those of priests (€1, free English flier, daily July–Aug 10:00–18:00, Easter–mid-May 11:00–16:00, mid-May–June and Sept 10:00–16:00, Oct 10:00–17:00—weather permitting, closed Nov–Easter, tel. 06134/8279).

▲**Hallstatt Museum**—This pricey little museum tells the story of Hallstatt. It focuses on the Hallstatt Era (800–400 B.C.), when this village was the salt-mining hub of a culture that spread from France to the Balkans. Back then, Celtic tribes dug for precious salt, and Hallstatt was, as its name means, the "place of salt." While its treasures are the countless artifacts excavated from prehistoric gravesites around the mine, you'll get the whole gamut—with displays on everything from the region's flora and fauna to local artists and the surge in Hallstatt tourism during the Romantic Age. Everything's in German, and the skimpy €3 English guide is worth borrowing, but not buying (€7.50, May–Sept daily 10:00–18:00, shorter hours off-season, adjacent to TI at Seestrasse 56, tel. 06134/8279).

▲**Lake Trip**—For a quick boat trip, you can ride the *Stefanie* across the lake and back for €4. It stops at the tiny Hallstatt train station for 30 minutes (note return time in the boat's window), giving you time to walk to a hanging bridge (ask the captain to point you to the *Hängebrücke*—HENG-eh-brick-eh—a 10-minute lakeside stroll to the left). Longer lake tours are also available (€7.50/50 min, €9/75 min, sporadic schedules—especially off-season—so check chalkboards by boat docks for today's times). Those into relaxation can rent a sleepy electric motorboat to enjoy town views from the water. There are two rental places: **Riedler,** next to ferry dock or across from Bräugasthof (tel. 06134/8320); or **Hemetsberger,** near Gasthof Simony or past the bridge before Bade-Insel (tel. 06134/8228). Both are open daily until 19:00 in-season and in good weather. Boats have two speeds: slow and stop (€11/hr, spend an extra €3/hr for faster 500-watt boats).

▲**Salt-Mine Tour**—If you have yet to tour a salt mine, consider visiting Hallstatt's, which claims to be the oldest in the world. First, you'll ride a steep funicular high above the town (€8.50 round-trip, €5.10 one-way, 4/hr, daily May–mid-Sept 9:00–18:00, mid-Sept–Oct 9:00–16:30, closed Nov–April). Then you'll hike 10 minutes to the mine (past excavation sites of many prehistoric tombs and a glass case with 2,500-year-old bones—but there's little to actually see). Report back 10 minutes before the tour time on your ticket, check your bag, and put on old miners' clothes. Then hike 200 yards higher in your funny outfit to meet your guide, who escorts your group down a tunnel dug in 1719. Inside the mountain, you'll watch a slide show, follow your guide through several caverns as you learn about mining techniques over the last 7,000 years, see a silly laser show on a glassy subterranean lake, peek at a few waxy cavemen with pickaxes, and ride the train out. The highlight for most is sliding down two banisters (the second one is longer and ends with a flash for an automatic souvenir photo that clocks your speed—see how you did compared to the rest of your group after the tour).

The presentation is very low-tech, as the mining company owns all three mine tours in the area and sees little reason to invest in the experience when they can simply mine the tourists. While the tour is mostly in German, the guide is required to speak English if you ask...so ask (salt-mine tour-€15.50, €21 combo-ticket for mine and funicular round-trip saves €3, you can buy mine tickets at cable-car station—note the time and tour number on your ticket, daily May–mid-Sept 9:30–16:30, mid-Sept–Oct 9:30–15:00, closed Nov–April, the 16:00 funicular departure catches the last tour at 16:30, no children under age 4, arrive early or late to avoid summer crowds, dress for the constant 47-degree temperature, tel. 06132/200-2400). If you skip the funicular, the scenic 40-minute hike back into town is (with strong knees) a joy.

At the base of the funicular, notice train tracks leading to the Erbstollen tunnel entrance. This lowest of the salt tunnels goes many miles into the mountain, where a shaft connects it to the tunnels you just explored. Today, the salty brine from these tunnels flows 25 miles through the world's oldest pipeline—made of wood until quite recently—to the huge modern salt works (next to the highway) at Ebensee.

▲**Local Hikes**—Mountain-lovers, hikers, and spelunkers who use Hallstatt as their home base keep busy for days (ask the TI for ideas). A good, short, and easy walk is the two-hour round-trip up the Echern Valley to the Waldbachstrub waterfall and back: From the parking lot, follow signs to the salt mines, then follow the little wooden signs marked *Echerntalweg*. With a car, consider hiking around nearby Altaussee (flat, 3-hour hike) or along Grundlsee to Toplitzsee. Regular buses connect Hallstatt with Gosausee for a pleasant hour-long walk around that lake. Or consider walking nine miles halfway around Lake Hallstatt via the town of Steeg (boat to train station, left along lake and past idyllic farmsteads, returning to Hallstatt along the old salt trail, *Soleleitungsweg*). The TI can also recommend a great two-day hike with an overnight in a nearby mountain hut.

Biking—The best two bike rides take nearly the same routes as the hikes listed previously: up the Echern Valley, and around the lake (bikers do better going via Obertraun along the new lakeside bike path—start with a ride on the *Stefanie*). Two places in town rent bikes: **Post Partner** (the stamp-selling place formerly known as the post office; €5/2 hrs, €9/half-day, €12/day, €30/weekend rental—Fri–Mon, open Mon–Fri 8:00–12:00 & 14:30–16:00, closed Sat–Sun, on Museum Square, tel. 06134/8201) and **Hotel Grüner Baum** (€2.50/hr, €9/half-day, €16/day, on Market Square, see "Sleeping").

Near Hallstatt

▲▲**Dachstein Mountain Cable Car and Caves**—For a refreshing activity, ride a scenic cable car up a mountain to visit huge, chilly caves.

Dachstein Cable Car: From Obertraun, three miles beyond Hallstatt on the main road (or directly across the lake as the crow flies), a mighty gondola goes in three stages high up the Dachstein Plateau—crowned by Dachstein, the highest mountain in the Salzkammergut (9,800 feet). The first segment stops at Schönbergalm (4,500 feet, runs May–Oct), which has a mountain restaurant and two huge caves (described next). The second segment goes to the summit of Krippenstein (6,600 feet, runs mid-May–Oct). The third segment descends to Gjaidalm (5,800 feet, runs mid-June–Oct), where several hikes begin. For a quick high-country experience, Krippenstein is better than Gjaidalm. From Krippenstein, you'll survey a scrubby, limestone,

Salzkammergut

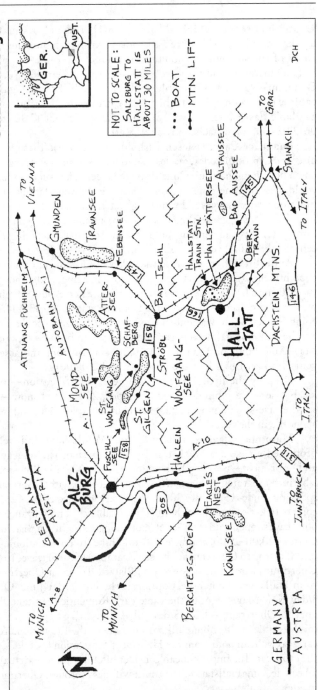

NOT TO SCALE: Salzburg to Hallstatt is about 30 miles

··· BOAT

↤↦ MTN. LIFT

Hallstatt

karstic landscape (which absorbs rainfall through its many cracks and ultimately carves all those caves) with 360-degree views of the surrounding mountains (round-trip cable-car ride to Schönbergalm and the caves-€15, to Krippenstein-€21.80, to Gjaidalm-€23.50; €23.70 combo-ticket covers the Schönbergalm cable car and entrance to both caves; cheaper family rates available, last cable car back down usually at about 17:00, tel. 06134/8400, www.dachsteinwelterbe.at).

Giant Ice Caves (Riesen-Eishöhle, 4,500 feet): These were discovered in 1910. Today, guides lead tours in German and English on an hour-long, half-mile hike through an eerie, icy, subterranean world, passing limestone canyons the size of subway stations. The limestone caverns, carved by rushing water, are named for scenes from Wagner's operas—the favorite of the mountaineers who first came here. If you're nervous, note that the iron oxide covering the ceiling takes 5,000 years to form. Things are very stable.

At the lift station, report to the ticket window to get your cave appointment. The temperature is just above freezing, and although the 600 steps help keep you warm, bring a sweater. Allow 90 minutes, including the 10-minute hike from the station (€9.30, €14.20 combo-ticket with Mammoth Caves, €23.70 combo-ticket covers the Schönbergalm cable car and entrance to both caves, open May–Aug, hour-long tours 9:00–16:00, stay in front and assert yourself to get English information, tel. 06134/8400).

Drop by the little free museum near the lift station—in a local-style wood cabin designed to support 200 tons of snow—to see the cave-system model, exhibits about its exploration, and info about life in the caves.

Mammoth Caves (Mammuthöhle): While huge and well-promoted, these are much less interesting than the ice caves and—for most—not worth the time. Of the 30-mile limestone labyrinth excavated so far, you'll walk a half-mile with a German-speaking guide (€9.30, €14.20 combo-ticket with ice caves, €23.70 combo-ticket covers the Schönbergalm cable car and entrance to both caves, open mid-May–Oct, hour-long tours in English and German 10:00–15:00, entrance a 10-min hike from lift station).

Getting to Obertraun: The cable car to Dachstein leaves from Obertraun, across the lake from Hallstatt. To reach Obertraun from Hallstatt, the handiest option is the bus (6/day June–Oct, 3/day Nov–May, direct to the cable car). Romantics can take the boat to Obertraun (€4.50, 5/day July–Aug, 4/day Sept–June, 15 min)—but it's a 30-minute hike from there to the lift station. You can also walk an hour from the Hallstatt train-station boat dock to the cable car. The impatient can consider hitching a ride—virtually all cars leaving Hallstatt to the south will pass through Obertraun in a few minutes.

Luge Rides (Sommerrodelbahn) on the Hallstatt–Salzburg Road—If you're driving between Salzburg and Hallstatt, you'll pass two luge rides. Each is a ski lift that drags you backward up the hill as you sit on your go-cart. At the top, you ride the cart down the winding metal course. It's easy: Push to go, pull to stop, take your hands off your stick and you get hurt. For more details, see "Luge Lesson" on page 114.

Each course is just off the road with easy parking. The ride up and down takes about 15 minutes. The one near Fuschlsee (closest to Salzburg, look for *Sommerrodelbahn* sign) is half as long and cheaper (€4/ride, 1,970 feet, tel. 06235/7297). The one near Wolfgangsee (look for *Riesenschutzbahn* sign) is a double course, more scenic with grand lake views (€6/ride, €40/10 rides, 4,265 feet, each track is the same speed, tel. 06137/7085). Courses are open Easter through October from 10:00 to 18:00 (July–Aug 9:30–20:00)—but generally close in bad weather. These are fun, but the concrete courses near Reutte are better (see page 114).

NIGHTLIFE

Locals would laugh at the thought. But if you do want some action after dinner, you have two options: **Gasthaus zur Mühle** (youth hostel with a rustic sports-bar ambience in its restaurant when drinks replace the food, open late, closed Tue Sept–mid-May, run by Ferdinand). Or, for your late-night drink, savor the Market Square from the trendy little pub called **Ruth Zimmermann,** where locals congregate with soft music, a good selection of drinks, two small rooms, and tables on the square (daily June–Oct 10:00–2:00 in the morning, Nov–May 11:00–2:00, tel. 06134/8306).

SLEEPING

Hallstatt's TI can almost always find you a room (either in town or at B&Bs and small hotels outside of town—which are more likely to have rooms available and come with easy parking). Mid-July and August can be tight. Early August is worst. Hallstatt is not the place to splurge—some of the best rooms are in *Zimmer,* just as nice and modern as the bigger hotels, at half the cost. A bed in a private home costs about €20 with breakfast. It's hard to get a one-night advance reservation. But if you drop in and they have a spot, one-nighters are welcome. Prices include breakfast, lots of stairs,

---

Sleep Code

(€1 = about $1.30, country code: 43, area code: 06134)
S = Single, **D** = Double/Twin, **T** = Triple, **Q** = Quad, **b** = bathroom,
s = shower only. Unless otherwise noted, credit cards are
accepted, English is spoken, and breakfast is included.

To help you sort easily through these listings, I've divided
the rooms into three categories, based on the price for a standard double room with bath:

$$$ Higher Priced—Most rooms €80 or more.
$$ Moderately Priced—Most rooms between €50–80.
$ Lower Priced—Most rooms €50 or less.

---

and a silent night. *"Zimmer mit Aussicht?"* (TSIM-mer mit OWS-
zeekt) means "Room with view?"—worth asking for. Unlike many
businesses in town, the cheaper places don't take credit cards. Ask
if your hotel has in-town parking when you book your room.

$$$ Hotel Grüner Baum offers the priciest beds in town. Its
22 rooms are huge, each with a separate living area with modern
furnishings on ancient hardwoods. The owner, Monika, moved in
from Vienna and renovated this stately old hotel with urban taste
(suite-like Db-€130–200, 8 percent discount if you book direct
with this book in 2008, family rooms, Internet access, laundry ser-
vice, bikes free for guests with this book in 2008, closed in Nov,
20 yards from boat dock and overlooking the lake and Market
Square, tel. 06134/82630, fax 06134/826-344, www.gruenerbaum
.cc, contact@gruenerbaum.cc).

$$$ Gasthof Zauner is run by a friendly mountaineer, Herr
Zauner, whose family has owned it since 1893. The 13 pricey, pine-
flavored rooms on the inland side of the main square are decorated with sturdy alpine-inspired furniture. Lederhosen-clad Herr
Zauner recounts tales of local mountaineering lore, including his
own impressive ascents (Sb-€57, Db-€98, Db with lakeview-€106,
cheaper mid-Oct–April, closed mid-Nov–mid-Dec, Marktplatz
51, tel. 06134/8246, fax 06134/82468, www.zauner.hallstatt.net,
zauner@hallstatt.at).

$$$ Pension Hallberg-Tauchergasthof (Diver's Inn), across
from the TI, rents five big, modern rooms above their antique
shop. The hallway is lined with a funky mini-museum of WWII
artifacts found in the lake and a chorus line of mounted fish heads
(Db-€70–120, rooms for up to five also available, price depends
on size, €10–20 less off season, breakfast-€5, cash preferred, tel.
06134/8709, fax 06134/20621, www.pension-hallberg.at.tf, hallberg
@aon.at, Gerda the "Salt Witch" and Eckbert Winkelmann).

Hallstatt

\$\$\$ Gasthof Simony is a well-worn, grandmotherly place on the square, with a lake view, balconies, ancient beds, creaky wood floors, slippery rag rugs, antique furniture, a lakefront garden for swimming, and a huge breakfast. Reserve in advance, ideally by phone or fax. To be safe, reconfirm your room and price a day or two before you arrive and call again if arriving late (S-€35, D-€55, Ds-€65, Db-€85, third person-€30–35 extra, cash only, kayaks for guests, Marktplatz 105, tel. & fax 06134/8231, www.hallstatt.net /gasthof/simony, Susanna Scheutz).

\$\$ Bräugasthof Hallstatt is like a museum filled with antique furniture and ancient family portraits. This creaky old place—a former brewery with eight clean, cozy rooms—is run by Virena and her daughter, Virena. Six of the rooms have gorgeous little lakeview balconies (Sb-€45, Db-€76, Db with balcony-€84, Tb-€120, free parking, just past TI on the main drag at Seestrasse 120, tel. 06134/8221, fax 06134/82214, www.brauhaus-lobisser.com, info@brauhaus-lobisser.com, Lobisser family).

\$\$ Gasthof Pension Grüner Anger is practical and modern—your best value in town for comfort—but located away from the medieval town center (a few blocks from the base of the saltmine lift, and a 15-minute walk from the Market Square). It's big and quiet, with 11 rooms and no creaks or squeaks (Sb-€41, Db-€72, Db-€69 for two or more nights, a little more July–Aug, third person-€15, non-smoking, Internet access and Wi-Fi, free loaner bikes, free parking, Lahn 10, tel. 06134/8397, fax 06134/83974, www.anger.hallstatt.net, anger@aon.at, Sulzbacher family). If arriving by train, have the boat captain call Herr Sulzbacher, who will pick you up at the dock. They run a good-value restaurant, too.

\$\$ Pension Sarstein, popular with students and other travelers, is a big, funky, flower-bedecked house heavy with lakeview balconies. You can swim from its plush and inviting lakeside garden (Db-€60, cash only, 200 yards to the right of boat dock at Gosaumühlstrasse 83, tel. 06134/8217, fax 06134/20635, www .pension-sarstein.at.tf, pension.sarstein@aon.at, Isabelle Fischer).

\$\$ Pension Seethaler is a dark, homey old lodge with 45 beds and a breakfast room mossy with antlers, perched above the lake. The confusing floor plan is like an M.C. Escher house with fire hazards. While overpriced, this place is a sleepable last resort (€22/person in S, D, T, or Q; €30/person in Db, Tb, or Qb; cash only, coin-op showers downstairs, closed Nov–May, Dr.-Morton-Weg 22, climb the stairs to the left of Seestrasse 116, tel. 06134/8421, pension-seethaler@aon.at).

\$ Helga Lenz's Zimmer rents two fine rooms a steep five-minute climb above the Pension Seethaler (look for the green *Zimmer* sign). This large, sprawling, woodsy house has a nifty garden perch, wins the "Best View" award, and is ideal for those who sleep well in tree houses and don't mind the ascent from town (Db-€50, Tb-€75; less for two or more nights: Db-€46, Tb-€69; family room, cash only, closed Nov–March, Hallberg 17, tel. & fax 06134/8508, www.hallstatt.net/privatzimmer/helga.lenz, haus-lenz@aon.at).

$ Two *Zimmer* are a few minutes' stroll south of the center, just past the bus stop/parking lot and over the bridge. **Haus Trausner** has four clean, bright, new-feeling rooms adjacent the Trausner family home (Ds/Db-€40, 2-night minimum for reservations, cash only, breakfast comes to your room, Lahnstrasse 27, tel. 06134/8710, trausner1@utanet.at, charming Maria Trausner makes you want to settle right in). **Herta Höll** rents out three spacious, modern rooms on the ground floor of her modern riverside house crawling with kids (Db-€50, Db-€46 for two or more nights, apartment for up to five-€60, cash only, Malerweg 45, tel. 06134/8531, fax 06134/825-533, frank.hoell@aon.at).

$ *Hostel:* **Gasthaus zur Mühle Jugendherberge,** below the waterfall, has 46 of the cheapest good beds in town (bed in 3- to 14-bed coed dorms-€14, D-€28, family quads, sheets-€3.50 extra, breakfast-€4, big lockers with a €15 deposit, closed Nov, reception closed Tue Sept–mid-May—so arrange in advance if arriving on Tue, below tunnel car park, Kirchenweg 36, tel. & fax 06134/8318, toeroe.f@magnet.at, Ferdinand Törö). It's also popular for its great, inexpensive pizza—see entry in "Eating."

EATING

In this town, when someone is happy to see you, they'll often say, "Can I cook you a fish?" While everyone cooks the typical Austrian fare, your best bet here is trout. *Reinanke* trout is caught wild out of Lake Hallstatt and served the same day. You can enjoy good food inexpensively, with delightful lakeside settings. Restaurants in Hallstatt tend to have unreliable hours and close early on slow nights, so don't wait too long to get dinner. The first four eateries listed below are also recommended under "Sleeping".

Restaurant Bräugasthof has great lakeside tables. You can feed the swans while your trout is being cooked. On a balmy evening, its lakeside dining offers the best ambience in town (three-course meals for €10–15, daily June–Sept 10:00–late, sporadic hours in May and Oct, closed Nov–April, Seestrasse 120, tel. 06134/8221).

Hotel Grüner Baum is another lakefront option (May–Oct daily 11:30–22:00; Dec–April Thu–Tue 11:30–22:00, closed Wed; closed Nov; at bottom of Market Square, tel. 06134/8263). Its **Restaurant zum Salzbaron** is a classy place with tables overlooking the lake inside and out (elegant service, €15–20 plates). Its **Kaiserstüberl** is more casual and rustic, with a folksy feel, no lake views, and €10 meals.

Gasthof Zauner's classy restaurant lacks a lakeside setting, but it's well-respected for its grilled meat with "cracklings" and its fish. The service comes in lederhosen, the ivy is real, and most agree that the food is worth the few extra euros (daily 12:30–14:30 & 17:30–22:00, closed mid-Oct–mid Dec, at top of Market Square).

Gasthaus zur Mühle serves the best pizza in town. Chow down cheap and hearty here with fun-loving locals and the youth-hostel crowd (€7 pizza, lots of Italian, some Austrian, daily in summer 11:00–14:00 & 17:00–21:00, closed Tue and no lunch Sept–mid-May, Kirchenweg 36, Ferdinand).

Strand Café, a smoky local favorite, is a 10-minute lakeside hike away, near the town beach, or Bade-Insel (€8–12 plates, plenty of alcohol, April–Oct Tue–Sun 10:00–21:00, closed Mon and Nov–March, great garden setting on the lake, Seelande 102, tel. 06134/8234).

Picnics and Cheap Eats: The **Zauner** bakery/butcher/grocer, great for picnickers, makes fresh sandwiches to go (Tue–Fri 7:00–12:00 & 15:00–18:00, Sat and Mon 7:00–12:00, closed Sun, uphill to the left from Market Square). The only **supermarket** is Konsum, in Lahn at the bus stop (Mon–Fri 7:30–12:00 & 15:00–18:00, Sat 7:30–12:00, closed Sun, July–Aug no midday break and until 17:00 on Sat, Sept–April closed Wed). The **hotdog stand** on the Market Square sells *döner kebab* and so on for €3 (tables and fine lakeside picnic options nearby).

TRANSPORTATION CONNECTIONS

For tips for drivers coming here from Salzburg, see the end of the Salzburg chapter.

From Hallstatt by Train: Most travelers leaving Hallstatt are going to Salzburg or Vienna. In either case, you need to catch the shuttle boat (€2, departs 15 minutes before every train) to the little station across the lake, and ride 90 minutes to **Attnang Puchheim** (hourly from about 7:00–18:00). Trains are synchronized, so after a short wait in Attnang Puchheim, you'll catch your connection to **Salzburg** (50 min) or **Vienna** (2.5 hrs). Day-trippers stopping by Hallstatt between Salzburg and Vienna can check their bags at the Attnang Puchheim station (follow signs for *Schliessfächer,* coin-op lockers are at the street, curbside near track 1, €2.50/24 hrs, a ticket serves as your key). Note: Connections can be fast—check the TV monitor. Hallstatt doesn't show up on schedules, but trains to Ebensee and Bad Ischl stop here. Train info: tel. 051-717 (to get an operator, dial 2, then 2).

By Bus: Some consider the bus ride from Hallstatt to **Salzburg** (with an easy change in Bad Ischl) more scenic than the train, and just as practical (9/day, allow 3 hrs, no bus in icy weather, www .ooevv.at or get details at Hallstatt TI).

INNSBRUCK AND HALL

Austria's Tirol region—in the country's panhandle, south of Bavaria—is a winter sports mecca known for its mountainous panoramas. In the region's capital, Innsbruck, the Golden Roof glitters—but you'll strike it rich in neighboring Hall, which has twice the charm and none of the tourist crowds.

Innsbruck

Innsbruck is world-famous as a resort for skiers and a haven for hikers...but when compared to Salzburg and Vienna, it's stale strudel. Still, a quick look is easy and interesting. Innsbruck was the Hapsburgs' capital of the Tirol, and its medieval center—now a glitzy, tourist-filled pedestrian zone—still gives you the feel of a provincial medieval capital. The much-ogled Golden Roof is the centerpiece.

ORIENTATION

(area code: 0512)

Tourist Information

Innsbruck has two TIs: **downtown** (daily 9:00–18:00, Burggraben 3, three blocks in front of Golden Roof, tel. 0512/5356, www.innsbruck -tourismus.com) and at the **train station** (daily 9:00–19:00, tel. 0512/583-766). At either one, you can pick up a free city map (the €1 map, with more information on sights, isn't necessary) or book a room (free).

Innsbruck and Hall

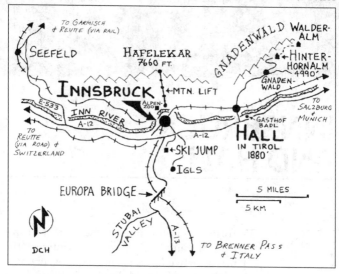

Innsbruck Card: The €24, 24-hour Innsbruck Card pays for itself if you take in four major sights and connect them with the bus or Sightseer minibus (easy to do, since the card is valid 24 hours.) Validate it in the early afternoon, visit two sights, climb the Stadtturm tower, and do two more the next day before your 24 hours expire. The Innsbruck Card is available at the TI and most participating sites, and includes the Mint Museum in Hall (but not the tower).

Walking Tours: The TI offers a basic one-hour city walk of Innsbruck (€8, €5 with Innsbruck Card, May–Oct daily at 14:00, July–Aug also daily at 11:00, Nov–April Fri–Sun at 14:00).

Arrival in Innsbruck

By Train: Some trains stop at Innsbruck's Westbahnhof, but stay on until you reach the main train station (Hauptbahnhof). The main station has lockers (€2–3.50), a post office (Mon–Sat 7:00–19:30, closed Sun), a supermarket (daily 6:00–21:00), and a *Reisezentrum,* where you can get rail information and tickets (Mon–Sat 6:00–21:30, Sun 6:30–21:30).

From the station, it's a 10-minute walk to the old town center. Leave by veering right to Brixnerstrasse. Follow it past the fountain at Boznerplatz where it turns into Meranerstrasse and go straight until it dead-ends into Maria-Theresa-Strasse. Turn right and head 300 yards into the old town (you'll pass the TI on Burggraben on your right), where you'll see the Golden Roof and Hotel Weisses Kreuz.

Helpful Hints

Laundry and Internet Access: Bubblepoint is a handy self-service launderette (€7/load, Mon–Fri 8:00–22:00, Sat–Sun 8:00–20:00, between train station and Golden Roof at Brixnerstrasse 1, tel. 0512/5650-0750, www.bubblepoint .com).

Bike Rental: Inntour has everything from city cruisers (€14/day) to mountain bikes (€28/day). For €4, they'll drop the bike off at your hotel or, even better, pick you up at your hotel for free and take you to their shop to get fitted for the proper bike (June–Sept Mon–Fri 9:00–18:00, Sat–Sun 9:00–17:00; May and Oct Mon–Fri 9:00–18:00, Sat 9:00–17:00, closed Sun except by request; closed Nov–April; Leopoldstrasse 4, by the Triumphal Arch, tel. 0512/5817-4217, if staying at Hotel Weisses Kreuz they will phone for you). Inntour is also a good contact for any adventure sports you might want to do (such as bungee jumping).

Getting Around Innsbruck

A single ticket for Innsbruck's buses or trams costs €1.70; a day ticket is €3.80. Buy tickets from the machine at the tram stop, at the TI, or at a tobacco shop *(Tabak);* single tickets can also be purchased from the driver. For transit information, call tel. 0512/530-7500 (Mon–Fri 7:30–18:00, closed Sat–Sun) or visit www.ivb.at.

A made-for-tourists minibus called the **Sightseer** follows two popular routes around town, connecting the key sights (€3 for any one-way trip, €4.50 round-trip to a particular sight and back, minimal headphone commentary in English, May–Oct 2/hr 9:00–17:30, Nov–April hourly 10:00–17:00). If visiting several outlying sights, you can buy a day ticket *(Tagesticket,* €8.80, includes funicular and transportation on the city bus system) and use the Sightseer as a hop-on, hop-off bus. It's pricey—more than twice the cost of a day pass on public transit—but convenient (for information and tickets, visit the TI, or buy directly from driver).

SIGHTS AND ACTIVITIES

Innsbruck's Old Town

▲▲**The Golden Roof (Goldenes Dach) and Herzog-Friedrich-Strasse**—The three-block pedestrian street (Herzog-Friedrich-Strasse) in front of the Golden Roof is Innsbruck's tourism central.

Stand in front of the Roof to get oriented. Emperor Maximilian I loved Innsbruck, and built a palace here—including the balcony topped with 2,657 gilded copper tiles. The Golden Roof (1494) offered Maximilian an impressive spot from which to view his medieval spectacles.

Most buildings along this street are Gothic (notice the entry arches), but across the street from the Golden Roof (to the left as you face the Roof) is the frilly Baroque-style **Helblinghaus** facade.

Above you is the bulbous **city tower** *(Stadtturm)*, with 148 steps you can climb for a great view (€3, daily June–Sept 10:00–20:00, Oct–May 10:00–17:00, tel. 0512/561-500). This was the old town watchtower. A prison was on the second floor. Like many Austrian buildings (including the nearby Hofkirche), the tower originally had a pointy Gothic spire—replaced with this onion-shaped one when Baroque was in vogue.

A block in front of the Golden Roof—next to the McDonald's—is the historic **Hotel Weisses Kreuz**. It's built on Roman foundations, but has only been hosting guests for the last 500 years. The white cross *(weisses Kreuz)* is the symbol of the Order of Malta—knights who opened up guest houses for Holy Land–bound pilgrims during the Crusades. In 1769, a 13-year-old Wolfgang Amadeus Mozart and his father stayed here on their way to Italy. A generation later, this hotel was one of the centers of resistance against Napoleon, and later still, against the Nazis (giving shelter to Jewish refugees). When the American soldiers moved in from Italy, they made the hotel their headquarters. Today, it's still a functioning hotel (see "Sleeping," page 636). It recently hosted Otto von Hapsburg, the Man Who Would Be Emperor, if his great-great-uncle hadn't started—and lost—World War I. Though Otto could have stayed in the fanciest place in town, he chose this historic, comfortable inn instead.

If you walk down the shop-lined Hofgasse (facing the Golden Roof, go right), you'll reach the Hofburg palace, Hofkirche, and Tirolean Folklife Museum (all described next).

Hofburg—This 18th-century Baroque palace, built by Maria Theresa, is only worth a visit if you aren't going to the much bigger and better palaces in Vienna, Munich, or near Füssen. The lone advantage is that, unlike those more famous palaces, you'll have this one virtually to yourself (€5.50, daily 9:00–17:00, last entry at 16:30; €10 includes entry and 1-hour guided tour in English—May–Oct daily at 12:15, plus June–Aug at 15:15; helpful €1.80 English booklet, tel. 0512/587-186, www.hofburg-innsbruck.at).

If you aren't visiting Salzburg or Vienna, get your *Sachertorte* fix here, at the local outpost of this venerable Viennese institution (Café Sacher, at Hofburg entrance, daily 8:30–24:00).

Innsbruck

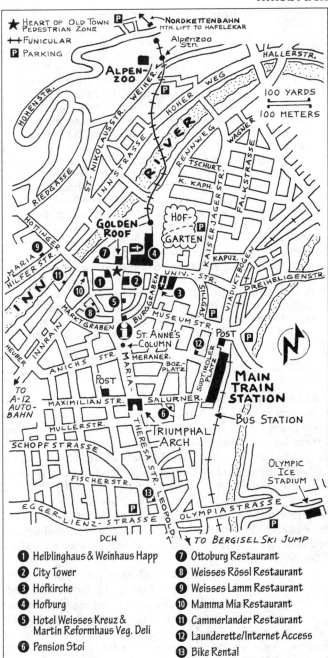

★ Heart of Old Town / Pedestrian Zone
✚ Funicular
P Parking

- ❶ Helblinghaus & Weinhaus Happ
- ❷ City Tower
- ❸ Hofkirche
- ❹ Hofburg
- ❺ Hotel Weisses Kreuz & Martin Reformhaus Veg. Deli
- ❻ Pension Stoi
- ❼ Ottoburg Restaurant
- ❽ Weisses Rössl Restaurant
- ❾ Weisses Lamm Restaurant
- ❿ Mamma Mia Restaurant
- ⓫ Cammerlander Restaurant
- ⓬ Launderette/Internet Access
- ⓭ Bike Rental

Emperor Maximilian I
(1459–1519)

The big name in Innsbruck is Emperor Maximilian I, who made this city a regional capital and built the Golden Roof. This Hapsburg emperor was a dynamic, larger-than-life Renaissance man—soldier, sculptor, and statesman (though not very good at any of these). At the same time, he clung to the last romantic fantasies of the Middle Ages; for example, he was the last Hapsburg who personally led his troops into battle.

Most people associate the Hapsburg Empire with Vienna, which was the capital of the empire's Eastern European holdings during its peak in the 17th and 18th centuries. But during Maximilian's time, two centuries earlier, the focus was on Italy—he took the "Roman" part of "Holy Roman Emperor" very seriously. This made Innsbruck very important, since it was the capital of Tirol (which then included much of today's northern Italy, and was on the Italian frontier).

This visionary emperor hoped that once all of Italy was his, Innsbruck would become the permanent capital of his empire. In reality, he was unlucky at war and ran up huge debts. But his strategic marriage to Mary of Burgundy set the stage for the large-scale expansion of the empire. Though he wanted to be a war hero, as with most Hapsburgs, his biggest victory came with a trip to the altar.

▲▲**Hofkirche**—Emperor Maximilian I liked Innsbruck so much, he wanted to be buried here, surrounded by 28 larger-than-life cast-bronze statues of his ancestors, relatives, in-laws...and his favorite heroes of the dying Middle Ages (such as King Arthur). They stand like giant chess pieces on the black-and-white checked-marble floor. The good €1 English book tells you who everyone is. Don't miss King Arthur (as you face the altar, he's the fifth from the front on the right, next to the heavy-metal dude) and Mary of Burgundy, Maximilian's first—and favorite—wife (third from the front on the left). Some of these sculptures, including that of König Artur, were designed by German Renaissance painter Albrecht Dürer.

That's Maximilian himself, kneeling on top of the huge sarcophagus. Sadly, the real Max isn't inside. By the time he died, Maximilian had become notorious for running up debts, and his men weren't allowed to bring his body here. Just inside the door to the church, you'll find the tomb of the popular Tirolean soldier Andreas Hofer, who fought against Napoleon (church entry-€3, Mon–Sat 9:00–17:00, Sun 12:30–17:00, Universitätsstrasse 2).

▲▲Tirolean Folklife Museum (Tiroler Volkskunst Museum)—
This museum, next door to the Hofkirche, will likely be closed for
renovation throughout 2008. When open, it offers the best look
anywhere at traditional Tirolean lifestyles. Fascinating exhibits
range from wedding dresses and gaily painted cribs and nativity scenes, to maternity clothes and babies' trousers. The upper
floors show Tirolean homes through the ages (if open—€5;
July–Aug daily 9:00–17:30; Sept–June Mon–Sat 9:00–17:00, Sun
10:00–17:00; hard to appreciate without the €2 English guidebook,
Universitätsstrasse 2, tel. 0512/5948-9510).

Maria-Theresa-Strasse—The fine, Baroque Maria-Theresa-
Strasse stretches south from the medieval center. **St. Anne's
Column** (Annasäule) marks the middle of the old marketplace.
This was erected in the 18th century by townspeople thankful that
their army had defeated an invading Bavarian army and saved the
town (it's the same idea as the plague columns you see throughout
Central Europe).

At the far end of the street, the **Triumphal Arch** is a gate
Maria Theresa built to commemorate a happy and a sad occasion.
The happy: Her son Leopold II, archduke of Tuscany, met and
married a Spanish princess here in Innsbruck—and Maria Theresa
and her husband Franz came for the ceremony. But Franz partied a
little too hard, and died the day after the wedding. (Maria Theresa
wore black for the rest of her life.) The south-facing side of the
arch—what you see as you approach the center—shows the inter-
locked rings of the happy couple. But the flipside, visible as you
leave town, features mournful statuary.

▲Slap-Dancing—For your Tirolean folk fun, Innsbruck hotels
offer an entertaining evening of slap-dancing and yodeling nearly
nightly at 20:30 from April through October (€20 includes a
drink with 2-hour show, tickets at TI). Every summer Thursday,
the town puts on a free outdoor folk show under the Golden Roof
(July–Sept, weather permitting).

Dom zu St. Jakob—Innsbruck's own cathedral is your typical
Baroque pastry: pink, frilly, and lots of gold. What makes it unique
is that the high altar houses one of Lucas Cranach's best-known
Madonna-and-Childs, the *Mariahilf* (free, Mon–Sat 10:15–18:30,
Sun 12:30–18:30, Domplatz 6, tram #1 or #3, tel. 0512/583-902).

▲Schloss Ambras—Just southeast of town is the Renaissance
palace Archduke Ferdinand II (1529–1595) renovated for his wife
(it was originally a medieval castle). Its extensive grounds are
replete with manicured gardens, a 17th-century fake waterfall, and
resident peacocks. Don't miss the armory, the "curiosities" collection that houses the archduke's assortment of the beautiful and
bizarre (*Kunst- und Wunderkammer,* ranging from stuffed sharks to
ancient Portuguese frocks), and the beautiful Spanish Hall (built

1569–1572), which is clearly the prize of the whole complex. Its intricate wooden ceiling and 27 life-size portraits of Tirolean princes make this a popular venue for classical music concerts (€8, daily 10:00–17:00, Aug until 19:00, closed Nov, audioguide-€1, Schlossstrasse 20, take the local TS bus or the Sightseer, tel. 0152/524-745, www.khm.at/ambras).

Into the Mountains

▲**Ski Jump Stadium (Bergisel)**—A new, modern ski jump has been built in the same location as the original one that was used for the 1964 and 1976 Olympics (demolished in 2000). It's an inviting side-trip with a superb view, overlooking the city just off the Brenner Pass road on the south side of town. Drivers follow signs to *Bergisel*. Walkers take tram #1 from the center and then walk uphill about 10 min, or have the Sightseer or the local

TS bus drop you near the parking lot. For the best view, hike to the Olympic rings under the dishes that held the Olympic flame, where Dorothy Hamill and a host of others who brought home the gold are honored. To get to the top of the ski jump, you can zip up in a funicular (2-min ride), then an elevator—or walk up the 455 steps—for a great view and a panorama café (€8.30 either way, includes Kaiserjäger Museum—described next, daily 9:30–17:00, until 18:00 in summer, last entrance 30 min before closing, funicular back down runs until 30 min after closing, tel. 0512/589-259, www.bergisel.info).

Near the ski jump parking lot is the **Kaiserjäger Museum** and a memorial to Andreas Hofer, the hero of the Tirolean battles against Napoleon. The museum is dedicated to the Hapsburg Emperor's infantry division, active from 1816 until 1918. Apart from two rooms honoring Hofer, the museum features paintings of important battles and officers, maps, battle plans, flags, uniforms, and weapons. Most interesting are the two upper floors, which contain black-and-white photographs and WWI weapons. Battle history buffs shouldn't miss this—since it's included in the ski-jump ticket, you might as well pop in. Ask to borrow the helpful English pamphlet (€3.50, or included in €8.30 ski-jump entrance, April–Oct daily 9:00–17:00, closed Nov–March, tel. 0512/582-312, www.kaiserjaegermuseum.org).

Mountain Lifts and Hiking—A popular mountain-sports center and home of the 1964 and 1976 Winter Olympics, Innsbruck is surrounded by 150 mountain lifts, 1,250 miles of trails, and 250

hikers' huts. One lift even goes right out of town. This lift system is being completely rebuilt, but is scheduled to re-open in early 2008 (see project updates on their website, www.nordpark.com). Still, the following details are subject to change.

The first stage, a **funicular** (called Hungerburgbahn, about €5, likely daily 8:00–18:00, every 15 min), goes directly from downtown (leaves from Congress Innsbruck, right behind the Hofburg) to the Alpenzoo (described next). From there, it connects to the cable cars that lead up into the mountains (€19, follow signs to *Nordkettenbahn Seegrube–Hafelekar,* daily 9:00–17:00, runs every 10–30 min). If it's sunny, consider riding the lift right out of the city to the mountaintops above (about €25 total; TI has exact times and prices).

Ask your hotel or hostel for a free Innsbruck Club card (different from the Innsbruck Card sold by TI), which offers overnight guests various discounts, bike tours, and free guided hikes in summer. Hikers meet in front of Congress Innsbruck daily at 8:45; each day, it's a different hike in the surrounding mountains and valleys (bring only lunch and water; boots, rucksack, and transport are provided; confirm with TI).

Alpenzoo—This zoo is one of Innsbruck's most popular attractions (understandable when the competition is the Golden Roof) and lets you have a look at all the animals that hide out in the Alps: wildcats, owls, elk, vultures, and more (€7, daily April–Oct 9:00–18:00, Nov–March 9:00–17:00, Weiherburggasse 37, tel. 0512/292-323, www.alpenzoo.at). The easiest way up is with the Hungerburgbahn funicular (described previously), but you can also walk (follow *Fussweg Alpenzoo* signs from the river) or take the Sightseer or local TS or W buses.

Near Innsbruck

▲▲**Alpine Side-Trip by Car to Hinterhornalm**—In Gnadenwald, a village sandwiched between Hall and its Alps, pay a €5 toll, pick up a brochure, then corkscrew your way up the mountain. Marveling at the crazy amount of energy put into such a remote road project, you'll finally end up at the rustic Hinterhornalm Berg restaurant (generally daily mid-May–Oct 10:00–19:00, closes later in summer—but entirely weather-dependent and often closed, closed Nov–mid-May, mobile 0664-211-2745). Hinterhornalm is a hang-gliding springboard. On good days, it's a butterfly nest. From there, it's a level 20-minute walk to Walderalm, a cluster of three dairy farms with 70 cows that share their meadow with the clouds. The cows ramble along ridge-top lanes surrounded by cut-glass peaks. The ladies of the farms serve soup, sandwiches, and drinks (very fresh milk in the afternoon) on rough plank tables. Below you spreads the Inn River Valley and, in the distance, tourist-filled Innsbruck.

Innsbruck

Sleep Code

(€1 = about $1.30, country code: 43, area code: 0512)
S = Single, **D** = Double/Twin, **T** = Triple, **Q** = Quad, **b** = bathroom,
s = shower only. Unless otherwise noted, credit cards are
accepted, English is spoken, and breakfast is included.

To help you sort easily through these listings, I've divided
the rooms into three categories, based on the price for a standard double room with bath:

   $$ Higher Priced—Most rooms €70 or more.
    $ Lower Priced—Most rooms less than €70.

SLEEPING

$$ Hotel Weisses Kreuz, near the Golden Roof, has been housing visitors for 500 years (see page 630). While its common spaces
still have an old-inn feel—with an airy atrium stairway, antique
Tirolean furniture, and big wood beams—its 40 rooms are newly
renovated and comfortable (S-€34–39, Sb-€58–62, D-€64–67,
small Db-€91–98, big Db at €101–115 is a better value, non-
smoking rooms, elevator, Internet access, parking €10/day—reserve
ahead, 50 yards in front of Golden Roof, as central as can be in the
old town at Herzog-Friedrich-Strasse 31, tel. 0512/594-790, fax
0512/594-7990, www.weisseskreuz.at, hotel@weisseskreuz.at).

$ Pension Stoi rents 17 pleasant, basic rooms 200 yards from
the train station (S-€34, Sb-€39, D-€54, Db-€62, T-€65, Tb-€75,
Q-€75, Qb-€86, cash only, no breakfast, reception open daily
8:00–21:00; walk left as you leave the station to Salurnerstrasse,
take first left on Adamgasse, then watch for signs in the courtyard
on the right, Salurnerstrasse 7; tel. 0512/585-434, fax 05238/87282,
pensionstoi@aon.at, Stoi family).

EATING

You'll find plenty of expensive places in the pedestrian zone around
the Golden Roof; locals favor **Weinhaus Happ,** offering standards
like *Wiener Schnitzel,* but also game, fish, and salads, all consumed
in a labyrinth of cozy, traditional *Stuben* (€9–22 plates, daily 11:00–
23:00, on the left as you face the Roof at Herzog-Friedrich-Strasse
14, tel. 0512/582-980), and the more elegant splurge, **Ottoburg**
(€16–22 entrées, Tue–Sun 11:30–14:30 & 18:00–22:00, closed
Mon, jog left down street in front of Roof to Herzog-Friedrich-
Strasse 1—it's the gray mini-castle with the red and white shutters,
tel. 0512/584-338).

Weisses Rössl is off the tourist track and, for culinary adventurers, features traditional Tirolean treats like oven-roasted liver and calf's head. Fear not: Schnitzels and steaks abound, as do the tasty *Grillteller* (an assortment of grilled meats) and *Pfandl*—meat, potatoes, and veggies served up in a cast-iron skillet (€9–18 plates, Mon–Sat 11:30–14:30 & 17:00–22:00, closed Sun; facing the Roof, go one block left to Kiebachgasse 8; tel. 0512/583-057). Or stroll across the Innbrücke (bridge over the Inn River) and go left a half-block along the waterfront street to the smoky, slightly seedy, but harmless and very local **Weisses Lamm** (€9–19 plates, Fri–Wed 8:00–24:00, closed Thu, hiding upstairs at Mariahilfstrasse 12, tel. 0512/283-156).

Mamma Mia, an escape from traditional fare, dishes up hearty portions of pizza and pasta (€6.50, indoor/outdoor seating, daily 10:30–24:00, Kiebachgasse 2, tel. 0512/562-902), while **Cammerlander** is *the* place for a steak fix or family-friendly pizza and pasta. Enjoy international cuisine in their sleek, candlelit dining room, on the glassed-in veranda, or riverside with a mountain view (€8–22 entrées, daily 9:00–21:00, Innrain 2, tel. 0512/586-398).

Martin Reformhaus, a health-food store with an eat-in or take-out deli, is where vegetarians can feast on tasty organic meals (daily soups and salads, €6 lunch specials Mon–Thu, open Mon–Fri 9:00–18:00, Sat 8:30–17:00, closed Sun, Herzog-Friedrich-Strasse 29).

TRANSPORTATION CONNECTIONS

From Innsbruck by Train to: Hall (hourly trains, 10 min, Hall is the second stop and is not always announced; also 4 buses/hr, 25 min, buses leave from stop marked with blue *H* in front of the orange building just south of the train station), **Salzburg** (every 2 hrs, 2 hrs), **Vienna** (every 2 hrs, 5 hrs), **Reutte** (every 2 hrs, 2.5 hrs, change in Garmisch, afternoon connection requires bus from Garmisch), **Füssen** (5/day, 4.25 hrs, change in Munich), **Bregenz** (nearly hourly, some with transfer in Feldkirch, 2.5 hrs), **Zürich** (3/day direct, every 1–2 hours with changes, 3.75 hrs), **Munich** (every 2 hrs, 2 hrs), **Paris** (3/day, none direct, 9 hrs), **Milan** (6/day, 5.5 hrs, most with change in Verona, fastest connections require seat reservation), **Venice** (1/day direct, 5 hrs; 7/day, 5–6 hours with changes). Night trains run to Vienna, Venice, and Rome. Train info: tel. 051-717 (to get an operator, dial 2, then 2).

Hall

Hall was a rich salt-mining center when Innsbruck was just a humble bridge *(Brücke)* town on the Inn River. Hall actually has a larger old town than does its sprawling neighbor, Innsbruck. Hall hosts a colorful morning scene before the daily tour buses arrive, closes down tight for its daily siesta, and sleeps on Sunday. There's a brisk farmers' market on Saturday mornings. (For drivers, Hall is a convenient overnight stop on the long drive from Vienna to Switzerland.)

ORIENTATION

Tourist Information

Hall's helpful TI offers lots of town information and brochures on a wide range of topics. If it's not too busy, they can also help you find a room (Mon–Fri 8:30–18:00, Sat 9:00–17:00, closed Sun, just off main square at Wallpachgasse 5, tel. 05223/455-440, regional info: www.regionhall.at, office@regionhall.at).

The TI organizes one-hour town **walking tours** in English (€6, includes admissions, €8 also includes Salt Museum tour, below; May–Oct usually daily at 10:00). The TI can also put you in touch with an English-speaking private guide (about €80/hr).

Arrival in Hall

By Bus: Coming from Innsbruck, get off at the Unterer Stadtplatz stop, just below downtown Hall. (If you're staying at Gartenhotel Maria Theresia, stay on the bus a few minutes more, as it makes a long loop beyond and then back into Hall, dropping you at the *Kurhaus* at the top of town.) From the Unterer Stadtplatz bus stop, you're a five-minute uphill walk from the town square and TI.

By Train: Hall's train station is a 10-minute walk from the town center (exit straight ahead up Bahnhofstrasse, turn right at the busy road, and you'll soon reach the fountain that marks the bottom of town).

By Car: Drivers approaching on the autobahn take the Hall-Mitte exit. You'll cross a big bridge, then you'll see two convenient parking lots (each one a 5-min walk from old center). Find parking immediately after the bridge in P5 (€1.20/hr, Mon–Fri 8:30–18:00, Sat 8:30–12:00, free on Sun), or go through the light to find P2 on the left (first hour free, €1/hr after that).

On Foot or Bike: Hall and Innsbruck are connected by a pleasant bike path along the Inn River and through some parks. From Innsbruck, cross the Inn River, then simply follow the river downstream along the *Inntal Radweg*, minding signs to *Hall*. A comfortable 30-minute pedal will get you there. If you want to carry on from Hall, the riverside, seven-mile bike path to Volders is a treat. (Unfortunately, there's no bike rental in Hall.)

SIGHTS AND ACTIVITIES

Main Square (Oberer Sadtplatz)—Hall's quaint main square at the top of town is worth a visit (TI just up the street). In the adjacent square (Pfarrplatz) is the Town Hall (Rathaus) and St. Nicholas Parish Church (Pfarrkirche St. Nikolaus). This much-appended Gothic church is decorated Baroque, with fine altars, a twisted apse, and a north wall lined with bony relics.

Hall Mint in Hasegg Castle (Münze Hall in Burg Hasegg)— Beginning in the 15th century, Hall began minting coins—most notably the *Taler* (which eventually became "dollar" in English). The former town mint, housed in Hasegg Castle, is between the river and the center at the south end of town. The Hall Mint Museum was renovated and expanded in 2003 to show off the town's proud minting heritage. The centerpiece is a huge, fully functioning replica of a 16th-century minting press—powered by water and made entirely of wood. The newly renovated tower *(Münzerturm)*, which contains a multimedia exhibit about the castle and the town, provides a medieval-style workout (202 steps) and a great view (€6 for mint museum, includes audioguide, €4 for tower, €8 combo-ticket for both; April–Oct Tue–Sun 10:00–17:00, closed Mon; Nov–March Tue–Sat 10:00–17:00, closed Sun–Mon; last entry 1 hour before closing, tel. 05223/585-5165, www.muenze -hall.at). The bus from Innsbruck drops you off right by the castle (stop: Unterer Stadtplatz, go through door marked #17 and *Burg Hasegg*); from Gasthof Badl, it's the first big building you'll see after crossing the old pedestrian bridge.

Salt Museum (Bergbaumuseum)—Back when salt was money, Hall was loaded. Try catching a tour at this museum, where the town has reconstructed one of its original salt mines, complete with pits, shafts, drills, tools, and a tiny but slippery wooden slide (€3.50, €8 town walk includes museum, English tours May–Sept at 11:30, no need to reserve, tel. 05223/455-440). The museum is a block south of the main square at Eugenstrasse.

Swimming—If you want to make a splash, check out Hall's magnificent *Freischwimmbad*, a huge outdoor pool complex with four diving boards, giant lap pool, big slide, and kiddies' pool, all surrounded by a lush garden, sauna, mini-golf, and lounging locals

(€3.50, mid-May–mid-Sept daily 9:00–19:00, closed Sept–mid-May, at campground northwest of Hall, follow *Schwimmbad* signs from downtown to Scheidensteinstrasse 24, tel. 05223/454-647, www.camping-hall.at or www.stadtwerke-hall.at/schwimmbad).

SLEEPING AND EATING

(€1 = about $1.30, country code: 43, area code: 05223)
Lovable towns that specialize in lowering the pulse of local vacationers line the Inn Valley. Hall, while the best town, has the shortest list of accommodations. Up the hill on either side of the river are more towns strewn with fine farmhouse hotels and pensions. Most *Zimmer* charge about €20 per person but don't accept one-night stays.

$$ Gartenhotel Maria Theresia, just a 15-minute walk from Hall's center, makes you feel a little bit like landed Tirolean gentry. This spacious, elegantly comfortable, family-run place is a fine splurge and makes a great hub from which to explore the Inn Valley (Sb-€70, Db-€110–130, Tb-€165, free parking, beautiful garden patio, restaurant, fine-dining room in wine cellar, ask about mountain-bike tours, Reimmichlstrasse 25, tel. 05223/56313, fax 05223/563-1366, www.gartenhotel.at, info@gartenhotel.at).

Getting to Gartenhotel Maria Theresia: If you arrive by **car** from Innsbruck, take the Hall-Mitte exit, go over the bridge, and through the light. At the roundabout, veer left (you'll already see signs) onto Speckbacherstrasse. Go left on Scheidensteinstrasse, right on Badgasse, and left on Reimmichelstrasse. If you are coming by **bus,** take it to the Kurhaus stop above town, then follow Stadtgraben (with the town on your left) to Kathreinstrasse, which feeds into Scheidensteinstrasse.

$ Gasthof Badl is a big, comfortable, friendly place with 25 rooms run by sunny Frau Steiner and her daughter, Sonja. I like its convenience, peace, big breakfast, easy telephone reservations, and warm welcome (Sb-€40–42, Db-€66–70, Tb-€96, Qb-€118, elevator, laundry-€7, Innbrücke 4, tel. 05223/56784, fax 05223/567-843, www.badl.at, info@badl.at). Hall's kitchens close early, but Gasthof Badl's **restaurant** serves excellent dinners until 21:30 (€7–11 entrées, closed Tue). They stock the essential TI brochures and maps of Hall and Innsbruck in English.

Getting to Gasthof Badl: It's easy for **drivers** to find: From the east, it's immediately off the Hall-Mitte freeway exit; you'll see the orange-lit *Bed* sign. From Innsbruck, take the Hall-Mitte exit and, rather than turning left over the big bridge into town, go straight. To reach Gasthof Badl from the Unterer Stadtplatz **bus stop,** go through the door next to the bus stop (marked #17 and *Burg Hasegg*), cut through a couple of courtyards until you're under the castle tower, then follow Münzergasse (marked by red-and-blue no-parking signs) across the creek. Go straight until you hit the train tracks, then go left to use the railroad underpass, which is about 10 yards away. Coming out of the underpass, go right up the ramp and, from there, cross the old wooden bridge to the hotel. From the **train station,** leave the station to the right, follow the tracks straight ahead, and as the street curves left, veer right on the footpath that follows the tracks to access the railroad underpass, then head straight across the old wooden bridge.

TRANSPORTATION CONNECTIONS

Innsbruck is the nearest major train station. Hall and Innsbruck are connected by train and bus. Trains do the trip faster but leave only hourly; bus #4 takes a bit longer (25 min, €2.80 each way) but leaves four times per hour and drops you closer to town (see "Arrival in Hall," earlier in this chapter). Buses go to and from the Innsbruck train station, a 10-minute walk from the old town center. Drivers staying in freeway-handy Hall can side-trip into Innsbruck on the bus.

Route Tips for Drivers
From Hall into Innsbruck and on to Switzerland: For old Innsbruck, take the autobahn from Hall to the Innsbruck Ost exit and follow the signs to *Zentrum,* then *Kongresshaus,* and park as close as you can to the old center on the river *(Hofgarden).*

Just south of Innsbruck is the new ski jump (from the autobahn take the Innsbruck Süd exit and follow signs to *Bergisel).* Park at the end of the road near the Andreas Hofer Memorial, and climb to the empty, grassy stands for a picnic.

Leaving Innsbruck for Switzerland, head west on the autobahn (direction: Bregenz). (If you're coming directly from Innsbruck's ski jump, go down into town along the huge cemetery—thoughtfully placed just beyond the jump landing—and follow blue *A-12/Garmisch/Arlberg* signs). The eight-mile-long Arlberg tunnel saves you 30 minutes on your way to Switzerland, but costs you lots of scenery and €8.50 (Swiss francs and credit cards accepted). For a joyride and to save a few bucks, skip the tunnel, exit at St. Anton, and go via Stuben.

After the speedy Arlberg tunnel, you're 30 minutes from Switzerland. Bludenz, with its characteristic medieval quarter, makes a good rest stop. Pass Feldkirch (and another long tunnel) and exit the autobahn at Rankweil/Feldkirch Nord, following signs for *Altstätten* and *Meiningen (CH).* Crossing the baby Rhine River, leave Austria.

From Hall or Innsbruck to Reutte: Go west (as above, direction: Switzerland) and leave the freeway at Telfs, where signs direct you to Reutte (a 90-min drive).

Side-Trip over Brenner Pass into Italy: A short swing into Italy is fast and easy from Innsbruck or Hall (45-min drive, easy border crossing). To get to Italy, take the great Europa Bridge over Brenner Pass. It costs about €8, but in 30 minutes you'll be at the border. (Note: Traffic can be heavy on summer weekends.)

In Italy, drive to the colorful market town of Vipiteno/Sterzing. **Reifenstein Castle** is a unique and wonderfully preserved medieval castle, just south of town on the west side of the valley, down a small road next to the autobahn. The lady who lives at the castle leads several tours a day in Italian and German, squeezing in whatever English she can (€5, open Easter–Oct; tours Sat–Thu at 10:30, 14:00, and 15:00; mid-July–mid-Sept also at 16:00, closed Fri; picnic spot at drawbridge; from Austria tel. 00-39-0472-765-879, from Italy tel. 0472/765-879).

GERMAN AND AUSTRIAN HISTORY

German History

There was no "Germany" before 1871, but the cultural heritage of the German-speaking people (of modern-day Germany and Austria) stretches back 2,000 years.

Romans (A.D. 1–500)

German history begins in A.D. 9, when Roman troops were ambushed and driven back by the German chief Arminius. For the next 250 years, the Rhine and Danube rivers marked the border between civilized Roman Europe (to the southwest) and "barbarian" German lands (northeast). While the rest of Europe's future would be Roman, Christian, and Latin, Germany would follow its own pagan, *Deutsch*-speaking path.

Rome finally fell to the Germanic chief Theodoric the Great (a.k.a. Dietrich of Bern, A.D. 476). After that, Germanic Franks controlled northern Europe, ruling a mixed population of Romanized Christians and tree-worshipping pagans.

Charlemagne and the Franks (A.D. 500–1000)

For Christmas in A.D. 800, the pope gave Charlemagne the title of Holy Roman Emperor. Charlemagne, the king of the Franks, was the first of many German kings to be called *Kaiser* ("emperor," from "Caesar") over the next thousand years. Allied with the pope, Charlemagne ruled an empire that included Germany, Austria, France, the Low Countries, and northern Italy.

Charlemagne (Karl der Grosse, or Charles the Great, r. 768–814) stood a head taller than his subjects, and his foot became a standard measurement. The stuff of legend, Charles the Great had five wives and four concubines, producing descendants with names like Charles the Bald, Louis the Pious, and Henry

Why We Call Deutschland "Germany"

Our English name "Germany" comes from the Latin *Germania*, the name of one of the "barbarian" tribes. The French and Spanish call it *Allemagne* and *Alemania* after the Alemanni tribe. Italians call the country *Germania*, but in Italy the German language is known as *tedesco*, after another Germanic tribe. Completely confused by all this, the Slavic peoples of Eastern Europe simply throw up their hands and call Germany *Německo* (Czech), *Niemcy* (Polish), *Németország* (Hungarian), or other variations of a word that means "mute."

To Germans, their country is *Deutschland*, a name used for at least 1,200 years. It probably derives from *Deutsch*—which is what eighth-century folks called the common language that developed in the eastern half of the Frankish empire. *Alles klar?*

the Quarrelsome. After Charlemagne died of pneumonia (814), his united empire did not pass directly to his oldest son but was divided into (what would become) Germany, France, and the lands in between (Treaty of Verdun, 843).

The Holy Roman Empire (1000–1500)

Chaotic medieval Germany was made of more than 300 small, quarreling dukedoms ruled by the Holy Roman Emperor. The title was pretty bogus, implying that the German king ruled the same huge European empire as the ancient Romans. In fact, he was "Holy" because he was blessed by the Church, "Roman" to recall ancient grandeur, and the figurehead "Emperor" of only a scattered kingdom.

Germany's emperors had less hands-on power than other kings around Europe. Because of the custom of electing emperors by nobles and archbishops, rather than bestowing the title through inheritance, they couldn't pass the crown father to son. This system gave nobles great power, and the peasants huddled close to their local noble's castle for protection from attack by the noble next door. There were no empire-wide taxes and no national capital.

When Emperor Henry IV (r. 1056–1106) tried to assert his power by appointing bishops, he was slapped down by the nobles, and forced to repent to the pope by standing barefoot in the alpine snow for three days at Canossa (in northern Italy, 1077).

Emperor Frederick I Barbarossa (1152–1190), blue-eyed and red-bearded (hence *barba rossa*), gained an international reputation as a valiant knight, gentleman, bon vivant, and lover of poetry and women. Still, his great victories were away in Italy and Asia (on the Third Crusade, where he drowned in a river), while back home nobles wielded real power.

This was the era of Germany's troubadours *(Meistersingers)*, who traveled from castle to castle singing love songs *(Minnesang)* and telling the epic tales of chivalrous knights (Tristan and Isolde, Parzival, and the Nibelungen) that would later inspire German nationalism and Wagnerian operas.

While France, England, and Spain were centralizing power around a single ruling family to create modern nation-states, Germany remained a decentralized, backward, feudal battle-ground.

Medieval Growth

Nevertheless, Germany was located at the center of Europe, and trading towns prospered. Several northern towns (especially Hamburg and Lübeck) banded together into the Hanseatic League, promoting open trade around the Baltic Sea. To curry favor at election time, emperors granted powers and privileges to certain towns, designated Free Imperial Cities. Some towns, such as Köln, Mainz, Dresden, and Trier, held higher status than many nobles, as hosts of one of the seven Electors of the emperor.

Textiles, mining, and the colonizing of eastern lands made Germany an economic powerhouse with a thriving middle class. In towns, middle-class folks (burghers), not the local aristocrats, began running things. In about 1450, Johann Gutenberg of Mainz invented moveable type for printing, an invention that would allow the export of a new commodity: ideas.

Religious Struggles and the Thirty Years' War (1500–1700)

Martin Luther—German monk, fiery orator, and religious whistle-blower—sparked a century of European wars by speaking out against the Catholic Church (see sidebar, page 646).

Luther's protests ("Protestantism") threw Germany into a century of turmoil, as each local prince took sides between Catholics and Protestants. In the 1525 Peasant Revolt, peasants attacked their feudal masters with hoes and pitchforks, fighting for more food, political say-so, and respect. The revolt was brutally put down.

The Holy Roman Emperor, Charles V (r. 1519–1556), sided with the pope. Charles was the most powerful man in Europe, having inherited an empire that included Germany and Austria, plus the Low Countries, much of Italy, Spain, and Spain's New World possessions. But many local German nobles took the opportunity to go Protestant—some for religious reasons, but also to seize Church assets and powers.

The 1555 Peace of Augsburg allowed each local noble to decide

History

Martin Luther
(1483–1546)

One of the most influential Germans of all time was Martin Luther, who defied the Catholic Church and forever divided its congregation. Luther was born on November 10, 1483, in Eisleben, south of Berlin. His dad owned a copper smelter, affording Luther a middle-class upbringing—a rarity in the medieval hierarchy of nobles, clergy, and peasants. At the University of Erfurt, Luther

 earned a liberal-arts degree, entered law school, and earned himself two nicknames—"the philosopher" for his wide-ranging mind, and "the king of hops" for his lifelong love affair with beer.

In 1505, while riding back to school after a trip home, a bolt of lightning knocked him to the ground. Terrified, he vowed to become a monk. By age 23, he was ordained a priest in Erfurt Cathedral, and was on the fast track to become a professor of theology.

Martin soon got a teaching job at a brand-new university in Wittenberg—the progressive city that would be his home for the rest of his life. Luther taught theology and mingled with the town's brightest thinkers and artists; he also spent hours alone in his cell (living quarters) in the Augustinian monastery. Consumed with the notion that he was a sinner, he devoured the Bible, looking for an answer and finding it in Paul's letter to the Romans. Luther realized that God makes sinners righteous through their faith in Jesus Christ, not by earning it through good deeds. As this concept of grace took hold, Luther said, "I felt myself to have been born again."

Energized, he began a series of Bible lectures at Wittenberg's twin-towered St. Mary's City Church. The pews were packed as Luther quoted passages directly from the Bible. Speaker and audience alike began to see discrepancies between what the Bible said and what the Church was doing.

Coincidentally, a representative of the pope arrived in Wittenberg to raise money by selling letters of indulgence promising "full forgiveness for all sins." Luther was outraged at the idea that God's grace could be bought, and thought the subject should be debated openly. On October 31, 1517, Luther approached Wittenberg's Castle Church and nailed 95 "theses"— or topics for discussion—to the door, which was then used as a public bulletin board. The theses questioned indulgences and other Church practices and beliefs. Luther's propositions were printed and circulated from Wittenberg's newfangled presses (some of Europe's first). It was the talk of Germany, and Luther became famous—or infamous—almost overnight.

The pope ordered Luther's writings to be burned and sent a letter excommunicating the rebellious monk. Luther was branded a heretic and ordered to Rome to face charges, but he refused to go. Finally, the most powerful man in Europe, Emperor Charles V, stepped in to arbitrate, calling an Imperial Diet (congress) at Worms (1521). Luther made a triumphal entry into Worms, greeted by cheering crowds.

The Diet convened, and Luther took his place in the center of the large hall, standing next to a stack of his books. Inquisitors grilled him while the ultra-Catholic Charles looked on from his throne. Luther refused to disavow his beliefs or books. "Here I stand," he told the assembly, "I can do no other. So help me God. Amen."

Given a few days to reconsider, Luther disappeared. Rumor was he was kidnapped, but in fact he'd escaped to safety in Wartburg Castle, overlooking his teenage home of Eisenach. Protected by a German prince opposed to Rome, he spent a year fighting depression and translating the New Testament from Greek into German. This "German King James Version" was revolutionary, bringing the Bible to the masses and shaping the modern German language. Finally, wearing a fake beard and disguised as a knight, Luther returned home to Wittenberg.

In 1525, 41-year-old Martin met 25-year-old Katherine von Bora, and within months, the ex-monk married the ex-nun in St. Mary's City Church. He and "Katie" moved from the monastery to their own house. Martin and Katherine had six children and raised four orphans.

Though living in Wittenberg under the protection of German princes, Luther traveled, spreading the Protestant message. In 1529, at Marburg Castle just north of Frankfurt, he attended a summit of leading Protestants to try and forge an alliance against Catholicism (1529). They agreed on everything except a single theological point: whether Christ was present in the wine and bread of Communion in a physical sense (according to Luther) or symbolic sense (per Ulrich Zwingli). The disagreement doomed the Protestant movement to splinter into dozens of sects.

In his 50s, Luther's health declined and he grew bitter, a fact made clear in such writings as "Against the Papacy at Rome Founded by the Devil" and "Of the Jews and Their Lies." He died on February 18, 1546, and was buried in Wittenberg. To this day, pilgrims bring flowers.

History

Germany Before Unification

the religion of his realm. In general, the northern lands became Protestant, while the south (today's Bavaria and Austria) remained Catholic.

Unresolved religious and political differences eventually expanded into the Thirty Years' War (1618–1648). This Europe-wide war, fought mainly on German soil, involved Denmark, Sweden, France, and Bohemia (in the modern-day Czech Republic), among others. It was one of history's bloodiest wars, fueled by religious extremism and political opportunism, and fought by armies of brutal mercenaries who worked on commission, and were paid in loot and pillage.

By the war's end (Treaty of Westphalia, 1648), a third of all Germans had died, France was the rising European power, and the Holy Roman Empire was a medieval mess of scattered, feudal states. In 1689, France's Louis XIV swept down the Rhine, gutting and leveling its once-great castles, and Germany ceased to be a major player in European politics until the modern era.

Austria and Prussia (1700s)

The German-speaking lands now consisted of three "Germanys":

Austria in the south, Prussia in the north, and the rest in between.

Prussia—originally colonized by celibate ex-Crusaders called Teutonic Knights—was forged into a unified state by two strong kings. Frederick I (the "King Sergeant," r. 1701–1713) built a modern state around a highly disciplined army, a centralized government, and national pride. His grandson, Frederick II "The Great" (r. 1740–1786), added French culture and worldliness, preparing militaristic Prussia to enter the world stage. A well-read, flute-playing lover of the arts and liberal ideals, Frederick also ruled with an iron fist—the very model of the "enlightened despot."

Meanwhile, Austria thrived under the laid-back rule of the Hapsburg family. Hapsburgs gained power in Europe by marrying it. They acquired the Netherlands, Spain, Bohemia, and Hungary that way—a strategy that didn't work so well for Marie-Antoinette, who wed the king of France.

In the 1700s, the Germanic lands became a cultural powerhouse, producing musicians (Bach, Haydn, Mozart, Beethoven), writers (Goethe, Schiller), and thinkers (Kant, Leibniz). But politically, feudal Germany was no match for the modern powers.

After the French Revolution (1789), Napoleon swept through Germany with his armies, deposing feudal lords, confiscating church lands, and forcing the emperor to hand over his crown (1806). After a thousand years, the Holy Roman Empire (or *Reich*) was dead.

German Unification (1800s)

Napoleon's invasion helped unify the German-speaking peoples by rallying them against a common foreign enemy. After Napoleon's defeat, the Congress of Vienna (1815), presided over by the Austrian Prince Metternich, realigned Europe's borders. "Germany" consisted of three Germanic nations—Prussia in the north, Austria in the south, and the German Confederation, a loose collection of small states in between. The idea of unifying these three nations into one began to grow, and by mid-century most German-speaking people favored forming a modern nation-state. The only question was whether the confederation would be under Prussian or Austrian dominance.

Economically, Germany was becoming increasingly modern, with railroads (1835), a unified trade organization (1834), mechanical-engineering prowess, and factories booming on a surplus of labor.

Energetic Prussia took the lead in unifying the country. Otto von Bismarck (served 1862–1890), the strong minister of Prussia's weak king, used cunning politics to engineer a unified Germany under Prussian dominance. First, he started a war with Austria, ensuring that any united Germany would be under Prussian

History

control. (The Austrian Empire would remain a separate country.) Next, Bismarck provoked a war with France (Franco-Prussian War, 1870–1871). This action united Prussia and the German Confederation against their common enemy, France.

Fueled by hysterical patriotism, German armies swept through France and, in the Hall of Mirrors at Versailles, crowned Prussia's Wilhelm I as Emperor *(Kaiser)* of a new German Empire uniting Prussia and the German Confederation (but excluding Austria). This Second Reich (1871–1918) featured elements of democracy (an elected *Reichstag,* or parliament), offset by a strong military and an emperor with veto powers.

A united and resurgent Germany was suddenly flexing its muscles in European politics. With strong industry, war spoils, overseas colonies, and a large and disciplined military, it sought its rightful place in the sun. *Volk* art flourished (Wagner's operas, Nietzsche's essays), fueled by nationalist fervor, reviving medieval German myths and Nordic gods. The rest of Europe saw Germany's rapid rise and began arming themselves to the teeth.

World War I and Hitler's Rise (1914–1939)

When Archduke Franz Ferdinand, the heir to the Austro-Hungarian Empire, was assassinated in 1914, all of Europe took sides as the political squabble quickly escalated into World War I. Germany and Austria-Hungary attacked British and French troops in France, but were stalled at the Battle of the Marne. Both sides dug defensive trenches, then settled in for four years of bloodshed, boredom, mud, machine-gun fire, disease, and mustard gas.

Finally, at 11:00 in the morning of November 11, 1918, the fighting ceased. Germany surrendered, signing the Treaty of Versailles in the Hall of Mirrors at Versailles. The war cost the defeated German nation 1.7 million men, precious territory, colonies, their military rights, reparations money, and national pride.

A new democratic government called the Weimar Republic (1919) dutifully abided by the Treaty of Versailles, and tried to maintain order among Germany's many divided political parties. But the country was in ruins, its economy a shambles, and the war's victors demanded heavy reparations. Communists rioted in the streets, fascists plotted coups, and a loaf of bread cost a billion inflated Marks. War vets grumbled in their beer about how their leaders had sold them out. All Germans, regardless of their political affiliations, were fervently united in their apathy toward the new democracy. When the worldwide depression of 1929 hit Germany with brutal force, the nation was desperate for a strong leader with answers.

Adolf Hitler (1889–1945) was a disgruntled vet who had spent the post–World War I years homeless, wandering the streets of Vienna with sketchpad in hand, hoping to become an artist. In Munich, he joined other disaffected Germans to form the National Socialist (Nazi) party. In stirring speeches, Hitler promised to restore Germany to its rightful glory, blaming the country's current problems on communists, foreigners, and Jews. After an unsuccessful coup attempt (the Beer Hall Putsch in Munich, 1923), Hitler was sent to jail, where he wrote an influential book of his political ideas, called *Mein Kampf (My Struggle)*.

By 1930, the Nazis—now wearing power suits and working within the system—had become a formidable political party in Germany's democracy. They won 38 percent of the seats in the *Reichstag* in 1932, and Hitler was appointed chancellor (1933). Two months later, the *Reichstag* building was mysteriously set on fire—an apparent act of terrorism with a September 11–size impact—and a terrified Germany gave Chancellor Hitler sweeping powers to preserve national security.

Hitler wasted no time in using this Enabling Act to jail opponents, terrorize the citizenry, and organize every aspect of German life under the watchful eye of the Nazi party. Plumbers' unions, choral societies, school teachers, church pastors, filmmakers, and artists all had to account to a Nazi Party official about how their work furthered the Third Reich.

For the next decade, an all-powerful Hitler proceeded to revive Germany's economy, building the autobahns and rebuilding the military. Defying the Treaty of Versailles and world opinion, Hitler occupied the Saar region (1935) and the Rhineland (1936), annexed Austria and the Sudetenland (1938), and invaded Czechoslovakia (March 1939). The rest of Europe finally reached its appeasement limit and World War II began (see sidebar, next page).

Two Germanys (1945–1990)

After World War II, the Allies divided occupied Germany into two halves, split down the middle by an 855-mile border that Winston Churchill called an "Iron Curtain." By 1949, Germany was officially two separate countries. West Germany (the Federal Republic of Germany) was democratic and capitalist, allied with the powerful United States. East Germany (the German Democratic Republic, or DDR) was a socialist state under Soviet control. The former capital, Berlin, sitting in East German territory, was itself split into two parts, allowing a tiny pocket of Western life in the Soviet-controlled East. Armed guards prevented Germans from crossing the border to see their cousins on the other side.

In 1948, Soviet troops blockaded West Berlin. The Allies responded by airlifting food and supplies into the stranded city, forcing the Soviets to back off. In 1961, the East Germans erected a 12-foot-high concrete wall through the heart of Berlin. The Berlin

---

Germany During World War II
(1939–1945)

1939 Soldiers singing *"Muss ich denn, Muss ich denn"* ("I must leave my happy home") march off to war. On September 1, Germany invades Poland, sparking World War II. Germany, Italy, and Japan (the Axis) would eventually square off against the Allies—Britain, France, the United States, and the Soviet Union.

1940 The Nazi *Blitzkrieg* (lightning war) quickly sweeps through Denmark, Norway, the Low Countries, France, Yugoslavia, and Greece. With fellow fascists ruling Italy (Mussolini), Spain (Franco), and Portugal (Salazar), all of the Continent is now dominated by fascists, creating a "fortress Europe."

1941 Hitler invades his former ally, the USSR. Bombastic victory parades in Berlin celebrate the triumph of the Aryan race over the lesser peoples of the world.

1942 Allied bombs begin falling on German cities. That autumn and winter, German families receive death notices from the horrific Battle of Stalingrad. On the worst days, 50,000 men died (by comparison, America lost 58,000 total in Vietnam). Back home, Nazi officials begin their plan for the "final solution to the Jewish problem"—systematic execution of Europe's Jews in specially built death camps.

Wall—built at the height of the Cold War between the United States and the USSR—was designed to prevent the westward flow of East German citizens. It came to symbolize divided Germany.

In West Germany, Chancellor Konrad Adenauer (who had suffered imprisonment under the Nazis) tried to restore Germany's good name, paying war reparations and joining international organizations of nations. Thanks to US aid from the Marshall Plan, West Germany was rebuilt, democracy was established, and its "economic miracle" quickly exceeded pre-WWII levels. Adenauer was succeeded in 1969 by the US-friendly Willy Brandt.

East Germany was ruled with an iron fist by Walter Ulbricht (who had been exiled by the Nazis). In 1953, demonstrations and protests against the government were brutally put down by Soviet—not German—troops. Erich Honecker (having endured a decade of Nazi imprisonment) succeeded Ulbricht as ruler of the East in 1971. Honecker was a kinder, gentler tyrant.

Throughout the 1970s and 1980s, both the US and the Soviet Union used divided Germany as a military base. West Germans debated whether US missiles aimed at the Soviets should be placed in their country. Economically, West Germany just got stronger while East Germany stagnated.

1943 Germany has to fight a two-front war: against tenacious Soviets on the chilly Eastern Front, and against Brits and Yanks advancing north through Italy on the Western Front. Germany's industrial output tries desperately to keep up with the Allies'. The average German suffers through shortages, rationing, and frequent trips to the bomb shelter.

1944 Hitler's no-surrender policy is increasingly unpopular, and he narrowly survives being assassinated by a bomb planted in an office. After the Allies reach France on D-Day, Germany counterattacks with a last-gasp offensive (the Battle of the Bulge) that slows but does not stop the Allies.

1945 Soviet soldiers approach Berlin from the east, and Americans and Brits advance from the west. Adolf Hitler commits suicide, and families lock up their daughters to protect them from rapacious Soviet soldiers. When Germany finally surrenders on May 8, the country is in ruins, occupied by several foreign powers, divided into occupation zones, and viewed by the world as an immoral monster.

In the war's aftermath, many German citizens learn for the first time of the mass killings and atrocities committed by their leaders.

On November 9, 1989, East Germany unexpectedly opened the Berlin Wall. Astonished Germans from both sides climbed the Wall, hugged each other, shared bottles of beer, sang songs, and chiseled off souvenirs. At first, most Germans—West and East—looked forward to free travel and better relations between two distinct nations. But before the month was out, negotiations and elections to reunite the two Germanys had already begun. October 3, 1990, was proclaimed German Unification Day, and Berlin re-assumed its status as German capital in 1991.

Germany Today (1990–present)

Differences between "Ossies" (rude slang for former East Germans) and "Wessies" remain, but they're diminishing as the two economies find equilibrium. Germany remains a major economic and political force in Europe. After a decade of a center-right government (under Chancellor Helmut Kohl), and a decade under the center-left Chancellor Gerhard Schroeder, Germany is at a crossroads. Elections in 2005 left no dominant political party, and the government is currently led by a loose coalition headed by a conservative Christian Democrat, Chancellor Angela Merkel. Germany is fully integrated into the international community as a

History

Benedict XVI, the German Pope

When Josef Ratzinger became the 265th pope in 2005, he introduced himself as "a simple, humble worker in the vineyard of the Lord." But the man has a complex history, a reputation for intellectual brilliance, a flair for the piano, a penchant for controversy for his unbending devotion to traditional Catholic doctrine...and a Bavarian accent.

Born in 1927 in the small Bavarian town of Marktl am Inn (southeast of Munich), young Josef went to school in nearby Traunstein, studying in the seminary. When Hitler took power, he lived life under Nazi rule as many Germans did—outwardly obeying leaders while inwardly conflicted. Like many Germans, he joined the Hitler Youth, was drafted into the Army, sprayed flak from anti-aircraft guns (guarding a BMW plant), and saw Jews transported to death camps. Near the war's end, he deserted, and subsequently spent a brief time in an American POW camp near Ulm.

After the war, Ratzinger became a priest and a professor of theology, first at Munster, then at the University of Tübingen. Originally a voice of liberal Catholicism, he became increasingly convinced that Church tradition was needed to offset the growing chaos of the world.

In 1977, he was made Archbishop of Munich. Ratzinger became Pope John Paul II's closest advisor and good friend. Every Friday afternoon for two decades, they met for lunch, intellectual sparring, and friendly conversation.

Under John Paul II, Ratzinger served as the Church's "enforcer" of doctrine, earning the nickname "God's Rottweiler." He spoke out against ordaining women, chastised Latin American priests for fomenting class warfare, reassigned bishops who were soft on homosexuality, reaffirmed opposition to birth control, and wrote thoughtful papers challenging the secular world's moral relativism.

The name of "Benedict" recalls both Pope Benedict XV (who healed World War I's divisions) and Europe's patron St. Benedict (c. 480–543), who symbolizes Europe's Christian roots.

member of the European Union—an organization whose chief aim was to avoid future wars with an aggressive Germany by embracing it in the economic web of Europe.

Austrian History

Austria's history marches in step with Germany's, but there are some differences that give Austria its own distinct culture.

c. A.D. 1 The Romans occupy and defend the "crossroads of Europe," where the west–east Danube River crosses the north–south Brenner Pass through the Alps.

c. 800 Charlemagne designates Austria as one boundary of his European empire—the "Eastern Empire," or *Osterreich*.

1273 An Austrian noble from the Hapsburg family (Rudolf I) is elected Holy Roman Emperor, ruling Austria, Germany, and northern Italy. From 1438 until 1806, every emperor but one is a Hapsburg. The Hapsburgs arrange strategic marriages for their children with other prominent royalty around Europe, gaining power through international connections.

1493 Maximilian I is crowned emperor. His marriage to Mary of Burgundy weds two kingdoms together, and their grandson, Charles V, inherits a vast empire.

1519 Charles V (r. 1519–1556) is the most powerful man in Europe, ruling Austria, Germany, the Low Countries, parts of Italy, and Spain (with its New World possessions). Charles is responsible for trying to solve the problems of all those lands, including battling Ottomans in Vienna and Lutherans in Germany. While many lands north of the Danube turn Protestant, Austria remains Catholic.

1522 Charles V gives Austria (and the Ottoman problem) to his little brother, Ferdinand, who, four years later, marries into the Bohemian and Hungarian crowns.

1529 Ottoman invaders from today's Turkey besiege Vienna, beginning almost two centuries of battles between Austria and the Ottoman Empire. In the course of the wars, Austria gains possession of Hungary and much of Eastern Europe.

1556 Charles V retires from the throne to enter a monastery, leaving his kingdom to his son (King Philip II of Spain), and the crown of Holy Roman Emperor to his brother, Ferdinand I of Austria. From now on, Austria's rulers would concentrate on ruling their eastern empire, which includes part or all of present-day Austria, Hungary, the Czech Republic, Slovakia, Romania, Slovenia, Croatia, Bosnia-Herzegovina, Serbia, northern Italy (Venice), and, later, parts of Poland.

1648 The Thirty Years' War ends, leaving the "Holy Roman Empire" an empire in name only; its figurehead emperor oversees a scattered group of

German-speaking people, mainly in Austria and Germany.

1683 Almost 200,000 Muslims from Ottoman Turkey surround the city of Vienna once again. The Ottomans are driven off, leaving behind bags of coffee that help fuel a beverage craze around Europe. Vienna's first coffee house opens.

1672–1714 Three wars with Louis XIV of France (including the War of the Spanish Succession) drain Austria.

1740 Maria Theresa (r. 1740–1780) has 16 children and still finds time to fight two wars in 25 years, defending her right to rule. Adored by her subjects for her down-to-earth personality, she brings Austria international prestige by marrying her daughters to Europe's royalty.

1781 Maria Theresa's son Josef II, who frees the serfs and takes piano lessons from Mozart, rules Austria as an "enlightened despot." Vienna becomes the world capital of symphonic music, home to Haydn (1732–1809), Mozart (1756–1791), and Beethoven (1770–1827).

1792 When Marie-Antoinette is imprisoned and (later) beheaded by revolutionaries in Paris, her nephew, Austria's Emperor Franz II, seeks revenge, beginning two decades of wars between revolutionary France and monarchist Austria.

1805 Napoleon defeats Austria at Austerlitz, his greatest triumph over the forces of monarchy. Napoleon forces Holy Roman Emperor Franz II to hand over the imperial crown (1806), ending a thousand years of empire, and he even marries Franz II's daughter, Marie-Louise.

1814–1815 After Napoleon is defeated once and for all, an Austrian, Chancellor Metternich, heads the Congress of Vienna—reinstalling kings and nobles recently deposed by Napoleon.

1848 Emperor Franz Josef (Emperor of Austria, not of the Holy Roman Empire) rules for the next 68 years, maintaining white-gloved tradition while overseeing great change—Austria's decline as an empire and entrance into the modern industrial world.

1849 Almost 100,000 Viennese attend the funeral of violinist Johann Strauss, responsible for the dance craze called the waltz. His son, Johann Strauss, Jr. (1825–1899), takes the baton of the Strauss Orchestra and waltzes on, writing "The Blue Danube."

1866 Prussia provokes war and defeats Austria, effectively freezing Austria out of any involvement in a modern German nation.

1867 To better suppress the huge Slavic population in its sprawling empire, and facing a low-morale moment after the war with Prussia, Austria gives partial control over its territories to Hungary. This creates the "Dual Monarchy" of the Austro-Hungarian Empire.

1914 Austria fires the opening shots of World War I to avenge the assassination of their heir to the throne, Archduke Franz Ferdinand.

1919 After its defeat in World War I, the Austro-Hungarian Empire is divided into separate democratic nations, with Austria assigned the small, landlocked borders that it has today.

1932 Mirroring events in Germany, a totalitarian government (of Engelbert Dollfuss) replaces a weak democracy floundering in economic depression.

1938 Nazi Germany—using the threat of force and riding a surge of Germanic nationalism—annexes Austria in the *Anschluss,* and leads it into World War II.

1945 Like Germany, a defeated Austria is divided by the victors into occupied zones, but Austria's occupation is short-lived.

1955 Modern Austria is born as a neutral nation, with the blessing of the international community.

1995 Austria joins the European Union.

2000 The European Union places sanctions on Austria (lifted a few months later) when the far-right Freedom Party—campaigning under the slogan *Überfremdung* ("Too many foreigners")—gains seats in Austria's parliament.

2002 The Freedom Party does badly in elections.

2004 Heinz Fischer, a center-left career politician, is elected president. Arnold Schwarzenegger, the Austrian-born "governor" of California, is criticized by Austrians for his historically questionable comments calling Austria "socialist." Still, "Ah-nolt" remains popular in his native land, a symbol of the small-town boy who made good.

2008 You arrive in Austria and make your own history.

APPENDIX

CONTENTS

RESOURCES

Tourist Information Offices

In the US

The German and Austrian national tourist offices in the US offer a wealth of information. Before your trip, get the free general-information packet and request any specifics you want (such as regional and city maps and festival schedules).

German National Tourist Office: They have maps, Rhine schedules, and information on castles, biking, genealogy, cities, and regions (tel. 800-651-7010, www.cometogermany.com).

Austrian Tourist Office: Ask for their "Austria Kit" with a map, and get information on cities, hiking, the wine country, and more (tel. 212/944-6880, www.austria.info).

In Germany and Austria

The tourist information office (abbreviated TI in this book) is your best first stop in any new town or city. Try to arrive, or at least telephone, before it closes. Throughout Germany and Austria, you'll find TIs are usually well-organized and have English-speaking staff.

As national budgets tighten, many TIs have been privatized. This means they become sales agents for big tours and hotels, and their "information" becomes unavoidably colored. While TIs are eager to book you a room, you should use their room-finding service only as a last resort. TIs can as easily book you a bad room as a good one—they are not allowed to promote one place over another. Go direct, using the listings in this book.

Resources from Rick Steves

Guidebooks and Online Updates

This book is updated every year in person. The telephone numbers and hours of sights listed in this book are accurate as of mid-2007—but even with annual updates, things change. For the very latest, visit www.ricksteves.com/update. Also at my website, you'll find a valuable list of reports and experiences—good and bad—from fellow travelers (www.ricksteves.com/feedback).

This book is one of more than 30 titles in my series on

European travel, which includes country guidebooks, city and regional guidebooks, and my budget-travel skills handbook, *Rick Steves' Europe Through the Back Door.* My phrase books—for German, French, Italian, Spanish, and Portuguese—are practical and budget-oriented. My other books are *Europe 101* (a crash course on art and history, newly expanded and in full color), *European Christmas* (on traditional and modern-day celebrations, including Germany's and Austria's), and *Postcards from Europe* (a fun memoir of my travels over 25 years). For a complete list of my books, see the inside of the last page of this book.

Public Television and Radio Shows

My TV series, *Rick Steves' Europe,* covers European destinations in 70 shows, with four episodes on Germany and three on Austria. My weekly public radio show, *Travel with Rick Steves,* features interviews with travel experts from around the world, including several hours on Germanic culture. All the TV scripts and radio shows (which are easy and free to download to an MP3 player) are at www.ricksteves.com.

Begin Your Trip at www.ricksteves.com

At our travel website, you'll find a wealth of free information on European destinations, including fresh monthly news and helpful tips from thousands of fellow travelers.

Our **online Travel Store** offers travel bags and accessories specially designed by Rick Steves to help you travel smarter and lighter. These include Rick's popular carry-on bags (wheeled and rucksack versions), money belts, totes, toiletries kits, adapters, other accessories, and a wide selection of guidebooks, planning maps, and DVDs.

Choosing the right **railpass** for your trip—amidst hundreds of options—can drive you nutty. We'll help you choose the best pass for your needs, plus give you a bunch of free extras.

Rick Steves' Europe Through the Back Door travel company offers **tours** with more than two dozen itineraries and 450 departures reaching the best destinations in this book... and beyond. We offer a 16-day tour of Germany, Austria, and Switzerland. You'll enjoy great guides, a fun bunch of travel partners (with small groups of generally about 25), and plenty of room to spread out in a big, comfy bus. You'll find European adventures to fit every vacation length. For all the details, and to get our Tour Catalog and a free Rick Steves Tour Experience DVD (filmed on location during an actual tour), visit www.ricksteves.com or call the Tour Department at 425/608-4217.

Free Audiotours

If your travels take you beyond Germany and Austria to France or Italy, take advantage of the free, self-guided audiotours we offer of the major sights in Paris, Florence, Rome, and Venice. The audiotours, produced by Rick Steves and Gene Openshaw (the co-author of seven books in the Rick Steves series) are available through iTunes and at www.ricksteves.com (Italy tours available after January 2008). Simply download them onto your computer and transfer

them to your iPod or MP3 player. (Remember to bring a Y-jack and extra set of ear buds for your travel partner.)

Maps

The black-and-white maps in this book, drawn by Dave Hoerlein, are concise and simple. Dave, who is well-traveled in Germany and Austria, has designed the maps to help you locate recommended places and get to the tourist offices, where you can pick up a more in-depth map (usually free) of the city or region. Better maps are sold at newsstands—take a look before you buy to be sure the map has the level of detail you want.

European bookstores, especially in touristy areas, have good selections of maps. For drivers, I'd recommend a 1:200,000- or 1:300,000-scale map for each country. Train travelers usually manage fine with the freebies they get with the train pass and from the local tourist offices.

Other Guidebooks

Especially if you'll be traveling beyond my recommended destinations, you may want some supplemental information. When you consider the improvements they'll make in your $3,000 vacation, $30 for extra maps and books is money well spent. Especially for several people traveling by car, the weight and expense are negligible. One good tip can save the price of an extra guidebook. Note that none of the following guidebooks are updated annually; check the copyright date before you buy.

Lonely Planet's guides to Germany and Austria are thorough, well-researched, and packed with good maps and hotel recommendations for low- to moderate-budget travelers. The similar Rough Guides are written by insightful British researchers.

Students and vagabonds like the highly opinionated Let's Go series, which is updated by Harvard students. Let's Go is best for backpackers who have railpasses, stay in hostels, and are interested in the youth and nightlife scene.

The popular, skinny, green Michelin Guides are excellent, especially if you're driving. Michelin Guides are known for their city and sightseeing maps, dry but concise and helpful information on all major sights, and good cultural and historical background. English editions are sold in Europe at gas stations and tourist shops.

Recommended Books and Movies

To get the feel of Germany and Austria past and present, consider these books and films:

Non-Fiction

Germany: A New History (Schulze) is a one-volume compendium covering 2,000 years. Albert Speer's *Inside the Third Reich*, based on 1,200 manuscript pages, is an authoritative account of 1933 through 1945. *Stasiland: True Stories from Behind the Berlin Wall*

(Funder) relays the secrets of the Stasi, the East German Ministry for State Security.

Germany and the Germans (Ardagh) is interesting if you'd like to know more about the 1990s reunification. For more on modern Germany, including cultural insights, pick up *Culture Shock! Germany* (Lord), *When in Germany, Do as the Germans Do* (Flippo), and *Of German Ways* (Rippley). Gourmets may want to grab *The Marling Menu-Master for Germany*.

Memoirs: Günter Grass stirred up controversy with his 2007 memoir, *Peeling the Onion*, which revealed he was a soldier in the dreaded Waffen-SS. *The Story of the Trapp Family Singers*, written by Maria von Trapp, tells the true story behind the musical phenomenon. *A Time of Gifts* (Fermor) tells of the author's walking tour of Europe—and Germany—in the 1930s. In *A Tramp Abroad*, Mark Twain recounts his amusing European adventures, including some in Germany.

Fiction

Classics of German fiction include the works of Thomas Mann (*Buddenbrooks* and *The Magic Mountain*) and Hermann Hesse (*Narcissus and Goldmund* and *Siddhartha*).

Some of the best modern German literature has wrestled with the country's warmongering past. *All Quiet on the Western Front*, a classroom classic by Erich Maria Remarque, speaks with eloquence about World War I. First published before World War II, *Address Unknown* (Kathrine Kressman Taylor) is a novella with a cautionary tone about what would follow. In *The Tin Drum*, Günter Grass broke the post-WWII silence, creating a landmark work of literature in the process. *The Silent Angel* is a complex love story set after the war (by Nobel Prize winner Heinrich Böll).

A book of science fiction and time travel, *1632* (Flint) sends West Virginians back to 17th-century Germany. *The Good German* (Kanon), set during the postwar years, is part thriller, part historical fiction. Mystery fans should also consider *Airs Above the Ground* (Stewart), with the Austrian Alps as the backdrop, and *A Death in Vienna* (Tallis), which involves a cover-up by the Catholic Church. *Berlin Noir* (Kerr) is filled with stories of secrets and crime.

For a recently written read, consider the following books, published since the mid-1990s. Esther Freud, the daughter of artist Lucien Freud, set *Summer at Gaglow* during the Great War. *Stones from the River*, the story of a dwarf in Nazi Germany, and *Floating in My Mother's Palm*, which takes place in a small town on the Rhine, have brought Ursula Hegi accolades. Told by a sympathetic narrator, *The Reader* (Schlink) challenges readers to think, "What if my loved ones had been Nazis?" *Saints and Villains* (Giardina) is the fictionalized account of Dietrich Bonhoeffer, a Protestant theologian who protested against Hitler's rise.

Films

Leni Riefenstahl's *Triumph of the Will* (1935) is infamous Nazi propaganda turned film classic. Orson Welles infuses *The Third Man* (1949, actually shot in a bombed-out and Soviet-occupied Vienna) with noir foreboding. *The Tin Drum* (1979) is based on Günter Grass' seminal novel (see previous page).

Other meditations on the war years—films filled with allegory and metaphor about the Nazis' rise to power—include *Mephisto* (1981) and Rainer Werner Fassbinder's The *Marriage of Maria Braun* (1979). *Downfall* (2004) tells of the Führer's final days. *Schindler's List* (1993)—about a factory owner's inspirational efforts to save his Jewish employees from deportation to concentration camps—won Steven Spielberg the Best Picture and Best Director Oscars.

Shoah (1985) is a 9.5-hour Holocaust documentary that includes no wartime footage, only interviews with those who lived through it. The well-respected *Das Boot* (1981) has a strong pacifist message, as do the films about the students who defied Hitler—and were ultimately sentenced to die: *The White Rose* (1982) and the beautiful, devastating *Sophie Scholl: The Final Days* (2005).

But German and Austrian film is not comprised of only dramatic, war-themed movies. The beloved musical *The Sound of Music* (1965) helped turn Julie Andrews into a star; *Cabaret* (1972, showing the crazy Berlin scene in the late 1920s) did the same for Liza Minnelli. Set in Berlin, *Wings of Desire* (1987) is Wim Wenders' best film, showing an angel who falls in love and falls to earth. *Amadeus* (1984) made Mozart into a flesh-and-blood man (who giggles), as did *Immortal Beloved* (1994) for Beethoven. For a list of films made about Sisi (a.k.a. Austria's Empress Elisabeth, a 19th-century Princess Diana), see page 480.

In *Before Sunrise* (1995), Ethan Hawke sees the sights, talks, romances, and talks some more with Julie Delpy in Vienna. *Run Lola Run* (1998) was an art-house phenomenon, combining action, love, and mobsters. Jewish refugees settle in 1930s Kenya in *Nowhere in Africa* (2001). *Good Bye, Lenin!* (2003) is a funny, poignant look at a son's struggle to re-create long-gone Eastern Europe for his mother, while the former GDR's harsh secrets are exposed in *The Lives of Others* (2006).

MONEY MATTERS

Damage Control for Lost Cards

If you lose your credit, debit, or ATM card, you can stop people from using it by reporting the loss immediately to the respective global customer-assistance centers. Call these 24-hour US numbers collect: Visa (410/581-9994), MasterCard (636/722-7111), and American Express (623/492-8427).

At a minimum, you'll need to know the name of the financial institution that issued you the card, along with the type of card (classic, platinum, or whatever). Providing the following information will allow for a quicker cancellation of your missing card: full card number, whether you are the primary or secondary cardholder, the cardholder's name exactly as printed on the card, billing address, home phone number, circumstances of the loss or theft, and identification verification (your birth date, your mother's maiden name, or your Social Security number—memorize this, don't carry a copy). If you are the secondary cardholder, you'll also need to provide the primary cardholder's identification-verification details. You can generally receive a temporary card within two or three business days in Europe.

If you promptly report your card lost or stolen, you typically won't be responsible for any unauthorized transactions on your account, although many banks charge a liability fee of $50.

Tipping

Tipping in Germany and Austria isn't as automatic and generous as it is in the US, but for special service, tips are appreciated, if not expected. As in the US, the proper amount depends on your resources, tipping philosophy, and the circumstance, but some general guidelines apply.

Restaurants: Tipping is an issue only at restaurants that have table service. If you order your food at a counter, don't tip.

At German and Austrian restaurants that have a wait staff, service is included, although it's common to round up the bill after a good meal (usually 5–10 percent; so, for an €18.50 meal, pay €20). Give the tip directly to your server. Rather than leaving coins, Germans and Austrians usually pay with paper, saying how much they'd like the bill to be (for example, for an €8.10 meal, give a €20 bill and say *"Neun Euro"*—"Nine euros"—to get €11 change).

Taxis: To tip the cabbie, round up. For a typical ride, round up about five to ten percent (to pay a €4.50 fare, give €5; or for a €28 fare, give €30). If the cabbie hauls your bags and zips you to the airport to help you catch your flight, you might want to toss in a little more. But if you feel like you're being driven in circles or otherwise ripped off, skip the tip.

Special Services: It's thoughtful to tip a euro to someone who shows you a special sight and who is paid in no other way. Tour guides at public sites often hold out their hands for tips after they give their spiel; if I've already paid for the tour, I don't tip extra, though some tourists do give a euro, particularly for a job well done. I don't tip at hotels, but if you do, give the porter about a euro for carrying bags and leave a couple of euros in your room at the end of your stay for the maid if the room was kept clean. In general, if someone in the service industry does a super job for you, a tip of a euro or two is appropriate...but not required.

When in doubt, ask. If you're not sure whether (or how much) to tip for a service, ask your hotelier or the TI; they'll fill you in on how it's done on their turf.

Getting a VAT Refund

As is the case throughout the European Union, wrapped into the purchase price of your souvenirs is a Value Added Tax (VAT) of 19 percent in Germany and 20 percent in Austria. If you make a purchase of more than a certain amount (€25 in Germany, €75.01 in Austria) at a store that participates in the VAT-refund scheme, you're entitled to get most of that tax back. Getting your refund is usually straightforward and, if you buy a substantial amount of souvenirs, well worth the hassle. If you're lucky, the merchant will subtract the tax when you make your purchase. (This is more likely to occur if the store ships the goods to your home.) Otherwise, you'll need to:

Get the paperwork. Have the merchant completely fill out the necessary refund document, called a "Tax-Free Shopping Cheque." You'll have to present your passport at the store.

Get your stamp at the border or airport. Process your cheque(s) at your last stop in the EU (e.g., at the airport) with the customs agent who deals with VAT refunds. It's best to keep your purchases in your carry-on for viewing, but if they're too large or dangerous (such as knives) to carry on, track down the proper customs agent to inspect them before you check your bag. You're not supposed to use your purchased goods before you leave. If you show up at customs wearing your new lederhosen, officials might look the other way—or deny you a refund.

Collect your refund. You'll need to return your stamped document to the retailer or its representative. Many merchants work with a service, such as Global Refund (www.globalrefund.com) or Premier Tax Free (www.premiertaxfree.com), which have offices at major airports, ports, or border crossings. These services, which extract a 4 percent fee, can refund your money immediately in your currency of choice or credit your card (within two billing cycles). If the retailer handles VAT refunds directly, it's up to you to contact the merchant for your refund. You can mail the documents from home, or quicker, from your point of departure (using a stamped, addressed envelope you've prepared or one that's been provided by the merchant)—and then wait. It could take months.

Customs for American Shoppers

You are allowed to take home $800 worth of items per person duty-free, once every 30 days. The next $1,000 is taxed at a flat 3 percent. After that, you pay the individual item's duty rate. You can also bring in duty-free a liter of alcohol (slightly more than a standard-size bottle of wine; you must be at least 21), 200 cigarettes, and up to 100 non-Cuban cigars. Food in cans or sealed jars is permissible, as long as no meat is included. Some, but not all, types of cheese are allowed. Fresh fruits and vegetables are prohibited. Note that you'll need to carefully pack any bottles of wine and other liquid-containing items in your checked luggage, due to the three-ounce limit on liquids in carry-on baggage. To check customs rules and duty rates before you go, visit www.cbp .gov, and click on "Travel," then "Know Before You Go."

TELEPHONES, EMAIL, AND MAIL

Telephones

Smart travelers learn the phone system and use it daily to reserve or reconfirm rooms, get tourist information, reserve restaurants, confirm tour times, or phone home.

Types of Phones

You'll encounter various kinds of phones on your trip:

Card-operated phones—where you insert a locally bought phone card into a public pay phone—are common in Europe.

Coin-operated phones, the original kind of pay phone (but now increasingly rare), require you to have enough change to complete your call.

Hotel room phones are sometimes cheap for local calls (confirm at the front desk first), but can be a rip-off for long-distance calls unless you use an international phone card (described below). But incoming calls are free, making this a cheap way for friends and family to stay in touch, provided they have a good long-distance plan for calls to Europe.

American mobile phones work in Europe if they're GSM-enabled, tri-band or quad-band, and on a calling plan that includes international calls. They're convenient, but pricey. For example, with a T-Mobile phone, you'll pay $1 per minute for calls.

European mobile phones run about $75 (for the most basic models) and come without contracts. These phones are loaded with prepaid calling time that you can recharge as you use up the minutes. As long as you're not "roaming" outside the phone's home country, incoming calls are free. If you're traveling to multiple countries within Europe, make sure the phone is electronically

Hurdling the Language Barrier

Germans and Austrians speak German (though each region has its own distinct dialect). Most young or well-educated Germans and Austrians—especially those in larger towns and the tourist trade—speak at least some English. Still, you'll get more smiles by using the German pleasantries. In smaller, non-touristy towns, the language barrier is higher. (See the "German Survival Phrases" on page 691.)

German—like English, Dutch, Swedish, and Norwegian—is a Germanic language, making it easier on most American ears than Romance languages (such as Italian and French). These tips will help you pronounce German words: The letter *w* is always pronounced as "v" (e.g., the word for "wonderful" is *wunderbar,* pronounced VOON-der-bar). In the vowel combinations *ie* and *ei,* you pronounce only the second letter, so *ie* sounds like the letter *e* (as in *hier* and *Bier,* the German words for "here" and "beer"), while *ei* sounds like the letter *i* (as in *nein* and *Stein,* the German words for "no" and "stone"). The vowel combination *eu* is pronounced "oy" (as in *treu* and *Deutsch,* the German words for "true" and "German"). To pronounce a vowel with an umlaut *(ä, ö, ü),* purse your lips when you say it. (In written German, these can be depicted as the vowel followed by an *e*—*ae, oe,* and *ue,* respectively.) The letter *Eszett (ß)* represents *ss.* Written German always capitalizes all nouns.

Give it your best shot. The locals will appreciate your efforts.

"unlocked," so that you can swap out its SIM card (a fingernail-sized chip that holds the phone's information) for a new one in other countries. For more information on mobile phones, see www.ricksteves.com/plan/tips /mobilephones.htm.

Using Phone Cards

Get a phone card for your calls. Prepaid phone cards come in two types: international and insertable (both described next).

Prepaid **international phone cards** are the cheapest way to make international calls from Europe (they also work for domestic calls). The cards are sold at small newsstand kiosks and hole-in-the-wall long-distance shops. Some international phone cards work in multiple countries—if traveling to both Germany and Austria, try to buy a card that will work in both places.

You can use international phone cards from any type of phone, even your hotel-room phone (if the phone is set on "pulse," switch it to "tone"), avoiding pricey hotel rates; make sure, however, that your hotel isn't overcharging you to dial the access number. These cards are such a good deal that the irritated German phone company is making them less cost-effective when you use them at pay phones. From a German pay phone, you'll get far fewer minutes for your money (for example, 10 min instead of 100 on a €5 card). No such pay-phone problem exists in Austria (at least, not yet).

There are many different brands of cards, so ask the clerk which one has the best rates to the States. Some cards are rechargeable; you can call up the number on the card, give your credit-card number, and buy more time. Because cards are occasionally duds, avoid the high denominations.

To use a card, scratch off the back to reveal your code. After you dial the access phone number, the message tells you to enter your code and then dial the phone number you want to call. A voice may announce how much is left in your account before you dial. Usually you can select English, but if the prompts are in German, experiment: Dial your code, followed by the pound sign (#), then the number, then pound again, and so on, until it works.

To call the US, see "Dialing Internationally," page 673. To make calls within Germany and Austria, dial the area code plus the local number; when using an international phone card, the area code must be dialed even if you're calling across the street.

To make numerous, successive calls with an international phone card without having to redial the long access number each time, press the keys (see instructions on card) that allow you to launch directly into your next call. Remember that you don't need the actual card to use a card account, so it's sharable. You can write down the access number and PIN (Personal Identification Number) in your notebook and share it with friends. Give the number of a still lively card to another traveler if you're leaving the country.

Insertable phone cards are a convenient way to pay for calls from public pay phones. Buy these cards at TIs, tobacco shops, post offices, and train stations. The price of the call (local or international) is automatically deducted while you talk. They are sold in several denominations starting at about €5. Calling the US with one of these phone cards is reasonable (about 2–3 min per euro), but more expensive than using an international phone card. Each European country has its own insertable phone card—so your German card won't work in an Austrian phone. Be aware that with the prevalence of mobile phones, public phones (especially the type that accepts phone cards) are getting harder to find, particularly in Austria.

European Calling Chart

Just smile and dial, using this key:
AC = Area Code, LN = Local Number.

European Country	Calling long distance within ...	Calling from the US or Canada to ...	Calling from a European country to ...
Austria	AC + LN	011 + 43 + AC (without the initial zero) + LN	00 + 43 + AC (without the initial zero) + LN
Belgium	LN	011 + 32 + LN (without initial zero)	00 + 32 + LN (without initial zero)
Bosnia-Herzegovina	AC + LN	011 + 387 + AC (without initial zero) + LN	00 + 387 + AC (without initial zero) + LN
Britain	AC + LN	011 + 44 + AC (without initial zero) + LN	00 + 44 + AC (without initial zero) + LN
Croatia	AC + LN	011 + 385 + AC (without initial zero) + LN	00 + 385 + AC (without initial zero) + LN
Czech Republic	LN	011 + 420 + LN	00 + 420 + LN
Denmark	LN	011 + 45 + LN	00 + 45 + LN
Estonia	LN	011 + 372 + LN	00 + 372 + LN
Finland	AC + LN	011 + 358 + AC (without initial zero) + LN	999 + 358 + AC (without initial zero) + LN
France	LN	011 + 33 + LN (without initial zero)	00 + 33 + LN (without initial zero)
Germany	AC + LN	011 + 49 + AC (without initial zero) + LN	00 + 49 + AC (without initial zero) + LN
Greece	LN	011 + 30 + LN	00 + 30 + LN
Hungary	06 + AC + LN	011 + 36 + AC + LN	00 + 36 + AC + LN
Ireland	AC + LN	011 + 353 + AC (without initial zero) + LN	00 + 353 + AC (without initial zero) + LN

European Country	Calling long distance within ...	Calling from the US or Canada to ...	Calling from a European country to ...
Italy	LN	011 + 39 + LN	00 + 39 + LN
Montenegro	AC + LN	011 + 382 + AC (without initial zero) + LN	00 + 382 + AC (without initial zero) + LN
Netherlands	AC + LN	011 + 31 + AC (without initial zero) + LN	00 + 31 + AC (without initial zero) + LN
Norway	LN	011 + 47 + LN	00 + 47 + LN
Poland	LN	011 + 48 + LN (without initial zero)	00 + 48 + LN (without initial zero)
Portugal	LN	011 + 351 + LN	00 + 351 + LN
Slovakia	AC + LN	011 + 421 + AC (without initial zero) + LN	00 + 421 + AC (without initial zero) + LN
Slovenia	AC + LN	011 + 386 + AC (without initial zero) + LN	00 + 386 + AC (without initial zero) + LN
Spain	LN	011 + 34 + LN	00 + 34 + LN
Sweden	AC + LN	011 + 46 + AC (without initial zero) + LN	00 + 46 + AC (without initial zero) + LN
Switzerland	LN	011 + 41 + LN (without initial zero)	00 + 41 + LN (without initial zero)
Turkey	AC (if no initial zero is included, add one) + LN	011 + 90 + AC (without initial zero) + LN	00 + 90 + AC (without initial zero) + LN

- The instructions above apply whether you're calling a land line or mobile phone.
- The international access codes (the first numbers you dial when making an international call) are 011 if you're calling from the US or Canada, or 00 if you're calling from virtually anywhere in Europe (except Finland, where it's 999).
- To call the US or Canada from Europe, dial 00, then 1 (the country code for the US and Canada), then the area code and number. In short, 00 + 1 + AC + LN = Hi, Mom!

Using Hotel Room Phones, VoIP, or US Calling Cards

The phone in your **hotel room** is convenient...but expensive. While incoming calls (made by folks back home) can be the cheapest way to keep in touch, charges for *outgoing* calls can be a very unpleasant surprise. Make sure you understand all the charges and fees associated with outgoing calls before you pick up that receiver. I find it handy for making local calls.

Dialing direct from your hotel room—without using an international phone card (described on page 668)—is usually quite pricey for international calls. Before you dial, get a clear explanation from the hotel staff of the charges, even for local and (supposedly) toll-free calls.

If your family has an inexpensive way to call Europe, either through a long-distance plan or prepaid calling card, have them call you in your hotel room. Give them a list of your hotels' phone numbers before you go. Then, as you travel, send them an email or make a quick pay-phone call to set up a time for them to give you a ring.

If you're traveling with a laptop, consider trying **VoIP (Voice over Internet Protocol).** With VoIP, two computers act as the phones, allowing for a free Internet-based call. The major providers are Skype (www.skype.com) and Google Talk (www.google.com/talk).

US Calling Cards (such as the ones offered by AT&T, MCI, or Sprint) are the worst option. You'll nearly always save a lot of money by paying with a phone card (see page 668).

How to Dial

Calling from the US to Europe, or vice versa, is simple—once you break the code. The European calling chart on page 670 will walk you through it.

Dialing Domestic Calls

Germany and Austria, like much of the US, use an area-code dialing system. If you're dialing within an area code, you just dial the local number to be connected; but if you're calling outside your area code, you have to dial both the area code (which starts with a 0) and the local number. For example, Munich's area code is 089 and the number of one of my recommended Munich hotels is 515-530. To call the hotel within Munich, you'd dial 515-530. To call it from Frankfurt, you'd dial 089/515-530.

Don't be surprised if local phone numbers in Germany and Austria have different numbers of digits within the same city or even the same hotel (for example, a hotel can have a 6-digit phone number and an 8-digit fax number).

Dialing Internationally

If you want to make an international call, follow these three steps:

1. Dial the international access code (00 if you're calling from Europe, 011 from the US or Canada).

2. Dial the country code of the country you're calling (49 for Germany, 43 for Austria, or 1 for the US or Canada).

3. Dial the area code (without its initial 0) and the local number.

For example, to call the recommended Munich hotel from the US, dial 011 (the US international access code), 49 (Germany's country code), 89 (Munich's area code without the initial 0), and 515-530.

To call my office in Edmonds, Washington, from Germany, I dial 00 (Europe's international access code), 1 (the US country code), 425 (Edmonds' area code), and 771-8303.

Useful Phone Numbers

Directory Assistance

Austria: National—tel. 16. International—tel. 08. Train info—tel. 051-717 (to get an operator, dial 2, then 2); ask for an English speaker.

Germany: National—tel. 11833. International—tel. 11834. Train info—tel. 11861 (€0.60/min); ask for an English speaker.

German Tourist Offices: Dial the local code, then 19433.

US Embassies

Austria (in Vienna): Boltzmanngasse 16, tel. 01/313-390, embassy @usembassy.at; consular services at Parkring 12, daily 8:00–11:30, tel. 01/313-397-535, www.usembassy.at, consulatevienna@state .gov

Germany (in Berlin): Neustädtische Kirchstrasse 4–5, tel. 030/83050; consular services at Clayallee 170, Mon–Fri 8:30–12:00, closed Sat–Sun, tel. 030/832-9233—Mon–Fri 14:00–16:00 only, www.usembassy.de, consberlin@state.gov

Email and Mail

Email: Many travelers set up a free email account with Yahoo, Microsoft (Hotmail), or Google (Gmail). Internet cafés are easy to find in big cities. Most of the towns where I've listed accommodations in this book also have Internet cafés. Many libraries offer free access, but they also tend to have limited opening hours, restrict your online time to 30 minutes, and may require reservations. Look for the places listed in this book, or ask the local TI, computer store, or your hotelier. Some hotels have a dedicated computer for guests' email needs. Small places are accustomed to letting clients (who've asked politely) sit at their desk for a few minutes just to check their email.

Wireless Internet access (Wi-Fi)—often called WLAN (VAY-lawn) in German—is available to laptop users for a minimal fee at Internet cafés, some post offices, and an increasing number of hotels.

Mail: Get stamps at the neighborhood post office, newsstands within fancy hotels, and some mini-marts and card shops. You can avoid standing in line at the post office by using the handy yellow stamp *(Briefmarke)* machines found just outside the building. Postcard stamps to the US or Canada cost €1 from Germany and €1.25 from Austria. Warning: These machines give change only in stamps, not in coins.

To arrange for mail delivery, reserve a few hotels along your route in advance and give their addresses to friends. Allow 10 days for a letter to arrive. Phoning and emailing are so easy that I've dispensed with mail stops altogether.

TRANSPORTATION

By Car or Train?

The train is best for single travelers, those who'll be spending more time in big cities, and those who don't want to drive in Europe. While a car gives you the ultimate in mobility and freedom, enables you to search for hotels more easily, and carries your bags for you, the train zips you effortlessly from city to city, usually dropping you in the center and near the tourist office. Cars are great in the countryside but a worthless headache in cities such as Munich, Berlin, Frankfurt, Salzburg, and Vienna.

Trains

Trains are generally slick, speedy, and punctual, with synchronized connections. They cover cities well, but some frustrating schedules make a few out-of-the-way recommendations (such as Bavaria's Wieskirche or the concentration camp at Mauthausen) not worth the time and trouble for the less determined. A new law makes it illegal to smoke on Germany's trains, buses, and taxis.

Schedules

For timetables, visit http://bahn.hafas.de/bin/query.exe/en (German Rail, but also good for much of Europe, including Austria) or www.oebb.at (Austrian Rail). At most train stations, attendants will print out a step-by-step itinerary for you, free of charge. You can also produce an itinerary yourself by using the computerized red-and-blue trackside machines marked *Fahrkarten*. The touch-screen display gives you an English option; choose

Public Transportation

"Timetable Information," indicate your point of departure and destination, and then hit "Print" for a personalized schedule, including transfers and track numbers. You can also buy tickets from these machines—cash only, since they don't accept non-European bankcards (for more information, see "Tickets," page 678).

Each country has train information numbers you can dial from anywhere in the country: for Germany—tel. 11861 (€0.60/min); for Austria—tel. 051-717 (to get an operator, dial 2, then 2). Ask for an English speaker.

Railpasses

Eurail's Germany and Austria–specific pass will probably be the

Railpasses

Prices listed are for 2007 and are subject to change. For the latest prices, details, train schedules, and easy online ordering, see my comprehensive *Guide to Eurail Passes* at www.ricksteves.com/rail. See Web site for more passes, including Germany-Benelux, Germany-Denmark, France-Germany, Germany-Poland, Germany-Czech, and European East passes.

"Saver" prices are per person for two or more people traveling together. "Youth" means under age 26. All passes for Germany cover KD Line boats on the Rhine and Mosel, 60% off Romantic Road and Castle bus ride.

GERMAN PASS

	Indiv. 1st Cl.	Indiv. 2nd Cl.	Twin 1st Cl.	Twin 2nd Cl.	Youth 2nd Cl.
4 days in 1 month	$316	$244	$245	$180	$201
Extra rail days (max 6)	44	29	29	22	15

Twin prices are per person for two traveling together. The fare for children 6–11 is half the individual fare. Kids under age 6 travel free. Five and ten-day versions available at some stations in Germany.

AUSTRIAN PASS

	1st Class	2nd Class
3 out of 15 days	$208	$142
Extra rail days (max 5)	28	26

The fare for children 6–11 is half the full fare. Kids under age 6 travel free.

GERMANY–AUSTRIA PASS

	Indiv. 1st Cl.	Indiv. 2nd Cl.	Saver 1st Cl.	Saver 2nd Cl.	Youth 2nd Cl.
5 days in 2 months	$378	$320	$320	$273	$273
6 days in 2 months	417	355	355	304	304
8 days in 2 months	498	422	422	365	365
10 days in 2 months	576	491	491	424	424

The fare for children 4–11 is half the adult individual fare or Saver fare. Kids under age 4 travel free.

SWITZERLAND–AUSTRIA PASS

	Individual 1st Class	Saver 1st Class	Youth 2nd Class
4 days in 2 months	$368	$314	$258
Extra rail days (max 6)	43	37	30

The fare for children 4–11 is half the adult individual fare or Saver fare. Kids under age 4 travel free.

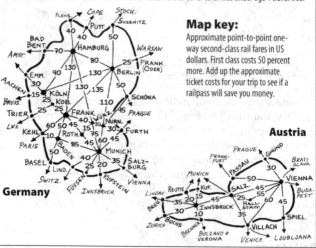

Map key:

Approximate point-to-point one-way second-class rail fares in US dollars. First class costs 50 percent more. Add up the approximate ticket costs for your trip to see if a railpass will save you money.

Germany

Austria

SELECTPASS

This pass covers travel in three adjacent countries. For four- and five-country options, please visit **www.ricksteves.com/rail**.

	Individual 1st Class	Saver 1st Class	Youth 2nd Class
5 days in 2 months	$429	$365	$279
6 days in 2 months	471	402	309
8 days in 2 months	562	478	365
10 days in 2 months	648	550	420

Selectpass diagram key:

A **Selectpass** can be designed to connect a "chain" of any three, four, or five countries in this diagram linked by direct lines. (Examples that qualify: Norway-Sweden-Germany or Germany-Austria-Switzerland.) "Benelux" is considered one country.

GERMANY–SWITZERLAND PASS

	Individual 1st Class	Saver 1st Class	Youth 2nd Class
5 days in 2 months	$401	$342	$281
6 days in 2 months	442	375	311
8 days in 2 months	524	447	368
10 days in 2 months	606	517	425

The fare for children 4–11 is half the adult individual or Saver fare. Kids under age 4 travel free.

GERMANY RAIL & DRIVE PASS

Any 2 rail days and 2 car days in 1 month.

Car Category	1st Class	2nd Class	Extra Car Day
Economy	$214	$177	$45
Compact	230	192	60
Intermediate	239	202	70
Small automatic	256	218	87

Prices are per person, two traveling together. Extra rail day $66 in first class, $47 in second class (max 3).

SELECTPASS RAIL & DRIVE

Any 3 rail days and 2 car days in 2 months within 3 adjoining countries.

Car Category	1st Class	Extra Car Day
Economy	$379	$53
Compact	397	72
Intermediate	407	81
Small Automatic	429	104

Prices are per person, two traveling together. Third and fourth persons sharing car get a 4-day out of 2-month railpass for approx. $326 (kids 4–11 $163). A fourth or fifth country each adds about $45 to these prices.

To order a Rail & Drive pass, call your travel agent or Rail Europe at 800-438-7245. *These passes are not sold by Europe Through the Back Door.*

best-value railpass if you are traveling exclusively in these two countries. If you're traveling in neighboring countries as well, consider the Eurail Selectpass, which gives you up to 15 travel days (within a two-month period) in three, four, or five adjacent countries—you could choose Germany, Austria, and any bordering country (some Eastern European countries—like the Czech Republic or Poland—are not eligible). If you're planning a whirlwind tour of Europe, another possibility is the 18-country Eurailpass. These passes are available in a Saverpass version, which gives a 15 percent discount on railpasses for two or more companions traveling together. Each country also has its own individual train passes that offer good value for trips limited to one country. But patchworking second-class country passes together is complicated and unlikely to save you money. To sort through the options, explore my online Railpass Guide at www.ricksteves.com/rail. You can purchase any of these railpasses from your travel agent or Rick Steves' Europe Through the Back Door.

Eurailers (including Eurail Select and single-country pass-holders) should know what extras are covered by their pass: for example, travel on any German buses marked "DeutscheBahn" or "DB" (run by the train company); travel on city S-Bahn systems (except in Berlin, where only S-Bahn lines between major train stations are covered); covered or discounted boats on the Rhine, Mosel, and Danube rivers; and a  60 percent discount on the Romantic Road bus tour. Flexipass-holders should note that discounted trips don't use up a flexi-day, but fully covered ("free") trips do. The "used" flexipass day can also cover your train travel on that day (but if you're not planning to travel more that day, it makes sense to pay for, say, a short boat ride rather than use up a day of your pass for it).

Note that if you take a night train between Germany and Italy, your railpass must also include Austria (which these trains pass through). This means you can no longer simply buy a separate ticket covering the Austrian segment; rather, you must buy a ticket for the entire route.

Tickets

People of any age buying individual tickets should remember that traveling in second class instead of first class provides the same transportation for 33 percent less. Ticket fares are shown on the map on page 676 and at http://bahn.hafas.de/bin/query.exe/en.

Deals: Look into local specials. In Germany, kids under 14 travel free when named on one of their parent's or grandparent's point-to-point ticket. Off-peak specials in Germany include a wild *Schönes Wochenende* ticket for €32; it gives groups of up to five people unlimited second-class travel on non-express trains all day Saturday or Sunday. *Länder-Tickets* are a similar deal (€27 for up to 5 people after 9:00 on weekdays on local trains within a single region, such as Bavaria). Those staying longer in Germany can get additional discounts for a full year by purchasing one of several BahnCards (starting at €50; see www.bahn.de).

Buying Tickets: Major German stations have a handy *Reisezentrum* (Travel Center) where you can ask questions and buy tickets. You can also buy tickets from machines (marked *Fahrkarten*, which means "tickets") at any train station. The red-and-blue computerized machines at larger stations sell short- and long-distance train tickets, and print schedules for free (see "Schedules," page 674). You can buy a ticket on board from the conductor for a long-distance journey (by paying a small markup), but if you're riding a local (short distance) train, you're expected to board with a valid ticket...or you can get fined.

To avoid being fined, it's helpful to know how to buy a ticket. It's easily done at the larger train stations (see above), but can be a challenge for tourists at the smaller, unstaffed stations like Bacharach's. Here's how to do it: Unstaffed stations have gray machines that sell same-day-only tickets to nearby destinations. To buy a ticket at one of these machines, press the flag button until it gives you a screen in English. Then look for your destination on the long list of towns on the left side of the machine. If your destination isn't on the list (because it's too far away), you can buy the ticket on board (let the conductor know where you boarded and you won't even have to pay the small markup for buying a ticket on the train). If your destination *is* on the list, note the four-digit code for your destination and enter it in the number pad. The machine will automatically issue you a ticket for a one-way *(Einfache)* second-class fare, but you can alter that with the buttons below the keypad (press *Hin- und Rückfahrt* if you want a round-trip ticket, *1./2. Klasse* for first class, and note the column of buttons for children's tickets). Feed the machine cash (it won't take your non-European credit card), then collect your ticket and change. *Gut gemacht!* (Well done!)

Train plus Bike

Hundreds of local train stations rent bikes for about $10 a day, and sometimes have easy "pick up here and drop off there" plans. For more on mixing train and bike travel, ask at stations for information booklets.

Car Rental

To rent a car for use in Germany, you must be at least 21 years old with a valid license; in Austria, the minimum age is 19. Drivers 24 and younger may incur a young-driver surcharge in both countries, and some companies restrict the type of vehicle you can rent if you're between 21 and 30. Car-rental companies in Germany and Austria generally don't have a maximum age limit, but if you are 70 or older, it's smart to confirm when you make your reservation. If you're considered too young or old, look into leasing, which has less-stringent age restrictions (see "Leasing," next page).

Research car rentals before you go. It's cheaper to arrange most car rentals from the US. Call several companies and look online to compare rates, or arrange a rental through your hometown travel agent. Two reputable companies among many are Auto Europe (www.autoeurope.com) and Europe by Car (www.europebycar.com). For the best deal, rent by the week with unlimited mileage (but for long trips, consider leasing).

Expect to pay about $750 per person (based on 2 people sharing the car) for a small economy car for three weeks with unlimited mileage, including gas, parking, and insurance. I normally rent a small, inexpensive model like a Ford Fiesta. For a bigger, roomier, more powerful but inexpensive car, move up to a Ford Focus or VW Polo. Minibuses are a great budget way to go for five to nine people.

If you want an automatic, reserve the car at least a month in advance and specifically request an automatic. You'll pay about 40 percent more to rent a car with an automatic instead of a manual transmission.

When you pick up the car, check it thoroughly and make sure any damage is noted on your rental agreement. Find out how your car's headlights, turn signals, wipers, and gas cap function.

Returning a car at a big-city train station can be tricky; get precise details on the car drop-off location and hours. When you return the car, make sure the agent verifies its condition with you.

If you drop your car off early or keep it longer, you'll be credited or charged at a fair, prorated price. But keep your receipts in case any questions arise about your billing.

Car Insurance Options

When you rent a car, you are liable for a very high deductible, sometimes equal to the entire value of the car. There are various ways you can limit your financial risk in case of an accident. You have three options: buy Collision Damage Waiver (CDW) coverage from the car-rental company, get coverage through your credit card (free, if your card automatically includes zero-deductible coverage), or buy coverage through Travel Guard.

CDW includes a very high deductible (typically $1,000–

1,500). When you pick up the car, you'll be offered the chance to "buy down" the deductible to zero (for $10–30/day; this is often called "super CDW").

If you opt instead for credit-card coverage, there's a catch. You'll technically have to decline all coverage offered by the car-rental company, which means they can place a hold on your card for the full deductible amount. In case of damage, it can be time-consuming to resolve the charges with your credit-card company. Before you decide on this option, quiz your credit-card company about how it works and ask them to explain the worst-case scenario.

Buying CDW insurance (plus "super CDW") is the easier but pricier option. Using the coverage that comes with your credit card saves money, but can involve more hassle.

Finally, you can buy CDW insurance from Travel Guard ($9/day plus a one-time $3 service fee covers you up to $35,000, $250 deductible, tel. 800-826-4919, www.travelguard.com). It's valid throughout Europe, but some car-rental companies refuse to honor it (especially in the Republic of Ireland and in Italy). Oddly, residents of Washington State aren't allowed to buy this coverage.

For more fine print about car-rental insurance, see www .ricksteves.com/cdw.

Leasing

For trips of two and a half weeks or more, leasing (which automatically includes CDW-type insurance with no deductible) is the best way to go. By technically buying and then selling back the car, you save lots of money on tax and insurance. Leasing provides you a new car with unlimited mileage and a 24-hour emergency assistance program. You can lease for as little as 17 days to as long as six months. Car leases must be arranged from the US. A reliable company offering 17-day lease packages for about $850 is Europe by Car (US tel. 800-223-1516, www.europebycar.com).

Driving

If you plan to drive in Austria, you are required to have an International Driving Permit (get through your local AAA office before you go; $15 plus two passport photos; www.aaa.com). For Germany, an International Driving Permit is recommended, but not required. Bring along your US driver's license for either country.

Austria charges drivers who use their major roads. You'll need to have a *Vignette* sticker stuck to the inside of your rental car's windshield (buy at the border crossing, big gas stations near borders, or a rental-car agency). The cost is €8 for 10 days, or €22 for two months. Dipping into the country on regular roads—such as around Reutte in Tirol—requires no special payment.

Learn the universal road signs (explained in charts in most

road atlases and at service stations). Seat belts are required, and two beers under those belts are enough to land you in jail.

Use good local maps and study them before each drive. Learn which exits you need to look out for, which major cities you'll travel toward, where the ruined castles lurk, and so on.

To get to the center of a city, follow signs for *Zentrum* or *Stadtmitte*. Ring roads go around a city. For parking, you can pick up a cardboard clock (*Parkscheibe*, available free at gas stations, police stations, and *Tabak* shops). Display your arrival time on the clock and put it on the dashboard, so parking attendants can see

you've been there less than the posted maximum stay (blue lines indicate 90-min zones on Austrian streets).

Every long drive between my recommended destinations is via the autobahn (super-freeway), and nearly every scenic backcountry drive is paved and comfortable.

The shortest distance between any two points is the autobahn. Signs directing you to the autobahn are green in Austria, blue in Germany. To understand the complex but super-efficient autobahn (no speed limit, toll-free), look for the *Autobahn Service* booklet at any autobahn rest stop (free, lists all stops, services, road symbols, and more). Learn the signs: *Dreieck* ("three corners") means a Y in the road; *Autobahnkreuz* is an intersection. Exits are spaced about every 20 miles and often have a gas station (*bleifrei* means "unleaded"), a restaurant, a mini-market, and sometimes a tourist information desk. Exits and intersections refer to the next major city or the nearest small town. Peruse the map and anticipate which town names to look out for. Know what you're looking for—miss it, and you're long autobahn-gone. When navigating, you'll see *nord, süd, ost,* or *west.*

Autobahns in Germany generally have no speed limit, but you will commonly see a recommended speed posted. While no one gets a ticket for ignoring this recommendation, exceeding this speed means your car insurance no longer covers you in the event of an accident. Speed limits in Austria, however, are enforced. Don't cruise in the passing lane; stay right. In fast-driving Germany, the

Driving: Distance and Time

backed-up line caused by an insensitive slow driver is called an *Autoschlange,* or "car snake." What's the difference between a car snake and a real snake? According to locals, "on a real snake, the ass is in the back."

Cheap Flights

While trains are usually the best way to connect places that are close together, a flight can save both time and money on longer journeys.

One of the best websites for comparing inexpensive flights is www.skyscanner.net. Other comparison search engines include www.kayak.com, www.mobissimo.com, www.sidestep.com, and www.wegolo.com.

Well-known cheapo airlines in Europe include easyJet (www .easyjet.com) and Ryanair (www.ryanair.com). Those based in Germany are Air Berlin (www.airberlin.com), Germanwings (www.germanwings.com), and TUIfly (www.tuifly.com).

Be aware of the potential drawbacks of flying on the cheap: nonrefundable and nonchangeable tickets, rigid baggage restrictions (and fees if you have more than what's officially allowed), use of airports far outside town, tight schedules that can mean more delays, little in the way of customer assistance if problems arise, and, of course, no frills. To avoid unpleasant surprises, read the small print—especially baggage policies—before you book.

HOLIDAYS AND FESTIVALS

This is a partial list of holidays and festivals. For more information, contact the tourist information offices listed at the beginning of this chapter. Vienna and Salzburg have music festivals nearly every month.

Jan	Perchtenlaufen (winter festival, parades), Tirol and Salzburg, Austria
Jan–Feb	Fasching (carnival season, balls, parades), throughout Austria and Germany
March 21	Good Friday
Easter	March 23 in 2008; Easter Festival, Salzburg
May 1	May Day with maypole dances, throughout Austria and Germany
May 9–12	Meistertrunk Show (medieval costumes, parties in the *Biergartens*, www.meistertrunk.de), Rothenburg, Germany
May 11–14	Dresden Dixieland Festival (www.dixieland.de), Dresden, Germany
May 12	Pentecost Monday (Pfingstmontag), southern Germany and Austria
Mid-May	Spring Horse Races (www.baden-galopp.de), Baden-Baden, Germany
May 22	Corpus Christi (Fronleichnam), southern Germany and Austria
May	Vienna Festival of Arts and Music
June 27–29	City Festival (www.elbhangfest.de), Dresden, Germany
June	Frankfurt Summertime Festival (arts)
Late June	Midsummer Eve Celebrations, Austria
July 12	Lichter Festival (fireworks and music, www.koelner-lichter.de), Köln, Germany
July 18–23	Kinderzeche Festival, Dinkelsbühl (www.kinderzeche.de)
Late July–Aug	Salzburg Festival (music)
Aug 15	Assumption (Mariä Himmelfahrt), Munich and parts of Austria
Late Aug	Fall Horse Races (www.baden-galopp.de),

2008

JANUARY						
S	M	T	W	T	F	S
		1	2	3	4	5
6	7	8	9	10	11	12
13	14	15	16	17	18	19
20	21	22	23	24	25	26
27	28	29	30	31		

FEBRUARY						
S	M	T	W	T	F	S
					1	2
3	4	5	6	7	8	9
10	11	12	13	14	15	16
17	18	19	20	21	22	23
24	25	26	27	28	29	

MARCH						
S	M	T	W	T	F	S
						1
2	3	4	5	6	7	8
9	10	11	12	13	14	15
16	17	18	19	20	21	22
$^{23}/_{30}$ $^{24}/_{31}$	25	26	27	28	29	

APRIL						
S	M	T	W	T	F	S
		1	2	3	4	5
6	7	8	9	10	11	12
13	14	15	16	17	18	19
20	21	22	23	24	25	26
27	28	29	30			

MAY						
S	M	T	W	T	F	S
				1	2	3
4	5	6	7	8	9	10
11	12	13	14	15	16	17
18	19	20	21	22	23	24
25	26	27	28	29	30	31

JUNE						
S	M	T	W	T	F	S
1	2	3	4	5	6	7
8	9	10	11	12	13	14
15	16	17	18	19	20	21
22	23	24	25	26	27	28
29	30					

JULY						
S	M	T	W	T	F	S
		1	2	3	4	5
6	7	8	9	10	11	12
13	14	15	16	17	18	19
20	21	22	23	24	25	26
27	28	29	30	31		

AUGUST						
S	M	T	W	T	F	S
					1	2
3	4	5	6	7	8	9
10	11	12	13	14	15	16
17	18	19	20	21	22	23
$^{24}/_{31}$	25	26	27	28	29	30

SEPTEMBER						
S	M	T	W	T	F	S
	1	2	3	4	5	6
7	8	9	10	11	12	13
14	15	16	17	18	19	20
21	22	23	24	25	26	27
28	29	30				

OCTOBER						
S	M	T	W	T	F	S
			1	2	3	4
5	6	7	8	9	10	11
12	13	14	15	16	17	18
19	20	21	22	23	24	25
26	27	28	29	30	31	

NOVEMBER						
S	M	T	W	T	F	S
						1
2	3	4	5	6	7	8
9	10	11	12	13	14	15
16	17	18	19	20	21	22
$^{23}/_{30}$	24	25	26	27	28	29

DECEMBER						
S	M	T	W	T	F	S
	1	2	3	4	5	6
7	8	9	10	11	12	13
14	15	16	17	18	19	20
21	22	23	24	25	26	27
28	29	30	31			

Baden-Baden, Germany

Aug 31–Sept 2 Imperial City Festival (fireworks), Rothenburg, Germany

Sept Berlin Festwochen (arts festival); Imperial City Festival (costumes, parade, fireworks on second weekend), Rothenburg, Germany

Sept 20–Oct 5 Oktoberfest (www.oktoberfest.de), Munich

Oct 3 German Unification Day (Tag der Deutschen Einheit), Germany

Oct 26 Austrian National Day (Nationalfeiertag)

Nov 1 All Saints' Day (Allerheiligen), southern Germany and Austria

Nov Berlin Jazz Festival; St. Martin's Day Celebrations (feasts), Austria and Bavaria

Dec St. Nicholas Day parades, Austria; Christmas Fairs, Austria and Germany

CONVERSIONS AND CLIMATE

Numbers and Stumblers

- Europeans write a few of their numbers differently than we do. 1 = 1, 4 = 4, 7 = 7.
- In Europe, dates appear as day/month/year, so Christmas is 25/12/08.
- Commas are decimal points and decimals commas. A dollar and a half is 1,50, and there are 5.280 feet in a mile.
- When counting with fingers, start with your thumb. If you hold up your first finger to request one item, you'll probably get two.
- What Americans call the second floor of a building is the first floor in Europe.
- On escalators and moving sidewalks, Europeans keep the left "lane" open for passing. Keep to the right.

Metric Conversions (approximate)

1 foot = 0.3 meter	1 square yard = 0.8 square meter
1 yard = 0.9 meter	1 square mile = 2.6 square kilometers
1 mile = 1.6 kilometers	1 ounce = 28 grams
1 centimeter = 0.4 inch	1 quart = 0.95 liter
1 meter = 39.4 inches	1 kilogram = 2.2 pounds
1 kilometer = 0.62 mile	32°F = 0°C

Climate

The first line is the average daily high; the second line, the average daily low. The third line shows the average number of days without rain. For more detailed weather statistics for destinations throughout Germany and Austria (as well as the rest of the world), check www.worldclimate.com.

	J	F	M	A	M	J	J	A	S	O	N	D
AUSTRIA • Vienna												
	34°	38°	47°	58°	67°	73°	76°	75°	68°	56°	45°	37°
	25°	28°	30°	42°	50°	56°	60°	59°	53°	44°	37°	30°
	16	17	18	17	18	16	18	20	18	16	16
GERMANY • Berlin												
	35°	37°	46°	56°	66°	72°	75°	74°	68°	56°	45°	38°
	26°	26°	31°	39°	47°	53°	57°	56°	50°	42°	36°	29°
	14	13	19	17	19	17	17	17	18	17	14	16
GERMANY • Munich												
	35°	38°	48°	56°	64°	70°	74°	73°	67°	56°	44°	36°
	23°	23°	30°	38°	45°	51°	55°	54°	48°	40°	33°	26°
	15	12	18	15	16	13	15	15	17	18	15	16

Appendix

Temperature Conversion: Fahrenheit and Celsius

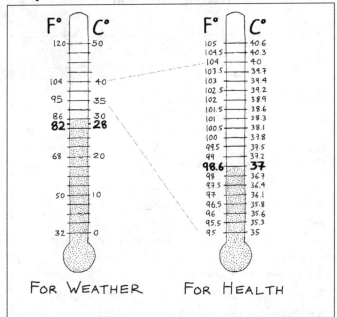

FOR WEATHER   FOR HEALTH

Europe takes its temperature using the Celsius scale, while we opt for Fahrenheit. For a rough conversion from Celsius to Fahrenheit, double the number and add 30. For weather, remember that 28°C is 82°F— perfect. For health, 37°C is just right.

Hotel Reservation

To: _____ _____
          hotel   *email or fax*

From: _____ _____
          name   *email or fax*

Today's date: _____ /_____ /_____
                    day   *month*   *year*

Dear Hotel _____ ,
Please make this reservation for me:

Name: _____

Total # of people: _____ # of rooms: _____ # of nights: _____

Arriving: _____ /_____ /_____ My time of arrival (24-hr clock): _____
                day *month* *year*   (I will telephone if I will be late)

Departing: ____ /____ /____
                 day *month* *year*

Room(s): Single____ Double ____ Twin ____ Triple ____ Quad____

With: Toilet ____ Shower ____ Bath ____ Sink only ____

Special needs: View____ Quiet ____ Cheapest ____ Ground Floor ____

Please email or fax confirmation of my reservation, along with the type of room reserved and the price. Please also inform me of your cancellation policy. After I hear from you, I will quickly send my credit-card information as a deposit to hold the room. Thank you.

_____
Name

_____
Address

_____
City   *State*   *Zip Code*   *Country*

Before hoteliers can make your reservation, they want to know the information listed above. You can use this form as the basis for your email, or you can photocopy this page, fill in the information, and send it as a fax (also available online at www.ricksteves.com/reservation).

Essential Packing Checklist

Whether you're traveling for five days or five weeks, here's what you'll need to bring. Remember to pack light to enjoy the sweet freedom of true mobility. Happy travels!

- ❏ 5 shirts
- ❏ 1 sweater or lightweight fleece jacket
- ❏ 2 pairs pants
- ❏ 1 pair shorts
- ❏ 1 swimsuit (women only—men can use shorts)
- ❏ 5 pairs underwear and socks
- ❏ 1 pair shoes
- ❏ 1 rainproof jacket
- ❏ Tie or scarf
- ❏ Money belt
- ❏ Money—your mix of:
  - ❏ Debit card for ATM withdrawals
  - ❏ Credit card
  - ❏ Hard cash in US dollars
- ❏ Documents (and backup photocopies)
- ❏ Passport
- ❏ Airplane ticket
- ❏ Driver's license
- ❏ Student ID and hostel card
- ❏ Railpass/car-rental voucher
- ❏ Insurance details
- ❏ Daypack
- ❏ Sealable plastic baggies
- ❏ Camera and related gear
- ❏ Empty water bottle
- ❏ Wristwatch and alarm clock
- ❏ Earplugs
- ❏ First-aid kit
- ❏ Medicine (labeled)
- ❏ Extra glasses/contacts and prescriptions
- ❏ Sunscreen and sunglasses
- ❏ Toiletries kit
- ❏ Soap
- ❏ Laundry soap (if liquid and carry-on, limit to 3 oz.)
- ❏ Clothesline
- ❏ Small towel
- ❏ Sewing kit
- ❏ Travel information
- ❏ Necessary map(s)
- ❏ Address list (email and mailing addresses)
- ❏ Postcards and photos from home
- ❏ Notepad and pen
- ❏ Journal

German Survival Phrases

When using the phonetics, pronounce ī as the long I sound in "light."

Good day.	Guten Tag.	**goo**-tehn tahg
Do you speak English?	Sprechen Sie Englisch?	**shprehkh**-ehn zee **ehng**-lish
Yes. / No.	Ja. / Nein.	yah / nīn
I (don't) understand.	Ich verstehe (nicht).	ikh fehr-**shtay**-heh (nikht)
Please.	Bitte.	**bit**-teh
Thank you.	Danke.	**dahng**-keh
I'm sorry.	Es tut mir leid.	ehs toot meer līt
Excuse me.	Entschuldigung.	ehnt-**shool**-dig-oong
(No) problem.	(Kein) Problem.	(kīn) proh-**blaym**
(Very) good.	(Sehr) gut.	(zehr) goot
Goodbye.	Auf Wiedersehen.	owf **vee**-der-zayn
one / two	eins / zwei	īns / tsvī
three / four	drei / vier	drī / feer
five / six	fünf / sechs	fewnf / zehkhs
seven / eight	sieben / acht	**zee**-behn / ahkht
nine / ten	neun / zehn	noyn / tsayn
How much is it?	Wieviel kostet das?	**vee**-feel **kohs**-teht dahs
Write it?	Schreiben?	**shrī**-behn
Is it free?	Ist es umsonst?	ist ehs oom-**zohnst**
Included?	Inklusive?	in-kloo-**zee**-veh
Where can I buy / find...?	Wo kann ich kaufen / finden...?	voh kahn ikh **kow**-fehn / **fin**-dehn
I'd like / We'd like...	Ich hätte gern / Wir hätten gern...	ikh **heh**-teh gehrn / veer **heh**-tehn gehrn
...a room.	...ein Zimmer.	īn **tsim**-mer
...a ticket to ___.	...eine Fahrkarte nach ___.	ī-neh **far**-kar-teh nahkh
Is it possible?	Ist es möglich?	ist ehs **mur**-glikh
Where is...?	Wo ist...?	voh ist
...the train station	...der Bahnhof	dehr **bahn**-hohf
...the bus station	...der Busbahnhof	dehr **boos**-bahn-hohf
...tourist information	...das Touristen- informationsbüro	dahs too-**ris**-tehn- in-for-maht-see-**ohns-bew**-roh
...toilet	...die Toilette	dee toh-**leh**-teh
men	Herren	**hehr**-rehn
women	Damen	**dah**-mehn
left / right	links / rechts	links / rehkhts
straight	geradeaus	geh-**rah**-deh-ows
When is this open / closed?	Um wieviel Uhr ist hier geöffnet / geschlossen?	oom **vee**-feel oor ist heer geh-**urf**-neht / geh-**shloh**-sehn
At what time?	Um wieviel Uhr?	oom **vee**-feel oor
Just a moment.	Moment.	moh-**mehnt**
now / soon / later	jetzt / bald / später	yehtst / bahld / **shpay**-ter
today / tomorrow	heute / morgen	**hoy**-teh / **mor**-gehn

In the Restaurant

I'd like / We'd like...	Ich hätte gern / Wir hätten gern...	ikh **heh**-teh gehrn / veer **heh**-tehn gehrn
...a reservation for...	...eine Reservierung für...	**ī**-neh reh-zer-**feer**-oong fewr
...a table for one / two.	...einen Tisch für ein / zwei.	**ī**-nehn tish fewr īn / tsvī
Non-smoking.	Nichtraucher.	**nikht**-rowkh-er
Is this seat free?	Ist hier frei?	ist heer frī
Menu (in English), please.	Speisekarte (auf Englisch), bitte.	**shpī**-zeh-kar-teh (owf **ehng**-lish) **bit**-teh
service (not) included	Trinkgeld (nicht) inklusive	**trink**-gehlt (nikht) in-kloo-**zee**-veh
cover charge	Eintritt	**īn**-trit
to go	zum Mitnehmen	tsoom **mit**-nay-mehn
with / without	mit / ohne	mit / **oh**-neh
and / or	und / oder	oont / **oh**-der
menu (of the day)	(Tages-) Karte	(**tah**-gehs-) **kar**-teh
set meal for tourists	Touristenmenü	too-**ris**-tehn-meh-**new**
specialty of the house	Spezialität des Hauses	shpayt-see-ah-lee-**tayt** dehs **how**-zehs
appetizers	Vorspeise	**for**-shpī-zeh
bread	Brot	broht
cheese	Käse	**kay**-zeh
sandwich	Sandwich	**zahnd**-vich
soup	Suppe	**zup**-peh
salad	Salat	zah-**laht**
meat	Fleisch	flīsh
poultry	Geflügel	geh-**flew**-gehl
fish	Fisch	fish
seafood	Meeresfrüchte	meh-rehs-**frewkh**-teh
fruit	Obst	ohpst
vegetables	Gemüse	geh-**mew**-zeh
dessert	Nachspeise	**nahkh**-shpī-zeh
mineral water	Mineralwasser	min-eh-**rahl**-vah-ser
tap water	Leitungswasser	**lī**-toongs-vah-ser
milk	Milch	milkh
(orange) juice	(Orangen-) Saft	(oh-**rahn**-zhehn-) zahft
coffee	Kaffee	kah-**fay**
tea	Tee	tay
wine	Wein	vīn
red / white	rot / weiß	roht / vīs
glass / bottle	Glas / Flasche	glahs / **flah**-sheh
beer	Bier	beer
Cheers!	Prost!	prohst
More. / Another.	Mehr. / Noch ein.	mehr / nohkh īn
The same.	Das gleiche.	dahs **glīkh**-eh
Bill, please.	Rechnung, bitte.	**rehkh**-noong **bit**-teh
tip	Trinkgeld	**trink**-gehlt
Delicious!	Lecker!	**lehk**-er

For more user-friendly German phrases, check out *Rick Steves' German Phrase Book and Dictionary* or *Rick Steves' French, Italian & German Phrase Book.*

INDEX

Travel smart…carry on!

The latest generation of Rick Steves' carry-on travel bags is easily the best—benefiting from two decades of on-the-road attention to what really matters: maximum quality and strength; practical, flexible features; and no unnecessary frills. You won't find a better value anywhere!

Rick Steves' Convertible Carry-On $99.⁹⁵

Our roomy, versatile 9"x 21"x 14" carry-on has a large 2600 cubic-inch main compartment, plus four outside pockets (small, medium and huge) that are perfect for often-used items. Wish you had even more room to bring home souvenirs? Pull open the full-perimeter expando-zipper and its capacity jumps from 2600 to 3000 cubic inches. When you want to use it as a suitcase or check it as luggage (required when "expanded"), the straps and belt hide away in a zippered compartment in the back. It weighs just 3 lbs.

Rick Steves' Classic Back Door Bag $79.⁹⁵

This ultra-light (1½ lbs.) version of our Convertible Carry-On features the same 9"x 21"x 14"dimensions and hideaway straps, but does not include a waistbelt or expandability. This is the bag that Rick lives out of for three months a year!

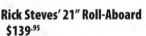

Rick Steves' 21" Roll-Aboard $139.⁹⁵

Our sturdy 21" Roll-Aboard is rucksack-soft in front, but the rest is lined with a hard ABS-lexan shell to give maximum protection to your belongings. We've spared no expense on moving parts, splurging on an extra-long button-release handle and big, tough inline skate wheels for easy rolling on rough surfaces. It features the same 9"x 21"x 14" carry-on dimensions, pocket configuration and expandability as our Convertible Carry-On—and at 7 lbs. it's the lightest roll-aboard in its class.

Prices and features are subject to change.

For great deals on a wide selection of travel goodies, begin your next trip at the Rick Steves Travel Store!

Visit the Rick Steves Travel Store at
www.ricksteves.com

Start your trip at
www.ricksteves.com

Rick Steves' website is packed with over 3,000 pages of timely travel information. It's also your gateway to getting FREE monthly travel news from Rick—and more!

Free Monthly Travel News

Fresh articles on Europe's most interesting destinations and happenings. Rick will even send you an email every month (often direct from Europe) with his latest discoveries!

Timely Travel Tips

Rick Steves' best money-and-stress-saving tips on trip planning, packing, transportation, hotels, health, safety, finances, hurdling the language barrier...and more.

Travelers' Graffiti Wall

Candid advice and opinions from thousands of travelers on everything listed above, plus whatever topics are hot at the moment (discount flights, politics, nude beaches, scams...you name it).

Rick's Guide to Eurail Passes

The clearest, most comprehensive guide to the confusing array of railpass options out there, and how to choo-choose the railpass that best fits your itinerary and budget.

Great Gear at Our Travel Store

In the past year alone, more than 50,000 travelers have enjoyed great online deals on Rick's guidebooks, maps, DVDs—and his custom-designed carry-on bags, day packs, and light-packing accessories.

Rick Steves Tours

This year, 12,000 lucky travelers will explore Europe on a Rick Steves tour. Learn about our 28 different one- to three-week itineraries, read uncensored feedback from our tour alums, and get our free Tour Experience DVD.

Rick on TV, Radio and Podcasts

Read the scripts from the popular Rick Steves' Europe TV series, and listen to or download your choice of over 100 hours of our Travel with Rick Steves radio show.

Respect for Your Privacy

Whether you buy something from us or subscribe to Rick's monthly Travel News emails, we'll never share your name or email address with anyone else. You won't be spammed!

Have fun raising your Travel I.Q. at
www.ricksteves.com

Rick Steves

More *Savvy*. More *Surprising*. More *Fun*.

COUNTRY GUIDES

Croatia & Slovenia
England
France
Germany & Austria
Great Britain
Ireland
Italy
Portugal
Scandinavia
Spain
Switzerland

CITY GUIDES

Amsterdam, Bruges & Brussels
Florence & Tuscany
Istanbul
London
Paris
Prague & The Czech Republic
Provence & The French Riviera
Rome
Venice

BEST OF GUIDES

Best of Eastern Europe
Best of Europe

As the #1 authority on European travel, Rick gives you inside information on what to visit, where to stay, and how to get there—economically and hassle-free.

www.ricksteves.com

PHRASE BOOKS & DICTIONARIES

French
French, Italian & German
German
Italian
Portuguese
Spanish

MORE EUROPE FROM RICK STEVES

Europe 101
Europe Through the Back Door
Postcards from Europe

RICK STEVES' EUROPE DVDs

All 70 Shows 2000–2007
Britain
Eastern Europe
France & Benelux
Germany, The Swiss Alps & Travel Skills
Ireland
Italy
Spain & Portugal

PLANNING MAPS

Britain & Ireland
Europe
France
Germany, Austria & Switzerland
Italy
Spain & Portugal

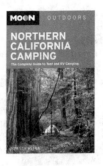

CREDITS

Researchers

To help update this book, Rick relied on…

Gretchen Strauch

Gretchen lived in Konstanz, Germany for three years, where she taught English, and became an expert on the *Eiscafes* of southern Germany. Raised in rural California, she now lives in Seattle and edits Rick Steves guidebooks. She still does not like sauerkraut.

Karoline Vass

Karoline was born and raised in Munich, Germany. Passionate about anything alpine, she made her way to Seattle via the Swiss Alps and the Rocky Mountains. When not researching guidebooks and leading tours, she makes her living as a freelance violist.

Contributor

Gene Openshaw

Gene is the co-author of seven Rick Steves books. For this book, he wrote material on art, history, and contemporary culture. When he's not traveling, Gene enjoys composing music, recovering from his 1973 trip to Europe with Rick, and living everyday life with his wife and daughter.

IMAGES

Location	Photographer
Germany	
Germany full-page: Munich's Marienplatz	Dominic Bonucelli
Munich: Marienplatz	Rick Steves
Bavaria and Tirol: Neuschwanstein Castle	Dominic Bonuccelli
Baden-Baden and the Black Forest: Baden-Baden	Cameron Hewitt
Rothenburg and the Romantic Road: Rothenburg	David C. Hoerlein
Würzburg: Würzburg Cityscape	Rick Steves
Frankfurt: Frankfurt Scene from Bridge	Rick Steves
Rhine Valley: Bacharach and the Rhine	Dominic Bonucelli
Mosel Valley: Beilstein	Cameron Hewitt
Trier: Market Square	Cameron Hewitt
Köln and the Unromantic Rhine: Köln's Cathedral	Cameron Hewitt / Cameron Hewitt
Nürnberg: Market Square	Rick Steves
Dresden: Zwinger	Cameron Hewitt
Berlin: Gendarmenmarkt	Cameron Hewitt
Görlitz: Church of St. Peter	Lee Evans
Austria	
Austria full-page: St. Peter's Church, Vienna	Cameron Hewitt
Vienna: Schönbrunn Palace	Cameron Hewitt
Danube Valley: Danube River	Rick Steves
Salzburg: Salzburg Overview	Dominic Bonucelli
Hallstatt and the Salzkammergut: Hallstatt	David C. Hoerlein
Innsbruck and Hall: Innsbruck	Rick Steves

Rick Steves' Guidebook Series

Country Guides

Rick Steves' Best of Europe
Rick Steves' Croatia & Slovenia
Rick Steves' Eastern Europe
Rick Steves' England
Rick Steves' France
Rick Steves' Germany & Austria
Rick Steves' Great Britain
Rick Steves' Ireland
Rick Steves' Italy
Rick Steves' Portugal
Rick Steves' Scandinavia
Rick Steves' Spain
Rick Steves' Switzerland

City and Regional Guides

Rick Steves' Amsterdam, Bruges & Brussels
Rick Steves' Florence & Tuscany
Rick Steves' Istanbul
Rick Steves' London
Rick Steves' Paris
Rick Steves' Prague & the Czech Republic
Rick Steves' Provence & the French Riviera
Rick Steves' Rome
Rick Steves' Venice

Rick Steves' Phrase Books

French
German
Italian
Spanish
Portuguese
French/Italian/German

Other Books

Rick Steves' Europe Through the Back Door
Rick Steves' Europe 101: History & Art for the Traveler
Rick Steves' Postcards from Europe
Rick Steves' European Christmas

(Avalon Travel Publishing)

Avalon Travel Publishing
a member of the Perseus Books Group
1700 Fourth Street
Berkeley, CA 96710, USA

Printed in the USA by Worzalla. First printing December 2007.

ISBN (10) 1-59880-135-X
ISBN (13) 978-1-59880-135-4
ISSN 1553-6866

For the latest on Rick's lectures, guidebooks, tours, public radio show, and public television
series, contact Europe Through the Back Door, Box 2009, Edmonds, WA 98020, tel.
425/771-8303, fax 425/771-0833, www.ricksteves.com, rick@ricksteves.com.

Thanks to my wife, Anne, for her support. Thanks to Gene Openshaw for writing the tours
of Munich's Alte Pinakothek and Vienna's Kunsthistorisches Museum; to Cameron Hewitt
for writing the original versions of the Dresden and Nürnberg chapters; and to Lee Evans
for writing the original version of the Görlitz chapter.

Europe Through the Back Door Senior Editor: Cameron Hewitt
ETBD Editors: Cathy McDonald, Jennifer Hauseman (Senior Editor), Gretchen Strauch
ETBD Managing Editor: Risa Laib
Avalon Travel Senior Editor and Series Manager: Madhu Prasher
Avalon Travel Project Editor: Kelly Lydick
Research Assistance: Gretchen Strauch, Karoline Vass
Copy Editor: Matthew Reed Baker
Indexer: Stephen Callahan
Proofreader: Janet Walden
Production & Typesetting: McGuire Barber Design
Cover Design: Kari Gim, Laura Mazer
Cover Art Manager: Laura VanDeventer
Maps & Graphics: David C. Hoerlein, Laura VanDeventer, Lauren Mills, Barb Geisler,
   Mike Morgenfeld
Photography: Cameron Hewitt, Rick Steves, Karoline Vass, Ian Watson, David C.
   Hoerlein, Pat O'Connor, Gretchen Strauch, Dominic Bonuccelli, Debi Jo Michael, Lee
   Evans,
Front Matter Color Photos: p. i, Bavarian beer maid © Rick Steves; Burg Eltz © Dominic
   Bonucelli
Cover Photo: front image, Berchtesgaden, Austria © Rick Steves; back image, Trier
   Market, Germany © Ian Watson